黄淮七省
考古论坛

# 黄淮七省考古新发现
## （2011—2017年）上

河南省文物考古研究院
山东省文物考古研究院
安徽省文物考古研究所
江苏省考古研究所
河北省文物研究所
陕西省考古研究院
山西省考古研究所

编著

大象出版社
·郑州·

中原出版传媒集团
中原传媒股份公司

图书在版编目(CIP)数据

黄淮七省考古新发现：2011-2017年：上下册 / 河南省文物考古研究院等编著. — 郑州：大象出版社，2019.7
ISBN 978-7-5347-9981-5

Ⅰ.①黄… Ⅱ.①河… Ⅲ.①考古发现—中国 Ⅳ.①K87

中国版本图书馆CIP数据核字（2018）第258488号

# 黄淮七省考古新发现（2011-2017年）
HUANGHUAI QISHENG KAOGU XINFAXIAN

河南省文物考古研究院等编著

| 出 版 人 | 王刘纯 |
|---|---|
| 责任编辑 | 郭一凡 |
| 责任校对 | 毛 路　张迎娟　马 宁　李婧慧 |
| 装帧设计 | 付铱铱 |

出版发行　大象出版社（郑州市郑东新区祥盛街27号　邮政编码 450016）
　　　　　发行科　0371-63863551　总编室　0371-65597936
网　　址　www.daxiang.cn
印　　刷　郑州新海岸电脑彩色制印有限公司
经　　销　各地新华书店经销
开　　本　889mm×1194mm　1/16
印　　张　44.75
字　　数　938千字
版　　次　2019年7月第1版　2019年7月第1次印刷
定　　价　528.00元（上下册）

若发现印、装质量问题，影响阅读，请与承印厂调换。
印厂地址　郑州市鼎尚街15号
邮政编码　450002　　　　电话　0371-86596155

# 前　言

　　黄河中下游地区及淮河流域地处中原腹地，是中华文明形成和发展的核心地区，近代中国考古学在此发端。秦、晋、豫、冀、鲁、皖、苏等黄淮七省地域相接，考古学文化相互交融，区域间学术交流合作也有着良好的传统与坚实的基础。

　　进入新世纪以后，随着全国经济区域协同发展的全面深化，省际、区域考古研究合作机制也蓬勃发展。为适应中国考古学发展的新趋势，进一步加强黄淮地区的考古区域合作，在国家文物局和权威专家积极倡导下，2011年7月，由河南省文物局倡议，在郑州召开了建立黄淮区域考古合作机制的筹备会，陕西、山西、河南、河北、山东、安徽、江苏七省的考古单位参加了会议。经过与会各方充分讨论和反复商讨，确定合作机制的名称为"黄淮七省考古论坛"，在七省轮流举办，旨在黄淮七省间建立起一种考古合作的平台和机制，探讨彼此间在课题、项目等方面的互动协作，创造良好的学术交流氛围，实现共同进步。自2011年9月首届"黄淮七省考古论坛"在郑州召开以来，先后在济南、合肥、南京、石家庄、西安、太原成功举办。七年来，论坛集中展示和交流了七省每年的主动课题研究、大遗址保护、基本建设抢救性考古发掘、科技考古、文物科技保护、公共考古等重要考古工作成果。论坛始终围绕黄淮地区在中华文明形成与发展中的重要地位和作用这一主题进行探讨，同时，论坛对相关工作也进行了广泛的交流和探讨。

　　"黄淮七省考古论坛"为展示黄淮地区考古工作成果、深化学术交流与合作提供了一个富有成效的平台，初步实现了开放包容，深化交流，务实灵活，推进合作，着眼于我国文化遗产保护事业大局，引导考古研究的方向和关注点的初衷。七年完成了一个圆满循环，成果丰硕，本次编撰的《黄淮七省考古新发现》就是七省合作交流成果的展现。

　　我们相信，"黄淮七省考古论坛"必定会行稳致远，在推动黄淮地区和中国文物考古事业发展中起到举足轻重的作用。

河南省文物考古学会会长　孙英民

2018年10月

# 目 录

## 七省考古成就综述

2011—2017年河南考古新收获　刘海旺 ·················003

2011—2017年山东省考古发现的主要收获　郑同修 ·················006

2011—2017年安徽省考古新进展　宫希成 ·················010

2011—2017年江苏省重要考古发现与收获　林留根 ·················014

搭建学术交流平台　促进考古研究发展
——河北省"黄淮七省考古论坛"考古发现综述　张文瑞 ·················018

熔古铸今　砥砺前行
——陕西省考古研究院2011—2017年考古工作述评　孙周勇 ·················022

山西考古七年回顾　王万辉 ·················026

## 人类的演化

### 自古在昔　先民有作

河北阳原泥河湾盆地马圈沟早更新世旧石器时代遗址群　刘连强　王法岗 ·················033

河北阳原泥河湾盆地马梁—后沟中更新世旧石器时代遗址群　王法岗 ·················037

河南栾川孙家洞旧石器时代遗址　顾雪军 ·················041

山西襄汾丁村旧石器时代遗址群　袁文明　王益人 ·················044

河北阳原泥河湾盆地侯家窑旧石器时代中期遗址　王法岗 ·················048

河南灵井许昌人旧石器时代遗址　李占扬　赵清坡……050
河北阳原板井子旧石器时代中期遗址　王法岗……053
山东青岛大珠山旧石器时代遗址　陈宇鹏……055
河北阳原油房旧石器时代中期和晚期遗址　梅惠杰……058
河北阳原西白马营旧石器时代晚期遗址　周振宇……061
山西陵川附城镇旧石器时代晚期洞穴遗址　任海云……064

# 文明化进程

## 骏惠维天　降幅之穰穰

江苏泗洪韩井遗址　于慧楠……071
江苏泗洪县顺山集新石器时代遗址　林流根　甘恢元　闫龙……073
安徽淮北相山区渠沟新石器时代遗址　张义中……077
河北尚义四台蒙古营遗址　王培生……080
安徽郎溪磨盘山新石器时代至商周时期遗址　赵东升……083
安徽含山凌家滩遗址及周边考古工作　吴卫红……087
江苏兴化、东台蒋庄新石器时代遗址　林流根　甘恢元　闫龙……092

## 且享且祀　以洽百之礼

山东即墨北阡遗址　王芬　栾丰实　林玉海　靳桂云……097
江苏沭阳万北遗址第四次考古发掘　甘恢元……100
山东泰安大汶口遗址　高明奎　梅圆圆……102
山东章丘焦家遗址　王芬　路国权　唐仲明　宋艳波……106
安徽萧县金寨新石器时代遗址　张小雷……111
江苏泗洪赵庄遗址第二、三次考古发掘　甘恢元……115
山东烟台午台遗址大汶口—龙山文化的新发现　王富强……119
安徽固镇南城孜遗址　余杰……123

| 安徽寿县丁家孤堆新石器—商周遗址　蔡波涛 | 126 |
| 山东章丘城子崖遗址 2013—2015 年度发掘概况　朱　超　孙　波 | 129 |
| 山东菏泽定陶十里铺北遗址的发掘　高明奎　王　龙 | 132 |

**日就月将　缉熙于明光**

| 河南舞阳贾湖遗址第八次发掘　蓝万里　魏兴涛 | 135 |
| 河北新乐何家庄遗址　张晓峥 | 140 |
| 山西临汾桃园新石器时代聚落遗址　郑　媛　武卓卓　薛新明 | 143 |
| 陕西西安高陵杨官寨遗址史前墓地　杨利平 | 147 |
| 河南淅川龙山岗遗址仰韶时代晚期城址　梁法伟 | 150 |
| 河南淅川下寨遗址仰韶至石家河文化时期墓地　曹艳朋 | 154 |
| 河南濮阳戚城龙山时代城址　李一丕 | 159 |
| 山西兴县碧村遗址龙山时期聚落　王晓毅　张光辉　王小娟　任海云 | 162 |
| 山西绛县周家庄遗址　田　伟 | 166 |
| 山西襄汾陶寺遗址宫城新发现　高江涛 | 170 |
| 陕西神木神圪垯梁龙山晚期遗址　郭小宁 | 174 |
| 陕西神木石峁遗址　邵　晶 | 177 |
| 安徽肥东刘墩新石器—商周遗址　陈小春 | 182 |

# 三代之礼　皇皇者华

**钟鸣鼎食　多姓一统**

| 河南偃师二里头遗址 5 号基址　赵海涛 | 187 |
| 安徽肥西县武斌大墩遗址　余　飞 | 191 |
| 河北肃宁县后白寺遗址　魏曙光 | 195 |
| 山东济南市榆林遗址　朱　超 | 199 |
| 安徽寿县斗鸡台遗址　蔡波涛 | 203 |

安徽和县章四科大城子遗址　余　飞 …………………………………………………… 207

安徽阜南县台家寺遗址　何晓琳 …………………………………………………… 211

安徽凤阳县古堆桥遗址　何晓琳 …………………………………………………… 215

山东济南市大辛庄遗址　郎剑锋 …………………………………………………… 217

陕西清涧县辛庄遗址　种建荣　孙战伟 …………………………………………… 221

山东济南市刘家庄遗址　郭俊峰　房　振　李　铭 ……………………………… 225

江苏镇江市孙家村遗址　何汉生 …………………………………………………… 229

陕西周原遗址　李彦峰 ……………………………………………………………… 233

江苏新沂市聂墩遗址　田二卫 ……………………………………………………… 237

河北行唐故郡遗址　齐瑞普　张春长 ……………………………………………… 241

山西榆社县偶尔坪遗址　王　俊 …………………………………………………… 245

## 作邦作封　翼翼四方

山东临淄范家遗址　赵益超 ………………………………………………………… 249

河南荥阳市官庄遗址　郜向平 ……………………………………………………… 253

河北满城要庄遗址　任雪岩 ………………………………………………………… 257

江苏苏州木渎古城　唐锦琼　孙明利 ……………………………………………… 261

山东鲁国故城　韩　辉 ……………………………………………………………… 265

山东临淄齐故城　赵益超　吕　凯　董文斌 ……………………………………… 270

山东邾国故城遗址　王　青　郎剑锋　路国权　陈章龙 ………………………… 275

河南新郑郑韩故城北城门遗址　樊温泉 …………………………………………… 279

河北邯郸赵王城　段宏振 …………………………………………………………… 283

河北雄安新区南阳遗址　张晓峥 …………………………………………………… 287

## 是飨是宜　继序思不忘

陕西宝鸡石鼓山商周墓地　丁　岩 ………………………………………………… 290

河南伊川县徐阳东周戎人墓地　吴业恒 …………………………………………… 294

河南南阳市夏响铺鄂国贵族墓地　崔本信 ……298

山西翼城县大河口西周墓地　王金平　陈海波 ……302

山西绛县雎村西周封国墓地　王金平　段双龙 ……306

陕西周原姚家墓地　赵艺蓬 ……310

山西洪洞县南秦村两周大型墓地　杨及耘　曹俊 ……314

山西襄汾县陶寺北两周墓地　王京燕　崔俊俊 ……318

陕西澄城县刘家洼春秋墓地　种建荣　孙战伟 ……323

陕西黄陵县寨头河战国戎人墓地　孙周勇　邵晶　孙战伟 ……327

山东沂水县纪王崮春秋墓葬　郝导华 ……331

安徽六安市白鹭洲战国墓　秦让平 ……335

山东济南市梁二村战国墓　刘秀玲　房振　郭俊峰　王惠明 ……339

河南信阳市城阳城址八号墓　武志江 ……343

安徽宁国市灰山土墩墓群　王峰 ……347

山西侯马市虒祁遗址东周祭祀坑　王金平　段双龙 ……351

河北黄骅市郛堤城瓮棺葬　雷建红　马小飞 ……355

### 龟卜筮占　吉金作钟

安徽省巢湖市城圩商周遗址　姚洁 ……359

山西闻喜县千金耙夏商矿冶遗址　李刚　南普恒 ……363

河南安阳市辛店村商代晚期铸铜遗址　孔德铭 ……366

### 煮海为盐　如玉如雪

近年来鲁北沿海地区盐业考古新发现　王子孟　党浩 ……370

# 秦汉一统　雄风万里

### 丝路迢迢　雄关开道

河南新安县汉函谷关遗址考古调查与发掘　王咸秋 ……377

## 巍巍之城　尽显其荣

陕西西安市秦都咸阳城考古新进展　许卫红 ……… 381

陕西西安市秦都咸阳城府库建筑遗址　许卫红 ……… 384

陕西西安市汉长安城北渭桥遗址　王志友 ……… 388

山东即墨故城遗址近年考古工作收获　郝导华 ……… 392

山东章丘东平陵城遗址 2009—2013 年考古发掘　张溯 ……… 396

河南汉魏洛阳故城 2012—2014 年考古新发现　钱国祥　刘涛　郭晓涛　莫阳 ……… 399

陕西靖边县统万城遗址的考古发现　邢福来 ……… 402

## 宏宏之穴　以象其生

河南三门峡市大唐火电厂墓地重要考古发现　马俊才　李辉　杨树刚　曹艳朋 ……… 406

山东龙口市西三甲墓群考古发掘重大收获　孙兆锋 ……… 410

安徽六安市十里铺战国—西汉土墩墓　王峰 ……… 414

陕西西汉帝陵考古（2011—2017 年）　焦南峰　马永赢　杨武站　曹龙　王东　赵旭阳
……… 418

江苏盱眙县大云山江都王陵　李则斌 ……… 422

江苏徐州市卧牛山 M2～M4 汉墓　刘超 ……… 426

河南南阳市百里奚西汉彩绘漆棺墓　王凤剑　翟京襄 ……… 429

山西蒲县曹家庄西汉匈奴墓　田建文　穆文军 ……… 433

河北石家庄市马鞍山汉代王侯墓　赵战护 ……… 436

山东青岛市土山屯汉墓群考古发掘　彭峪 ……… 439

山东定陶王陵 M2 近年来考古发现　崔圣宽　王江峰 ……… 448

河南洛阳市东汉帝陵考古调查与发掘　王咸秋 ……… 452

陕西靖边县杨桥畔渠树壕东汉壁画墓　段毅 ……… 456

2012 年河北安平县汉王公园东汉墓葬　张晓峥 ……… 460

安徽广德县南塘汉代土墩墓　陈超 ……… 463

山西太原市开化墓地　马　昇　张光辉 ……………………………………………… 467

　　河南洛阳市西朱村曹魏墓　王咸秋 ………………………………………………… 471

　　安徽当涂县"天子坟"孙吴墓　叶润清 …………………………………………… 475

　　江苏邳州市新河煎药庙西晋墓地　马永强 ………………………………………… 478

### 天地鬼神　享礼之尊

　　陕西凤翔县雍山血池秦汉祭祀遗址　陈爱东　田亚歧 …………………………… 481

### 灼铁烁金　铸刚锻韧

　　陕西杨凌邰城铸铁作坊遗址　赵艺蓬 ……………………………………………… 486

### 亭里乡间　布衣炊烟

　　山东枣庄市海子汉代遗址考古发掘　吕　凯 ……………………………………… 488

## 唐风宋韵　气象万千

### 运河悠悠　润千载文明

　　隋代大型仓储遗址的考古调查与发掘　刘海旺　王　炬 ………………………… 493

　　安徽柳孜唐宋时期运河遗址第二次考古发掘　陈　超 …………………………… 497

　　江苏淮安市板闸遗址　胡　兵　赵李博 …………………………………………… 501

　　京杭大运河山东段考古　李振光　吴志刚　王春云　吴双成 …………………… 505

　　江苏镇江市中华路明清京口闸遗址　霍　强 ……………………………………… 512

### 航琛越水　宝船佳瓷

　　河北黄骅市海丰镇遗址　雷建红　马小飞 ………………………………………… 516

　　江苏苏州市太仓樊村泾元代遗址　张照根　张志清　孙明利 …………………… 520

### 绿堤春草　脉脉九河流

　　河北邢清干渠威县北宋"鲧堤"　佟宇喆 ………………………………………… 524

### 灵明宝藏　收在水晶宫

　　河北水下文化遗产保护　雷建红 …………………………………………………… 527

## 万里江山　自古竞繁华

山西蒲州故城遗址发现北朝至唐代城墙　刘　岩　赵　辉 …………………………… 529

江苏南京市花露岗唐至五代遗址的考古发掘　李　翔 …………………………………… 532

江苏盱眙县泗州城唐代至清代遗址　朱晓汀　甘恢元 …………………………………… 536

河北肃宁县后白寺唐宋时期遗址　雷建红 ……………………………………………… 540

山西晋阳古城2012—2018年考古发现及主要收获　韩炳华 …………………………… 542

江苏东台市辞郎村遗址　高　伟　李光日 ……………………………………………… 546

山西绛州州署遗址的考古发现　杨及耘　曹　俊 ……………………………………… 550

河南开封北宋东京城顺天门遗址　葛奇峰 ……………………………………………… 553

河北张家口市崇礼太子城遗址金代行宫　黄　信　任　涛　魏慧平 ………………… 557

安徽凤阳县明中都遗址　王　志 ………………………………………………………… 561

山东济南市宽厚所街遗址明代郡王府　李　铭　房　振　郭俊峰 …………………… 565

## 梵庭钟磬音　职奉三清隐终南

山西大同市云冈石窟窟顶遗址发掘　白曙璋 …………………………………………… 568

陕西西安市周陵镇杨家村发现北朝佛教造像　肖健一　胡松梅 ……………………… 571

定国寺、龙兴寺、天齐大王行宫
　——山东东阿大秦村北朝唐宋宗教遗址发掘概述　李宝军　郑同修 ……………… 574

河北正定县开元寺南广场遗址　陈　伟　翟鹏飞　佘俊英　房树辉 ………………… 577

江苏南京清凉寺遗址考古发掘　龚巨平 ………………………………………………… 581

山东烟台市严因寺遗址发掘　朱　超　吕　凯 ………………………………………… 585

山东济南市神通寺遗址的勘探和发掘　房　振　郭俊峰　邢　琪　李　铭　王　峰 …… 588

## 幽室冥冥　事死以象生

江苏南京市栖霞区狮子冲南朝陵园考古概况　许志强 ………………………………… 591

2015年山西侯马市新月小区北魏裴氏家族墓　王金平　段双龙 ……………………… 595

山西忻州市九原岗北朝壁画墓　白曙璋　张庆捷 ……………………………………… 598

江苏苏州市虎丘路新村土墩砖室墓群　张铁军　何文竞 ............ 601

江苏扬州市隋炀帝墓　束家平 ............ 605

河北邢台市唐祖陵调查、勘探与发掘　郭济桥 ............ 609

陕西唐代帝陵近年来的工作和新发现　张　博 ............ 613

陕西华阴市唐敦煌县令宋素墓　刘呆运　赵占锐 ............ 616

陕西咸阳市唐昭容上官氏墓　李　明　耿庆刚 ............ 619

山西临汾市西赵唐代墓葬　王金平　陈海波 ............ 623

陕西长安郭庄唐宰相韩休墓　刘呆运　赵占锐 ............ 626

河北平山县王母村唐代崔氏墓　韩金秋 ............ 630

河北曲阳县田庄大墓　张春长 ............ 634

江苏南京市西天寺墓园宋墓　王　宏 ............ 638

安徽南陵县铁拐宋墓　张　辉 ............ 642

山西昔阳县宋金墓葬考古发掘　刘　岩　史永红 ............ 646

山西长治县沙峪村宋至明清古墓群　杨林中 ............ 649

山西汾西县郝家沟金代纪年壁画墓　武俊华 ............ 653

河南荥阳市明代周懿王墓　孙　凯 ............ 657

## 百卉千葩　巧艺夺天工

河北邢窑历次考古工作、收获与特点　王会民 ............ 661

河北井陉县隋至清代瓷窑址　黄　信　胡　强 ............ 663

安徽萧县白土寨唐宋瓷窑址　蔡波涛 ............ 665

安徽繁昌县骆冲窑遗址　罗　虎　汪发志　徐　繁　崔　炜 ............ 669

安徽繁昌窑柯家冲瓷窑遗址　罗　虎 ............ 672

山西河津市固镇宋金瓷窑址　高振华　王晓毅　贾　尧 ............ 676

河南禹州神垕镇瓷窑发掘概况　李　辉 ............ 680

安徽凤阳县乔涧子明代琉璃窑遗址　罗　虎　唐更生　朱　江 ............ 683

江苏南京市栖霞区官窑村明代窑场遗址　杨平平 ········································· 687

陕西渭南市尧头窑明清瓷窑遗址调查与发掘　于春雷 ····································· 691

## 汲井岁榾榾　出车日连连

河北黄骅市大左庄唐代盐业遗址　雷建红　马小飞　曹　洋 ························· 694

**编后记** ······································································································· 698

# 七省考古成就综述

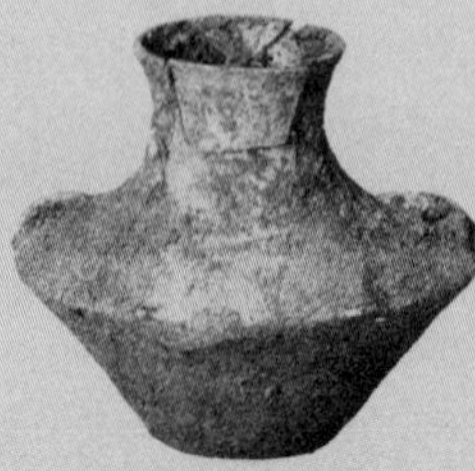

# 2011—2017年河南考古新收获

自2011年首届"黄淮七省考古论坛"在郑州召开以来，河南考古工作的重心仍然集中在为配合基本建设而进行的抢救性考古发掘上。同时，围绕丝绸之路与大运河申报世界文化遗产、大遗址保护与考古遗址公园建设、重大学术课题等方面进行了较多的主动性考古调查与发掘工作。在包括配合基本建设考古发掘在内的重要考古工作中，加强了学术课题意识，运用各类新技术多方获取信息，多学科全过程联合发掘，保护与利用理念贯穿发掘过程，积极展开与国内外科研机构合作研究等。在2011—2017年间，河南考古取得了重要收获。

## 一、旧石器时代

旧石器时代遗址考古发掘与研究，除了继续对灵井许昌人遗址进行考古发掘外，又在洛阳栾川、淅川丹江库区、三门峡等地开展了调查与发掘工作，取得了新的发现和成果。在灵井许昌人遗址又首次发现了2块古人类肢骨化石；新发现了大量经过压制法制作的、具有欧洲旧石器时代中期特色的石器。在对位于洛阳栾川距今约40万年的孙家洞旧石器遗址的考古发掘中，出土了包括门齿、臼齿及颌骨残块在内的古人类化石，从牙齿发育看存在幼年个体，这是首次在河南省境内发现的、有明确地层的中更新世时期古人类牙齿化石。

## 二、新石器时代

七年来，河南省的新石器时代遗址的考古发掘工作主要为配合考古遗址公园建设而进行。2013年对贾湖遗址进行了第八次考古发掘，较为特别的是在集中分布的近10座墓中出土有大量绿松石串饰，这在贾湖遗址历年的发掘中是首次发现。濮阳戚城龙山时期城址位于太行山脉与鲁中南山地之间的黄河冲积平原上，其城墙的夯筑使用了先进的版筑法，城址之下还叠压有龙山早期的环壕聚落。在配合南水北调中线工程丹江库区建设的考古工作中，一些新石器时代遗址得到了较大面积的发掘，如淅川龙山岗遗址、下寨遗址等。龙山岗遗址（黄楝树遗址）主要包含仰韶文化、屈家岭文化、石家河文化、王湾三期文化等时期遗存，特别是发现了疑似始建于仰韶时代晚期的城址。下寨遗址最重要的是发现了仰韶文化晚期至石家河文化时期的一处墓地。

## 三、商周时期

二里头遗址、偃师商城、郑州商城、安阳殷墟等都城遗址一直是河南夏商考古工作的重心。二里头遗址近年重要的收获是明确了属于二里头二期的5号基址的平面布局、结构、年代变迁等内涵，展示了二里头文化早期都邑格局的特征。2016年在安阳殷墟宫殿宗庙区北约10千米处发现了一处商代晚期铸铜作坊遗址，该遗址与已发现的殷墟铸铜遗址同为当时重要的青铜礼器铸造作坊，但相距较远，这扩大了对殷墟范围的新认识和对殷墟铸铜手工业规模的新认识。

## 四、两周时期

荥阳官庄遗址是近年河南两周时期城址考古发掘的重要成果。该城址时代为西周中晚期至战国时期，系由大小城构成，较为重要的是在大城中北部发现了丰富的春秋时期制陶、铸铜、制骨手工业遗存。郑韩故城的重要考古成果是北城门遗址的发现。该门址始建于春秋时期，由城墙、道路、水渠和城壕组成，至战国时期增设了两条道路，加筑了瓮城城墙。南阳夏响铺西周晚期至春秋早期鄂国贵族墓地是两周墓葬考古重要收获，发掘清理该时期墓葬60余座，出土青铜器等随葬器物上千件，其中40余件青铜器带有"鄂侯""鄂伯""鄂姜"等铭文。伊川徐阳东周戎人墓地为东周时期，该墓地共清理春秋中晚期墓葬48座，陪葬车马坑10座，墓葬随葬器物组合及特征，都与洛阳地区东周时期墓葬随葬器物特征相似，但陪葬车马坑均葬有大量马、牛、羊头或蹄等，与西北地区戎人葬俗类似，该墓地的发现与文献记载的东周时期陆浑戎人曾在伊洛河流域活动和居住相吻合。信阳城阳城址战国中期八号墓的发掘是近年河南境内楚墓的新发现，该墓为大型土坑竖穴木椁墓，椁室分为7部分，尽管遭到盗掘，但仍出土了较多数量的漆木器、仿铜彩绘陶礼器、髹漆竹席、丝织品、铜兵器等。

## 五、秦汉时期

三门峡地区是河南秦文化墓葬发现最多的地区。2014年在配合三门峡大唐火电厂建设工程中，共发掘清理了属于战国晚期至西汉早期的750余座秦人墓，绝大多数为竖井墓道侧向或顺向洞室墓；墓地分南北两区，北区为战国晚期小型墓，排列密集有序，葬式多为屈肢葬，南区分布有属秦至西汉初的较大型的围沟墓和积石墓；出土有铜蒜头壶、鍪等较为典型的秦文化器物。南阳百里奚路西汉墓是近年来河南省境内少见的汉墓考古发现，在其中一座墓道朝南的墓葬中出土了一具保存较为完好的彩绘漆棺，棺的外侧四周分别在黑漆上用红白色彩绘出朱雀（北）、玄武（南）、白虎（东）、青龙（西）的图案，棺盖上绘有阳乌和蟾蜍，四周填绘卷云纹。2005年以来，对洛阳东汉帝陵及其陵园遗址开展了大规模的考古调查勘探工作，并对北陵区朱仓M722、南陵区百草坡村M1030帝陵陵园进行了考古发掘，确认了东汉帝陵的分布及基本特征，对东汉帝陵陵园布局有了较为清晰的认识。

## 六、魏晋南北朝

魏晋南北朝考古重要的发现主要有洛阳西朱村曹魏帝后级大墓和洛阳汉魏故城太极殿遗址。2015年在洛阳西朱村发现两座东西排列的大型墓葬（M1、M2），并对其中的M1进行了抢救性考古发掘。该墓由墓道、甬道、前室、后室组成，长斜坡墓道西向，砖券墓室前室砖壁上残存有人物、瑞兽、宴饮、祥云等壁画。在所见的随葬器物中，较为独特的是出土了数量较多的铭刻石牌，这些石牌的尺寸、书体、格式、内容等与曹操高陵出土的石牌高度一致。2012年以来，随着对洛阳北魏宫城太极殿及宫院的考古勘探系统而全面的展开，以及对太极殿遗址东半部的较大规模的考古发掘，对太极殿和两侧东西宫殿建筑群的平面布局及殿基形制、规模有了明确的认识，确认宫殿群始建于曹魏，北魏和北周等时期相继增修和沿用。

## 七、隋唐宋金元明时期

近年河南隋唐时期考古工作主要是围绕丝绸之路和中国大运河"申遗"而进行的，较为重要的是对同属地下储粮仓窖的隋代回洛仓与黎阳仓的考古勘探与发掘。回洛仓与黎阳仓两座仓城均由仓城城墙、仓窖、道路、漕渠、管理区等组成。黎阳仓是依托大运河而建的具中转性质的大型官仓，仓窖口大而较浅，便于粮食的储备与转运。回洛仓属于为都城提供战略储备和最终消费的超大型官仓，仓窖大而深，容量更大，数量更多。

北宋时期的考古工作除了对宝丰清凉寺遗址、汝州张公巷遗址等瓷窑址持续进行考古发掘外，最重要的是第一次大规模对北宋东京城外城西墙正门——顺天门遗址进行了考古发掘，确认了顺天门的形制、规模、基础建筑方法及其瓮城的平面布局等内涵。

河南省金元明清时期考古工作在配合基本建设工作中较前有了突破和重要发现，除了在开封城内不断发现明代建筑遗址外，还完成了禹州神垕镇瓷窑遗址和荥阳明代周懿王壁画墓的发掘。

在七年间，河南的考古工作紧紧围绕全省的经济建设、文化建设大局而开展，在中国考古学进入全面快速发展的背景下，取得了丰硕成果，为社会发展和学科发展做出了应有的贡献。

河南省文物考古研究院院长

2018年10月

# 2011—2017年山东省考古发现的主要收获

2011—2017年，基本建设中的文物保护工作仍然是山东考古工作的重心和主要任务，国家考古遗址公园、大遗址保护、课题性考古等主动性工作日渐成为新的重点和亮点，且均取得重要收获。

## 一、旧石器时代考古开启新篇章

自20世纪以来，山东地区的旧石器工作开展较少，且多为零星的地面调查。但自2011年以来，多家科研机构联合工作，调查了日照沿海、莱西与平度大沽河流域、沂沭河流域等区域，新发现多处旧石器地点，确认旧石器时代晚期胶东丘陵及东部沿海地区有古人类活动，并了解了该时期遗存的分布特点，填补了旧石器遗存分布的区域性空白。在德州确认旧石器遗存的存在。发掘了日照黄泥梁、胶南大珠山、临沂凤凰岭三处遗址，较重要的是均找到了旧石器晚期原生文化堆积，这对以往山东地区已知旧石器遗存信息多来自地表采集而言，在发现和认识上均属重要突破。黄泥梁和大珠山遗址均属北方石片工业系统，凤凰岭遗址属细石器文化系统，大珠山遗址测年距今6万～5万年，凤凰岭遗址测年距今1.9万～1.5万年，黄泥梁遗址时代当晚于大珠山遗址。

## 二、新石器时代考古突破和深化

### （一）新石器早期文化探索取得新进展

山东新石器时代后李—北辛—大汶口—龙山文化的发展谱系在20世纪90年代初建成，但新石器时代早期仍有缺环，而沂源扁扁洞遗存的发现则填补了这一段空白。扁扁洞遗址测年为距今9800～9600年，是一处典型的新石器早期洞穴遗址。另外，在沂源县通过调查又发现两座类似洞穴遗址，均见石制品和陶片；济南张马屯发现的房基测年距今9200～9000年，出土平底陶器，同类遗存还见于临淄锡腊营、诸城陆吉庄子。上述发现，为探索山东新石器时代文化的起源及早期发展提供了重要线索，同时对研究旧石器向新石器时代文化的过渡也具有重要意义。

### （二）大汶口文化阶段聚落与社会的认识进一步深化

考古遗址公园的建设和有关课题的连续开展，使得同一遗址得以多年大范围揭露，这为深入认识聚落形态及其反映的社会状况提供了重要契机。在大汶口遗址中揭露了两个居住区的20多座房基，该居住区布局明显经过规划，但房基规模大小有别，居住区间也有差别，显示出中心性聚落内部社会成员间的分化及社会的复杂性；即墨北阡大汶口文化早期聚落基本被全面揭露，该聚落的格局是以两个相邻的小广场为中心，100多座房基和197座墓葬围绕广场分布，是目前所获资料最丰富、最完整的大汶口文化阶段的聚落资料；章丘焦家遗址是大汶口文化中晚期泰山北侧的中心性聚落，由于这次发现取得了自20世纪发掘泰安大汶口遗址以来大汶口文化阶段最重要的考古新收获，为认识黄河下游史前社会的转变及复杂化的程度，提供了前所未有的新资料，入选"2017年度全国十大考古新发现"。

### 三、夏商周考古多项突破性发现改变了固有认识

（一）岳石文化城址和环壕聚落

岳石文化两处城址、一处环壕聚落的发现，是近年山东考古工作的重要亮点。在章丘城子崖遗址发现存在着两周岳石文化城墙，应为岳石文化时期的区域性中心；定陶十里铺北遗址为一座新发现的小城址，虽然规模不大，但由于地处东西方文化交会的鲁西南地区，彰显了以岳石文化为代表的东方势力在夏商时期各种力量东西对峙、南北交会背景中的影响力和控制力；章丘榆林遗址属城子崖遗址聚落群内二级环壕聚落，对于认识城子崖聚落群的地位及内部的社会结构具有重要价值。上述发现，有助于改变以往有关岳石文化衰落和社会不发达的认识，其在华夏文明形成中地位和作用有待深入研究。

（二）商代城址与墓葬

商代考古的两项突出成就就是在齐国腹心及鲁西南地区分别发现商代晚期的小城。临淄小范家是山东省发现的首座商代城址，北距齐故城约2.8千米，为探讨商代晚期的央地关系、早期齐文化的形成和齐国早期都城提供了重要线索。定陶十里铺北商城是在岳石文化夯土墙基础上增筑而成，可能是殷商在经略东方路线上的重要据点。

济南刘家庄墓地是山东商代考古需关注的重要地点，出土多件晚商族徽铭文铜器，是一处包含不同氏族的贵族墓地。其与大辛庄间距不到10千米，但随葬陶器组合及族徽均有明显不同，二者之间的关系及所反映的晚商区域政治格局耐人寻味。

（三）周代都城考古逐步深入，大型墓葬令人瞩目

在新的工作理念和工作方法指引下，我们相继对曲阜鲁国故城、临淄齐故城开展了新一轮系统考古工作，均取得重要收获。

有关齐、鲁两座都城的始建年代一直是学界关注的首要问题，通过解剖城墙，可初步判断齐故城大城年代可早到西周中期，而鲁故城大城约建于西周晚期。对两城的宫殿区及城内局部都做

了重点勘探和发掘，廓清了齐故城10号大型宫殿建筑基址的形制、规模及年代。确认了鲁故城周公庙高地为春秋晚期—战国时期的宫城，通过勘探摸清了周公庙宫殿区基本建筑布局，揭露了一座战国时期大型夯土建筑基址。

沂水纪王崮春秋大墓是近年山东地区社会关注度最高的周代考古发现，入选"2013年度全国十大考古新发现"。墓葬位于易守难攻的崮顶，规模较大、规格较高且结构特殊，出土青铜器、玉器等各类文物近200件，仍有许多谜团待解。

### 四、汉代考古新收获精彩纷呈

近几年山东汉代考古空前繁荣。

城址考古重要收获有：确认平度即墨故城形制、规模和年代，外城墙体主要为汉代建成，近长方形，总面积约14.4平方千米；章丘平陵城内揭露一座大型回廊式夯土基址，面阔9间，进深5间，回廊外为散水和甬道，始建于西汉中晚期，沿用至东汉；邾国故城中发现秦汉时期的仓储区，在一座水井（J3）中出土了8件新莽度量衡铜器，对研究王莽托古改制和我国度量衡发展史有重要价值。

手工业考古实现了历史性突破。在章丘东平陵城发现了制铁作坊，主要由夯土地基、熔铁炉及锻炉、烘范窑、储泥池、藏铁坑等遗迹组成，其中熔铁炉10多座。临淄齐故城阚家寨遗址为战国至西汉的冶铸工场作坊，并且存在着陶窑、铜镜铸造、制铁不同作坊的区划，这是首次发现的汉代铜镜铸造作坊遗址。

在配合基本建设中清理了大量墓葬，为研究汉代基层社会提供了丰富的实物材料。在枣庄庄里水库，已完整揭露前台、前台北、沃里等墓地，墓葬数量近600座。在上述墓地附近，还发掘了相当于"里"的海子汉代聚落，该聚落与上述数处墓地为汉代基层社会的研究提供了难得的宝贵资料。青岛土山屯墓群是汉代中下层官吏的家族墓葬，出土保存完好的公文木牍、大量漆木器、丝织品等珍贵文物，为北方汉代考古所罕见。

对大型黄肠题凑汉墓——定陶王陵2号墓的发掘又取得重要进展。在封土下发现状如"覆斗形"大型版筑夯土台、墓道及阙台等遗迹，这些现象可能共同构成一座大型礼仪性建筑。如此结构的地上大型封土建筑，在国内尚属首见。

### 五、北朝以来宗教遗存的新发现

东阿大秦、烟台严因寺、济南神通寺遗址的发掘收获，则是山东宗教考古的新突破。

大秦遗址是山东地区首次完整揭露的宋代院落建筑群，据出土碑文载为北周—宋初的天齐大王行宫，曾是北魏、北齐的定国寺，唐代的兴隆寺，并出土不同时期的石造像、经幢、碑刻等大量珍贵文物。严因寺为宋代及明清时期的佛教寺院遗址，发掘清理出了宋代的塔院、明代早期位于一条南北轴线上的三座大殿基址、明晚期至清代的三处东西并列相通的院落，建筑布局紧凑有序。对神通寺的发掘共清理15座房基及相关遗迹，基本廓清了明清时期该寺庙的基本布局。

### 六、明清大运河水利设施发掘助推申遗成功

为配合南水北调东线工程及大运河"申遗"工作，我们对京杭大运河山东段河道及水工设施进行了多年的调查、勘探，并对汶上县南旺枢纽遗址、南旺柳林闸、寺前铺闸、阳谷县七级码头、东昌府区土桥闸、临清戴闸进行发掘。通过对南旺枢纽遗址的发掘，弄清了分水龙王庙建筑群的形制、规模、布局，确认了小汶河与运河交接处分水口的位置及结构，搞清了连通南旺湖与运河的邢通、常鸣两个斗门及沟通小汶河与蜀山湖的徐建口斗门的位置、结构。通过对上述四处船闸的发掘，了解到运河船闸的形制、结构、规模、建筑材料、工序基本一致，大多始建于明成化年间，清乾隆年间曾经维修过，充分体现了运河漕运设施管理建造的统一性。扎实的考古材料，为成功"申遗"提供了翔实、科学的基础资料。

山东省文物考古研究院院长 郑同修<br>
2018年10月

# 2011—2017年安徽省考古新进展

2011—2017年以来，安徽地区的考古工作仍以建设工程中的抢救性发掘为主，同时，主动性发掘项目和配合大遗址保护及国家考古遗址公园建设的考古工作也取得很大突破。主要收获有以下几个方面。

## 一、旧石器时代考古取得重大发现

2014年以来，对东至县华龙洞旧石器时代遗址的发掘，已累计发现包括1件较完整的古人类头骨化石在内的20余件古人类化石，古人类制作使用的石器及大量具有人工切割或砍砸痕迹的骨片，以及20余种脊椎动物化石。这是在中国新发现的一处重要的包含有头骨化石的直立人（猿人）化石地点，是近年中国古人类学研究取得的一项重大进展，对于探讨中国直立人的分布、演化、变异具有重要的价值。根据动物群的组成，初步判断华龙洞古人类生存时代在更新世中期，与安徽和县直立人年代接近或更早。

## 二、新石器时代考古取得重要进展

2012—2017年间发掘的淮南小孙岗遗址、蚌埠双墩遗址、淮北渠沟遗址、肥东南院遗址和定远军大古堆遗址，距今8000～6000年，特征与以往发现的宿州小山口、淮北石山子、蚌埠双墩、定远侯家寨等遗址接近，丰富了我们对安徽北部地区新石器时代较早阶段文化面貌的认识，对于理清此阶段本地区的文化谱系和文化面貌有重要意义。

通过2012年至2015年对固镇南城孜遗址的勘探发掘，发现较完整的大汶口文化聚落和丰富的龙山时代早期遗存。2016—2017年对萧县金寨遗址的发掘，揭露出一处大汶口中晚期墓地，墓地位于一处土台上，堆土为纯净的黄褐土，清理墓葬20多座，均为竖穴土坑墓，多为单人葬，少数为二人葬、三人葬、七人葬。随葬品在5～30余件不等，器物组合以鼎、豆及壶为主，另有鬶、盉、杯、背壶、罐、盆、钵、尊和纺轮等，有少量小型玉器，主要位于人骨的头部，有玉珠、小玉环、绿松石坠、玉坠、锥形器、三联璧、牙璧和耳珰等。此外，在丁家孤堆和斗鸡台遗址还发现了大量龙山文化阶段的遗存。这些新资料，对探讨黄淮地区新石器时代晚期的文化内涵、文化交流、聚落结构及文明化进程具有重要意义。

2015—2016年，在郎溪县磨盘山遗址发现了马家浜晚期、崧泽晚期—良渚早期、良渚末期—钱山漾时期三个阶段的古文化堆积，发现崧泽晚期—良渚早期阶段墓地，已清理发掘墓葬166座，随葬品以陶器、石器为主，可见少量玉器。陶器器形以壶、罐、豆、杯、鼎及纺轮为大宗，也有少量的盉、动物形异形器等。石器以锛、凿、镞为主。玉器有璜、管、蝴蝶形挂饰、璧、坠及镯等。这是在安徽省东南地区首次进行的大规模发掘，对认识该地区的史前文化面貌及其与环太湖地区古文化的联系至关重要。

### 三、夏商时代考古取得重大突破

2014—2016年，对阜南县台家寺商代遗址进行了勘探发掘，共发掘了16座商代房址，273个商代灰坑，7座商代墓葬，确定了以台家寺遗址为代表的淮河流域的商文化属于中原商文化系统。遗址的年代自早商时代晚期延续到晚商早期，其中在相当于洹北商城时期是其最为发达的时间段。发现了完整的方形围沟、奠基坑、祭祀坑及贵族墓葬，特别是大型建筑基址和铸铜作坊等重要遗迹出土的大量遗物，揭示了商代高等级贵族在淮河流域的生产、生活、埋葬的场景，是近年来安徽省考古工作取得的重大成果之一。在2012年发掘的凤阳县古堆桥、蚌埠市钓鱼台等遗址中，均发现了丰富的商代遗存，其文化面貌和年代均与台家寺遗址基本相同。

此外，2014年在寿县丁家古堆和斗鸡台遗址、2016年在肥西县武斌大墩遗址和肥东县刘墩遗址，均发现了丰富的夏代时期的遗存。2017年发掘的萧县前白遗址，发现了典型的岳石文化遗存。

上述夏商遗存的发现，对于进一步认识安徽地区夏商时代文化面貌和谱系，及其与黄河流域的文化联系具有重要意义。

### 四、瓷窑遗址考古取得良好开局

安徽现存瓷窑遗址数量众多，但以往仅限于零星的调查与试掘。2013年以来，安徽省考古研究所有计划地开展了系统的瓷窑遗址考古工作。

2013—2016年，对繁昌窑柯冲、骆冲2处地点进行发掘，发现较完整的龙窑3座及制瓷作坊，出土大量瓷器及窑具。繁昌窑产品以青白瓷为主，创烧于五代，主要烧造时代为北宋早期。其中骆冲一号龙窑内设4道隔墙，将窑室分割为5段，是我国古代分室龙窑的最早形式之一，是研究分室龙窑的起源和发展的重要资料。

2015年、2017年分别发掘了萧县欧盘窑址和白土窑址。在欧盘窑址共清理出瓷窑址6座、料池

4座、房址15座，出土器物近万件。在白土窑址共计清理出唐宋时期窑址3座、料池4座、储灰池7座、房址10座，出土文物约800件。同时，还对萧窑窑址的分布情况开展了系统调查。根据前期调查和发掘，初步判断萧窑始烧自隋唐，一直延续至宋元时期，欧盘窑址主要烧造时代为隋至盛唐时期，白土窑址则以北宋时期为主。

### 五、运河考古取得丰硕成果

运河通济渠段自西北向东南横贯安徽省境，长180多千米，绝大部分现已淤塞湮没于地下。1999年在濉溪县百善镇柳孜遗址进行的抢救性考古发掘，拉开了运河考古的序幕。2012—2013年，因运河保护和大运河申报世界文化遗产的需要，又对柳孜遗址进行了第二次发掘，揭露出34米长的一段河道，发现两岸河堤、石筑桥墩及道路等重要遗迹，发现唐代沉船8艘、宋代沉船1艘。在河道中出土唐宋时期瓷器、陶器、石器、骨器、铜器及铁器等文物1万余件。又分别在泗县、灵璧县曹苗等多处地点对运河河道与河堤进行解剖发掘，并组织对运河安徽段全线开展了详细的调查勘探。通过以上考古工作，对安徽段运河本体的情况有了比较全面的认识。

1. 通过考古勘探和发掘，已经可以准确划定安徽段运河本体的走向和具体位置，在重点保护的地段都设立了界桩和保护标志。大致上，运河线路大部分与今S303省道公路并行，部分河段还被压在公路下。运河从河南省永城市入安徽境，自西北向东南，经濉溪县铁佛、柳孜、百善、五铺、四铺，埇桥区西二铺、宿州市城区、朱仙庄、宋庙、大店，灵璧县葛店、娄庄、灵城、虞姬，泗县长沟、关庙、泗城、草庙，向东进入江苏省泗洪县。

2. 根据考古勘探发掘结果可知，早期运河河道宽约40米，两岸河堤各宽约20米，堤顶宽在13米左右。但是，河道内的泥沙淤积速度比较快，使河床不断抬高，需要不断清淤才能保证正常通航。因此，河道内会留下大量遗物和一层层泥沙，河堤也留下一次次增筑的痕迹。在淤积严重的时候，在局部河段也采取缩窄河道、加高河堤的办法以保证通航。为使不断增高的河堤能够稳固，使用了"木岸狭河"技术。即打入密集排列的木桩以加固河堤，填充泥土或沙石，木桩连接为"木岸"。这样，河床由斜坡改为陡壁，使河床束窄，水深加大，水流加快，以改善航运状况，还可起到一定的清淤效果。已解剖的河堤坡度约45°，河坡中发现有成排的、但已腐朽的木桩，纵横交错，十分密集，印证了"木岸狭河"的记载。

3. 在柳孜遗址，发现了分列于南北两岸的石筑台墩，长约14米，宽约9米，高约5米，依托河堤用石块砌筑，临水面陡直，在石块之间填充支山石并用碎土石整平，局部用白灰黏合。在北河堤外侧，还发现了约14米宽的道路，直接通达北台墩。根据种种迹象判断，这南北相对的2座石筑台墩应该是桥墩。

4. 共发现沉船10艘。唐代船8艘，其中有2艘独木舟，其余6艘为木板平底货船。宋代船2艘，均为木板平底货船。唐代货船船体修长窄狭，平头方艄，通体架设空梁，不设桅杆且无帆，其动力主要靠背纤。造船用榫钉与油灰捻缝技术相结合，列板缝线非常密实。船体结构严密、工艺精良、用材合理，反映了当时的运河漕船造船工艺的特点。

5. 发掘出土文物已超过1万件。按质地分有陶器、瓷器、铁器、铜器、石器、骨器及木器等七大类。其中瓷器数量最多，初步统计有定窑、长沙窑、吉州窑、磁州窑、建窑、钧窑、越窑、耀州窑、龙泉窑、萧窑、巩县窑、繁昌窑、景德镇窑、鹤壁集窑等，基本包含了唐宋时期南北方各主要窑口的产品，反映了因运河的开通而带来的商贸和文化交流的频繁。

安徽省文物考古研究所副所长 宫希成

2018年10月

# 2011—2017年江苏省重要考古发现与收获

近年来，江苏始终遵循探索地域文明、保护文化遗产、服务社会公众的宗旨，积极有效地开展考古工作，工作重点基于做好基本建设工程中的文物保护、建立和完善江苏考古学文化时空框架体系以及研究解决社会历史的复原与重建。2011—2017年是江苏考古发掘与研究事业迅速发展的七年，江苏考古工作者高质量地完成了一系列重要遗址和墓葬的考古发掘工作，特别是围绕考古学术课题研究、大遗址保护工程及基本建设中的文物保护等取得了一批重要成果，考古工作的社会关注度越来越高、公众参与意识不断加强，重大考古发现成为热点话题。

## 一、新石器时代考古

淮河中下游新石器时代早中期考古发掘与研究工作，在20世纪八九十年代取得较大突破，但该区域新石器时代早中期考古学文化谱系尚不十分清晰，相应年代框架尚未完全建立。2011—2017年，江苏淮河流域新石器早中期考古取得突破性进展：泗洪顺山集遗址作为同时期该区域面积最大的环壕聚落遗址，其延续时间长，文化内涵丰富，在同类遗存中具有典型代表性，为本区域该时期的考古学文化研究建立了可资参考的标尺，以顺山集遗址一、二期遗存为代表的顺山集文化，为江苏迄今发现时代最早的考古学文化，填补了淮河中下游地区史前考古学文化的空白；在泗洪赵庄遗址中所揭露出的壕沟、较高等级墓葬、大型水井、陶窑及整理的猪狗等重要遗迹，结合遗址聚落布局及整体规模，无不表明赵庄遗址所具备的区域性中心聚落属性。同时该遗址大汶口文化遗存较为单纯，少见同时期的良渚文化因素，将有助于我们更深入探讨良渚文化跨江北上之后的路线图及其与大汶口文化发生碰撞、交流、融合的时空坐标；泗洪韩井遗址是继顺山集遗址以后，在淮河中游地区发现的又一处新石器时代中期的环壕聚落，于其中发现的距今8500至8000年前的水稻田以及炭化稻、驯化小穗轴稻遗存，是迄今已知的世界最早人工稻作遗迹，为研究新石器时代中期淮河流域的生业经济，提供了不可多得的资料。沭阳万北遗址所在区域是海岱历史文化区的重要组成部分，其北辛、大汶口、岳石文化遗存的发现为更进一步认识该区域史前及夏时期文化面貌，探讨南北文化交流与融合提供了重要线索。兴化—东台蒋庄遗址是在长江以北地区首次大规模发掘的良渚文化聚落，突破了以往学术界认为良渚文化分布范围北不过长江的传统观点，对全面、深入研究良渚文明与良渚社会提供了新资料，填补了长江以北地区良渚文化考古发现的空白。

## 二、商周考古

近年来，本省的商周考古工作开展较多，可以镇江孙家村铸铜遗址和多年持续工作的苏州木渎古城为代表。镇江孙家村遗址保存较好，外侧挖有环壕，台地边缘堆筑土垣，中心位置堆筑大土台，其周边堆筑多个圆形或椭圆形小土台，出土较多的铜器及少量陶范、坩埚等与铸铜有关的器物，这为吴国青铜器找到了一处生产地，是近年来吴文化考古的一次重要发现。近年对苏州木渎古城开展了持续性的钻探、发掘和研究工作，发掘者认为古城更有可能是未构筑完成的城墙体系，是在山口处因地制宜构筑的防御设施，它利用周边的山体作为天然的城墙，从而构筑起较为完备的防御体系。城址所在区域有着复杂的发展演变过程：西周晚期—春秋早期为小型城址，春秋晚期出现了大型城址，沿用至战国时期并有所增益，而大量汉代遗存则反映了该城址或可延续到西汉时期。

## 三、秦汉考古

2011—2017年秦汉考古的重要发现以苏北地区高等级墓葬为代表。经过全面勘探与发掘，于盱眙大云山揭示出一处比较完整的西汉江都王陵园，出土了大量陶器、铜器、金银器、玉器、漆器等各类文物一万余件（套），许多文物均为首次发现，收获巨大。对徐州卧牛山M2、M3、M4等"凿山为藏"的大型横穴式崖洞墓的发掘，充实了西汉楚王陵墓考古工作成果，对西汉楚王陵墓墓主、陵墓制度等综合性研究及汉代楚国的政治、经济等诸多方面提供了极为重要的参考资料。邳州煎药庙西晋贵族墓地的发现弥补了徐州地区西晋考古的空白，使鲁南、苏南的西晋时期考古建立了地域空间上的联系，随葬品中的鹦鹉螺杯与玻璃碗显示出了海上贸易与东西方文化的交流；南方青瓷与北方酱釉瓷器的共出反映了西晋时期南方青瓷的北传，以及以南北商品的流转为代表的文化交流与融合。

## 四、六朝考古

江苏是六朝考古的重要区域。经过详细的考古工作，确认南京市栖霞区狮子冲南朝陵园为梁昭明太子萧统及其生母丁贵嫔的墓葬。墓葬、陵墙、石刻及神道同属一体，构成了一座南朝陵园，对于同时期的陵墓研究具有极为重要的学术意义。

苏州地区曾是三国孙吴政权的早期政治中心。虎丘路新村土墩考古出土文物精美且丰富，墓室体量巨大，保存基本完整，出土的"吴侯"印文砖，对于孙吴早期器物学研究、孙吴早期宗室丧葬制度研究、六朝时期考古学研究以及长江南北文化交流研究均具有重要价值。

## 五、唐宋考古

江苏的唐宋时期考古发现较为丰富，以城址和墓葬为主。

盱眙泗州城遗址是我国目前发现的唯一一座"州城"遗址。泗州城内的行政机构、文化教育机构、礼制祠祀场所、商市、居民区及军事机构等埋没于泥沙之下，因而得到了较好的保存。

镇江京口闸遗址，对于研究大运河的水工设施、运河沿岸的物质文化习俗、南北经济、运输、商贸等方面交流与沟通有着重要意义，遗址中出土的两件元代青花海水龙纹、云龙纹三足香炉，烧造工艺奇特，十分珍贵。

南京花露岗唐至五代遗址建筑群规模宏大、格局基本完整，可能与南唐时期合署办公有关，对于研究南唐时期南京历史文化具有重要的意义。

扬州隋炀帝墓是中国隋唐考古的重要发现，是中国历史上废弃帝王墓葬的难得的实物样本，印证了历史文献记载，意义非凡。

南京西天寺墓园宋墓墓葬形制为仿木结构雕砖壁画墓，与北方宋金时期的壁画墓类似，该类具有北方因素的墓葬在南京的发现，应是南迁北人的传统丧葬习俗的反映和体现，对我们了解两宋之际的南京居民构成、南北文化的交流与交融提供了极其珍贵的材料。

## 六、元明清考古

元明清时期的重要考古发现以遗址为主。

苏州太仓樊村泾遗址为元代中晚期大型院落基址及仓储遗存、居住生活基址，且道路、水系完整，建筑基址分布有序，并且出土了数以吨计、具有商品属性的瓷器，又紧邻有大元第一码头之称的"太仓港"，故推测该遗址是元朝在江南地区经营的一处以龙泉青瓷为主的瓷器贸易集散地及仓储遗存，填补了苏南地区元代大型遗址的空白。

基本摸清了明代南京清凉寺北部的总体布局，对于复原明代寺院具有重要意义；悟空禅师墓塔的发现，补充了文献记载的不足，对于探讨南唐时期清凉大道场的范围具有重要意义。

南京明代窑场遗址的发现学术价值极高：在砖上发现了丰富的铭文，为明初行政管理体制、户籍制度以及书法艺术等研究提供了重要材料；为研究南京地区、全国乃至整个东亚地区的窑业技术丰富了材料，为后续研究提供基础；疑似石构码头的石头面遗存和水系交通是该窑场整体布局的重要组成部分，大大丰富了窑场面貌和内涵。

淮安"板闸"是目前全国唯一一座木板衬底的水闸遗址，它是淮安段大运河闸运体系的重要组成部分，发挥着调节水位和疏通河道的重要作用，直到发轫于明代中期、成熟于清康乾时期的清口水利枢纽全面建成后，板闸逐渐失去了它的作用。

江苏省的考古工作随着时代发展而不断进步，课题意识逐步增强，发掘方法和出土遗迹保护技术屡屡创新，科技考古的比重逐渐增大，考古工作全盘协作的观念不断增强，工作理念也在不断转变，从单纯的考古发掘转变为与大遗址保护紧密结合，通过详尽的考古调查、勘探和考古发掘为大遗址保护规划编制提供科学有效的证据、奠定坚实可靠的基础。

今后，江苏省考古工作将继续坚持以保护文化遗产为最高要求，以争取课题为工作追求，以增强协调协作能力为具体要求，以社会的整体效益为最终目标，抓住机遇、转变理念、拓展思路、创新方法、服务社会。

江苏省考古研究所所长 林流根

2018年10月

# 搭建学术交流平台　促进考古研究发展
## ——河北省"黄淮七省考古论坛"考古发现综述

"黄淮七省考古论坛"走过了7个年头。在这七年的时间里，河北省考古工作者在省文物局的领导下，以经济建设为中心，本着"既有利于文物保护，又有利于经济建设和提高人民群众生活水平"的原则，积极主动参与国家经济建设，在做好基本建设工程考古工作的同时，突出考古工作主动性、科学性，有计划地开展考古课题研究工作，在一些学术领域取得突破，新发现一批重要考古学文化遗存。

### 一、旧石器时代考古取得新进展

泥河湾发现、命名于20世纪20年代。自1965年发现第一处旧石器遗址以来，经过50多年的持续调查、发掘，已成为我国旧石器考古的重点区域。2013—2017年，马圈沟遗址连续调查、发掘，新确认文化层9个，将同一剖面文化层的数量增至15个，时代最早的为176万年前，最晚的晚于130万年前。遗址除发现大量人工特征明显的石制品，还发现丰富动物化石。草原猛犸象除发现化石，还在文化层内发掘出脚印遗迹，能够辨识出清晰的脚趾结构，它的发现将该种猛犸象的起源时间向前推进了约50万年，并改变了过去草原猛犸象起源于欧洲的认识。

同时还开展广泛的旧石器调查，将遗址数量增至380余处；侯家窑遗址发掘，重新确认了文化遗物的埋藏类型，结合新的光释光测年结果，其时代为距今20万～16万年；扳井子、西白马营等遗址的发掘对文化层有了新的认识，新的年代测试结果确认其时代分别为8.6万年、4.5万年，并发现了多处古人类活动面；油房遗址的发掘确认了石叶技术在该遗址的存在，为探讨中西方文化交流提供了依据；蔚县、怀来的旧石器调查、发掘，则将研究扩大到外围的广大地区。

通过系列工作，构建起泥河湾盆地的旧石器文化序列，重建了古人类的演化过程，为探讨古人类的出现、演化及对环境的适应方式、生计模式、石器技术的演变等问题提供了基础资料。

### 二、新石器时代考古获得新发现

四台蒙古营遗址是我省新发现的一处新石器中期早段文化遗存，位于北方长城地带北侧蒙古高原与华北平原的交界地带。经过考古勘察试掘，发现房址4座。F1出土各类石铲9件、石斧4件、石磨盘5件、石磨棒4件以及素面筒形陶罐1件。经$^{14}$C测定，四台蒙古营遗址房址年代为距今7670～7580年。经过对石器附着植硅粉样本检测，当时主要有粟、黍、藜属和小麦族等类植物。

四台蒙古营遗址是继磁山文化之后，河北省新石器时代考古学文化的又一重大发现，出土的素面筒形陶罐和有肩石铲十分接近辽西地区的小河西文化。器表饰压印锯齿纹的大口尖底罐，目前在已知的新石器时代遗址中尚未发现，而这类器形与俄罗斯外贝加尔地区的卡林加河口、南西伯利亚阿凡纳谢沃文化普遍存在的尖底罐十分接近，为探讨我国新石器时代早期与北方草原文化的交流提供了重要线索。

### 三、夏商周考古取得新突破

为配合引黄入冀补淀工程而发掘的后白寺遗址发现了先商、早商、晚商三个时期的文化遗存。先商文化遗存包含了下七垣文化、大坨头文化、先商文化下岳各庄类型三种文化因素，为探索该地区文化内涵、三种文化因素分布范围具有重要意义。

经过勘探发掘，确认满城要庄遗址为西周早期的城址。北城垣和西城垣底部保存相对较好，南城垣底部现仅余西段，东城垣全段被现民房占压、破坏殆尽。城垣周围环绕着护城壕。要庄西周早期城址是我国商周考古的一项重要发现，将河北地区古代城址的历史提早到西周早期，填补了河北缺乏早期城址的空白。从历史背景来看，该城址很可能与西周封国甚至燕国分封等密切相关，具有重大的学术价值。

### 四、春秋战国时期考古取得新收获

行唐故郡遗址清理出墓葬37座、车马坑7座、水井50眼、灰坑520余座、窑址2座、灰沟2条及城垣1段。出土青铜、陶、金、玉石、骨角、蚌器等遗物千余件（组）。墓葬以积石墓居多，有中部置棺椁，四周砌石或顶部及四周砌石，底部及四周砌石等三种形制。部分墓葬设壁龛，龛内置器物或羊的头蹄，个别墓葬有腰坑，内置青铜器。2号车马坑东西长约20.85米、宽3.9～4.2米，车马坑内纵列摆放五辆车，辀东向，坑中部两侧各有一壁龛，龛内各殉一成年男性。五号车置于坑内最东端，未见系驾动物，车轮卸下后放置在车舆下。一至四号车为驷马独辀车，16匹马杀死后摆放在车辆系驾位置。车轮卸下扣置于车舆上。自辐条间露出的部分车舆可知各车表面有红、黑、白色漆绘装饰，三、四、五号车舆还贴饰有金箔。

故郡遗址从时空及文化内涵来看，与鲜虞、中山国关系密切。年代自春秋晚期延续至战国中晚期，为城址、墓地、居址共存，多种文化因素在此交融，强烈地反映出北方族群文化与华夏系统文化之间的融合与嬗变的过程，其考古发现与研究，填补了中山国考古及历史研究的空白。同时，为研究戎狄等北方族群的华夏化进程与中华民族多元一体格局形成，提供了极为珍贵的实物资料。

### 五、汉代考古增添新内容

在黄骅郭堤城发现110座儿童墓葬，葬具组合方式多达二十多种，年代为战国晚期至西汉早期。从目前国内的发现来看，战国、秦、汉时期的瓮棺葬主要集中发现于中国北方尤其是环渤海地区，不仅数量多而且分布密集。黄骅郭堤城发现的瓮棺葬，特色鲜明，不仅是该地区的首次发现，也是国内战国、汉时期最具代表性的瓮棺葬墓群之一，对于深入研究这一具有鲜明时代特色和地域特色的文化现象，进一步探索瓮棺葬对东北亚文化交流的深远影响，具有重要意义。

### 六、唐代考古收获新资料

曲阳田庄大墓为晚唐时期墓葬中结构最复杂、规模最大的砖筑结构墓葬。综合多方因素，墓主人应为地方节度使。据此，有学者推断该墓为范阳节度使安禄山之墓，亦有学者推断为成德军节度使李宝臣或义武军节度使王处直的儿子王都的墓葬。田庄大墓的发掘，为探索晚唐时期唐朝社会结构、意识形态、墓葬制度、物质文化、艺术成就等方面提供了重要的实物资料。

平山王母村唐代末年（904年）壁画墓，墓葬形制、仿木构建筑保存完整。其房形椁室系唐墓中的首次发现。墓中的山水画是目前我国发现最早的一幅通屏水墨山水画，填补了唐、五代、北宋时期山水画发展序列的缺环，树立了中国早期山水画的标尺。

经考古发掘证实黄骅大左庄煮盐遗址，是目前所见的北方地区最为完整的唐代制盐作坊，填补了河北地区盐业考古的空白，且从实物上佐证了黄骅地区有着上千年的盐业发展史。

对内丘步行街邢窑遗址的考古发掘不仅批量出土了隋、唐时期成组和单体窑炉，还首次出土了"官""盈"字款器物残片，证明了内丘城关窑场是"官""盈"产品的主产区，是邢窑制瓷核心所在。该考古发现被评为"全国十大考古新发现"。

### 七、辽宋金元考古扩展新领域

在开元寺南广场遗址，发现晚唐、五代、北宋、金、元、明及清等7个时期的文化遗存，出土石器、陶器、骨器、瓷器、铜器及建筑构件等可复原文物3000余件。其中晚唐、五代时期的建筑遗存，当为本次考古重要发现，为研究正定古城城市建造史、发展史提供了重要资料。

经勘探发掘，崇礼太子城遗址为一座平面为长方形的城址，从城址结构、布局，及城址内出土"尚食局"款瓷器，"内""宫""官"字款铭文砖看，并结合文献记载，推断该遗址为金代皇家行宫遗址。曾入选"2017年度全国重要考古发现"名录。

海丰镇遗址的发掘，对于研究金代瓷器的产出、交通运输以及对外贸易等都具有重要意义。同时，该遗址为研究北方海上丝绸之路的形成和发展具有举足轻重的作用。

## 八、水下考古拓宽新视野

河北省是全国11个沿海省市之一（除港澳台），大陆海岸线长487千米，岛岸线长178千米，其中秦皇岛、唐山、沧州三市濒临渤海。为做好水下文化遗产保护工作，成立河北省水下文化遗产保护机构；开展沿海水下文化遗产资源调查；与国家文物局水下文化遗产保护中心合作，对唐山东坑坨沉船进行水下重点调查。借此，河北水下文化遗产保护工作借着国家"一带一路"战略的东风，已经扬帆启航。

## 九、雄安考古迈进新时代

中共中央设立河北雄安新区，是千年大计、国家大事。为切实做好雄安新区文物保护和考古工作，全力支持新区建设，根据国家文物局、河北省文物局的部署和要求，河北省文物研究所联合中国社会科学院考古所、故宫博物院、国家博物馆等单位组成联合考古队于2017年6—12月对雄安新区全域进行了考古调查，全面掌握了雄安新区境内文物遗存总体分布情况，并对南阳遗址进行考古勘探和试掘，初步判定南阳遗址为一处战国、汉时期中型城址。为弘扬新区优秀传统文化，延续新区历史文脉，服务新区建设及发展提供了有力支撑。

河北省文物研究所在这7年的时间里，更为重要的是培养了一批年轻有为、甘于工作在第一线的考古人，是他们在推动河北考古学研究的不断深入，是他们促进河北考古研究的不断发展。同时，我们也清醒地认识到，与其他6省兄弟单位相比，我们做得还远远不够，无论从考古梯队建设、人才培养，还是考古学研究方面还相差太远，我们还没有完全融入国家考古战略体系，在河北考古领域，考古学年代序列还存在着缺环；一些地区，仍然是一片处女地，等待我们考古人去涉足；一些国内顶尖的学术课题，等待着我们去发掘研究。现在，新的起点，已经踏在我们脚下；新的征程，已经摆在我们面前，借着"黄淮七省考古论坛"的东风，让我们迈开步伐，迈向新时代，去开创河北考古新局面。

河北省文物研究所所长 张文瑞

2018年10月

# 熔古铸今　砥砺前行

## ——陕西省考古研究院 2011—2017 年考古工作述评

2011年，在河南省文物局倡议下，首届"黄淮七省考古论坛"在郑州召开，豫、鲁、皖、苏、冀、秦、晋七省联合成立"黄淮七省考古论坛"。论坛采取按省份轮值举办，集中推介年度各省的考古发现最新成果，交流学术心得，建立区域合作新机制。首轮论坛于2017年在太原顺利落下帷幕，会后七方代表一致认为，论坛运行富有成效，密切了作为中华文明形成发展核心地区——黄淮区域的考古研究联动机制，推动了学术研究和成果共享。河南文物考古研究院同人不辞劳苦，编撰2011—2017年的七省考古成果，厥功甚伟。

首届黄淮论坛我院学者提交研讨论题涉及大遗址8处10项、基本建设考古项目6项、抢救性发掘3项及主动性发掘4项，大致反映了过去七年间陕西考古的概貌：大遗址考古阶段性成果令人瞩目；基本建设考古如火如荼，重大发现层出不穷；主动性考古学术方向明确，预期目标初步实现。

田野考古工作始终是考古研究机构的立院之本。七年间，陕西考古工作者的足迹踏遍三秦大地，发现上迄旧石器，下至宋元明清，共开展考古调查、勘探、发掘工作600余项，其中发掘遗址近100处、古墓葬5000余座。这沉甸甸的数字背后凝聚着全体职工、技师辛勤努力的汗水。值此著作付梓之际，应海旺院长邀请，对过去七年间论坛提交的陕西重要考古发现与研究成果做一评述，回顾成绩，反思不足，与有荣焉。

### 一、保护与传承：大遗址考古

在国家经济逐步进入新常态的社会背景下，近年间考古工作的主要形式与十年之前相比也发生了一定变化，即主动性考古快速增加，逐渐占据更加重要的地位，成为田野考古转型发展的重要趋势。

为了顺应这种新变化，在国家文物局的大力支持和省文物局的领导下，我们及时调整工作思路，结合我省文化遗产资源丰富，大遗址数量多、面积大、种类全、等级高的特点，主动谋划、精心组织实施了一批大遗址考古和课题性考古项目。在课题的设计安排上，既考虑到每个具体项目的学术价值和意义，又兼顾到全省考古工作分布时空范围的均衡性。

本书收集史前聚落、都城或帝王陵园在内的大遗址考古项目成果10篇，涉及杨官寨、石峁、周原、秦雍城、秦咸阳城、西汉帝陵、统万城、唐代帝陵等遗址。在大遗址的考古工作实践中，针对遗址范围广、蕴含丰富、综合性强的特点，逐步摸索出"深入调查、全面勘探、精确测绘、小面积发掘"的田野工作思路，总结出了注重聚落功能区的划分与相互关系的"聚落结构调查法"、依据抽样调查原理设计的"条带式钻探法"以及能够更好地把握堆积单位状况和形成过程的"开放式发掘法"。其中，杨官寨、周原、秦雍城、秦咸阳城等项目取得突破性进展，基本厘清了聚落布局、功能区划及重要遗存分布等信息。基本完成了对西汉帝陵、唐代帝陵的勘探工作，全面掌握了陵园布局及周边重要遗存分布情况，由野外工作转入资料整理与综合研究阶段。特别值得一提的是伴随着黄淮论坛启动的石峁遗址考古工作，是"十二五"期间新增一处大遗址项目，首次确认了中国北方地区龙山晚期一处早期王国都邑，尤为引人注目。

在考古发掘过程中借助科技设备与手段，大力推广使用无人机航拍、航测、RTK测绘及GIS信息录入、三维扫描、近景及延时摄影测绘等方法，极大地提高了考古测绘的精度和资料的信息化程度，保障了全面获取古代人类与社会信息。2012年扶风姚家西周墓地的发掘就是一次成功的实践，在发掘过程中以这一思路为指导，以墓地的钻探、发掘为工作重心，还采用"条带式钻探法"钻探周边重点区域，用"聚落结构调查法"大范围调查周原遗址东部区域，基本实现了厘清墓地所在的周原遗址东部边缘区域聚落结构的总体目标。

这些主动性考古项目所获的丰富成果不仅有力地促进了中华文明起源研究、古代都城制度、古代陵寝制度等重大学术课题研究的进展，亦为文化遗产价值的评估、保护规划的制定与实施提供了科学依据和基础资料，为深入研究以及遗址保护与展示利用提供了重要基础资料，在国内乃至国际上产生了较大的影响。

## 二、探幽寻微：主动性及抢救性考古

针对热点学术问题，近年来开展了近30项主动性的课题项目，特别是之前匮乏的大遗址工作平台及工作力量薄弱的夏商、魏晋南北朝、宋元明清考古方面。本书收录的清涧辛庄遗址、长安城北渭桥遗址、唐代韩休墓、尧头明清瓷窑址调查与发掘等课题性项目就成为了陕西商代考古、汉唐长安交通系统、唐代家族墓地及明清手工业研究方面的有益补充。

抢救性考古项目也取得了较大的收获，如宝鸡石鼓山商周墓地、澄城刘家洼两周墓地等均在学术界产生了较大影响。2012年，宝鸡石鼓山村民在宅基地发现一座商周时期墓葬，我院联合地方文物部门开展抢救性发掘，并对墓葬所在区域进行全面勘探，发现并清理商周时期墓葬14座以及与墓葬年代同期的灰坑数座。该墓地是迄今所知高领袋足鬲文化圈内等级最高的墓地，入选

"2013年度全国十大考古新发现",科技手段与传统方法相结合的又一成功范例,荣获了2011—2015年度"田野考古奖三等奖"。

在开展各项抢救性考古发掘和配合基本建设考古工作的同时,并没有停留在简单的随工清理阶段,而是在考古实践中融入课题意识,将一批保存较好、学术价值较高的抢救性或配合基本建设项目培育为课题性考古项目。肇始于2016年的刘家洼两周墓地,由最初被盗而开展的抢救性发掘,到联合地市文物部门组成联合考古队对墓地进行全面勘探与抢救性发掘,直至依托刘家洼遗址建立"渭南考古基地",就是这一思路的积极探索,激发了地方政府保护文物的积极性,实现文物保护与经济发展和谐共进,推动该区域文化旅游事业和经济社会实现新的发展。

### 三、抢救与保护:基本建设考古

近年来配合基本建设而进行的考古工作日益繁重,且呈现出区域不平衡的特点。一方面,我们要做到守土尽责,提高考古工作的前瞻性和科学性,另外一方面要积极处理好文物保护与经济建设的关系,争取达到二者双赢互利。针对以往配合基本建设的考古工作大多缺乏明确学术目标的现状,提出了"基本建设考古与课题研究相结合"的思路,强调了在基本建设考古中的课题意识。要求每一个项目在组织实施前,先由业务管理部门大致根据以往考古资料对建设工程所涉区域进行分析,然后结合专业人员研究方向及相邻区域正在进行考古项目,安排项目负责人并组建发掘及文物保护队伍,使被动的基建考古融入主动的课题研究范畴,达到了"两利"的效果。

七年来,我院共开展了各类调查、发掘项目600余项,其中包括了黄韩侯铁路、宁西铁路复线、西成高铁、吴定高速、南门沟水利枢纽、大保当榆神工业移民安置、西咸新区一大批国家和省级重点建设项目,有效地保护了文化遗产,也为各类项目的顺利开展及国民经济和社会发展提供了有力的保障。例如,神木木柱柱梁遗址首次发现了陕北地区的史前环壕聚落;黄陵寨头河墓地系西北地区首次全面揭露的战国时期戎人墓地;杨凌邰城西汉铸铁作坊系目前唯一正式发掘的西汉冶铁作坊。许多发现不仅填补了学术空白,还创造了多个"首次"和"第一"。

### 四、熔古铸今 砥砺前行

近年来,我国考古事业的突飞猛进,中国考古融入了世界考古大舞台,中国力量在世界考古领域稳步崛起。陕西考古的发展也迎来了巨大变革和重要转型时期。考古发掘与研究中新技术、新方法的全面推广与使用、理念和手段的不断创新,促使田野发掘水平和质量稳步提升,重大考古新发现层出不穷,呈现出良好的发展态势和鲜明的时代特点。弹指一挥,倏忽十年。我院产生的众多考古成果也获得了国内外同行的认可,其中神木石峁遗址获得"世界重大田野考古发现", 2012年度石峁遗址,2013年度石鼓山商周墓地、长安城渭桥遗址,2015年度周原遗址,

2016年度血池秦汉祭祀遗址，2017年度杨官寨遗址等先后入选当年"全国十大考古新发现"。西汉帝陵调查、石峁遗址考古调查与发掘、凤栖原西汉家族墓地、宝鸡石鼓山、韩休墓等多个项目获得田野考古奖。

陕西考古极大地促进了陕西文化、社会、经济建设的飞跃提升，扩大了陕西在国内外的知名度。陕西因为考古发现走向世界，中国的文化遗产因为陕西的重要发现而增光添彩。随着一大批教育程度高、装备精良的考古工作者走上考古工作岗位，陕西考古发展进入了全新的阶段，其规模前所未有，田野考古出现了空前的繁荣和发展。

陕西省考古研究院院长

2018年10月

# 山西考古七年回顾

山西省位于黄河中游，是中国古代文明的重要发祥地之一。自1926年李济主持西阴考古工作以来，近百年的山西考古为中国考古学做出了突出贡献，著名的丁村遗址、侯马盟誓遗址、晋侯墓地、虞弘墓等闻名遐迩。系统的考古工作也使中华文明的进程更加具体，完整的山西考古学文化序列也更好地阐释了山西在历史上的特殊地位。从2011年始，进入了国民经济建设的"十二五"时期和"十三五"时期，到目前已有七年，其间我们工作的重点集中在三个方面：一是重大课题的主动探索，二是积极做好经济建设中的考古工作，三是及时完成被盗墓葬的抢救性文物保护工作。这七年，我们在田野考古、资料整理、文物保护、信息化建设与考古服务社会等各个方面都取得了前所未有的成绩。

## 一、人类起源与早期人类文化多样性探索

从2011年开始，为了探索早期人类起源、农业起源等重大问题，我们在芮城西侯度遗址、丁村遗址以及太行山麓的陵川县附城镇西瑶泉村后河洞和麻吉洞两处洞穴遗址开展了为期多年的考古调查与发掘，其中发现旧石器时代地点近百处。其中，丁村遗址的再发掘意义重大，极大地扩展了丁村遗址群的时空分布范围，使丁村遗址年代由旧石器时代中期扩大到旧石器时代早中晚期，形成了完整的旧石器文化序列。

## 二、文明起源与早期国家形成的探索

围绕"中华文明起源和早期发展综合研究"和"河套地区的聚落与社会研究"国家重大课题，主要对新石器时代的重要聚落和遗址开展连续的考古工作。以陶寺遗址、周家庄遗址和碧村遗址成果最为显著。

陶寺遗址经过5年的持续发掘，基本廓清了宫城城墙堆积、结构、年代、发展演变等问题，并较为全面地揭露了宫城南东门址和东南拐角处的侧门，确定了陶寺宫城基址保存较为完整，自成体系，规模宏大，形制规整，并具有突出的防御性质，是目前考古发现的中国最早的宫城。周家

庄遗址确认了遗址的北、西环壕，还在遗址中部偏东南区域进行了大规模发掘。从聚落形态的角度看，周家庄遗址在晚期形成一处大型中心聚落。碧村遗址与陕西石峁遗址隔河相望，是龙山时代晚期一处规模较大的石城聚落，作为国家文物局"十三五"期间重大课题之一，近年通过大量的考古工作，已经明确了碧村周边史前遗存的空间分布信息与聚落结构。这些都为早期文明起源与国家形成提供了重要的资料。

### 三、商周方国考古

2017年启动的闻喜酒务头墓地发掘，是晋南地区晚商考古的重大突破。该墓地共发现晚商时期墓葬12座，其中甲字形大墓5座，中小型墓葬7座，车马坑6座。特别是其中一座甲字形大墓未遭盗扰，发掘出土各类青铜器123件，证实这里是一处晚商时期侯伯一级的墓地，为深入研究殷墟时期政治地理格局提供了极为重要的考古资料。

自绛县横水墓地、黎城西关墓地、翼城大河口墓地发现后，山西西周时期封国考古成为近年山西商周考古工作的重点。七年工作主要是对翼城大河口墓地进行持续性发掘、绛县雎村墓地抢救性发掘、长子西南呈墓地开展抢救性发掘。2011年至2016年，对翼城大河口墓地进行了持续性考古发掘，彻底搞清了墓地的范围和分布状况。2015年至2017年，对绛县卫庄镇雎村墓地进行了大规模的考古发掘工作，共清理墓葬854座，这是新发现的西周方国墓地。

### 四、晋文化考古

由于盗墓频发，2014年开始对襄汾陶寺北两周墓地开展抢救性发掘。这个墓地是晋文化的重要墓地，位于陶寺村北约800米处。到目前为止，已发掘春秋时期竖穴土坑墓葬186座，其中的墓祭遗存、丧葬遗迹、保存较完整的"荒帷"遗迹等，是研究晋国及晋文化的重要资料。洪洞县广胜寺镇南秦村南秦墓地也是因屡次发生盗掘古墓行为而进行抢救性发掘的，尽管发掘面积不大，但南秦墓地反映了该地区不同时期、不同种群、不同阶层人类的生活情况，是一处历时久长、内涵丰富、保存较为完整的大型墓地，对研究晋南地区不同时期的埋葬制度、人群族属、社会生活等提供了新的资料。

另外，因经济建设而发掘的多个墓地与遗址也对晋文化研究有所贡献。2014年9月到2015年7月间，在侯马市冶炼厂新月小区建设中，对晋国都城遗址中的虒祁遗址进行了第九次发掘，该遗址的发掘为研究晋都新田废弃前后的文化发展提供了极为珍贵的资料；2017年，在太焦高铁建设中，榆社县河峪乡西周村西南发掘偶尔坪遗址，这个遗址时代上从战国早期延续到晚期，推测与春秋战国时期晋国的"涅氏"有关。

## 五、匈奴考古

匈奴考古是近年来汉代考古的重要方向，中国境内发现的西汉匈奴墓，有陕西长安客省庄、铜川枣庙、宁夏同心倒墩子、内蒙古伊克昭盟补洞沟、西沟畔墓地等。2016年底2017年初，在配合基本建设过程中，黄河东岸的山西蒲县曹家庄发掘墓葬42座，其中有18座西汉晚期（汉武帝以后）的匈奴人墓葬。这批匈奴墓，应是匈奴首领被俘后，被汉武帝封为"骐侯"，于封地"骐县"所留下的遗存，是目前识别出的最早的一批南匈奴墓葬，是近年来我国匈奴考古的重要收获。

## 六、手工业考古

手工业考古是考古学的重要组成部分，研究古代社会离不开手工业考古。近几年，我们主要对青铜器生产的原料产地和陶瓷生产作坊进行了考古调查与发掘。首先是开展了"中条山地古代矿冶遗址遥感考古调查与研究"项目。2011年9月至2012年8月对闻喜千金耙矿冶遗址进行了抢救性考古发掘，该遗址的发现初次为含高放射性成因铅的早期青铜器找到了一处原料产地。随后，在2016年3月至9月，对晋南地区宋金时期重要的烧瓷窑场之一——河津固镇窑址进行了抢救性发掘。该窑址发掘，是山西乃至全国陶瓷考古的一次重要突破，入选"2016年度全国十大考古新发现"。

## 七、建筑与城市考古

建筑与城市考古是2011年以来我所主动性考古项目中的重点，经过七年的田野工作，取得了一些重要成果。晋阳古城和蒲州故城的发掘，是国家大遗址保护和国家考古遗址公园建设的重要内容，通过考古工作，对这两个城市的布局有了一定的认识，使城市的沿革更加清晰，为国家考古遗址公园的建设提供了重要的资料。

值得一提的是，为配合云冈石窟窟顶防渗水工程，2011年，在云冈石窟窟顶发掘了一处北魏至辽金的建筑遗址及辽金铸造场所，本次考古发现被评为"2011年度全国十大考古新发现"，有助于了解北魏前期云冈寺院的布局和范围。

## 八、北朝至明清墓葬抢救性发掘

忻州九原岗北朝壁画墓位于忻州市忻府区兰村乡下社村东北，共清理壁画240余平方米，出土大量陶俑残片、陶器等，墓主人身份显赫、位高权重，其年代应是东魏至北齐早期。

该墓壁画面积较大，内涵极为丰富，许多题材在同时期墓葬壁画中属首次发现，是研究北朝社会生活、历史文化和军事制度等方面的珍贵材料。万荣西思雅北魏薛怀吉墓葬的发掘，是太原以南发现的规模最大、等级最高的北朝墓葬，为研究北魏晚期的墓葬制度、社会历史具有重要意义。除此以外，为配合"太原市铁路枢纽西南环工程"的建设，在太原开化村清理汉代墓葬26座，北齐墓葬21座。对临汾三星凤凰府项目建设施工范围内的西赵遗址12座唐墓进行了发掘。以上这些北朝至唐代墓葬的发掘，揭示了不同地区、不同时代的墓葬埋葬习惯和丧葬礼俗，为研究当时社会增添了重要资料。

宋金以后的考古发掘也有一定的特色。主要有以下几个墓地。一是在昔阳县发掘了7座宋金时期仿木构砖室墓葬，填补了这一时期墓葬资料的空白，为研究宋金时期墓葬提供了宝贵的资料。二是汾西郝家沟金代纪年壁画墓，墓主葬于金大定二十二年（1182年），是临汾北部山区首次发现的金代纪年壁画墓，为金墓断代研究又提供了一座标尺型墓葬。三是长治县沙峪村宋至明清古墓群，此次发掘所获取的墓葬形制结构、随葬品，以及随葬品的制作工艺等综合信息，为研究上党地区宋、明、清时期的生产力发展水平、生活方式等提供了宝贵的实物资料。

在紧张的田野工作之余，我们还完成了积压考古报告的整理和出版，主要有《清凉寺史前墓地》《汾阳东龙观宋金壁画墓》《长治分水岭东周墓地》《晋西商代青铜器》等20余部，发表简报与学术论文300余篇。同时，我们在文物保护、科技考古、遗址保护规划、考古传播等方面也有突出成绩，如较早地成立了考古数字化团队，配置了最先进的设备，形成了全方位的信息交换与共享，完成了众多重大课题；保护规划重视特色与深度研究，使学术研究与社会实用密切结合；创建了"考古汇"新媒体平台，获得社会强烈反响，考古公益性越来越强，服务社会的能力显著提高。

当然，尽管我们取得很多显著成果，但是相比较国内同行，我们还有很多不足。在未来的考古工作中，我们会秉承考古大志，吸取教训，革故鼎新，把山西考古推向一个新的高度。

山西省考古研究所所长

2018年10月

# 人类的演化

约在45亿年前宇宙爆炸，地球横空出世！经过数亿年的演化，这颗星球出现了海洋生命，尽管只是单细胞生物，但之后地球上的一切生命，皆与之密切相关。

那么，现今居于生物链顶端的人类，尤其是处于欧亚大陆东面的中国版图的黄淮流域，其间的人类是如何起源、如何演化，如何拥有独特的文化，如何由聚落发展至集权制国家的？

1929年，裴文中先生在北京房山区周口店龙骨山下发现的一颗保存完整的猿人头盖骨化石，成为人类栖居亚洲的直接证据。

冀西北保存丰富第四纪地层堆积的泥河湾盆地得到中外学者广泛关注，学者纷至沓来，寻找人类生活的证据。他们虽然没有得到上天的眷顾，与人类化石或遗物擦肩而过，但这些科学探索，将泥河湾呈现在世人面前。1965年，发现第一处旧石器遗址，揭开了泥河湾盆地旧石器考古的序幕。几十年来，学者们在这个盆地先后发现了一批旧石器时代遗址，其中的马圈沟遗址被普遍认为是东亚地区早期人类生存之地，其生物地层学显示它的年代在距今200万年前后，其后的考古学序列完整，石器面貌展现了北方石器工业的特征，并在200多万年的历史长河里贯穿始终。

有关人类的进化，不仅仅体现在泥河湾盆地的马圈沟、虎头梁，在泾渭流域、黄淮平原，旧石器遗址随着时间的推进呈现出逐渐增多的趋势，而且遗存也愈加丰富。当我们以一种宏观的、区域性的视角多方审视这些分散零碎的遗址时，就会发现随着时间、环境的变化，这些遗址由点成线，由线成片，居于其间的古人类最终跨越了人类演化过程中的关键点，进化成为了地球上的主宰，同时也开启了新石器时代的历程。

# 自古在昔　先民有作

## 河北阳原泥河湾盆地马圈沟早更新世旧石器时代遗址群

◎ 刘连强　王法岗

马圈沟遗址位于河北阳原县大田洼乡岑家湾村西南约1千米处，泥河湾盆地东缘、马圈沟的南段。遗址发现于1992年，通过以往的工作，确认了马圈沟第Ⅰ～Ⅵ文化层，连同剖面上部1990年发现的半山遗址，该区域有7个文化层得到确认，时代最早者距今175万年，最晚的距今134万年，成为东亚地区最重要的早更新世遗址群。

2014年，河北省文物研究所在2005年发掘C区探方北侧的Ⅵ层以下近1米处，发现了第Ⅶ文化层的存在，这也是泥河湾盆地目前已确认的层位最低的古人类文化遗存。同时，在D区发掘29平方米，在第Ⅰ文化层和半山遗址文化层之间确认两个新文化层：马圈沟遗址Ⅰa、Ⅰb文化层。

2016年，在鱼咀沟1号地点进行了发掘，又新发现第Ⅲ文化层、第Ⅴ文化层。

2017年，对鱼咀沟2号地点进行了发掘，共发现4个文化层，第Ⅳ文化层为主文化层，层位与半山遗址相同。新发现鱼咀沟第Ⅰ～Ⅲ文化层。

该遗址群的7个发掘点皆分布于马圈沟内，处于同一剖面，地层早晚关系清晰，该区域得到确认的古人类文化遗存有15层，由早及晚依次为：马圈沟遗址第Ⅶ、第Ⅵ、第Ⅴ、第Ⅳ、第Ⅲ、第Ⅱ，鱼咀沟1号地点第Ⅴ，马圈沟遗址第Ⅰ（鱼咀沟1号地点第Ⅳ），鱼咀沟1号地点第Ⅲ，马圈沟遗址Ⅰa（鱼咀沟1号地点第Ⅱ），马圈沟遗址Ⅰb（鱼咀沟1号地点第Ⅰ），半山遗址（鱼咀沟2号地点第Ⅳ），鱼咀沟2号地点第Ⅲ、第Ⅱ、第Ⅰ文化层。

马圈沟遗址群地点多，层位关系清晰，延续时间长，文化遗物丰富，石制品人工特征明确，基本建立起早更新世中晚期古人类演化的文化序列。证明早更新世中晚期古人类反复在该区域活动，是早期人类在华北地区出现、演化的直接证据，为研究早期人类在东亚地区的出现、演化、扩散等问题提供了实物资料，为研究东亚地区早期人类的石器技术、行为模式提供了直接材料。

马圈沟遗址群分布图（上为西）

鱼咀沟2号地点发掘平面（上为北）

鱼咀沟2号地点剖面及出土遗物（北—南）

鱼咀沟1号地点剖面（西南—东北）及出土遗物

马圈沟Ⅰb文化层石片

马圈沟第Ⅶ文化层化石

马圈沟第Ⅶ文化层石制品

Majuangou Site was discovered in 1992 and has experienced continuous archaeological surveys and excavations carried out by archaeologists from Hebei Provincial Institute of Cultural Relics. By 2017, the total excavated area had exceeded 500 square meters and the sum of unearthed objects, mainly stone artifacts and animal fossils, was over 7000.

As sites complex, Majuangou is featured with numerous densely distributed spots, rich cultural layers, clear stratigraphic relations, and long time span (1.75 million to 1.34 million years ago). Abundant cultural remains and stone objects with apparent artificial traits were recovered. Based on the discoveries, its cultural sequence of hominid evolution in the middle and late phases of early Pleistocene Period has been established. It proves that there were repeated human activities in this area at that time, providing direct evidence for the emergence and evolution of ancient humans in North China.

# 河北阳原泥河湾盆地马梁—后沟中更新世旧石器时代遗址群

◎ 王法岗

马梁—后沟遗址位于河北阳原县大田洼乡东谷坨村北200米处，泥河湾盆地的东缘，分布于一条南北向冲沟（后沟）东西两侧的梁上（西侧为马梁）。该区域发育了丰富的中更新世泥河湾层堆积，其中埋藏有丰富的旧石器时代文化遗物，马梁遗址埋藏于B-M界限（78万年）以下约1米的地层内，后沟遗址埋藏于泥河湾层的顶部，三棵树遗址则埋藏于马梁遗址与后沟遗址中间的位置。

2013年以来，河北省启动东方人类探源工程，马梁—后沟一带是建立完善泥河湾盆地中更新世古人类演化序列的重点工作区域。数年来，河北省文物研究所持续在该区域开展旧石器专题调查，先后发现旧石器时代遗址20余处，获得了准确的完整地层剖面，发现一批石制品、动物化石，确认该区域为中更新世古人类活动频繁的重要区域。

依古地磁测年结果显示：剖面下部的马梁遗址（ML），年代接近于79万年；剖面顶部后沟遗址（HG）的年代为39.5万年，与光释光测得的36万年的结果较为接近，基本可以反映该剖面下部、顶部的年代。依据周围地层的对比及古地磁测年数据，最下部的马梁8号地点时代可能在80万～90万年，马梁6号地点、5号地点接近于B-M界限，在78万年前后，ML3、HG5（ML2）、SKS、HG则在上述年代之间。依据该区域相近剖面泥河湾层顶部与上覆地层之间接近20万年的沉积间断推测，马梁6号地点的时代则接近20万年。

该遗址群始于早更新世之末，结束于中更新世之末，贯穿整个中更新世，基本建立起泥河湾盆地中更新世古人类演化的文化序列，证明在东亚地区中更新世古人类的演化具有很强的连续性，展现了中更新世旧石器考古的巨大潜力。

马梁—后沟遗址远景及文化序列

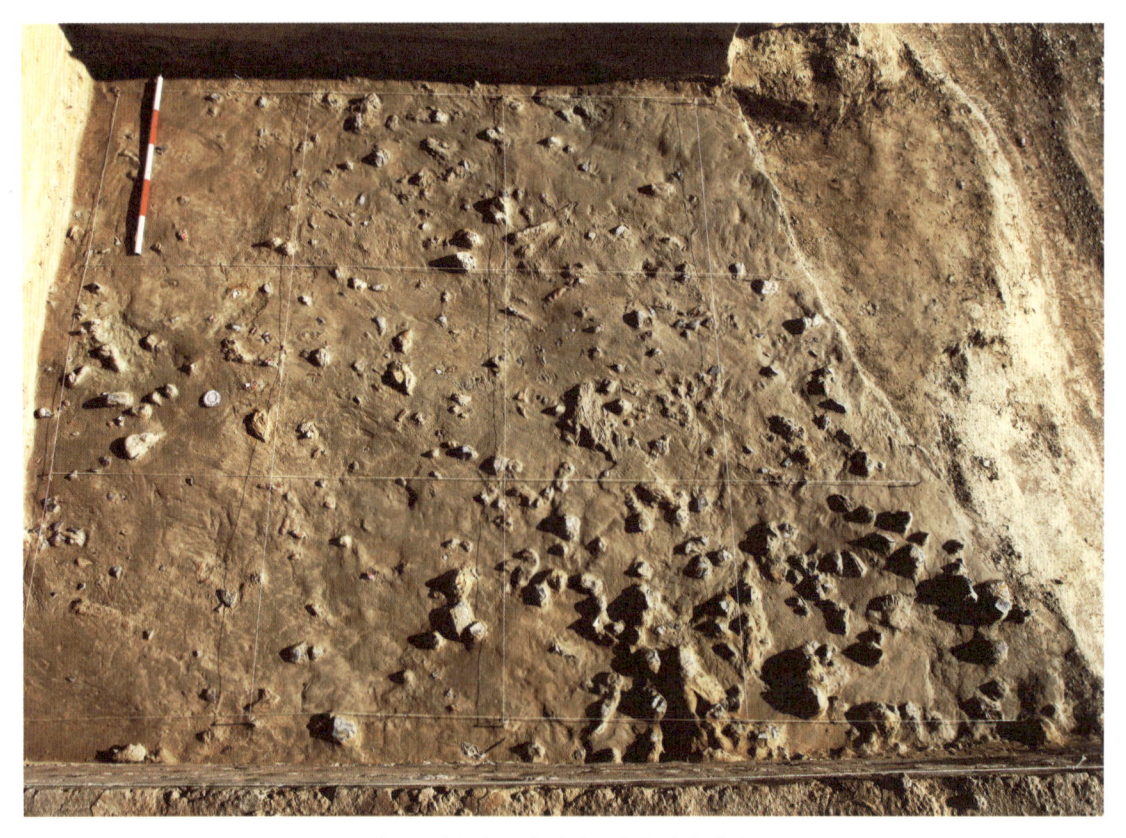

后沟5号地点古人类活动面全景（上为北）

后沟8号地点（西—东）
及出土石制品

马梁10号地点（南—北）
及出土石制品

后沟5号地点动物化石

后沟5号地点石制品

后沟8号地点石制品及动物化石

In 2013, a project, aiming to trace the origin of ancient human in the East, was initiated in Hebei Province and has been carried out since then. In the northern area of Maliang-Hougou in Donggutuo Village, Datianwa Township, Yangyuan County, archaeologists from Hebei Provincial Institute of Cultural Relics continuously conducted paleolithic investigations and test excavations, confirming more than 20 paleolithic sites, discovering a batch of stone implements and animal fossils, and revealing an accurate and complete stratigraphic section.

Maliang-Hougou sites complex started in the final phase of early Pleistocene Period, existed throughout middle Pleistocene Period, and ended in the last phase of middle Pleistocene Period. Numerous sites, continuous cultural layers and abundant cultural remains all illustrate that this area witnessed frequent human activities in middle Pleistocene Period. The basically established cultural sequence of hominid evolution in Nihewan Basin in middle Pleistocene Period proves that hominid evolution in East Asia had a strong continuity and displays the great potential of archaeological work concerning middle Pleistocene Period in Paleolithic Age.

# 河南栾川孙家洞旧石器时代遗址

◎顾雪军

孙家洞旧石器遗址位于栾川县栾川乡湾滩村哼呼崖的断崖上，北边紧邻伊河。原有洞口朝北，呈扁长形椭圆状，宽2.65米，高0.70米。

2012年洛阳市文物考古研究院联合栾川县文物管理所对该洞穴进行了抢救性考古发掘，发掘位置在距离现在进出的洞口约10米处，发掘面积约有3平方米，深4.60米左右，厚度为0.50～1.80米，方向320°。发掘出土遗物包括动物化石、石制品、人牙化石等。

孙家洞遗址出土的石制品较少，类型简单，主要包括石核、石片和断块，未见到有加工成器的石制品。石核有单台面石核、双台面石核、盘状石核和砸击石核，石片有远端断片和裂片。石制品原料以脉石英为主，打片方法以锤击法为主，仅发现一件砸击制品。

该遗址出土了上万件动物骨骼，这些化石主要属于中国鬣狗、熊、大熊猫、狼、獾、貘、肿骨大角鹿、葛氏斑鹿、李氏野猪、牛、梅氏犀以及豪猪、竹鼠、刺猬等小哺乳类。

另外，在孙家洞遗址内还发现了古人类牙齿化石，经过鉴定包括门齿、臼齿及颌骨残块，从牙齿发育看存在幼年个体；从牙齿大小和形态看，有不同于现代人的原始特征。

经初步测定，孙家洞遗址的年代为距今40万年左右，是中国新近发现的一个重要的旧石器时代早期遗址。出土的古人类化石，是河南省境内首次在考古发掘中有明确出土地层的中更新世时期古人类牙齿化石，对于研究人类起源及演化有着重要的科学意义。该遗址的动物化石非常丰富，对于研究中国中更新世时期该过渡区域动物群的种类及特征有着重要的作用，同时为动物地理区系演化及古气候环境变迁提供了重要的信息。

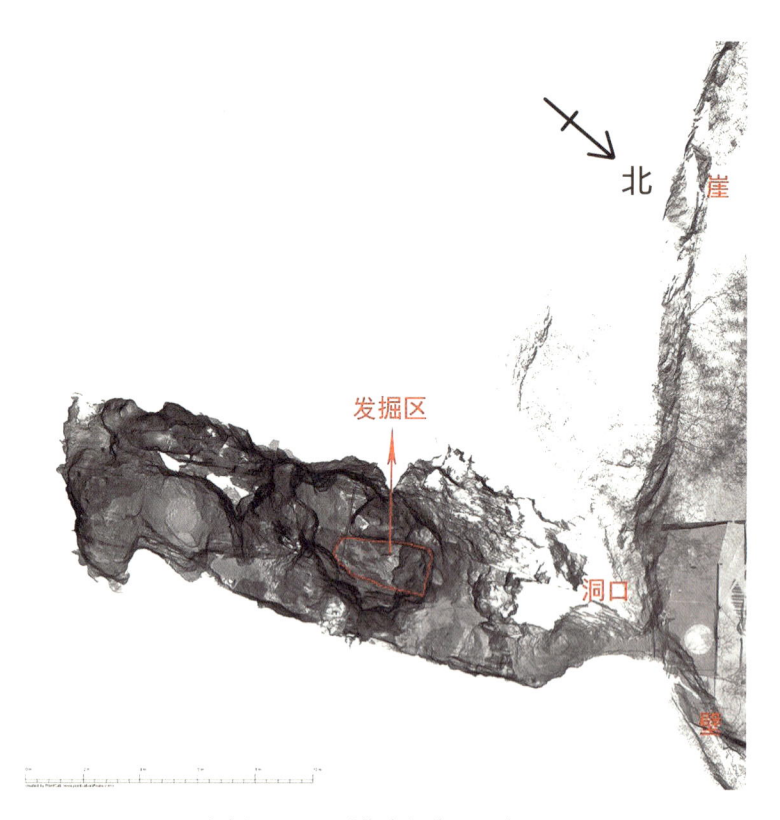

孙家洞旧石器时代发掘位置示意图

地层堆积

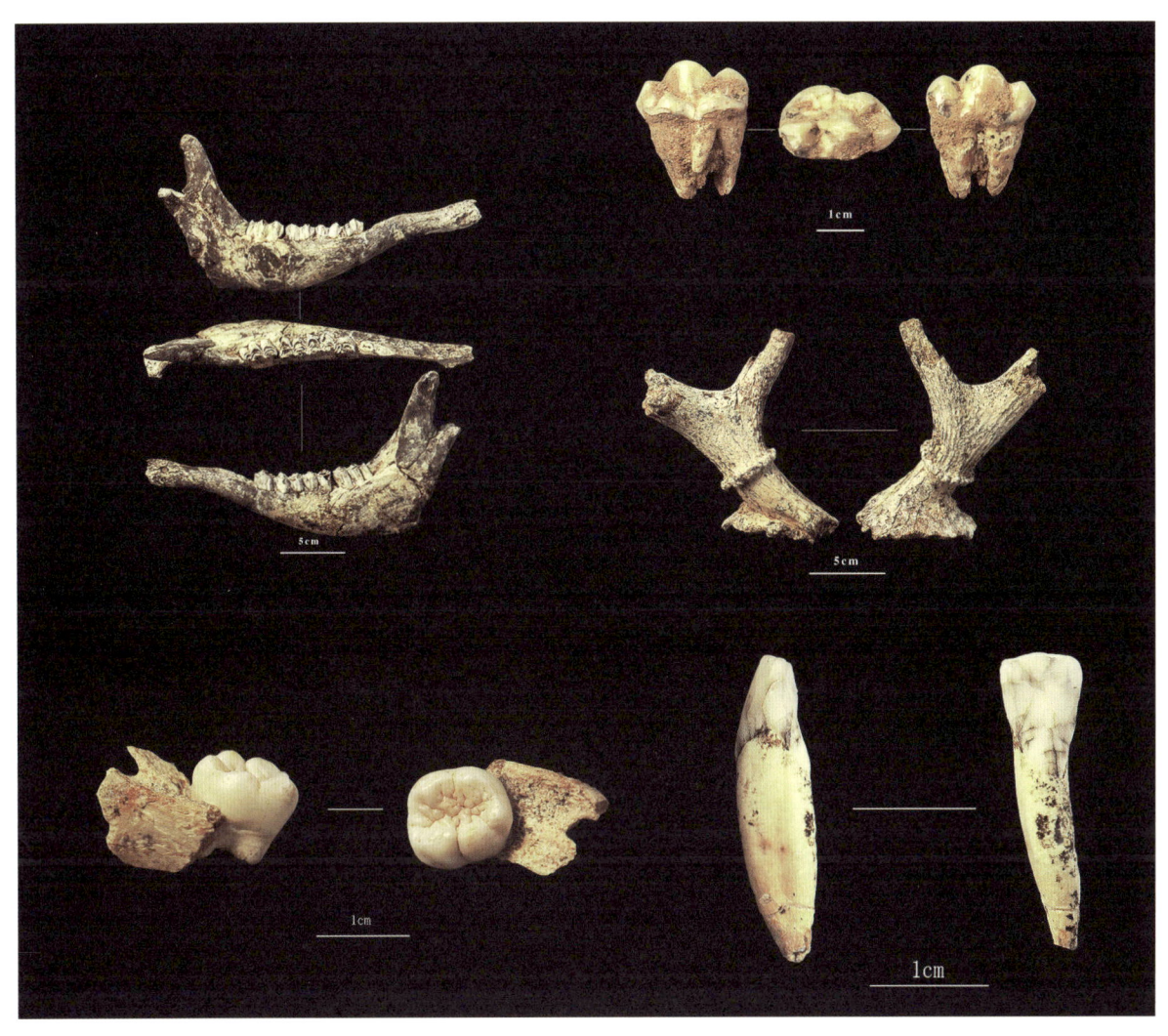

出土化石

Sunjiadong Paleolithic Site is located on an escarpment of Henghu Cliff in Wantan Village, Luanchuan Township in Luanchuan County. In 2012, a salvage archaeological excavation was carried out in this cave site, unearthing objects including animal fossils, stone implements, fossils of human teeth, etc. Dating tests results proved that the site, a significant one of early Paleolithic Age, formed and developed around 400,000 years ago.

It was for the first time in Henan Province that archaeologists discovered fossilized human teeth, which were of mid-Pleistocene Period and whose stratal position could be accurately determined. This discovery is of great scientific value for the study of the origin and evolution of human beings. Meanwhile, the great number of excavated animal fossils play an important role in researching species and characteristics of fauna in this transitional region in mid-Pleistocene Period and simultaneously contribute important information to studying geographical evolution of the fauna and ancient climate changes.

# 山西襄汾丁村旧石器时代遗址群

◎袁文明　王益人

2011—2017年对襄汾丁村遗址群进行的调查发掘，是丁村遗址发现以来的第三次大规模田野调查发掘。

2012年年底，在柴庄对岸的石沟村采沙场发现一块人类枕骨化石。2014年在老虎坡遗址中首次发现人类活动的遗迹。2015年以来，我们对丁村遗址群东部约40平方千米的黄土台塬进行了跨年度分区域考古调查，结果显示：丁村遗址群不仅局限于汾河河谷地带，遗址东侧塔儿山向汾河谷地过渡的山前台塬区，亦是丁村远古人类的重要活动区。

2013—2017年，山西省考古研究所与丁村民俗博物馆、襄汾县博物馆先后对襄汾石沟遗址、老虎坡遗址、过水洞遗址、九龙洞遗址和洞门遗址进行了连续发掘，收获颇丰。石沟遗址发现地震裂缝遗迹，以及数量丰富的石制品和动物化石。九龙洞遗址在不同层位连续发现多个石器打制现场以及用火遗迹等重要遗迹现象，表明九龙洞遗址是丁村人进行原料采集、石器打制、食物分享等活动的重要场所。2015年在对老虎坡遗址的发掘中，发现在同一平面上密集分布着200余件角页岩和花岗岩砾石，其分布显示出了一定的结构，疑为有意识建造的"营地"或石铺地面。并于该层中发现数个石制品拼合组，显示了人类在此进行石器打制并从事了一定的生产活动，为我们认识10万年前的丁村人生存模式提供了新材料、新视角。在过水洞遗址中则发现了大量动物化石与石制品、炭堆、炭屑、红烧土块同时出现在同一水平面黄土地层中的现象，表明这里可能是一处与人类活动密切相关的临时营地。根据地层堆积判断：遗址形成年代为距今30万～20万年前。

本阶段考古工作，扩大了丁村遗址群的时空范围，空间上由汾河谷地扩展至黄土台塬区，时代上由旧石器时代中期为主扩展到旧石器时代早中晚期，形成了完整的旧石器文化序列。特别是在石沟、老虎坡、过水洞、九龙洞等遗址发现的诸如古人类化石、人工性质的"建筑遗迹"、石器制作现场、用火遗迹等重要遗物和遗迹，为研究远古丁村人的演化、生存模式、行为链条、认知能力等提供了宝贵的材料，具有重要意义。

丁村遗址群调查石制品

过水洞遗址用火遗迹

老虎坡遗址"建筑遗迹"俯瞰

九龙洞遗址石器打制现场（东—西）

九龙洞遗址石制品拼合组

For years, archaeological work concerning paleolithic Dingcun Sites has been carried out mainly in the stratified deposits on terraces along Fenhe River; while little attention has been paid to earth strata outside the terraces. On account of these facts, from 2011 to 2017, archaeologists conducted the third large-scale fieldwork and excavations at Dingcun Sites in Dingcun Village, Xiangfen County.

Numerous paleolithic sites were discovered on the loess tableland. The discovery per se greatly expands the spatial and temporal distribution of Dingcun Sites. Besides, the era, in which Dingcun Sites formed and developed, is prolonged from mere mid-Paleolithic Age to early, middle and late Paleolithic Age. As a result, Dingcun Culture turns out to be a complete paleolithic cultural series. Fossilized bones of homo sapiens, venues for stone implements making, remains of fire, artificial architectural ruins and other important objects and traces, discovered in Laohupo Site, Guoshuidong Site, Jiulongdong Site, etc., are of great significance and provide valuable materials for the study of Dingcun Man in ancient times.

# 河北阳原泥河湾盆地侯家窑旧石器时代中期遗址

◎王法岗

侯家窑遗址是指许家窑人遗址的74093地点，位于泥河湾盆地西部，河北阳原县侯家窑村西南。发现于1974年，1976、1977、1989年连续进行发掘，发现被命名为"许家窑人"的古人类化石20件，石制品、动物化石上万件。目前，对其年代分歧巨大，自不足2万年前到四五十万年前，各时期皆有。

为解决有关许家窑人年代的争议，河北省文物研究所先后多次在遗址周围区域开展专题调查，确认遗址所在的梨益沟发育了三级阶地，新发现旧石器时代遗址15处，皆分布于梨益沟的第二、三级阶地内，为正确认识侯家窑遗址年代、建立区域文化序列打下了基础。

2007—2013年连续在以往发掘区西北角开展考古发掘，发掘面积约12平方米，发掘总深度近16米，获得了完整地层剖面。共发现两个文化层，上文化层距地表深7.50～10米，发现石制品、动物化石2500余件；下文化层距地表深12.60米，厚20～30厘米，埋藏于黑色粉砂质黏土夹的粗砂层中，发现少量石制品、动物化石。在黑色粉砂质黏土之下、距地表约14.50米处发现一不整合接触面，其下为顶部被侵蚀呈高低不平、水平层理发育的黏土、粉砂质黏土，为泥河湾层。

本次发掘地层与20世纪70年代的发现在文化层深度、地层厚度、土质土色有稍许差异，但两者的地层序列、文化层分布基本一致，可以确认20世纪70年代出土的古人类化石埋藏于上文化层；文化遗物埋藏于不整合接触面之上，即形成于泥河湾层被侵蚀后形成的河流相堆积中，而非最初认定的泥河湾层。

文化遗物埋藏于泥河湾层之后的堆积中，与泥河湾层沉积时间存在未知的沉积间断，基本可以排除古地磁测年结果认为该遗址时代古老的认识。根据动物化石绝灭种为45%、人类化石属于古老型人类、铀系法测年数据、新的光释光测年序列，确认许家窑人的生存时代在距今20万～16万年之间，对解决许家窑人的演化地位、泥河湾古湖的演变过程等都具有重要价值。

侯家窑遗址2003—2013年发掘地层剖面（东—西）

Since 2003, in order to fully understand geological and geomorphological features of Xujiayao Site, to map the distribution of ancient human cultural remains and to disperse confusion caused by chronological gap concerning Xujiayao Man, archaeologists from Hebei Provincial Institute of Cultural Relics have successively carried out specific investigations on geological, geomorphological and paleolithic approach in the western part of Xujiayao Basin in which Houjiayao Site is located.

From 2007 to 2013, an unconformity contact surface, which was above the stratified deposits of Nihewan Layer and under that of the fluvial terrace layer, was confirmed 4 to 5 meters below the cultural layer. Combining archaeological work done in the 1970s, it has been further confirmed that hominin fossils were concealed in fluvial sediment, not in the primarily identified sludge of lacustrine facies in Nihewan Layer. Taking into account the geomorphological development of both banks of Liyigou River, it has been determined that fossils of Xujiayao Man were buried on the third level of river terrace. It is believed that Xujiayao Man lived about 200,000 to 160,000 years ago, the time corresponding to early oxygen-isotope stage 6.

# 河南灵井许昌人旧石器时代遗址

◎李占扬　赵清坡

灵井许昌人遗址位于河南许昌市西北约15千米的灵井镇。遗址地层为湖相沉积，面积约3万平方米。已发掘的堆积物深度为9米，自上而下堆积物可分为11层，第5层发现有细石器、早期陶片、雕刻艺术品等，$^{14}$C年代测定为距今1.3万年左右。著名的人类头骨化石"许昌人"就出自第11层T9之中，年代为距今12.5万～10.5万年。

2011年，在对第11层发掘时出土了一批具有刻划痕迹的骨片，其刻划痕和以往出土的因割肉或肢解动物遗留的痕迹有所区别。同时出土一批石器和骨器，有些种类是以往发掘未曾见到的。

在2012年度的考古发掘中，于遗址上部残存地层发现数10块泥质和夹砂的陶片，经送日本东京大学进行加速器$^{14}$C等年代测定，其年代范围在距今11,131～10,372年（经过树轮校正），这是目前已知的中原地区最早的陶器。

2013年，比较重要的收获是出土10余件精致的骨器。2014年3—5月，新出土了27块古人类头骨化石断块——"许昌人2号头骨"。骨骼多数可拼接复原。2015年5月首次发现2块古人类肢骨化石。上面残留的齿痕可能是古人类留下的。这2件古人类化石可能属同一个体。除了古人类化石，在第11层还发掘出土了1000多件哺乳动物化石和加工精美的石器。

2016年，在灵井许昌人遗址考古发掘中发现了大量石器，这些石器多用压制法制作，具有欧洲旧石器时代中期石器的特征。2017年在灵井许昌人遗址发掘9平方米，出土约4000件动物化石和石器。

经初步研究，许昌人生活时期的沉积环境经历了三个阶段，总体来看，不同阶段的考古遗存都属于水下埋藏环境。石制品的尺寸分布显示，小于2厘米的石制品所占比例最高（占全部石制品的69.5%），但仍低于模拟实验结果（87.1%），表明文化遗物经历了一定程度的筛选和搬运。化石和石制品呈现NE方向的优势长轴方向，倾角集中在0°～10°，指示遗物在形成过程中经历了低能量水流动力的扰动。

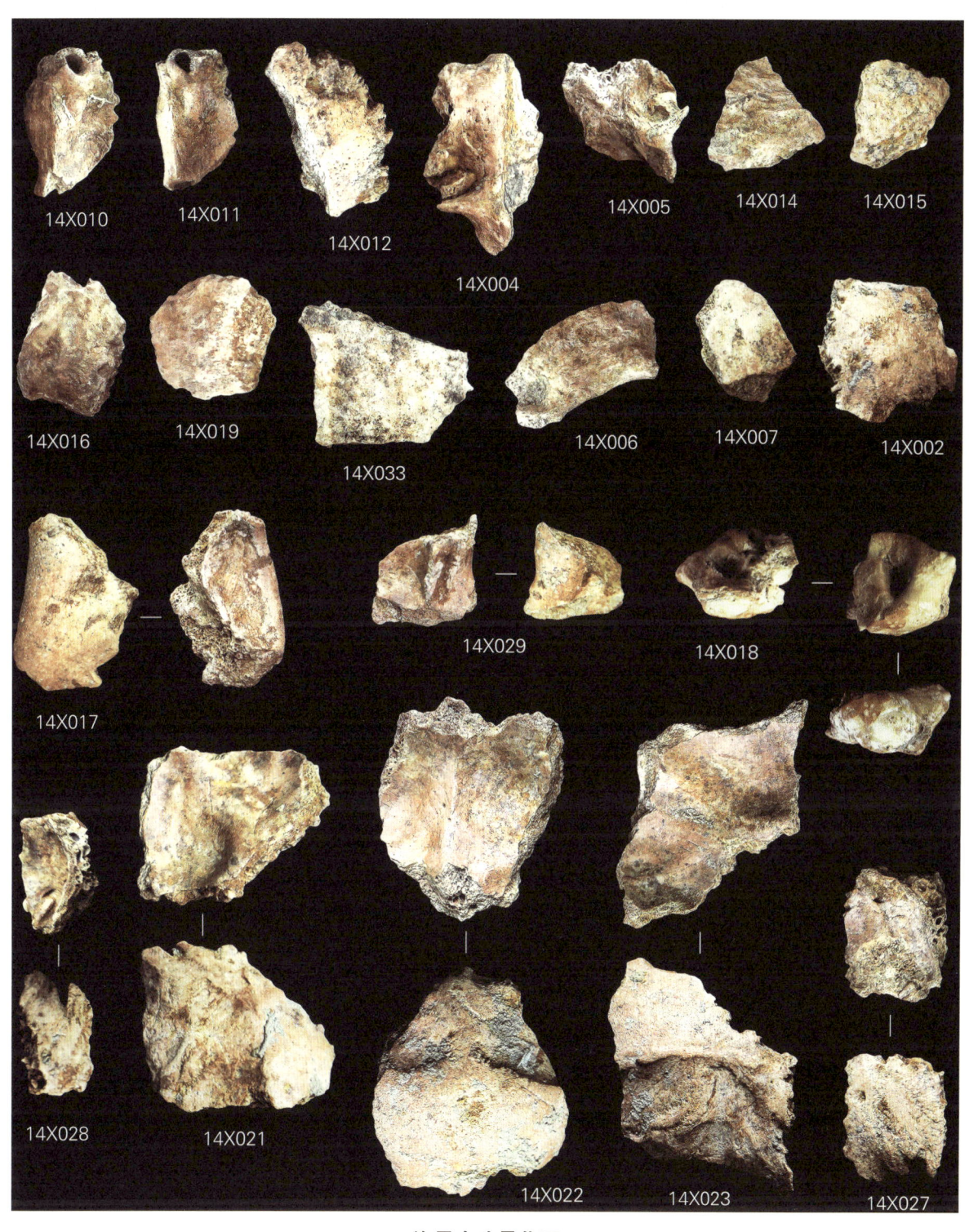

许昌人头骨化石

灵井许昌人遗址发掘现场（南—北）

    Lingjing Xuchang Man Site is located in Lingjing Township, about 15 kilometers, northwest of Xuchang City in Henan Province. The site covers approximately 30,000 square meters, with a 9-meter-thick stratified deposit that can be divided into 11 layers. $^{14}$C tests results prove that the 5th layer dates back to 13,000 years ago and the fossils of Xuchang Man, unearthed from the 11th layer, are 105,000 to 125,000 years old.

    Microlithic implements, fragments of pristine clay wares, carved artworks, etc. were unearthed from the 5th layer; while numerous animal fossils, over 20,000 pieces of stone implements, and abundant fragments of animal bones were excavated from the 11th layer and the lower part of the 10th layer. On the 11th layer of exploration ditch T9, pieces of fossilized human skull, named as Xuchang Man, were discovered. Later in the western part of exploration ditch T13, stone implements, crafted by a secondary process, were found in quantity. Most of these stone tools were made by pressing process and featured with similar characteristics of those made in late Paleolithic Age in Europe. This discovery per se will change conventional perception of middle paleolithic culture in China.

# 河北阳原板井子旧石器时代中期遗址

◎王法岗

板井子遗址位于河北省阳原县板井子村北的高台地上，这里为泥河湾盆地东端，桑干河的北岸。遗址发现于1984年，先后进行过5次大规模发掘，共发掘两个地点，发现石制品、动物化石近万件，是泥河湾盆地旧石器时代中期最重要的遗址之一。

为了解遗址的范围及周围区域古人类遗存的分布状况，2013年以来，河北省文物研究所多次在遗址周围区域开展旧石器专题调查，新发现旧石器地点12处，使该区域旧石器地点的数量达到14处。这些地点分布密集，文化遗物的埋藏部位、层位接近，表明该区域存在一处分布集中的旧石器时代中期遗址群，是古人类活动频繁的区域，为研究盆地内旧石器时代中期古人类的石器技术、生存模式等提供了新材料。

为了进一步确认文化遗物的埋藏状况，2015年，中国科学院古脊椎动物与古人类研究所等单位对板井子遗址进行了发掘，发掘面积约36平方米。发掘获得石制品1900余件、动物骨骼化石700余件、动物牙齿320余件、鸵鸟蛋碎片6件。石制品原料以燧石为主，类型主要有石锤、石核、石片、石器、断块、碎屑等，剥片方法主要采用硬锤锤击法，存在一些典型的盘状石核，部分石核具有预制现象。石器类型以边刮器为主，片状毛坯居多，主要采用硬锤锤击修理，存在大量加工精制的石器标本。

对板井子遗址的年代测定以往采用铀系法测得结果为距今10.8万～7.4万年间，新的光释光测年结果为8.6万年。作为旧石器中期的典型遗址，新的发掘全面采集遗址信息，为研究遗址堆积的形成过程、古人类在不同时段对遗址的占用方式、石器技术演变等问题提供了可能，为讨论旧石器时代中期在中国存在与否提供新的看法。为探讨华北地区现代人的起源与演化过程提供了重要资料，也为建立泥河湾盆地旧石器时代文化序列补充了重要环节。

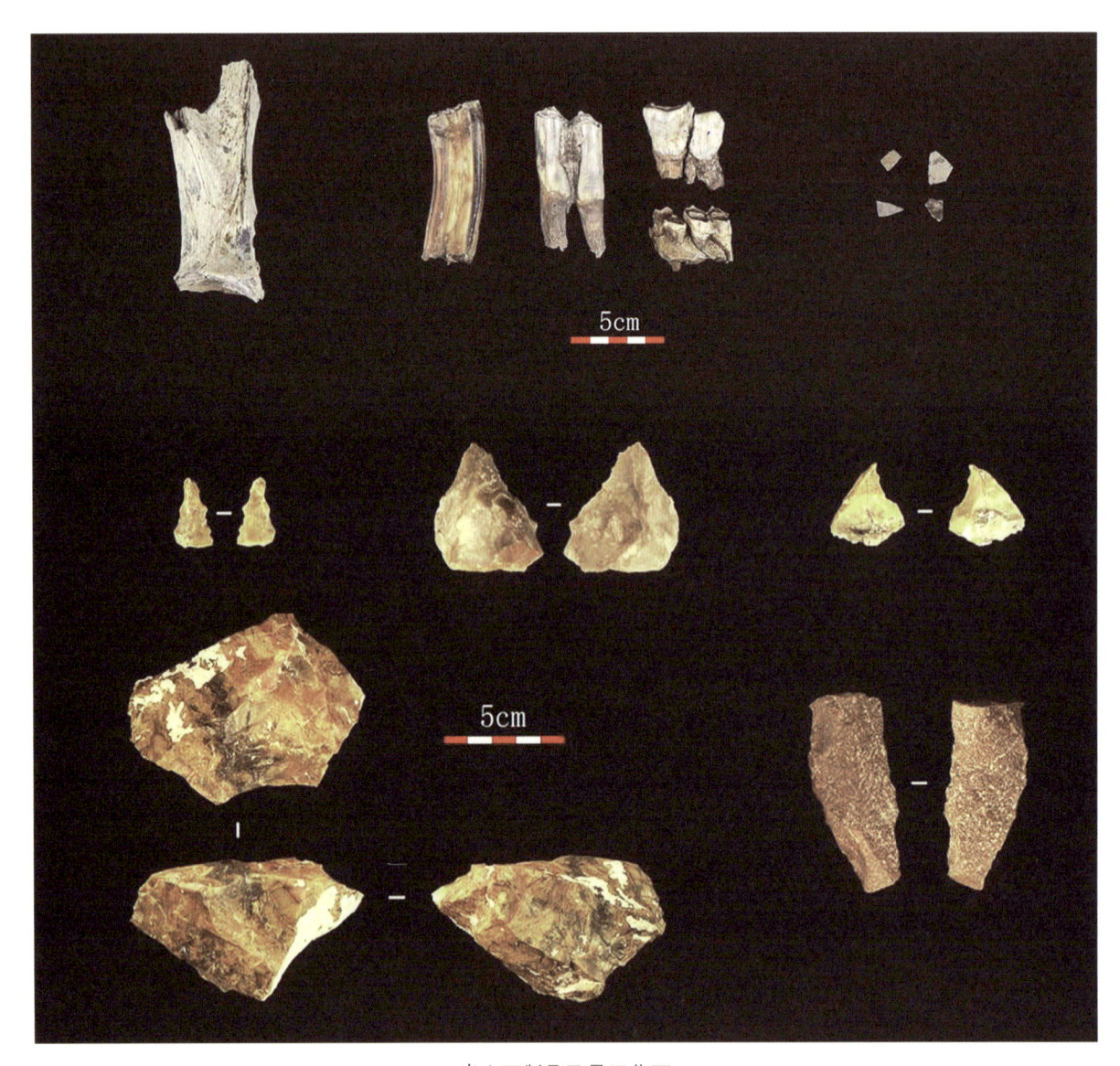

出土石制品及骨牙化石

In 2015, archaeologists from Institute of Vertebrate Paleontology and Paleoanthropology of Chinese Academy of Social Sciences and other institutes excavated Banjingzi Site, in Banjingzi Village in Yuanyang County. The excavation area covered approximately 36 square meters and revealed more than 1900 stone artifacts, over 700 fossils of animal bones, 320 animal teeth and 6 pieces of broken ostrich eggs. The latest dating tests results prove that Banjingzi Site dates back to 86,000 years ago.

The latest excavation carried out on Banjingzi Site, which is a typical one that formed and developed in middle Paleolithic Age, has made it possible for explorations into the formation of the stratified deposits, the ways in which ancient human occupied the site at different times, and the evolution of stone-implement-making skills, etc.

# 山东青岛大珠山旧石器时代遗址

◎陈宇鹏

大珠山旧石器时代遗址位于青岛市黄岛区乔家洼社区以西约1千米的大珠山东麓，东距海岸线约2千米。2013年10—11月，中国科学院古脊椎动物与古人类研究所和青岛市文物保护考古研究所合作，对该遗址进行了一次系统的考古发掘，获得了重要的考古发现。

本次考古发掘面积约30平方米，发掘深度距地表4.20～4.50米。众多的石制品、动物化石、植物遗存等共出于晚更新世地层中，地层、时代归属明确，是山东半岛为数不多的具有明确地层的旧石器考古新发现，不仅有助于研究山东沿海地区古人类行为的适应模式，同时为古气候、古生态环境研究提供了良好的材料。

大珠山遗址出土的石制品类型包括石器、石核、石片和断块等，大部分为中小型石器，人工打制痕迹明显，加工技术成熟，属于中国北方的小型石片石器文化。石器的打片和修整技术主要为锤击法，第二次加工技术成熟，多为陡刃加工，且多向背面加工，其中有少部分石片石器为错向加工。在大珠山遗址中发现的细石器遗存中，中型石器所占比例较大，遗址的绝对年代为距今6万～5万年前，属于晚更新世中晚期。

大珠山遗址出土大量动物化石和一些植物残体，以及丰富的孢粉等微体植物遗存，且标本保存非常好，几乎没有被石化，腐蚀也非常轻微，文化层的孢粉组合反映了较为暖湿的区域环境。

通过测年得到了各文化层土样的光释光测年数据，经与动物骨骼标本、植物残体的 $^{14}$C 测年数据比较，共同指示大珠山遗址文化层的年代在距今6万～5万年间，地质年代属于晚更新世。

大珠山旧石器遗址埋藏环境特殊，同时该遗址也是目前距离当今海岸线最近的具有明确时代和地层的遗址，为讨论中国沿海地区古人类的适应生存与海岸线变迁的关系等提供了重要素材。

工作现场

出土石制品

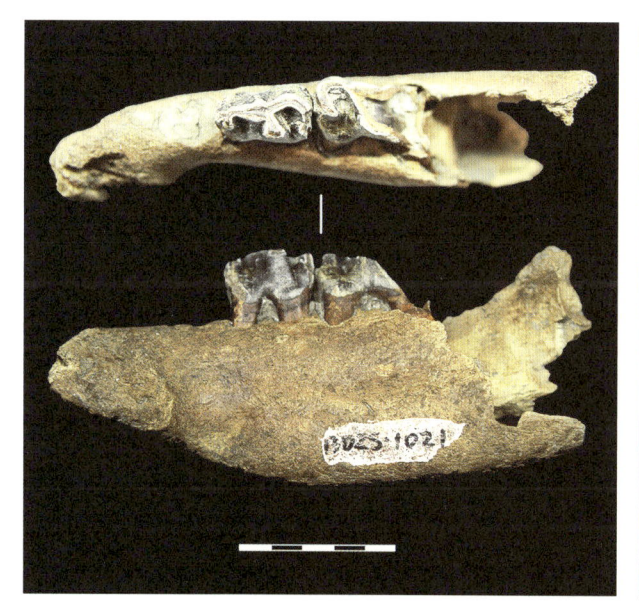

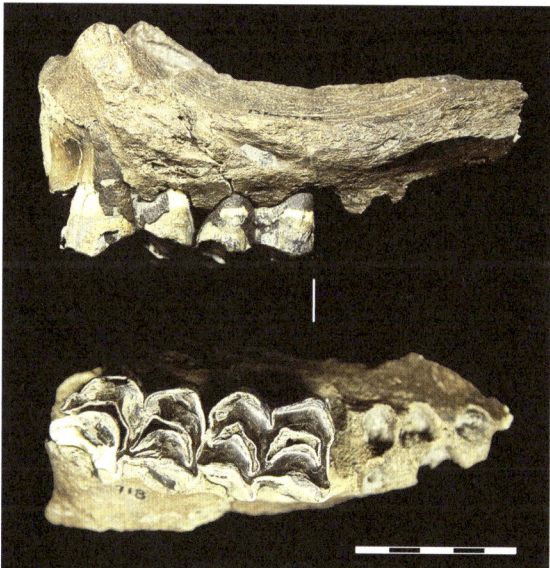

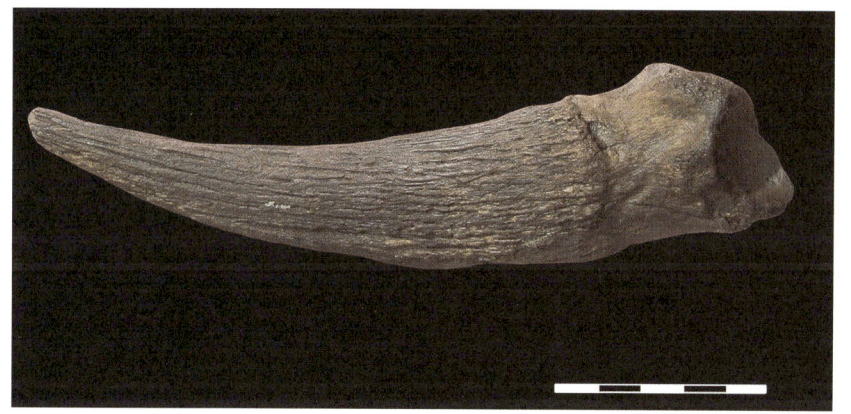

出土动物化石

Dazhushan Paleolithic Site is located in the eastern piedmont region of Dazhushan, about 1 kilometer west of Qiaojiawa Community in Huangdao District, Qingdao. In 2013, a systematic archaeological excavation was carried out at the site, unearthing abundant paleolithic stone artifacts, animal fossils, specimens of plant remains, etc. Dating tests results proved that the cultural layer of Dazhushan Site dates back to 60,000 to 50,000 years ago and its geological age dates from late Pleistocene Period.

Most of the stone artifacts unearthed in Dazhushan Site are small and medium-sized stone tools, showing obvious traces chipped by humans and reflecting mature processing skills. These stone implements indicate this cultural as the category of small-scale stone-flake tools in North China. Meanwhile, a large number of animal fossils, remains of plants, residues of spores, pollens and other micro-plants, are of great significance for reconstructing contemporary ecological environment and analyzing the relationship between natural environment and human culture. As a site which is the closest to today's coastline and whose age and stratal position can be accurately determined, Dazhushan provides archaeologists with important materials for the discussion of the connection between ancient human's survival in coastal areas and changes of the coastline in China.

# 河北阳原油房旧石器时代中期和晚期遗址

◎梅惠杰

油房旧石器时代遗址位于河北阳原县油房村南，地处泥河湾盆地东缘，发现于1984年，1986年试掘。该遗址以典型的细石器工业为特点，石器类型丰富。

2013—2016年，为解决遗址的年代、层位序列和文化序列，华北地区石叶和细石叶工业的出现及其相互关系，以及现代人的起源和扩散等问题，河北师范大学等单位对该遗址开展了连续的考古发掘，出土石制品、烧骨、装饰品及动物化石等遗物逾万件，清理出古人类石器加工和用火遗迹。首次明确了泥河湾盆地石叶工艺制品的原生层位及其与细石叶工艺制品的层位关系。采集古环境分析样品360个，$^{14}$C和光释光等年代学样品近百个。遗址区的地貌演化和沉积成因基本清晰。

该项考古发掘融合了多个学科，提取多方面的考古信息，并揭露出该遗址完整的地层剖面。在对油房遗址的传统认识的文化层下部新发现多个文化层，划分出包含华北传统石片石器文化的下文化层（旧石器时代中期），以典型石叶和细石叶工业为代表的上文化层（旧石器时代晚期）。从而将油房遗址的年代上限大为提前，填补了距今5万～2万年泥河湾盆地史前考古学文化研究的空白，揭示出一场重大的技术变革。初步测年结果显示，油房遗址的时代正处于深海氧同位素第3阶段，对于研究华北晚更新世的气候变化及其与古人类文化演变的对应关系具有重要意义，也为探讨东亚地区现代人的扩散和文化交流提供了新的资料。

清理石器加工现场

出土石叶

出土石制品及拼合

From 2013 to 2016, archaeologists from Hebei Normal University and other institutes carried out continuous archaeological excavations on the paleolithic Youfang Site, located in the south of Youfang Village in Yangyuan County. Over 10,000 objects were unearthed, including stone artifacts, bone articles, burnt bones, ornaments, animal fossils, etc. The range and core area of the site were determined. The primary position of stone blade implements was located; and its relative position with stone artifacts made with micro-blade craftsmanship was also determined. Meanwhile, multidisciplinary and comprehensive researches were underway to collect archaeological information from various aspects.

Newly discovered cultural layer underneath has drastically advanced the start of Youfang Site, filling in the gap on the cultural study of prehistorical archaeology concerning Nihewan Basin in 50,000 to 20,000 years ago. It has been revealed that Youfang Site was on the third stage of marine oxygen isotope and the site witnessed the last glaciation maximum. All these new important materials have been contributed to the study of climate changes in the late Pleistocene period and to the relationship between these changes and the evolution of hominid culture in North China.

# 河北阳原西白马营旧石器时代晚期遗址

◎周振宇

西白马营旧石器时代晚期遗址位于河北阳原县西白马营村南，河北文物研究所于1985年调查并试掘，1986年正式发掘，发现丰富的石制品、动物化石，石制品数量多，类型丰富，石器类型丰富，加工精致，属于小石器工业类型。依据骨化石的铀系法测年结果为1.8万年±0.1万年、1.5万年±0.1万年，处于旧石器时代晚期的末段。

2015—2017年，中国社会科学院考古研究所等单位持续对该遗址进行发掘。发掘分三个发掘区进行，1号地点位于西白马营村南，即1985年发掘区，文化层较厚，遗物丰富。地层基本上为水平状分布，仅第⑫⑬层受水动力侵蚀致层面不甚平整。文化遗物原地埋藏特征明显，第⑨层内出土动物化石、石制品极其丰富，石核、石片、断片及工具类比较集中，并同时拌有少量的烧骨、鸵鸟蛋皮等，可能为古人类活动面。2号地点位于1号地点西侧，揭露一处古人类生活面，发现有大型动物肋骨及脊椎骨，周边分布有大型砾石砍砸器，以及可用作石砧的大型砾石，推测为古人类猎杀解肢动物的场所。3号地点位于东白马营村东南约50米处，发现于1995年，采集到大量石制品、动物化石。本次发掘揭露出数个古人类活动面，以用火遗迹、大型石板、砾石砍砸器为中心，周边分布有大量动物化石、石制品。

发掘确认了遗址分布于桑干河北岸、西白马营、东白马营之间的广大区域；明确了其埋藏类型，文化遗物埋藏于自熊耳山（北山）流向桑干河的支流上，而非以往认识的桑干河的第二级阶地内；文化多为原地埋藏类型，揭露出多处古人类生活面，文化遗物丰富，为探讨古人类生存模式、技术类型提供了基础资料。结合新的 $^{14}C$、光释光测年数据，该遗址最早也是最丰富文化层的年代为距今4.5万年前后，这也是"单一地区起源论"认为现代人扩散至东亚地区的时间，而该遗址的石器工业继承于泥河湾盆地长期存在的小石器工业，体现了区域内技术的连续演化，对探讨东亚地区现代人的起源具有重要价值。

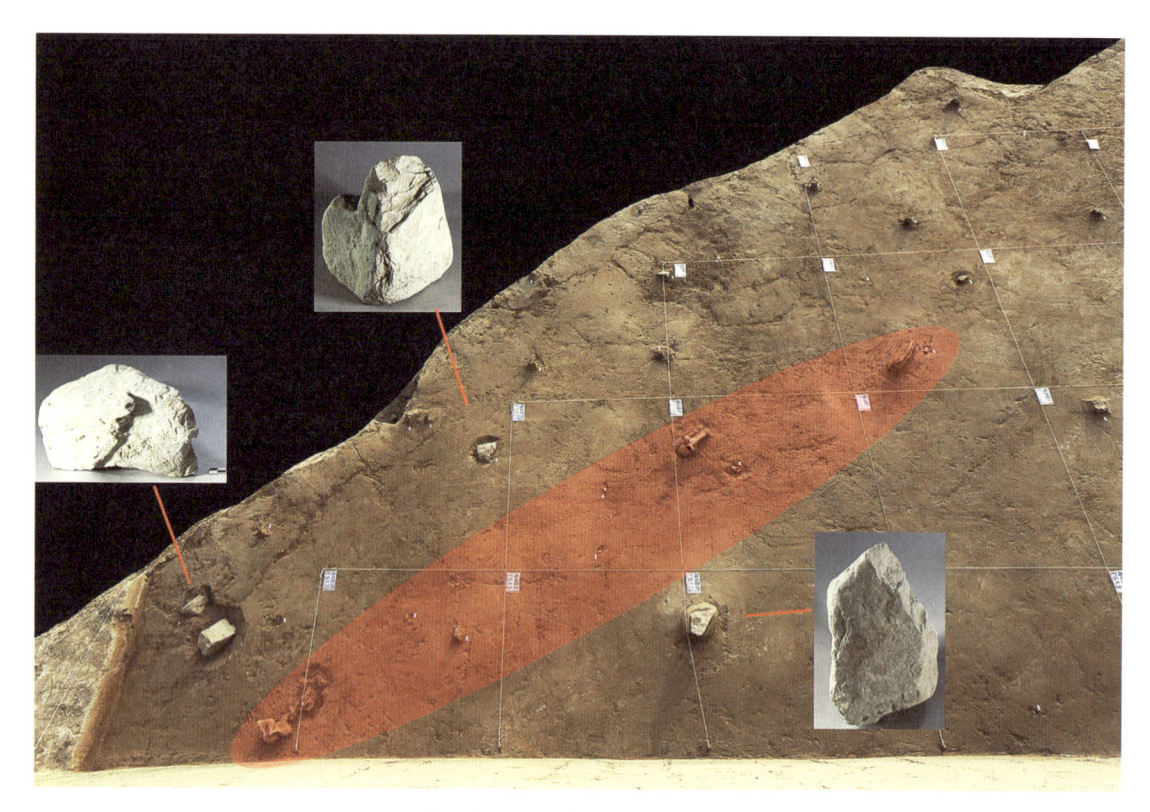

2号地点发现的人类活动面（上为南）

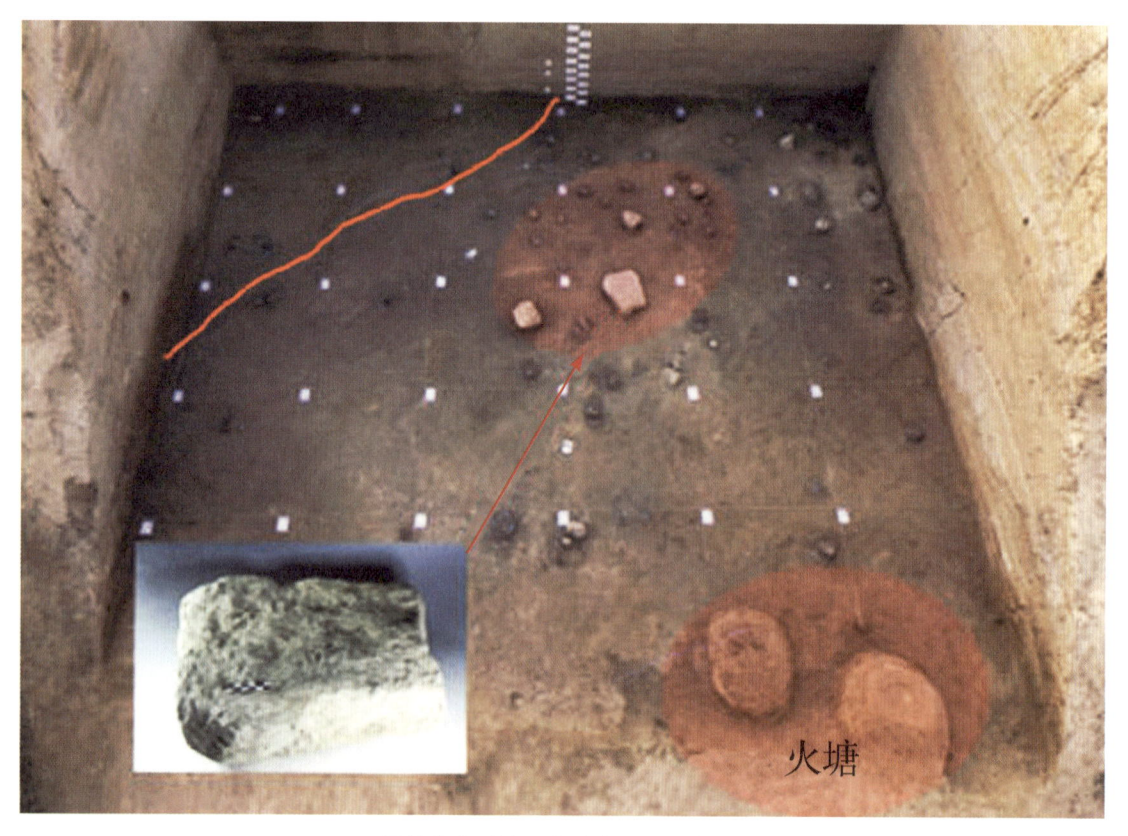

3号地点发现的人类活动面（上为西）

火塘

西白马营旧石器时代遗址分布图（南—北）

From 2015 to 2017, archaeologists from Institute of Archaeology of Chinese Academy of Social Sciences, working with those from Hebei Provincial Institute of Cultural Relics, formally excavated the paleolithic site in the south of Xibaimaying Village in Yangyuan County. The excavation uncovered a number of spots showing traces of human lives, including remains of fire, large stone slabs, pebble choppers, abundant stone implements and animal fossils. Photoluminescence dating tests results proved that the site formed and developed around 46,000 years ago.

Years of archaeological work has not only brought about a more comprehensive understanding on the distribution, burial types, properties and stone-implement-making skills of West Baimaying Site, but also provides important information for the exploration of ancient humans' living pattern in Nihewan Basin 50,000 years ago.

# 山西陵川附城镇旧石器时代晚期洞穴遗址

◎ 任海云

2012年10月至11月，山西省考古研究所在陵川县附城镇丈河流域调查旧石器洞穴遗址，并对其中两处石灰岩洞穴遗址——后河洞和麻吉洞，进行了为期一个月的抢救性发掘。

后河洞遗址位于西瑶泉村北约4千米处，发掘区域在洞口南壁处，发掘面积约9平方米，深度0.40～0.50米，共发现石制品、动物化石、烧骨及用火遗迹1处。

清理出的用火遗迹面积近2平方米。根据发掘区域的种种迹象，推测完整的用火遗迹呈椭圆形，面积在5平方米左右。石制品和骨头集中分布在用火遗迹外围，主要是西南、北侧和南侧即靠近洞南壁位置。共清理出石制品1405件，包括石核62件、石片275件、石器224件，其他（断块、断片、碎屑等）844件。其中各类刮削器数量最大，三棱小尖状器、"塔水河尖状器"和凹缺刮器是较具特色的三类器物，尖状器有一定数量，琢背小刀、石镞、锥钻形器数量少。锤击法被广泛应用在剥片和石器加工中，同时修理石器时运用了软锤压制技术。骨样品未获得有效年代数据，从石制品类型、石料、毛坯选择及打制技术等方面看，后河洞遗址与塔水河遗址的石制品特征高度相似，二者年代相当，均为旧石器时代晚期遗址。

麻吉洞遗址位于西瑶泉村西北约1.5千米处，文化堆积位于洞口，当地老百姓1970年代垒砌的石墙下方，呈斜坡式分布。

在该遗址清理出4层用火遗迹面，其中第4层用火遗迹面厚度最厚。第1层用火遗迹面之上为黄色粉砂土堆积，此层之下为细砂层，之下是第2个用火遗迹面。按照这一规律，我们共清理出用火遗迹面4处。每个用火遗迹面上出土的石制品、化石或烧骨均较少，在用火遗迹面之下与细砂粒层相接部位出土了丰富的文化遗物。观察与统计的石制品共计929件，包括石核、石片、石器和680件断块、断片、碎屑等四大类。工具有各类型刮削器13件，尖状器和砍砸器各1件。石料以燧石为主，其次是硅质灰岩和石灰岩。石器加工法与后河洞遗址相似。从骨样品的测年数据（未经校正）看，该遗址的年代不晚于3万年前，是一处重要的旧石器晚期早段人类反复活动的临时性营地。

麻吉洞遗址用火遗迹面及遗物分布

后河洞遗址发掘位置（西—东）

后河洞遗址遗物分布
（西南—西北）

后河洞遗址出土牙齿化石（左）及石制品（右）

后河洞出土的尖状器　　　　　　　　　　　麻吉洞出土的燧石制品

From October to November in 2012, archaeologists from Shanxi Provincial Institute of Archaeology conducted careful reconnaissance and reexamination in paleolithic caves within an 8-kilometer radius of Zhanghe River Basin, Fucheng Town, Lingchuan County. Among the cave sites, two—Houhe Cave Site and Maji Cave Site—were confirmed to be of late Paleolithic Age.

After comparisons, Houhe Cave Site dates back to the late Paleolithic Age. Dating tests results indicate that Maji Cave Site became into existence more than 30,000 years ago. Maji Cave, used as a major temporary camp, witnessed repeated human activities in early late Paleolithic Age. The obtained materials and preliminary chronological data are very important for following archaeological work in this region. The work done here is the first step in the regional paleolithic study in Taihang Mountains.

# 文明化进程

更新世末期，由于气候变暖，环境性生产力大为提升。在公元前9500—前6500年，人类安居、农作物栽培，相当规模的农业村落先后出现。其中最早的含酒精饮品就出现在黄淮流域的河南舞阳贾湖遗址中。

在舞阳贾湖遗址所属的新石器时代中期阶段的裴李岗文化，黄淮流域还分布着磁山文化、老官台文化、后李文化及马家浜文化。据这些遗址的考古资料显示，随着农业经济的发生发展，各级聚落同步扩大，农业经济及低下的生产水平基本能够满足社群的自给自足，各聚落间缺乏关联。但就在这缓慢的发展中，祖先们已经不知不觉地踏上了文明化进程。

审视考古材料，会发现生产的发展改变着原本单一的社会，出现了和多级血亲组织相匹配的多级所有制。由于各地区所处地域的气候环境的差异，发展模式不尽相同，出现了以中原北方地区为代表的旱作农业，以及东部的稻作农业。作为社会演进中的基本动因——社会生产力，它发展的高低缓急，在社会小型化及社会成员的阶层分化程度上都有明确的反映，从而导致社会在发展过程中表现出不同面貌。

史前社会的文明化约始自公元前4000年，在文明发展的进程中，各地呈现出多元化的面貌。海岱地区的大汶口文化、龙山文化，中原及北方地区的仰韶文化庙底沟类型以及以陶寺为代表的龙山时代，异彩纷呈，遥相辉映。但从长远来看，如上的多元中存在着一体化的趋势——中原龙山文化。对整个中国历史而言，以中原为中心历史趋势的出现意义非凡。它占据地利，同时在经过了数千年的发展已于其周边形成了多重空间的文化构架；对内为了建立起新秩序、新权威，不惜动用各种资源和手段；对外需要处理同各方的关系，这就决定了它的集权性，并贯穿于整个中国古代史。

## 骏惠维天　降幅之穰穰

### 江苏泗洪韩井遗址

◎ 于慧楠

2014年春，通过对泗洪县梅花镇和归仁镇的区域系统调查，初步确认韩井遗址为一处顺山集时期的环壕聚落。2014年至2016年，由中国国家博物馆、南京博物院、泗洪县博物馆合作对该遗址进行了三次发掘工作。

通过解剖遗址北部的环壕G14，得知其始建年代不晚于顺山集文化二期，在三期时形成了三个活动面，和由密集红烧土颗粒铺垫的长条形似道路堆积，至三期时彻底废弃。在遗址的东南部和壕沟处，还发现顺山集文化时期水沟20多条、灰坑200余座，以及由洼地和水沟组成的"水稻田"遗迹1处。水稻田S1为一期时使用并废弃，在稻田遗迹东侧，以生土埂相隔的G16则比S1略晚或者同时形成，其内堆积，则为二期时逐渐形成，同时在顺山集文化一期和二期的20多个灰坑中发现了炭化稻，个别灰坑内发现了驯化类型的炭化小穗轴，是韩井遗址先民对水稻进行栽培的直接证据。在水沟和洼地组合遗迹的填土中发现了较多的水稻扇型和水稻双峰型植硅体，故推测此组遗迹应当是当时的"水稻田"。

选用韩井遗址浮选出土的6份炭化水稻的残块和2014年发掘灰坑内出土的木炭，进行加速器质谱$^{14}$C测年，经过拟合后显示一二期年代集中分布在距今8450～8200年，处于顺山集文化一至二期的年代范畴（距今8500～8000年），属于连续发展的时期，两期的分界放在距今8400年比较合适，而第三期的年代在距今7800年左右，与遗址的一期、二期之间有着长时间的缺环。

韩井遗址是继顺山集遗址以后，在淮河中游地区发现的又一处新石器时代中期的环壕聚落，其文化遗存的发现，不但丰富了顺山集文化的内涵，为研究顺山集文化以及淮河中游与长江流域的文化交流，也为研究新石器时代中期淮河流域的生业经济，提供了不可多得的资料。

水稻（H140）　　　炭化小穗轴　　　骨器（S1填土）　　　骨器（S1填土）

石器（S1填土）　　　陶甑（G16）　　　磨石（G16）

The National Museum of China, Nanjing Museum and Sihong County Museum cooperated in 2014. Preliminary drillings and explorations were conducted on Hanjing Site. An east-west major ditch, with abundant and diversified cultural relics, was discovered. After the excavation and subsequent probings and drillings, the site was identified as a moated settlement site dating back to Shunshanji Culture period. From 2015 to 2016, excavations were once more carried out in the southeastern part of the site and also in the ditches.

After excavations, it has been preliminarily determined that Hanjing Site, after Shunshanji Site, is another moated settlement of mid-Neolithic Age in the middle reaches of Huaihe River. The discovery has enriched the cultural content of Shunshanji Culture. It also has provided rare materials not only for the study of Shunshanji Culture and cultural exchanges that happened in the middle reaches of Huaihe River and Yangtze River Basin, but also for the researches of living conditions and production in Huaihe River Basin in mid-Neolithic Age.

# 江苏泗洪县顺山集新石器时代遗址

◎林畅根　甘恢元　闫　龙

顺山集遗址位于江苏省泗洪县梅花镇赵庄及前老行政村，南距泗洪县城约15千米。2010年、2011年、2012年南京博物院考古研究所与泗洪县博物馆联合对其进行了三次考古发掘工作，共清理新石器时代墓葬、房址、灰坑、灶类遗迹、红烧土堆积及狗坑等各类遗迹，出土陶、石、玉、骨器近400件。依地层叠压、器物演变与组合关系，将该遗址新石器时期遗存分为三个时期，二期遗存最为丰富，共清理出环壕、房址、墓地、灰坑及一处大面积烧土堆积。

依据$^{14}$C测年数据分析，顺山集遗址第一期遗存上限当在距今8500~8400年，第二期遗存下限当在距今8000年前后。第三期遗存年代在距今8000年至7500年之间。

顺山集遗址第一、二期遗存具有明显的前后传承关系，应视为同一文化不同发展阶段。我们将之命名为顺山集文化。顺山集一、二期遗存与周边时代相同的后李文化、裴李岗文化、贾湖文化及彭头山文化存在某些方面的联系，但更多的是时代共性。该区域目前已发现与顺山集文化面貌接近或时代相当的遗址有近10处，主要包括江苏泗洪韩井、半城，安徽泗县于庄、唐圩、张集、淮北石山孜、宿州小山口及古台寺等。

顺山集遗址第三期遗存文化内涵与一、二期遗存有着明显差异，但与分布于钱塘江流域的跨湖桥文化，在器物组合与制陶工艺上存在诸多相同或相似的文化因素。跨湖桥文化的源头在本地上山文化中找到了线索，顺山集第三期遗存虽有少量顺山集文化特征，但主体文化因素尚未在本地找到来源。仅就目前考古材料推断，顺山集第三期遗存可能来源于跨湖桥文化的跨区域迁徙，抑或是受其强烈影响。

顺山集作为同时期该区域面积最大的环壕聚落遗址，其延续时间长，文化内涵丰富，在同类遗存中具有代表性，为本区域该时期的考古学文化研究建立了可资参考的标尺，填补了空白。

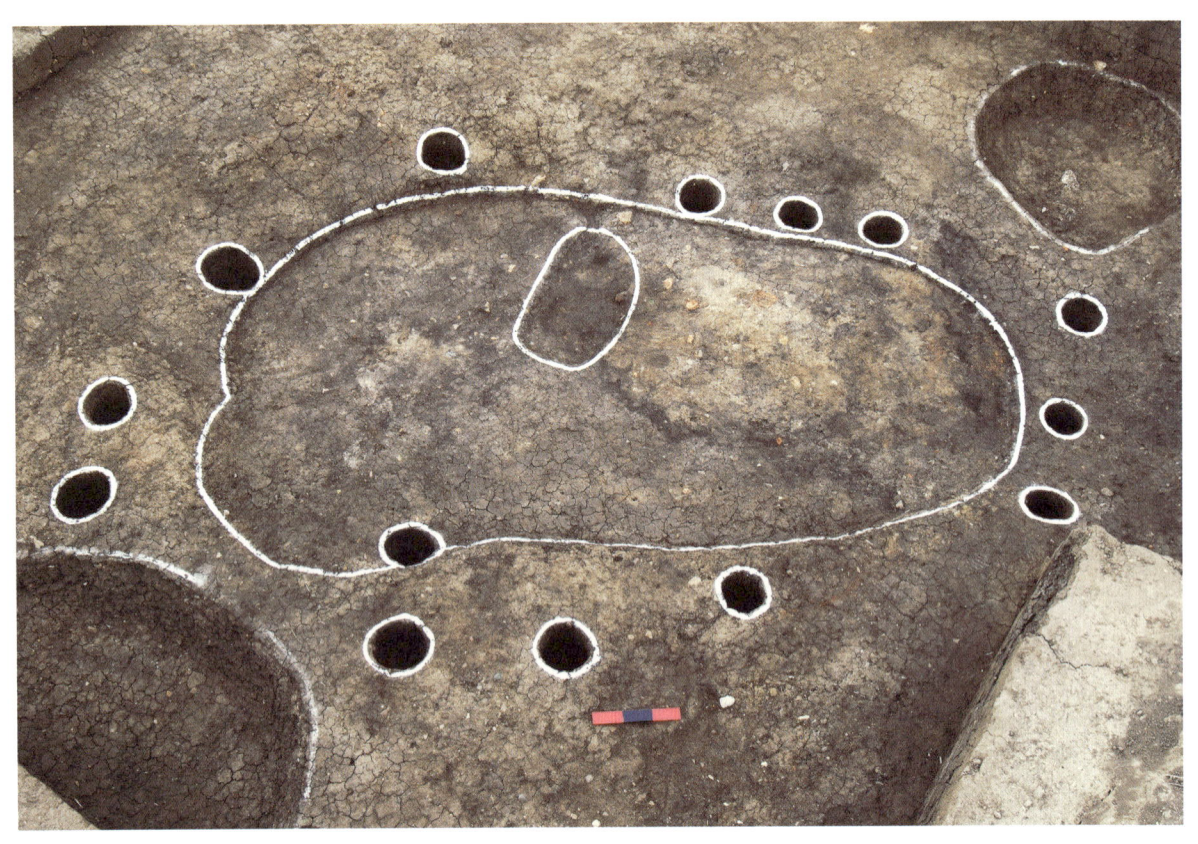

一期房址F1全景（东北—西南）

二期墓地全景（南—北）

文明化进程 075

陶釜　　　　　　　　　陶盆

陶壶　　　　　玉管　　　　石磨球

顺山集一期遗物

陶壶　　　　　陶釜　　　　　陶罐

陶塑猴面　　　石磨盘与石磨球　　陶支脚

顺山集二期遗物

陶釜　　　　　　　　陶豆

陶壶　　　　　　　　陶圈足盘　　　　　　玉锛

**顺山集三期遗物**

Shunshanji Site is located in Zhaozhuang Village and its former administrative village, Meihua Town, Sihong County, Jiangsu Province. Archaeological excavations have been carried out three times since 2010. The total excavated area is 2750 square meters. The excavation and preliminary analyses indicate that the Neolithic remains of Shunshanji Site are of three eras. $^{14}$C tests results show that the site is 8500 years (the uppermost age limit of the first phase) to 7500 years (the age of the third phase) old.

Obvious inheritable features have been observed from the first and second phases of Shunshanji Site and these two phases should be regarded as different development stages of the same culture; while remains of the third phase is possibly the result of a cross-regional spread of Kuahuqiao Culture, or these remains might have been heavily affected by Kuahuqiao Culture. Shunshanji Site is the largest moated settlement site of early and middle Neolithic Age in the middle and lower reaches of Huaihe River. The site is a representative of its kind and helps to fill the gap with standards that can be referred to in archaeological cultural study of this period in this region.

# 安徽淮北相山区渠沟新石器时代遗址

◎张义中

渠沟遗址位于安徽省淮北市相山区渠沟路与西山路交叉口西北，2016年2月至9月，安徽省文物考古研究所与淮北市文旅体委、淮北市博物馆联合组队，对遗址展开抢救性考古发掘。

据勘探资料，遗址主体可分为两部分，即位于遗址南部和东部的墓葬区，和位于北部的遗址区。从发掘情况来看，遗址地层共分为14层，其中第5~14层为新石器时代。

发现各类新石器时代遗迹总计533处，有灰坑、灰沟、柱洞、房址及灶坑，还有陶片堆积2处、红烧土遗迹3处、墙基2处。出土器物可辨器形的有石斧、石锛、石杵、石磨棒、石磨盘，骨针、骨锥、骨镞、骨哨、角锥及陶釜、陶支座等。

房址共17处，根据形状结构不同可分两类。有以F1为代表的半地穴式，由门道、房间主体、灶和柱洞四部分组成。房址地穴斜弧壁，壁面粗糙，底部土质较硬，结构紧密，无明显加工夯打痕迹。F1内形成了厚薄不一的5层堆积。F4则为地面式建筑，由房间主体和柱洞两部分组成。居住面土色系灰白色，柱洞围绕在房间周围，共计10个，推测为平地开挖柱洞后立柱围墙搭顶。

墙基共2处。Q2位于发掘区西北部，TG3中东部。开口于⑪层下，平面大体呈长条形，南北走向，残长7.01米，宽0.19~0.54米。在其南段和中段基槽内有6个柱洞，北段基槽内有3个柱洞。三段基槽内堆积情况相同。包含有少量兽骨残片、石块、烧土粒和炭粒。

淮北市渠沟遗址新石器时代遗存，与同在濉河流域的石山子遗址文化内涵相似，年代相当，可初步判断为新石器时代中期偏早或早期偏晚，距今8000~7000年。遗址文化层较厚，面貌独特，内涵丰富，是了解安徽乃至淮河流域史前文化发展不可多得的珍贵材料。

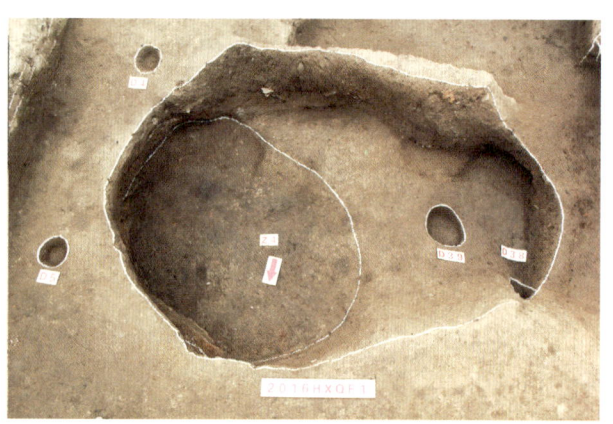

半地穴式房址内的堆积　　　　　　　　　清理完毕的半地穴式房址

地面式房址

墙址　　　　　　　　　　　　　　　　灶坑内的堆积

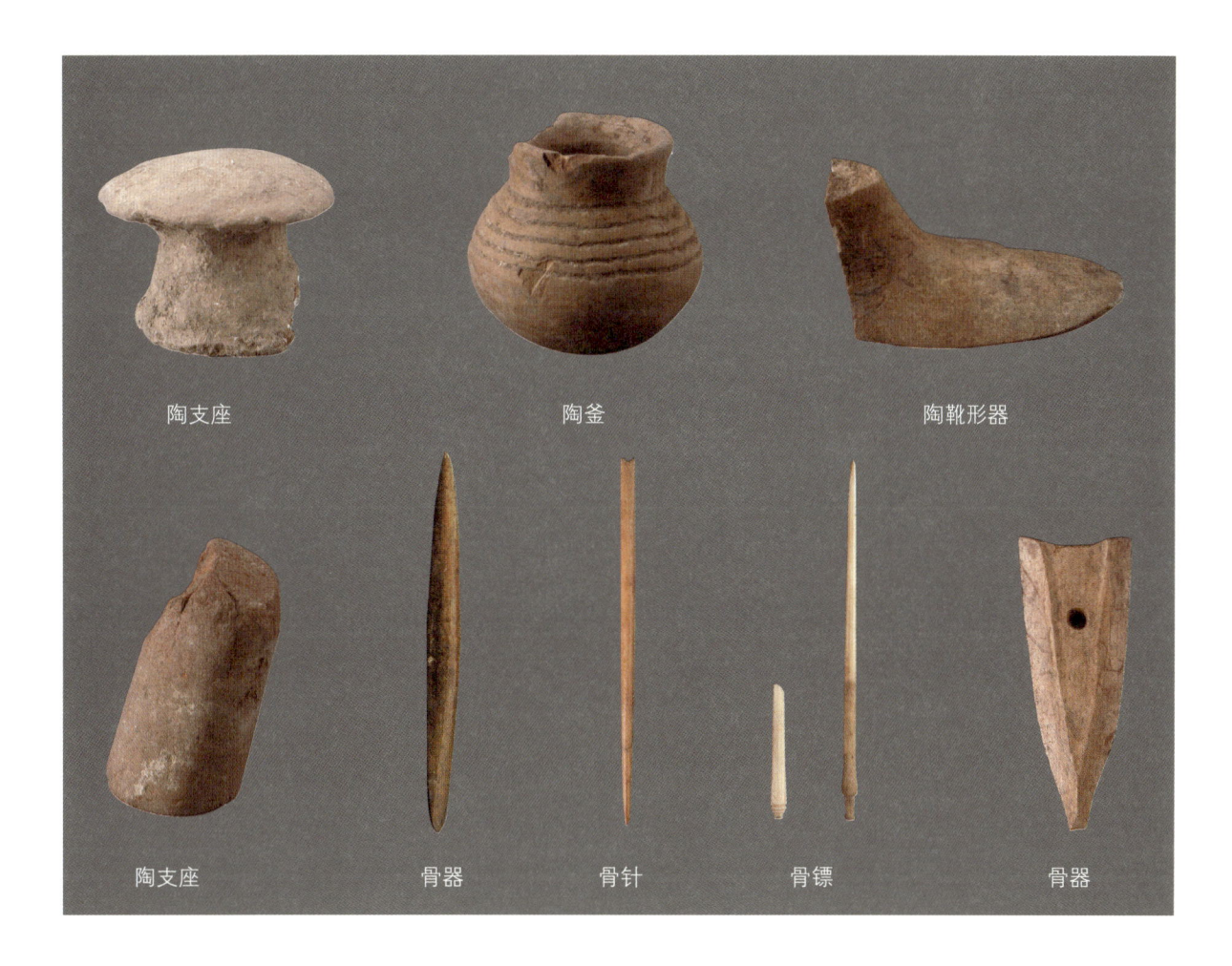

| 陶支座 | 陶釜 | 陶靴形器 |
| 陶支座 | 骨器 | 骨针 | 骨镖 | 骨器 |

Qugou Site is located in the northwest of the intersection of Qugou Road and Xishan Road in Xiangshan District, Huaibei City, Anhui Province. In 2016, archaeologists from Anhui Provincial Institute of Cultural Relics and Archaeology and other institutes carried out salvage excavations on the site.

Excavations and preliminary analyses indicate that Neolithic remains discovered on Qugou Site and those unearthed from Shishanzi Site, which is also located in the Suihe River Basin, are not only culturally identical but also of equivalent chronological age. It has been preliminarily determined that the remains of two sites date back to early middle Neolithic Age or late early Neolithic Age, approximately 7000 to 8000 years ago. The cultural layer of Qugou Site, which is thick, unique and with diversified contents, provides rare and precious materials for the understanding of prehistorical cultural development in Anhui Province and even in the Huaihe River Basin. It is of great significance for in-depth study and clarification of the Neolithic cultural features in the middle and lower reaches of Huaihe River. Important clues have been provided for the study of ancient cultural exchanges and population migration in the Huaihe River Basin and even in eastern China.

# 河北尚义四台蒙古营遗址

◎ 王培生

四台蒙古营遗址位于河北张家口市尚义县石井乡四台蒙古营村西南1000米处，属北方长城地带北侧蒙古高原与华北平原的交界地带，总面积约3万平方米。遗址中部由西向东被冲出一条最深约15米，长约500米的沟壑，自断崖上可见零星暴露的人骨和红烧土，在沟底可采集到细石器、残石磨盘、石磨棒等石质工具。

2014年7月，张家口市文物考古研究所在调查时，认定这是一处年代较早的新石器时代遗址。2015年5月初，对该遗址进行了考古勘探及抢救性清理，清理面积290平方米。

遗址文化层可分5层，其中第④层为新石器时代堆积层，发现少量细石器、夹砂黑褐陶片和器表饰压印锯齿纹的大口尖底罐1件。有4座方形房址开口于第④层下，均不完整，所幸尚保存了灶坑和部分柱洞。第⑤层为生土层。4座房址除F2出土1件残陶罐外，其他3座房址出土遗物都十分丰富。F1既出土各类石铲9件、石斧4件、石磨盘5件、石磨棒4件以及素面筒形陶罐1件。另外，在该房址东侧还发现两具焚烧过的人骨。

经美国贝塔实验室对房址出土木炭$^{14}$C测定，房屋年代为距今7670～7580年；经中科院地理科学与资源研究所对房址土样浮选和淀粉粒样本检测，遗址年代距今7500年。同时还对房址出土的石器上附着的淀粉粒样本检测，当时的植物有粟、黍、藜属和小麦族等植物。另外，由河北师范大学从遗址5个层位分别提取的孢粉样本检测，显示遗址曾有乔木、灌木、草本、蕨类等草原类型植物。气候特征分别为温凉偏干—寒冷干燥—温凉偏干。

四台蒙古营遗址的重要性在于，粟、黍、藜属和小麦族等农作物得到初步确认，出土的素面筒形陶罐和有肩石铲十分接近小河西文化，晚于房址的第④层出土的压印锯齿纹大口尖底罐，和俄罗斯外贝加尔地区的卡林加河口、南西伯利亚阿凡纳谢沃文化普遍存在的尖底罐十分接近，这无疑为探讨我国新石器时代早期与北方草原文化的交流提供了重要线索。

文明化进程　081

出土遗物

尚义四台蒙古营新石器时代遗址遗存

Sitai Mengguying Site is located 1000 meters southwest of Sitai Mengguying Village, Shijing Township, Shangyi County, Hebei Province.

The site dates back to comparatively early Neolithic Age and it was found by archaeologists from Zhangjiakou Institute of Cultural Relics and Archaeology in July 2014. In 2015, archaeological reconnaissances covered 2000 square meters near an escarpment. Meanwhile, salvage excavations were carried out in exposed areas, clearing up 290 square meters.

It has been confirmed that Sitai Mengguying Site, after Cishan Site and Peiligang Site, is another major early Neolithic site discovered in Hebei Province. Since the site is located in the southern area of Inner Mongolia Plateau, the discoveries of crops like millet, sorghum, quinoa, wheat, etc., and unearthed unglazed cylinder-shaped clay jars, big-mouthed and pointed-bottomed jars with sawtooth pattern pressed on the surface, and shouldered stone shovels are of extreme academic values. These have provided important clues for the study of exchanges between Chinese culture and that of nomadic tribes on the northern grassland in early Neolithic Age.

# 安徽郎溪磨盘山新石器时代至商周时期遗址

◎赵东升

磨盘山遗址位于安徽郎溪县飞鲤镇幸福社区新法村磨盘山自然村南漪湖东岸的山前阶地上。

2015年至2016年，南京大学考古文物系与安徽省文物考古研究所合作对遗址进行了全面钻探，并选择了遗址西部的一处高台地作为发掘地点，两次发掘面积分别为800平方米和400平方米。

文化堆积可分为四个时期：马家浜晚期（第⑥层）、崧泽晚期—良渚早期（第⑤层）、良渚末期—钱山漾时期（第④层）及二里头—春秋时期（第③层）。生土为网纹红土。马家浜文化主要分布在较高区域的外围，崧泽晚期—良渚早期文化主要分布于发掘区较高位置，良渚末期—钱山漾时期遗存则分布于发掘区的东部，二里头—春秋时期遗存分布范围较广，尤其是在地势偏低的区域尤为深厚。

马家浜时期以居住遗存为主，分布有大量的红烧土堆积和房址。崧泽晚期—良渚早期以墓葬遗存为主，并利用了马家浜时期的红烧土作为基础。良渚末期—钱山漾时期和二里头—春秋时期也以居住遗存为主，多以经过处理的多层铺垫土建造，有的还以石块作为房屋基础。

两个年度的发掘共出土各类完整及可修复文物2500余件。

随葬品以陶器、石器为主，有少量玉器。陶器以壶、罐、豆、杯、鼎、纺轮为大宗，也有少量的盉、动物形异形器等。石器以锛、凿、镞为主。玉器有璜、管、蝴蝶形挂饰、璧、坠、镯等。

生活遗存中所见遗物以陶器和石器为主，陶器中网坠和结网工具陶"觿"的数量可占三分之一，说明当时古人对水的依赖性较大。石器的数量也较多。玉器的数量不多且体型不大。

通过对磨盘山遗址的两次发掘，主要认识如下：

1.第一期遗存和第二期遗存与马家浜文化和崧泽文化同属一个文化区，马家浜时期与太湖西部同时期文化面貌更为接近，有平底釜和鼎，与溧阳神墩遗址、宜兴西溪遗址非常相似。崧泽时期文化与神墩遗址和昆山遗址更为接近，都有太湖东部地区不见的浅盘豆形器和带把鼎。崧泽遗存中有少量的多孔石刀，可能与西部的薛家岗文化存在着一定的交流。一些小型的三足器和带把器可能也表明与北阴阳营文化有一定的互动关系。马家浜因素可能是目前所见遗址中最为偏西的地点，崧泽因素也较为偏西。

2.这里的古环境属于山前湖边地区，通过湖区较为平静的水路可与太湖周边地区相连。

3.良渚末期文化在太湖东南部地区被称为钱山漾文化，在这里也发现有部分鱼鳍形鼎足与钱山漾文化相似，说明当时应该存在交流。

4.可见岳石文化和湖熟文化的因素，说明这个时期与北方和宁镇地区的关系最为密切。

5.大量网坠和织网工具的发现，说明当时这片区域渔猎发达。大量墓葬所表现出的等级分化不明显。加之文化遗存均为各考古学文化的晚期或末期，故而推测此遗址可能是古人在各考古学文化发展末期作为避难之处所使用的。

马家浜文化晚期遗物

崧泽晚期至良渚早期遗物

良渚末期—钱山漾文化时期遗物

商周时期遗物

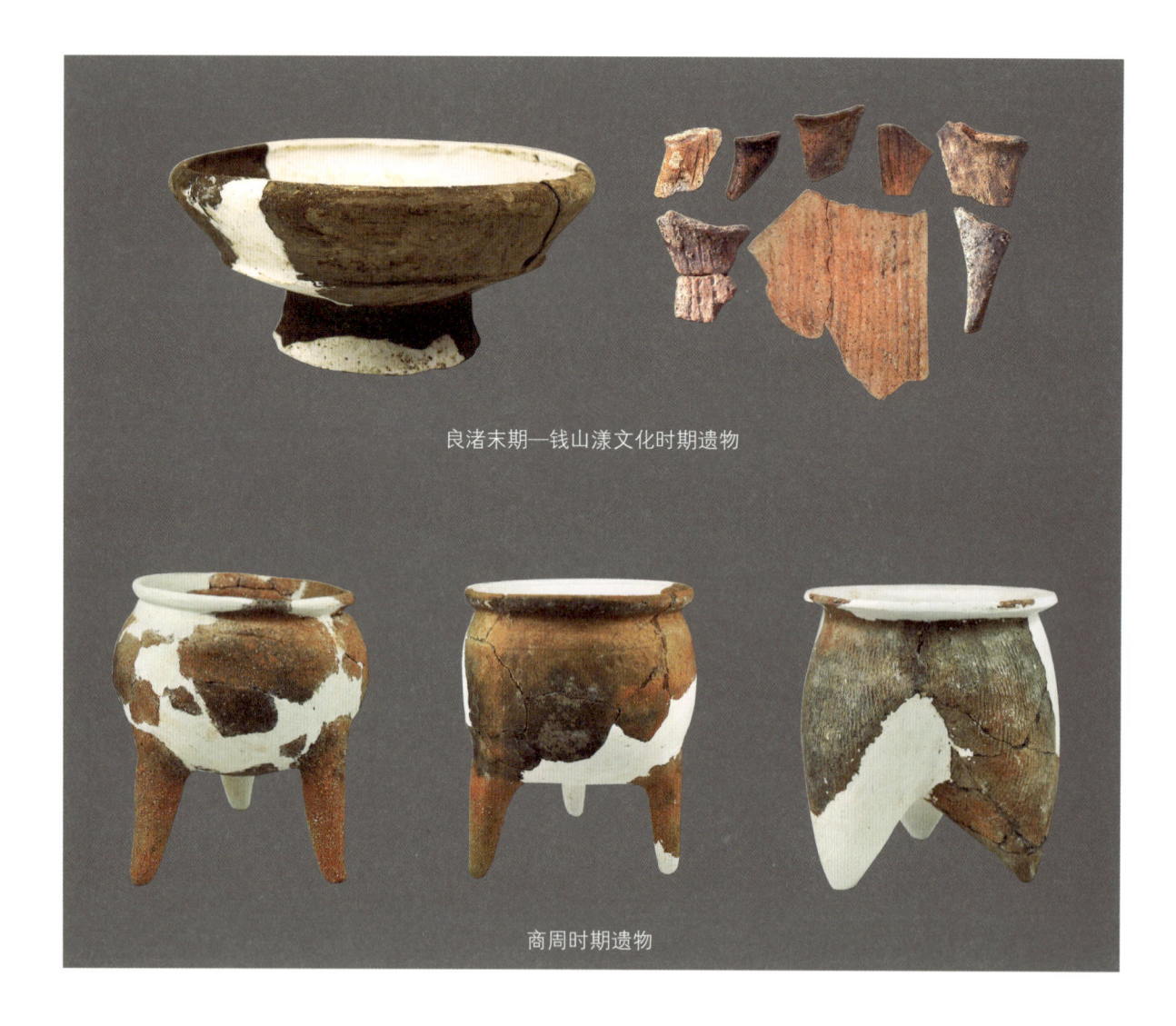

Mopanshan Site is located on the piedmont terrace of the east bank of Nanyi Lake in Mopanshan Unincorporated Village, Xinfa Village, Xingfu Community, Feili Town, Langxi County, Anhui Province. From 2015 to 2016, a joint team, consisting of archaeologists from Nanjing University and Anhui Province, conducted formal excavations, protection and researches on the site.

Archaeological reconnaissance showed that the key area of the site, covering approximately 49,565 square meters, appeared to be an irregular ellipse. Culturally the stratified deposits of Mopanshan Site formed and developed during four periods, i.e. late Majiabang Culture period, late Songze Culture period to early Liangzhu Culture period, the final phase of Liangzhu Culture period to Qianshanyang Culture period, and Erlitou Culture period to early Spring & Autumn period. Early remains of Mopanshan Site date back to Majiabang Culture period and Songze Culture period and these remains are located the western most on the distribution map of these two cultures. The hierarchal gradation reflected by a large number of tombs is extremely inconspicuous. Graves, in which jade burial accessories have been excavated, are not "outstanding" in terms of the quantity of unearthed antiquities or the tomb size.

# 安徽含山凌家滩遗址及周边考古工作

◎吴卫红

2008—2017年，凌家滩遗址的考古工作理念实现了"从玉器到聚落"的转变，以"探寻活着的世界"为目标，对凌家滩遗址及周边进行了多年连续性的调查、勘探、发掘工作。

在约400平方千米范围内共发现先秦遗址70余处，其中与凌家滩大体同时期的遗址20处左右，但面积都只有1万～4万平方米，大多数遗址略早于凌家滩以墓葬为主体的年代，少数延续至凌家滩墓葬出现的时代，各遗址的重复利用程度很低。特别是在凌家滩遗址周边、裕溪河北岸一片被山岗环抱的约40平方千米的半封闭区域，还有6处以上的同时期遗址，年代单纯。

据目前所知，凌家滩遗址周边大体同时期的遗址面积均较小，基本上在1万平方米左右，个别分布较散的也只有3万平方米左右，而凌家滩遗址的面积约140万平方米，有内、外两重壕沟，是该区域内面积最大的聚落。

内壕沟全长2000多米，大体呈梯形，与裕溪河（后河）围成一个封闭空间，南北宽400多米，东西最长1200多米。在圩区中的壕沟现存宽约8～17米，深1米多，个别地段更宽，底部较平。沟内靠近生活区的位置遗物较多，而其他位置少见遗物。北段的壕沟呈东—西向，主要穿过山岗，将岗地明显切断分为南、北两个区域，现存宽度20～40米，最深超过6米，底部与山岗的坡度相合，呈斜坡状。墓地位于壕沟的北侧，其南侧有一缺口可与生活区相连。

外壕沟仅在遗址的西北部发现，东、南部未发现。西段呈东北—西南走向，在北段近山岗处改为东西向，一般宽20多米，在山岗的高处有一缺口。

生活区主要在内壕沟以内，面积近50万平方米。发现了大量的红烧土层堆积，面积可达10万平方米，分布较密集，大小不一，最大者可达几百平方米，小者仅10平方米左右，根据以往的情况分析，多数应与房址有关，部分或为红烧土坑，灰坑大小不一，大者径长有10余米，多数应与生活垃圾有关。

文化层主要分布在壕沟以内，且多数区域离沟越近则遗物越少或不见，沟外则基本不见。村东的石头圩区域内遗物丰富的分布范围由北往南渐厚，以靠近河边为多，说明居住区具有沿河而居的特点。

2013—2017年，在调查勘探的基础上，对凌家滩外围的韦岗遗址和凌家滩本体进行了数次发掘，发掘总面积1600多平方米。

韦岗遗址发掘于2013年10月，发掘面积约230平方米。经发掘，遗址可分新石器时代、汉代、唐宋—明清三个时期。新石器时代的堆积最为丰富，发现了一批新石器时代的灰坑、柱洞以及1条沟状遗迹、陶片堆等。

新石器时代遗物以陶器为主，基本不见完整器，其中以陶鼎、陶缸数量最多，另有陶豆、陶盘、陶钵、陶纺轮、陶饼及陶丸等。在陶土中夹杂石英、植物碎末是其明显特点，陶器表面施红色陶衣，少量陶器表面还装饰有简单的彩绘图案。

出土的石器数量较少，仅有少量锛、斧、凿，且均有残损，但出土砺石较多。此外，动物骨骼也较多，包括牙齿、颌骨、角等[①]。

通过多次对凌家滩遗址的考古发掘，使得其壕沟结构、聚落的功能分区基本明晰。发掘出土了一批与墓葬随葬品明显有异的生活用品，石器中的砺石数量最多，另有少量残石钺、石镞等，玉器极少发现，但出土了较丰富的陶片、动物碎骨等。陶器以鼎、豆、壶、盆为主，在略晚的时期出土了一定量的觚形杯底、刻槽盆、鬶把手等，这些器物组合，表现出与以往不同，或许反映出当时的生活方式发生了较大变化。

在较多的红烧土块中，都发现了水稻颖壳印痕，通过对浮选的大植物遗存及植硅体分析，发现了芦苇、水蕨等指示水体或潮湿环境的植硅体，以及可能与水稻相关的植硅体，推测当时的环境温暖湿润，存在小幅暖—冷变化，植被有以栲属、栎属、榛属和榆属为主的亚热带常绿—落叶阔叶树种，以禾本科、蒿属和藜科为代表的草丛，另有竹亚科植物，而香蒲和芦苇等生长在浅水沼泽等湿地处。

截至目前，凌家滩遗址是裕溪河流域规模最大、等级最高的史前聚落，整个区域内大体同时期的聚落密度不大，绝大多数面积较小，但存在数处小聚落群。对凌家滩遗址本身生活区的确认、大量生活用品的出土和壕沟的发现则为最重要的收获。

---

[①] 详见《安徽含山县韦岗新石器时代遗存发掘简报》，《文物》2015年第3期。

凌家滩遗址及周边遗址分布示意图

2015年凌家滩南半坎地点发掘现场（东北—西南）

夹砂陶鼎　　　　　　　　夹石英陶缸

陶纺轮　　　　　　　　　陶鼎足

砺石　　　　　　石凿　　　陶轮形器

**韦岗遗址出土遗物**

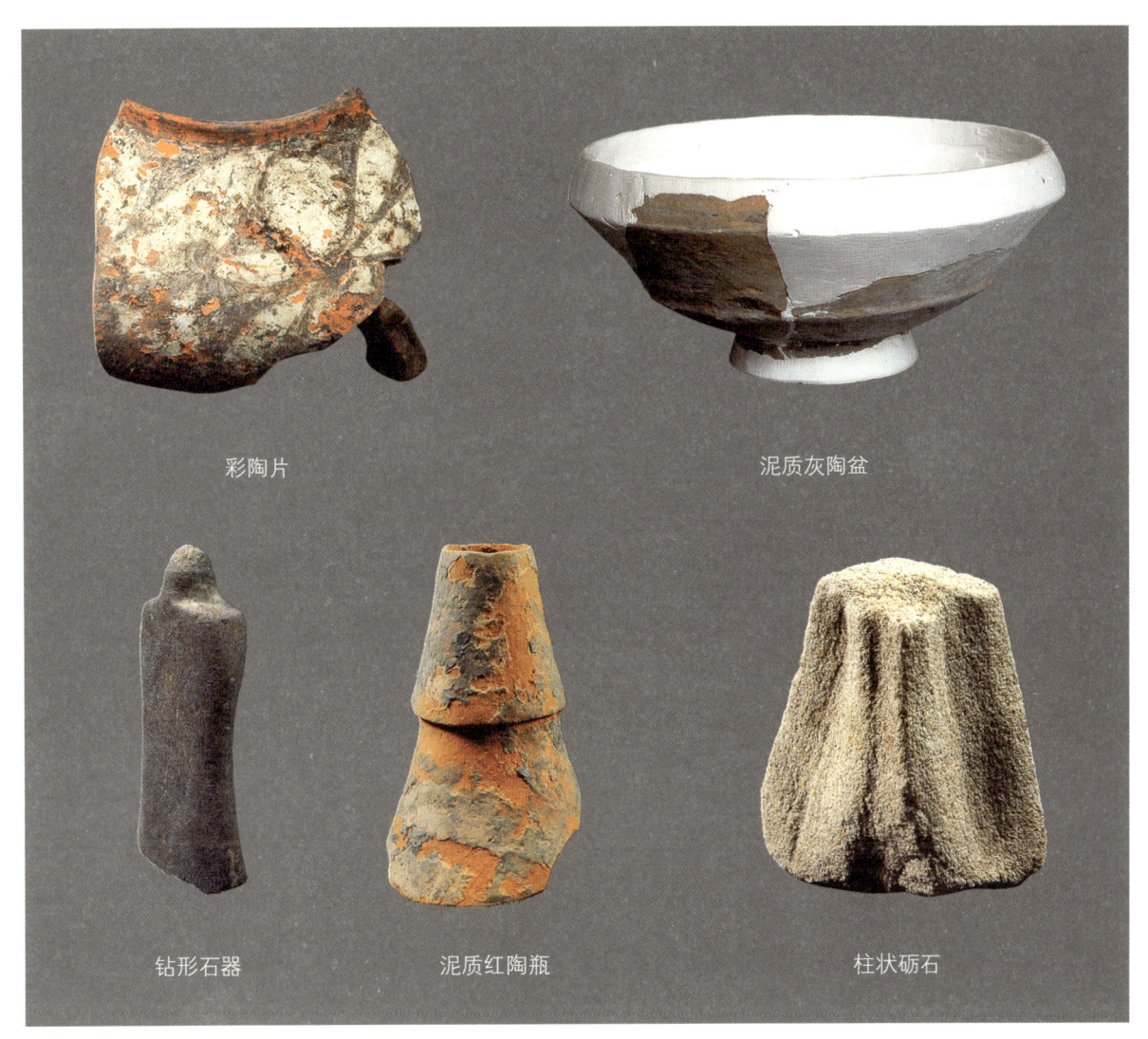

| | |
|---|---|
| 彩陶片 | 泥质灰陶盆 |
| 钻形石器 | 泥质红陶瓶 | 柱状砺石 |

**凌家滩遗址出土遗物**

Lingjiatan Site is located in Lingjiatan Village in Hanshan County, Anhui Province. In the 1980s, this Neolithic site was discovered, and archaeological work has been carried out in continuity since then. From 2013 to 2017, based on the discoveries of investigations and reconnaissances, several excavations were conducted on Lingjiatan Site itself and Weigang Site, which is peripheral to Lingjiatan Site. The total excavated area was over 1600 square meters.

After years of investigations, probings and test excavations, it is known, at least, that Lingjiatan Site is the largest and highest-ranking prehistorical settlement in the Yuxi River Basin. In the entire region, other settlement sites, which existed roughly in the same period, are found in low density and most of them cover a comparatively smaller area. However, there are several small settlement cluster sites. The confirmation of the living area in Lingjiatan Site per se, the great number of unearthed articles for daily use and the discovery of moats are the most important achievements.

# 江苏兴化、东台蒋庄新石器时代遗址

◎林流根 甘恢元 闫 龙

2011年10月至2015年12月，南京博物院对位于江苏兴化、东台两市交界处的蒋庄新石器时代遗址进行了抢救性考古发掘，共发掘面积3500平方米，揭露良渚文化聚落一处。目前已清理墓葬284座、房址8座、灰坑110余座以及水井、灰沟等遗迹。出土玉、石、陶、骨器等遗物近1200件。

此次发掘的良渚文化墓地，是蒋庄遗址良渚文化聚落最为重要的内容。墓地位于聚落东北部，为一处公共墓地，有着持续而稳定的使用过程。另外，墓葬间等级分化严重，随葬玉璧、玉琮的高等级墓葬主要集中于墓地南部，而"平民墓"主要位于墓地中北部。这种不同等级墓葬间明显的分区，体现了社会分层现象。

墓葬形制均为长方形竖穴土坑，葬式多样，一次葬与二次葬并行。头向东，主要分布于墓地的中北部。二次葬分烧骨葬与拾骨葬两种，随葬玉琮、玉璧的较高等级墓葬均为二次葬。

墓葬共出土玉、石、陶、骨器等随葬品700余件。还见木胎漆器，但与墓葬等级高低并无直接关联。其中石钺、锛、凿与陶纺轮不同出，随葬前者的为男性，随葬后者的为女性，反映了墓主性别与社会分工的差异。

同时，还发现了8座良渚时期房址，均为挖基埋柱的平地起建式，平面形状有圆形及长方形两种，并见多间联排式房址。

蒋庄遗址是在长江以北地区首次经大规模发掘的良渚文化聚落，其中良渚文化墓地是在长江以北首次发现随葬琮、璧等玉质礼器的高等级墓地，突破了以往学术界认为良渚文化分布范围北不过长江的传统观点，是迄今为止发现保存骨骸最为完整和丰富的良渚文化墓地资料。

其远离良渚文化核心区，出土的各类陶鼎的鼎足各异，具有鲜明的自身特点，显示出这类遗存可能属于良渚文化的又一地方类型，是良渚与当地文化因素融合后的产物。

良渚文化墓地（西—东）

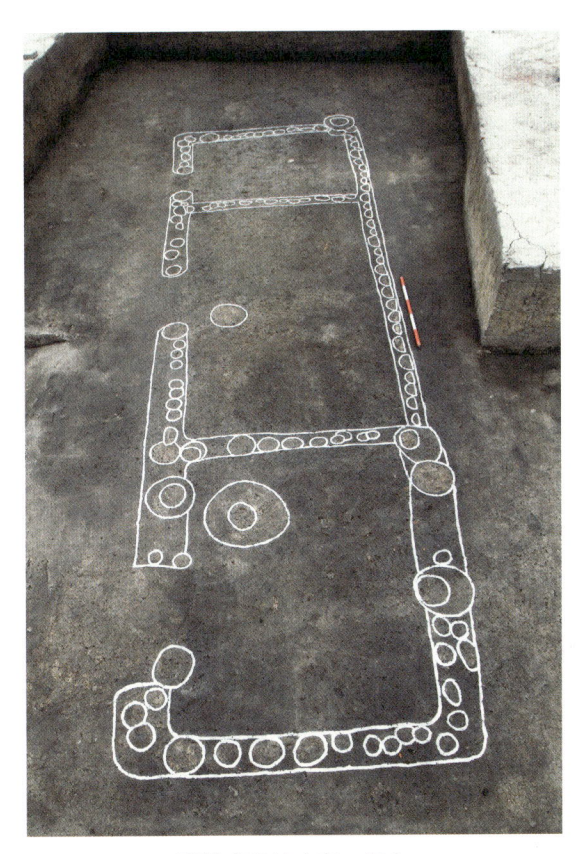

联排式房址（东—西）

M158全景（北—南）

M45全景（西—东）

M100玉器组合

M110玉器组合

陶鼎　　　　　　　　　　　　　　　陶鼎

双鼻陶壶　　　陶鼎　　　　　　　陶鬶

陶鼎　　　　　　　　　　　双鼻陶壶

**良渚文化陶器**

刻纹玉璧

玉琮

石钺

石锛

**良渚文化遗物**

Jiangzhuang Site is located on the border of Dongtai City and Xinghua City in Jiangsu Province. From 2011 to 2015, archaeologists from Nanjing Museum conducted salvage excavations on the site. The excavation was carried out mainly in the west section and a settlement of Liangzhu Culture period was revealed.

The cemetery excavated this time is of Liangzhu Culture. It is the first time that high-ranking cemetery of Liangzhu Culture, in which there were burial accessories like Cong, Bi and other jade ritual vessels, was discovered north of Yangtze River. Conventionally, in academic circles, it was believed that all the sites of Liangzhu Culture were distributed south of Yangtze River and none was located beyond the river in the north. Now, the regional distribution confinement has been broken through. Jiangzhuang Site is located north of Yangtze River and in the area which was an important passage for the northward spread of Liangzhu Culture. The site per se, far away from the core area of Liangzhu Culture, has its own distinctive features. It is indicated that such sites, as products of combined Liangzhu Culture and native cultural elements, may be a localized type of Liangzhu Culture. The excavation of Jiangzhuang Site is of great significance for the establishment of prehistorical archaeological cultural pedigree in the eastern area of Yangtze River-Huaihe River Region and for the study of the relationship between Liangzhu Culture and Dawenkou Culture in the north.

## 且享且祀 以洽百之礼

## 山东即墨北阡遗址

◎王 芬 栾丰实 林玉海 靳桂云

北阡遗址位于胶东半岛南岸西部，隶属于即墨市金口镇，遗址面积5万余平方米。现地表散布大量的陶片、红烧土块及牡蛎壳屑等。该遗址于1979年被发现。2007—2013年，山东大学考古学系和青岛市文物保护考古研究所先后进行四次发掘，累计发掘面积为2450平方米，文化遗存主要包括西周晚期到春秋时期、北辛文化晚期到大汶口文化早期阶段两大时期。

发掘工作基本上完整揭露了北阡大汶口文化聚落。聚落的格局大体是以两个小的室外活动广场为中心，在广场周围房址（柱洞）和墓葬呈现分组分布的特点。而且这种格局延续性较强，在同一地点打破关系极为复杂。另外，在聚落东北部还发现一处时代较早的垃圾沟。

两处广场规模不大，广场1位于东南部，面积约200平方米，广场2位于西北部，面积约100平方米，两广场相距约15米。广场的堆积均为层层筑打而成，中间夹杂有成层的红烧土铺垫层，十分坚硬。广场的堆积比较简单，与周边遗迹呈现出的错综复杂的打破、叠压情况完全不同。广场上基本没有遗迹分布，而广场周围则分布着较多的房址和墓葬。

大汶口文化房址比较复杂，从结构上看，有地面式建筑、半地穴式建筑。地面式建筑主要分为基槽式、柱洞式建筑，有的还有前后分间现象。四个年度发现的房址多达一百多座。房址面积大小不一，大的可达20多平方米，小的还不足10平方米。

共发现墓葬197座，其中多人二次合葬墓51座，单人二次葬1座，迁出葬137座，火烧葬8座，没有发现其他地区同时期流行的单人一次埋葬现象。可鉴定的埋葬人数近三百人。

二次葬墓分为二次合葬和二次单人葬两种类型，以二次合葬最为多见。二次合葬墓形制较为复杂，平面形状以长方形最多，也有近方形、椭圆形和不规则形者。墓坑一般较浅，墓葬内的人骨多为单层放置，也有分二层和三层摆放的现象。除个别合葬墓的人骨放置较为规则之外，绝大多数墓葬的人骨摆放得十分凌乱，似无规律可循。从后期的整理和鉴定情况看，每一个个体的人骨缺失均十分严重。多数墓葬没有随葬品，有者也极少，种类有鼎、鬶、罐、觚形杯等陶器和少量石器、骨器。

迁出墓葬的平面形状以长方形为主，也有少数椭圆形者，有接近一半数量的迁出墓的长度较短，多在1.50米之内。墓葬内部往往遗有少量零碎骨骼，如指(趾)骨等。有的墓葬还有个别随葬品等。

该遗址还发现较为丰富的周代遗存。遗迹类型有：代表围墙的基槽、沟、窑、窖穴和灰坑等。在遗址中部位置，发现一处周代围墙，现仅存基槽部分。在围墙使用期间，有一次大规模的重建过程，表现为在早期基槽外侧又另挖建一条晚期基槽。在基槽的外围发现至少两周环壕，其中内侧环壕打破基槽。由于基槽和环壕围拢起来的面积不大，墙体内侧总面积约1200平方米，所以居住于其内的人口不会太多。

除了基槽和环壕，周代遗存还包括一批颇具规模的大窖穴，多为圆筒形，口径在1~2米，大者超过4米的也不在少数。有的灰坑两侧和底部还保留有清晰的木板灰痕迹，有的还发现了埋人现象。大部分灰坑出土大量陶片和贝类遗存等。

5座周代墓葬的规模略大，多有一椁一棺，均为单人葬，头向东。其中等级最高的M1，随葬有青铜鼎和成组陶礼器。这批周代墓葬，应该具有一定的等级，大约可以与文献记载的士一级相对应。所以，周代的即墨地区如果是一个小的诸侯国，那么北阡遗址的等级和规模大体相当于一处二或三级聚落。

陶鼎　　　　　　　　　　觚形杯

房址（西—东）

房址垫土里的石块、贝壳及骨片（东—西）

G7内的贝类遗存（上为北）

多人二次合葬

Beiqian Site is located in the western area of the south coast of Jiaodong Peninsula. It is affiliated to Beiqian Village, Jinkou Town, Jimo City, in the northeastern corner of Qingdao City.

From 2007 to 2013, archaeologists from Department of Archaeology of Shandong University and other institutes conducted successive excavations four times on the site. The total excavated area is 2450 square meters. Cultural remains are of two major eras, i.e., Zhou Dynasty and prehistorical periods. The prehistorical periods mainly cover the time from late Beixin Culture period to early Dawenkou Culture period. On Beiqian Site, a settlement site dating back to Dawenkou Culture period was revealed basically complete and intact. Overall, the settlement had two small outdoor squares as its center. Around the squares, dwelling sites (postholes) and tombs were distributed in groups. Based on archaeological excavations, multidisciplinary researches centering on Beiqian Site were carried out by joint efforts.

# 江苏沭阳万北遗址第四次考古发掘

◎甘恢元

万北遗址位于江苏省宿迁市沭阳县万匹乡万北村，南距沭阳县城15千米。遗址于1987年春经由南京博物院考古调查发现，确认其为一处主体为新石器时代至商周时期遗址。

2015年3月至11月，南京博物院考古研究所与沭阳县文广新局组成联合考古队对万北遗址进行了第四次考古勘探与发掘。发掘显示，遗址文化堆积时代涵盖新石器、岳石文化、商、西周、汉及唐宋等不同时期。

相当于大汶口文化早期遗存出土遗物最为丰富，陶器分泥质陶与夹砂陶两类，以红陶为主，其次为灰陶。器表以素面为主，并见一定数量的内彩陶片。器类主要有鼎、釜、钵、罐、盆、纺轮、网坠等。石器主要有锛和砺石。骨器有镖、镞及锥等，多通体打磨光滑。大汶口文化中晚期遗存陶器主要为泥质陶与夹砂陶两类，以灰陶为主，其次为红陶。器表以素面为主。器类主要有鼎、豆、壶、罐、钵、网坠及纺轮等。发掘所获大汶口文化中晚期遗存石器见有锛、斧等。骨器有镞、镖及锥等。（在大汶口中期地层中同出典型崧泽文化亚腰柄陶豆，大汶口晚期地层中则出土较多的良渚文化鱼鳍形鼎足及少量双鼻壶。）

新石器时期动物遗存极为丰富，种类以鹿科为主，其次为猪、狗及水生的鱼、龟鳖、蚌类，地层及遗迹中见大量的动物粪便。植物遗存亦十分丰富，种类主要有水稻、菱角、芡实、菰、粟、狗尾草属、蓼属、马唐属、苋/藜科等。

陶豆

水晶

骨镖

出土遗物

In 2015, the fourth archaeological reconnaissances and excavations were carried out by a joint team, consisting of archaeologists from Institute of Archaeology of Nanjing Museum and other institutes.

This time, the unearthed cultural remains and relics are of various eras, including Beixin Culture period, Dawenkou Culture period, Yueshi Culture period, Shang Dynasty, Western Zhou, Han Dynasty, Tang Dynasty, Song Dynasty, etc. The excavated Neolithic remains are of Beixin Culture and Dawenkou Culture. Antiquities dug from remains of Beixin Culture are the most diversified. The range and quantity of stone implements and bone implements of Dawenkou Culture, are comparatively limited and just a few. The strata dating back to Yueshi Culture period is thin and not consistent; therefore, the overall cultural landscape of this period is not very clear.

The area in which Wanbei Site is located is an important part of Haidai Historical and Cultural District. During the middle Dawenkou Culture period, this area became gradually under the influence of Songze Culture, which existed in Circum-Taihu Lake Cultural District. When it came to late Dawenkou Culture period, the impact of south-originated Liangzhu Culture reached its zenith. It provides important clues for the exploration of cultural exchanges and integration between the north and the south.

# 山东泰安大汶口遗址

◎高明奎　梅圆圆

从2012年冬季开始至2017年，我们对作为黄河下游新石器时代最重要的古文化遗址之一的大汶口遗址启动了新一轮的考古发掘工作。总发掘面积达2800平方米，发掘区域主要集中于汶河北岸、省道S801东侧、保护碑北侧。2012年冬首次发现7座排列有序的大汶口文化早期房基，其规模大小、建筑形式、间距基本一致，显然经过有意规划。2014年，在7座房基的南侧又揭露了2座房基，与上述7座的规模一致，从布局上分析，应为同一居住区。之后在靠近省道S801的西部又揭露了7座房基，但布局和规模不同于在东部发掘的9座房基。2016—2017年，在1978年发掘区的东边缘，向东、北侧又揭露了600平方米，也发现了大量居住遗迹。

连续五年的发掘，获取了一批新的居住址材料，尤其是保存较好、布局有序的10多座房基，对了解大汶口文化早期房址的形制、结构及聚落内部的布局提供了宝贵的实物资料。

北区是新发现的居住区。在2200平方米的范围内揭露16座房基，除一座为长方形外，其余基本都呈正方形，方向大体一致，皆为地面式建筑，有的墙基挖浅基槽，四面墙基皆有柱洞，墙体应为木骨泥墙。

南区清理出大量柱洞或柱坑，彼此间存在叠压打破关系，许多柱洞间的关系难以缀连，分布得较为零乱。该区的房址经过多次营造、修整、重建，大致可分为前后两个阶段。

通过观察，得知在大汶口早期阶段的房屋墙体以木骨支撑，以草拌泥经烘烤成硬面为主体结构，内部生活居住面经烘烤形成硬面，门道部位也被仔细修整，房址内部功能已规划出活动区、食物加工区，灶址的分布规整、合理。这对于研究大汶口文化居址形态、社会生活等各个方面具有难得的价值。

以前对大汶口文化的考古发现以墓葬为主，而本次发掘揭露出相对完整的大汶口居址区，极大地丰富了人们对海岱地区大汶口文化的认识。

文明化进程　103

2012—2016年发掘区（上为北）

北区房址F8

南区房址F19

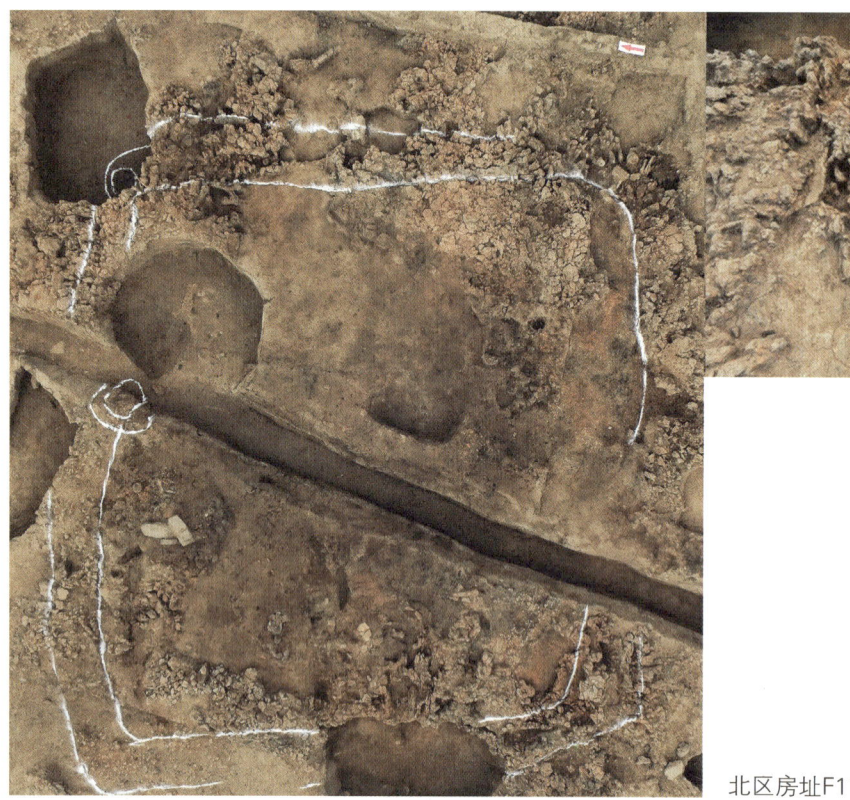

北区房址F11（上为东）

F11门道剖面

F11器物（上为西南）

F11残存墙体

陶器盖　　　石磨盘棒

陶鼎　　　陶鼎

    Dawenkou Site in Tai'an is one of the most important ancient cultural sites of the Neolithic Age in the downstream area of Yellow River. The site is located in Tai'an City, on the border of Dawenkou Town of Daiyue District and Ciyao Town of Ningyang County.

    Most previous knowledge about Dawenkou Culture was limited to researches of tombs. From 2012 to 2017, excavations were carried out on the site. Newly discovered dwelling sites, especially over ten well-preserved and orderly arranged foundations, are valuable materials for the study of the shape and structure of dwelling sites dating back to early Dawenkou Culture period, and the layout inside these settlements.

# 山东章丘焦家遗址

◎王 芬 路国权 唐仲明 宋艳波

焦家遗址位于济南市章丘区西北20千米处，主要分布于焦家、苏官、董家和河阳店等村庄之间的农田区域，遗址总面积超过100万平方米。焦家遗址延续时间较长，主要遗存为大汶口文化中晚期阶段，下限为汉代。

2016—2017年春夏，为探讨该聚落的布局、结构和内涵等问题，山东大学历史文化学院考古学与博物馆学系结合学生的考古实习，对遗址进行了详尽调查、勘探和发掘工作。以贯穿遗址东西的道路为界，发掘区分为南北两区，发现了丰富的大汶口文化中晚期遗存，包括1圈夯土墙和壕沟、215座墓葬、116座房址和1座陶窑等。另外，在发现的974座灰坑中，大部分属于大汶口文化，此外还有少量属于龙山文化、岳石文化和汉代的遗存。

从聚落演变的角度考察南、北两个发掘区，可以看出其阶段性特征非常明显，从早到晚都经历了早期居住址—墓地—晚期居住址三个发展阶段。

早期居住址的房址多是半地穴式，也见少量的单间基槽式房屋。面积在5~15平方米之间，门道方向不固定，房屋在空间上有分群分组的现象。

墓地共发现墓葬215座。墓葬成排成列分布的特点明显。墓葬形制都为土坑竖穴墓，从墓葬体量、葬具、随葬品等情况来看，可分为大、中、小型墓葬，已经表现出明显的社会分化。根据随葬品形制推断，大部分墓葬的年代在大汶口文化中期晚段到晚期早段，只有少数墓葬可以到晚期晚段。在南区大墓附近还集中分布有20多座祭祀坑，坑内堆满打碎的陶器，器形多见陶鼎、陶罐、陶壶等。也有坑内埋葬整狗和整猪的现象。

位于发掘区南部的夯土墙和外侧壕沟，目前已经基本探明壕沟的走向和分布范围，夯土墙可以分为两期，第一期的夯层局部见版筑迹象，第二期应属于夯土墙的增筑部分，没有发现版筑现象。

除此之外，通过筛选和水洗浮选等方法，收集了大量的各种自然遗物标本，系统采集土样进行检测和分析，相关专家开展环境、地貌、土壤、水文等专题调研，为全面研究当时的聚落与社会、生态环境、生业结构、人地关系等奠定了坚实基础。

文明化进程　107

居住址分布图

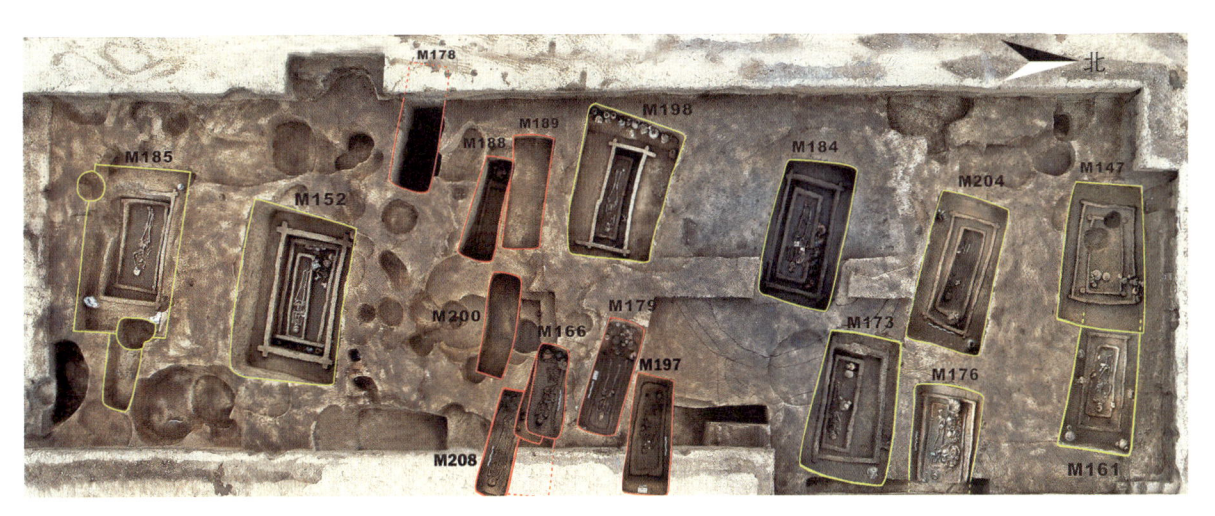

晚期阶段居住期：　晚段　中段　早段

南区墓葬分布图

北区墓葬分布图

M152（上为西）及其随葬品

文明化进程 109

祭祀坑　　　　　　　　　　　　　动物祭祀坑

狗

M66　　　　M70　　　　M5

中型墓葬　　　　　　　　　　　　小型墓葬

墓葬出土陶器

In the springs and summers of 2016 and 2017, in order to explore the layout, structure and content of the settlement, archaeologists from School of History and Culture of Shandong University carried out excavations on Jiaojia Site. Major remains of the site dated back middle and late Dawenkou Culture period. Examined from the perspective of settlement development, the south and north exploration pits both represent their phased features. Chronologically the site experienced three major developmental stages. In the early stage, it was used as a dwelling area, then as a cemetery, and later in the final stage it was again a dwelling area. Most early settlement sites were semi-subterranean and spatially distributed in groups. From the middle stage to the last stage of Dawenkou Culture period, the hierarchal gradation of tombs was increasingly intensified. The site of the rammed earthen city wall can be divided into two sections. There is a method of building walls by stamping earth between board frames. In the first section, it is observed from parts of the rammed layers that this exact method was applied during construction. The second section should be an added part to the wall and there is no trace indicating the application of the building method mentioned above.

# 安徽萧县金寨新石器时代遗址

◎ 张小雷

金寨遗址位于安徽宿州市萧县庄里乡毵沟行政村金寨自然村周边，总面积约60万平方米。遗址主体年代相当于新石器时代大汶口文化中晚期至龙山文化中期。2015年春，安徽省文物考古研究所对该遗址核心区进行了钻探，2016年、2017年持续进行发掘。

2016年度东区发掘区文化堆积较浅，属于新石器时代，遗迹有墓葬、房址、灰坑等。上部有少量龙山早中期的房址和灰坑，之下有少量大汶口晚期至龙山早期的墓葬，保存较差，其下为大汶口中晚期集中墓地。共清理墓葬26座，均为竖穴土坑墓，墓向均为东稍偏南，人骨保存较差，多为单人葬，少数为二人葬、三人葬、七人葬。葬具大多无存。随葬品多寡不一。代表性器物有泥质黑陶瓦形足折腹盆形鼎、夹砂红陶壶形鼎、背壶、实足鬶、圈足镂孔豆、盉、双鼻壶、圈足尊、盂形器、盅、长筒形器等。发现少量小型玉器，主要位于人骨的头部，其中一座墓葬人骨胳膊上套有2件石环。石器有石锛、石凿、石斧、石钺、砺石等。

2016年度发掘西区位于"玉石塘"的东部和南部，在东部偏北位置发现一条壕沟遗迹。开口宽12米，沟底宽4米，深2米，沟内堆积以灰褐土和红烧土为主，出土较多的陶片和少量动物骨骼。在南部发现一座大型红烧土坑，其内填满红烧土块，包含较多陶片和少量动物骨骼。

2017年发掘西区位于遗址西部偏北，该区堆积丰富，从大汶口文化中期至晚期，发现有排房基址及大汶口晚期为单间、双间和多间房址，有4座大汶口晚期墓葬，与房址杂处，随葬品为1~10件陶器不等。

两个年度的发掘结果显示，该遗址从大汶口中期一直延续到龙山文化中期。大汶口文化中期时，遗址西部为居住区，东部为墓葬区。大汶口文化晚期时，遗址西部主体是居住区，有少量墓葬，东部有少量墓葬。到了龙山文化时期，整个聚落向东部推进。

金寨遗址地处苏鲁豫皖交界处，其文化面貌与鲁南地区的大汶口文化、龙山文化较为一致，同时与豫中地区、沿淮地区、江汉地区、环太湖地区都有一定程度的交流。其大汶口文化中期墓葬随葬品带盖鼎与鲁南邹县野店遗址出土基本一致。其随葬的瓦足盆形鼎多见于新沂花厅、郑州大河村、江汉平原屈家岭文化的一些遗址中。其随葬的双鼻壶为良渚文化的典型器。

金寨遗址遗迹

2016年发掘区
2017年发掘区

大汶口文化房址（西南—东北）

大汶口文化灶（南—北）

大型红烧土坑（西—东）

龙山时期房址（西—东）

文明化进程 113

大汶口文化七人葬（西—东）及随葬品

大汶口文化单人葬（北—南）

大汶口文化双人葬（南—北）

大汶口文化三人葬（北—南）

出土陶器　　　　　　　　　　　　出土玉器

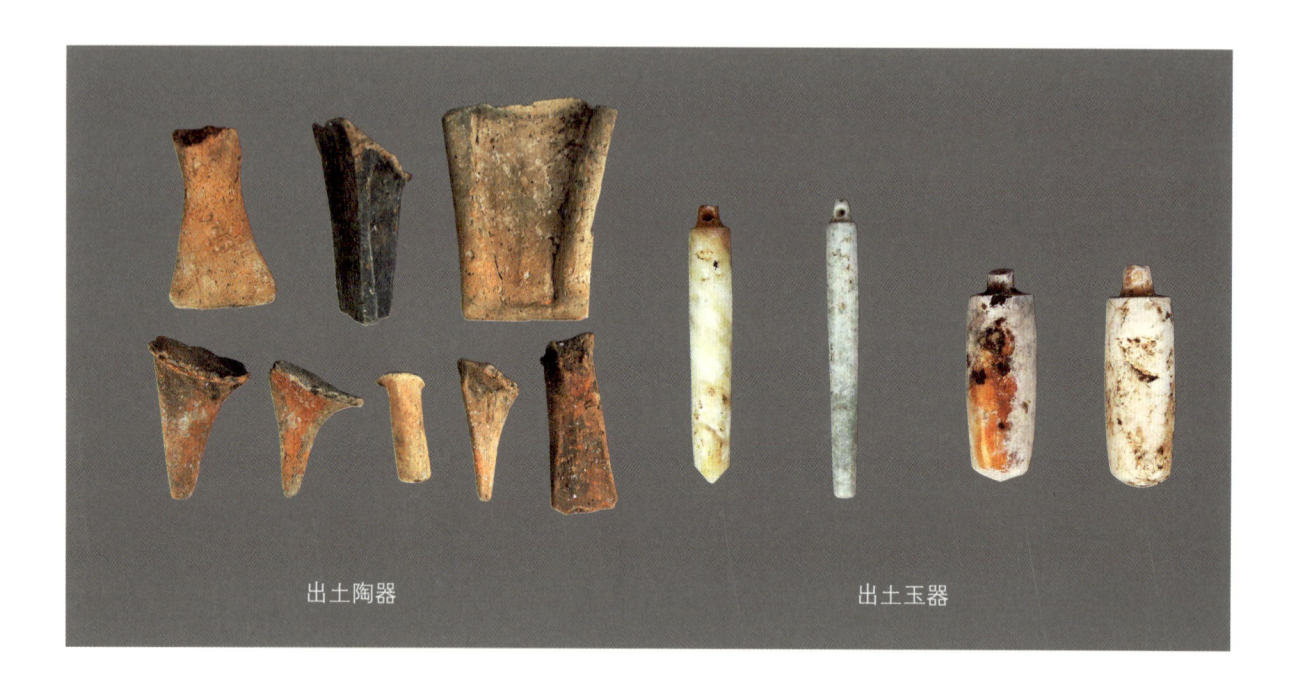

In 2016 and 2017, a joint team, consisting of archaeologists from Anhui Provincial Institute of Cultural Relics and Archaeology and Xiaoxian Museum, carried out excavations on the Jinzhai site.

The excavation results indicate that Jinzhai Site started from the middle Dawenkou Culture period and existed throughout the time till middle Longshan Culture period. There are a small number of ruins dating back to Zhou Dynasty and Han Dynasty. In middle Dawenkou Culture period, the western part of the site was a dwelling area and the eastern part was used as a cemetery. In late Dawenkou Culture period, the western part of the site was mainly a dwelling district with a small number of tombs; and only a few tombs were sited in the eastern part. When it was Longshan Culture period, the entire settlement spread eastwards. The excavation of Jinzhai Site is of great significance for the exploration and discussion concerning cultural content, settlement structure and the process of civilization in the region of Yellow River-Huaihe River Basin in late Neolithic Age.

# 江苏泗洪赵庄遗址第二、三次考古发掘

◎甘恢元

赵庄遗址位于江苏省宿迁市泗洪县梅花镇赵庄村，于20世纪60年代初由尹焕章等先生调查发现，距顺山集遗址直线距离不足1千米。（根据勘探结果，我们将之前分别命名的龟墩遗址、赵庄遗址统一命名为赵庄遗址。）2016年和2017年，南京博物院联合宿迁市博物馆、泗洪县博物馆先后对遗址进行了考古发掘。

两次考古发掘取得重要收获，确认大汶口文化遗存有壕沟、房址、墓葬、灰坑、灰沟、陶窑、兽坑及水井。出土玉、石、骨、陶等各类质地遗物共计500余件。大汶口文化晚期遗存是这两次考古发掘的主要收获。

壕沟已确认区段位于遗址东部、发掘区的西侧，宽度普遍在20米左右、深2.50米。沟内堆积夹杂大量的陶片与灰烬，陶窑及兽坑多位于沟内。

大汶口文化墓葬普遍使用木制葬具（仅存痕迹）。几乎所有有葬具的墓葬均发现墓底有横置枕木的现象。以大陶鼎为葬具的"鼎棺葬"所葬均为婴儿。墓葬间随葬品数量差异大，有木制葬具的墓葬无论在墓坑尺寸还是随葬品数量上均远胜于无葬具者，儿童墓葬均不见随葬品。随葬陶器有陶鼎、豆、壶、高柄杯、觚形杯、尊、盆、鬶、盉等。石器有石钺，玉器有环、锥形饰、坠等，未见随葬骨器现象。除鼎棺葬葬具为大陶鼎外，其他墓葬中陶鼎出土概率低，且为高度仅10厘米左右的非实用器，与之相对应，灰坑及地层中陶鼎属最常见器物，均为有明显使用痕迹的实用器。

经区域考古调查表明，赵庄遗址所在的洪泽湖西北部地区分布着多处大汶口文化遗址，但其规模远不及赵庄遗址，表明赵庄遗址具备了区域性中心聚落的属性。其文化面貌具有自身特色，与邳州梁王城等大汶口文化遗址高度相似，为大汶口文化的地方类型之一。

赵庄遗址大汶口文化遗存较为单纯，少见同时期的良渚文化因素，与阜宁东园遗址、陆庄遗址差异明显。通过对赵庄及周边遗址的考古发掘研究，将有助于我们更深入探讨良渚文化跨江北上之后的路线图及其与大汶口文化发生碰撞、交流、融合的时空坐标。

赵庄遗址发掘全景（上为北）

大汶口文化陶窑（西南—东北）

大汶口文化猪坑（西—东）

M43（南—北）

陶鼎　　　　　　　刻纹陶纺轮　　　　　　陶壶

瓦足陶鼎　　　　　　刻符大口尊

陶盉　　　　　双鼻陶壶　　　　陶鬶

M15随葬品

Zhaozhuang Site is located in Zhaozhuang Village, Meihua Town, Sihong County, Suqian City, Jiangsu Province. The site contains remains and relics of the Neolithic Age (the period of Dawenkou Culture), Shang and Zhou Dynasties, Han Dynasty, Tang Dynasty, Song Dynasty, etc. The settlement site of late Dawenkou Culture period encompasses over 300,000 square meters. In 2016 and 2017, two excavations revealed 1100 square meters and the discovery of remains dating back to late Dawenkou Culture period was a major achievement.

Regional archaeological surveys indicate that there are many sites of Dawenkou Culture in the northwestern area of Hongze Lake where Zhaozhuang Site is located. Various remains excavated from Zhaozhuang Site all illustrate that the site per se was qualified as a regional central settlement. Cultural features of Zhaozhuang Site are unique. The site itself, as an example of localized types of Dawenkou Culture, is highly identical with other sites of Dawenkou Culture like Liangwangcheng Site in Pizhou City.

# 山东烟台午台遗址大汶口—龙山文化的新发现

◎王富强

午台遗址位于烟台市莱山区初家街道办事处午台村村东河滨台地上，现存面积近10万平方米。烟台市博物馆考古队于2011年10月—2012年1月、2013年3—5月先后两次对公路占压的南部边缘进行考古发掘，发掘面积1000余平方米。

文化堆积厚1.20~1.50米，可分6层，包含了三个时期的文化堆积，即大汶口文化时期、龙山文化时期和春秋时期，其中龙山文化时期堆积最厚。发掘区域最丰富的遗迹位于④⑤之下，无论柱洞还是墓葬，其分布密度均较大，应该是该聚落遗址最为繁荣的时期。从出土的遗物看，⑤层下的部分遗迹和⑥层大约为大汶口文化晚期，其他大部分则为龙山文化早中期遗物。

此次发现的大量形制各异的柱洞大致分为10余组群，这些组群经过多次构建，这一点与日照、青岛以及烟台等同时期遗址非常相同，可能与沿海地区海洋季风有关，午台遗址更为密集，且构筑形态也复杂多样，这对认识沿海地区的聚落形态具有重要意义。

此次清理出的46座墓葬均为小型墓，葬式为仰身屈肢葬，屈肢的幅度比较大，随葬品以明器为主，以罐、壶、杯为基本组合，随葬品多置于二层台或墓主人腰部、脚部，反映了胶东地区在这个时期的葬制葬俗。屈肢葬和合葬墓多属于大汶口文化晚期墓葬。由于土质原因，人骨保存较好，我们将对收取的24具人骨进行科学检测，分析研究当时人的体质特征等相关课题。

在⑤层下零散分布的贝壳堆积可能与胶东地区贝丘堆积有一定渊源，出土的遗物虽然不多，但与贝丘遗址的晚期遗物接近，填补了胶东文化谱系的空白。

⑤层下和⑥层的贝壳堆积等反映了该区域因离海较近，海洋采集和渔捞活动仍比较活跃。通过检测和分析，发现该遗址当时在开展粟、稻、小麦混作农业的同时，海洋采集、渔捞所占的比重较大。

东发掘区域（上为西）

西区墓葬分布图（上为北）

文明化进程　121

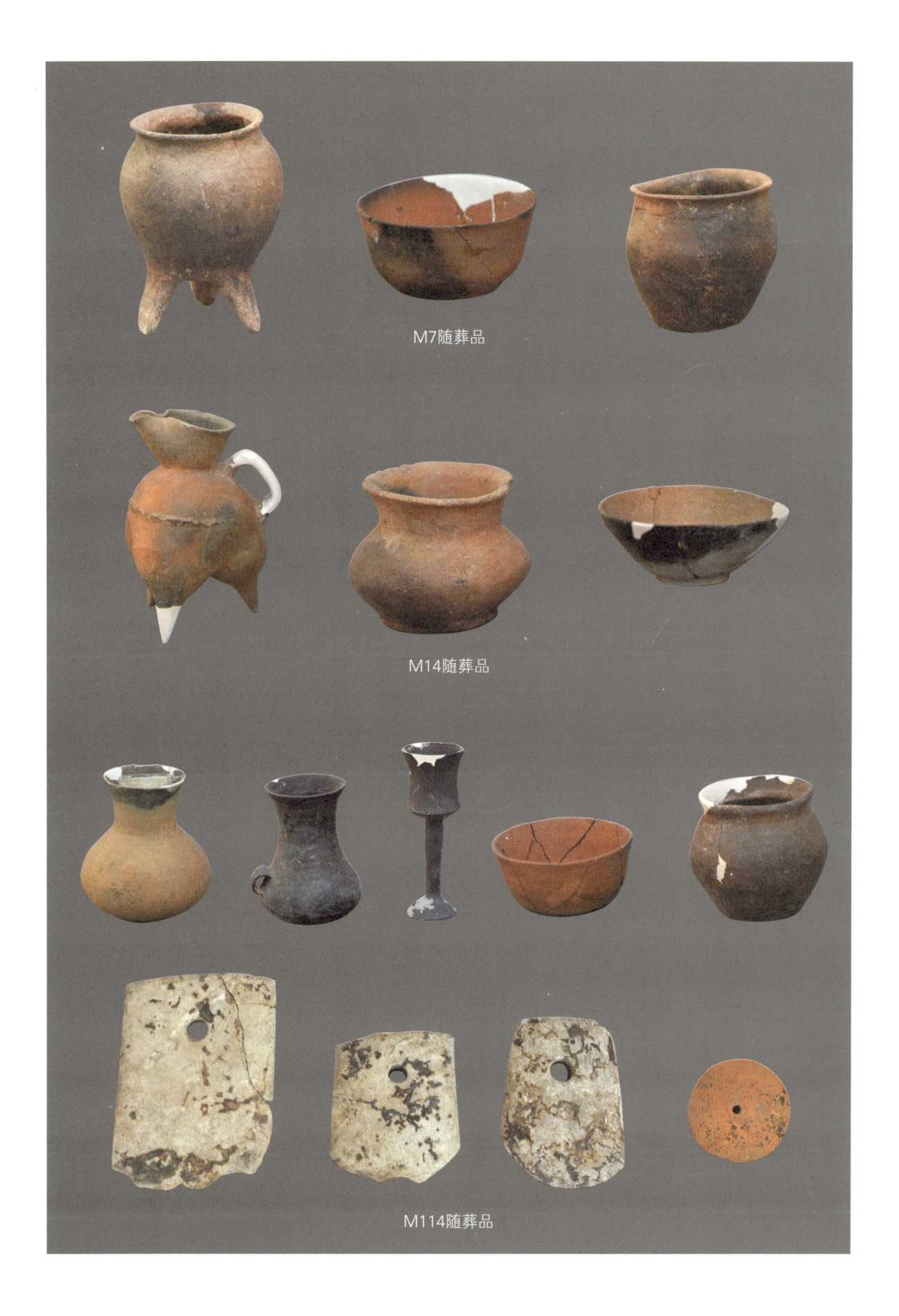

M7随葬品

M14随葬品

M114随葬品

房址F1　　　　　　　　　　　　　柱洞

地层剖面图

Wutai Site is located on the riverside terrace east of Wutai Village, Chujia Community, Laishan District, Yantai City. From 2011 to 2012 and in 2013, Yantai Museum twice carried out excavations on the southern edge which was occupied by capital construction sites.

After excavations on Wutai Site, it has been preliminarily found out that there are remains of three major eras, i.e. Dawenkou Culture period, Longshan Culture period, and Spring & Autumn Period. Stratified deposit dating back to Longshan Culture period is the thickest. Unearthed tombs prominently reflect contemporary special burial rites and customs in eastern Shandong Province. Densely distributed and elaborately structured postholes are of great value for the understanding of the layout of coastal settlements. In Longshan Culture period, in terms of production in Wutai, apart from millet-rice-wheat mixed cropping, oceanic harvesting and fishing took up a large proportion.

# 安徽固镇南城孜遗址

◎余 杰

南城孜遗址位于固镇县西南部的马楼村与杨圩村交界处。2012—2015年，安徽省文物考古研究所与武汉大学考古系合作，对该遗址进行了为期四个年度的考古发掘与勘探工作。发现了大汶口文化遗存、王油坊类型遗存、岳石文化遗存、商代遗存、西周遗存、东周遗存及秦汉遗存。本文主要介绍史前遗存。

重要收获可概括为两方面，一是出土了一批年代跨度长且序列较为完整的遗存，二是大致摸清了大汶口文化时期聚落的宏观结构。

大汶口文化遗存的分布范围遍及整个发掘区，堆积保存较为完好，所见遗迹与出土遗物丰富，为大汶口文化晚期。王油坊类型遗存仅见于遗址东南部堌堆上，岳石文化遗存仅见于遗址中部堌堆上，二者均只见灰坑。

大汶口文化聚落有壕沟隔离的台地，台地间及台地外围壕的"壕沟"，位于2号台地东、北侧的曲尺形建筑等处。

1、2、3号台地现存厚度为1.50至2米，为不同阶段多次堆筑而成。三者底部的台基可能为同时堆筑而成。

曲尺形建筑由黄土堆筑，宽17～26米，年代晚于2号台基。堆积分为内、外两部分，靠近台地的内侧堆积向外侧"壕沟"方向隆起，外侧堆积则向内侧隆起，形成一种近似墙体的存在。

通过解剖"壕沟"发现有大汶口文化时期堆积，其内侧的"护坡"堆积叠压着台基，显示前者的年代晚于台基。

在1、2、3号台地中，发现有房屋、灰坑、墓葬等遗迹。其中，房屋均为地面式建筑，多数仅保留有房屋垫土层、柱洞或墙基，因目前发掘面积有限，少有完整揭露者。墓葬见有成人墓与未成年人墓葬两种，未成年人墓葬均采用瓮棺葬。

南城孜遗址的文化遗存为距今4900年至距今2000年。在淮河流域目前已发掘的同时期遗址中，以南城孜遗址包含的文化序列最为完整，对于探索淮河流域古代社会与文化的变迁具有重要价值。

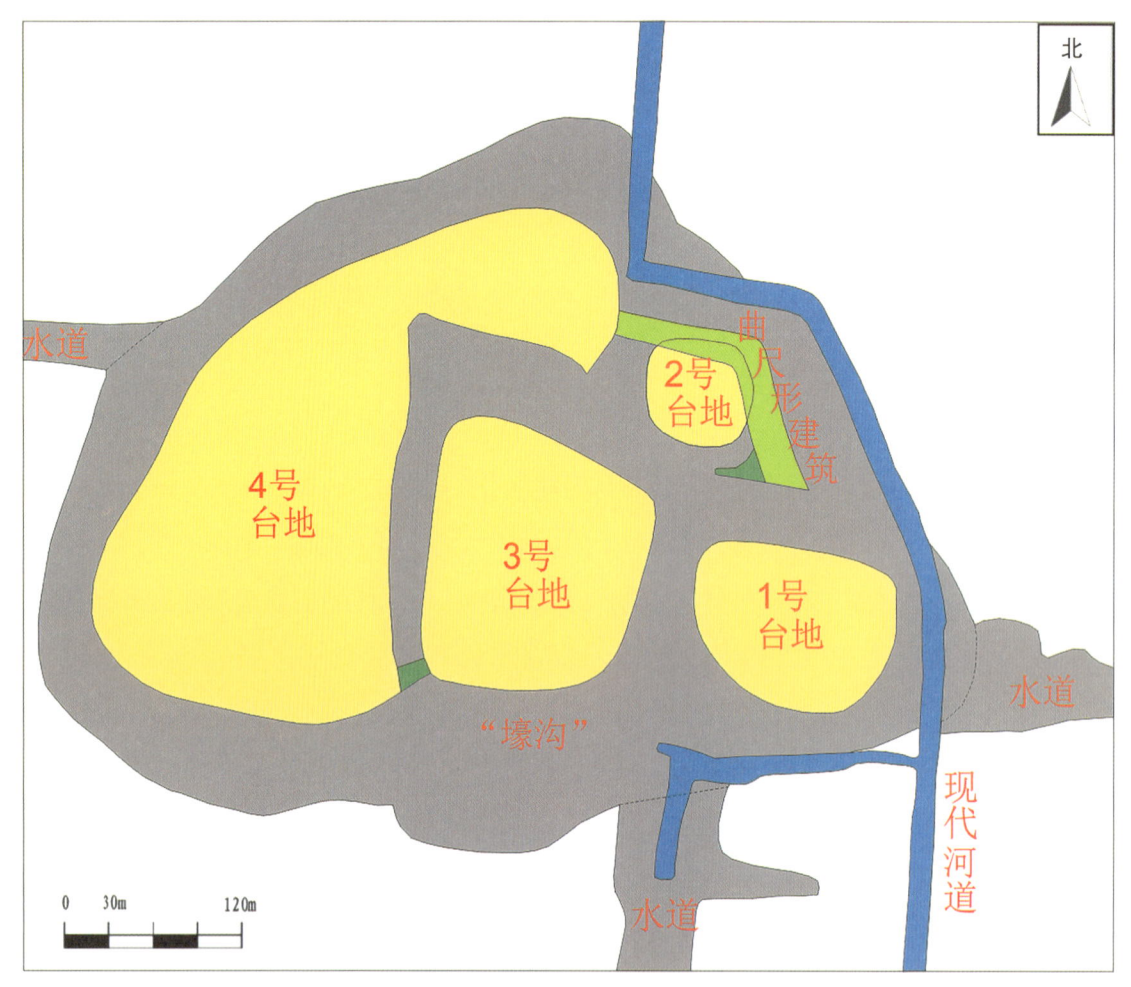

大汶口文化聚落结构图

H1出土陶器

壕沟出土遗物

Nanchengzi Site is located on the border of Malou Village and Yangwei Village, in the southwest of Guzhen County, Anhui Province. From 2012 to 2015, a joint team, consisting of archaeologists from Anhui Provincial Institute of Cultural Relics and Archaeology and Department of Archaeology of Wuhan University, devoted four years to the excavations and archaeological reconnaissances of the site.

Major achievements of archaeological work done on this site can be summarized in two aspects. One is the excavation of a series of relics that lasted a long time span and in a relatively complete sequence. The other is a rough understanding of the macroscopic structure of the settlement in Dawenkou Culture period.

Remains unearthed from Nanchengzi Site roughly existed 4900 to 2000 years ago. Compared with many contemporary sites excavated in the Huaihe River Basin, the cultural sequence contained in Nanchengzi Site is the most complete. Besides, comparatively abundant relics have been discovered from every phase. It is of great value for the exploration of ancient social and cultural changes in the Huaihe River Basin.

# 安徽寿县丁家孤堆新石器—商周遗址

◎蔡波涛

丁家孤堆遗址位于寿县堰口镇青莲寺村丁家孤堆村民组北部。2014年，安徽省文物考古研究所联合寿县文物管理局对丁家孤堆遗址进行了抢救性考古发掘。该遗址呈不规则圆形台地状，是江淮地区商周时期典型的"堌堆型"遗址。

在遗址的最下层堆积中发现有少量相当于大汶口文化晚期至典型龙山文化早期的遗存，代表器类有饰宽横篮纹、正装扁凿形足的鼎、长颈壶以及红陶鬶等。

丁家孤堆遗址龙山时代晚期遗存有灰坑、零星柱洞式房址，以及较多类似冲沟，推测本次发掘的区域可能为龙山时期遗址的外围区，这些冲沟很可能具备当时聚落的环壕性质。该时期的遗物以陶器为主，另有石器、骨角器和少量玉器等。该期遗存分布较广泛，基本覆盖整个发掘区。

岳石文化遗存则数量较多，典型器类有素面的鼎、盆和橄榄形罐等，说明岳石文化在江淮地区西部的分布较为强劲。本次发现的岳石文化遗存，对于深入探讨该文化西进具有重要意义。

本次发掘还获得了一批二里头文化时期的遗物包括豆、深腹罐和爵等。

遗址所发现的典型商文化遗存较少，只有零星的遗物或少量地层堆积，可辨识典型器类为尖锥状鬲足和假腹豆等。

丁家孤堆遗址西周时期的聚落主体即居住址主要位于遗址整个台地的北部区域。

丁家孤堆遗址堆积丰富，是江淮西部地区龙山文化晚期至二里头文化的复合型遗址。它的发掘，将完善本地区从龙山时代早期到西周的编年序列。

丁家孤堆遗址发掘区航拍图（上为北）

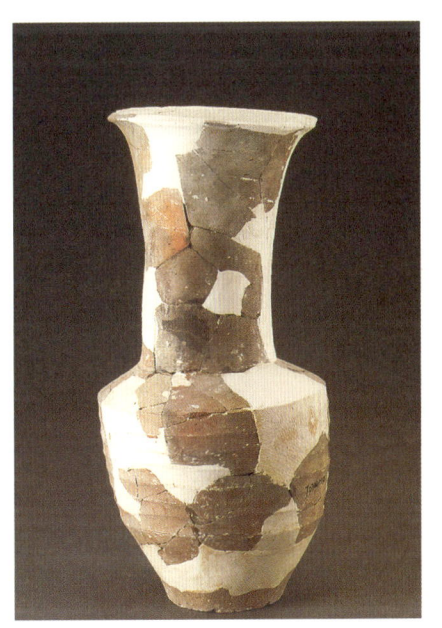

红陶鬶　　　　　　　　长颈壶

陶鼎　　　　陶鼎　　　　陶鼎

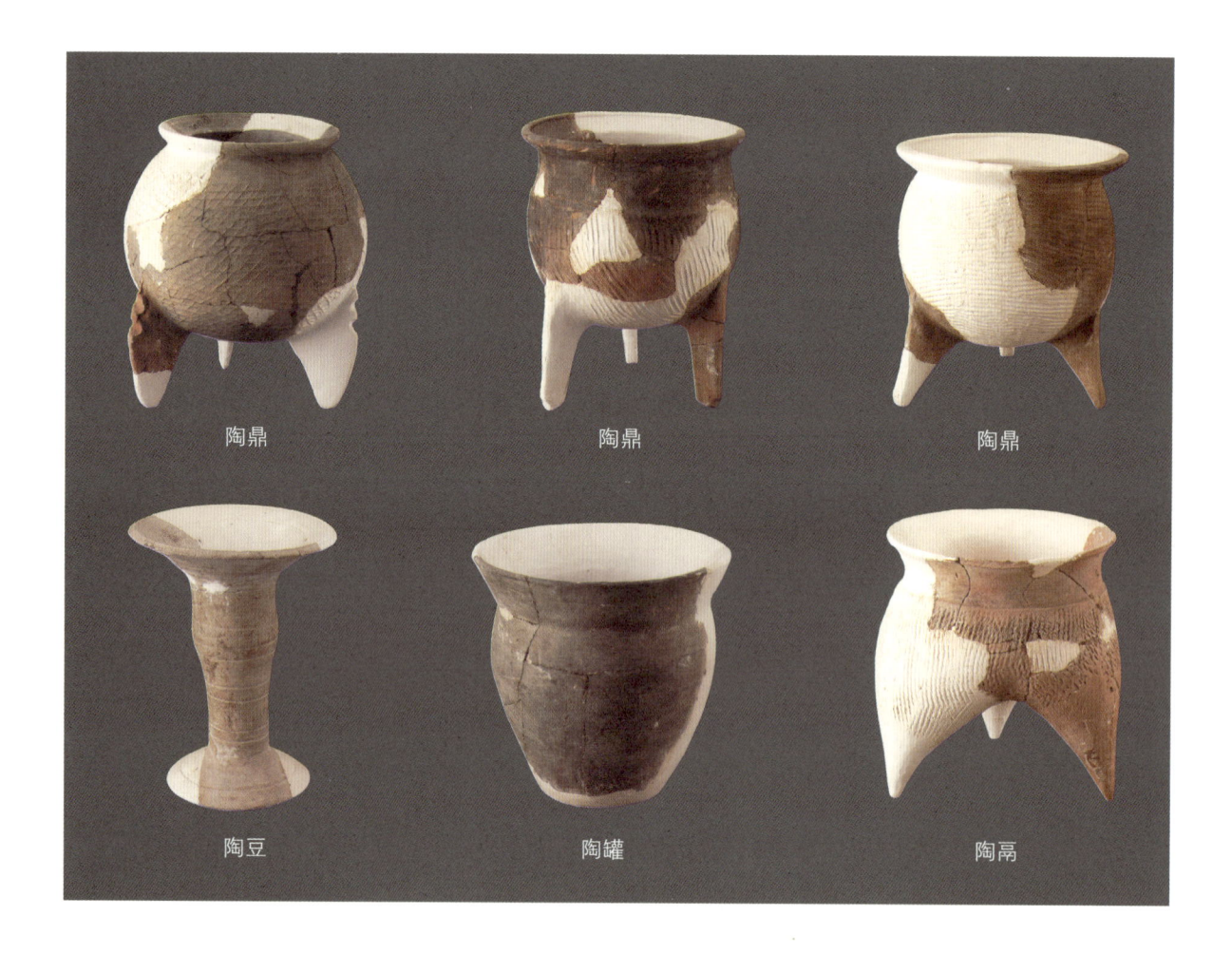

陶豆　　　　陶罐　　　　陶鬲

Dingjiagudui Site, which is just 5 kilometers away from the well-known Qingliansi Site, is located in the northern part of Dingjiagudui Villagers' Group in Qingliansi Village, Yankou Town, Shouxian County, Anhui Province. In 2014, a salvage excavation was carried out on the site. The excavation has revealed that the site mainly contains remains of four eras. Most of the remains date back to Western Zhou and to the late Longshan Culture period; some others date back to Shang Dynasty and Erlitou Culture period.

What is more important is the discovered remains of typical Yueshi Culture. The discovery is of great significance for further exploration of the westward spread of Yueshi Culture and other issues. Stratified deposits on Dingjiagudui Site are diversified. The site per se, the same with Doujitai Site, is a compound site which contains remains of multiple eras in the southern area of Yangtze River-Huaihe River Region. The excavation of Dingjiagudui Site helps to establish the regional cultural sequential framework from early Longshan Culture period (it was late Dawenkou Culture period in the northern area of Huaihe River Basin) to Western Zhou. It also benefits the study of cultural pedigrees.

# 山东章丘城子崖遗址 2013—2015 年度发掘概况

◎朱　超　孙　波

城子崖遗址位于山东省章丘市龙山街道龙山四村东北、山城村北邻，东距章丘市区约15千米，西临巨野河。遗址地貌呈台状，面积20余万平方米。2010—2015年为配合"中华文明探源工程"课题研究和国家考古遗址公园建设，山东省文物考古研究所（今山东省文物考古研究院前身）联合北京大学考古文博学院对遗址进行了新的调查和试掘。

2010—2011年为前期调查。共记录遗址49处，其中除已发掘或先前记录在案的2处遗址外，新发现遗址47处。其中大汶口文化、龙山文化、岳石文化三个阶段的发现与本课题有关。

大汶口文化时期遗址共发现6处，在巨野河上、中、下游均有分布，于下游干流较为密集，遗址面积数万平方米不等，仅焦家1处超过50万平方米。龙山文化时期遗址数量成倍增加，共发现12处，面积从一两万至20多万平方米不等。绝大多数遗址分布于城子崖以北河段，以南仅发现2处。在下游干流遗址明显增多的同时，另有一半以上遗址迤逦东去。岳石文化时期遗址共发现8处，此期遗址下部地层多为龙山文化遗存，故数量虽较之有所回落，其沿河分布特征却基本没有改变，也是下游干流较为密集。遗址面积从一两万到20余万平方米不等。商代文化遗址仅发现4处，数量急剧减少，面积多数超过10万平方米。整体沿河道呈线性分布，距离河道较近。

2013—2015年的考古发掘可分两部分，主要是对纵中探沟的复掘发掘及岳石文化晚期南城门区域的发掘。

1930年，在对纵中探沟发掘时曾布设了45段探沟，长度450米，实际发掘了340米。这次复掘，除了将部分原来没有发掘的段落补上，还各向南北两端延伸了20米，以将南北城墙包括进来，合计长度490米。后对南部区域进行了小面积发掘，收获如下：

1.城子崖遗址经历了龙山、岳石、早商、周代四个阶段。

2.探沟南北端都发现龙山文化和岳石文化城墙。其中，龙山文化城墙保留较差，基本被岳石文化城墙破坏殆尽；岳石文化城墙分为两道，分别位于龙山文化城墙内、外侧。岳石文化外侧城墙打破龙山城墙外坡，最后被岳石文化晚期壕沟打破。岳石文化内侧城墙仅存基槽部分，可能与打破外侧岳石文化城墙的岳石文化晚期壕沟相对应，属于新筑城墙，反映了新的建筑方式和特点，墙与壕分开，城墙的防护效果不再像从前一样主要依赖城壕的宽度与深度，而主要来自垣墙自身。

3.遗址南部发现的缺口为岳石文化晚期城墙城门，据路土残宽及形态判断，城门宽约4米。紧贴城门内侧发现岳石文化大型夯筑基址，面积达1000平方米，不甚规整，为多次使用堆积形成。在1座大型灰坑内发现埋人现象，可能与祭祀活动有关。基址被二里岗上层早段的墓葬打破，墓葬兼具岳石文化和商文化因素，可能是城子崖遗址岳石文化结束时期的最后遗存。

4.有关遗址中部1930年代揭示的胶泥堆积。这些淤土应该为湖沼相堆积，分属龙山、岳石、周代三个阶段，应该是在漫长历史时期内逐步堆积形成的。

5.在遗址中部淤土范围北侧，发现较多大型遗迹现象，包括龙山、岳石、周代三个阶段的大型沟状遗迹和周代夯筑基址。特别是沟状遗迹，形制规整，体量较大，在岳石阶段，被反复开挖。对其形制的探明还需进一步工作。

6.遗址北部发现龙山文化壕沟，比较规整，向东西两侧延伸，与遗址北部略呈舌形外凸部分外缘的壕沟连接，围成一个略呈椭圆形的区域。目前资料显示可能是龙山城内的一片特殊的地方。

7.初步结果显示，城子崖龙山文化、岳石文化阶段农业遗存有粟、黍、稻等，以粟占绝对优势，余者均甚少。两个阶段除了岳石文化发现大豆，其余无论种类还是占比变化不大。

城子崖遗址发掘现场

岳石文化大型夯土基址夯层剖面（北—南）　　　　　岳石文化祭祀坑（西—东）

岳石文化早期北城墙基槽剖面（北—南）　　　　　岳石文化晚期北城墙剖面（南—北）

Chengziya Site is located in the northeast of Longshansi Village, Zhangqiu City, Shandong Province. From 2010 to 2015, a joint team, consisting of archaeologists from Shandong Provincial Institute of Cultural Relics and Archaeology and School of Archaeology and Museology of Peking University, carried out new investigations and conducted trial diggings on the site.

Basic conditions of the cultural stratified deposits have been generally understood. Remains of city walls, which were of Longshan Culture period and Yueshi Culture period, were revealed at the north end and the south end of the exploration ditch. The gap discovered in the southern part of the site is the gate on the city wall dating back to the late Yueshi Culture period. In the 1930s, mud deposits (afterwards it was proved to be an area of silt that covered approximately 10,000 square meters, and its nature was unknown) were excavated from the middle area of the site. New excavations carried out this time indicate that the deposits are of lacustrine facies. The formation and development of these deposits happened in three phases, i.e. Longshan Culture period, Yueshi Culture period and Zhou Dynasty. In addition, ring-shaped ditches dating back to Longshan Culture period were among the discoveries.

# 山东菏泽定陶十里铺北遗址的发掘

◎高明奎　王　龙

十里铺北遗址位于山东菏泽市定陶区仿山镇十里铺村北约100米处，山东省文物考古研究院联合菏泽市历史与考古研究所和原定陶县文物局于2014年下半年和2015年春季两次对此进行了考古发掘。

两次发掘最大的收获是发现了岳石文化和商代晚期的夯土城墙。

城址坐落于北部土丘高地上，平面近圆形，面积约3万平方米。现存约2/3周的夯土墙，剖面处显示出墙体的建筑和使用可分三大期。

第Ⅰ期墙体为岳石文化时期。

第Ⅱ期可能始建于岳石文化时期，沿用至商代晚期。

第Ⅲ期系商代晚期增补加固而成，到东周时期可能仍在沿用。

在堌堆遗址的东北部边缘，还清理出大量灰坑、窖穴、墓葬，及少量的房基和陶窑等遗迹，其中以龙山文化、岳石文化、商代晚期遗存最为丰富。

十里铺北遗址是鲁西南地区现存古文化延续时间最长、保存最完整、发掘面积最大的堌堆遗存，是研究、展示6000年以来该区域环境和社会演变的绝佳实例。

之前在鲁西南地区已知最早的史前文化为大汶口文化晚期，而此次发掘不仅确认了大汶口文化中期的人类生活遗存，还发现了大汶口早期或更早阶段的遗物，填补了该区域距今6000~5000年人类发展的一段空白，进一步完善了鲁西南地区史前文化发展的链条。

该区域是新石器时代晚期至夏商时期东夷文化与中原文化接触地带，是夏商时期东西势力碰撞、冲突、融合的关键地域，可能与《史记·殷本纪》所载汤伐夏桀"还亳"途经的"泰卷陶"有关。

发掘区域航拍图（上为东）

龙山文化房基

龙山文化窖穴

南部墙体解剖（南—北）

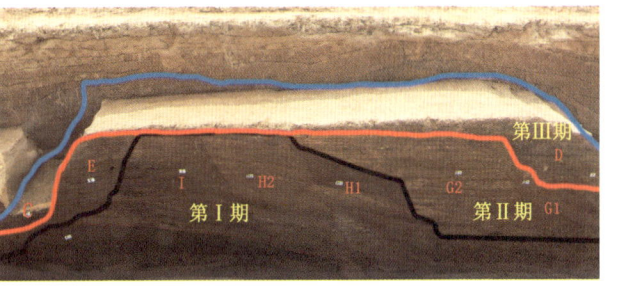

南探沟东剖面局部示意图

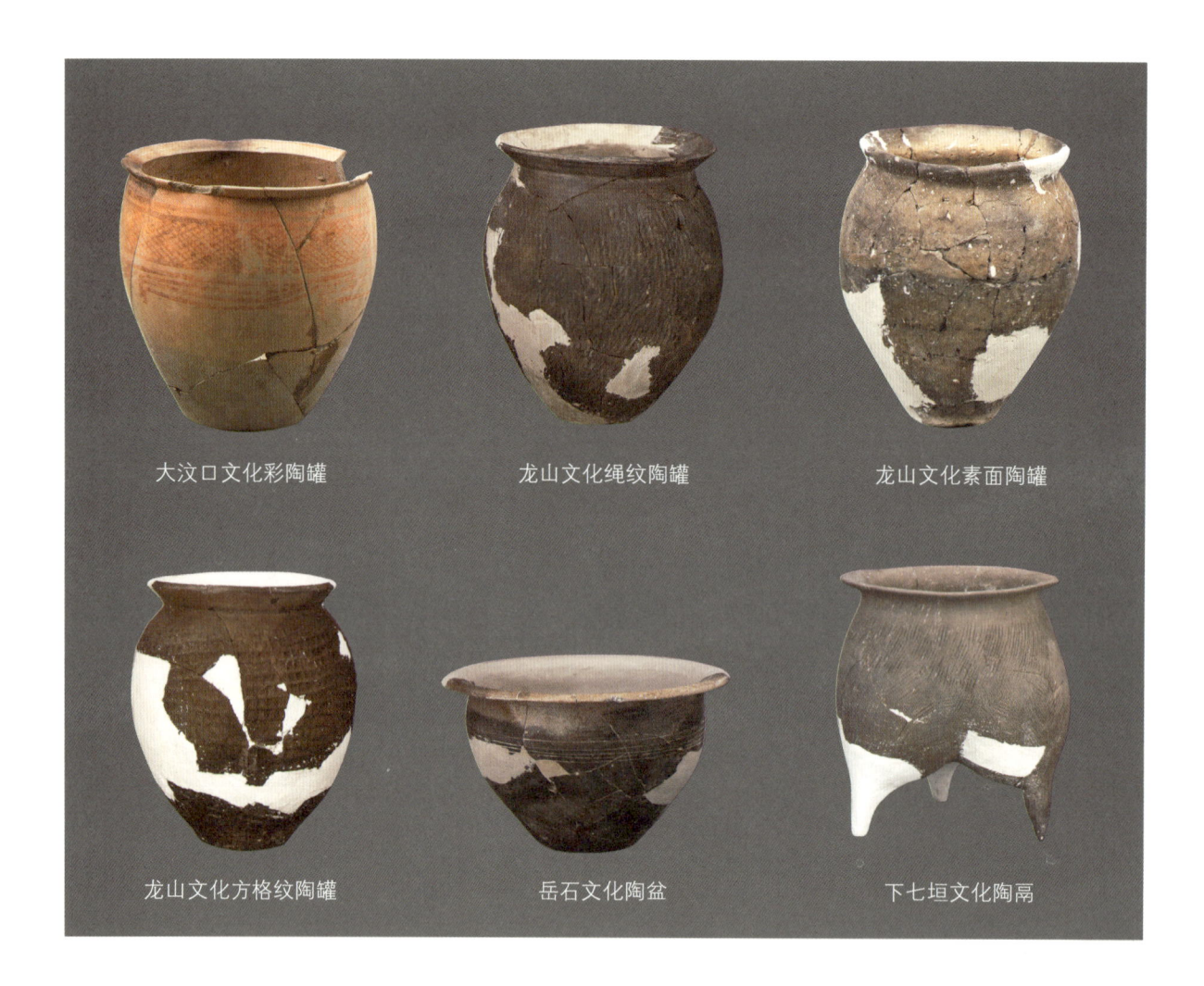

大汶口文化彩陶罐　　龙山文化绳纹陶罐　　龙山文化素面陶罐

龙山文化方格纹陶罐　　岳石文化陶盆　　下七垣文化陶鬲

North Shilipu Site is about 100 meters north of Shilipu Village, Fangshan Town, Dingtao District, Heze City, Shandong Province. In 2014 and 2015, archaeologists from Shandong Provincial Institute of Cultural Relics and Archaeology and other institutes twice carried out excavations on the site.

After excavations, the greatest achievement is the discovery of a rammed earthen wall dating back to Yueshi Culture period and late Shang Dynasty. Apart from digging exploration ditches and dissecting the city wall, on the northeastern edge of Gudui Site (heap remains), archaeologists also cleared up many ash pits and storage pits, more than 10 tombs and a small number of foundation sites, kiln sites, etc. Remains dating back to Longshan Culture period, Yueshi Culture period and late Shang Dynasty were the most impressive in terms of quantity and range.

North Shilipu Site consists of heap remains which are of the longest time span, the best preserved and intact, and with the largest excavation area in southwestern Shandong Province. The site is a perfect example for the study of regional environmental changes and social evolution in the past 6000 years.

# 日就月将 缉熙于明光

## 河南舞阳贾湖遗址第八次发掘

◎ 蓝万里 魏兴涛

贾湖遗址位于河南漯河市舞阳县北舞渡镇贾湖村，该遗址自20世纪60年代初被发现以来先后经历了7次考古发掘，取得了一系列有重要影响的学术成果。

2013年9月至12月，为了配合贾湖遗址考古公园的建设，河南省文物考古研究院与中国科学技术大学科技史与科技考古系及舞阳县博物馆合作，对该遗址进行了第8次考古发掘。此次发掘区域位于遗址中部偏北，发掘面积300平方米。清理出房址8座、灰坑24座、墓葬97座，出土了丰富的陶、石、骨、牙制品及大量绿松石装饰品等。

在贾湖遗址墓葬中首次发现随葬数量较多的绿松石串饰，且分布范围集中，表明当时可能在墓葬等级和分区上已经有了一定程度的分化。还首次发现在墓葬中随葬象牙雕板的现象，该类器物的用途目前尚不清楚。制作精美的象牙雕板，其形制在新石器时代遗址中极为罕见。此外，除了在前7次发掘中出现过的骨笛、骨叉形器、龟甲、带流陶壶等，本次发掘还发现了非正常死亡、一墓三笛等很多新的重要现象。

本次发掘的墓葬与前7次发掘相比还有一个明显的特点，就是基本不见二次葬和多人合葬的现象。可能标志着贾湖与裴李岗这两支亲缘文化之间存在着密切的联系。

这次发掘经浮选发现了丰富的各类植物遗存，在贾湖先民的食物资源结构中，采集是获取食物的主要方式，稻、粟所占比重较小，农业在生业结构中仍处于次要和补充地位。

本次发掘取得的上述新发现，不仅进一步丰富了贾湖遗址的文化内涵，深化了对贾湖文化的认识，同时还为开展中原地区和淮河流域新石器时代人类文化交流、生业结构等研究提供了丰富的新资料。

房址（东—西）

灰坑

墓葬（东—西）　　　　墓葬（北—南）

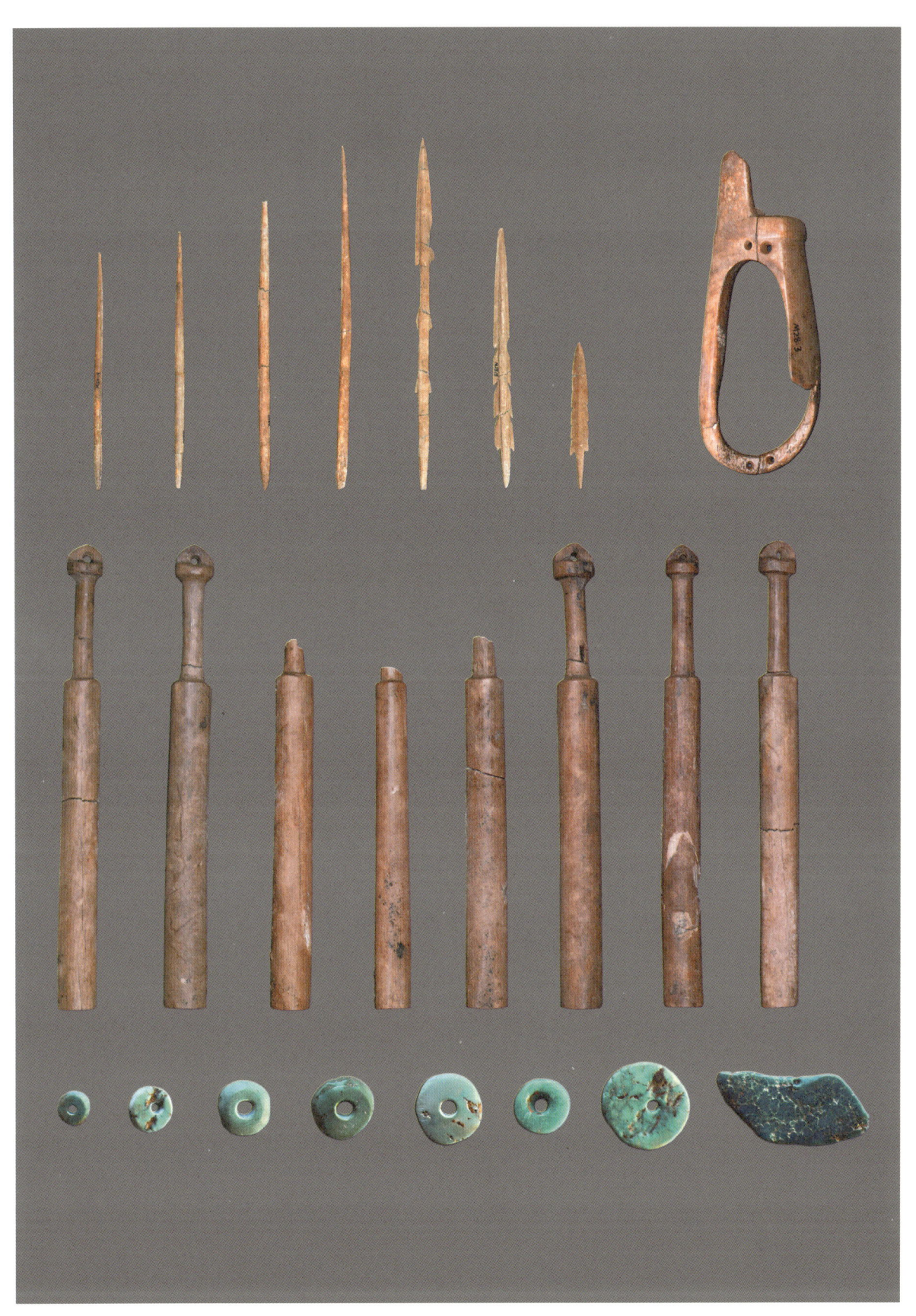

骨器及绿松石饰品

骨笛

象牙雕板

出土陶器

Jiahu Site is located in Jiahu Village, Beiwudu Town, Wuyang County, Henan Province. From September to December in 2013, the eighth excavation was carried out on the site, revealing 300 square meters. 8 dwelling sites, 24 ash pits, 97 tombs were cleared up. A wide range of potteries, stone implements, bone tools, artifacts made of ivory or animals' teeth, a great number of turquoise ornaments, etc. were unearthed.

New discoveries include Funeral objects like exquisitely cared ivory tablets, but twice burial and joint burials were not found this time. These discoveries not only enrich cultural contents of Jiahu Site and deepen the understanding of Jiahua culture, but also provide abundant new materials for the studies of civilization exchanges in Central China and Huaihe River Basin in Neolithic Age, contemporary living conditions, production structure, etc.

# 河北新乐何家庄遗址

◎张晓峥

何家庄遗址位于新乐市长寿镇何家庄村北，面积120000平方米。河北省文物研究所于2016年11月至2017年6月，对何家庄遗址进行考古发掘，揭露遗址面积1200平方米，发现灰坑、陶窑及墓葬等遗迹，出土遗物有陶、石、骨等类，年代分别为仰韶时代、龙山时代、夏时期、东周时期等。

何家庄遗址仰韶时代文化遗存器物组合为勾沿盆、敛口钵、小口双耳平底壶、直口缸、侈口罐等。其文化面貌归属于庙底沟文化。该文化面貌与太行山东麓庙底沟文化钓鱼台类型共性较多；但该遗存缺少庙底沟文化重要器物——卷沿曲腹盆，而宽沿内勾敛口盆比较有特色，这一器形应为庙底沟文化东传的一个地方文化类型。龙山时期文化遗存较少，但出土器物较为丰富，与冀南豫北地区后岗二期文化遗存共性较多，其遗存年代为龙山时代晚期，文化面貌为华北平原龙山文化。

此次发现的夏代文化遗存较为丰富，可分早、晚两期。早期文化遗存其年代为夏时期早期，相当于二里头文化二期。晚期文化遗存其年代为夏时期晚期，相当于二里头文化四期。东周文化遗存较为简单，折沿粗绳纹深腹平裆鬲、折沿圜底盆、平盘豆等器物组合与灵寿故城同时期器类基本一致，年代为春秋晚期至战国中期，文化面貌为中山文化。

此次考古发现的何家庄遗址时间跨度大，文化内涵丰富，是太行山东麓中部山前地区一处重要遗址，尤其是仰韶时代晚期遗存是研究庙底沟文化东传的重要节点。龙山时代晚期遗存是首次在大沙河流域经科学考古发现的，基本揭示出该流域龙山时代文化面貌，为先商文化起源提供重要考古学资料。夏文化遗存是大沙河流域的重要发现，应为一种具有地方特色文化类型"北放水类型"，是研究先商文化源流重要的考古学资料。

仰韶文化晚期遗物

仰韶文化晚期遗物

夏文化遗物

仰韶文化陶窑（南—北）

夏文化陶窑（东—西）

Hejiazhuang Site is located north of Hejiazhuang Village, Changshou Town, Xinle City. The site covers 120,000 square meters. From November 2016 to June 2017, archaeologists from Hebei Provincial Institute of Cultural Relics carried out excavations and revealed 1200 square meters of the site. Ash pits, kiln sites, 1 tomb and other cultural remains were discovered. Respectively they are of Yangshao Culture period, Longshan Culture period, the era of Xia, Eastern Zhou, etc.

Its remains are featured with long time span and diversified cultural contents. In particular, remains dating back to late Yangshao Culture period have been discovered and this discovery is a milestone for the study of the eastward spread of Miaodigou Culture. The revealed remains dating back to late Longshan Culture period is the first scientific archaeological discovery in Dashahe River Basin. Generally, these remains represent contemporary cultural features in this region and provide archaeological materials concerning the origins of culture before Shang Dynasty. Cultural relics dating back to the era of Xia are important ones in Dashahe River Basin, and they contribute important archaeological materials to the study of the source and spread of culture before Shang Dynasty.

# 山西临汾桃园新石器时代聚落遗址

◎郑　媛　武卓卓　薛新明

临汾桃园遗址位于临汾市尧都区贾得乡南部桃园村，与襄汾县邓庄镇寺头村北交界处的黄土台地上。2016年7月底至12月底，山西省考古研究所、山西大学、临汾市文物考古工作站、襄汾县文化局等单位对桃园遗址进行了考古发掘。本次发掘区域位于寺头村界内，根据地形分为三区进行发掘，发掘面积共计2500平方米。

本次发掘的遗迹遗物的年代主要集中于新石器时代庙底沟文化时期。遗迹以各种类型的灰坑居多，同时发现半地穴房址4处，残窑1处，出土了丰富的红陶钵、盆、尖底瓶、平底瓶，彩陶盆、钵、罐，夹砂罐等陶器残片，均为庙底沟文化时期典型的陶器，另有磨制石斧、石铲、骨锥、陶刀、陶纺轮、陶环等遗物。综合分析，这里应为一处庙底沟文化时期聚落遗址。其中，F1、F2、F5这3处房址地面结构保存相对完整，均为半地穴房屋，地面经夯打或涂抹处理为硬面，残存贴壁柱洞和室内中心柱洞。房址内均有火塘，在F1火塘的东边有一不规则圆洞，疑为保持火种之处；F2火塘由F5火塘多次修整移位形成，且火塘西南带有一条向下的烟道。其中F2呈五边形，室内面积近90平方米，应系在F5基础上扩建而成。同时期同类大型房址在河南灵宝西坡遗址、陕西华阴泉护村遗址、陕西彬县水北遗址等地均有发现，是研究当时聚落结构、建筑特点、技术水平等方面的考古材料。

本次考古发掘地点位于晋南豫西庙底沟文化这一核心区域，聚落遗迹丰富且保存较完整，它为深入了解庙底沟文化时期的社会结构、生产生活、文化面貌等提供了一批非常珍贵的实物资料，同时该遗址的发掘对今后认识同时期的同类聚落遗址具有指导意义。

F5（上为东北）

红陶钵　　　　小口尖底瓶　　　　葫芦口平底瓶

文明化进程　145

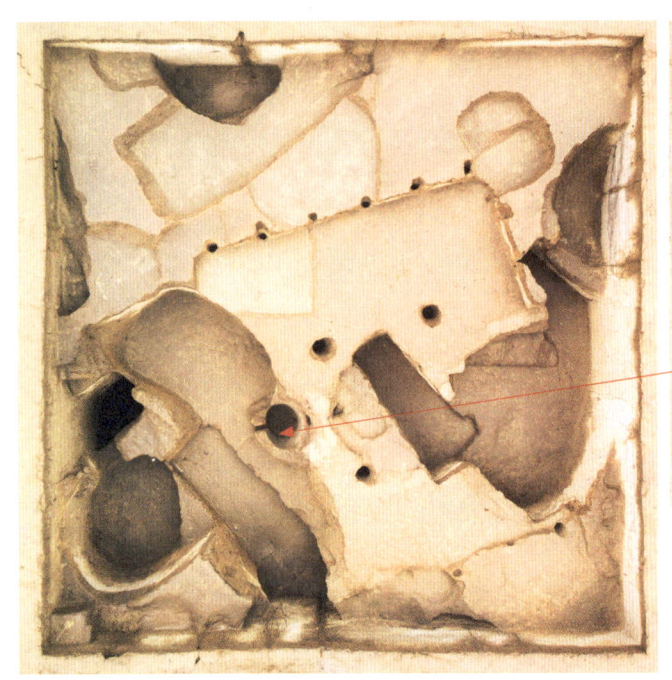

F1（上为西北）俯视图及其南部火塘

F2（上为西北）及其火塘壁草木灰、柱洞、火塘

彩陶

红陶刀　　　陶环　　　石斧

Linfen Taoyuan Site is located on the loess tableland on the border of southeastern Taoyuan Village (in Jiade Township, Yaodu District, Linfen City) and northern Sitou Village (in Dengzhuang Town, Xiangfen County, Linfen City). The site is on the slope of the west piedmont of Ta'er Mount.

From July to late December in 2016, comparatively large-scale archaeological excavations were carried out on Taoyuan Site. Most of the discoveries date back to Miaodigou Culture period in Neolithic Age. Most of the remains are ash pits of varied types. From semi-subterranean dwelling sites and kiln remains, a great number of relics were unearthed, including terra-cotta pateras, pots, flat-bottomed vases, and pointed-bottomed vases, painted pottery pots and pateras, jars made of pottery mixed with sand, pottery knives, pottery spinning wheels, pottery rings, etc. Taoyuan Site should be a settlement site dating back to Miaodigou Culture period. There are three dwelling sites with relatively complete superstructures. These are rare archaeological materials for the study of contemporary settlement structures, architectural features, building techniques, cultural styles, etc.

# 陕西西安高陵杨官寨遗址史前墓地

◎杨利平

杨官寨遗址位于陕西西安高陵区姬家街道杨官寨村四组东侧，南距现泾河河道仅1千米，遗址总面积100多万平方米，是关中地区仰韶中晚期一处特大型中心聚落遗址。自2004年首次发现以来，陕西省考古研究院在此持续开展考古发掘工作，取得了一系列重大考古发现和收获。2015年，为了进一步探索遗址东部区域的功能区划，以及聚落布局状况，我们在杨官寨遗址环壕聚落外东北部开展了针对性的考古发掘工作，发现了一处大型史前公共墓地。

目前已发掘的数百座墓葬规格普遍相近，均为小型墓，墓葬方向基本为东西向，且同期墓葬之间未见打破关系，在部分墓葬开口的东端或西端发现有圆形的疑似柱洞遗迹。墓葬形制可分为洞室墓和竖穴土坑墓两类。前者可分为偏洞室墓和半洞室墓两型，均建有长方形竖穴墓道。竖穴土坑墓根据有无二层台可分为两型。尚未发现木质葬具，个别墓葬中在人骨周围发现有疑似编织物包裹的痕迹，据分析，推测在下葬死者时可能存在用芦苇类编织物进行敛尸的现象。另外在清理墓葬时还发现，在相当数量的墓葬中出现尸骨手指骨移位的现象，它们有的摆放在头骨或盆骨附近，有的则与尺骨整体分离0.20米，这一现象疑似当时流行的某种割体葬仪。

在墓葬内出土了重唇口尖底瓶、卷沿曲腹彩陶盆、泥质筒形斜腹罐、夹砂鼓腹罐等陶器，具有庙底沟文化的典型特征，而且墓葬的$^{14}$C测年数据与环壕的测年结果完全吻合，因此我们判断该批墓地的年代为庙底沟文化时期，是国内首次确认的庙底沟文化大型墓地，填补了该时期考古发现的空白。

本次发掘的杨官寨遗址东区墓地，墓葬规格普遍较小，未见有显著的等级差异。且很少出土随葬品，与环壕聚落西门址两侧出土大量成层分布的完整陶器形成了极为鲜明的对比。因此，推断该批墓葬应是杨官寨遗址普通居民的公共墓地。本次发现的偏洞室墓葬当属目前所知最早的同类遗存，将其出现年代提前了600多年，为该类墓葬的起源与传播，以及关中地区与中国西部地区、乃至西方文化的交流与影响提供了珍贵的考古材料，具有十分重要的学术意义。

杨官寨东区墓地航拍图

偏洞室墓

半洞室墓

竖穴土坑墓

带二层台竖穴土坑墓

彩陶盆　　　　　　泥质筒形罐

夹砂鼓腹罐　　　　彩陶壶　　　　　小口尖底瓶

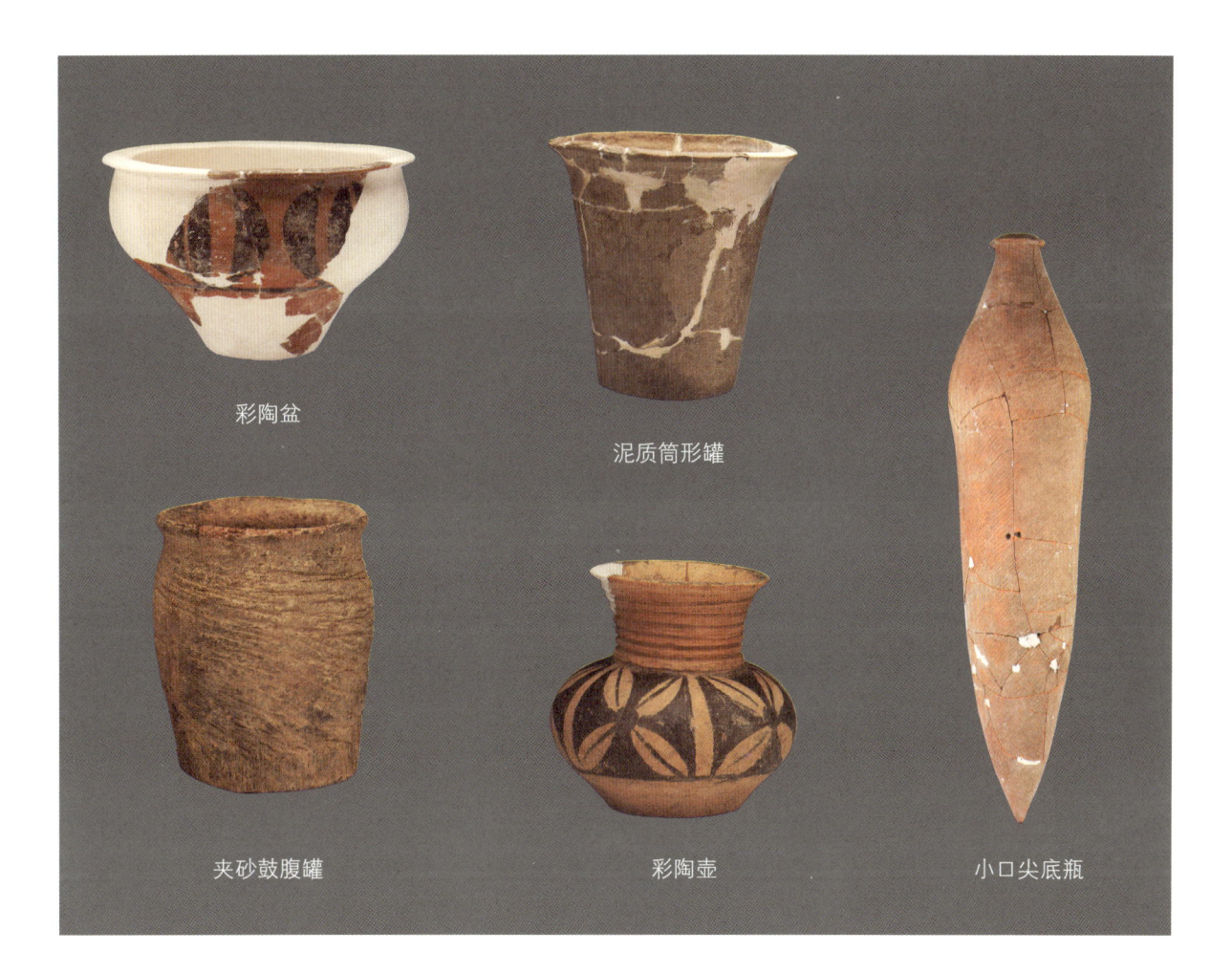

Yangguanzhai Site is located east of the Fourth Villagers' Group in Yangguan Village, Jijia Community, Gaoling District, Xi'an, Shaanxi Province. The site is on the first level of river terrace on the north bank of Jinghe River. The site, covering a total area of over 1,000,000 square meters, was preliminarily discovered in 2004. It is the site of an extreme large-scale central settlement dating back to middle and late Yangshao Culture period on Guanzhong Plain.

After years of excavations, the total excavated area has exceeded 25,000 square meters. A series of major archaeological discoveries and achievements have been made. The discoveries include the only well-preserved and intact large-scale moat dating back to Miaodigou Culture period, the site of a big pool in the center of a moated settlement, the only large-scale adult cemetery dating back to Miaodigou Culture period, a pottery-making workshop dating back to the fourth phase of Banpo Culture period, etc. Important issues like cultural nature of the site, distribution of the remains, layout of the settlement, etc. have been gradually clarified.

# 河南淅川龙山岗遗址仰韶时代晚期城址

◎梁法伟

龙山岗遗址曾被称为黄楝树遗址，位于河南淅川滔河乡黄楝树村西。该遗址自1957年发现以来，前后经过数次发掘，发现了丰富的仰韶时代晚期（朱家台文化）、屈家岭文化等新石器时代遗存。2008年5月—2012年10月，河南省文物考古研究所（现河南省文物考古研究院）对该遗址进行了大规模考古勘探和发掘，发掘面积13600平方米。

该遗址堆积丰富，以新石器时代遗存为主，包含仰韶时代晚期、屈家岭文化、石家河文化、王湾三期文化等时期遗存，发现有城墙、壕沟、河道及房址、路、祭祀遗存、陶窑、灰坑、沟、瓮棺葬等遗迹。出土铜、陶、石、骨等各类遗物上千件。其中，始建于仰韶时代晚期的城址的发现是本次发掘最重要的收获。

城墙依遗址当时所处的地理环境而建，共修筑两段，一段位于遗址东北部边缘，沿古河道修建，呈东南—西北走向。另一段城墙位于遗址的东南部边缘，呈东北—西南走向，和遗址东北部城墙大体垂直。城墙外有壕沟。道路位于遗址中北部，呈东北—西南走向，同时期遗存分布于道路两侧，和道路鲜有打破关系。大型分间式房屋共发现3座，每座房屋的建筑面积均在100平方米以上。祭祀坑位于遗址现存范围的西部，坑内埋葬的猪下颌骨数量不等，有的还有用火烤过的痕迹。

屈家岭文化的遗迹有房址、灰坑、墓葬、瓮棺葬等。发掘表明，这一时期城墙和壕沟尚未废弃，仍在使用。石家河文化时期的遗存数量明显减少，且至该时期，城墙及壕沟的防御功能已经不复存在。王湾三期文化时期，聚落规模显著缩小。这一时期的遗存集中分布在遗址北部，分布范围1万余平方米。

从长江中游地域环境来看，龙山岗仰韶时代晚期城址是其众多城址之中始建年代较早、位置最靠北的一座，也是汉水中上游发现的唯一一座新石器时代城址。该城址的发掘和研究对于认识长江中游地区史前城址相关问题无疑具有重要意义。

龙山岗遗址航拍图（上为北）

遗址东南部城墙内护坡剖面

仰韶时代晚期祭祀遗存

仰韶时代晚期道路（东北—西南）

仰韶时代晚期F4、F10、F16航拍图（上为北）

仰韶时代晚期房址（上为东北）

石家河文化灰坑

屈家岭文化墓葬

仰韶时代晚期遗物

屈家岭文化陶杯

屈家岭文化陶簋

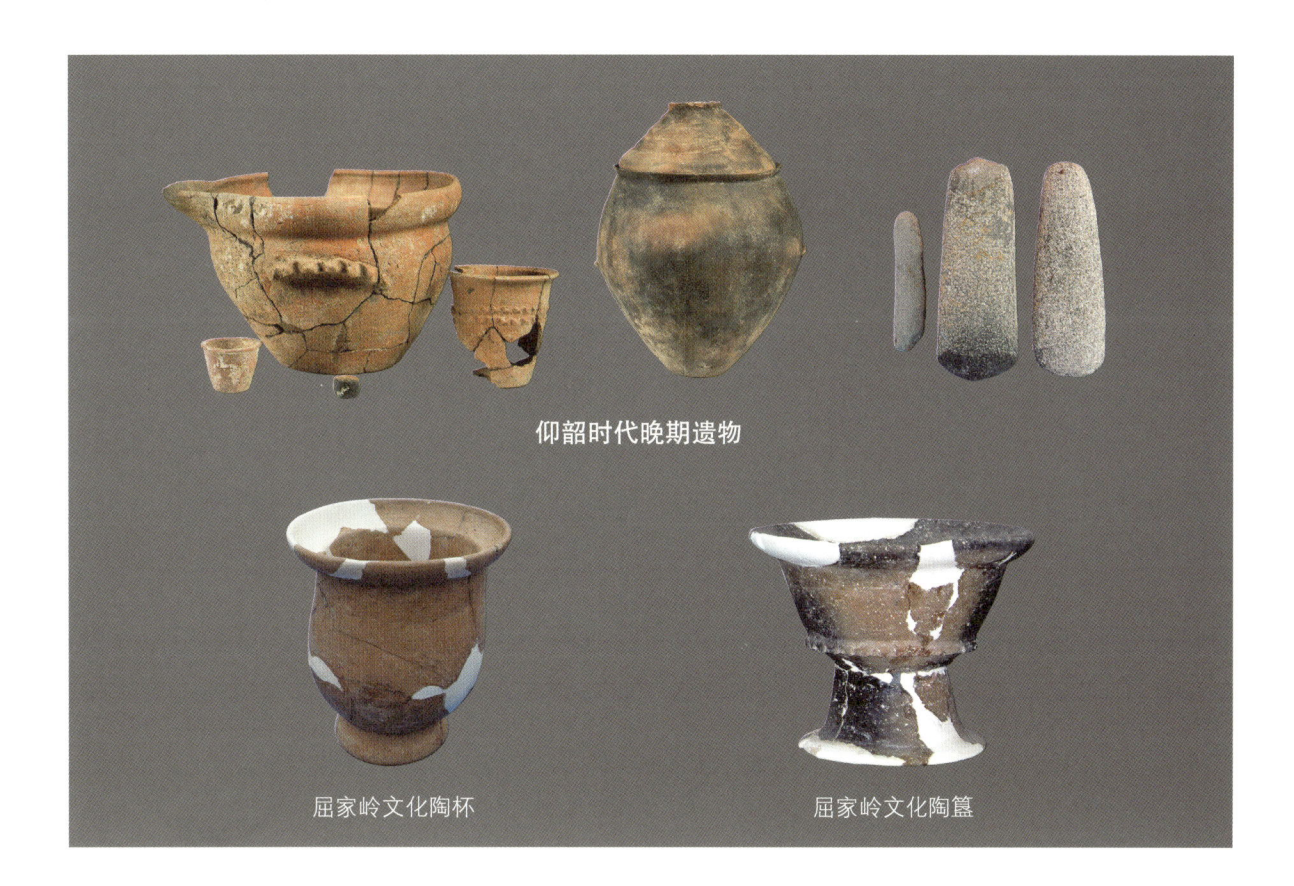

Longshangang Site used to be known as Huanglianshu Site. It is located west of Huanglianshu Village, Taohe Township, Xichuan County, Henan Province. From May in 2008 to October in 2012, large-scale archaeological reconnaissances and excavations were carried out on the site.

After reconnaissances and excavations, the revealed Neolithic stratified deposits cover approximately 136,000 square meters. These deposits are remains of late Yangshao Culture period, Qujialing Culture period, Shijiahe Culture period, the third phase of Wangwan Culture period, etc. There are also a small number of remains dating back to Western Zhou, Han Dynasty, Song Dynasty, Yuan Dynasty, Ming Dynasty, Qing Dynasty, etc. Discovered remains include city walls, moats, canals, dwelling sites, roads, ritual sites, kiln sites, ash pits, ditches, urn burials, etc. Thousands of relics of a wide range were unearthed. Among these, the discovery of a city site that was initially built in late Yangshao Culture period is the most important achievement.

Among the great number of city sites discovered in the middle reaches of Yangtze River, this one was built comparatively early and located the northernmost. It is also the only Neolithic city site found in the upper and middle reaches of Hanjiang River. The discovery of the site and relevant researches are of great academic value not only for the exploration into regional settlement changes and development patterns in every phase of Neolithic Age, but also for the understanding of the cultural features and nature in the intermediary area between the South and the North.

# 河南淅川下寨遗址仰韶至石家河文化时期墓地

◎ 曹艳朋

下寨遗址位于河南淅川县滔河乡下寨村东北，遗址地处两河交汇处的河谷地带，现存面积约60万平方米。河南省文物考古研究院于2009—2013年对其进行了发掘，揭露面积19000平方米。遗址主要堆积为仰韶文化、石家河文化、王湾三期文化和东周时期遗存。最重要的收获是发现了仰韶晚期至石家河文化时期的墓地一处，发掘长方形土坑竖穴墓葬133座。共出土各类随葬品148件，计有陶器、玉石器和蚌片。这些墓葬按照墓主头向的不同可分为甲、乙、丙、丁四类。

甲类墓葬头向大致朝南，共59座，时代应为仰韶文化晚期。乙类墓葬头向大致朝西，共55座。这类墓葬主体年代为石家河文化早期或略早。丙类墓葬头向大致朝东，仅4座。埋葬方法和器物形制同乙类墓葬一致。其时代与前者也大致相同。丁类墓葬头向大致朝北，共15座。根据随葬陶器的组合与特征分析，这类墓葬主要为石家河文化早期，M207可能晚至石家河文化中期。从墓葬之间的打破关系来看：朝南的墓葬分别被朝西、朝东以及朝北的墓葬所打破，证明甲类朝南的墓葬年代最早。

这四类墓葬墓主的头向不同，但并非各自成片，而是处于同一墓葬区。甲类墓葬布局相对集中，大致呈东西向成排分布。乙类墓葬分布范围最广，大致呈南北向成排分布。丙类墓葬数量最少，且分布零散，可与乙类墓葬归为一类。丁类墓葬暂时难以考察其布局规律。除上述后三类墓葬有少量打破甲类墓葬外，同一朝向的墓葬之间绝无叠压打破关系。这从一定程度上说明，虽然各类墓葬共用同一墓区，但是在不同的时期，墓地是经过布局和规划的。

甲类墓葬随葬品主要为玉石钺，乙、丙类墓葬随葬品主要为陶器，而丁类墓葬随葬品则陶器和玉石钺各占一定的比例。后三类墓葬在陶器埋葬方式、组合和钵底凿孔等习俗方面，都具有高度的一致性，属于同一文化传统。甲类墓葬和后三类墓葬之间具有较为明显的差异性，分别属于中原地区的仰韶文化系统和江汉地区屈家岭—石家河文化系统。

下寨遗址发现的仰韶时代晚期至石家河文化时期墓地，表现出的文化面貌印证了豫陕鄂三省交会地带文化因素的多元和性质的复杂，特别是乙类墓所代表的腰坑葬习俗，时代较早，为探索腰坑葬的起源提供了线索。单独随葬玉石钺的墓葬以往在这一地区罕见，对于相关问题的研究有重要意义。

仰韶晚期至石家河文化时期墓地航拍图（上为南）

仰韶文化晚期出土器物

156　黄淮七省考古新发现

乙类墓腰坑

丁类墓腰坑

甲类墓出土遗物

文明化进程　157

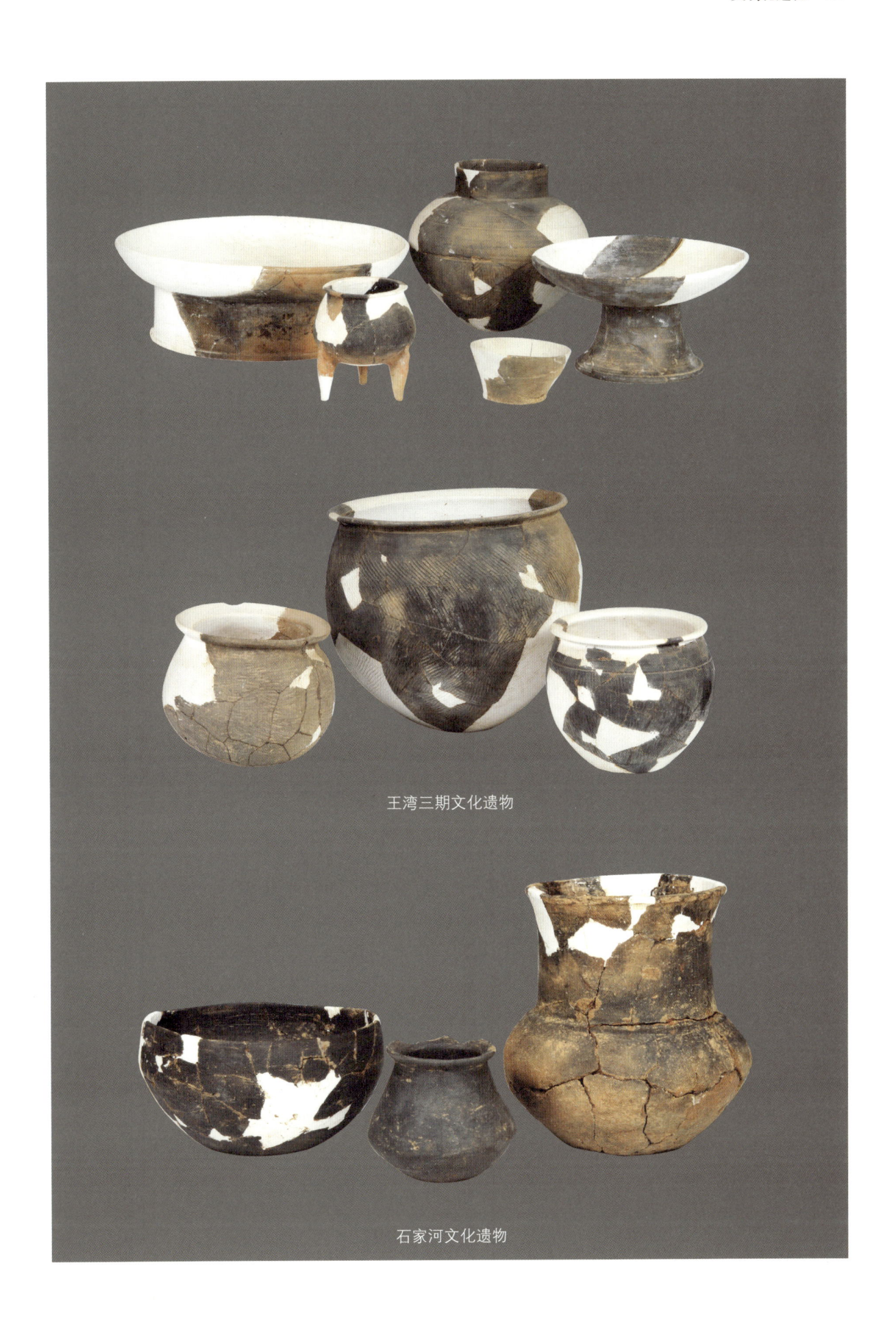

王湾三期文化遗物

石家河文化遗物

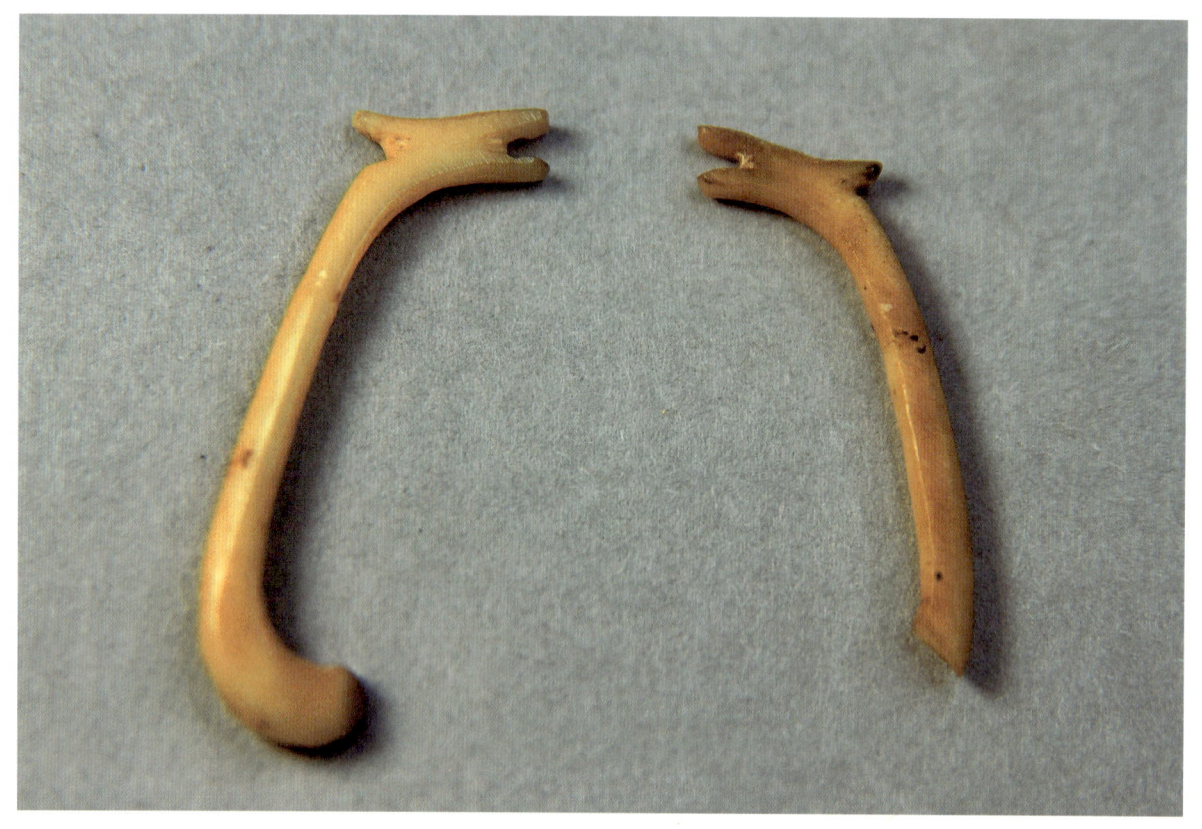

王湾三期文化骨龙

Xiazhai Site is located northeast of Xiazhai Village, Taohe Township, Xichuan County, Henan Province. At present, the site covers approximately 600,000 square meters. From 2009 to 2013, excavations were carried out on the site, revealing 19,000 square meters. It has been discovered that major stratified deposits are of Yangshao Culture period, Shijiahe Culture period, the late third phase of Wangwan Culture period to early Erlitou Culture period, Western Zhou and Eastern Zhou, and Han Dynasty to Tang Dynasty.

The most important archaeological achievement is the discovery of a cemetery dating back to late Yangshao Culture period to middle Shijiahe Culture period. The cemetery was in use for a long time and represented certain continuity. In the cemetery, there were concentrated burials and densely distributed tombs. The discovery of this cemetery fills an archaeological gap since no similar remains had been found in southwestern Henan Province or northwestern Hubei Province. (According to a burial custom, a small pit was dug under the waist of the tomb occupant. In the pit, there were funeral articles, sacrificial objects, or even human sacrifices.) Especially the burial rite, as it is represented in tombs in which the occupants' heads point to the west, provides clues for the exploration of the origins of this burial custom.

In the southwestern part of the site, remains dating back to the late third phase of Wangwan Culture period to early Erlitou Culture period were discovered.

# 河南濮阳戚城龙山时代城址

◎李一丕

戚城龙山时代城址位于河南濮阳市华龙区古城路与京开大道交会处一带，地表现存晚期城址一座，龙山时期城址与其大体重合。近17万平方米（含城垣）。

该城址东部，城墙淤埋较浅，保存相对较差。西部保存相对较好。戚城龙山时代城墙一般残高1~5米。从发掘情况看，龙山城墙东墙顶部残宽约14.30米，底部残宽约28米，残高约3.05米；西墙顶部残宽约5.55米，底部残宽约22.40米，残高约4.70米。

戚城龙山城墙在修建过程中使用了版筑法。在发掘中，发现有版筑过程中形成的台阶状立面。版块之间的立面上亦发现有较为平整的夹板痕迹。版块既见有纵向排列的，亦有横向分布的。此外，戚城龙山城墙主墙体和内护坡均普遍使用了夯筑法修筑堆积层。仅在内护坡局部见有堆筑法修建的堆积层。

龙山城址城外分布有一周宽窄不一的护城壕沟。

戚城龙山城址之下叠压有龙山早期的环壕聚落。龙山城址废弃之后，东周时期，修筑三重城防，成为一座具有都邑性质城址聚落。汉代时期，原东周内城被修补使用，其他城防设施废弃。北宋时期，戚城城墙再次被修补使用。

戚城龙山时代城址是一座时代明确、结构清楚、建造有序、筑法考究的龙山城址，也是濮阳地区首座经过考古发掘证实了的龙山城址。20世纪80年代，考古工作者在濮阳西水坡发现了著名的仰韶文化时期蚌塑龙虎墓。戚城龙山时代城址的发现、发掘与研究，再次表明以濮阳为代表的豫东北地区也是探索中原地区文明起源与发展的重要区域之一，具有十分重要的意义。

龙山时代城墙黄沙堆筑层

城墙版块平面

台阶状版块立面（东—西）

城墙夯窝

版筑夹板立面遗痕

打破龙山时代城墙的H1出土陶器

打破龙山时代城墙的H5出土陶器

Qicheng Site dates back to Longshan Culture period. The site is located near the junction of Gucheng Road and Jingkai Avenue in Hualong District, Puyang City, Henan Province. It covers nearly 170,000 square meters (including ramparts). After excavations, the structure and construction process of the city wall of Qicheng Site have been understood. It has been proved that the construction of the city wall was meticulously planned. Outside the city site, there is a moat whose width varied from part to part.

Qicheng Site is also the first site of Longshan Culture period excavated in Puyang and its existence has been proved by archaeological evidence. The discovery of Qicheng Site, its excavations and relevant researches again illustrate that the northeast of Henan Province, with Puyang as a representative, is one of the key zones for the exploration of the origins and development of the civilization in Central China.

# 山西兴县碧村遗址龙山时期聚落

◎王晓毅　张光辉　王小娟　任海云

碧村遗址是近年山西史前考古的一个重要地点，该遗址地处蔚汾河与黄河的交汇处的兴县高家村镇碧村村北，是龙山时期一处规模较大的石城聚落，总面积达75万平方米。

经过2015—2017年的工作，首先明确了台地中心小玉梁在当时所处的核心地位，并基本了解了该地点在龙山时代晚期的聚落结构与演变，初步确认该台地在龙山时期经历了半地穴房址和石砌排房早晚两大阶段，同时从宏观上掌握了碧村周边史前遗存乃至整个晋西新石器末期的空间分布信息。

在小玉梁四周还发现一周包砌台地边缘的护墙，它们依靠台地边缘顺势而建，各段墙体及各层墙体基础并不完全在同一个平面上，起到护坡包边作用。

出土遗物以陶器为主，常见鬲、蛋形瓮、折肩罐、敛口斝、管流盉、圈足盘、细柄豆等，主要见于灰坑之内，也发现部分骨针、卜骨、蚌饰、细石器等。此外，还发现零星玉器残片及绿松石、蚌饰。

截至目前，在碧村所在的黄河吕梁山沿线，经调查发现龙山时期聚落10余座，可与陕北、内蒙古中南部石城连成一片。其中，白崖沟遗址达120万平方米，与内蒙古清水河县后城嘴遗址面积接近，规模大于同处于蔚汾河下游的碧村遗址，是目前在晋西发现的面积最大的龙山时期石城聚落，其南抱蔚汾河，东、西、北三面依地势修建城墙，居民点位于沟谷两侧，普遍流行在房址白灰面上装饰黑彩的地画，时代主要集中龙山前期，略早于碧村，这为探索龙山时期蔚汾河流域的社会格局及其变迁提供了可能。

文明化进程

柳林八盘山遗址（西—东） 　　　　　　兴县冯家沟遗址（西—东）

兴县古城岭（北—南） 　　　　　　河曲石城遗址（西—东）

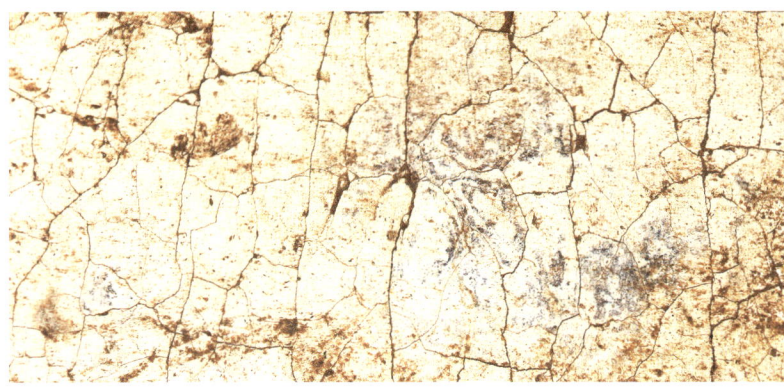

F5西南角 　　　　　　F6∶1

F6西北角　　　　F6中西角 　　　　F4∶1

蚌串饰

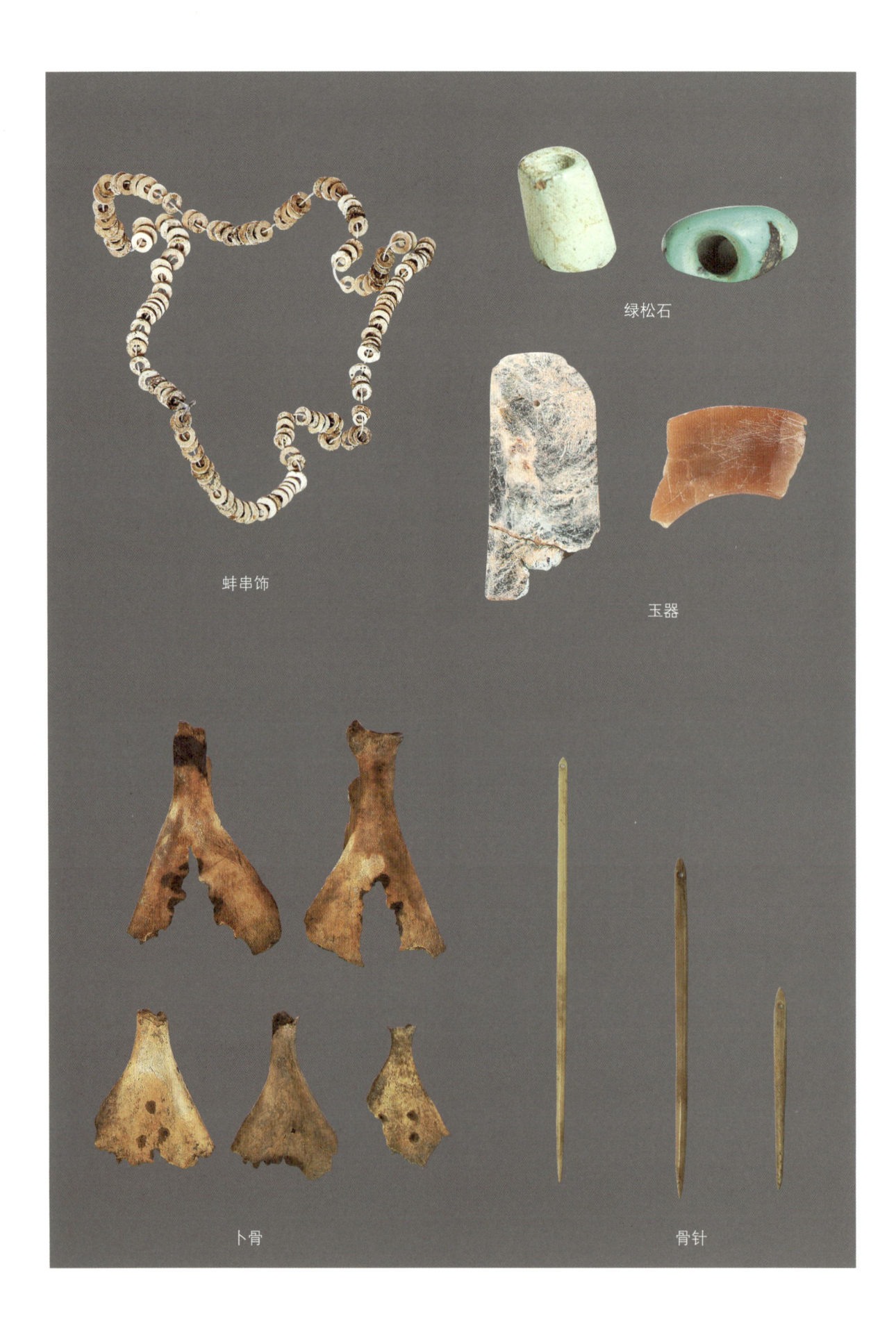

绿松石

玉器

卜骨

骨针

出土陶器

Bicun Site is a relatively large stone settlement dating back to late Longshan Culture period.

From 2015 to 2017, initial trial diggings confirmed the importance of Xiaoyuliang, which is a strip-shaped loess hill, and discovered large-scale dwelling sites and remains of the east city wall. Over 10 prehistorical stone cities were revealed as reconnaissances reached Weihe River-Fenhe River Basin. In 2016 and 2017, excavations centering on Xiaoyuliang were carried out. Stone dwelling sites and contemporary remains were entirely revealed. This discovery was the evidence proving the core status of Xiaoyuliang. The development of Xiaoyuliang reached its zenith at the time during which newer stone terraced houses were constructed. At the same time, protective walls around the terrace were gradually established. As a result, a typical terrace-centered city came into existence. Bicun Site is the counterpart of the outer city wall on a hill, known as Chengqiang Geduo, which is in the east of the site. The excavations conducted on Bicun Site have made it possible for the exploration of social structure and changes in Weihe River-Fenhe River Basin in Longshan Culture period.

# 山西绛县周家庄遗址

◎ 田 伟

绛县周家庄遗址地处运城盆地东北部、涑水河北岸黄土台塬上，总面积500余万平方米，其中以龙山时期遗存最为丰富。2011—2017年，我们继续在该遗址开展工作，取得了丰硕的成果。

新发现的北环壕起于遗址东北，与先前发现的东环壕北端相接，向西则与西部的大型冲沟相连，形成了一个较为封闭的环境。可初步确定大型环壕形成于龙山晚期，是该聚落发展到兴盛时期的产物。

继2007年秋发掘揭露出龙山时期的房址和墓葬后，我们又在"房址、墓葬集中分布区"发现龙山期灰坑100余座、房址30余座、陶窑10余座及墓葬200座。经初步分析，可知该区域在早期是与生产陶器关系密切的居址，至晚期变为墓地。墓葬包括竖穴土坑墓与瓮棺葬两类，大都为东北—西南向，均成排、成组分布，相互间少见叠压打破关系。其中，瓮棺葬位于墓地中部，被土坑墓环绕。此现象鲜见于同时期的龙山墓地。所有墓葬几乎都不见随葬品。

在遗址北部的崔村发现了居址、墓葬遗存。居址时代较早，种类包括房址、陶窑、灰坑等。居址废弃后形成墓地。

2015年春季，我们发掘了遗址西北部一片被壕沟环绕的区域，发现一批龙山晚期至二里头初期遗迹，出土大量陶、石、骨器。龙山时期遗迹包括房址、灰坑、陶窑等。

周家庄遗址龙山时期遗存的文化面貌与陶寺文化（或称陶寺类型）接近，修正了陶寺文化只局限于临汾盆地，而运城盆地属于"三里桥文化（类型）"的分布范围的认识。从现有材料看，周家庄遗址早期遗存的分布范围仅限于遗址中南部地区。至周家庄晚期阶段，遗址面积急剧增加，向北扩展至崔村一带。代表着公共权力的大型环壕也在晚期形成，标志着周家庄遗址成为一处大型中心聚落。通过多年的工作，我们了解到遗址内部存在多处设施完备、且相对独立的居住生活区或墓地。这些较为完备的功能区共同构成了周家庄遗址。

规模较大的周家庄龙山期墓地排列有序，在规模上存在差异，或可表明出现家族墓以及等级分化。这些资料对研究晋南乃至中原地区龙山时期的葬制、社会都有着重要的意义。

出土陶器

半地穴式房址及其部分剖面（东北—西南）

地穴式房址（西南—东北） 　　　　　陶窑（西—东）

墓葬（东北—西南） 　　　　　瓮棺葬（东南—西北）

出土陶、骨、蚌及石器

Zhoujiazhuang Site in Jiangxian Town is located on the loess tableland on the north bank of Sushui River, in northeastern Yuncheng Basin. There are remains dating back to Yangshao Culture period, the second phase of Miaodigou Culture period, Longshan Culture period, Erlitou Culture period, Erligang Culture period, Zhou Dynasty, Han Dynasty, Song Dynasty, etc. Zhoujiazhuang Site covers over 5,000,000 square meters. Among the remains, those dating back to Longshan Culture period are the most plentiful.

From 2011 to 2017, based on the previously discovered the east moat and tombs of Longshan Culture period, archaeological work was carried out. Now it has been preliminarily determined that the large-scale moat was dug in the late Longshan Culture period. The moat per se is an accomplishment of the era during which the settlement flourished. Obviously, the comparatively large-scale cemetery of Longshan Culture period was well planned. Scales of the shaft tombs vary, and this fact indicates that a hierarchical system had been established among tomb occupants. The above materials are important for the study of society and burial conventions back in Longshan Culture period in southern Shanxi Province and even in Central China.

# 山西襄汾陶寺遗址宫城新发现

◎高江涛

陶寺作为一处大型都邑类遗址有着其明确的功能分区，其中最为核心的宫殿区一直是学界关注的区域。2012年我们对宫殿区一带进行钻探，结果表明其周边存在围垣遗迹。若其真为宫城城墙，学术意义之重大不言而喻。自2013年3月31日始，中国社会科学院考古研究所与山西省考古研究所联合，持续对陶寺遗址疑似宫城城墙进行发掘。经过5年的持续发掘，至2017年6月，联合考古队基本廓清了宫城城墙堆积、结构、年代、发展演变等问题，并较为全面地揭露了宫城南东门址和东南拐角处的侧门，取得重大收获。

陶寺宫城位于陶寺遗址东北部，即原来认为的宫殿区的外围。陶寺宫城呈长方形，东西长约470米，南北宽约270米，面积近13万平方米。方向大体北偏西45°左右，与陶寺大城方向基本一致。通过对宫城四面城墙的解剖发掘，基本厘清了墙基的早晚关系及门址的形制。

陶寺遗址宫城及其门址的发掘取得重要成果，意义重大，经多次专家现场会讨论得到以下认识：一是陶寺宫城基址保存较为完整，自成体系，规模宏大，形制规整，并具有突出的防御性质，是目前考古发现的中国最早的宫城。二是这一城址历时较长，始建于陶寺文化早期，陶寺文化中期继续使用，并因陶寺大城的修建使其成为了真正意义上的宫城。在陶寺文化晚期有重建现象，在其偏晚阶段彻底废弃。三是陶寺宫城的发现，使得陶寺遗址"城郭之制"完备，陶寺很可能是中国古代都城制度重要内涵的源头或最初形态。四是陶寺宫城东南角门，在形制结构上与石峁遗址外城东门址有些相近，陶寺城墙建筑形制对同期其他地区考古学文化可能有着深远影响。而陶寺南东门址形制特殊，结构复杂，具有较强的防御色彩，又与后世带有阙楼的门址如隋唐洛阳应天门等有些类似，对后世影响深远悠长。

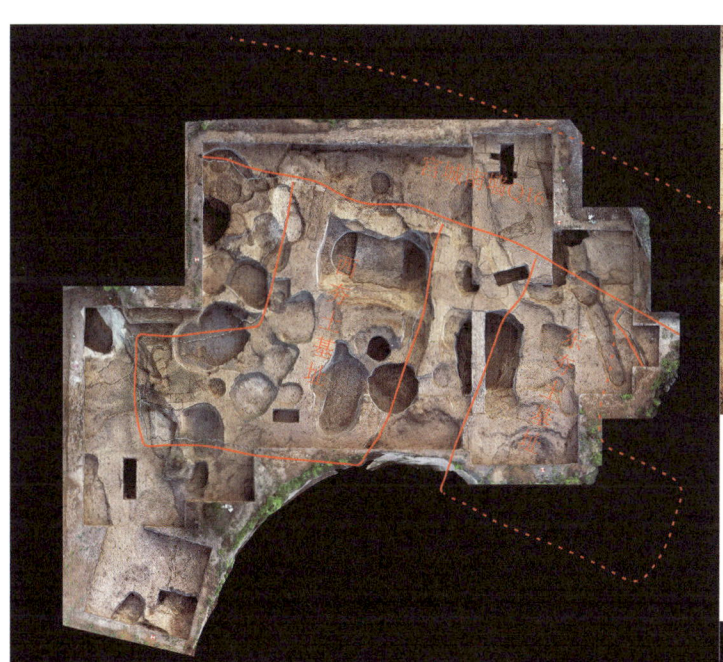

南东门址路土及其下夯土层

南东门址示意图

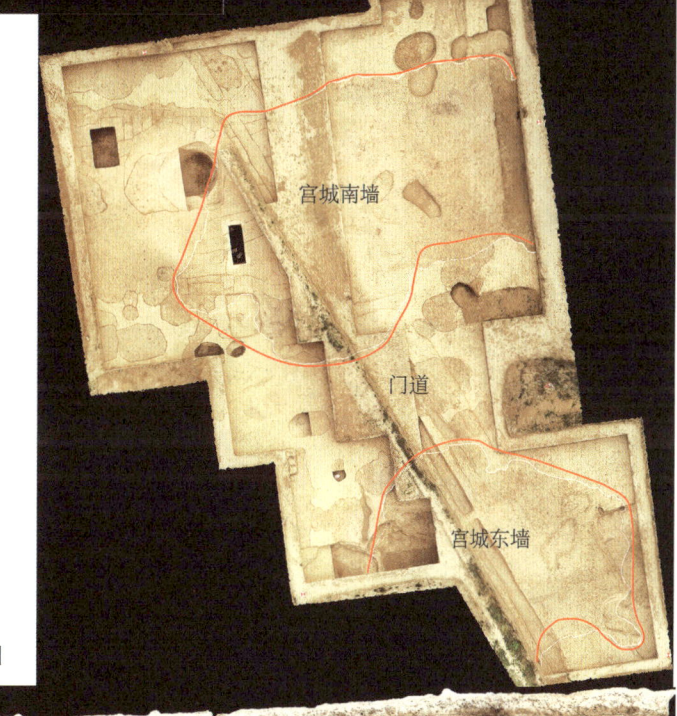

东南角门示意图

Q10北壁上的夯土基槽

172　黄淮七省考古新发现

陶片上的刻划符

宫殿南墙出土陶支垫

陶"楔形器"

石臼

玉器

As the site of an ancient capital, Taosi Site was divided into multiple zones and each zone had its specific function. The core palace zone has drawn most academic attention. In 2012, drillings conducted in the palace zone indicated the existence of surrounding ramparts. From 2013, a jointed team of archaeologists from the Institute of Archaeology of Chinese Academy of Social Sciences and Shanxi Provincial Institute of Archaeology had been continuously excavating remains that seemed to be a palace wall on Taosi Site. Till June in 2017, the stratified deposit, structure, age, development of the palace wall and other issues had been generally clarified by the joint team. The sites of the east gate which is in the south of the palace and the side gate around the southeast corner had been basically completely revealed. These were among the major archaeological achievements that had been made.

# 陕西神木神圪垯梁龙山晚期遗址

◎ 郭小宁

神圪垯梁遗址位于陕西神木县大保当镇野鸡河村六组的神圪垯梁南部缓坡上，面积不到5万平方米。2013—2014年，陕西省考古研究院联合榆林市文物考古勘探工作队、神木县文管会等单位对该遗址进行了考古发掘。

这次发掘共发现各类遗迹163个，其中有灰坑、房址、墓葬、陶窑、灶、沟及夯土遗迹。

发现的28座墓葬以M7规模最大，是迄今为止发现的陕北地区龙山晚期最大的、保存完整的墓葬。该墓为竖穴土坑墓，由墓室和壁龛两部分组成。墓室平面呈长方形，在北壁距墓口1.40米处有一壁龛，龛内有6件陶器。墓底中部有一具棺木，棺内的人骨上涂有两层朱砂，一层与身体相接，其外裹有织物，于织物上再涂一层朱砂。朱砂均从头部覆盖到脚部。经鉴定，人骨为男性，年龄为35～39岁。在墓室底部、棺西侧有一人骨，侧身屈肢，头向东，面朝南，四肢呈捆绑状。此具人骨应为墓主殉葬。经鉴定，人骨为女性，年龄为20～25岁。M8为竖穴土坑墓，墓主为女性，在人骨一侧有一完整猪骨架。

房址除两座为地面式房址外，其余均为半地穴式。灰坑多不规整，分布不规律，一般出土陶片较少，动物骨骼较多。

在发掘中还发现有陶窑、壕沟、夯土等遗迹，特别是夯土遗迹，位于整个遗址位置偏低的地方。该夯土遗迹形状不规则，似由3条长条形夯土组成，在对夯土解剖的探沟内未发现陶片等遗物。

神圪垯梁遗址年代为龙山晚期，处于陕北北部，而陕北地区在该时期为晋陕高原、内蒙中南部的中心。它的发现，为研究陕北地区在这一时期的生业、环境、人地关系、社会组织、墓葬习俗等提供了较充实的资料。

大型墓葬（东南—西北）
及其随葬品

地面式房址（东—西）

半地穴式房址（东—西）

文明化进程　175

小型墓葬（北—南）及其殉猪

Shengedaliang Site is located on a gentle slope in southern Shengedaliang, in the area of the Sixth Villagers' Group of Yejihe Village, Dabaodang Town, Shenmu County, Shaanxi Province. From 2013 to 2014, archaeologists from Shaanxi Provincial Institute of Archaeology and local units of cultural relics conducted excavations on the site. Revealed remains include dozens of shaft tombs, unequal numbers of ash pits, dwelling sites, kiln sites, etc.

Shengedaliang Site dates back to late Longshan Culture period. At that time, the northern part of Shaanxi Province was the center of an area encompassing Shanxi-Shaanxi Plateau and the central and southern Inner Mongolia. In recent years, quite a number of sites dating back to late Longshan Culture period have been discovered one after another on the northern part of Shaanxi Province. These discoveries provide substantial materials for the study of contemporary living conditions, production, environment, man-land relationship, social structure, burial rites, etc.

# 陕西神木石峁遗址

◎ 邵 晶

石峁遗址位于神木市高家堡镇，地处黄土高原北部的黄河西岸，毛乌素沙漠南缘，坐落在黄河一级支流秃尾河北岸的梁峁上。陕西省考古研究院2011年开始对石峁遗址进行了区域系统考古调查。自2012年起，重点发掘了外城东门址、韩家圪旦墓地、樊庄子"哨所"、皇城台等重要地点，取得了重要收获。作为石峁遗址的主要组成部分，石峁城址面积逾400万平方米，由皇城台、内城、外城三座基本完整并相对独立的石构城垣组成。另外，城外还分布有数座人工修筑的"哨所"类建筑遗迹。

皇城台位于内城偏西的中心部位，为一座底大顶小、四面包砌层阶状石墙的台城，顶部面积8万余平方米，系大型宫殿及高等级建筑的分布区域。内城将皇城台包围其中，面积约210万平方米。城内密集分布着居址、墓地、窑址等遗迹。外城系利用内城东南部墙体向东南方向再行扩筑的一道弧形石墙形成的封闭空间，城内面积约190万平方米，亦分布有一些居址和墓地。

2012至2013年，重点发掘了外城东门址，揭露出一座结构复杂、筑造技术先进的城门遗址，出土了玉铲、玉钺、玉璜、玉璋、陶器、壁画、纴木和石雕等大量重要遗物，发现了"人头奠基"（祭祀）、"藏玉于墙"等重要现象。

2014年发掘的韩家圪旦地点位于内城中部偏东的一处东西向"舌形"山峁之上，与皇城台隔沟相望。清理的遗迹包括房址、墓葬、灰坑及窑址，出土器物包括陶器、石器、玉器、骨器等，发掘表明，韩家圪旦地点的聚落功能有变化，早期为一处以窑洞为重要居住方式的居址，晚期变为一处大型墓地。

2015年发掘了城外东南方向的樊庄子地点，揭露出一座上中部为石砌方围、一侧下方有弧形石碓的"高台式"建筑，根据上部方围内壁均匀分布的壁柱槽判断，可能为一处"哨所"类建筑，与城外另几处类似建筑共同构成石峁城外的预警体系。

2016年开始重点发掘皇城台。皇城台为一处四围包砌台阶状石砌护墙相对独立的台城。2016至2017年发掘了皇城台门址及东护墙北段上部，收获重大。皇城台门址是目前皇城台确认的唯一一处城门遗址，位于皇城台东侧坡下偏南。皇城台门址规模宏大、结构复杂、保存良好，自外而内的主要组成部分包括广场、外瓮城、墩台、内瓮城及"主门道"等。非常重要的是，在覆盖东护墙北段墙体的文化堆积内，遗物数量惊人，特别是以骨针为代表的骨器数量已逾万件。

皇城台出土了骨、陶、石、玉及铜等各类遗物，骨器除针外，还有镞、锥、铲、凿、卜骨、几何纹饰片及骨料等，陶器以敞口盆、喇叭口折肩罐、三足瓮、高领鬲、斝、豆、盉等为主要器形，石器多见斧、刀、杵、锄等器物，另外还有少量石范，玉器有钺、璋、璜、环、镞等，铜器主要环首刀、镞、锥等小件器物。另外，还有陶鹰、筒瓦和板瓦残片、壁画残块、布块等重要遗物。

石峁遗址地处沿黄河南下进入中原地区的中介地带，皇城台铜器和石范的发现为冶金术自北方传入中原的观点提供了关键性的支持证据，为探索早期冶金术在中国的传播路线提供了关键的连接点。皇城台骨针"制作链"为找寻骨器作坊提供了重要线索。在皇城台东护墙北段上部弃置堆积内的大量兽骨中发现了完整的骨针制作链，这一发现预示着皇城台顶上偏东北可能存在骨器作坊，以生产骨针为主，同时也兼顾其他骨器。皇城台门址相较于外城东门址结构更为复杂、规模更为宏大，巍峨壮观的台阶状石砌护墙更是彰显了皇城台的特殊地位，加之筒瓦、板瓦、壁画残块的发现，意味着皇城台顶部建筑可能存在着的覆顶形式。这些发现是深入认识皇城台性质的重要物证，皇城台或许已经具有早期"宫城"的意义。皇城台是公元前2000年前后东亚地区保存最好的宫城遗址，由内、外城拱卫宫城的布局开创了东亚地区古代都城格局的先河。

石峁城址存续于公元前2300至公元前1800年左右，城内面积超过400万平方米，系国内已知规模最大的上古时期（龙山晚期至夏代早期）城址。石峁城址的社会功能不同于一般原始聚落，已经步入中国北方早期国家都邑行列，是中国北方距今4000年前后早期国家的统治中心和权力象征，为中国国家起源的研究提供了有力实证。

韩家圪旦航拍图（上为北）

石峁遗址遗迹分布图（东—西）

皇城台门址航拍图（上为西）

皇城台东护墙北段

玉钺

骨针　　　　　　　　石范　　　　陶筒瓦

Shimao Site is located in Gaojiabu Town, Shenmu City, Shaanxi Province. Regional systematic archaeological researches have been underway since 2011. Since 2012, excavations have been carried out at a number of key spots. A series of major archaeological achievements have been made. As a major part of Shimao Site, the city site, consisting of three basically complete and independent stone ramparts, i.e. "the terrace of the imperial city", the inner city and outer city, covers over 4,000,000 square meters. In addition, outside the city, there are several architectural remains that look like "sentry posts".

Archaeological work done from 2011 to 2017 shows that the city site, as a major part of Shimao Site, dates back to 2300 B.C. to 1800 B.C. This city site is the largest known city site of ancient times (late Longshan Culture period to early Xia Dynasty) in China. Social functions of the city differ from those of average primitive settlements. The city was among the early capitals in North China. About 4000 years ago, it was the center of ruling and symbol of authority among those early countries in North China. The discovery of the city site provides convincing evidence for the study of China's origin.

# 安徽肥东刘墩新石器—商周遗址

◎陈小春

刘墩遗址位于安徽肥东县店埠镇定光社区刘墩村东约500米处。遗址整体呈墩台形，总面积约4500平方米。2012年刘墩遗址由肥东县人民政府公布为县级文物保护单位。2016年12月至2017年3月，由安徽省文物考古研究所等单位对该遗址进行考古发掘工作。

本次发掘区主要位于遗址的中部和北部，共发掘面积994平方米。遗址文化层厚度在1.30米至2.50米之间，依据地层和出土器物，初步判断刘墩遗址可分为龙山文化时期、二里头文化时期、西周和清代四个时期。各时期均发现数量不等的遗迹遗物，在此重点介绍早期遗存。

龙山文化时期人类活动范围较大，地层堆积较厚，遗迹遗物多。共发现房址、灰坑、柱洞及墓葬，出土遗物有陶器和石器，其中陶器多为夹砂陶，器形有鼎、鬶、罐等，石器有石斧和石锛。F1开口于⑧层下，打破第⑩层，平面呈不规则形，填土为黑色黏土，含较多红烧土颗粒和少量红烧土小块，土质疏松，房址表面平且硬，周围分布有6个柱洞，洞中均填红烧土及少量炭屑。出土少量陶片，有夹砂红、黑陶，部分有绳纹，发现数个鼎足。

二里头时期人类活动范围缩小，地层堆积薄，遗迹遗物较少。共发现灰坑、窑及墙。出土陶片数量较少，器形包括陶鼎、陶罐、陶豆、陶斝、陶盆等。Y2开口于⑤a层下，打破第⑧层，北部为窑室，南部则为火膛，壁面上部为红色烧土，下部为青色烧土，向内倾斜，圜底，窑室填土为浅黄色，夹少量红烧土，火膛中填土为黑色，夹杂大量炭屑和少量烧土颗粒。窑中出土少量陶片，有夹砂红、黑陶，无纹饰。Q1开口于⑩层下，打破第⑪⑫层，平面呈弧形，东西向，中部向北凸出，未见明显的下挖墙基迹象，堆土主要为黄、红色交杂的黏土，土层之间有明显的剥离现象，但未见夯窝及夯层。堆土中出土的陶片，多为夹砂灰陶、红陶，可辨器形有口沿、斝足等，纹饰有按窝纹，亦可见类小泥圆饼似眼的装饰。

此次发掘，基本弄清了刘墩遗址的堆积结构，为江淮地区这一类型遗址的研究补充了资料。二里头时期遗迹遗物的发现，填补了该地区这一时期的空白。

文明化进程 183

龙山文化房址 　　　　　　　　　　二里头时期窑

西周时期灰坑 　　　　　　　　　　二里头时期灰坑

龙山文化陶鬶　　　　　　　　　　龙山文化石斧

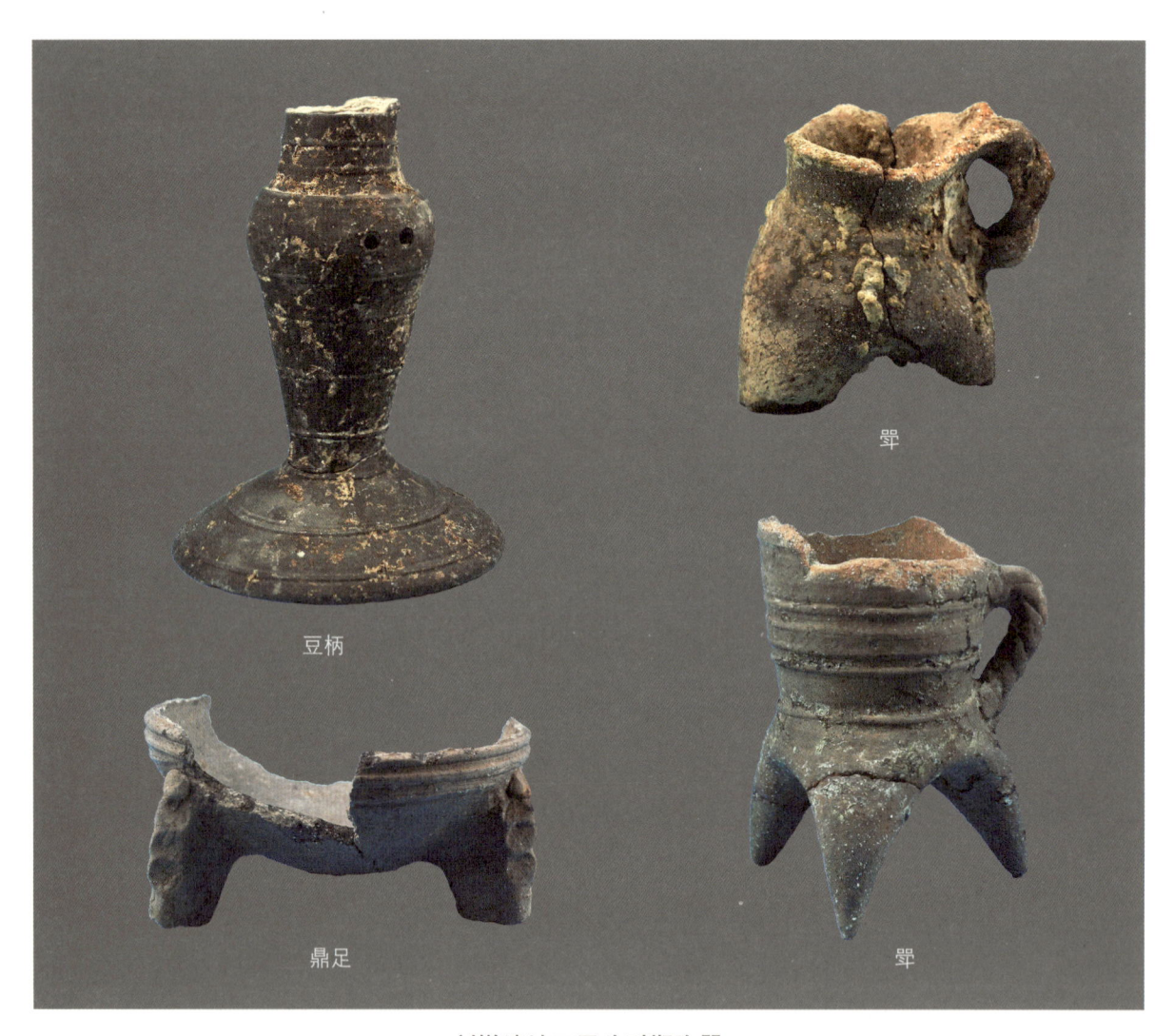

刘墩遗址二里头时期陶器

Liudun Site, covering approximately 4500 square meters, is located about 500 meters east of Liudun Village in Dingguang Community, Dianbu Town, Feidong County, Anhui Province. In 2016, salvage excavations were carried out on the site.

This time, excavations were conducted mainly in the central and northern parts of the site, encompassing 994 square meters in total. It has been preliminarily determined that cultural remains unearthed from Liudun Site are of four periods—Longshan Culture period, Erlitou Culture period, Western Zhou and Qing Dynasty. During Longshan Culture period, Liudun Site witnessed human activities in a vaster area; and there are comparatively thicker stratal stratified deposits and more ruins and objects dating back to this period. During Erlitou Culture period, on Liudun Site, the area of human activities shrunk; the stratal stratified deposits were thinner and there were fewer ruins and objects. In the epoch of Western Zhou, the site was revitalized and flourished again. As a result, in this era, the area of the site was the vastest, the stratal stratified deposits were the thickest and the number of ruins and objects was the largest.

三代之礼　皇皇者华

苏秉琦先生说，中国国家的起源，经由古国—方国—帝国三部曲，古国在三代之前，三代属于方国，帝国是秦汉帝国。而三代时期也是早期中国第一次从分裂走向西周的大一统，再到东周列国林立的大治大乱之世。

黄淮流域作为早期中国的文明中心之一，时代的特征在这里展现得淋漓尽致。宗教祭祀方面，既有安徽巢湖城圩商周遗址等发现的卜骨、卜甲，也有山西侯马虒祁遗址、山西襄汾陶寺北两周墓地等发现的动物祭祀坑、玉石器祭祀遗迹。文字方面，既有山西榆社偶尔坪遗址发现的陶文及刻划符号，也有山东刘家庄遗址商墓等发现的青铜器铭文。宫室建筑方面，不但有河南偃师二里头遗址5号基址、陕西周原凤雏5号基址这类大型宫殿建筑，也有陕西清涧辛庄发现的一堂三室建筑以及江苏新沂聂墩发现的普通圆形房址。城市作为文明的重要要素，在这一地区发现的早期商周城址有山东临淄范家遗址、河南荥阳官庄遗址、河北满城要庄遗址等。东周时期的城市发展已较为成熟，山东的鲁国故城、临淄齐故城、邾国故城以及河北的邯郸赵王城都是这一时期的典型代表。河南郑韩故城遗址北城门的发掘，发现战国时期的瓮城，这在东周时期的王城中是首次发现。

青铜器作为商周时期的"金"，主要用于礼乐和征伐。河北行唐故郡遗址、山东纪王崮春秋墓葬都发现有大气古朴的青铜礼乐器。而玉器不仅是中国典型的奢侈品和装饰品，也是商周时期贵族见面用"币"中最重要者。山东纪王崮春秋墓葬、陕西周原姚家墓地、山西襄汾陶寺北两周墓地等发现的玉器都十分精致华美。另外，河南信阳城阳城八号墓发现了许多保存较好的楚国贵族漆木器、彩色髹漆竹席，墓主人全身敷裹的织物也十分罕见。

手工业方面，安徽巢湖城圩商周遗址是一处聚落内负责祭祀、制骨等活动的核心功能区，山西闻喜千金耙夏商矿冶遗址是早期青铜器的一处原料产地，而河南安阳市辛店铸铜遗址则是目前发现的殷墟之外唯一的一处商代晚期铸铜遗址。近年来鲁北地区的盐业考古所获材料也为我们探讨不同时期山东北部沿海地区的制盐工艺、制盐规模、运作模式等提供了真实可靠的资料。

# 钟鸣鼎食　多姓一统

## 河南偃师二里头遗址5号基址

◎赵海涛

2001—2002年，中国社会科学院考古研究所二里头工作队在遗址宫殿区东中部发现东西并列的3号和5号基址，二者中间以通道和暗渠间隔。3号基址由至少3进院落组成，院内发现2排5座贵族墓葬，出土包括绿松石龙形器在内的较多精美文物，为全面、深入了解二里头文化早期大型夯土基址的形制、结构、年代变迁，以及相近区域的遗存分布情况和历时性变化、宫室营建制度等提供了丰富的实物资料。2010—2011年、2014—2017年工作队对5号基址进行了多次发掘，主要收获包括：

首先，明确了5号基址的布局和构成。台基最上层夯土总面积超过2700平方米，由至少4进院落组成。每进院落包括主殿、院内路土，第2～4进院落内共发现3排5座同期的贵族墓葬。各进院落的主殿均为以窄墙间隔成不同房间的连间排房，南侧多有门道，部分主殿北侧有门道。多数南北向墙体中间有缺口，缺口中间有东西向窄墙，东西向窄墙与南北向隔墙垂直但不相连。

其次，再次确认5号基址使用时期院内存在贵族墓葬。5号基址的2、3、4进院内，分别发现2、2、1座贵族墓葬。这些墓葬均打破院内的夯土基址和使用时期的路土，其上又被稍晚的使用时期路土所叠压，确证这些贵族墓葬与夯土基址为同一时期。这些墓葬属于二里头文化墓葬的第Ⅰ等级，随葬品丰富且规格较高，一般都出土有漆器、绿松石器、陶礼器和一般陶器，部分墓葬中还有玉器和铜器，为认识二里头文化时期的墓葬制度、研究5号基址的时代和性质等问题提供了重要资料。

再次，初步判断5号基址的修建、使用和废弃年代均为二期。多组地层关系表明，5号基址始建于二里头文化二期早段，使用至二期晚段。

最后，5号基址与3号基址展现了二里头文化早期都邑格局的独特特征。5号基址是目前发现的保存最好的二里头文化早期多进院落的大型夯土基址，是中国后世多院落宫室建筑的源头。其与3号基址的这种外围无围墙、多进院落、院内有贵族墓葬的建筑格局和内涵，构成了二里头文化早期宫室建筑、宫殿区布局的独特特征，与二里头文化晚期宫殿区内以1号、2号基址为代表的外围有围墙、廊庑，院内无同时期的贵族墓葬的四合院式建筑，以4、7、8号基址为代表的单体夯土台基式建筑的格局和内涵的差别较大，其背后反映了怎样的社会背景，值得深入探究。

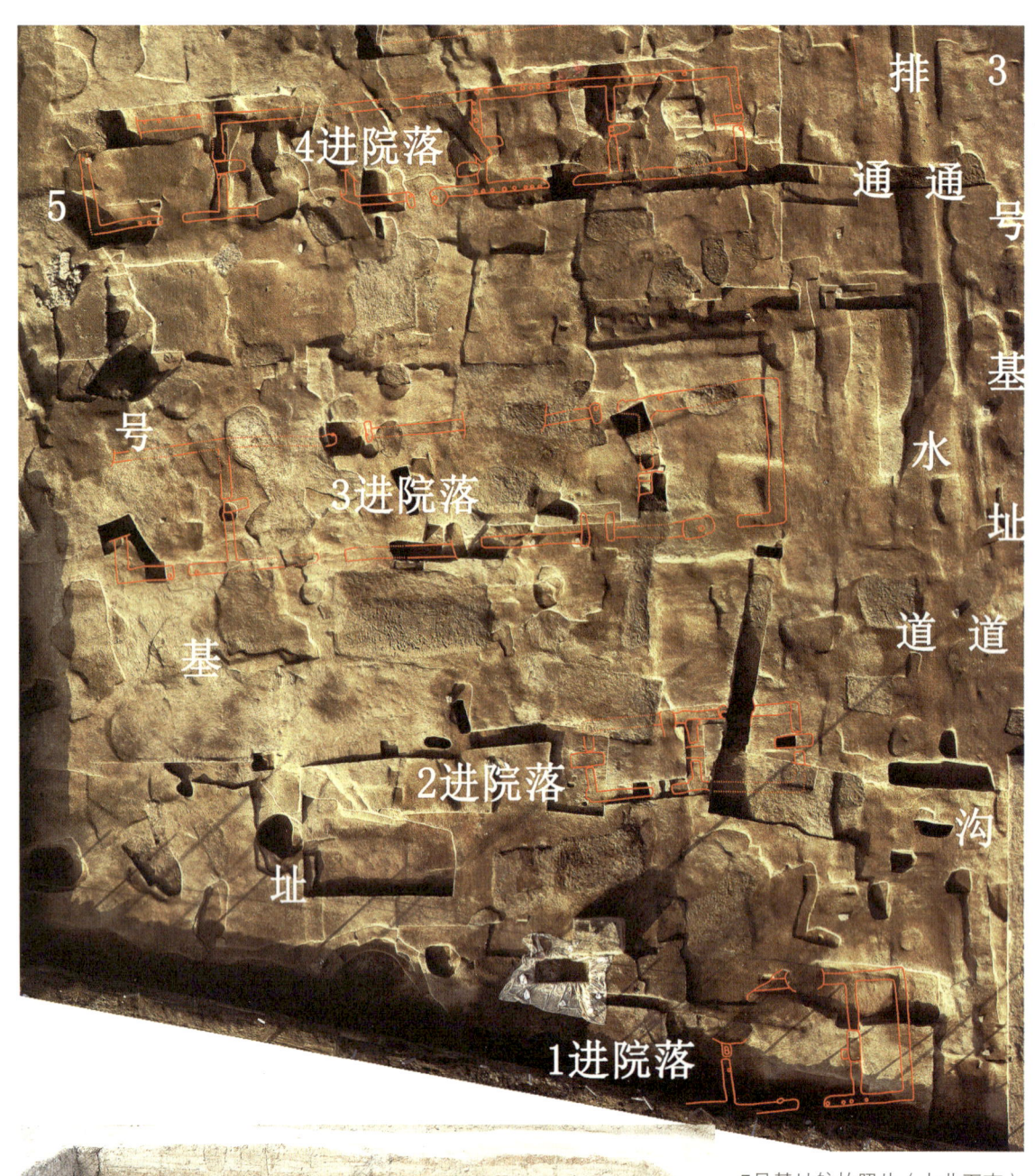

5号基址航拍照片（上北下南）

5号基址夯土结构

三代之礼　皇皇者华　189

5号基址夯面、夯窝

5号基址3号院局部（上北下南）

5号基址2号院西部（上北下南）

From 2010 to 2011 and 2014 to 2017, archaeologists from Institute of Archaeology of the Chinese Academy of Social Sciences conducted several excavations on the Foundation Site No. 5 in the middle eastern area of the palatial zone on Erlitou Site. The following are major discoveries: Layout and structure of Foundation Site No.5 have been clarified, i.e. it was south-facing and consisted of at least 4 courtyards. It has been confirmed again that there were aristocratic tombs in the courtyards when Foundation Site No.5 was in use. It has been preliminarily determined that the construction, use and disuse of Foundation Site No. 5 all happened in the second phase of Erlitou Culture period. Foundation Site No. 5 is presently the best-preserved multi-courtyard large-scale rammed earthen foundation site dating back to early Erlitou Culture period. As the origin of multi-courtyard palatial architectures in China, Foundation Site No.5 shows the unique features of the layout of a capital city in early Erlitou Culture period.

# 安徽肥西县武斌大墩遗址

◎余 飞

武斌大墩遗址为椭圆形台地，位于安徽省合肥市肥西县上派镇北张社区武斌村民组西。因肥西县市政道路建设需要，2015年7月至2016年9月，安徽省文物考古研究所对武斌大墩遗址进行了发掘。

武斌大墩遗址文化层堆积基本可以分为三个时期：二里头文化三、四期文化遗存，西周中期和西周晚期。

二里头文化时期的堆积较薄，发现的遗迹和出土器物均较少。遗迹主要是灰坑和灰沟。出土的二里头文化时期器物基本为陶器。足跟上部带按窝的鼎足以及斝等陶器显示武斌大墩遗址该时期文化因素与寿县斗鸡台文化三期极为相似，应属斗鸡台文化范畴，地方特征明显，同时兼有二里头文化和岳石文化特点。

西周时期遗迹主要有灰坑、灰沟、房屋基址、墓葬等。发现灰坑69个，在遗址中分布密集。房屋基址3处，可以分为两类：一类是以一定数量基槽构成，基槽内一般有柱洞；另一类则直接埋设具有一定规律和数量的柱子。清理墓葬14座，其中成人墓7座、未成年人墓7座，部分墓葬有用石头压在死者肩部的习俗。出土的西周早期和中期以绳纹陶器为主的器物特征表明武斌大墩遗址早期以周文化为主，地方文化因素开始逐渐增强的特点；西周晚期大量出现的折肩鬲、素面高柱足鬲等器物表明该时期的文化特征已发展到以地方文化因素为主，同时兼有周文化和其他地区文化的特点。

肥西武斌大墩遗址的发掘对于安徽江淮地区周代聚落典型的台形遗址的营建过程也具有非常重要的意义。通过发掘发现台形遗址是由有夯打痕迹的、截面呈梯形的土埂人工堆筑而成，该土埂环绕成闭合的不规则椭圆形，土埂每次的堆筑均有一个较长时期的生活堆积倾斜叠压于土埂内坡上。并且在土埂的内坡发现了较多的柱洞，这些柱洞与斜坡下的柱洞形成完整的面，虽经后期扰乱破坏，仍可判断出此应为搭建简易建筑留下的遗迹。土埂内外的地层堆积大多是在土埂堆筑完成后持续生活留下的生活堆积，并最终形成了土台的形状。周代的台形聚落遗址广泛分布于安徽江淮地区，土埂结构的建筑遗迹展示了先民的聪明和智慧，外可抵御水患和猛兽，内可方便居住。

发掘航拍图（上东北下西南）

压有大石块的俯身直肢葬

二里头文化时期陶斝　　　西周中期铜凿

三代之礼　皇皇者华　193

陶拍

残陶范

西周墓出土陶豆

西周墓出土陶鬲

西周中期绳纹鬲

西周晚期陶钵

西周晚期原始瓷钵

西周晚期折肩罐

有随葬品的侧身直肢葬

未成年人墓葬

Wubin Dadun Site is in the west of Wubin Villagers' Group, Beizhang Community, Shangpai Town, Feixi County, Hefei City, Anhui Province. From 2015 to 2016, archaeologists from Anhui Provincial Institute of Cultural Relics and Archaeology conducted excavations on the site. The excavated area was 900 square meters. Its cultural stratified deposit can be generally divided into three phases which respectively date back to late Western Zhou, middle Western Zhou and the third and fourth phases of Erlitou Site. The majority of the stratigraphic accumulation of Dadun Site formed during Western Zhou. Features of unearthed objects that date back to early Western Zhou and middle Western Zhou indicate that Zhou Culture used to play a dominating role on Dadun Site and gradually local cultural elements became active. When it came to late Western Zhou, local cultural elements prevailed; Zhou Culture and other regional cultures also existed. The layer of stratified deposit of Erlitou Culture period excavated this time is comparatively thin and just a small number of remains and relics have been revealed from it.

# 河北肃宁县后白寺遗址

◎魏曙光

为配合引黄入冀补淀工程建设，河北省文物研究所会同河北大学历史文化学院、肃宁县文物保管所组成联合考古队，于2017年3—11月对肃宁县后白寺遗址实施抢救性考古发掘。

后白寺遗址位于沧州市肃宁县梁村镇后白寺村西北，小白河东岸。遗址文化堆积厚，遗迹、遗物丰富，清理出房址、柱洞、灰坑、灰沟等各类遗迹，复原陶器70余件，并出土有丰富的石、骨、角、蚌器。遗址大体包含三个时期的文化遗存：第一期为下七垣文化遗存，遗迹主要有房址、灰坑、灰沟、柱洞等；第二期为早商时期文化遗存，此时期遗存未发现文化层，仅发现少量灰坑；第三期为晚商文化遗存，此期发现有较多的灰坑，并有少量的房址、灶、条带状堆积等。另外，遗址出土了丰富的鱼类骨骼、鱼鳞以及丰富的蚌壳，有时蚌壳成堆堆放，个体大小多样，最大个体长度达22厘米，体现了优良的水环境。

后白寺遗址位于古黄河—山经河一线附近，此区域古文化遗存埋葬较深，夏商时期文化遗存发现极少。后白寺夏商文化遗存的发现与研究，对于认识该区域的夏商时期的文化面貌具有重要意义。后白寺遗址第一期文化遗存的文化面貌与豫北冀南的下七垣文化漳河型和冀中的下岳各庄类型都有联系，同时又受岳石文化与大坨头文化影响，而其夹粗砂厚胎敛口罐、素面磨光鼓腹鬲、夹砂厚胎直口缸等器物体现了其自身特色。第二期文化遗存，为沧州地区首次发掘到该时期的遗存，对于研究早商时期商文化在河北地区的发展态势具有重要意义。第三期遗存为晚商遗存，与东先贤五期文化面貌基本一致，为商末周初的商文化遗存，对于研究商代末年商文化的北部疆域具有重要学术意义。后白寺遗址夏商时期的三期遗存，正是夏商时期河北古文化相对繁盛的三个阶段，对于完善河北地区特别是冀中东部地区夏商文化序列具有重要学术价值。另外，遗址中丰富的水产品遗存和丰富的捕捞工具，对于研究冀中平原东部地区古生态环境和人们的生业方式都具有重要意义。

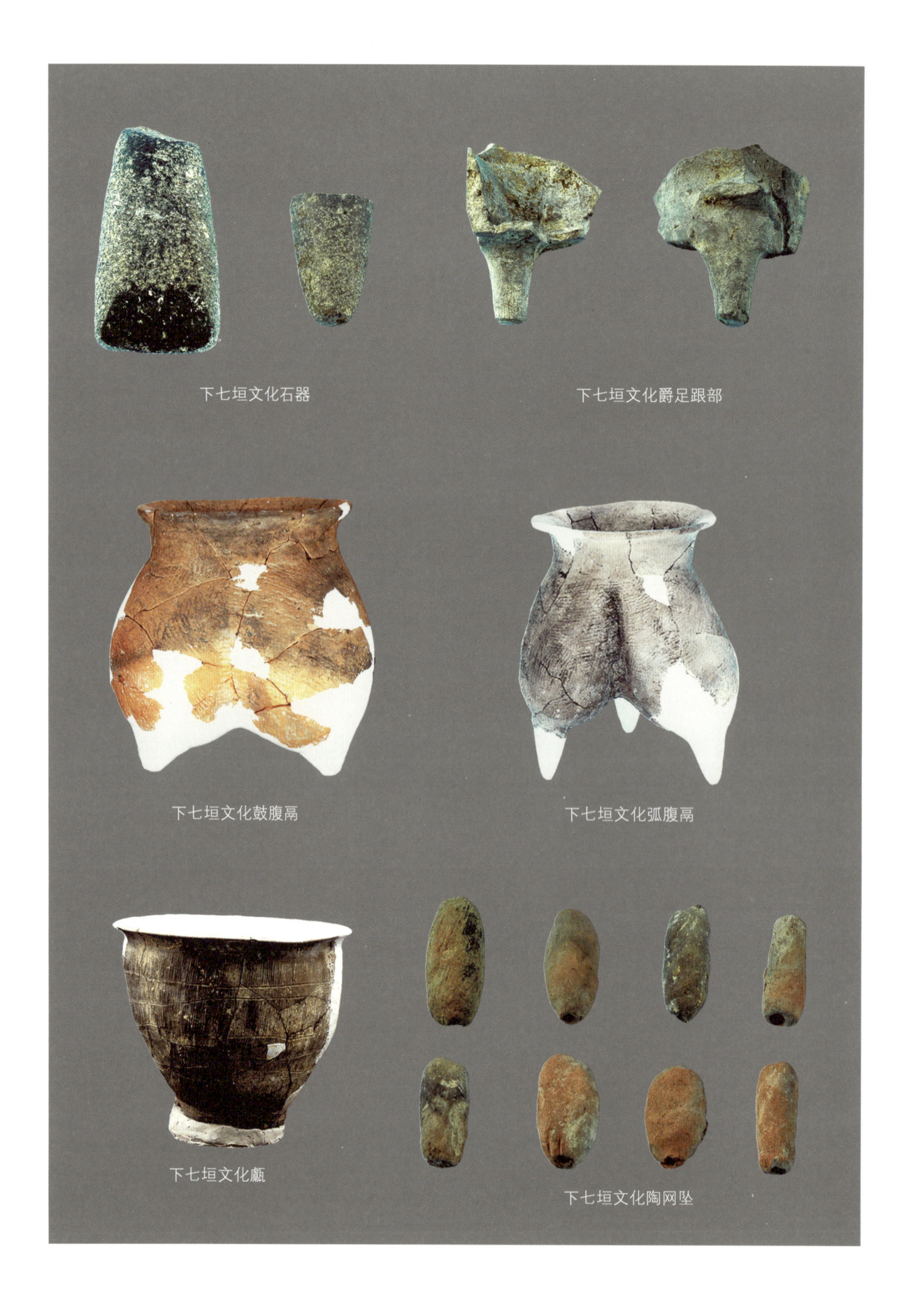

下七垣文化石器　　　　　　　　　下七垣文化爵足跟部

下七垣文化鼓腹鬲　　　　　　　　下七垣文化弧腹鬲

下七垣文化甗　　　　　　　　　　下七垣文化陶网坠

下七垣文化高柄陶豆　　　　　　　　　下七垣文化夹砂陶罐

早商文化陶豆　　　　　　　　　　　　早商文化陶豆

早商文化陶钵　　　　　　　　　　　　晚商文化陶鬲

晚商文化陶簋　　　　下七垣文化器钮　　早商文化卜骨

后白寺夏商遗址发掘平面（上南下北）

Houbaisi Site is in the northwest of Houbaisi Village, Liangcun Town, Suning County, Cangzhou City. From March to November in 2017, archaeologists from Hebei Provincial Institute of Cultural Relics and other organizations carried out salvage excavations on the site. The majority of the site consists of remains that could be date back to three historical periods, i.e. Xiaqiyuan Culture period, early Shang Dynasty, and late Shang Dynasty. These three periods are exactly the three phases during which ancient culture flourished in Hebei Province in Xia Dynasty and Shang Dynasty. Archaeological discoveries made on Houbaisi Site are of considerable academic value since they help fill in blanks and complete cultural sequence of Xia Dynasty and Shang Dynasty in Hebei Province, especially in the middle and eastern regions of Hebei Province. In addition, abundant remains of aquatic products and a wide range of fishing tools unearthed from the site are of great significance for the study on paleoecological environment and people's living conditions and production on eastern Central Hebei Plain.

# 山东济南市榆林遗址

◎朱 超

榆林遗址位于山东省济南市章丘区绣惠镇榆林村南500米处，西侧紧临绣江河，南距章丘城区约10千米，为章丘市级文物保护单位。整个遗址地势略高于周边，呈低台状。为配合济青高速铁路项目建设，山东省文物考古研究院于2016年5—9月对该遗址南缘偏西位置进行抢救性考古发掘。

遗址内堆积非常丰富，时代自早至晚分别为大汶口文化、龙山文化、岳石文化、早商、东周、唐、辽金、明清几个阶段。其中大汶口文化仅发现零星遗迹，龙山文化、岳石文化、早商、东周时期堆积最为丰富。

本次发掘最为重要的发现为岳石文化时期的夯土基槽及壕沟。两者紧邻，分布于西区东端，因道路限制壕沟未能完全揭露。根据发掘及勘探情况来看，已揭露的壕沟应该为门道北侧的一段，方向近南北向，呈斜壁平底沟状。贴近门道处的壕沟内壁及底部均铺砌有石块，局部可见明显垒砌迹象，铺砌所用石块多为扁平状，可分为大、小石块两类，小石块主要用于填塞缝隙。从壕沟内堆积情况分析，该壕沟沿用时间较长，开挖于岳石文化时期，早商时期可能仍在使用，至春秋时期完全废弃。夯土基槽位于壕沟西侧，其东侧局部被壕沟打破，方向大致呈东南—西北向。经局部解剖可知，该基槽夯筑应存在分段夯筑情况，根据不同位置夯层解剖情况看，结构差异较大。通过分析壕沟与夯土基槽的位置及相互关系，仅能得知壕沟在建造时间上晚于夯土基槽，目前还无法完全判断两者是否存在同时使用的关系。

榆林遗址应属于城子崖遗址聚落群范围内一处极为重要的二级聚落。疑似城墙性质的夯土基槽是除城子崖遗址外在岳石文化分布区域发现的另一处城墙类相关遗迹，其重要性不言而喻，为了解岳石文化城墙修筑形式提供了不可多得的新材料。壕沟内壁铺砌石块的做法在海岱地区岳石文化时期也是首次发现，该种修筑形式明显是门道两侧位置的加固设施，较龙山城址的壕沟有了显著进步，该种新技术是交流引入的结果或其就是本地自发创造的，值得思考。

西区发掘航拍图（上南下北）

东区发掘航拍图（上南下北）

三代之礼　皇皇者华　201

岳石文化壕沟

局部疑似人工垒砌石块

夯土基槽剖面

龙山文化陶瓮　　　　　龙山文化陶壶

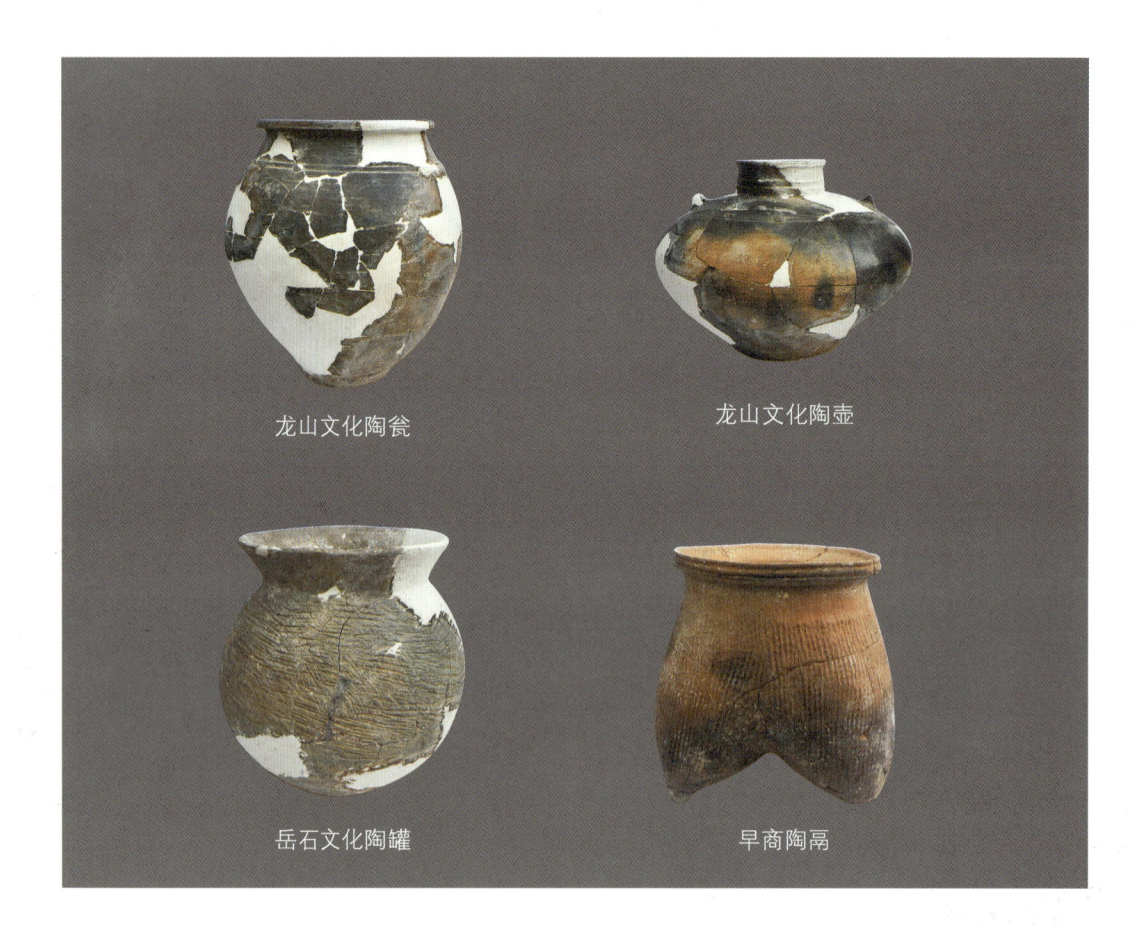

岳石文化陶罐　　　　　早商陶鬲

Yulin Site is located 500 meters south of Yulin Village, Xiuhui Town, Zhangqiu District, Jinan City, Shandong Province. The site is a low tableland, slightly higher than its surrounding area. From May to September in 2016, archaeologists from Shandong Provincial Institute of Cultural Relics and Archaeology conducted salvage excavations on the western part of its southern margin. A rammed earthen foundation trench and a moat both dating back to Yueshi Culture period are the most important discoveries this time. According to excavations and archaeological reconnaissance, the discovered moat remains should be the part that used to be on the north side of the doorway. Close to the doorway, on the inner side and the bottom of the moat remains here, paved stones have been revealed and obviously piled up stones can be seen at some spots. The way in which the stones were arranged has never been observed on other sites dating back to Yueshi Culture period in Haidai Area. The rammed earthen foundation trench, which is suspected to be part of the city wall, is located on the west side of the moat and part of its east side overlaps with the moat. This foundation trench provides rare new materials for the study of city wall construction pattern in Yueshi Culture period.

# 安徽寿县斗鸡台遗址

◎蔡波涛

2014年度斗鸡台遗址考古发掘的重要发现主要有以下几点：第一，江淮地区西周时期遗址形态均为台地型，房址等居址类遗迹均主要分布于台地的周围，而台地中部为较纯且厚的地层堆积，斗鸡台遗址西周时期聚落的布局形式符合这一规律。第二，西周时期的房址发现较多，但多不完整，平面多为方形，结构一般为基槽柱洞式，也有部分房址仅有柱洞而无基槽。第三，与房址的分布相似，西周时期墓葬也主要发现于台地外围的探方内。从墓主年龄来看，以未成年人墓居多，成人墓较少；墓内均未发现随葬品。第四，另发现西周时期有几种可能为祭祀类的遗迹，一是T0402内发现的由多个动物坑群组成的祭祀遗迹，每个坑内均有一具羊或狗类尸骨堆积，坑群东北部有一儿童墓，未发现有明显墓圹，且人骨头部被一动物所压，其余骨坑似有围绕该儿童墓分布的迹象；二是蚌壳堆塑遗迹。第五，本次发掘发现比较重要的商代遗迹当属灰坑H47和H53以及房址F15、F20。H47打破的地层为该遗址较具代表性的商代垫土层；F15即是建在该层垫土上，其平面呈分间状，结构上有房基存在；H53也打破了属于商代的垫土层，且从出土陶器的形制来看，该坑的年代应与二里岗上层时期相当；F20为保存较好的商代分间式房址，为江淮地区首次发现。第六，以H75为代表，可能属斗鸡台文化的典型遗迹。且H75出土了较多骨器，此外还发现有两件牛肩胛骨，其中一件保存较好，其上有灼烧的痕迹，未发现钻痕和钻孔，应为卜骨无疑。另外还发现有龟甲的残片，推测该坑应为占卜祭祀类遗迹。第七，F22和F30代表了该遗址龙山时代晚期房址的两种形式。F22的建造也是铺垫一层垫土，再挖基槽，而基槽底部并不连通；基槽内填土分层版筑而成，墙基以上为墙体，从剖面观察墙基要宽于墙体，墙体也应为版筑而成。F30的建造方式应为先挖柱坑，后立柱，再填土以固定木柱。

斗鸡台遗址2014年度考古发掘获得了一批重要的考古资料，为学界进一步探讨以斗鸡台文化为核心的相关问题积累了新的研究素材。就居住的房址来说，从龙山时代晚期至西周时期均主要分布在台地周围，即本次发掘区的外围探方内；而就这些房址的走向来看，其方向多为东南—西北向，具有高度一致的传承性。从众多的与祭祀类相关遗迹和遗物的发现情况来看，至少在商周这一重视祭祀礼仪文化的时期，斗鸡台遗址在该地区应具有较高的地位。

西周早期房址

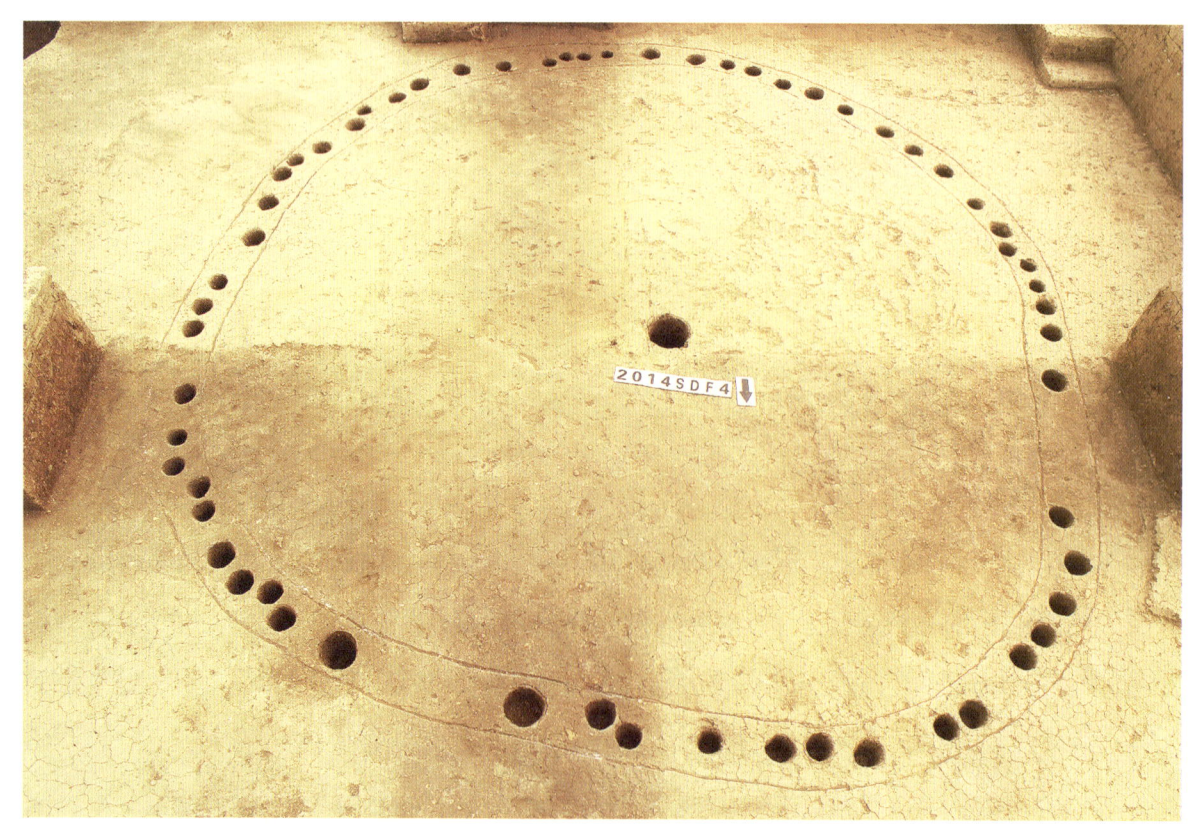

西周晚期圆形房址

三代之礼　皇皇者华　205

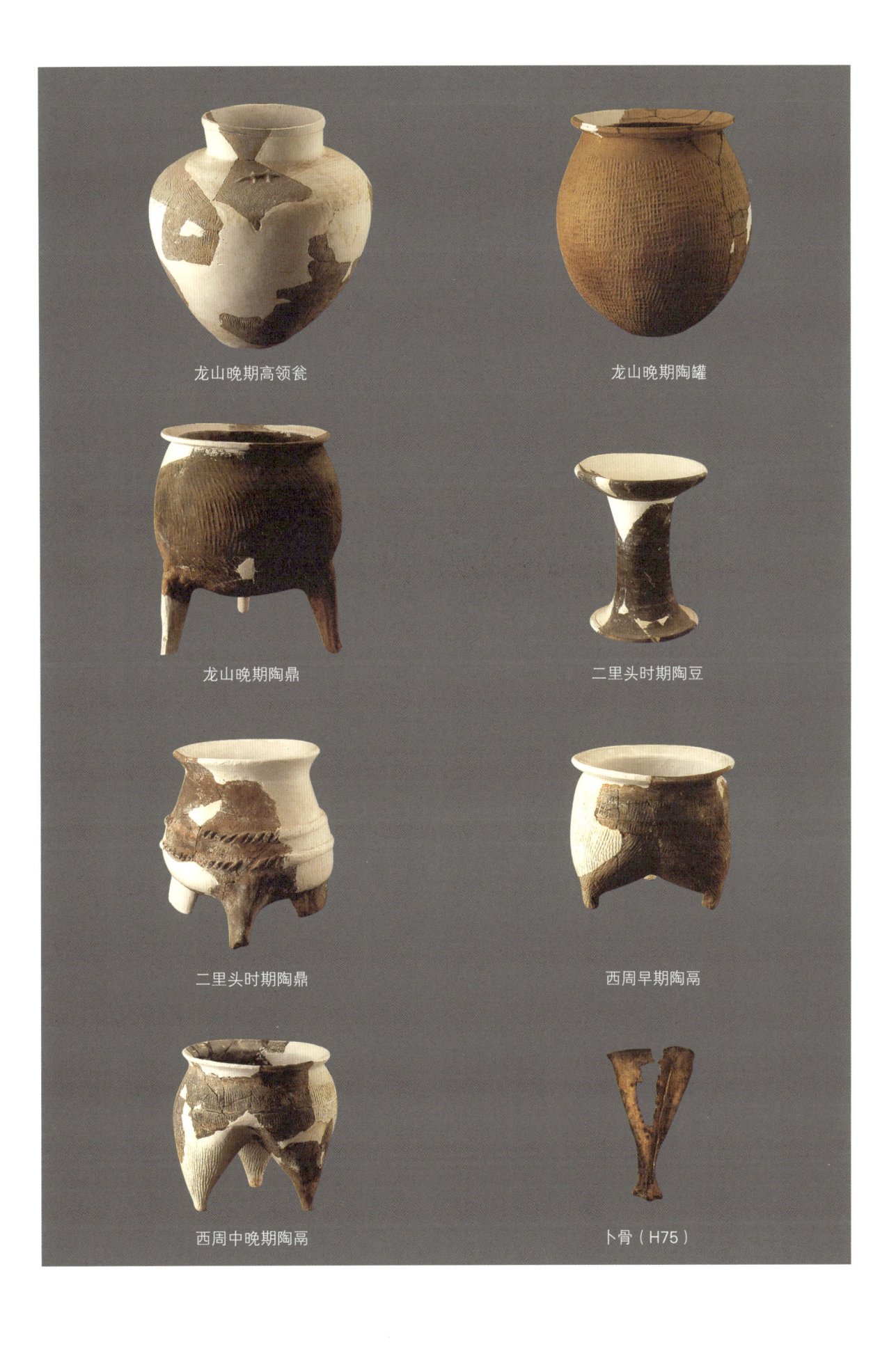

龙山晚期高领瓮　　　　　　　　　　龙山晚期陶罐

龙山晚期陶鼎　　　　　　　　　　二里头时期陶豆

二里头时期陶鼎　　　　　　　　　　西周早期陶鬲

西周中晚期陶鬲　　　　　　　　　　卜骨（H75）

西周早期祭祀遗迹

西周晚期灰坑H12内蚌壳堆积

Doujitai Site is located in the west of Dijia Xiaoying Villagers' Group, Shuangqiao Town, Shouxian County, Anhui Province. The following are major outcomes of archaeological excavations carried out in 2014. The settlement site discovered on Doujitai Site dates back to Western Zhou and this settlement used to be on a terrace. Its layout is in accordance with the pattern adopted by other sites of Western Zhou in Yangtze-Huaihe River Region. Generally speaking, foundation trenches and postholes are usually found on dwelling sites of Western Zhou. Tombs are mainly found on the periphery of the terrace. There are several remains that might be venues for sacrificial ceremonies back in Western Zhou. Dwelling site F20, as a relatively well-preserved partitioned residence dating back to Shang Dynasty, is the first one of its kind that has ever been discovered in Yangtze-Huaihe River Region. Oracle bones and other vestiges related to sacrificial ceremonies all indicate that Doujitai Site should enjoy a relatively superior status in terms of sacrificial rituals in this region.

# 安徽和县章四科大城子遗址

◎余 飞

章四科大城子遗址位于安徽省马鞍山市和县香泉镇龙塘行政村章四科自然村。遗址呈椭圆形台地，顶部地面平坦，相对高度约6米。2013年7月至2014年1月，为配合基本建设，安徽省文物考古研究所对该遗址西部进行了发掘。

发现各类遗迹235个，主要是灰坑、灰沟，有少量墓葬、房基、兽坑和窑等。出土器物主要有石器、陶器、原始瓷器和铜器等。根据地层堆积和出土器物判断，章四科大城子遗址主要经历了新石器晚期、二里头文化、商和西周四个阶段。

第一阶段遗存年代属新石器时代晚期，应属良渚文化范畴。典型陶器有饰有刻划凹弦纹的侧扁三角足深腹圜底盆形鼎、侧扁三角足垂鼓腹鼎、宽折沿浅弧腹盆等。

第二阶段遗存属二里头文化三、四期。典型遗物有宽折沿鼓腹大袋足鬲、凸棱豆等。以和县章四科大城子和含山大城墩遗址为代表的滁河流域以及往南的沿江江北地带该时期遗存中均受到二里头文化、岳石文化、马桥文化等几种考古学文化的共同影响，这几种考古学文化因素在此融合，并有了相当范围的分布。

第三阶段遗存属商文化时期。该阶段遗存延续性较强，从早商至晚商基本未间断。出土遗物可见典型的商式陶器如附加堆纹鼓腹袋足鬲、斜腹袋足鬲等，也可见到与宁镇地区、太湖流域互见的鼎式鬲、锥足盘形鼎等。这说明遗址该阶段与长江下游地区江南地带的交流更为频繁，而且这种交流并非单向而是相互的。

第四阶段遗存年代属西周时期。这个阶段的文化从西周早期一直延续至西周晚期，出土遗物文化特征经历了从西周早期以中原周文化为主，到西周中期的周文化特征变弱，吴文化和地方文化增强，再到西周晚期的地方文化进一步加强并与周文化和吴文化融合形成具有特色的地方文化类型。文化特征的演变也揭示了周王朝势力和地方势力在安徽江淮东部沿江地区的变化。

和县章四科大城子遗址具有从新石器时代至周代连续而完整的文化遗存，同时文化内涵多样，充分展现了各时期的文化交流与融合，又由于其承东启西、连通南北的特殊地理位置，对于安徽江淮东部和沿江江北地区的新石器时代晚期和夏商周时期区域文化研究具有重要意义。

房址

窑址

灶

三代之礼　皇皇者华

骨器

袋足鬲

砺石、陶拍

澄滤器

陶鼎

兽坑（狗骨架）

墓葬

Zhangsike Dachengzi Site is located in Zhangsike Unincorporated Village, Longtang Incorporated Village, Xiangquan Town, Hexian County, Ma'anshan City, Anhui Province. The physical appearance of the site is an oval tableland. From 2013 to 2014, archaeologists from Anhui Provincial Institute of Cultural Relics and Archaeology conducted excavations on the site, discovering ash pits, ash ditches, as well as a small number of tombs, pits buried with animals, dwelling sites, kilns, etc. There is a continuous and complete sequence of cultural remains dating back to the time spanning from Neolithic Age to Zhou Dynasty on Zhangsike Dachengzi Site in Hexian County. A wide range of cultural contents revealed from the site fully demonstrate cultural exchanges and diffusion in every era. Because of its special geographical location, the site used to connect the East and the West as well as the South and the North. Therefore, it is of great importance for the study of regional culture in late Neolithic Age and Xia, Shang and Zhou dynasties in eastern Yangtze-Huaihe River Basin in Anhui Province and the riverside area north of Yangtze River.

# 安徽阜南县台家寺遗址

◎何晓琳

台家寺遗址位于安徽省阜阳市阜南县朱寨镇三河村白庄自然村，是省级文物保护单位。2014—2016年，安徽省文物考古研究所和武汉大学历史学院考古系组成台家寺考古队，在台家寺遗址进行考古发掘工作。发掘确定了台家寺遗址的年代和文化面貌，探明了台家寺遗址的聚落结构，发现了完整的方形围沟、大型建筑、铸铜遗存、奠基坑、祭祀坑、贵族墓葬等重要遗迹，出土了大量遗物，揭示了商代高等级贵族在淮河流域的生产、生活以及埋葬的场景。

目前，考古队共发掘商代房屋建筑16座，灰坑273个，墓葬7座，确定了以台家寺遗址为代表的淮河流域的商文化属于中原商文化系统。台家寺商代遗址的年代自早商时代晚期延续到晚商时代早期，其中洹北商城时期是其文化最为发达的时期。

以台家寺遗址为代表的墩台形遗址是整个淮河流域和江淮地区龙山时期至春秋时期居址的主流形态，其发掘成果将推进对这一类遗址的时代和布局的综合研究。

台家寺遗址贵族居住区北部大型台基及3座大型建筑，属于典型的商文化建筑。在规模上，它是商代在南方地区仅次于三星堆和盘龙城的大型宫殿建筑。东部的大型建筑平面呈"品"字形布局，这在商文化中是首次发现，将推进对于夏商周时期建筑的研究。

台家寺遗址的铸铜手工业遗存发现的遗迹、遗物十分丰富。铸铜作坊F16和大量铜容器陶范使其铜容器铸造活动证据链完整，这是在商代两处都城遗址以外的地区的首次发现。同时，遗址内发现的陶范数量和铸造器类也是在两处都城以外最多的。其铜容器铸造技术，也是商代最为尖端的技术。台家寺遗址的考古发现证明了铜容器在商代可以在都城以外制作，且技术水准不逊于都城，同时也为商代金属资源的控制与分配、铸铜技术的控制与传播提供了最为重要的直接资料。台家寺遗址所在的淮河流域缺乏铸铜活动所需要的各种金属资源，这里的铸铜手工业的重要发现不仅为中国青铜时代早期的青铜铸造手工业的布局和管理提出了新的课题，也为探索中国青铜文明提供了重要线索。

发掘区航拍（上北下南）

贵族居住区北部台基与大型建筑（上北下南）

铸铜作坊内半地穴浇铸场地的石灰铸铜平面

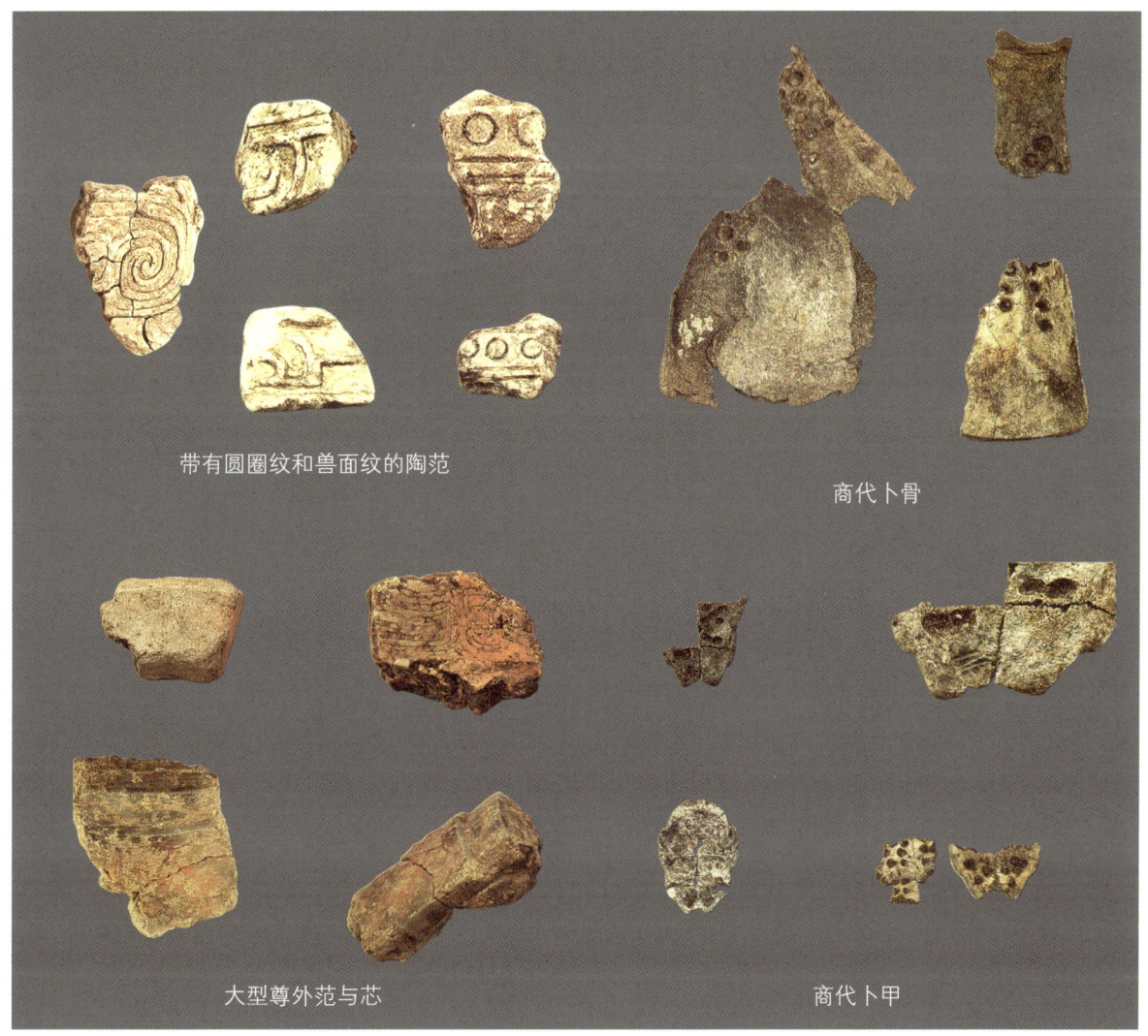

带有圆圈纹和兽面纹的陶范

商代卜骨

大型尊外范与芯

商代卜甲

商代墓葬（M3、M6）

M3铜爵出土情况

Taijiasi Site is located in Baizhuang Unincorporated Village, Sanhe Village, Zhuzhai Town, Funan County, Fuyang City, Anhui Province. From 2014 to 2016, archaeologists from Anhui Provincial Institute of Cultural Relics and Archaeology and other organizations conducted excavations on the site. The following are major outcomes. Taijiasi Site, as a site of Shang Dynasty, existed throughout the time from late early Shang Dynasty to early late Shang Dynasty. It reached its zenith during the time when Huanbei, a capital of Shang, formed and developed. Relatively complete remains of massive buildings, distributed in the aristocratic residential area, have been revealed. Tombs of Shang Dynasty are all located on a terrace-like mound. Such layout of a dwelling site prevailed during the time from Longshan Culture period to Spring & Autumn Period in the entire Huaihe River Basin and Yangtze-Huaihe River Region. Bronze casting sites dating back to Shang Dynasty are all located in the residential area of the nobles.

# 安徽凤阳县古堆桥遗址

◎何晓琳

古堆桥遗址位于安徽省凤阳县府城镇卫前村东部，其主要年代为商周时期。2012年9月至2013年1月，安徽省文物考古研究所和武汉大学历史学院考古系联合对该遗址进行了详细调查和发掘工作。遗址位于淮河南岸的河流冲积平原上，大体呈椭圆形，现地表最高处高出周边农田3～4米。其南部和东部为濠河支流唐河所环绕。

此次发掘共清理灰坑207个，房址9座。出土遗物非常丰富，包括陶器、卜甲、铸铜遗物等。古堆桥遗址有较丰富的商时期文化遗存，年代上从中商一直延续到晚商偏早，弥补了淮河流域商文化序列的空白。

古堆桥遗址的商时期文化，具有很强的中原文化特征，如遗址发现有折沿鬲、甗、假腹豆等器物。但口沿外侧呈台阶状的陶鬲、陶尊等器物也有很强的自身特点。同时古堆桥商文化的陶器演变没有完全与中原商文化同步，比如晚商早期在中原比较少见在陶鬲上饰有旋纹的现象，但在古堆桥商文化中这一现象却一直从中商延续到晚商。花园庄期起，中原商文化开始流行真腹豆，且假腹豆豆盘变深，但古堆桥却一直只有浅盘假腹豆这一个器类贯穿始终。

与江淮地区南部商文化的主要代表大城墩类型相比，以古堆桥遗址为代表的淮河流域商文化的位置更靠北。在皖北的淮河支流地区一些遗址的普查资料里也可以看到比较典型的折沿鬲的口颈部标本，可见淮河流域商文化的分布是围绕淮河干流及其支流的。它们是沟通中原商文化和江淮地区及长江下游商时期文化的桥梁。从现在已发掘和调查得到的材料看，淮河及其支流所在地区商文化的年代是相对固定的，都属于二里岗上层至大司空村一期。这些遗址的商文化面貌都与中原商文化相对接近，古堆桥遗址即是其中最为典型的遗址之一。

古堆桥遗址西周遗存不如其商时期遗存丰富，但也能表现出一些特点。尤其是，它与以霍邱堰台遗址为代表的江淮地区西部西周遗存和以滁州何郢遗址为代表的江淮地区东部西周遗存均不相同。古堆桥西周遗存明显拥有更多的中原周文化因素。这对探索中原周文化与江淮地区的交流也具有十分重要的意义。

熔炉残壁　　陶范

卜甲　　卜骨

Guduiqiao Site is in the eastern part of Weiqian Village, Fucheng Town, Fengyang County, Anhui Province. From September in 2012 to January in 2013, archaeologists from Anhui Provincial Institute of Cultural Relics and Archaeology and other organizations carried out thorough investigations and excavations on the site. A wide range of relics were unearthed, including potteries, oracle bones, bronze casting remains, etc. Comparatively abundant cultural relics and remains dating back to Shang Dynasty were discovered from Guduiqiao Site. Blanks of a cultural sequence of Shang Dynasty in Huaihe River Basin was filled in since these relics and remains date from the time spanning from middle Shang Dynasty to early late Shang Dynasty. A small number of remains dating back to Western Zhou were discovered. Showing obvious cultural features of Zhou Dynasty in Central Plains, these remains are of importance for the exploration into cultural exchanges between the Central Plains and Yangtze-Huaihe River Region in Zhou Dynasty.

# 山东济南市大辛庄遗址

◎ 郎剑锋

大辛庄遗址位于山东省济南市历城区王舍人街道办事处大辛庄村东南。遗址内的文化堆积是一处以商文化为主，另有少量史前时期和历史时期的文化遗存。2014年3—7月，山东大学联合山东省文物考古研究院、济南市考古研究所对大辛庄遗址进行考古发掘。

本次发掘区位于蝎子沟以东，发掘面积近700平方米。发掘商代的文化遗存种类多，数量大，是此次发掘的主要收获。发现的遗迹包括灰坑、墓葬、建筑、水井、陶窑等。灰坑的数量最多，少量灰坑平面为圆形或长方形，多数灰坑平面形状不规则，规模较大，打破关系非常复杂。与灰坑数量相比，墓葬数量有限，且规模较小，随葬品也较为贫乏。除墓葬外，在较为大型的灰坑内还发现了较为完整的人骨架，死者的身份很值得注意。建筑遗迹破坏较甚，保存状况不佳，平面形状不明，部分建筑遗迹内还发现人骨架，可能与奠基等祭祀行为有关。水井平面呈圆形，剖面呈梯形，上大下小，井壁保存完好，加工痕迹明显，但未发现用于上下的脚窝。陶窑仅发现1座，保存状况较好，结构明确，包括操作间、火门、火膛、窑室、窑箅等。陶窑内出土的陶片数量不多，可辨器形包括鬲、盆、甗等。需要特别指出的是，若干灰坑内出土了少量的陶范。

大辛庄遗址本次考古发掘具有多方面的学术价值：首先，此次发掘又获得大批包括陶器在内的商文化遗存，年代多集中于中商至晚商早期，为进一步完善大辛庄遗址的文化序列奠定了基础；其次，发掘出土大量人工遗物，采集了大量自然标本，可以有效开展有关古代社会的技术、经济、人地关系等方面的研究；再次，发掘获得了包括灰坑、墓葬、建筑遗存、水井、陶窑在内的多种遗迹，跨越不同的文化阶段和时期，为深入探讨大辛庄遗址的文化内涵、聚落布局和聚落形态的演变提供了丰富的资料。

灰坑

陶范

陶范

陶觚（J002）

墓葬

J002及其出土的陶鬲、陶鼎

陶窑

Daxinzhuang Site is located in the southeast of Daxinzhuang Village, Wangsheren Neighborhood, Licheng District, Jinan City, Shandong Province. The majority of the stratified deposit dates back to Shang Dynasty. From March to July in 2014, a joint team consisting of archaeologists from Shandong University, Shandong Provincial Institute of Cultural Relics and Archaeology and other organizations conducted excavations on the site. The following are major outcomes of archaeological work done in 2014. This time, volumes of cultural relics, including potteries, dating back to Shang Dynasty, mainly from middle Shang Dynasty to early late Shang Dynasty, had been unearthed. This laid the foundation for further perfecting the cultural chronicle of Daxinzhuang Site. Various remains had been excavated, including ash pits, tombs, buildings, wells, and kilns of varied cultural phases and historical periods. They are materials for further discussion on cultural contents, changes of settlement layout and structure of Daxinzhuang Site.

# 陕西清涧县辛庄遗址

◎种建荣　孙战伟

辛庄遗址位于无定河下游支流川口河上游的辛庄村，是在第三次文物普查时首次发现的，其文化堆积以商代晚期为主，文化面貌与李家崖、绥德薛家渠、山西柳林高红同时期遗存相同，总面积约10万平方米。2012年由于遗址内墓葬遭受盗掘，受陕西省文物局指派，由陕西省考古研究院联合市县文物部门对被盗7座墓葬进行抢救性发掘。随后对该遗址进行了详细调查和重点勘探，发现有夯土基址、房址、灰坑、包边夯土墙等重要遗迹。2013年经报国家文物局批准，对该遗址展开了有计划、有目的的考古发掘工作。经过连续五年的考古发掘工作，发掘揭露出一座规模宏大的晚商城址。

辛庄遗址发现有大型礼仪性夯土建筑，以及其他中、小型下沉式夯土建筑，铸铜作坊，灰坑，墓葬等遗迹，出土器物包括陶器、石器、骨器、铜器等，年代主要为商代晚期。辛庄遗址是继李家崖、高红等遗址的发掘之后，对陕晋高原地区商时期遗址进行的又一次大规模考古发掘项目。这些发现为进一步认识陕晋高原地区商代考古学文化面貌特征、生活习俗、经济形态提供了重要资料。不同形式建筑设施的揭露和较多石刀、石斧等与农业相关的生产工具的发现，反映了以辛庄遗址为代表的李家崖文化先民应该是以山地农业经济为主，并经营少量畜牧活动，可能将明显改变过去普遍认为的我国北方早期青铜文化属于所谓草原牧业文明的观念。特别是发现的重楼环屋式建筑群，以复杂的结构、独特的设计、宏大的规模、考究的营造乃至修饰，显示了该文化在中国古代建筑方面所取得的显著成就，建筑物室内铺设木质地板的形式，可谓独树一帜，应在古代建筑史上具有重要的地位。

发现的陶范和铸铜作坊，也是陕北商周考古的又一突破，不仅证明陕北以往发现的大量晚商青铜器部分应为本地制造，而且证明部分和殷墟一样的铜礼器应也是本地所造。从另一个角度反映了这一文化在当时已发展到相当高的文明水准，也说明中原和陕北可能存在着铸铜技术和铜料的流动，对理解这一文化青铜器、铸铜业以及由此而反映出的社会组织结构等问题，提供了十分珍贵的材料。

F1北包边墙

廊道木地板

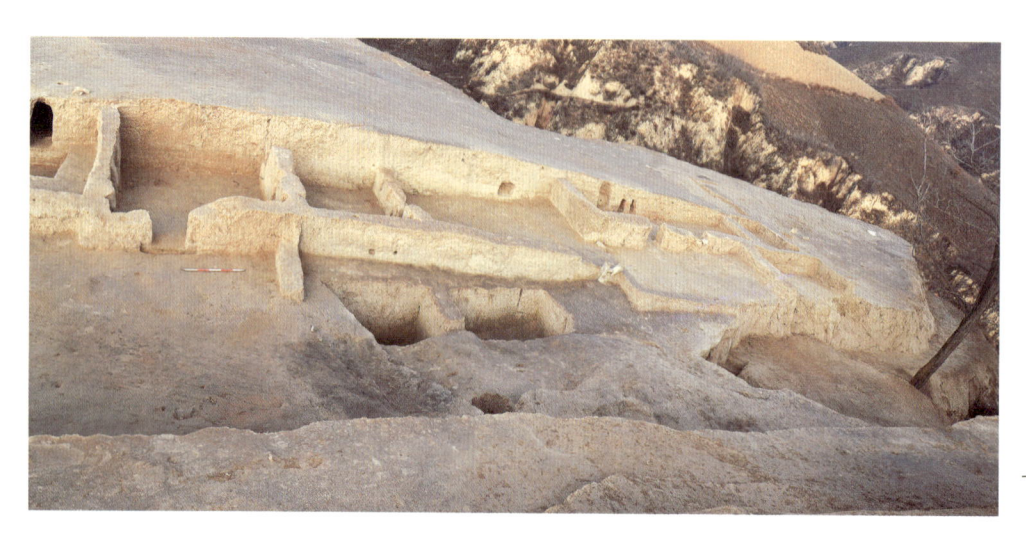

一堂三室建筑
（上北下南）

铃模　　　　　　　　　　　陶范

小口折肩罐　　　　　　　　陶鬲

三足瓮　　　　　　　　　　小口折肩罐

遗址东南角夯土（左南右北）

Xinzhuang Site is located in Xinzhuang Village, upper reaches of Chuankou River, a tributary of the lower reaches of Wuding River. Since 2013, archaeologists from Shaanxi Provincial Institute of Archaeology had launched planned and goal-oriented archaeological excavations on the site. Discoveries included remains of large-scale rammed earthen ceremonial architectures, medium-sized and small sunken buildings made of rammed earth, bronze casting workshop, ash pits and tombs. Important unearthed objects included potteries, stone implements, bone implements, bronzes and other relics of late Shang Dynasty. These discoveries are important materials for further understanding of cultural features, customs and economic forms on Jin-Shan Plateau in Shang Dynasty.

# 山东济南市刘家庄遗址

◎郭俊峰 房 振 李 铭

刘家庄遗址位于济南市古城区西北约3千米的刘家庄村，是一处商周和唐至明清时期的遗址。2010年6月至2011年2月，为配合该区域的棚户区改造工程，济南市考古研究所对其进行了抢救性考古发掘，共清理墓葬122座、灰坑169个，其中以77座商代晚期墓葬和141个商周灰坑等遗迹的发现最为重要，另发现少量唐至清代的墓葬、灰沟、窑址等遗迹。

商代墓葬共发现77座，大多比较分散，部分相对集中。墓葬规模较小，墓向不固定，其中三分之一有葬具一棺，个别棺外有椁。半数见随葬品，且多为陶器，个别还有戈、镞等兵器；极少数墓出土鼎、觚、爵等青铜器，其中3座数量较多。M121墓葬规模最大，随葬品最多，共91件（组）。该墓出土有铭铜器9组3类，铭文分别为"🚩""戈""✧"。M122与M121东西并列，出土青铜器残损严重，似为埋葬时故意损毁，器形完整及可辨者43件。该墓出土有铭青铜器3组3类，铭文分别为"🚩""🔲""✧"。发现商周灰坑141个，少数灰坑内放置整头的牛或猪；个别出土卜骨，其中部分灰坑应为当时的窖穴和祭祀坑。

刘家庄商墓出土了大量有铭青铜器，是济南市区内首次发掘的商代遗址，成为继大辛庄、长清小屯后又一处重要遗址。发掘表明，晚商时期刘家庄地区居住着至少一支与商都殷墟有密切关系的氏族，为山东地区商代晚期政治、经济格局的研究提供了新材料，对研究商代晚期商王朝对东方的经略也有重大意义。

初步分析，商代晚期墓葬主要应属殷墟三期、四期。从出土铭文及墓葬分布推测，发掘东区南部为该地统治阶层"🚩"族贵族墓葬区，葬制、葬俗与殷墟基本一致；东区北部和西区大部为平民墓葬区，氏族较多，除少量墓葬方向和葬式不同外，其余大多文化面貌相近，既有殷商文化因素，又有鲁北地区文化因素；西区西端为子姓商族"子工"族墓葬区（目前仅M56一座），其墓主人可能被派遣至此监视其他氏族或另有任务。

此外，刘家庄遗址与大辛庄遗址仅相距约10千米，有着相同时期的文化遗存，但出土陶器组合却有差别，前者以簋、豆、罐较常见，鬲少见，且两地铜器铭文亦无相同者。因此，二者之间的关系也有待进一步研究。

M121（上西下东）及出土铜器铭文拓片

M109（上西下东）

三代之礼 皇皇者华

铜爵　　　　　铜斝　　　　　铜觚

铜鼎　　　　　　　　　铜鼎

铜鼎　　　　　　　　　铜簋

铜提梁卣　　　　　　　　　铜壶

Liujiazhuang Site is located in Liujiazhuang Village, approximately 3 kilometers northwest of Gucheng District of Jinan City. The site dates back to Shang Dynasty, Zhou Dynasty and a period spanning from Tang Dynasty to Ming Dynasty and Qing Dynasty. From 2010 to 2011, Jinan Institute of Archaeology carried out salvage excavations on Liujiazhuang Site. The most important discoveries are remains of Shang Dynasty and Zhou Dynasty, including 77 tombs dating back to late Shang Dynasty, ash pits, etc. Those tombs, dating back to late Shang Dynasty were mainly constructed during the third and fourth phases of Yinxu Culture period. There was a cemetery of the nobles, a civilian cemetery and a cemetery of "Zigong" clan who were descendants of Shang people with the family name of Zi. A great number of bronzes, many of which are with inscriptions, have been unearthed from tombs of Shang Dynasty on Liujiazhuang Site. As the first site of Shang Dynasty that has been discovered and excavated in the urban area of Jinan City, Liujiazhuang Site provides new materials for the study of the political situation and economic pattern of late Shang Dynasty in the place that is now Shandong Province.

# 江苏镇江市孙家村遗址

◎何汉生

孙家村遗址位于镇江市新区丁岗镇原孙家村西侧。遗址由环壕和台地构成，外侧为环壕，内侧为台地。台地平面近椭圆形，顶部近平，高于周边地面约4.5米。2015年11月至今，南京博物院、镇江博物馆，对其进行了考古发掘，面积为4650平方米。

发掘显示遗址外侧为环壕，环壕内侧台地边缘为土垣，土垣内侧有土台、墓葬、灰沟、灰坑、窑等。环壕位于台地外侧，底部中间有一条生土坎将其分为内、外两部分，壕内为淤土层。环壕开挖于西周时期，沿用至春秋中晚期，遗址废弃后仍为浅沟状，以后逐渐被淤埋于地下。土垣为人工堆筑而成，堆土以黄土为主，由下而上、由外向内堆积。上部截面呈梯形，底部开挖基槽，斜壁，平底。土垣筑于西周早期，内侧在使用过程中逐渐加高，春秋中晚期的土台顶面与之大致持平。土台42个，其中西周时期3个、春秋时期39个。多个土台台面上发现有圆形坑，每组4个，大致呈正方形分布，直壁，平底，填土多为纯净的黄土，十分密实。此坑暂被称为柱坑，应为房屋建筑的基础结构。其他发现包括墓葬2座、灰沟1条、窑4座、灰坑45个。

孙家村遗址出土可复原遗物1000余件，大多属春秋时期，少量为西周遗物。出土遗物以陶瓷器为主，有夹砂陶、泥质陶、硬陶、原始瓷。另发掘出土多件与铸铜有关的器物，有陶范、石范、坩埚、吹火筒、石锤、砺石等。出土铜器104件，另出土较多铜块及较多铜渣。从出土的陶范、石范及铜器分析，其主要用于铸造兵器及生产工具。

孙家村遗址保存较好，外侧挖环壕，台地边缘堆筑土垣，中心位置堆筑大土台，其周边堆筑多个圆形或椭圆形小土台，这一布局从西周早期遗址最初使用时即已形成，并保持至春秋中晚期。遗址布局完整，与以往宁镇地区发掘的同时期遗址布局明显不同的是，土台上发现了4座窑，位于遗址中心大土台上，其余土台散布于周边；多个土台上发现烧结坑、烧结面，地层中发现大量红烧土、木灰、倒塌的窑壁，出土了较多的铜器及少量陶范、坩埚等与铸铜有关的器物，可见此遗址曾存在铸铜活动。孙家村遗址的发掘为吴国青铜器找到了一处生产地，是近年来吴文化考古的一次重要发现，为吴文化研究及古代冶金考古研究提供了新的资料。

土垣(上南下北)

土台及房址(上南下北)

三代之礼 皇皇者华 231

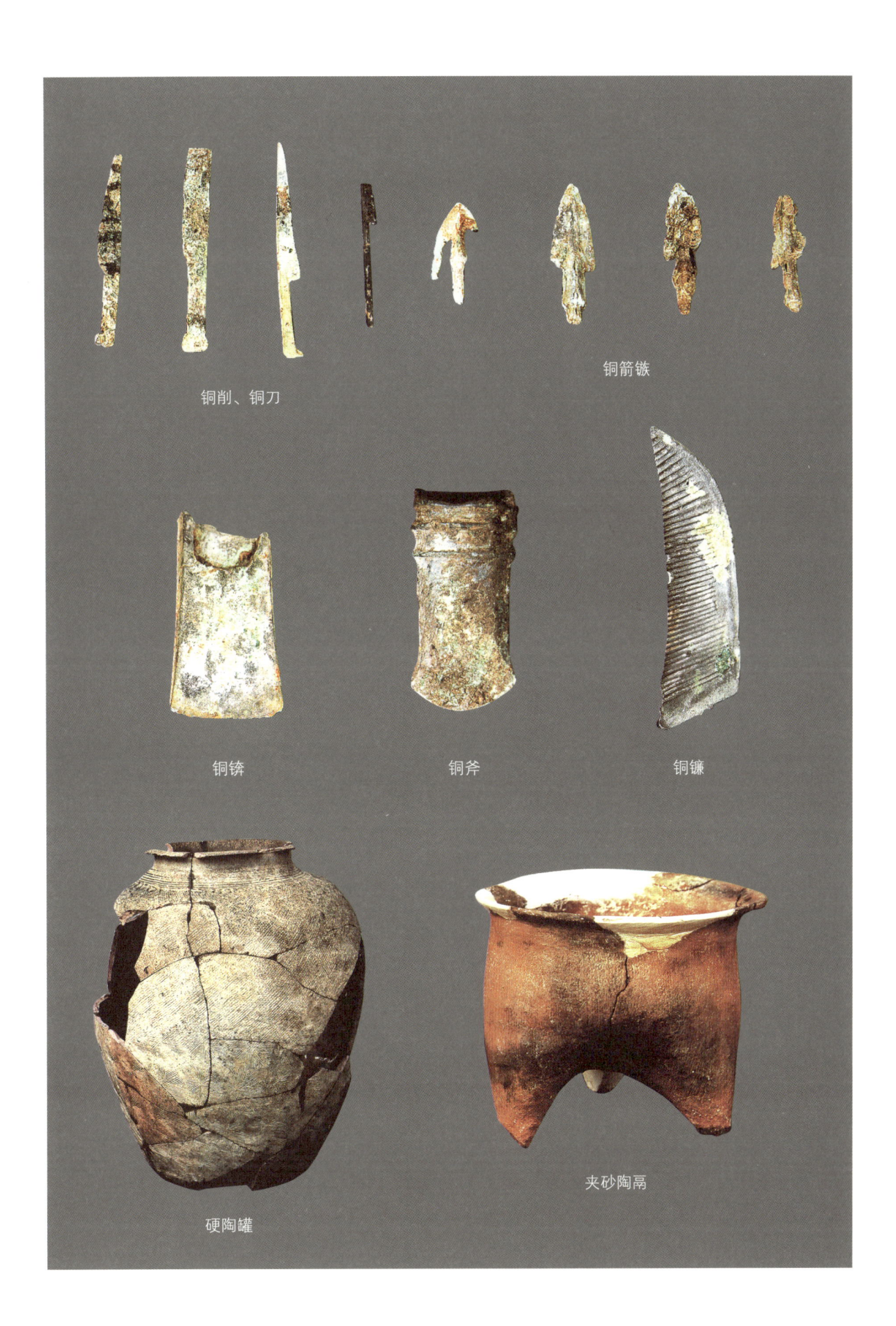

铜削、铜刀　　　　　　　　　　铜箭镞

铜锛　　　　　铜斧　　　　　铜镰

　　　　　　　　　　　　夹砂陶鬲

硬陶罐

陶范

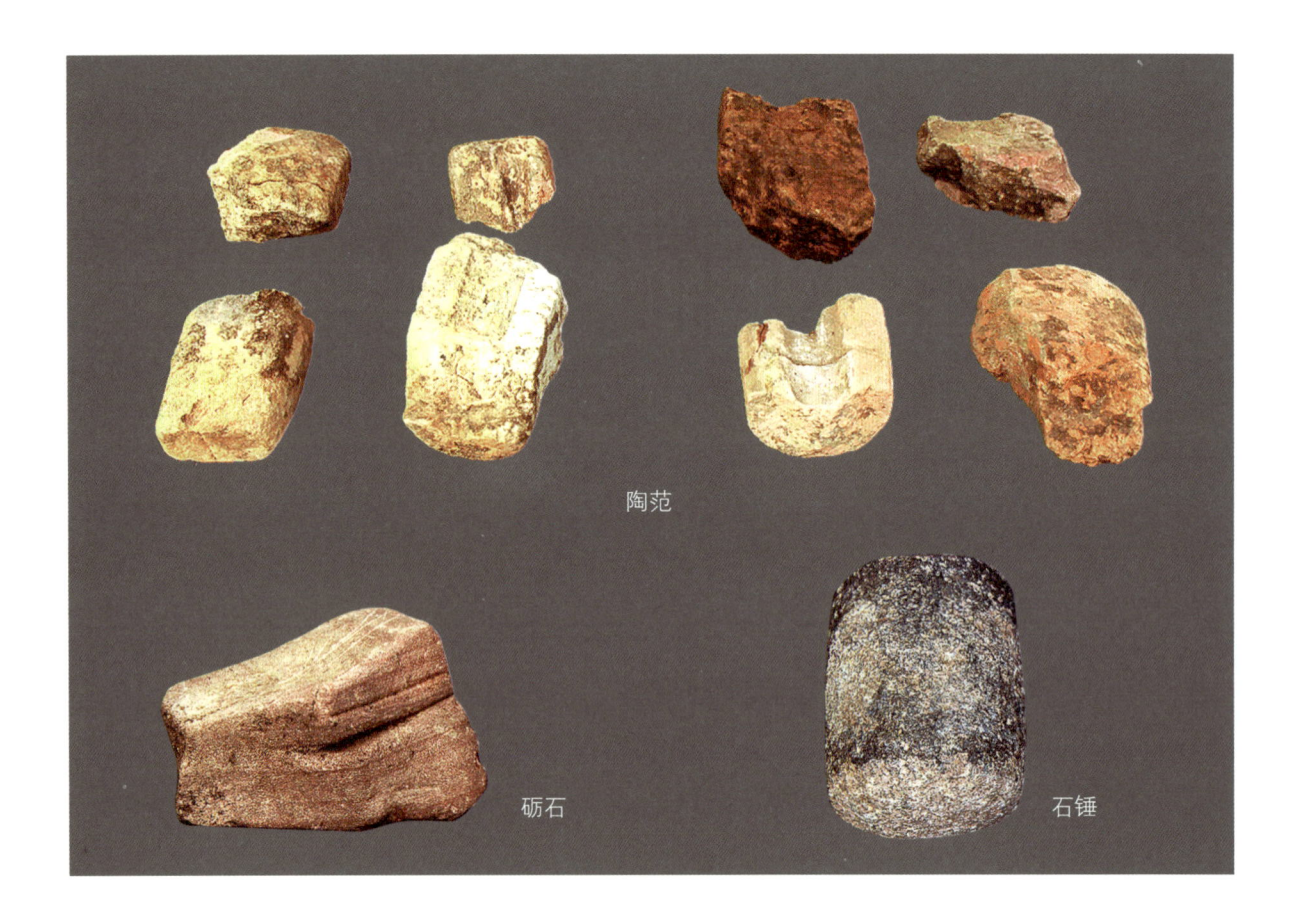

砺石　　　　　　　　　石锤

Sunjiacun Site is located in the west of an area that used to be Sunjiacun Village, Dinggang Town, in the New District of Zhenjiang City. The site is on an almost elliptical terrace, approximately 4.5 meters higher than its surrounding area. A joint team consisting of archaeologists from Nanjing Museum and Zhenjiang Museum has been conducting excavations on the site since November in 2015. There is a moat outside the site. Inside the moat, an earthen wall was built on the rim of the terrace. Inside the earthen wall, there used to be earthen platforms, tombs, ash ditches, ash pits, kilns, etc. Most of the relics that have been unearthed so far date back to Spring & Autumn Period; a small number of them are of Western Zhou. Four kilns discovered on the site, along with many unearthed bronzes and a small number of pottery molds, crucibles and other objects used for bronze casting, all indicate that there used to be bronze casting activities in this place. Excavations carried out on Sunjiacun Site have proved the site as a provenance of bronzes of Wu State. Sunjiacun Site, as an important discovery of Wu Culture archaeology in recent years, provides new materials for the study on Wu Culture and archaeological researches on metal smelting in ancient times.

# 陕西周原遗址

◎李彦峰

2014—2015年，由陕西省考古研究院、北京大学考古文博学院、中国社会科学院考古研究所三家单位组成的周原考古队，对周原遗址进行新一轮的勘探发掘。

2014年度，考古队发掘清理出2座夯土基址，即凤雏三号基址和四号基址。其中四号基址位于三号基址东南角，可能为三号基址的附属部分，二者相距9米。三号夯土基址北距1976年发掘的凤雏甲组、乙组基址约40米。基址主要部分的形状呈"回"字形，四面为夯土台基，包括北面的主体台基、东西两侧的台基及南面门塾的台基。中间的庭院为长方形，四周发现散水遗迹。庭院的中部偏西有一处长方形的铺石遗迹，由较大的砾石块铺砌而成。紧贴铺石的北侧，正中为一青灰色砂岩质长方体立石。根据地层关系和出土遗物特征，可以判定凤雏三号基址始建于西周早期，于中期前后曾遭大面积失火，西周晚期彻底废弃。

2015年还重点针对水系遗迹进行了大规模勘探，并对刘—庞家淤土遗迹和4条沟渠遗迹进行了解剖发掘。根据勘探和试掘情况推测，刘—庞家淤土遗迹或为一处与人工有关的蓄水设施，其北侧的G4、G5可提供稳定的水源。而G6自东向西的流向，亦具有将东侧水源引入的功能。结合"云塘—齐镇—召陈池渠"遗存的考古成果，可以初步认为周原遗址内存在着自然水系与人工水系、蓄水池与引水渠、干渠与支渠等不同层次的水系遗存，共同构成了周原遗址的水网系统。

凤雏三号基址是继1976年凤雏甲组基址之后的又一次重大发现，也是迄今发掘的最大规模的西周单体建筑遗存，进一步丰富了凤雏建筑群的内涵。其"回"字形的平面布局是西周时期建筑中的首次发现，为本已形式多样的西周建筑又增一新例，为研究西周时期建筑形制发展演变规律提供了实例；基址庭院内的立石、铺石遗迹更是以往西周考古中未曾见到过的特殊遗存，依据文献资料推测可能为一处"社祀"遗存。

周原遗址内水网系统的发现与确认，进一步强化了以往所发现的诸多重要遗迹之间的有机联系，加深了以往对周原遗址聚落扩张过程与水源关系的认识，与丰镐遗址的"昆明池"等池渠一起填补了周代都邑性遗址给水（池苑）系统的空白。最为重要的是，这一系列工作，尤其是以淤土遗存为线索，为旨在探寻聚落结构的田野工作提供了一条较为切实可行的途径。

凤雏三号基址全景（上东下西）

G6剖面正射影像图

立石、铺石遗迹正射影像图（上南下北）

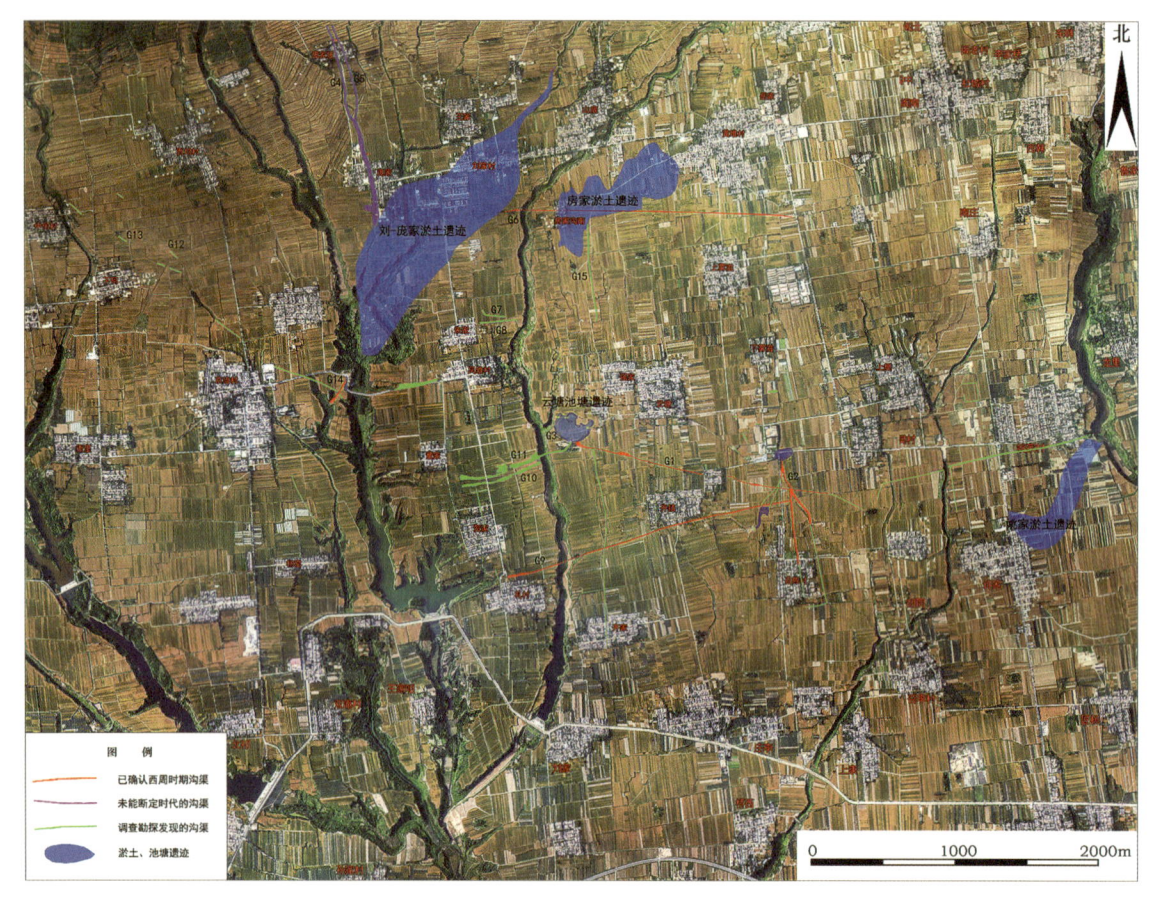

周原遗址池渠遗存平面分布图

The following are major outcomes of archaeological work done by an archaeological team based at Zhouyuan Site from 2014 to 2015. Successive excavations were carried out in Hejiabei Area centering with Fengchu Building Complex. 2 rammed earthen foundation sites, 1 chariot pit, 24 tombs and 130 ash pits that overlap with the tombs were revealed. These discoveries have further enriched the volume of relics of Western Zhou unearthed from Hejiabei Area. In the process of tracing remnants of a water system, one of Framework Relics, 3 large patches of silt sites and 13 ditch sites were newly discovered by examining silt deposits. After excavating and examining remains of ponds and canals that had been revealed on Zhouyuan Site and combing previous archaeological findings, it has been preliminarily determined that there used to be a relatively established water network on Zhouyuan Site. It provides new materials for the study on Wu Culture and archaeological researches on metal smelting in ancient times.

# 江苏新沂市聂墩遗址

◎ 田二卫

聂墩遗址位于江苏省新沂市瓦窑镇瓦窑中学西约700米的农田中，与西聂墩相望。遗址呈墩形，漫坡状，墩心高出周围约2米。其东缘被现代水渠破坏，时代为西周至汉代。2015年10月，徐州博物馆、新沂博物馆组建联合考古队对其进行抢救性考古发掘，共清理汉墓46座、灰坑9座。

遗址主要包含早、晚两期遗存，其中早期西周文化层共发掘300平方米。2016年度发掘共揭露遗迹58处，其中房址12座、灰坑43个、灰沟3条，并收集大量文化遗物与动植物标本。房址皆为地面式建筑，F1为木骨泥墙建筑，复原后为长方形建筑；F2仅存一道基槽，全貌不明；F3~F11为近圆形房址，多由基槽与柱洞构成，少数无基槽，其中F3、F5等可见全貌；F12为早期主要建筑，由众多巨型柱洞构成，多两两成组，整体近方形，其西侧一排柱洞呈东北—西南向延伸，现将少数代表遗迹举例如下：

F1分布于T0305、T0306、T0406中，保存较差，为遗址主要建筑。主体呈东北—西南向延伸，南部与西部残见部分木骨泥墙，据残存墙体复原后，平面近"L"形，可见4间，南端向东延伸。未发现门道痕迹。房内残存大量红烧土块，北部房内出土一件夹砂灰陶敛口豆，中部与南部出土大量夹砂灰陶残片，多饰绳纹。器形可见鬲、甗、盆、罐等。房内堆积清理后，地面呈褐色，较坚硬，推测为木骨泥墙建造过程中为加固墙体于室内纵火焚烧所致。

F12分布于T0305、T0405、T0406中，平面近方形，由43个柱洞构成，呈内外两重，向东延伸入T0405、T0406东壁，未作完整揭露。柱洞多较为巨大，平面有圆形、椭圆形、圆角方形三种。第10层叠压于F12的柱洞之上，为灰黄色沙土，土质较硬，纯净，无包含物，且在3个探方中皆有分布，且F12的木柱柱窝在10层表面可见，应为刻意铺垫而成，推测该层为F12的活动面堆积。另第9层为灰黑色粉土，土质疏松，含有大量黑色灰烬与灰陶片，或为F12的使用堆积。

238 黄淮七省考古新发现

遗址航拍图（上东下西）

房址位置图（上东下西）

F1（上东南下西北）

F3（上西北下东南）

F5（上东北下西南）

F12（上南下北）

Niedun Site, facing Xinie Mound, is located in the farmland approximately 700 meters west of Wayao Middle School in Wayao Town, Xinyi City, Jiangsu Province. From 2015 to 2016, archaeologists from Xuzhou Museum and other organizations carried out salvage excavations on Niedun Site. The site itself was first discovered by archaeologists from Nanjing Museum in 1962. Looking like a mound, the site existed throughout the time from Western Zhou Dynasty to Han Dynasty. The majority of the remains are of two phases, i.e. the early phase and the late phase. 46 tombs of Han Dynasty and 9 ash pits were revealed from the cultural layer dating back to late Han Dynasty. Among the 46 tombs, 45 were shaft tombs and 1 was a brick-chambered tomb. From the cultural layer dating back to early Western Zhou, remains, including 12 dwelling sites, 43 ash pits and 3 ash ditches, were discovered at 58 spots.

# 河北行唐故郡遗址

◎ 齐瑞普　张春长

故郡遗址位于河北省行唐县故郡村北，地处太行山东麓山前平原地带，东临大沙河，主体年代为东周时期，居址、墓地与城址共存。截至目前，发掘共清理东周墓葬37座（其中积石墓28座），车马坑7座，水井50眼，灰坑520余座，窑址2座，灰沟2条，城垣1段。

其中，东周时期的二号车马坑为积石墓M53的车马坑，坑内纵列摆放5辆车，坑中部两侧各有1壁龛，龛内各殉1成年男性。五号车置于坑内最东端，未见系驾动物。一至四号车为驷马独辀车，16匹马杀死后摆放在车辆系驾位置。车轮皆卸下覆盖车舆之上，三至五号车舆表面部分贴金彩绘。东侧殉牲坑以充填卵石的沟槽与车马坑相通，坑内分三层埋放牛、羊、马等动物头、蹄。

故郡遗址年代为春秋晚期至战国中、晚期，大致可分为三期。第一期以南北向土坑墓及J39、J47等为代表，典型器物为夹砂灰陶鬲，折沿鼓腹、裆近平或略外鼓、三乳足根，年代为春秋晚期，不晚于春秋战国之际。第二期以积石墓、车马坑为代表，年代为战国早期。第三期以J1、J6等带井圈水井及遗址第④层为代表，典型器物为陶釜、鼓腹罐，年代为战国中期，部分遗存或可延至晚期。

故郡遗址从时空及文化内涵来看，与鲜虞、中山国密切相关。遗址文化面貌显示其既深受华夏系统文化的影响，同时又具有鲜明的北方族群特色。墓葬以积石墓为主，随葬器物既有中原、燕、齐等华夏系统文化因素的铜器、兵器、车马器，同时又有具有鲜明北方族群特色的铜鍑、金盘丝耳环及大量的玛瑙、绿松石饰品。墓葬普遍使用殉牲且多用马、牛、羊等动物头、蹄，同时又使用车马衬葬制度。有的填土中有猪下颌、猪腿骨、狗骨，有的棺上置动物肩胛骨，有的壁龛内殉羊头、蹄等。五座车马坑内葬车马或车，其东侧有单独的殉牲坑，二者共用一生土梁并以填砌卵石的沟槽相通，殉牲坑内分层埋葬马、牛、羊等动物头、蹄，这种独特的车马-殉牲坑形制，系考古中首次发现。

故郡遗址自春秋晚期延续至战国中、晚期，城址、墓地与居址共存，多种文化因素在此交融，强烈地反映出北方族群文化与华夏系统文化之间的融合与嬗变，其考古发现与研究，填补了冀中地区同期考古及历史研究的空白，不但可以补充和完善春秋战国史的缺环，而且也为研究戎狄等北方族群的华夏化进程与中华民族多元一体格局的形成，提供了极为珍贵的实物资料。

二号车马坑（上北下南）

GH04左侧栏间金箔

GH03左骖马头颈海贝编串的络辔

二号车马坑殉牲坑第三层牛、羊、马等动物头、蹄

铜鼎

铜鸟盖瓠壶

铜豆

铜敦

错金铜镦

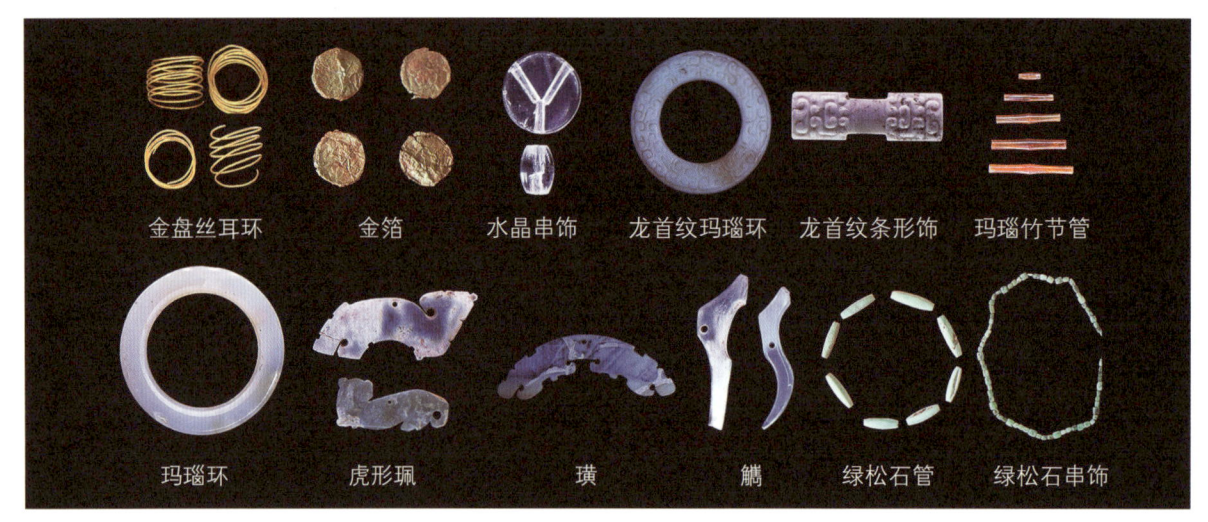

| 金盘丝耳环 | 金箔 | 水晶串饰 | 龙首纹玛瑙环 | 龙首纹条形饰 | 玛瑙竹节管 |
| 玛瑙环 | 虎形珮 | 璜 | 觿 | 绿松石管 | 绿松石串饰 |

金器和玉器

| 当卢 | 鎏金铜泡 | 陶鬲 |

Gujun Site is in the north of Gujun Village, Xingtang County, Hebei Province. From 2015 to 2017, archaeologists from Hebei Provincial Institute of Cultural Relics and other organizations carried out archaeological reconnaissances and excavations on the site. Gujun Site existed from late Spring & Autumn Period to middle and late phases of Warring States Period. The coexistence of city sites, tombs and dwelling sites, along with cultural fusion, strongly reflected integration and evolvement between the culture of northern ethnic groups and that of Chinese cultural system. Archaeological discoveries made on Gujun Site and relevant studies have filled in the blank of contemporary archaeological and historical researches in central Hebei Province. These discoveries can be used to supplement and complete historical records of the period from Spring & Autumn Period to Warring States Period. Besides, extremely rare materials have been provided to the study of Chinesization progress of northern ethnic groups and formation of the pluralistic integrative Chinese nation.

# 山西榆社县偶尔坪遗址

◎王 俊

榆社县隶属山西省晋中市，地处太行山中段西麓，浊漳河西源两岸，古为北上党地区北端门户地带。2017年，为配合太焦高铁榆社段的地下文物保护工作，山西省考古研究所组织联合考古队对先期勘探发现的古代遗址积极开展了考古发掘。偶尔坪遗址位于榆社县河峪乡西周村西南的冲沟间台地上，目前发掘工作仍在进行中。

遗址地层堆积比较简单，但文化内涵极为丰富，发现遗迹有灰坑、灰沟、小型墓葬、灰坑葬、陶窑、土坑灶、半地穴式房址、地下建筑基址及部分夯土城墙等，时代上从战国早期延续到战国晚期。

战国早期墓葬主要为长方形小型竖穴土坑墓，南北向居多，东西向仅2座，一棺一椁，单人葬。小型土坑墓成排成组，应是血缘家庭的族墓地。墓葬时代推测均在战国早期，墓主身份应为下士。

灰坑、灰坑葬、陶窑等晚期遗迹及文化层中出土物主要为泥质灰陶片，包括建筑构件、生活器具和工具。器物陶片上发现不少陶文，包括戳印文字、刻划文字和刻划符号三种，戳印文字主要有"隋徻""公""家""士"等，刻划文字有"东盾""丁"等，刻划符号有"＋""×"等。

地下建筑基址共发掘4座，位于发掘区西部，现主要残存地下部分。石砌建筑3座，建造方法是在长方形土圹内用河卵石垒砌石墙和积石基础。夯土木构建筑1座，是在长方形土圹内中部起建，周边夯土填实，活动面是在铺平的河卵石基础之上再平铺木板，墙壁由竖排的木板和圆木立柱组成，转角处存有板状石柱础或磉墩。夯土基址位于发掘区东部，目前共发现2处，均呈北偏西走向。二者大致并排，初步判断东侧为夯土城墙，东缘紧临冲沟，被破坏严重；西侧为夯土基址，分段夯筑。两组夯土基址的边缘还发现有多处成排倚立的扣合整齐的筒瓦及板瓦用以包边，性质不明。此类建筑遗迹现象在以往的考古发掘中极为罕见，对战国时期地上、地下建筑的形制、工艺及使用功能具有极高的研究价值。

我们推测遗址可能与春秋战国时期晋国的"涅氏"有关，或可能为"涅氏"的一个邑，具体结论还需要进一步论证。

地下建筑遗存F1~F4位置关系图（上西下东）

F2和F3打破关系（北为F2，南为F3，上北下南）

F4内建筑遗存地面解剖图（上东下西）

发掘区东部一号夯土基址及夯土城墙（上东下西）

夯土城墙东缘倚立的成排扣合的筒瓦及板瓦（上西下东）

陶片上的文字和刻划符号拓片

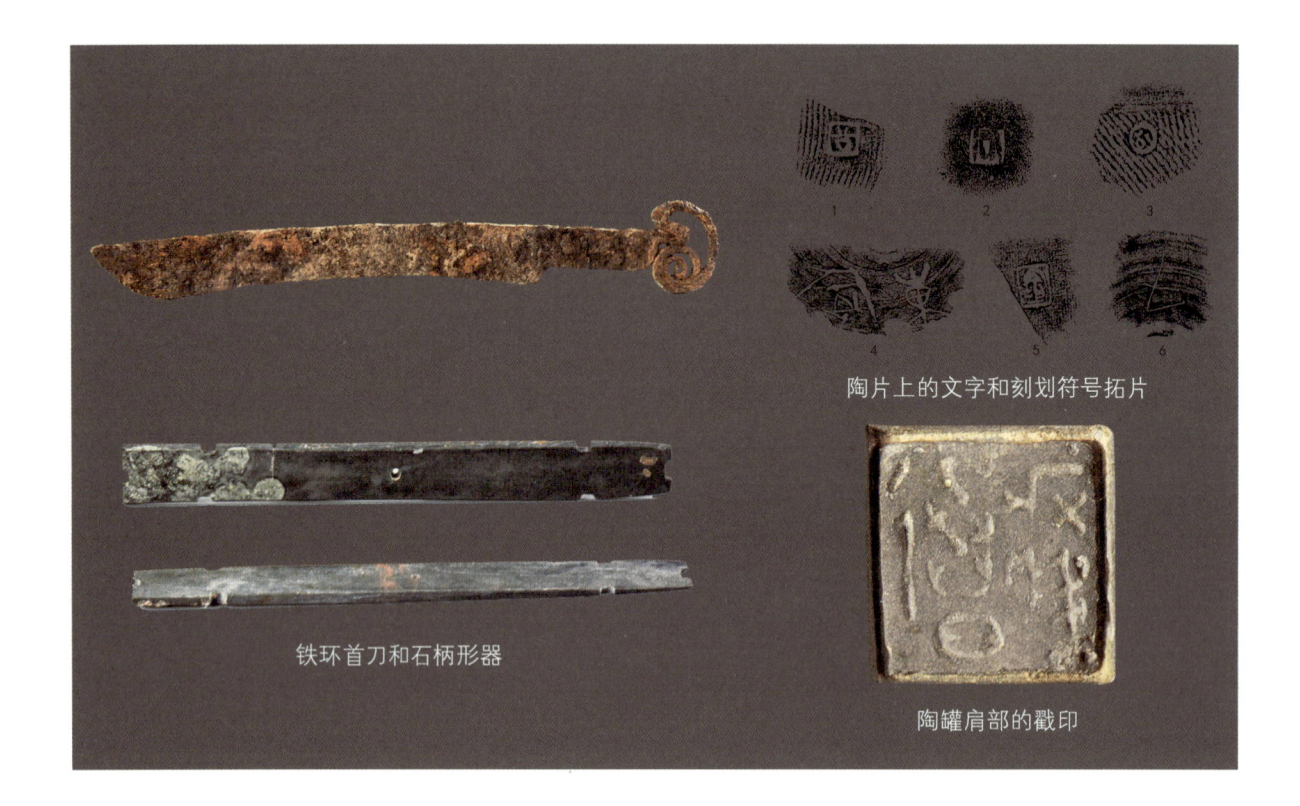

铁环首刀和石柄形器

陶罐肩部的戳印

Ouerping Site is in the southwest of Xizhou Village, Heyu Township, Yushe County, Jinzhong City, Shanxi Province. Archaeologists from Shanxi Provincial Institute of Archaeology and other organizations have been conducting archaeological reconnaissances and excavations on the site since May in 2017. Discovered remains date back to the epoch spanning from early to late Warring States Period. The foundation sites of subterranean architectures and above-ground rammed earthen foundation sites are the most important discoveries made this time. In total, there are four excavated foundation sites of subterranean architectures, all located in the western part of the excavated area; three of them are stone buildings. Two northwestward above-ground rammed earthen foundation sites are located in the eastern part of the excavated area. It has been preliminarily determined that in the east of the above-ground foundation sites there are remains of the rammed earthen city walls. These architectural remains are extremely valuable for studies on shapes, building techniques, and functions of above-ground and subterranean architectures in Warring States Period.

# 作邦作封　翼翼四方

## 山东临淄范家遗址

◎ 赵益超

范家遗址位于山东省淄博市临淄区稷下街道办事处范家新村以北约200米处，遗址中心隆起，高出周边地区约2米。根据山东省文物考古研究院及淄博市文物局进行的勘探和发掘，我们初步认为其为一座城址。城址大致呈圆角方形。城墙年代不早于商代晚期，西周早期已废弃。遗址存在内外两条壕沟，内侧壕沟较宽，外侧壕沟略窄。夯土堆积分布于内壕沟内侧，可分为两期，分别编号夯Ⅰ、夯Ⅱ，夯Ⅰ应为对夯Ⅱ的修补。

范家遗址是山东省境内首次发现的商代城址，意义重大。另外，由于其特殊的地理位置和时间节点，为探讨商代晚期的央地关系、早期齐文化的形成和齐国早期都城提供了重要线索。

商王朝与山东地区一直有着密切的联系，虽与夷人关系时有反复，但商文化势力在鲁北地区表现出极强势的一面。商代末期商王朝政权逐渐式微，但鲁北地区这一时期的商文化因素反而是有所加强的。范家城址的出现正是商晚期中央对鲁北地区经略控制的一种直观反映。从我们发现的城墙和两条平行紧密分布的深壕沟所反映出的较强的防卫性特征来看，这可能与商晚期中央对鲁北地区的征伐有某种关联。范家遗址处淄河西岸，鲁北泰沂山北麓的山前平原地带，向西可直抵济水而转向中原，东有淄河天险可与东夷势力周旋，北可直达海盐生产基地。从其地理交通和战略位置考虑，也符合其属于当时某种战略重心的推测。

在范家城址废弃后的西周早期墓葬中，我们发现了素面袋足鬲和"夷式簋"的组合，正反映了武王灭商后鲁北地区在商残余势力、夷人土著势力和周人势力三股较强势力的角逐中逐渐形成了比较复杂的考古学文化风貌。早期齐文化正是在这种角逐、斗争、妥协下产生并发展的。

从另一层面上看，城址在西周初年的废弃也可能说明，商亡之后，新的中央政权主导的战略重心已经发生了转移。居于范家遗址北部不足3千米的临淄齐故城是否为新政权主导下的战略重心是非常值得怀疑的，这也为我们探讨齐国早期都城——营丘的地望提供了有益的线索。

Ⅰ期夯土

内侧壕沟全貌

南墙夯土夯层及夯窝

打破城墙的西周墓分布（上北下南）

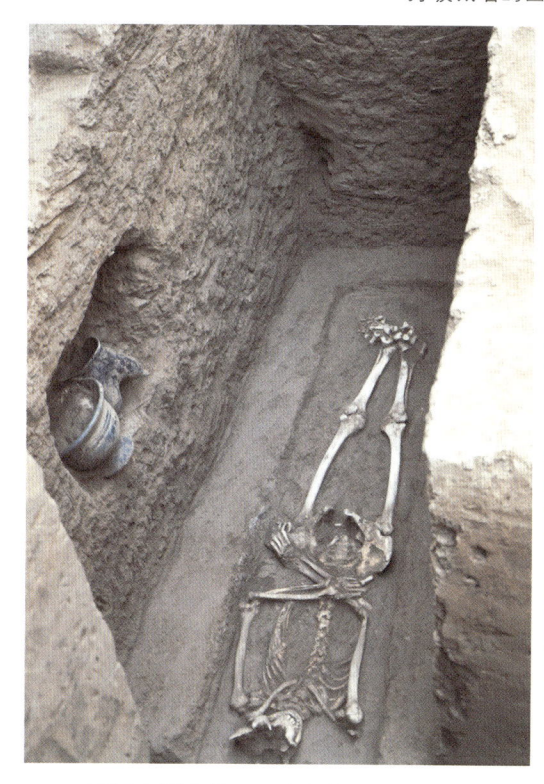

西周早期墓葬M18（上东南下西北）　　　　　西周早期墓葬M4（上北下南）

商代晚期灰坑H21、H29

Fanjia Site is located about 200 meters north of Fanjia Xincun Village, Jixia Neighborhood, Linzi District. In January, 2013, archaeologists from Cultural Relics Bureau of Linyi District conducted a preliminary archaeological excavation on the site. The site was then confirmed to be a city site. From September to December in 2013, archaeologists from Shandong Provincial Institute of Cultural Relics and Archaeology carried out trial diggings in a southerly area of its east wall, discovering remains dating back to Longshan Culture period, Shang Dynasty, Zhou Dynasty, Han Dynasty, Song Dynasty and Yuan Dynasty. Fanjia Site is a square with rounded corners and there used to be an inside moat and an outside moat. Rammed earth discovered during archaeological reconnaissance has been confirmed to be remains of the city wall, which was on the inner side of the early moat and closely clung to it. Severely damaged in later years, the city wall dates back to the time as early as late Shang Dynasty and it was abandoned in early Western Zhou. Fanjia Site is the first city site dating back to Shang Dynasty that has ever been discovered in Shandong Province. Its special geographical location and history provide important clues to central-local government relationships, formation of early Qi Culture and of the early capital city of Qi State.

# 河南荥阳市官庄遗址

◎ 郜向平

官庄遗址位于河南省荥阳市高村乡官庄村西部，该遗址包含龙山、两周、汉、唐、宋时期的遗存，其中以两周时期遗存最为丰富。2011年以来，郑州大学历史学院、郑州市文物考古研究院、荥阳市文物保护管理中心联合对该遗址进行了系统的勘探和发掘。

官庄两周城址由外壕及外壕内的大、小城构成。大、小城南北相连，呈"吕"字形。其中大城位于外壕内中部，有一重环壕，平面呈东西长方形。大城环壕与小城外壕相通，环壕内侧为一周红褐色生土条带，表面平整，其上局部发现有残存的夯土层，应为大城城墙所在。小城位于外壕内北中部，大城之北，平面近方形，由两重环壕环绕。内、外环壕之间为生土带。内环壕的内侧为红褐色生土条带，应是小城城墙所在。在小城南壕中部发现一处出入口遗迹，呈舌状突出，其上发现有柱洞及建筑基槽，应存在城门建筑。在小城内出土的一些东周时期陶豆上发现有"格氏左司工""格氏右司工""格氏"等陶文。

2015年以来，在大城中北部发现了丰富的手工业遗存，包括春秋时期的制陶、铸铜、制骨手工业遗存，以及汉代砖瓦窑、铁器窖藏等。春秋时期的手工业遗存以青铜器铸造为主，兼有制陶和制骨生产。结合附近钻探出土的铁渣来看，此地在汉代可能有冶铁作坊。

根据对出土遗物的初步整理，官庄城址小城的始建不晚于两周之际，大城及外壕大致同时或稍晚，大、小城的环壕至战国早期方被填平。遗址两周之际至春秋时期的遗存丰富，为完善郑州地区两周时期考古学文化序列提供了重要资料。遗址内多重环壕，大、小城南北并列的结构非常独特，小城南城门及相关出入设施为此前周代城址所未见，为相关研究提供了新的资料。结合勘探和发掘来看，春秋时期官庄大城北部存在综合性的手工业生产区，铸铜、制陶、制骨等多种手工业活动集中分布，相互间又有一定界限。其中铸铜作坊的年代正处于春秋早中期新的铜器风格的形成时期，对于探讨西周至春秋青铜器风格及生产方式的转变有重要意义。该区域在汉代很有可能再次成为一处手工业生产活动集中地，这为研究汉代荥阳地区的铁器生产等提供了重要资料。根据文献记载，两周时期郑州地区有管、东虢、郑、韩等封国。官庄遗址的发掘和研究，对于深入探讨郑州地区两周时期考古学文化的发展演变，厘清东虢、郑、韩相关历史具有重要意义。

小城内东北部墓葬区（上南下北）

小城南门（上北下南）

三代之礼　皇皇者华

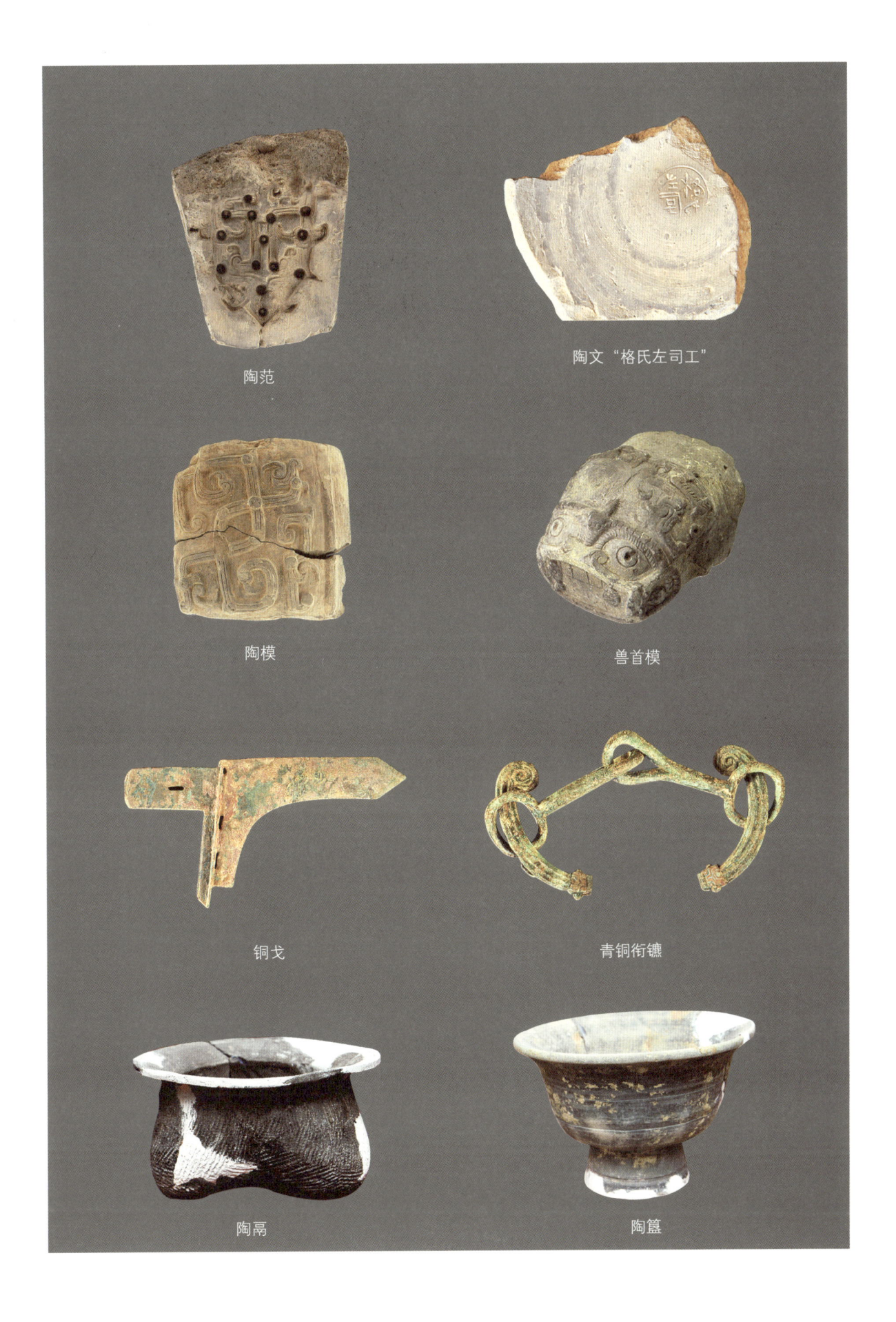

陶范

陶文"格氏左司工"

陶模

兽首模

铜戈

青铜衔镳

陶鬲

陶簋

陶窑　　　　　　　　　　　　　　　　　　灰坑中的殉马

制陶泥料坑

Guanzhuang Site is in the west of Guanzhuang Village, Gaocun Township, Xingyang City, Henan Province. Since 2011, a joint team consisting archaeologists from School of History of Zhengzhou University and Zhengzhou Institute of Cultural Relics and Archaeology have been carrying out systematic archaeological reconnaissances and excavations on the site. A wide range of remains and relics, dating back to the epoch from Western Zhou and Eastern Zhou to Spring & Autumn Period, have been unearthed from the site. On the site, special multiple ring-shaped ditches have been revealed. The north-south paralleling layout of the Big City and Small City are extremely unique. Previously, nothing like the south gate of the Small City and its access facilities has been discovered from a city site dating back to Zhou Dynasty. During Spring & Autumn Period, in the northern part of the Big City, there was a comprehensive handicraft production area. In this area, sites for bronze casting, pottery making, bone implements making, and various kinds of handicraft industry were densely distributed with certain boundaries between each other.

# 河北满城要庄遗址

◎任雪岩

要庄遗址位于河北省保定市满城区要庄乡要庄村，地处太行山东麓的平原地带。该遗址于1977年发现，为进一步弄清遗址的文化内涵、性质、年代等问题，2014年3月至2016年10月，河北省文物研究所与保定市文物管理所、满城区文物保管所、吉林大学边疆考古研究中心、河北大学历史学院等单位联合组队，对要庄遗址进行了考古勘探和发掘。

本次考古工作首次确认了要庄遗址西北区域是一处西周时期城址。城垣的始建年代不晚于西周中期，其使用年代基本应在西周早期范围内。2015年11月至2016年7月，选择城址西北角进行发掘，该区域位于北城垣与西城垣转角处。初步推断城垣直接起建于生土之上，有分层建筑现象。最外侧为护城壕，城壕内侧边缘有加固处理现象。勘探表明，护城壕剖面呈梯形圜底状，环绕城墙分布。2016年6—10月，选择北城墙中部进行发掘。发掘表明，该区域为北城墙水门处，大致明晰了城内排水沟与城外护城壕的连接情况以及水门的局部形态。

要庄遗址大致可分为三大区域，即西北区、西南区和东南区。西北区为城址区，经钻探，城址内有夯土遗迹现象6处、道路1条、淤积沟1条、窑址2处、灶9处及大量灰坑等；西南区的工作，清理出6座两周时期的陶窑，推测该区域应为手工业作坊区；东南区基本为墓葬区，本次考古钻探工作发现了12处相对独立的墓葬群，进一步确认了遗址东南部分作为墓葬区的功能。

此次发掘对要庄遗址的文化内涵和发展序列的认识更为清晰。长期以来，学界对要庄遗址文化内涵的认识主要基于1982—1983年的发掘收获，即基本对应于西周时期的文化遗存。近三年考古工作则获得了多个时期的文化遗存，其中以西周、东周和汉三大时期的文化内容最为重要。

从出土遗存来看，要庄遗址当属两周文化重要的区域中心性聚落，遗址年代为西周至东汉时期，其中尤以两周时期最为重要。要庄城址的确认，将河北地区城址的历史提早到西周早期，在一定程度上填补了河北缺乏早期城址的空白。从历史背景来看，该城址很可能与西周封国甚至燕国分封等密切相关，具有重大的学术价值。另外，钻探与发掘获得的翔实资料及其可建构的文化序列对于深入认识燕文化及两周文化、汉文化以及区域历史发展等提供了重要的实物资料。

要庄遗址西北角整体揭露（上西下东）

要庄城址北墙中部水门（上南下北）

周代陶窑

西周墓葬

周代陶鬲、陶罐

西周陶豆、陶簋

西周水井

西周乱葬坑

铜爵　　　铜爵上刻族徽　　　铜觯

Yaozhuang Site is located in Yaozhuang Village, Yaozhuang Township, Mancheng District, Baoding City, Hebei Province. From 2014 to 2016, archaeologists from Hebei Provincial Institute of Cultural Relics and other organizations carried out archaeological reconnaissances and excavations on the site. The following are major discoveries. It was for the first time that a city site of Western Zhou was confirmed to be in the northwestern area of Yaozhuang Site. There was a general understanding of the function divisions and cultural heritage composition of Yaozhuang Site, i.e. the northwestern area was the city site, the southwestern area was for handicraft industry, and the southeastern area was basically used as a cemetery. Unearthed remains all illustrated that Yaozhuang Site should be a prominent central settlement in Western Zhou and Eastern Zhou. The settlement was mainly in use from Western Zhou to Eastern Han and it played the most important role during Western Zhou to Eastern Zhou.

# 江苏苏州木渎古城

◎唐锦琼　孙明利

苏州木渎古城的考古工作始于21世纪初。2010年起，由中国社会科学院考古研究所与苏州市考古研究所组成的联合考古队对该城址及其周边地区展开了持续性的钻探、发掘和研究工作。

关于城址的范围。2010年在北侧发现五峰段城墙，南侧发现新峰段城墙。古城更有可能是未构筑完整的城墙体系，而是在山口处因地制宜地构筑防御设施，利用周边的山体作为天然的城墙，构筑起较为完备的防御体系。

关于城址的布局。我们在城内多处地点发现古代遗存，最主要的包括五峰地点、新峰地点和合丰地点等。五峰地点位于城址北侧，处于一处"几"字形盆地中，五峰段城墙即在此处。在城墙外侧有城壕环绕，并经东南侧水门流入城内。新峰地点位于城址东南侧，位于尧峰山和皋峰山之间山口处，新峰段城墙即在此处北侧。新峰段城墙为"两墙夹一河"的基本结构布局，此段城墙及河道继续向南延伸，横贯整个山口。合丰地点位于木渎古城西南部，其中最重要的发现是合丰小城。其他遗存如廖里地点为一处规模宏大的生活居址，马巷上遗址为一处石器加工作坊区，南野竹遗址发现有制陶遗存等。这些遗存的发现，为深入探讨城址的各功能分区提供了线索。另外。我们在城外的清明山南麓还发现了千年寺小城。城址平面呈方形，城址外侧有城壕环绕，是遏制木渎古城与太湖之间的交通要道。

通过历年来的工作，我们认为：木渎古城是以周边山地作为天然屏障，仅在山口处构筑人工城墙和其他防御设施。城址内遗存分布有大散居、小聚居的特点，遗存较多地分布在山前地点。各地点间可能有着一定的功能分区，在各地点间是大片湿地，或是人们的生产区域。木渎古城所在区域有着复杂的发展演变过程：西周晚期至春秋早期出现小型城址，春秋晚期出现大型城址，战国时期继续沿用并有所增益，大量汉代遗存反映了城址或可延续到西汉时期。木渎古城性质的最终确定还需将其置于吴、越、楚在长江下游历史进程中加以探讨。

五峰城墙与周边山体

五峰地点水门

新峰地点河道

马巷上遗址石质遗物堆积状况

三代之礼　皇皇者华　263

山渚头M1出土陶器、原始瓷器

廖里遗址陶器

廖里遗址陶器

善山遗址M7出土遗物

合丰小城城墙内出土陶罐

合丰小城东城墙及城壕（上南下北）

合丰地点D161上大量汉墓（上西下东）

Site of Mudu City is located in an intermontane basin. A joint team consisting of archaeologists from Institute of Archaeology of the Chinese Academy of Social Sciences and Suzhou Institute of Archaeology has been carrying out successive trial drillings, excavations and researches on the site and in its adjacent area. In Mudu City, there might be surrounded by an incomplete city wall. Instead, taking the advantage of the favorable geographical position of Mudu City, people constructed defense facilities at the mountain pass and accomplished a relatively established defense system by using surrounding mountains as the natural city wall. Inside Mudu City, small settlements were sparsely distributed with a certain function division between each other. Large patches of wetlands around the settlements might be the production area. Mudu City emerged as a small city during the time from late Western Zhou to early Spring & Autumn Period and became a larger one in late Spring & Autumn Period. It existed throughout the time and expanded in Warring States Period. Volumes of remains dating back to Han Dynasty indicated that Mudu City might be still in use in Western Han.

# 山东鲁国故城

◎ 韩 辉

鲁国故城是周代和汉代鲁国的都城，位于山东省曲阜市市区及周边。2011年以来，围绕曲阜鲁国故城国家考古遗址公园建设等，山东省文物考古研究院做了大量工作，取得一系列重要收获。

考古勘探工作包括：2012—2015年，全面、重点勘探郭城和宫城等120万平方米。勘探确认位于鲁故城中部，全城最高处的周公庙台地建筑群夯筑基址区为鲁故城宫城，呈长方形，西北角略内折。城墙、城壕环台地周边，西门、南门、东门各有与之相配的道路。城内夯土建筑基址目前辨识81座，属东周和汉代，为基槽及地面式，呈院落式布局。还发现陶质排水管道系统、大量水井等。宫城西部西周遗存仅见面积较大的坑状堆积。重新确定了郭城城墙、城壕范围，壕沟至少分为三期，并新发现了内侧壕沟。城墙未见明显基槽，晚期城墙叠压在早期城壕之上。城壕可粗分为两期，时代为春秋、战国。内城壕沿城墙内侧一周，与城内水系相连。2016年对宫城西南部周公庙村西夯土建筑基址进行勘探，发现春秋时期遗迹包括灰坑7个、井2个、夯土基址3处，多呈基坑式；发现战国时期墓葬8座，分布相对集中。汉代遗迹有水井、灰坑、墓葬、夯土基址等。这些基址修筑、废弃过程均与宫城类似，始建于春秋时期，汉代再次兴建。推测该区域应为贵族居住区。其中夯8为院落式建筑群，东西严格对称，院墙包裹房屋，整个院落为东西长方形，房屋分为三间，东西两小间，中间一大间，推测其为宗庙建筑院落。

考古发掘工作包括：对鲁故城宫城发掘确认了其年代、性质。2012—2014年全面揭露发掘了宫城西南部大型夯土基址F8和西城门，解剖了南、北城墙。城墙仅余基槽部分，其内侧有战国取土坑和水井。城壕时代为春秋晚期到汉代。壕沟外侧上部有路土，年代为战国晚期至汉代早期，为城壕废弃之后的环城大路。东南部城墙发掘发现东周夯土城墙1期、汉代城墙2期。城墙底部预埋有五边形陶管道，沟通城内外。北面为一蓄水池，与管道相连。战国始建，沿用至汉代。城墙与城壕之间还发掘3座战国中晚期小型墓葬。西城门宽约12米，路土时代从春秋时期延续至唐代，其中东周路土最宽，南侧分布有水沟，为城门排水设施。东周大型夯土建筑基址F8位于周公庙北部，现仅存墙基部分。汉代大型房址F6筑于东周夯土基槽之上，现尚存残墙、前披厦，发现有石柱础、散水。唐代揭露一组院落式建筑遗迹叠压打破F8、F6建筑基址，与周、汉房址方向、中轴线基本一致，推测它们是有延续承继关系的，启后世宋、明、清周公庙于此处。

2012—2013年发掘南东门，发现门道及两侧高大的阙台基。门道两侧的夯土台基当为门阙的基础。目前看至少分两大阶段：第一阶段约属春秋时期，夯土台基略小；第二阶段为战国时期，台基增宽筑高，这是目前我国所发现最早的门阙实例。南东门可能与文献中记载的稷门、南门和高门有关。

关于郭城城墙，2012—2017年解剖三处，为南、东、东北城墙。确认郭城城墙始建于两周之际或春秋早期，至春秋早期晚段形成了现在所知的规模。南东门东部发现春秋早期M13打破一期城墙，该段城墙或早至西周晚期始建。北东门东部城墙初步分为五期。春秋早期始建，总体呈南高北低倾斜状。一期城墙平地起建在生土之上，被春秋早期H9打破。东北城墙于2017年解剖发掘，城墙由内向外扩建，计6次建筑活动，在春秋早期之后，又有春秋中期、春秋晚期，战国早、中、晚期城墙增筑。城墙内外各有一条壕沟。外城壕与各期城墙对应，内侧壕沟应为战国晚期取土砌墙形成的。鲁故城东北角居址位于城墙下部及内侧，遗迹丰富，其窑址、灰坑、墓葬存在共存关系，是一处春秋早期到春秋晚期以生产活动为主的遗址。

2017—2018年发掘老农业局遗址，以春秋时期遗迹最为丰富，聚族而居，聚族而葬，居葬相近。西北部为窖穴区，杂有水井，再向北应为居址区。东北部为大型水域，应为战国时期人工所挖。遗址南部为一处春秋晚期到战国早期的墓地。

2013年配合孔府西苑建设项目，发掘位于明故城内孔府西部的原曲阜一中北院区域。发现西周中晚期、春秋、战国、汉代、宋元、明清文化堆积。其中春秋晚期到战国时期遗存最为丰富，有灰坑、墓葬、井、沟等，另以发现战国大型堆筑建筑台基较为重要。

林家村遗址位于曲阜市城南约3千米，发现有大汶口、龙山、岳石、商代、春秋、战国、汉代、唐代、清代遗迹遗物。其中商代大约为商代二里岗上层至殷墟一期，为解决商奄等问题提供了线索。

近年来考古工作的收获及意义：确认鲁故城宫城，初步判断宫城始建于春秋晚期，战国晚期废弃，汉代重修，最终废弃于魏晋，最初的修建原因可能与仲孙、叔孙、季孙"三家侈张"有关。发现东周、汉、唐代大型建筑，与宋、明、清周公庙对应。推测此处可能为东周太庙区域。汉代割取鲁故城西南，西汉、东汉均再利用、重建原宫城。春秋早期建成了诸侯国最大的郭城之一，到战国晚期逐渐增筑。年代或可与鲁僖公筑城、越国北上、楚国灭鲁等历史大事件相对应。春秋晚期，以周公庙区宫城建设为标志，礼仪性的南东门址、宫城和舞雩台形成了鲁国故城中轴线布局。"府第"建筑、一般居址、手工业作坊址规划严谨，反映了对自然资源因地制宜的利用，也是鲁国"尊尊亲亲"治国方略在布局中的直接反映。

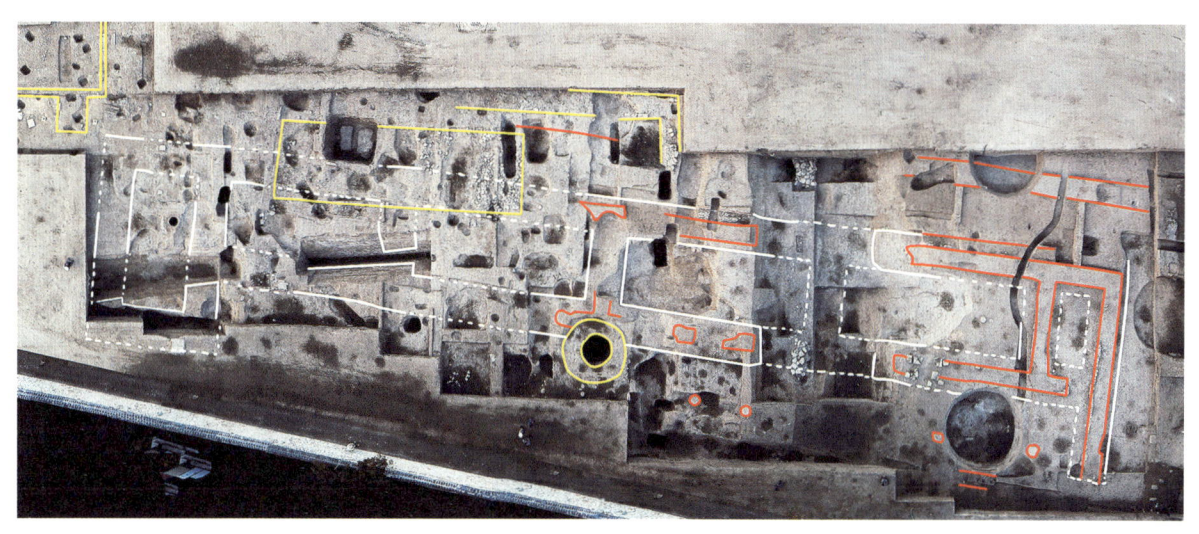

宫殿建筑基址（上北下南，东周F8—白线，汉代F6—红线，唐代F4、F5—黄线）

外郭城北城墙分段夯筑（上北下南）

宫殿南城墙底部预埋管道沟（上西下东）

南东门打破一期城墙的春秋早期M13

战国城墙夯土穿棍

宫城J2出土战国花纹砖　　　　　宫城J2出土战国瓦当　　　　　宫城T201地层出土瓦当

宫城J4出土汉代散水砖　　　　　　宫城F6出土汉代铺地砖

宫城J2出土遗物　　　　　　　　　宫城H117出土西周陶罐

老农业局墓地M6出土铜鼎　　　　老农业局墓地M7出土铜戈

北城墙（北向南）

Site of the Lu State Capital used to be the capital city of Lu State back in Zhou Dynasty and Han Dynasty. The site is in the locality of Qufu City and its adjacent area. Excavations that have been carried out in recent years include the excavation of a large-scale rammed earthen foundation site F8 in the southeastern part of the palace zone, the excavation of the west palace gate, the dissection of three exploration ditches at the south city wall and the north city wall, the excavation of the southeast gate and the discovery of its doorway and foundation sites of two tall side towers, the dissection of south, east and northeast sections of the outer city wall, etc. The following are archaeological discoveries that have been made on Site of the Lu State Capital and relevant researches in recent years. It has been basically confirmed the palace was built in late Spring & Autumn Period, abandoned in late Warring States Period, rebuilt in Han Dynasty and finally deserted in Wei and Jin dynasties.

# 山东临淄齐故城

◎赵益超　吕　凯　董文斌

临淄齐故城是周代齐国的都城，位于今山东省淄博市临淄区中部。临淄城由大城和小城两部分组成，小城的东北部嵌入大城的西南角，平面呈西南部外凸状的不规则长方形，总面积约15.75平方千米。城墙用土夯筑而成。东、西城墙临河修筑，因河岸蜿蜒曲折，致使城墙多拐角。勘探中发现城门11座，其中小城5座（东、西、北门各1座，南门2座）、大城6座（东、西门各1座，南、北门各2座）。城墙下有4处石砌排水道口。城内探明了10条交通干道，并发现较大的炼铁遗址6处、冶铜遗址2处、铸钱遗址2处、制骨遗址多处。宫殿建筑遗址经探明的有2处，均在小城内。2011年以来，临淄齐故城的考古工作主要围绕四个方面：第一，小城宫殿区的布局、结构和年代；第二，冶铸手工业考古；第三，临淄齐故城城墙的营建年代、构筑方式；第四，小城北门发掘。

宫殿考古方面，我们主要围绕临淄齐故城目前已探明的两处宫殿建筑（群）展开工作。一处位于小城西北的桓公台周围，一处为小城东北部的10号建筑。桓公台位于小城的北部偏西，西距小城西墙约300米，其周边密布建筑基址。2014年年底至2015年年初，我们对桓公台及周边建筑进行勘探。首先，桓公台底部台基的形状较规整，呈南北向长方形，南端中间位置可能有一通道。其次，该区域周边有大面积厚砖瓦层，从目前情况看，夯土建筑分布较为密集，且形制较为规整，这对于了解齐国都城的宫殿、建筑形式及布局方式都大有裨益。发现夯土台基10余处，有大有小，布局错落，且有的夯土存在早晚分期。再次，夯土台基及周边新发现有多条较窄的道路，这对了解建筑之间的关系有重要帮助。最后，本次勘探除了证实先前所探淤土沟的存在，还在小城西墙东侧新发现一条淤沟。10号宫殿遗址位于小城的东北部，西南方向不远处为著名的桓公台宫殿建筑遗址区。2011—2016年，我们先后对10号建筑遗址进行勘探和两次考古发掘。遗址中央为战国时期修的夯土台基建筑，规模宏大；台基仅一层，高度在3米以上，且周围壁面立柱镶板，装饰完善；台上建筑已无法复原，但出土的高大华美的彩绘木门以及纹饰繁复的铜构件，反映了建筑具有相当高的规格。台基周围堆积的大量烧红的夯土墙体、瓦片、木炭及熔化变形的铜构件表明，台上建筑曾经历大火。这座建筑是否为田齐宗庙及其烧毁是否与战争有关，尚待进一步的研究来证实。

手工业考古方面，2011—2012年，我们与中国社会科学院考古研究所合作在临淄齐故城进行考古调查、勘探，并选定阚家寨B区，分三个地点进行试掘。其中第Ⅰ地点主要着眼于与窑址有关的遗存，第Ⅱ地点主要着眼于与铜镜铸造有关的遗存，第Ⅲ地点主要着眼于与冶铁有关的遗存。主要收获包括：第一，初步摸清了阚家寨B区的文化堆积状况，即下部是春秋时期的文化堆积，并且有可能存在大型建筑遗存，但大多已毁坏；中、上部为战国秦汉时期的堆积。第二，确认阚家寨遗址B区为战国至西汉的冶铸工场作坊分布区，并且存在着明显的分区，即第Ⅰ地点为陶窑作坊，第Ⅱ地点为铜镜铸造作坊，第Ⅲ地点为冶铁或铸铁作坊。第三，首次科学发掘了汉代铜镜铸造作坊遗址，清理出铜镜铸造遗迹，出土一批铜镜铸范及相关遗物，说明临淄可能为当时的铸镜中心之一。

城墙年代方面，2014—2015年分两次对临淄齐故城大城东墙北段进行解剖。发掘部分城墙结构比较清晰，由晚到早分别编号为夯Ⅰ~夯Ⅸ。从层位关系可以对城墙年代进行初步推断，第一期城墙年代不会晚于西周晚期，第二期城墙年代应为春秋时期，第三、四期城墙年代应为战国时期。城内西周早中期灰坑H11内有一完整牛骨架（后期被M4破坏），可能与祭祀活动有关，离第一期城墙不远（不足8米），或与城墙建筑有关。城墙是否可早到西周中期以前目前尚不确定。

大城西墙北段的发掘是配合临淄齐故城排水道口展示项目开展的。发掘工作分为两次进行。第一次主要发现城墙的基槽部分。基槽向南深入地面以下，其西侧有5段夯土，可能与祭祀有关，构筑年代为春秋晚期至战国早期。第二次发掘利用残存城墙断面对排水道口北侧约90米的西城墙进行解剖，由主体、护坡组成，护坡西侧为城壕。城墙主体夯筑于生土层之上，底部较平，未见基槽，自东向西夯土板块编号为夯Ⅰ~夯Ⅴ。护坡紧邻夯Ⅴ西侧，呈斜坡状。城壕位于城墙西侧。

小城北门遗址位于小城北墙中部偏西，西距大城、小城接合处约90米。2017年6—12月进行考古发掘，共发现南北向道路4条，与早期城门建筑有关的遗迹为L1，南北向，与城墙基本垂直；堆积顶部四层为近代、金元、唐代时期道路，底部四层为战国至西汉道路；早期道路两侧均为夯土，可认定此处为齐故城小城北门。北侧出入口位置道路变宽，根据勘探可知北向有3条道路，南侧出入口两侧为大型长方形夯土建筑基址，均呈南北向长方形。

临淄齐故城目前还存在很大的短板，主要就是缺乏非常明确的时空框架。目前我们已明确了解齐故城始建于西周中期之前，且存在扩建的过程。但是其营建年代的上限目前尚不清晰，且是否存在一个早期城圈我们尚不知晓，遑论早期城圈的范围了。我们了解，目前的小城是田齐的宫城，那么西周和春秋时期的姜齐宫城在什么位置、布局如何、是否存在宫城城墙，这些问题都是摆在我们面前亟待解决的。

10号建筑遗址夯土台基壁面角柱痕迹

10号建筑遗址壁柱痕迹及石柱础

10号建筑夯土台基南部铺石地面

10号建筑战国彩绘木门痕迹

大城东城墙北段城墙剖面（左北右南）

大城西城墙北段城墙外侧"基槽"（上北下南）

大城东城墙北段夯8、夯9关系（左北右南）

大城东城墙北段打破夯Ⅷ的M11（上西下东）

Site of the Qi State Capital in Linzi used to be the capital city of Qi State back in Zhou Dynasty. The site is located in the middle of Linzi District in Zibo City, Shandong Province. The following are major outcomes of archaeological work done in recent years. In terms of palace archaeology, the archaeological reconnaissance has been carried out around Huangong Terrace in the northwest of the Small City. Discovered remains include rammed earthen foundation bases, layers of bricks and tiles and roads. Excavations have also been conducted in parts of Building No. 10, whose foundation base is massive, in the northeastern of the Small City. Unearthed items include colored wooden doors and bronze structural components. In terms of smelting and casting industry, an area of smelting and casting workshops dating back to an era spanning from Warring States Period to Western Han has been discovered. These workshops used to be kilns and places for bronze mirror molding, iron smelting or iron casting. Excavations carried out at the north gate of the Small City have revealed four south-north roads. Massive rectangular rammed earthen architectural foundation sites have been found at both sides of the south entrance/exist. The city wall of the Qi State Capital was initially built before middle Western Zhou. Construction of the Small City started late early Warring States Period.

# 山东邾国故城遗址

◎ 王 青　郎剑锋　路国权　陈章龙

邾国故城遗址位于山东省邹城市峄山镇纪王城村周围，地处峄山南麓，平面略呈长方形，面积约6平方千米。其四周城墙保存基本完好，城外大部分地段还有城壕。根据相关文献记载，该遗址是东周时期邾国都城所在。2015—2017年，山东大学考古队对其进行了两次考古发掘，并对城址中部的宫殿区进行了重点勘探，对城内南部进行了系统调查。

城内中部为宫殿区，北部为贵族墓地，中部偏西为仓储区，其余大部为居住区和手工业区。其中宫殿区为高出地表3～4米的高台（俗称"皇台"），勘探发现数十处夯土基址，外围有2～3米的窄墙，但分布不连续，应为各院落的围垣，暂未发现宫墙。台下四周发现城壕，依地势由北向南，南侧还发现东西向道路。2017年在"皇台"中部偏北的F3工作区东南部发掘，其中一座西汉水井（J3）出土了8件新莽度量衡铜器，对研究王莽托古改制和我国度量衡发展史有重要价值。综合分析，发掘区在战国时期应是官营冶铸作坊区，汉代为官署区的组成部分。

仓储区位于皇台下西南三四百米处，共清理遗迹单位757个，主要为灰坑（窖穴），另有少量水井、房址、炼炉等。年代可分为春秋、战国、秦汉三个时期。结合相关文献记载，这些窖穴应是仓廪之类储粮设施。这些窖穴的废弃堆积包含大量板瓦、筒瓦及少量小陶鸟，推测应是仓廪顶部的建筑遗留。经综合分析，此处应是战国至秦汉时期的仓储区，同时出土的10余件陶量则应是官府籴粜谷物粮食的量器。发掘区内10余口水井呈"一"字形排列，推测应是仓储区的防火设施。发掘中采集了大批动植物标本和其他检测样品，经初步的检测分析我们发现，2015年发掘区出土的动物遗骸中谷物以小麦为主，占有绝对优势，另有少量粟、黍、大豆等；老鼠的数量从东周至汉代逐渐增多，尤其汉代老鼠的数量增加明显，这与此处是仓储区的判断是相符合的。此外，此次出土的考古遗存主要属于春秋至汉代，不仅与遗址作为邾国都城和邹县县治的时期相符，也和春秋中期邾文公迁都至此的史料大致符合，为建立该遗址的文化序列提供了丰富的基础资料。另出土了刻划有战国时期的陶文的陶器200余件，为相关研究提供了珍贵的第一手资料。

276　黄淮七省考古新发现

诏版铭文局部

衡杆铭文

三代之礼 皇皇者华 277

卅斤权（J3）

仓储区出土的
战国时期陶量

货版（J3）　　　诏版（J3）　　　诏版（J3）

衡杆（J3）

环权（J3）　　环权（J3）　　环权（J3）　环权（J3）

东周窖穴及谷物朽灰

汉代灰坑

小麦

粟　黍

东周、汉代的谷物遗骸

Site of the Zhu State Capital is located around Ji-wang-cheng Village, Yishan Town, Zoucheng City, Shandong Province. From 2015 to 2017, archaeologists from Shandong University carried out focused archaeological reconnaissances and excavations on the site. Now there is a general understanding of the city layout and its development. The central palace zone is a terrace, three to four meters high above the ground, commonly known as the Imperial Terrace. In the Warring States Period, state-run smelting and casting workshops were located in the northern central part of the Imperial Terrace. From a well dating back to Western Han, eight pieces of bronze weight and measurement tools have been unearthed. These tools are valuable for the study of Wang Mang's Reformation by referring to old doctrines and development history of Chinese weight and measurement tools. The storage area is located 300 to 400 meters southwest of the Imperial Terrace. Apart from over 200 engraved clay fragments, excavated sites in this area are mainly ash pits. They are valuable first-hand materials for relevant researches.

# 河南新郑郑韩故城北城门遗址

◎ 樊温泉

郑韩故城位于今河南省新郑市，都城选址于古溱水与古洧水交汇处。故城内有一条南北走向的隔城墙，将故城分为东西两城：西城为宫城，东城为郭城。2016—2017年，河南省文物考古研究院对位于隔城墙与北城墙交会处东侧缺口的郑韩故城北城门遗址进行了考古发掘，发掘清理出春秋战国至明清时期带车辙的道路，春秋战国时期的城壕、水渠、瓮城等重要遗迹。

城墙墙体系用五花土分层夯筑而成，夯面上有圆形圜底夯窝。城墙的主体部分是春秋时期修建的，这一时期的夯层较厚，夯窝小而密集；战国时期对墙体有大面积的修补，此时的夯层较薄，夯窝大而疏散。

截至目前，已发现各个时期的道路16条，其中可以确定时代的道路9条，包括春秋时期1条、战国时期2条、汉代1条、唐宋时期2条、明清时期3条。此次发掘中，在春秋时期道路的东侧发现了1条呈西南—东北向的水渠，这条水渠和道路并行进入了城内。我们推测这条水渠对应的北城墙缺口处可能就是当时郑国的"渠门"所在。

通过发掘，在城墙缺口外侧约50米处，发现了1处大致呈西北—东南走向的夯土建筑。这处夯土建筑与北城墙突出部分共同构成了瓮城，战国道路在往北通过夯土建筑的地方明显变窄，推测此处可能是瓮门。在瓮城外侧约10米处，发现有1条西北—东南走向的城壕，城壕下层发现有黑色淤积层，其底部发现有大小不均的料姜石块。

根据遗迹层位关系及出土遗物，我们初步判断北城门形成于春秋时期，由北城墙、春秋道路、水渠和城壕组成，结构较为简单。战国时期，在春秋时期原有城门结构基础上，增设了2条战国道路，同时加筑了瓮城城墙，从而构成了一套完整的军事防御体系。

此次发掘是历史上第一次科学发掘郑韩故城城门，厘清了春秋时期水陆并用的城门结构，是国内发现的先秦时期唯一的渠门类遗址，对研究中国古代城市规划与建设有极其重要的意义。战国时期以瓮城为中心的军事防御体系在东周时期王城遗址中是首次发现。此外，不同时期带车辙的道路，不仅为研究新郑城市的变迁提供了实物资料，而且也是研究中国古代交通史的重要材料。

北城门航拍（上北下南）

隔城墙与北城墙（左南右北）

瓮城墙体范围（上东下西）

水渠与道路（上东下西）

各时期道路遗迹图（上东下西）

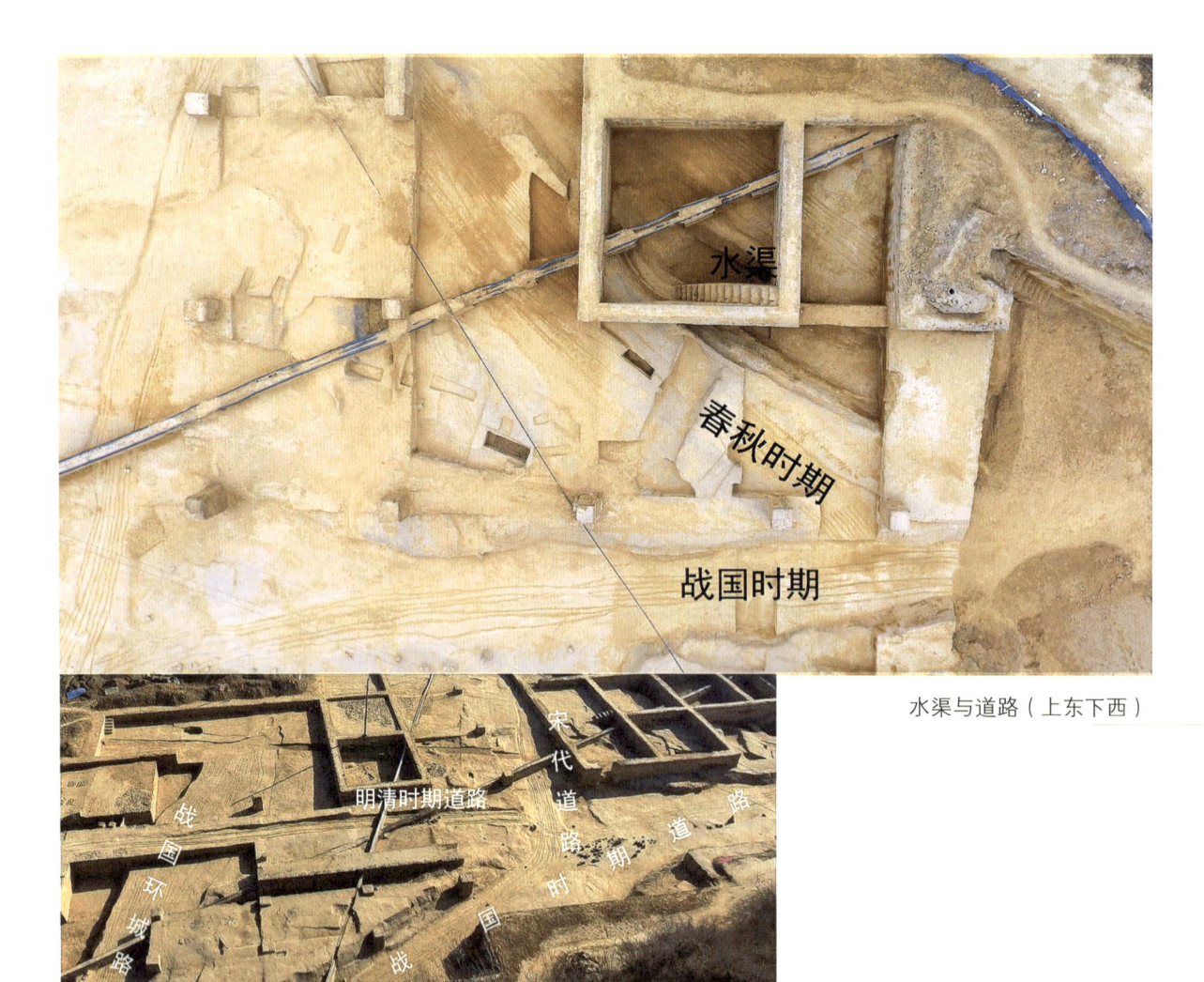

    From 2016 to 2017, archaeologists from Henan Provincial Institute of Cultural Relics and Archaeology excavated the site of the north gate of Zheng and Han States Capital in Xinzheng City. The site is located at the intersection of the partition wall and the north city wall of this ancient capital. Important excavated remains, dating back to the time from Spring & Autumn Period and Warring States Period to Ming and Qing dynasties, include roads with ruts, moats, canals, walls of the barbican entrance, city gates, drainage pipes, deposition layers that recorded human activities, ash pits, wells and tombs. This is the first time in history to scientifically excavate the city gate of Zheng and Han States Capital. The structure of an amphibious city gate of Spring & Autumn Period, which is the only canal gate site constructed before Qin Dynasty that has been discovered in China, has been figured out. It is extremely important for the study of urban planning and construction in ancient China. The military defense system which was established in Warring States Period and centered with a barbican entrance, is the first one that has been discovered on an imperial city site dating back to Eastern Zhou.

# 河北邯郸赵王城

◎段宏振

赵王城遗址是赵邯郸故城遗址的宫城部分，现保存有大部分的地面城垣遗迹。2010—2016年，河北省文物研究所与邯郸赵王城文物管理处组成考古队，对赵王城遗址进行了大规模的勘察和测绘，同时对西城南垣、东城东垣、北城西垣等地点进行了解剖发掘；对西城西垣的城门遗址（编号4号城门）、西城3号宫殿基址外围区进行了考古发掘，主要发现包括城墙建筑、城门建筑及宫殿基址等。

作为赵王城防御屏障的城垣建筑系统，依结构及功能可分为三个建筑单元：城垣本体即墙体部分，包括基座、主墙、附加墙等；城垣内侧的防雨排水设施，属于城垣附属建筑设施，包括散水、铺瓦、排水槽等；城垣外侧防御壕沟系统，包括内壕和外壕。西城南垣墙体内侧壁面上保存有清晰的麻布纹印痕，上面还有捶打的小窝状痕迹。这一城垣表面加固处理原始痕迹的完整发现，是东周城市建筑考古的重要收获。城垣内侧的形制结构呈多级台阶状内收至顶，其目的是在台界面铺设瓦层，即城垣的防雨排水设施。这种形式的城垣内侧结构，是东周城市城垣建筑形式的唯一实例。

西城门建筑基址包括4个单元，自前向后依次为：城壕、阙台、门道、城垣内侧防雨排水设施（防雨铺瓦和排水槽道）。城门外的城壕呈弓形环绕围护着城门阙，阙台基址对称分列于城门外南、北两侧，北阙台基址西北端台基边以西11米处，发现一条南北向排水管道，向北直通城壕，应与北阙台前端排水有关。城门的主体建筑为门道及附属建筑，包括门道两侧壁体基础及所连接的主城墙、内外附城墙、柱石坑、墩台、隔墙基础、路面等。赵王城西城西门的建筑形式独特，门外两侧建有双阙，这是目前考古实证所见最早的城门阙实例，对研究中国早期阙台建筑的结构和形式具有重要意义。另外，根据现有的发现推测，赵王城西门的门洞壁体设立柱，顶部架梁，或有城楼；门洞呈矩形或近梯形，一门两道、双扇重门。这些都为研究东周城门建筑提供了新资料。

西城3号宫殿基址南距2号宫殿基址约200米，是西城中轴线建筑群最北面的一座夯土台式建筑基址。初步考古勘察和发掘表明，3号夯土台基址北台属于一座高台式宫殿建筑，坐北朝南，为该区域主体建筑，前方有宽大的庭院，庭院南侧另建有大型平台式附属性建筑即南台。对3号夯土台宫殿基址的考古发掘，将有助于了解赵王城宫殿建筑的形式与结构。

3号宫殿基址前的庭院

排水槽

西城南垣墙体麻布纹

排水槽及铺瓦

三代之礼　皇皇者华　285

板瓦

瓦当

陶碗

铜镞

陶罐

陶豆

陶釜

陶鼎

赵王城西门全景航拍（上东下西）

Site of the Imperial City of Zhao State is part of the palace site on Site of the Zhao State Capital in Handan. From 2010 to 2016, archaeologists from Hebei Provincial Institute of Cultural Relics and other organizations carried out a large-scale archaeological reconnaissance and mapping on Site of the Imperial City of Zhao State. The following are the major outcomes. In terms of city wall construction, traces of fabric cloth and depressions rammed by pestles found on the surface of the ramparts all indicate reinforcement; the inner side of the ramparts turns out to be a stepped structure with an apron slope, tiled facilities and drainage gullies; the outside of the ramparts used to be surrounded by two concentric moats. Such unique architectural features become an empirical basis for the study of Site of the Zhao State Capital in Handan and urban archaeology of Eastern Zhou. In terms of city gate construction, outside the west gate of the western part of the Imperial City of Zhao State, there used to be a side tower on each side. It has been confirmed that both side towers are the earliest ones that have ever been discovered. On Palace Foundation Site No.3, which is in the western part of the Imperial City of Zhao State, the northern terrace used to be a part of a palatial architecture built on a high platform. This particular palatial architecture was the main building in this region. In the front of this palatial architecture, there was a spacious courtyard; on the south, there was the South Terrace, a vast terrace-like auxiliary building. These archaeological discoveries all help understand the shape and structure of the palatial buildings in the Imperial City of Zhao State, which was established in Warring States Period and centered with a barbican entrance, is the first one that has been discovered on an imperial city site dating back to Eastern Zhou.

# 河北雄安新区南阳遗址

◎ 张晓峥

南阳遗址位于河北省雄安新区容城县晾马台镇南阳村南20米。其北部为台地，由东北部向南逐渐低缓平展。南阳遗址是雄安新区内保存面积最大、文化内涵较丰富的一处古遗址，19世纪六七十年代，遗址周围出土"西宫"铭文蟠螭纹铜壶、长方形附耳蹄形足铜鼎等，有学者指出其可能为东周时期燕国南部城邑"临易"或"易"。为廓清遗址的分布范围、遗存堆积状况，2017年6月至12月，河北省文物研究所对南阳遗址进行考古勘探和试掘，解剖东西向南城垣1处，清理灰坑42个，沟3条，窑址1座，墓葬5座，道路1条，发现其文化遗存主体年代为西汉时期。

2017年考古队对南阳遗址进行区域性考古调查，发现以南阳遗址为中心面积达18平方千米的东周、汉代遗址聚落集群区。勘探发现城址1座，夯土建筑台基23处，灰坑461座，路3条。城址平面大致呈方形，地上城垣基本不存，仅余地下夯土基槽，南城垣保存较好，东城垣破坏严重，西、北城垣大部分被南阳村占压。经对城址南城垣解剖得知：地下基槽叠压于第③层下，打破生土。在基槽底部南、北两侧各分布2个"倒梯形"基槽；自北至南地下基槽大致由6块夯土版块错落叠压，依次分别夯筑而成，夯土夹杂遗物较少，可辨器形为长方形素面砖块、绳纹板瓦残片（内饰麻点纹）、圆唇翻沿上翘夹蚌红陶釜残片、方唇折沿盆口沿等，我们推测城垣年代上限不早于战国末期。

西南发掘区域经初步整理，文化遗存可分为早、晚两段。早段文化遗存的典型器物有尖圆唇翻沿上翘筒腹釜、方唇卷沿弧腹圜底釜、方唇宽折沿釜、深腹碗形豆、尖圆唇浅腹平盘豆、折腹碗等。其相对年代为战国末期至西汉早期。晚段文化遗存的典型器物有圆唇折沿筒腹釜、方唇卷沿斜腹圜底釜、厚叠唇溜肩小口瓮、折沿内三足炉、折腹碗等，其相对年代为西汉中晚期至两汉之际。

南阳遗址为一处战国、汉代时期的中型城址，以南阳遗址为核心的东周、汉代聚落集群区的新发现，为东周、汉代城市考古的研究提供了新的考古学资料。南阳遗址较为丰富的战国、汉代时期文化遗存，初步构建了该区域战国末期至两汉之际的考古学序列，遗址东周燕文化、汉代文化是雄安新区千年历史文化的重要组成部分，探索其城市聚落演变与生态环境互动关系、生业演进模式，对雄安新区规划建设发展具有重要意义。

288　黄淮七省考古新发现

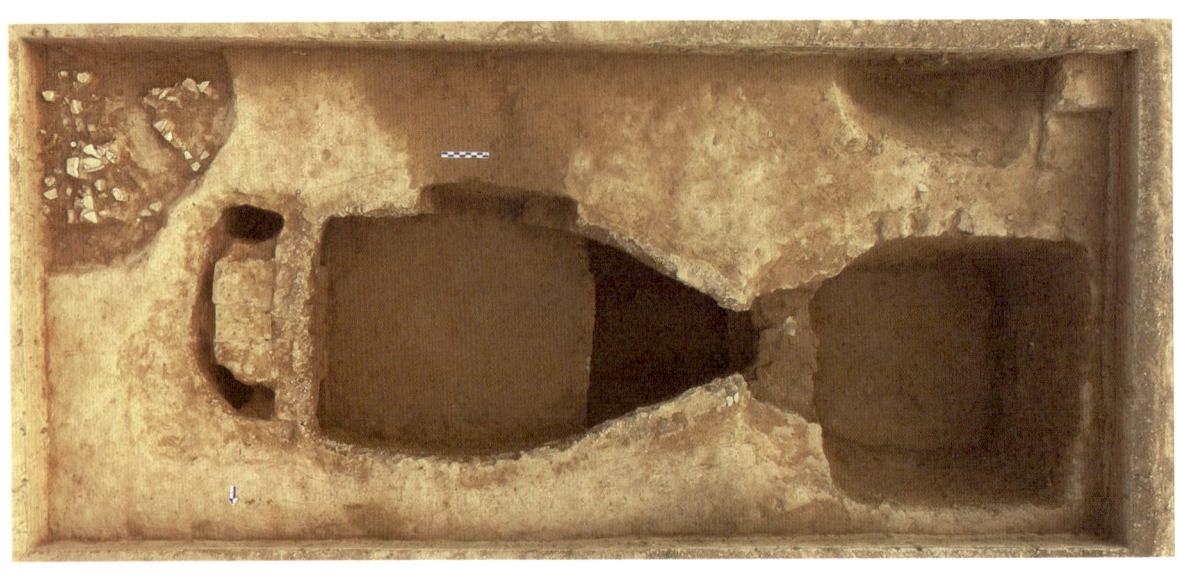

瓮棺葬板瓦

盆形釜

"匋(陶)攻(工)某"陶文陶片

筒形釜

陶窑(上南下北)

南阳遗址西南发掘区域航拍（上东下西）

From June to December in 2017, archaeologists from Hebei Provincial Institute of Cultural Relics and other organizations conducted archaeological investigations in the entire area of Xiong'an New District and carried out archaeological reconnaissances and trial drillings on Nanyang Site. It has been found out that the majority of the cultural relics discovered there date back to Western Han. Nanyang Site, dating back to the Warring States Period and Han Dynasty, is a medium-sized city site with relatively rich cultural contents within Xiong'an New District. A settlement cluster with Nanyang Site as its core has been discovered. It dates back to Eastern Zhou and Han Dynasty. The discovery of this settlement cluster marks the beginning of urban archaeology on Nanyang Site and provides important archaeological outcomes for urban archaeology of Zhou Dynasty and Han Dynasty.

# 是飨是宜　继序思不忘

## 陕西宝鸡石鼓山商周墓地

◎丁　岩

宝鸡石鼓山商周墓地位于陕西省宝鸡市市区、秦岭北麓山前台地的石鼓山区域，其北临渭河。2012年3—6月，石鼓山村四组村民在宅基地建设中发现3座商周时期墓葬，陕西省考古研究院、宝鸡市考古研究所、宝鸡市渭滨区博物馆随即组建考古工作队进行考古发掘，至2013年年底，发现并清理商周时期墓葬14座以及与墓葬年代同期的灰坑数座。

发现的14座商周墓葬在分布上具有大稀疏、小聚集的特点，可划为北区和西南区。北区有中型墓3座、小型墓4座、形制不明确的墓葬2座，西南区有小型墓5座。该墓地是迄今所知高领袋足鬲文化圈内等级最高的墓地，其中型墓葬集中分布在北区，且处于核心区域，小型墓葬在两区均有分布且处于边缘地带。两种规格的墓葬，同处一地，等级差异又十分明显，显示出这里存在高等级贵族与一般平民两个层级的人群。

依据墓葬形制、规模和随葬品内涵等因素推测，石鼓山两座中型墓葬M3、M4的墓主很可能是宝鸡地域内级别很高的首领。对比西周早期燕侯、晋侯、曾侯、应侯等墓葬的情况，认为其墓葬级别约略低于侯或侯夫人。两墓距离很近，且在形制、规模、棺椁结构、葬式、随葬器物和一些随葬器物的特定摆放位置以及同出高领袋足鬲等方面极其相似，两墓墓主极有可能是夫妻关系。

墓地的中型墓葬设有壁龛且随葬高领袋足鬲，有宽的二层台，其中三号墓葬还是车人同穴，随葬陶器以高领袋足鬲、圆肩罐为主。这是宝鸡市区第一次集群性出土此种鬲，为认识刘家文化提供了面貌明确的高级别贵族墓葬的新资料。

在墓地M3、M4出土的青铜礼器上，共发现数十组不同的殷商族群的族徽或曰名，表明这些青铜器来源于殷商系统的多个"家族"。由此，这些青铜礼器应该是通过武王灭商或者周公平乱的战争方式进入关中地区，进而显示两墓的年代已经进入西周初期，成为少有的时代明确的典型的西周初期墓葬。随葬的这些青铜礼器，也成为该时期典型的成组的青铜礼器。

石鼓山商周墓地的发现与发掘，在推进商末周初考古学文化的研究方面具有极其重要的价值，不仅为宝鸡地区商末周初刘家文化的深入研究提供了更为丰富的考古材料，也为以高领袋足鬲代表的刘家文化和以联裆鬲代表的姬周文化的更替过程等多方面研究提供了前所未有的翔实资料。

M3（上北下南）及所出铜禁

M4东壁壁龛

M4八号壁龛

铜簋（M4）

球腹簋（M4）

陶鬲（M4）

户彝（M3）

Shigushan Cemetery is located in Shigu Mountain, on the northern piedmont terrace of Qinling Mountains, Baoji City, Shaanxi Province. From 2012 to 2013, archaeologists from Shaanxi Provincial Institute of Archaeology and other organizations discovered and excavated 14 tombs of Shang and Zhou dynasties and several ash pits of the same age. The discovery and excavation of Shigushan Cemetery are of great value in promoting the cultural study of late Shang Dynasty and early Zhou Dynasty. Shigushan Cemetery has provided more archaeological materials for in-depth study of Liujia Culture back to the epoch from late Shang Dynasty to early Zhou Dynasty in Baoji. Liujia Culture is represented by Li, which is a vessel featured with a high-neck and bag-like crotched legs; Ji-Zhou Culture is represented by Li which has low crotches between its legs. Shigushan Cemetery has also contributed unprecedented materials to studies like the replacement process of the above two cultures.

# 河南伊川县徐阳东周戎人墓地

◎吴业恒

徐阳墓地位于洛阳市西南伊川县鸣皋镇徐阳村。墓葬主要分布在以徐阳村为中心的顺阳河及其支流两岸台地上。2013—2017年，洛阳市文物考古研究院对墓地进行抢救性考古发掘，共清理西周时期墓葬6座，房址1座，祭祀坑1座；东周时期墓葬48座，陪葬车马坑10座，马坑1座；宋墓6座。

发现西周墓6座，随葬陶器为陶鬲或鬲、罐组合，个别伴出铜戈等铜器。随葬遗物均放置在头部上方，普遍有在人的足部、头部或口内放置贝币的现象。东周墓48座，其中大型墓葬5座，随葬遗物主要有铜、石礼器、陶器、玉器、金器、玛瑙饰件、漆器等；中型墓葬7座，大部分被盗扰，出土遗物以铜器为主；小型墓36座，部分墓中还发现有用狗或马、牛、羊头殉牲现象。随葬品以陶器为主，均为生活用具。其他发现包括：车马坑10座，马坑1座，房址1座，祭祀坑1座。祭祀坑内近底北、东、西、南四面各发现人骨1具，无葬具。从骨架放置情况看，东部人骨疑被腰斩下葬，其余三人疑似捆绑下葬。

徐阳墓地已发掘遗存以春秋中晚期墓葬及陪葬车马坑为主体遗存，其春秋中晚期墓葬出土器物组合及特征等与洛阳地区东周时期墓葬出土遗物特征相似，而陪葬车马坑东北角或北部均放置了大量马、牛、羊头蹄等，则与西北地区戎人葬俗类似。

据文献记载，伊洛河流域很早以前就有戎人部族活动。据考证，陆浑戎分布的大致范围在今伊阙、鹿蹄山以南，伏牛山以北，熊耳山以东区域内，涓水（今顺阳河）流域为其中心地带。陆浑戎活动的中心地域与徐阳墓地所在的涓水地理位置相符。陆浑戎自公元前638年迁入晋国"南鄙"之地伊川，至公元前525年陆浑国灭，立国伊川凡114年。陆浑戎在伊河流域活动时间也与徐阳墓地的时代基本吻合。陆浑戎虽然身份不太高，但也是一个小诸侯国，具有一定的经济实力，陪葬的车马坑规模与其身份相符。

综上所述，徐阳墓地无论从时间、地域、规模、习俗等都可以与春秋时期活跃在这一区域的陆浑戎形成对应关系。因此徐阳墓地应为陆浑戎贵族墓地，其附葬的车马坑应为陆浑戎国君或高级贵族墓的陪葬。徐阳墓地的发现证实了陆浑戎迁伊川的历史事件，是研究中原地区少数民族迁徙和融合的重要资料。

M2（上北下南）

牛马坑（上西下东）

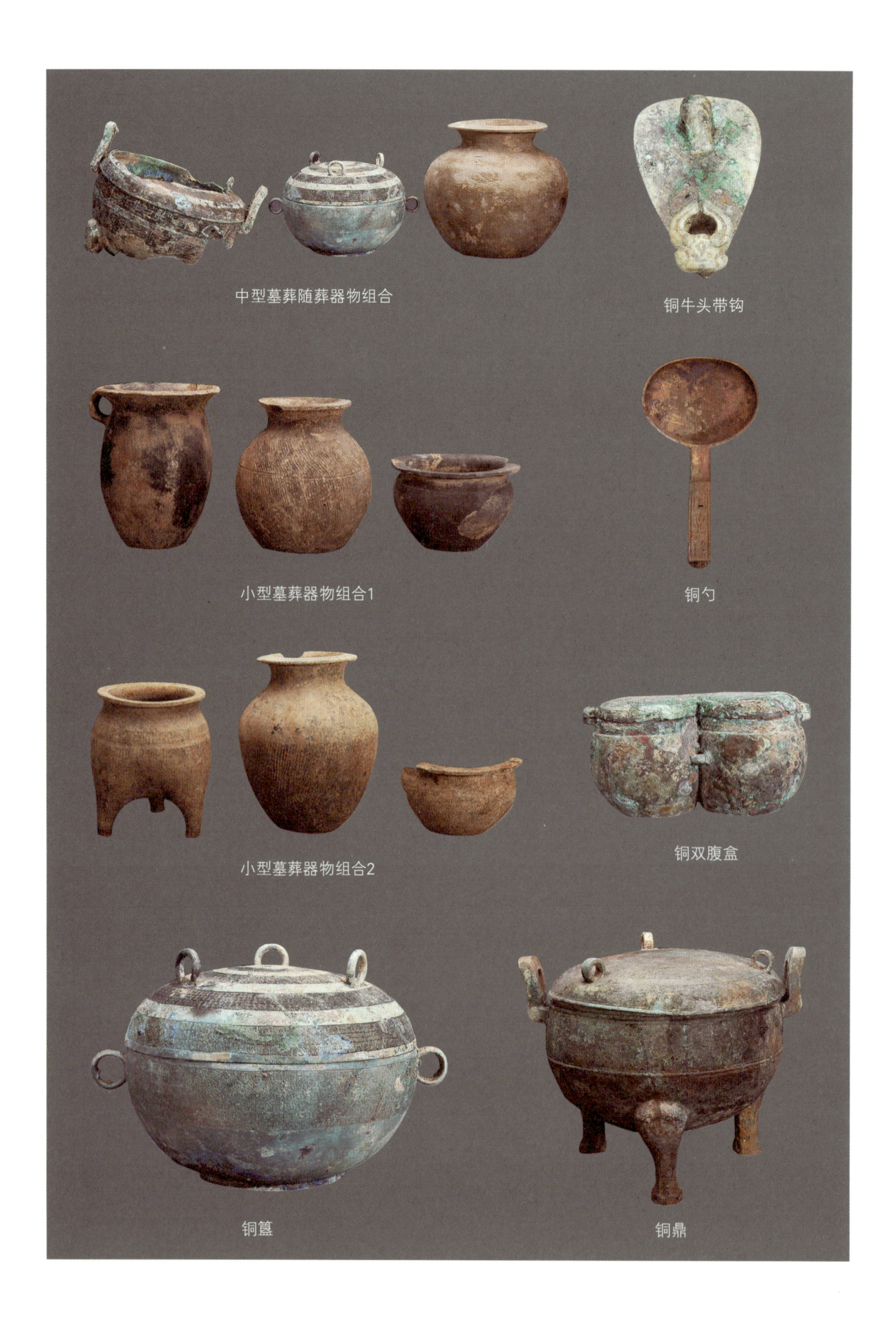

中型墓葬随葬器物组合　　　　　　　　　　　铜牛头带钩

小型墓葬器物组合1　　　　　　　　　　　　铜勺

小型墓葬器物组合2　　　　　　　　　　　　铜双腹盒

铜簋　　　　　　　　　　　　　　　　　　　铜鼎

牛马坑（上北下南）

    Xuyang Cemetery is located in Xuyang Village, Minggao Town, Yichuan County, southwest of Luoyang City. From 2013 to 2017, archaeologists from Luoyang Institute of Cultural Relics and Archaeology excavated 6 tombs, 1 dwelling site and 1 sacrificial pit of Western Zhou, 48 tombs, 10 satellite chariot pits and 1 horse pit of Eastern Zhou, 6 tombs of Song Dynasty. The majority of sites excavated in Xuyang Cemetery are tombs and satellite chariot pits of middle and late Spring & Autumn Period. Sets of antiquities that have been unearthed from tombs of middle and late Spring & Autumn Period and their features are similar to those revealed in tombs of Eastern Zhou in Luoyang district. At the northeastern corner and northern part of the satellite chariot pits, there are volumes of heads and hooves of horses, cows and sheep, etc. This burial custom is similar to that of the Rong People in northwestern China. It has been preliminarily determined that Xuyang Cemetery should be an aristocratic cemetery of Luhun Rong and the chariot pits were satellite pits of tombs in which rulers or high-ranking nobles of Luhun Rong Kingdom were buried. The discovery of Xuyang Cemetery has confirmed Luhun Rong's migration and relocation to Yichuan and has provided important materials for the study of migration and integration of ethnic minorities on the Central Plains.

# 河南南阳市夏响铺鄂国贵族墓地

◎ 崔本信

夏响铺鄂国贵族墓地位于南阳市区东北10千米，南阳新区新店乡夏响铺村北西边距白河1.5千米的一道南北向高岗上。其东边即先秦时代贯通黄河、长江流域的南北要道"夏路"。该墓地于2012年南水北调干渠施工时发现，鄂侯夫人墓M1已被严重破坏。2012—2013年，南阳市文物考古研究所对夏响铺鄂国贵族墓地进行考古发掘，清理出西周晚期至春秋早期墓葬60多座，出土带铭文青铜器40余件，铭文有"鄂侯""鄂伯""鄂姜""养伯""上鄀太子平侯""卫"等，我们判断这是一处西周晚期到春秋早期鄂国贵族墓地。

鄂国贵族墓地按墓主人身份、地位、从属关系等有序排列，整个墓地分三个区域，最北部第一个区域为一排8座小型墓葬，可能为鄂侯陪葬墓。往南第二区域一排共7座墓葬，可能为四代鄂侯及配偶墓葬，形制在墓地中规模最大，随葬品最为丰富。最南部的第三区域应为鄂侯亲属墓葬区。

M1被盗掘到底，破坏严重，仅从墓内填土和挖出的土堆上清理、拣选出一批青铜器、玉器等。发现列鼎7件，形制一样，纹饰相同，大小不同，其中6件上有"鄂侯作夫人行鼎"铭文；仅发现2件铜簋盖，上铸有"鄂侯夫人"铭文；铜鬲3件，形制、纹饰相同，口沿上有"鄂侯夫人"铭文；铜方壶盖2件，形制、纹饰相同，上有"养伯"铭文；铜盘匜1套，匜残片上有铭文。玉器有璧、戈、璜、玦、玉虎等。

夏响铺鄂国贵族墓地的发现与发掘，改变了我们对鄂国及鄂国历史的传统认识。M1、M5、M6、M16、M19、M20等墓葬出土青铜器上有"鄂侯""鄂侯夫人""鄂"的铭文，从墓葬大小、结构、距离看，M1为鄂侯夫人墓，M5和M6、M7和M16、M19和M20均为异穴夫妻合葬墓。这样看来，夏响铺鄂国贵族墓地至少有四代鄂侯在此埋葬，这对研究西周晚期到春秋早期鄂国的地望、历史以及鄂、养、鄀、卫等古国关系等学术问题提供了弥足珍贵的实物资料。

从夏响铺鄂国贵族墓地的发掘与发现来看，西周晚期到春秋早期鄂国仍然存在于南阳，应是周王朝灭鄂国后，把鄂国王族置于周王朝统治范围内。初步判断M5、M6的时代为西周晚期晚段，在墓地范围内时代应为最早。鄂国在西周中晚期被周王朝灭掉，到M5、M6这个时代中间有缺环，相信以后的考古发掘和研究对解决这个问题应有重要价值。

三代之礼　皇皇者华　299

M6

编钟

300　黄淮七省考古新发现

盘匜　　　　　　　　　　　　铜鼎

铜彝　　　　　　　　　　　　铜尊

铜鹤首

方壶盖　　　　　　　　　　　铜簠铭文

玉器

Xiaxiangpu Aristocratic Cemetery of E State is on a south-north hillock, 1.5 kilometers east of Baihe River, north of Xiaxiangpu Village, Xindian Township, Nanyang New District, Nanyang City, Henan Province. From 2012 to 2013, archaeologists from Nanyang Institute of Cultural Relics and Archaeology carried out excavations in the cemetery, excavating over 60 tombs dating back to a period spanning from late Western Zhou to early Spring & Autumn Period. More than 40 pieces of inscribed bronzes have been unearthed. It has been preliminarily determined that this cemetery should be a superior aristocratic cemetery of E State during the time from late Western Zhou to early Spring & Autumn Period. According to inscriptions on the bronzes and tomb structure, it has been inferred that at least four generations of marquises who ruled E State were buried here. The cemetery has provided extremely valuable materials for the study on issues like the geographical location and history of E State, the relationship between ancient countries during the time from late Western Zhou to early Spring & Autumn Period.

# 山西翼城县大河口西周墓地

◎王金平　陈海波

大河口墓地位于山西翼城县城以东约6千米处大河口村北的高台地上。墓地包括大量不同等级的西周墓葬和附属车马坑，以及晚于墓葬的灰坑。墓地于2007年5月被盗发现，自2007年9月至2016年12月，山西省考古研究所等单位先后多次对墓地进行了大规模、全方位的考古勘探与发掘，墓地贯穿整个西周时期，为研究霸国的文化面貌提供了极为珍贵的资料。2014年7月至2016年12月，我们对墓地七区至十三区进行了考古发掘。目前已经将大河口墓地现存的墓葬全部发掘完毕。

发现墓葬1660座，全部为土圹竖穴墓，分布无明显规律性，个别墓葬之间存在打破关系。葬具大多数为单棺，少数为双棺或一棺一椁。部分墓葬发现有木质葬具痕迹，部分葬具下有垫木和腰坑，有的腰坑内发现有动物遗骨，个别能辨明为狗。绝大多数为熟土二层台，个别为生土二层台。墓主人头向整体上看，西向墓占大多数，部分为东向墓，个别为北向墓。面向方面各种情况都存在，看不出有明显的规律性。以仰身占绝大多数，也有部分为侧身，仅两例为俯身。部分人骨上发现有衣物或编织物残尸的痕迹。本次发掘没有发现殉人现象。

随葬器物种类有陶器、青铜器、蚌贝器、玉石器、骨器、漆器、锡器等，以陶器和蚌贝器为大宗。陶器以陶鬲和陶罐为代表的陶容器为主，一般置于墓主人头端二层台之上。青铜器包括礼器、兵器、工具、饰品、车马器等，其中铜礼器21件，一般置于墓主人头端二层台之上或棺椁之间，也有个别放置于墓主人脚端；兵器、工具、饰品、车马器一般置于棺内墓主人身旁，也有部分置于二层台之上或葬具盖板之上。蚌贝器以蛤蜊和海贝为多数，蛤蜊一般为装饰品，放置于墓主人身上，海贝有在口内做口含的情况，但更多的是放置在墓主人身上做装饰品。出土的玉石器数量较少，有的是作为工具放置于二层台之上，有的是作为装饰品放置于墓主人身上，也有个别作为口含放置于墓主人口内。骨器的数量也较少，其中出土的两件卜骨尤为引人注目。

大河口墓地是西周时期非姬姓封国之霸国墓地，贯穿整个西周时期。在本次发掘工作完成之后，我们基本搞清了墓地的范围和分布状况，这也是继山西绛县横水倗国墓地之后，又一处全部揭露完毕的西周时期封国墓地，对推动西周考古研究、推动晋文化研究具有重要意义。

房址（左北右南）

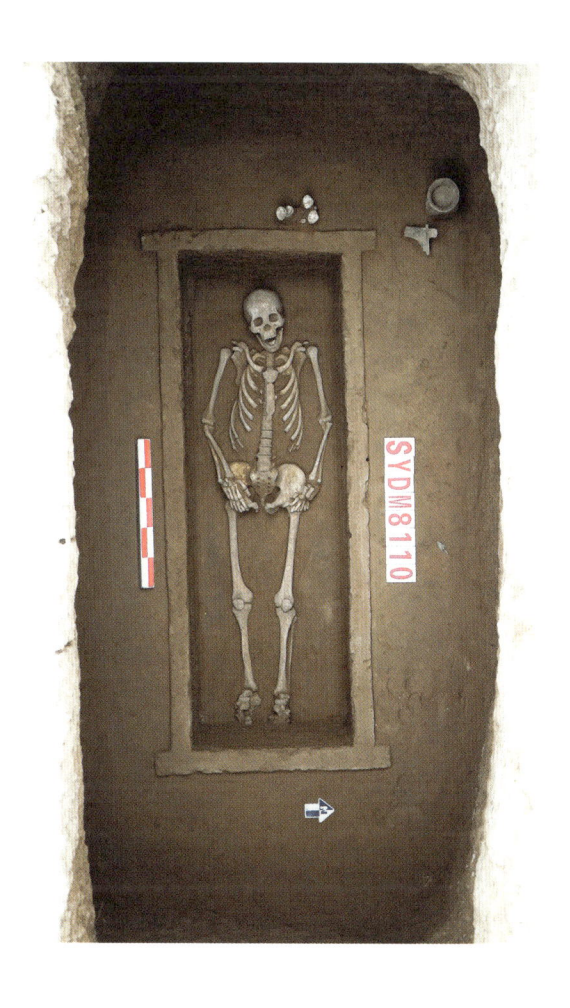

墓葬（左南右北）

铜器

陶器

Dahekou Cemetery is located on the tableland north of Dahekou Village, approximately 6 kilometers east of Yicheng County, Shanxi Province. From 2014 to 2016, archaeologists from Shanxi Provincial Institute of Archaeology and other organizations carried out excavations on the site. In total, 1660 tombs and over 10,800 sets of antiquities of Western Zhou were excavated. Dahekou Cemetery, which existed throughout the time of Western Zhou, was used by the Vassal State of Ba, ruled by people who were not from the Ji clan. The cemetery has provided extremely rare materials for the study of cultural features of the Vassal State of Ba. After Hengshui Cemetery of the Vassal State of Peng in Jiangxian County in Shanxi Province, Dahekou Cemetery is another wholly revealed cemetery of a vassal state dating back to Western Zhou. Materials obtained are of great significance for promoting archaeological researches on Western Zhou and cultural studies of Shanxi Province.

# 山西绛县雎村西周封国墓地

◎王金平　段双龙

雎村墓地位于绛县卫庄镇雎村北500米的台塬地上，西距绛县县城约5千米，距横水墓地约20千米。墓地地势平坦，南望中条山，西北依紫金山，西面为季节性河流，属浍河水系。

2011年6月，墓葬因被盗而被发现。经对被盗墓葬的初步调查和追缴文物的鉴定，判定雎村墓地为一处西周时期墓地。2015年7月至2018年1月，雎村考古队对墓地进行了大规模的考古发掘工作，共清理西周墓葬854座，其中大型墓葬10座，但全部遭盗掘，无一幸免。其他发现包括车马坑1座、马坑1座、灰坑5座、陶窑2座。出土文物有铜器、陶器、漆器、海贝、毛蚶、蚌泡等器物共计11000余件。其中铜器560余件，包括鼎24件、簋7件、甗1件、戈46件、铜铃28件及车马器等百余件；陶容器828件，包括鬲、罐、簋、壶、豆、盆、大口尊等；漆器30余件，因腐朽挤压，绝大部分器形不识。其他海贝、毛蚶、蚌器、蛤蜊等器物9600余件。

通过发掘基本厘清了墓地的布局，了解了墓地的文化面貌。从目前发掘的资料显示，墓地时代从西周早期延续至西周晚期。墓葬特征明显，均为东西向的圆角长方形竖穴土坑墓；墓主人以头向西为主，其次为头向东；葬式以仰身直肢为主，其次为俯身直肢；发现有腰坑、殉人；在3座大墓四角发现有斜洞。

雎村墓地的发现与发掘，是晋南地区在倗（绛县横水墓地）、霸（翼城大河口墓地）之外发现的又一个区域中心（封国）。从现有的材料看，该处墓地人群单纯，应是与天马—曲村相区别的，属于以横水、大河口墓地为代表的文化。其与绛县横水墓地相距仅15千米，且在墓葬形制、头向、葬式、随葬品及墓葬附近的柱洞、斜洞、腰坑、殉人等墓葬特征方面共性明显，而其与无殉人现象的大河口墓地略显不同。

从空间位置与属性等方面看，其价值与意义也非常重要，对于研究西周分封制与政体具有重要的价值。雎村墓地的发现与发掘将有利于推动西周时期晋南及当时整个社会组织结构的探讨与争论，同时也将有助于对该时期族群迁移、融合及各个区域中心的性质及其之间关系的研究。

M1022（上北下南）

簋（M1022）

鼎（M1022）

M1029二层台（上西下东）

车马坑（上北下南）

铜车辖、铜轴头饰

马坑（上东下西）

M1073（上北下南）

Suicun Cemetery is located on a tableland, 500 meters north of Suicun Village, Weizhuang Town, Jiangxian County. From July 2015 to December 2018, an archaeological team based in Suicun Village conducted large-scale excavations in this cemetery. In total, 854 tombs, 1 chariot pit, 1 horse pit, 5 ash pits and 2 kilns were excavated. The cemetery was in use from early Western Zhou to late Western Zhou. After vassal states of Peng (Hengshui Cemetery in Jiangxian County) and Ba (Dahekou Cemetery in Yicheng County), another regional center (vassal state) in southern Shanxi Province was revealed because of the discovery and excavation of Suicun Cemetery. The discovery and excavation of Suicun Cemetery have promoted investigation and discussions concerning its contemporary societal structure in not only southern Shanxi Province but also the entire country in Western Zhou, and have contributed to studies on contemporary migration and integration of ethnic groups as well as natures of regional centers and the relationships between each other.

# 陕西周原姚家墓地

◎赵艺蓬

周原姚家墓地西距许家村400米，东距美阳河约500米。2010年5月，陕西省考古研究院已故技师史浩善同志据当地群众提供的线索发现了该墓地。为进一步了解墓地特征，陕西省考古研究院于2011年11月至2012年12月，在姚家墓地及其周邻区域开展了大规模的考古钻探、调查与发掘。以往在周原遗址仅发现1座带墓道的西周大墓，而此次姚家墓地2座带墓道大墓的发现，有助于我们更深入地研究周原遗址各墓地的等级与性质。

姚家墓地性质单纯，可分为南、北、西三区。经过以往对周原遗址商周时期墓葬形制和随葬器物及组合的研究，判断西区和北区应为姬姓周系墓群，南区为东土集团的殷遗民系统。三区不同墓向墓葬共居一个墓地的现象，未见于以往周原地区西周时期墓地中。三区周围并无其他墓葬，表明其人群关系非常紧密，但又不属于同一族系，其间应为统治和附庸的关系。

南、北区墓地共发掘44座墓葬、1座马坑和1座车马坑，包括不同墓向、不同等级及不同墓列的墓葬。墓地起始年代不早于西周中期偏早阶段，延续使用至西周晚期。中小型墓葬特征基本相同于周原以往发掘墓葬，但个别墓葬随葬陶鬶、陶丸、椭圆形小石子等特征系周原地区首见。发掘墓葬虽均遭严重盗扰，但仍出土了大量的青铜器、玉石器、骨蚌器、原始瓷器和陶器等。一些中型墓中出土了不少精美的玉器与原始瓷簋、觯、尊等，这在周原地区乃至全国尚属首次发现，同时也为探讨北方原始瓷器产地问题提供了新的资料。

西区墓地发掘的2座带墓道大墓M7和M8，形制较为特殊。M7墓室四角各有一条窄而短的斜道，该特征以往在周原地区并未发现，经比较，其特征与北京琉璃河遗址M1193更为接近。M1193被认为是燕侯墓，所以从墓葬形制看M7为姬姓；M8墓道整体呈弧形弯曲，呈"香蕉形"，此形制墓道以往仅在商系殷墟西区M93与周系的应国墓地M232和张家坡M152发现过，而M8其他墓葬特征亦与殷墟大墓不同，所代表的不是商系主流，因此"香蕉形"墓葬更可能是姬姓周系的。

在发掘姚家墓地之余，我们对周原遗址东部边缘区域进行了详细调查，发现周原遗址东部边缘区域的聚落形态属"居葬分离"模式，其性质应为"许家北居址区"居民的公共墓地，不同于周原遗址西周聚落中心区域"居葬一处"的聚落特征。

玉鹦鹉

圆雕玉伏兽

原始瓷簋

原始瓷尊

龙凤纹玉牌

M7南墓道（上南下北）及墓道东壁葬车轮痕

Yaojia Cemetery is located 1 kilometer southwest of Xujia Village, Famen Town, Fufeng County. This area is the eastern margin of Zhouyuan Site. From 2011 to 2012, archaeologists from Shaanxi Provincial Institute of Archaeology conducted a large-scale archaeological drilling, reconnaissance and excavation in Yaojia Cemetery and its adjacent area. In total, 44 tombs, 1 horse pit and 1 chariot pit were revealed in Yaojia Cemetery. This cemetery came into existence no later than early middle Western Zhou and had been in use until late Western Zhou. A considerable number of exquisite jade implements and primitive porcelain that were unearthed in some medium-sized tombs are new materials for the investigation into issues like the provenance of primitive porcelain in the North. The special structure of large tombs M7 and M8, in which there are tomb tunnels, indicates that both tombs should belong to occupants who were descendants of Zhou Dynasty and from the Ji clan. The appearance of the tomb tunnel in tomb M8 is a banana-shaped curve. The excavated area could be divided into 11 function divisions. They help determine the pattern and nature of settlements on Zhouyuan Site in Western Zhou.

# 山西洪洞县南秦村两周大型墓地

◎杨及耘  曹 俊

南秦墓地位于山西省洪洞县广胜寺镇南秦村西南的一处台地之上，北距永凝堡遗址约1千米，东北距坊堆遗址约2.5千米，南10余千米处为东周洪洞古城遗址。2016年5月，由山西省考古研究所、临汾市文物旅游局和洪洞县文物旅游局三家单位组成联合考古发掘队，对墓地进行抢救性发掘，清理出不同时期的墓葬9座、灰坑4处。经初步推断，有春秋墓2座、战国-秦墓葬3座、清代墓4座。其中未被盗掘的2座春秋时期墓葬M4、M6为此次发掘的重要发现。

两墓皆为竖穴土坑墓，平面呈长方形，东西向，南北并列，M4位于M6南侧。M4墓内填土有夯打痕迹。葬具为一椁一棺，有熟土二层台。棺内发现人骨1具，保存状况较差，仅存牙齿数颗。另在头骨右侧发现一具兽骨。随葬器物从材质上见有陶、铜、金、漆、石、骨器等，不见玉器，皆位于棺椁间。M6墓内填土未见夯打痕迹，偶见鹅卵石、木炭、青膏泥等。墓壁与椁之间围以积石二层台，二层台之上有积炭。葬具为一椁两棺，人骨保存较差。出土有陶、铜、金、玉等各类器物150余件，残损严重。其中铜容器皆置于棺椁间东部，乐器置于棺椁间南部偏西，兵器、车马器多置于棺椁间西侧和东南部，陶器位于棺椁间南部靠中间的位置，玉器置于人骨头部和脚端。

从墓葬形制及出土器物来看，大致可推断M6的墓葬时代为春秋中期偏晚，M4的年代应为春秋晚期。墓主级别为贵族阶层，或为卿大夫。M6、M4为夫妻异穴合葬墓的可能性较大。墓葬所反映的葬俗为非姬姓，南秦村地处洪洞与赵城交界，或许与赵氏有关。其他墓为不同时期的平民墓葬。

南秦墓地反映了该地区不同时期、不同种群、不同阶层人们的生活情况，是一处历时久长、内涵丰富、保存较为完整的大型墓地，为研究晋南地区不同时期的埋葬制度、人群族属、社会生活等提供了新的资料。

三代之礼　皇皇者华　315

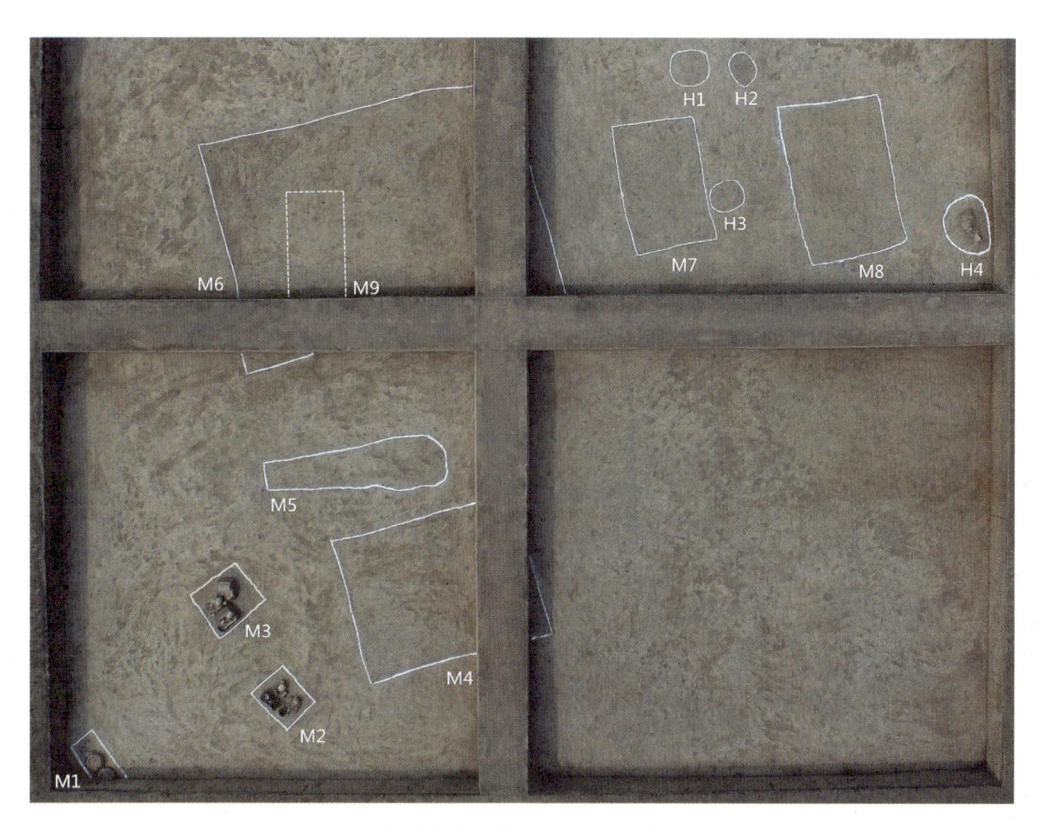

墓葬分布情况（上北下南）

M4

M6南壁抹泥 　　　　　　　　　M6出土编钟、编磬

M6出土鎏金铜泡 　　　　　　　M6出土铜豆

M6

M9（打破M6）

修复中的铜甗

    Nanqin Cemetery is located on a tableland southwest of Nanqin Village, Guangshengsi Town, Hongdong County, Shanxi Province. In May 2016, archaeologists from Shanxi Provincial Institute of Archaeology and other organizations carried out excavations on the site. As many as 9 tombs dating back to different eras were excavated: 2 were of Spring & Autumn Period, 3 were constructed during the epoch from Warring States Period to Qin Dynasty, and 4 were built in Qing Dynasty. Occupants buried in the tombs of Spring & Autumn Period were not members of the Ji clan. They were possibly linked with the Zhao clan since Nanqin Village was located on the border of Hongdong County and Zhaocheng Town. Nanqin Cemetery reflects the living conditions of people who were of varied ethnic groups and different classes during different historical periods in this region. As a relatively well-preserved large-scale cemetery with a long history, Nanqin Cemetery provides new materials for the study concerning issues like the funerary system, ethnic groups, social life of different historical periods in southern Shanxi Province.

# 山西襄汾县陶寺北两周墓地

◎王京燕　崔俊俊

陶寺北两周墓地位于陶寺村北约800米处。据历年发掘情况推测墓葬总数在10000座左右。墓葬由早到晚从西北向东南排列，从两周之际延续到战国时期。2014年山西省考古研究所开始对其进行抢救性发掘，迄今已发掘春秋时期竖穴土坑墓葬256座，其丰富的地下文物是构筑晋国史的宝贵资料。

墓地春秋早期的重要发现有墓祭遗存和丧葬遗迹。从陶寺北墓地近几年的发掘情况来看，发现的祭祀遗存仅限于大中型墓葬，年代集中在春秋早期。2014M7北部发现玉石器祭祀掩埋层，多为碎石圭，也有少量玉圭、玉璧、玉环、玉玦等。2014M7人骨已朽不能鉴定性别，从随身玉器多串饰，无兵器的特点判断墓主人应是位女性。2017年发掘区内，在M2009、M2010周边的祭祀遗存中发现动物祭祀坑30个，多数集中在M2010的北部，且30个祭祀坑没有打破关系，殉马均在小型祭祀坑的外围，显示祭祀前对祭祀动物的位置是有预先安排的。陶寺北墓地中的玉石器祭祀遗存仅限于春秋早期的女性墓葬。这种针对某座墓葬的祭祀活动在当时并不是普遍的现象，仅见于部分贵族墓葬中，其中原因仍待研究。2017年Ⅱ区8座大中型墓葬中，除最东边的M2008外，其余7墓墓口的北部均有两个大致圆形的坑。M2010的两个圆形坑叠压于玉石器祭祀层之下，可见这类坑形成于祭祀活动之前。《礼记·丧大记》载："君葬用辁，四綍缕，二碑，御棺用羽葆。大夫葬用辁，二綍，二碑，御棺用茅。"墓葬北部的圆坑可能就是用来立碑的，下葬以后，填土夯实。

墓地春秋晚期的重要发现有卫国编钟和"荒帷"遗迹。M3011出土的甬钟是目前卫国唯一存世的春秋时期的实用刻铭编钟，从中或可领略到见于史籍的"郑卫之音"。甬钟在棺椁之间的南部，共13件，形制相同，大小相次。其中11件钟的钲、鼓部可见刻铭，9件钟上铭文相同，共18个字："卫侯之孙申子之子書擇吉金乍鑄龢鍾六堵"；另2件钟上铭文也相同，共177个字。钟上的刻铭无疑是珍贵的历史、文字资料。2017年发掘的M3015、M3014是东西并列的"对子墓"。M3015墓主人是士一级的低等贵族。M3014外棺南、北两端局部暴露出红色的纺织品痕迹，应为"荒帷"遗迹。其上绘黑、黄色"巳"形图案，或即是两"巳"相背的蔽纹。陶寺北墓地M3014中的荒帷遗迹，在目前北方地区两周时期是第三次发现，是唯一的保存较完整的春秋晚期荒帷实物资料。

三代之礼 皇皇者华 319

M3014荒帷局部

M7北部玉石器祭祀遗存

M1出土铜鼎、铜鬲

M1东南角出土鼎、壶

M3011（上西下东）

M3011西南角青铜器

M3011西南部的甬钟

M3011棺椁之间北部的漆器

M3011出土的鼓座

三代之礼　皇皇者华　321

铜鼎

玉璜　　　　　　　　　玉璜

玉玦　　　　　　　　　玉玦

玉神面　　　　　　　　玉饰

丧葬遗址（上北下南）

Tao-si-bei Cemetery, dating back to Western Zhou and Eastern Zhou, is located approximately 800 meters north of Taosi Village, Xiangfen County, Shanxi Province. From 2014 to 2017, archaeologists from Shanxi Provincial Institute of Archaeology carried out successive excavations on this site. In total, 256 tombs built in Spring & Autumn Period were excavated. Besides, sacrificial remains like sacrificial pits of animals and jade ware of early Spring & Autumn Period were discovered. The jade ware was only found in tombs of early Spring & Autumn Period buried with female tomb occupants. From tomb M3011, as many as 13 Yong Zhong, which are bells with a cylindrical handle on top, were unearthed, and 11 of them were engraved with inscriptions. These bells make up the only inscribed Bian Zhong, a chime of bells, that was utilized and left by the Vassal State of Wei in Spring & Autumn Period. In tomb M3015, traces of red fabrics, exposed at parts of the south and north ends of the outer coffin, are the only relatively intact materials of palls dating back to late Spring & Autumn Period.

# 陕西澄城县刘家洼春秋墓地

◎种建荣 孙战伟

刘家洼墓地位于陕西澄城县王庄镇刘家洼村西鲁家河东岸塬边。这里地处洛河与黄河之间的渭北黄土台塬北部，是关中与北方的交流通道，宗周与晋来往的交通要冲，秦与三晋争锋的重点区域，地理位置关键而重要。该墓地因2016年年底被盗而发现。经国家文物局批准，2017年2月以来，陕西省考古研究院与渭南市、澄城县相关单位联合组成考古队，对墓地进行了全面勘探与抢救性发掘。

首先，确认了带两条墓道的高等级贵族大墓。经钻探，刘家洼墓地共有墓葬56座，车马坑2座，马坑1座。其中最引人瞩目的是2座"中"字形大墓（M1与M2），东西并列，居于墓地中部偏东处。特别是M1，规模宏大，墓室大小仅次于同时期、同形制的甘肃礼县大堡子山的秦公大墓M2与M3。大墓墓主人身份亦当为诸侯国国君级别，地位不亚于大国诸侯。其余墓葬皆为南北向长方形竖穴土坑墓，与大墓墓向一致，以大、中型墓葬为主。因此推定，刘家洼墓地应是包括最高统治者在内的一处贵族公共墓地。其次，出土了大量青铜器等各类珍贵文物。目前已经完成20座中、小型墓，共出土各类材质的文物300余件（组），其中青铜器占大宗，主要包括青铜礼器、车马器、兵器三大类。除发掘所获外，已追缴的该墓地被盗文物多达402件（组），其中铜器最多，仅铜礼器多达60余件。再者，发现夯土墙、陶范、陶窑、板瓦建材等居址遗存。

根据出土器物以及墓葬形制、葬俗等特征初步判断，刘家洼墓地是一处春秋早期前后的周文化系统贵族墓地。刘家洼墓地与居址在空间上相邻或靠近分布，年代上接近，功能上互补，等级上匹配，可见墓地与居址为同一聚落的不同构成部分，这里有可能是春秋早期某一周系高级贵族的封国或采邑。

刘家洼墓地这一封国或采邑的发现，不仅增添了我们对关中东部周代遗存的了解，也有助于对周代采邑、封国的城邑形态、居葬模式、生业方式、社会组织等问题进行深入探讨。这一发现加上以往的考古线索，使我们初步认识到：在关中东部特别是渭北台塬区，沿洛河与黄河的支流上可能分布着多个或源于西周贵族采邑，或从西部东迁而来的小封国。

墓室（上西下东）

青铜器

漆器

三代之礼　皇皇者华　325

铜簋　　　　　　　　　　　　玉琮

棺环　　　　　　　　　　　　陶埙

石磬　　　　　　　　　　　　玉玦

发掘航拍（上南下北）

Liujiawa Cemetery is located on the bank of Lujiahe River, west of Liujiawa Village, Wangzhuang Town, Chengcheng County, Shaanxi Province. Ever since February in 2017, a joint team consisting of archaeologists from Shaanxi Provincial Institute of Archaeology and other organizations has been conducting comprehensive archaeological reconnaissances and salvage excavations on the site. Up till now, 19 medium-sized and small tombs have been excavated. Systematic archaeological reconnaissance has been carried out in the adjacent area. Remains of rammed earthen walls, clay molds, kilns, building materials like plate tiles and other advanced dwelling sites have been discovered. It has been preliminarily determined that, in early Spring & Autumn Period, this area should be a vassal state or a fief belonging to a high-ranking aristocrat who was a descendant of Zhou Dynasty.

# 陕西黄陵县寨头河战国戎人墓地

◎孙周勇　邵　晶　孙战伟

2011年4—12月，在延安市南沟门水利枢纽工程建设过程中，陕西省考古研究院对库区范围内的黄陵县阿党镇寨头河村战国墓地展开了全面系统的考古发掘，共清理墓葬90座、马坑2座及殉埋青铜短矛的方坑1座。

寨头河墓地位于洛河支流——葫芦河北岸一处舌形坡地上，西南凸向河床。该坡地人工修整为数阶台地，墓葬分布于其中的四层台地上。面积在2~6平方米之间，葬具分为一棺一椁、单棺和无葬具三种。葬式分为仰身直肢葬、曲肢葬、二次葬和解体葬，其中仰身直肢葬80座。墓向绝大多数为东西向。墓室内多有马、牛、羊头骨及前肢骨等随葬，放置于棺椁上或壁龛内。

随葬品有陶、铜、铁、骨、玉、石、料器等多种，数量逾千件。依等级差异，墓葬内随葬器物差别明显。一般而言，小型墓葬仅随葬日用陶器和配饰铜器，中型墓葬内兼葬有骨镳、铜衔等车马器以及铜鼎、铜剑等礼器和兵器，大型墓葬则多见玛瑙、绿松石、海贝等串饰。

寨头河墓地出土的陶器大致分为"甘青"和"中原"两个系统。结合与甘青系统陶器共存的豆、罐等中原式陶器及魏"梁半钅斤"和"阴晋半钅斤"等钱文，将这批墓葬的时代确定于战国中晚期，族属推测为戎人。

寨头河墓地出土的铜鼎外腹装饰的套索纹及贝纹是东周时期三晋地区常见的装饰风格，短肥援铜戈也是三晋常见之器形。加之中原式陶器的战国时期魏国文化特征以及墓地中发现的魏国布币，初步认为寨头河墓地战国先民的国别当属魏。

寨头河墓地是陕北地区首次全面清理的战国墓地，也是延安地区第一次系统的考古工作，发掘意义重大。首先，战国中晚期的陶器特征的确认，为延安地区陶器序列的建立填补了重要的一环，同时"凿空"了内蒙古西南部——榆林地区、甘肃陇东地区这两大文化区与关中地区商周考古研究的阻障。其次，使寺洼文化的东界翻越子午岭，到达洛水之滨，为研究寺洼文化的流布提供了翔实可靠的考古学新材料。最后，墓地族属和国别的初步确认，是研究民族融合、历史地理的新素材。

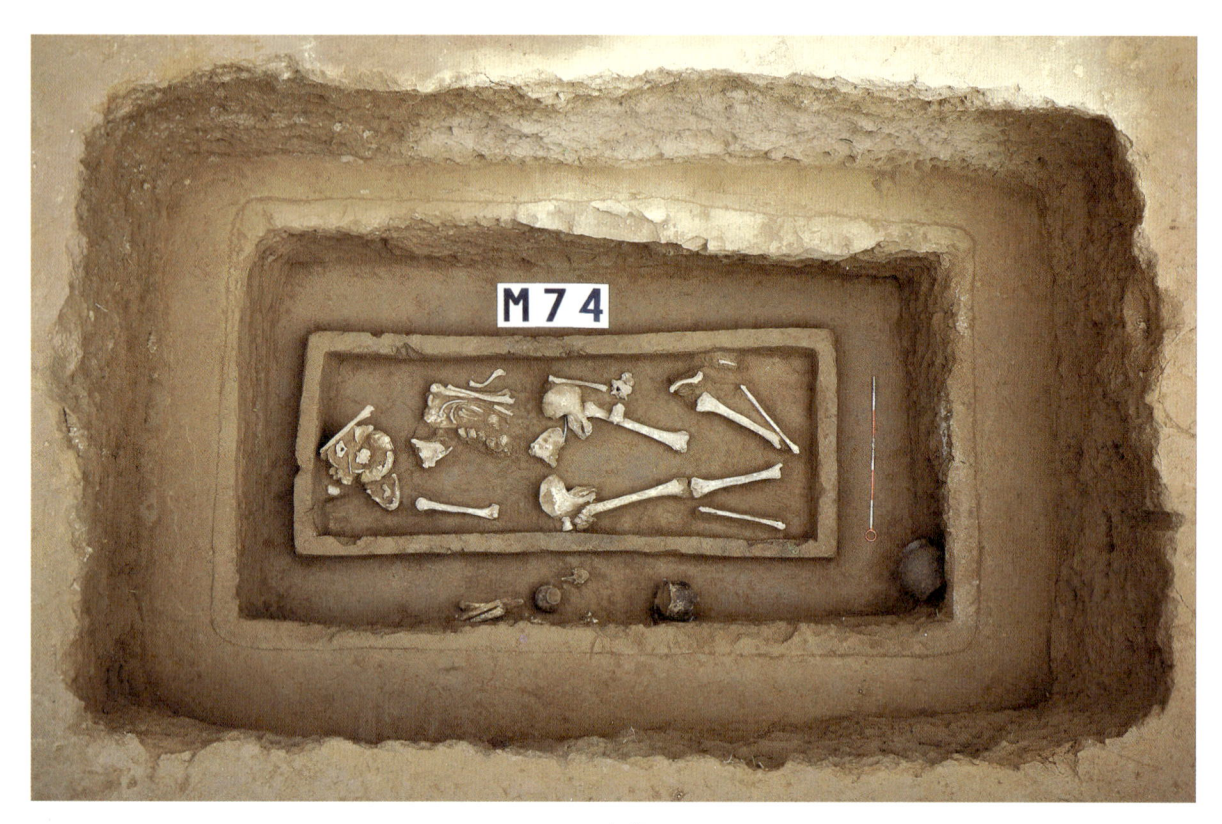

二次葬

解体葬

三代之礼　皇皇者华

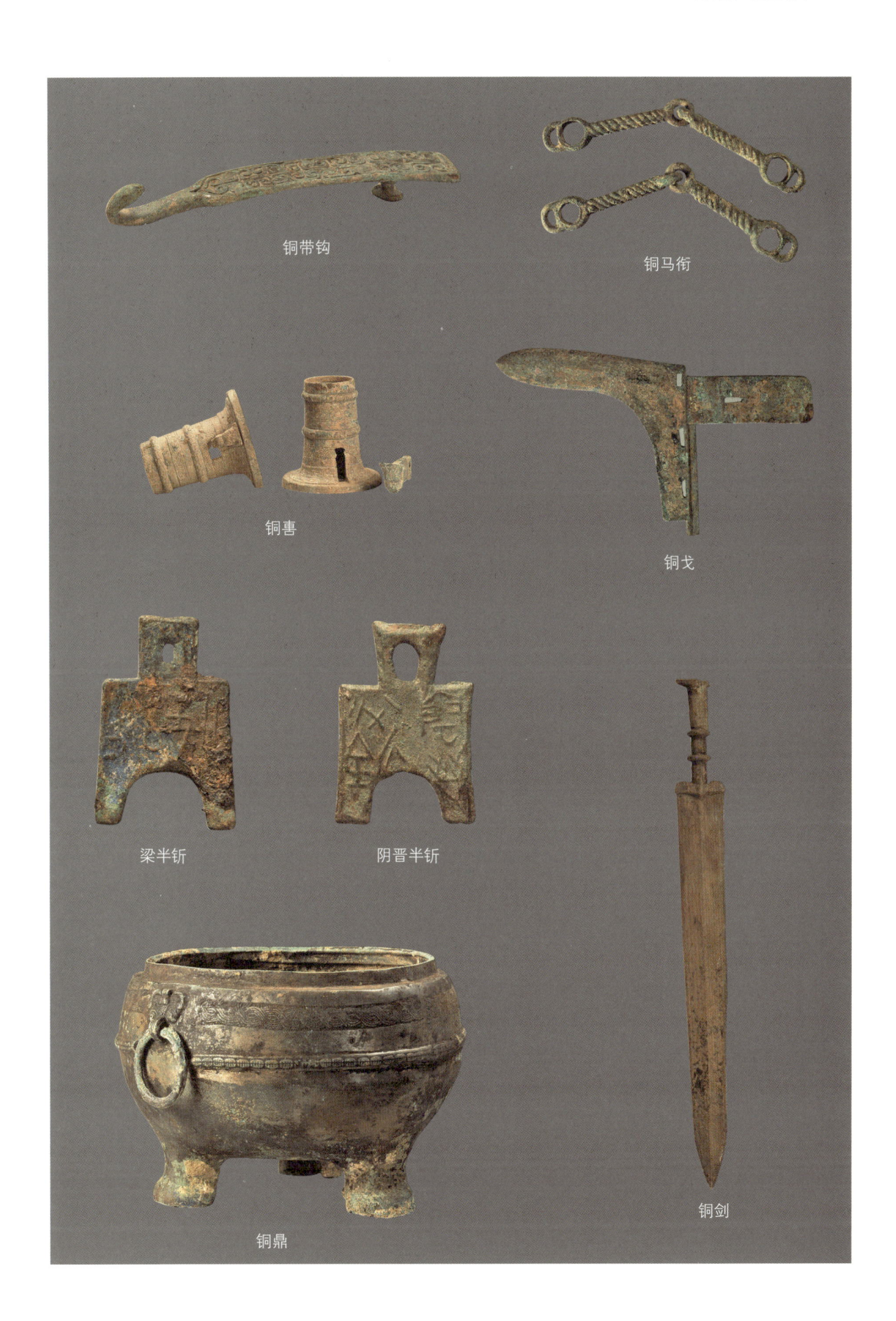

铜带钩　　　　　　　　　铜马衔

铜䡇　　　　　　　铜戈

梁半釿　　　阴晋半釿

铜剑

铜鼎

中原式陶器组合

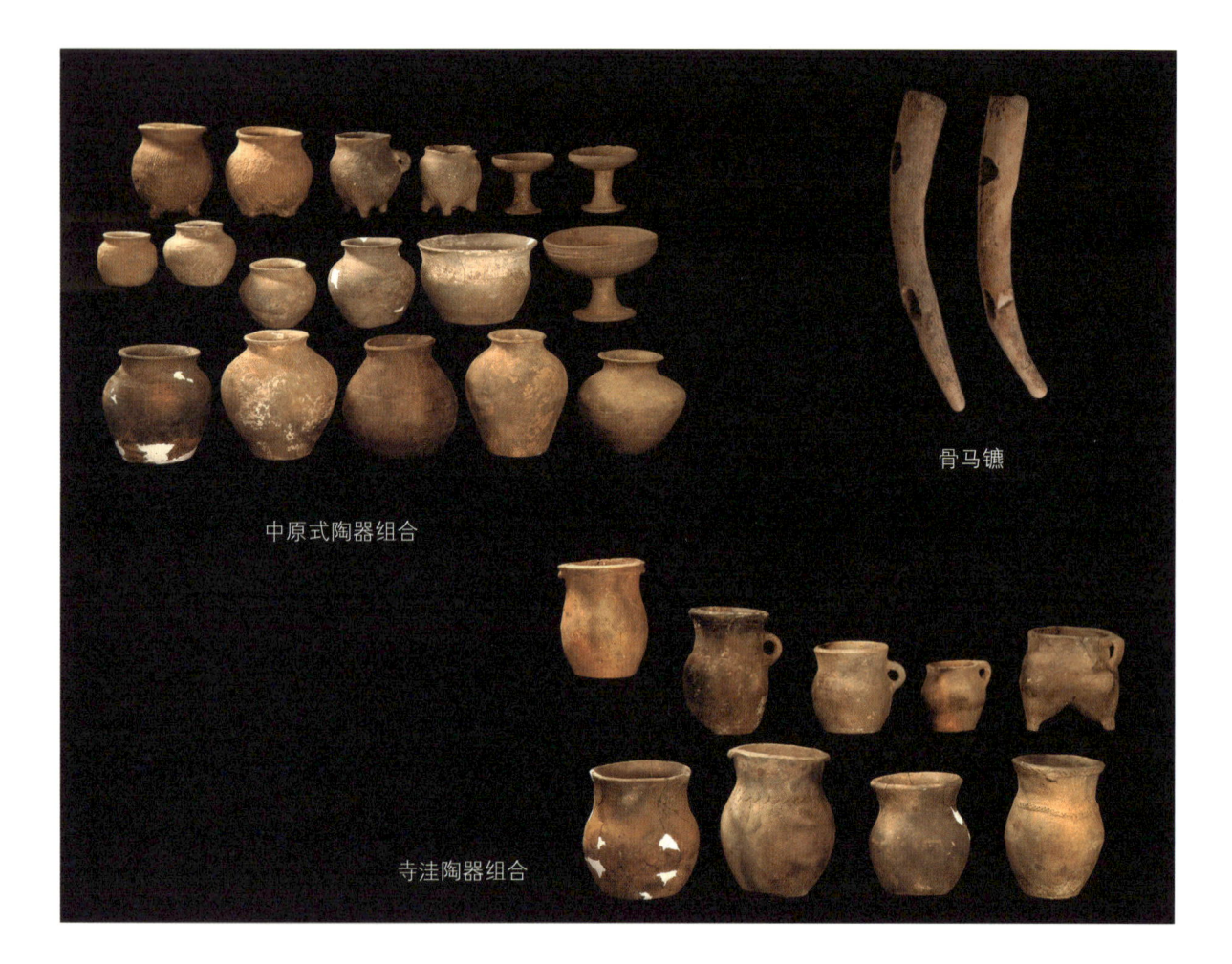

骨马镳

寺洼陶器组合

Zhaitouhe Cemetery, dating back to Warring States Period, was discovered in Zhaitouhe Village, Adang Town, Huangling County, in the locality of Nangoumen Water Conservancy Project in Yan'an City. From April to December in 2011, archaeologists from Shaanxi Provincial Institute of Archaeology carried out comprehensive and systematic excavations in this cemetery, revealing 90 tombs, 2 horse pits and 1 square pit buried with bronze spears. Zhaitouhe Cemetery is the first thoroughly excavated and revealed cemetery of Warring States Period in northern Shaanxi Province. Unearthed potteries, which were confirmed to be of middle and late Warring States Period, have turned out to be an important part of the earthenware sequence that has been established in the district of Yan'an. Preliminarily determined ethnic groups and nationalists of the tomb occupants are new materials for the study of ethnic integration and historical geography.

# 山东沂水县纪王崮春秋墓葬

◎郝导华

纪王崮墓葬位于山东省沂水县城西北约40千米处的"纪王崮"崮顶，隶属泉庄镇，号称"沂蒙七十二崮之首"。现整个山崮已被开发为旅游景区，名"天上王城"。2012年2—7月，山东省文物考古研究院与临沂市文物考古队、沂水县博物馆组成考古队，对墓葬M1进行了抢救性考古发掘。

M1形制较为特殊，墓室与车马坑共凿建于一个岩坑之中。墓葬虽被破坏较为严重，但主墓室部分保存较好。根据残存部分判断，墓圹呈长方形，南部为墓室，北部为车马坑。斜坡墓道位于岩坑东南部，已残，东向，其西部正对内椁室。内椁南、北侧各有一个器物箱，在内椁和器物箱之间及内椁室西侧共发现三个殉人坑，殉人皆有一棺。墓主棺室为重棺，位于内椁之内。在内棺的底部铺有一层厚约6厘米的朱砂。人骨已腐朽，头向东，其他葬式不清。在棺椁以下，发现殉犬一只，但未发现腰坑。车马坑位于墓葬的北侧，破坏较为严重。残存车四辆，每辆车有两匹马驾驭，在2号车内出土有鼎、鬲、敦三件车载青铜礼器，这种现象非常少见。在棺室、器物箱、车马坑及殉人坑中共出土文物近200件，主要包括青铜器、陶器、玉器、海贝、骨器、玛瑙珠、绿松石饰及骨珠等。根据器物形制特点推断，该墓的年代为春秋中晚期。

在M1南部，另发现一座墓葬，编号M2。考古队于2013年9—10月，对二号墓进行了抢救性考古发掘。该墓为岩坑竖穴墓，呈阶梯状倾斜。由墓葬中处处留有施工中的杂乱痕迹等种种迹象推测，二号墓应是一座正在开凿中的大型春秋墓葬，可能由于某种突发事件凿墓过程突然终止。

纪王崮春秋墓墓葬与车马坑规模大、规格高，结构特殊、出土遗物丰富，是山东近年来东周考古最重要的发现之一。墓葬位于易守难攻的崮顶，而且墓室与车马坑凿建在一个岩坑中，是一种全新的类型，丰富了我们对该地区东周贵族埋葬制度的认识，具有十分重要的学术价值。墓内的玉器有的还未雕刻完成，有的发现起稿的痕迹，有的甚至只制成粗坯，这其中的原因不但耐人寻味，还为我们研究当时玉器的制造工艺、佩戴方式及陪葬方式等提供了实物资料。这次考古新发现对研究该地区春秋时期的政治、经济、文化以及工艺技术、墓葬制度，对历史复原、传说印证及考古学与历史学的整合等均具有重要作用和意义。

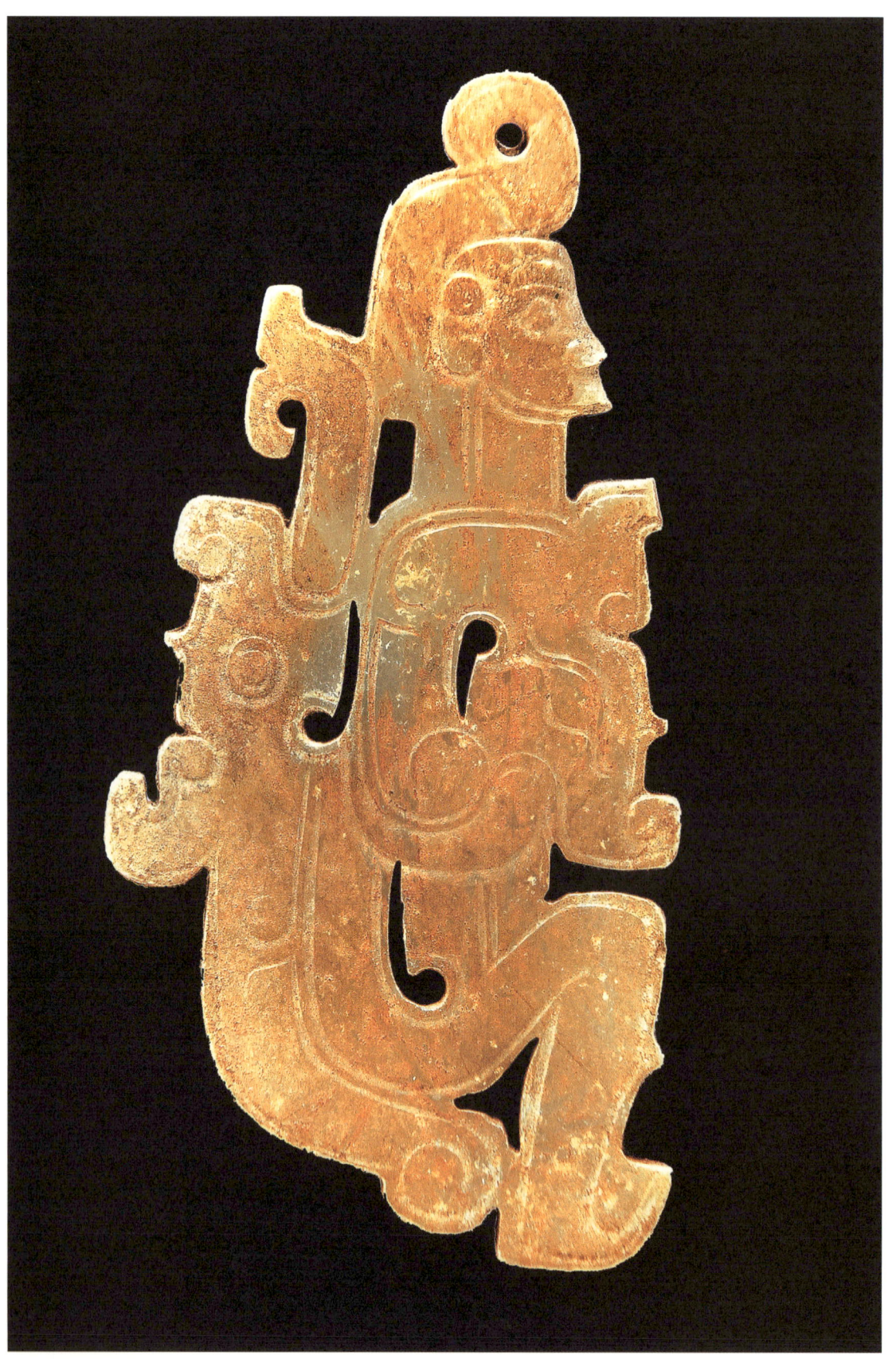

玉人

三代之礼　皇皇者华　333

铜鼎　铜鬲

铜敦

铜壶

铜錞于　铜镈钟　铜钮钟

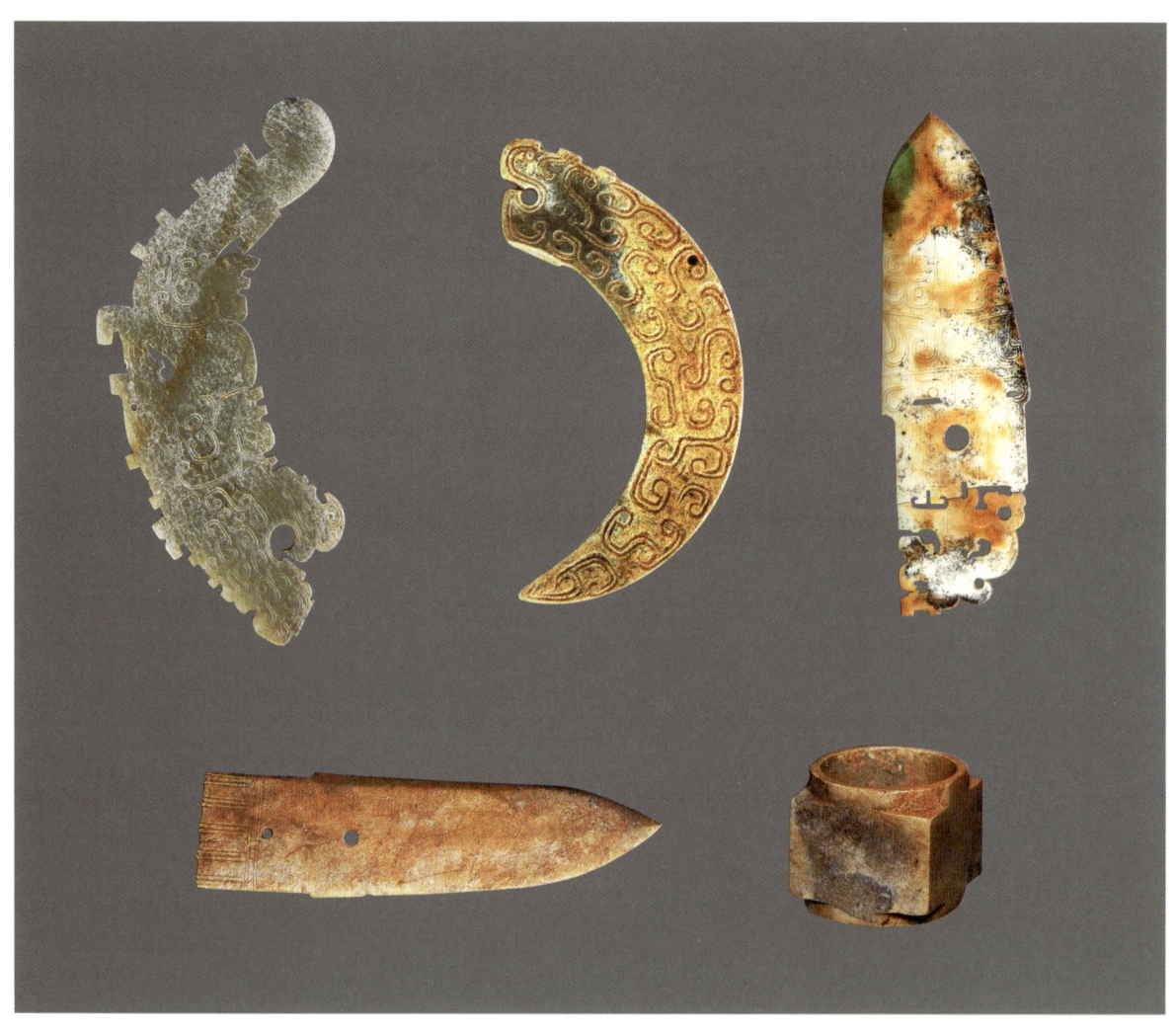

M1出土玉器

Jiwanggu Tombs, dating back to Spring & Autumn Period, are located on the top of a mesa named as Jiwanggu, Quanzhuang Town, about 40 kilometers northwest of Yishui County. From 2012 to 2013, archaeologists from Shandong Provincial Institute of Cultural Relics and Archaeology and other organizations carried out salvage excavations in two tombs here. Tomb M1 was constructed in a special structure, i.e. the coffin chamber and chariot pit were built in the same rock pit. This discovery has enriched our knowledge about aristocratic burial customs back in Middle and Late Spring & Autumn Period in this region. Volumes of antiquities have been unearthed from tomb M1. The construction of tomb M2, which could have been a large-scale one, was suddenly terminated possibly due to some unexpected events. New archaeological findings are of great significance for the study of regional politics, economics, culture, craftsmanship, techniques and burial customs. They also play an important role in restoring history, confirming legends, integrating Archaeology and History, etc.

# 安徽六安市白鹭洲战国墓

◎ 秦让平

2011年3月至4月，安徽省文物考古研究所与六安市文物局对位于六安市城东白鹭洲的两座战国墓葬进行了抢救性发掘。两座墓葬保存情况完好，葬具结构完整，随葬品丰富，人骨保存较好，为安徽地区战国晚期楚文化的研究提供了珍贵的资料。两座墓葬位于白鹭洲中心地带的岗垄上，南北并列，相距10米。

两墓均为带斜坡墓道的"甲"字形土坑木椁墓，墓道位于墓室东侧。M566葬具由外藏室、椁室、三重棺室组成。椁室高于外藏室，椁室顶部盖有南北向的横板，有三重棺。随葬器物主要放置于外藏室中，内棺可见一部分贴身玉器随葬。M585葬具由外藏室、椁室及棺室组成。外藏室分北、东、南、西四个，边上每隔一段有立柱承托横梁，横梁上盖有望板。内棺盖板上方覆盖菱形纹饰的纺织物。除中棺盖板及两侧站板外弧之外，椁室及外棺、内棺均为长方形盒状。随葬品放置于四周的外藏室内。

M566棺内人骨保存较为完整，头部及身上有纺织物覆盖，均已腐烂。头发保存完好，发髻形态可辨。牙齿整齐，略呈黑色。M585内棺内人骨较为散乱，经后期整理拼对后发现躯干骨骼基本完整，未发现头骨及其残片。

两墓共出土文物241件（套），包括铜器、陶器、漆木器、玉器及角器等。随葬器物大多位于外藏室内，仅M566内棺出土一组玉器，M585内棺无任何随葬品。

据史书记载，六安在春秋中期并入楚国版图，直至战国末期一直处于楚国统治之下。随着楚国向东扩张，楚文化也从江汉平原传至江淮之地。两墓所出器物及组合形式具有典型的楚式风格，应当为战国时期六安地区有代表性的楚墓。根据出土器物特征，可推测两墓的年代相近，当属战国晚期。

两墓的葬具均使用一椁三重棺，其墓主身份应不低于大夫级。两墓之间的关系以及在整个墓地中所处的地位有待进一步研究和探讨。两墓的发现也为研究楚国入主江淮之后历史和文化的变迁提供了新的资料。

龙形玉佩

铜灯　　　　　六山纹镜

三代之礼　皇皇者华　337

铜匜

铜鼎　　　　　　　　　　铜罍

陶器

M566盖板揭去后（上西下东）

From March to April in 2011, archaeologists from Anhui Provincial Institute of Cultural Relics and Archaeology and other organizations conducted salvage excavations in two tombs dating back to Warring States Period in Bailuzhou, in the eastern part of Lu'an City. Unearthed antiquities indicate that both tombs are almost of the same age. In both tombs, there is a triple-layered inner coffin in an outer coffin. It can be inferred that the occupants should rank higher than Dafu. Sets of antiquities unearthed from the tombs are all in typical Chu style. As representatives of tombs of Chu style dating from Warring States Period in Lu'an district, both tombs have provided new materials for the study of the history and culture changes after Chu State became in charge of Yangtze-Huaihe River Region.

# 山东济南市梁二村战国墓

◎刘秀玲 房 振 郭俊峰 王惠明

为配合山东省济南市新东站片区安置房建设工程，济南市考古研究所于2016年8月至2017年7月对历城区梁二村发现的三座战国墓和两座春秋时期的木构水井进行了抢救性发掘。

M1形制为"甲"字形竖穴土坑积石木椁墓。墓室最下层填土之上的东南、西南角各有一只殉狗。椁室内四周以大型石块垒砌，石块间填以卵石和蚌壳。前期征缴出土器物40余件（组），多已残损，初步统计相对完整的有青铜镈钟、钮钟、句鑃、盖豆、罍、镜，另有盒形、罐形明器、铜器残片若干。M2位于M1西侧约150米，亦为竖穴土坑积石木椁墓，仅存底部椁室部分。随葬品8件，均置于椁内棺外东、西两侧，包括铜镈、铜戈、骨雕、圆形铜盒、铜镜、铜剑。另于北部卵石中发现铁锛1件。M3位于M1东侧约15米，与M1形制大体一致。由于早期盗扰破坏，棺椁、人骨等均被扰乱无存，残存木椁灰痕。随葬品发现很少，仅在盗洞内发现铜盖弓帽、铺首、熨斗等小器物十余件。M1、M3两墓规模较大，墓壁台阶内收，刷有白灰层，二层台宽大，椁室以大石块垒砌、卵石填缝，这些都是战国时期齐国贵族墓的典型特征。另据出土器物初步推测这三座墓的年代为战国中期偏晚。

另外，在M1发掘过程中，发现其东壁和北侧各打破一座水井。两井形制一致，上部均被破坏，土圹平面近椭圆形，内部保存有较为完整的木构井框，由略经加工的木材层层搭叠而成，两木相交处砍有凹槽。根据出土器物形制及碳14测年，两座水井的年代为春秋中早期。

出土器物中，句鑃、圭形铜片、璧形铜环这三种器物在山东地区发现较少。句鑃作为单独乐器，是吴越地区的典型器类，具有很强的地域性，时代多为春秋时期。此次该器物组合的发现也有利于对齐文化与吴越文化交流的研究。

梁二村战国墓虽被严重破坏，但结构相对完整、随葬品较为丰富。M1、M3是济南乃至山东地区近年来发现的规模最大的战国墓，根据墓葬形制和出土器物推测，两墓主人当为大夫一级贵族，其或为夫妻并穴合葬。M2为士一级贵族，与M1、M3或属同一家族。此次发掘为研究齐国葬俗、齐国边邑、齐文化变迁、齐国历史等提供了重要资料。保存相对完整的春秋木构水井在山东地区也较为罕见，对研究当地的环境变迁、聚落形态等有重要意义。

M3（上东下西）

铜熨斗

木构水井

M1墓道西壁北端填土台阶（北向南）

铜剑

玉瑗

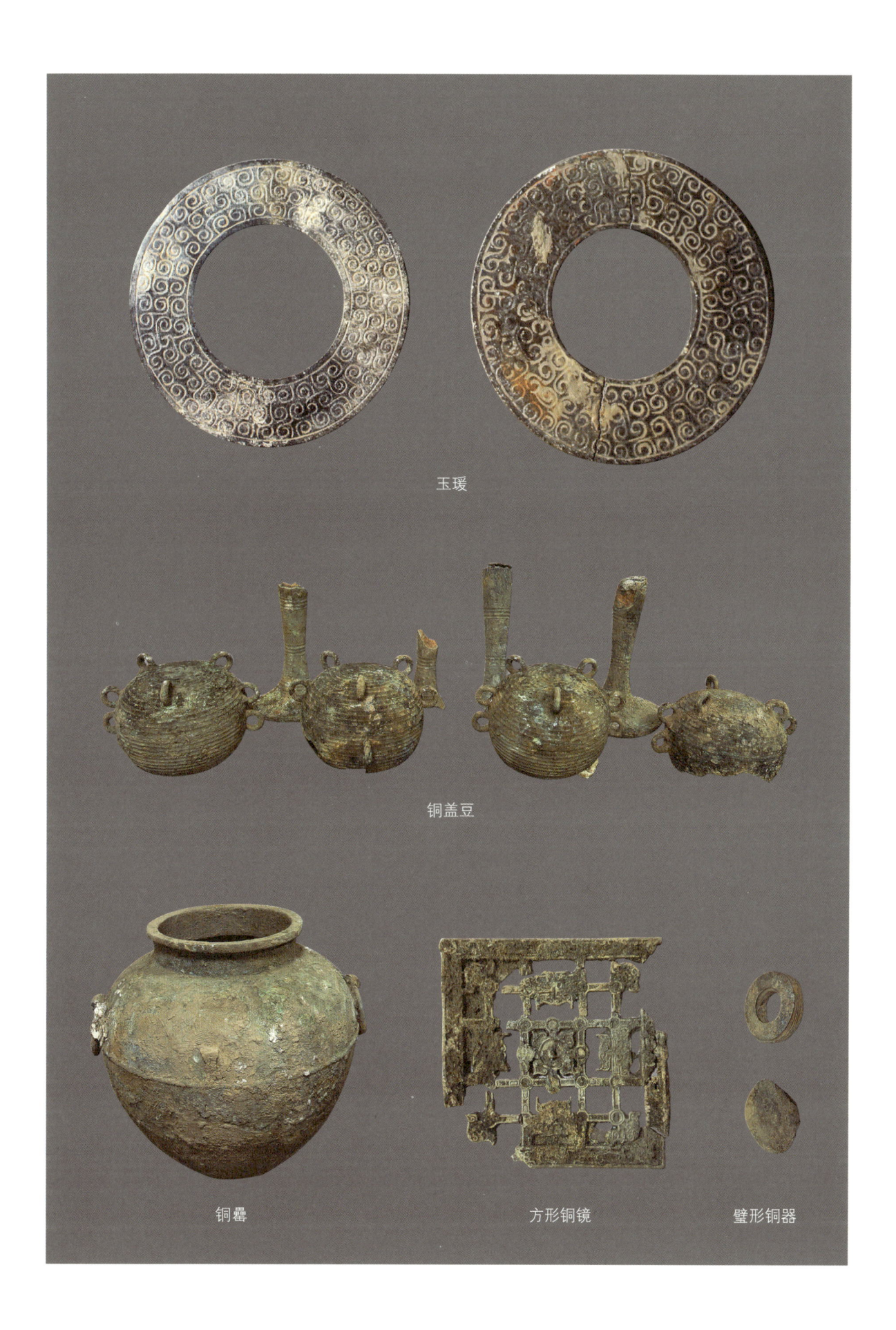

铜盖豆

铜罍　　　　　方形铜镜　　　璧形铜器

钮钟

镈钟　　　　　　　　　　　　　　　石磬

Three tombs of the Warring States Period and two wood-structured wells of Zhou Dynasty were discovered in Liang'er Village, Licheng District, Jinan City. From 2016 to 2017, archaeologists from Jinan Institute of Archaeology conducted salvage excavations on the above sites. Tomb M1 and tomb M3 are the largest tombs of the Warring States Period that have been discovered in Jinan and even in Shandong Province in recent years. According to tomb structure and unearthed objects, the occupants of both tombs should be nobles ranking as Dafu. Both tombs might be joint burial tombs. The occupant buried in tomb M2, a noble ranking as Shi, and the occupants of tomb M1 and tomb M3 might from the same family. Excavations carried out this time have provided important materials for the study of burial customs, border cities, cultural changes, history and other aspects of Qi State. Relatively well-preserved wood-structured wells of Spring & Autumn Period which are rare even in Shandong Province are of great significance for the study of local environmental changes.

# 河南信阳市城阳城址八号墓

◎武志江

城阳城址八号墓位于河南省信阳市平桥区城阳城址保护区。从20世纪50年代起，该地区陆续发掘了8座大型楚墓，包括著名的长台关一号墓、二号墓以及七号墓。八号墓位于七号墓南部20米，2015年8月至2016年2月，河南省文物考古研究院对其进行发掘。

八号墓平面呈"甲"字形，坐西向东，由墓道、墓室两部分组成。墓室平面大致呈方形，自上而下呈阶梯状逐层内收，共发现5级台阶。椁室平面呈长方形，由主室、前室、南侧室、北侧室以及北后室、中后室、南后室组成。前室和南、北侧室被盗严重，主室和后室保存完好。椁板上部发现覆盖物，目前大致可确定有两层：上层为成束的竹叶，下层为芦苇茎秆编织的席子。椁室与墓壁之间用成束的植物填充。

主室居中，有两层盖板，之下为一椁二棺。外棺盖板上部为弧形，北部外侧发现织物（多朽），盖板下部较平，内侧髹朱漆。内棺盖板平，表面有红色彩绘，内侧髹朱漆。墓主人头向东，头部及全身被织物敷裹，织物纹样依稀可辨。南后室陶壶和陶鬲可确定为战国中期楚文化遗存，与七号墓的年代相当。其他诸如彩色髹漆竹席、长柄矛、耳杯、案、几等漆木器十分精美。特别是墓主人全身敷裹的织物，是信阳地区乃至河南省战国时期楚墓的首次发现。在全国楚文化墓葬中，这样完整织物的发现也十分罕见。

从墓葬形制来说，八号墓为大型土坑竖穴木椁墓，主室为一椁二棺，显示出墓主人生前具有较高的级别。这一点与该区域（西南岗墓葬区）发现的战国时期高等级楚墓基本一致。墓葬外围发现有排列整齐的圆形夯土圈，在该地区之前的墓葬考古发掘中没有发现过，为研究当时的筑墓活动或者祭祀行为提供了参考。随葬品摆放有序，各室器物存在明显的功能区别，如南室主要是生活起居用品，北室则为征战出行用品，前室则多为代表墓主人身份等级的仿铜陶礼器和耳杯。根据出土器物形态与出土木炭测年结果推测八号墓的年代应为战国中期晚段。八号墓出土文物精美，以漆木器最具代表性，如彩色髹漆竹席、长柄矛、耳杯、案、几等。此外，铜剑、车軎与车辖、玉璧等也非常有代表性，为研究战国时期楚国手工业发展提供了重要的考古材料。

八号墓南侧室

三代之礼　皇皇者华　345

南侧室竹席

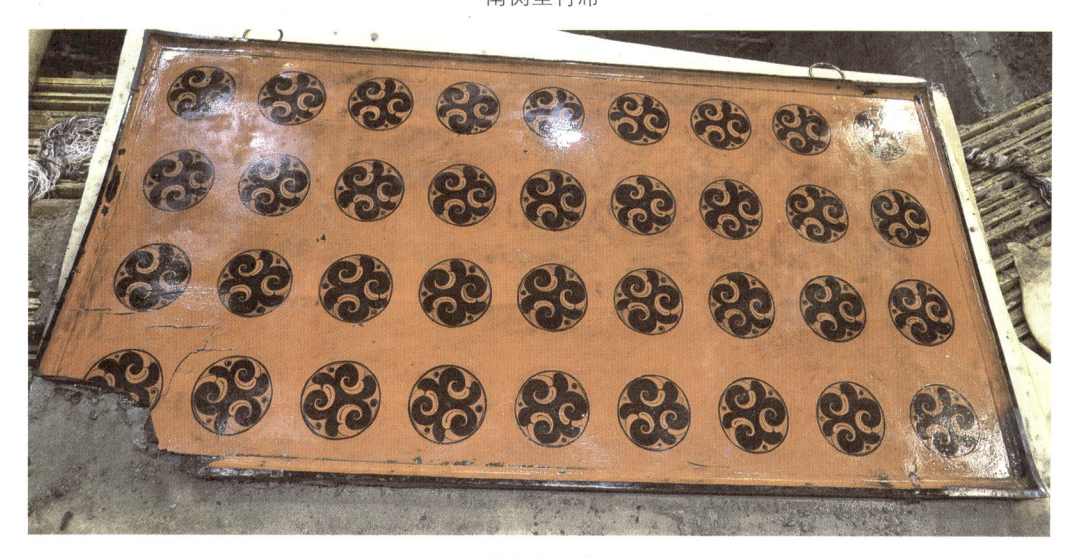

前室漆木案

前室耳杯 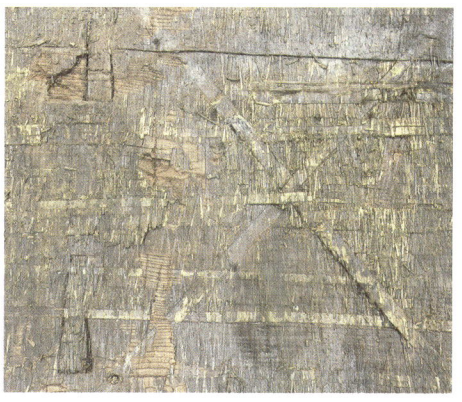　　　　　　　　　椁板覆席

八号墓主室（上东南下西北）

Tomb No. 8 of Chengyang City Site is located in the Preservation Area of Chengyang City Site, Pingqiao District, Xinyang City, Henan Province. Eight large-scale tombs of Chu State, including the well-known Changtaiguan Tomb No. 1, Tomb No. 2 and Tomb No. 7, have been successively excavated in this area since the 1950s. Tomb No. 8 is 20 meters south of Tomb No. 7. From 2015 to 2016, archaeologists from Henan Institute of Cultural Relics and Archaeology carried out excavations in Tomb No. 8. According to the unearthed objects, this tomb should be one of Chu Culture dating back to middle Warring States Period and it is as old as Tomb No. 7. The main coffin chamber is well preserved and there is a double-layered inner coffin inside a double-layered outer coffin. The cover of the outer coffin is found covered with fabrics, most of which are rotten now. There are red-colored paintings on the cover of the inner coffin. The tomb occupant's head points to the east and the head and entire body are covered with fabrics, whose patterns are still visible. Such fabrics are the first ones that have been discovered in tombs of Chu State of Warring States Period in Xinyang District and even in Henan Province.

# 安徽宁国市灰山土墩墓群

◎ 王　峰

灰山土墩墓群位于安徽省宁国市港口镇灰山村，该地位于皖南山区北麓向沿江平原过渡的丘陵地带。土墩墓群位于一处高山脚下相对平缓的山冈上，且多数土墩位于冈脊上。由于植被覆盖茂密，整个土墩墓群的数量及分布情况尚不明确。2012年5—11月，因宁国港口生态工业园平整土地，安徽省文物考古研究所对其中的部分土墩墓进行了抢救性发掘，共发掘土墩36个。

每一个土墩的外观都近似汉墓封土，大小不一，除3个可能因为晚期破坏严重没有发现单体墓葬外，其余33个土墩内共发现单体墓葬85座。有一墩一墓和一墩多墓两类，一墩多墓的往往为2～3个单体墓，一墩内有4个单体墓以上的土墩仅8个，最多的为一墩七墓。土墩内单体墓葬往往普遍有较浅的长方形墓坑，多数墓坑从平面上难以判断，往往是发现器物后再仔细判断，发现墓坑内的填土确实与其外的堆土有细微的区别。因此推测部分浅坑单体墓在埋葬时或许并没有挖坑，只是在下葬过程中对墓葬边缘区域进行堆土和踩踏，由于葬具等有机物的腐烂，才形成单体墓坑内外土质土色的细微差别。这种情况其实与所谓的"平地掩埋"类似。从发掘结果看，一墩多墓的形成过程，往往是先有一个单体墓的土墩后，在这个土墩的边缘区域再次下葬，然后叠加封土，形成所谓的"向心式"布局。随着单体墓葬的增多，土墩也随之增大。

在其中5个土墩中央位置分布的5座单体墓葬中，发现有用石块铺底的情况，或称棺床。5个土墩中一墩一墓1座，一墩多墓4座。而有石棺床的单体墓的随葬品数量往往多于同一墩内的其他墓葬，或有某种身份差别。这5座石棺床的单体墓中，D6M4还在石棺床墓坑周边发现9个柱洞环绕一周，柱洞开口界面与石棺床相当，显示该墓在形成之初或许有临时性的墓上建筑。

多数单体墓葬有随葬品，少则1件，多则10件左右，极少数无随葬品，表明个体之间等级差别不大。比较江浙地区周代土墩墓出土同类器物的器形、纹饰，大致判断宁国灰山土墩墓群的年代为西周—春秋时期。安徽境内的土墩墓多发现于长江以南的宣城、广德、南陵、繁昌地区，一般认为该地区的土墩墓为南方吴文化遗存。此次宁国灰山发现的土墩墓群，与南陵地区一样，均位于皖南山区北麓向沿江平原过渡的丘陵地带。南陵、宁国一线再往南，历史上是人口稀少的大山地区。因此南陵、宁国一线，或可认为是吴文化的西部边陲。

D33M1～M4在土墩中的位置

D6M2

夹砂红陶鼎

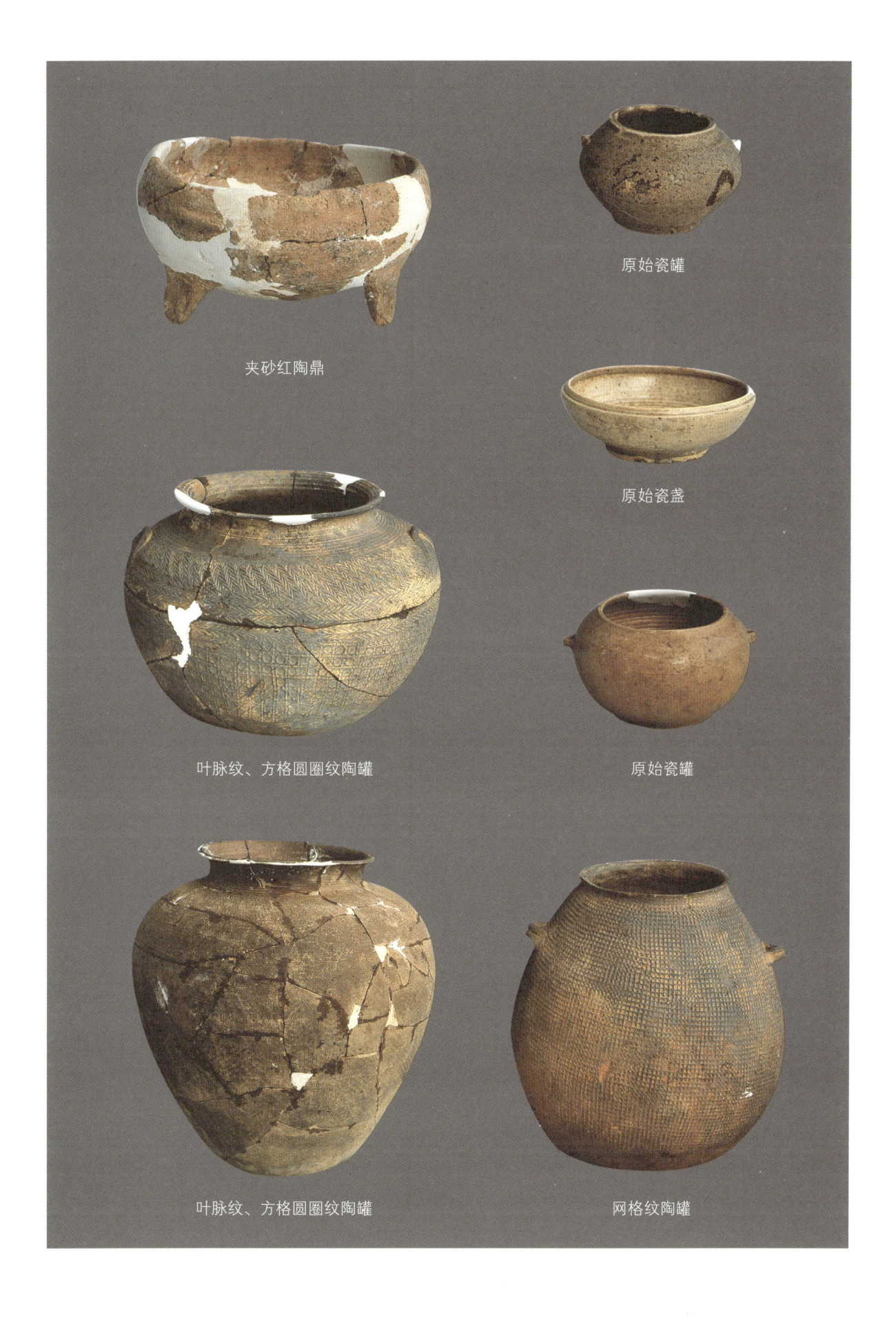

原始瓷罐

原始瓷盏

叶脉纹、方格圆圈纹陶罐

原始瓷罐

叶脉纹、方格圆圈纹陶罐

网格纹陶罐

D6M4周围柱洞　　　　　　　　　　　　D2M3石棺床

Huishan Mound Tombs are located in Huishan Village, Gangkou Town, Ningguo City, Anhui Province. From May to November in 2012, archaeologists from Anhui Provincial Institute of Cultural Relics and Archaeology carried out salvage excavations in some of these mound tombs. In total, 36 mounds were excavated. In three of the excavated mounds, there was no single tomb because of possible later serious damages. A total number of 85 tombs were discovered from the remaining 33 excavated mounds. They could be classified into two burial types: one tomb in a mound and multiple tombs in a mound. In one mound, as many as seven tombs were discovered. Funerary objects, mainly impressed hard potteries and pristine porcelain, were unearthed from most mounds that contained a single tomb. Very few of this kind of tomb was buried with no funerary objects. It is indicated that hierarchical differentiation among the individuals buried in the tombs was not that huge. It has been preliminarily determined that Huishan Mound Tombs in Ningguo City, as remnants of Wu Culture in the South, could be dated back to the epoch from Western Zhou to Spring & Autumn Period.

# 山西侯马市虒祁遗址东周祭祀坑

◎王金平　段双龙

　　虒祁遗址位于山西省侯马市高村乡虒祁村西北约1.5千米处，北距台神古城约2千米，地处浍河北岸。遗址从东至西由夯土建筑、墓地、祭祀遗迹三部分组成。1996年8月至2012年8月，山西省考古研究所先后对该遗址进行了八次大规模的科学发掘，为研究晋都新田废弃前后的文化发展提供了极为珍贵的资料。2014年9月到2015年7月间，为配合侯马市冶炼厂新月小区建设，山西省考古研究所侯马工作站对建设区域内的祭祀坑和墓葬进行了科学发掘。本次发掘系虒祁遗址第九次发掘。

　　本次发掘分南北两区进行发掘，共清理祭祀坑822座，墓葬37座，其中西汉墓6座，东汉墓2座，北魏墓4座，宋金墓25座。822座祭祀坑多为长方形竖穴土坑，方向多为南北向或稍偏东西，也有个别东西向者。在部分坑壁的南北两壁发现有脚窝以及工具修整的痕迹。在南区祭祀坑中多发现有壁龛，一般开口于祭祀坑的北壁底部中央，在壁龛内多置有玉石器1至2件。坑内填土较疏松，未经夯打。祭祀坑底部多数不平整，部分发现有二层台。埋牲种类有牛（89例）、羊（275例），另有无牲坑458座，未发现马。葬式有侧卧、仰卧、俯卧、蹲坐几种，多呈四蹄捆绑状。在该祭祀地点发掘的祭祀坑中发现了大量的玉石器、少量陶器，未发现铜器。玉器上面多数有切割痕迹，其中3件玉片上发现有墨书的字迹。南北两区祭祀坑特征明显，北区多长方形圆角形坑，少见或不见壁龛，出土器物成形者较多；南区则多长方形方角形坑，多见壁龛，出土器物薄如纸片，且多数不成形。

　　从20世纪50年代开始，在侯马晋都新田遗址范围内相继发现煤灰制品厂、呈王路、省建一公司机运站、省水文二队、西南张、虒祁村、热力公司、西高、秦村、公路枢纽货运中心10处春秋晚期至战国早期的祭祀和盟誓遗存，它们分布在晋都的东、南、西三个方位，本次发掘位于遗址西部。近年来关于该地区祭祀地点的性质出现了新的观点，本次822座祭祀坑的科学发掘，为进一步确定祭祀坑的年代、性质，揭示和研究晋都的规制和宗教礼仪制度提供了新的资料。

玉饰

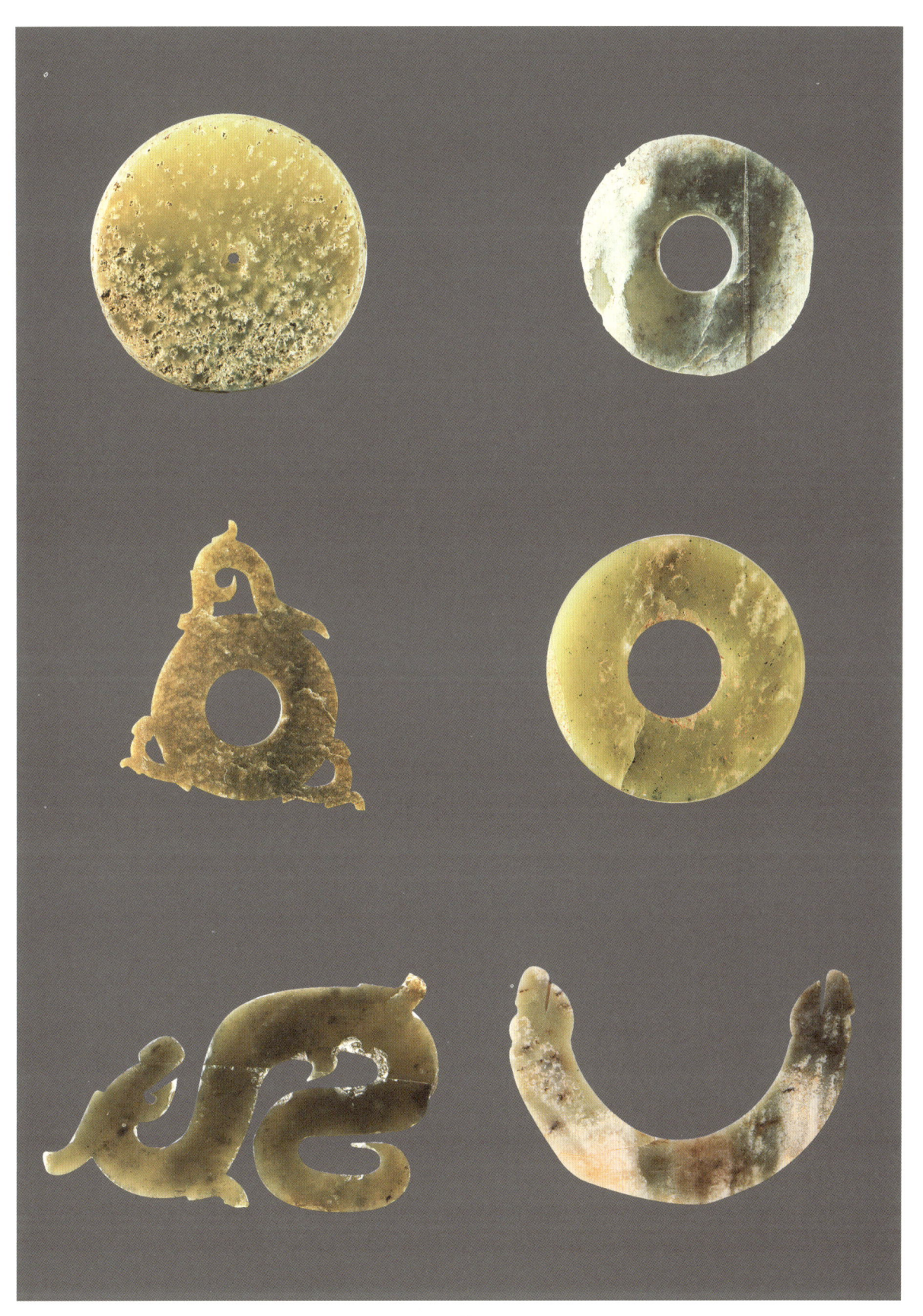

玉饰

祭祀坑（均为上东下西）

Siqi Site is located approximately 1.5 kilometers northwest of Siqi Village, Gaocun Township, Houma City, Shanxi Province. From 2014 to 2015, archaeologists from Shanxi Provincial Institute of Archaeology and based in Houma City carried out scientific excavations in sacrificial pits and tombs in Xinyue Community. Some important remains were relocated for protection and preservation. It was the ninth excavation of Siqi Site. In total, 822 sacrificial pits, 37 tombs, several kilns, rammed earthen wall bases and bronze casting sites were unearthed. They date back to the period from late Spring & Autumn Period to Han Dynasty. Excavation conducted in the sacrificial pit has provided new materials to further determination of the age and features of sacrificial pits in the locality of Xintian Site, which used to be the capital of Jin State, in Houma City. These new materials also benefit the revelation and study of regulations and religious etiquette system used in the capital of Jin State.

# 河北黄骅市郛堤城瓮棺葬

◎雷建红　马小飞

瓮棺葬群位于河北省黄骅市主城区北部。2016年6月底至10月初，河北省文物研究所和黄骅市博物馆共同组队，对该处瓮棺葬群进行大面积抢救性发掘，共计发现战国至汉代时期瓮棺葬113座，另发现灰坑10余个。发现的113座瓮棺葬，排列无规律，但相互之间无叠压打破关系，除个别被施工破坏外，大部分墓葬保存比较完整。用作瓮棺的陶器，最常见的有红陶釜、盆、筒形瓮、筒形器，次之为小口瓮或罐、板瓦、钵，极少量为甑、陶管，另外发现个别轮盘及残陶器等。所用的陶器既有日常生活实用器，大多数器物有使用痕迹，也有专门烧制用作葬具的陶容器，如筒形瓮、筒形器，发现的数量还比较多。

按墓葬的葬具材料，可将其分为瓮棺葬和砖瓦棺葬，包括瓮棺葬106座、砖瓦棺葬7座，其中砖瓦棺2座、砖棺3座、瓦棺2座。葬具组合方式达20多种，以两器组合和三器组合最多见，也有少数四器组合，未见单器瓮棺。此处发现的113座墓葬，不仅有儿童瓮棺葬，还发现一批成人瓮棺葬，两者各有其分布的区域，说明有分组现象。成人瓮棺人骨相对保存较好，儿童瓮棺人骨保存很差。所有已清理的墓葬中均未发现随葬品。

从层位关系及陶制形制来看，推测这批瓮棺葬的年代为战国中晚期到西汉时期。瓮棺葬是以陶容器作为葬具的一种特殊埋葬形式，起源于新石器时代，战国秦汉时期较为流行，此后不同时期和地区比较少见。战国秦汉时期的瓮棺葬主要集中发现在中国北方尤其是环渤海地区，不仅数量多而且分布密集。近年来，战国秦汉时期的瓮棺葬在环渤海各地又有不少新发现，本次黄骅郛堤城发现的113座瓮棺葬，规模庞大，类型多样，分布密集，年代清楚，是战国秦汉时期最具代表性的瓮棺葬墓地之一。除儿童瓮棺葬外还有一批成人瓮棺葬，具有明显的地方特色，这对研究当地两千多年前的丧葬习俗极为重要。瓮棺葬群和郛堤城址并存发现，可以更全面地从"生"和"死"两个方面研究当地古代社会状况，也证明了在战国末年，最晚到西汉初年，汉王朝对这个地方已经进行有效统治和管理开发。战国后期随着燕文化东渐，瓮棺葬这一埋葬习俗传播到东北地区和东亚地区，产生了深刻的影响，郛堤城瓮棺葬正是这种丧葬文化传播带上的重要一环。

砖瓦葬

瓦棺葬

盆、筒形器、筒形器、盆组合

盆、筒形器、筒形器、瓮组合

钵、陶管、釜组合 　　　　　　　　　　　盆、罐组合

罐、筒形器、盘组合 　　　　　　　　　　釜、罐组合

盆、筒形器、釜组合 　　　　　　　　　　盆、盆组合

瓮、瓮、瓮组合 　　　　　　　　　　　　盆、釜组合

瓮棺葬人骨（上西下东）

Fudicheng Urn Tombs are located in the north of the downtown area of Huanghua City, Hebei Province. The tombs are near Fudicheng Site, one of the Historical and Cultural Monuments under Provincial Protection in Hebei Province. From June to October in 2016, archaeologists from Hebei Provincial Institute of Cultural Relics and other organizations carried out large-scale salvage excavations in Fudicheng Urn Tombs. The excavated area was approximately 1200 square meters. 106 urn tombs and 7 brick-and-tile-chambered tombs dating back to the epoch from Warring States Period to Han Dynasty were discovered. Besides, more than 10 ash pits were revealed. Large in scale, diverse in type, densely distributed and age clearly determined, Fudicheng Urn Tombs have formed the most representative cemetery buried with funerary urns dating back to the era from Warring States Period to Han Dynasty. Apart from funerary urns for children, there were funerary urns for adults, with obvious local features. Fudicheng Urn Tombs also reflect cultural diffusion and exchanges with the eastward spread of Yan Culture during the late Warring States Period.

# 龟卜筮占　吉金作钟

## 安徽省巢湖市城圩商周遗址

◎ 姚　洁

　　城圩遗址位于巢湖市西北15千米的夏阁镇成子圩村，为台地墩形遗址。2016年5月至2017年4月，为配合商合杭高铁建设，安徽省文物考古研究所对该遗址展开了勘探和发掘工作，出土陶器、玉器、石器、骨器、甲骨、铜器等标本800多件，发现遗迹包括灰坑、作坊遗存、建筑使用堆积、墓葬等。

　　另外，此次发掘共出土龟甲594件，其中有人工痕迹的龟甲、鹿角和骨器共117件，钻、凿、灼兼施的卜甲、卜骨共64件。出土龟甲的上部地层均伴生大量的螺壳、蚌壳。龟甲分布以遗址边缘分布较多，中心地带略少。

　　城圩遗址龟甲埋藏密集度之大在南方地区是比较罕见的，其多样的钻凿方式是值得注意的。这些甲骨的发现为研究该区域考古学文化特征、占卜制度以及与中原地区商周时期的联系等提供了新资料。凌家滩遗址曾发现1枚玉龟，由背甲和腹甲两部分组成，合成整龟后形成一个空腹。在城圩遗址不仅发现了大块完整的腹甲，在同一堆积单位也发现了相应的背甲，是天然宇宙模型还是与原始先民的占卜习俗有关值得思考。该遗址卜骨、卜甲特殊的埋藏方式和分布特点改变了学术界原先一致认为的卜骨和卜甲不同坑，以及南方多用龟卜、北方多用骨卜的观点，也为中国甲骨学研究提供了一个全新的思路。

　　初步判断该遗址上限应不晚于二里岗上层，可能到早商时期，且根据目前该遗址出土资料和周边调查情况初步认为，该遗址可能为一处聚落内负责祭祀、制骨等活动的核心功能区。

　　该遗址中商、晚商、西周文化遗存的发掘丰富和完善了环巢湖地区商周时期考古学分期体系和文化谱系。城圩遗址的发现，其出土资料与活跃于商周之际的古巢国是否存在联系是值得我们去研究探讨的。巢湖流域文化的延续性、独特性、交融性体现了先秦时期巢湖文化是一个独具个性的地方文化谱系，城圩遗址的发现，使我们目前对该地区先秦文化有了突破性的认识。基于该遗址出土的丰富而系统的考古资料，可望初步建立起淮河以南环巢湖流域先秦时期考古学文化时空框架及文化谱系，对建立安徽省从二里岗时期到西周时期的时间框架也是不可或缺的重要环节。

墓葬 灰坑

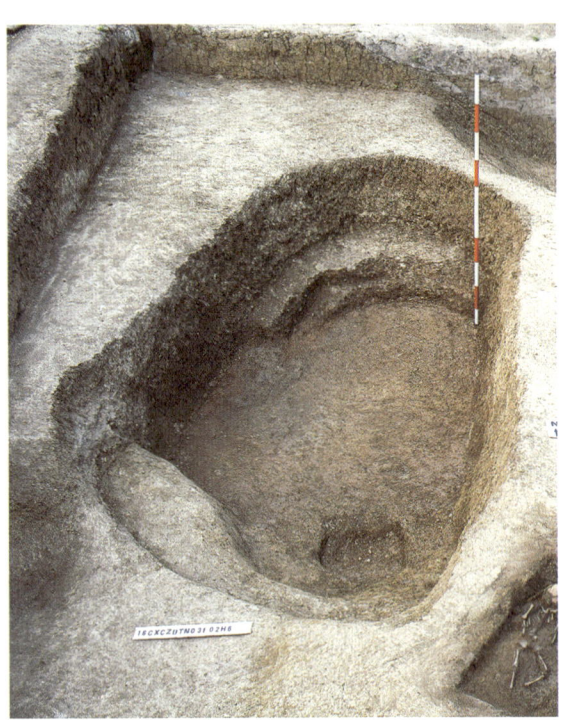

柱洞、红烧土堆积

出土骨器标本

出土石器标本

出土铜器及生产工具标本

玉器　　　　　　　　　　　　　　卜骨

卜甲

Chengwei Site is in Chengziwei Village, Xiage Town, 15 kilometers northwest of Chaohu City. From 2016 to 2017, archaeologists from Anhui Provincial Institute of Cultural Relics and Archaeology carried out archaeological reconnaissances and excavations on the site. It has been preliminarily determined that Chengwei Site is as old as the uppermost layer of Erligang Site, possibly dating back to early Shang Dynasty. In total, 594 pieces of tortoise shells have been unearthed from Chengwei Site. 117 pieces of tortoise shells, antlers and bone implements are with artificial marks. They are new materials for the study of regional cultural features, divination system, regimes and liaison on the Central Plains in Shang and Zhou dynasties. According to remains and relics that have been unearthed from the site and investigations carried out in the surrounding area, it has been preliminarily determined that Chengwei Site might be a core functional zone for ritual ceremonies, bone-implement making and other activities inside a settlement.

# 山西闻喜县千金耙夏商矿冶遗址

◎ 李 刚　南普恒

自古至今，中条山脉一直是中国重要的铜矿产地之一，而邻近中条山的临汾盆地、运城盆地及黄河中游地区分布有诸多较大规模的青铜文化遗址，其铜矿来源与早期青铜文化起源密切相关。

闻喜千金耙遗址是"中条山地古代矿冶遗址遥感考古调查与研究"项目发现的一处重要的夏商时期采冶遗址。2011年9月至2012年8月，中国国家博物馆和山西省考古研究所组成联合考古队对其进行了抢救性考古发掘，两次发掘面积共约400平方米，清理采矿竖井、斜井、平巷、灶、灰坑、炭窑等遗迹若干，出土亚腰形石锤、石臼、石刀等石器200余件，以及炉壁残块、炼渣、矿石、炭屑等与采矿及冶炼相关的标本若干。发现矿井巷遗迹16处，部分井巷的接续关系因部分山体被取土毁坏，已无法判断。其中较为重要的是仅见早期遗物的J2和出土采矿工具的H26。

千金耙遗址坐落于富含高放射性成因铅的铜矿体之上，其含铅矿物的铅同位素比值与部分含此种特殊铅的夏商时期青铜器相近，出土的陶器残片与东下冯及郑州商城遗址的陶器特征类同，并与此处的采矿工具伴出。该遗址的发现初次为含高放射性成因铅的早期青铜器找到了一处原料产地，为中条山作为夏、商早期青铜原料产地之一的立论提供了考古学和地球化学的双重证据。遗址内发现的双亚腰、三亚腰石锤和石钎是国内首次发现的古代矿业工具，为研究欧亚大陆早期铜矿采冶技术的交流互动提供了新的资料。

环中条山铜矿带的运城盆地、临汾盆地及黄河中游地区分布着诸多夏商时期的青铜文化遗址，近年来在中条山北麓地带的新石器时代遗址中也发现有含铜氧化物。可见，中条山铜矿带与黄河中下游流域青铜文化的起源和发展具有密切的联系。从千金耙遗址的发掘及闻喜、垣曲等地区的考古调查可知，自夏商时期，历经周秦汉唐，乃至近现代，中条山的铜矿生产只有小间歇，而无长时间停顿。

千金耙遗址临近闻垣路，其向东不足10千米可至流经垣曲盆地的亳清河，借水路、陆路皆可达垣曲商城，再沿黄河而下极为便利。向西经横榆可达白家滩的汤王山，向西偏北可经酒务头、河底到达闻喜，由河底向西南不足9千米即东下冯商城。运城盐池向南出中条山则有平陆前庄遗址，亦可能是商前期的军事要塞。中条山断裂带以西至运城盐池，有着极为重要的矿产资源，这一区域在商代前期应已处于商人的严密控制之下。

南北向排列的四座木炭窑（上南下北）

H26

千金耙遗址 I 区部分遗迹（上北下南）

亚腰形石锤、石钎、石坠

素面锥形鬲足　　　　亚腰形石锤　　　　铁钎

Wenxi Qianjinba Site used to be a place of mining and smelting. The site is located in Yupo Village, Shimen Township, Wenxi County, Yuncheng City, Shanxi Province. From 2011 to 2012, a joint team consisting of archaeologists from National Museum of China and the Shanxi Provincial Institute of Archaeology conducted salvage excavations on the site. Excavated remains included mining shafts, inclined shafts, gateways, stoves, ash pits and charcoal kilns. Qianjinba Site is the very first raw material source that has been ever found for the early bronzes containing high-radioactive lead. This fact is seen as evidence proving the argument that Zhongtiao Mountains were the provenance of raw materials for some early bronzes dating back to Xia Dynasty and Shang Dynasty. Stone borers and stone hammers which with one groove or two grooves are the first ancient mining tools that have been discovered in China. They are new materials for the study on exchanges of early bronze mining and smelting techniques in Eurasia.

# 河南安阳市辛店村商代晚期铸铜遗址

◎孔德铭

2016年5月,安阳市文物考古研究所为配合安阳市西北绕城高速公路建设,在安阳市辛店村西南发现一处商代晚期大型铸铜遗址。此次发现的铸铜遗迹主要有房址、阴范坑、烘范窑、灰坑、窖穴、井等,另有商代房址5处,商代窑址2处,商代道路2条,商代墓葬40座,其中出土青铜礼器的墓葬有5座。出土商代晚期陶范1000余块,青铜礼器、兵器、工具及陶器、玉石器、漆器等共计100余件。

根据遗址和墓葬内出土青铜器、陶器、陶范等器物形制初步推断,该遗址的时代为商代晚期,约相当于殷墟文化的二期至四期。整个遗址延续时间长,面积大,各种铸铜要素齐全,保存较好,是殷墟"居、葬、生产合一"社会形态的体现,具有重要的学术意义,对于研究商代晚期青铜手工业的布局、管理、分期和青铜铸造技术的传承、发展、传播等具有重要的价值。

从考古发掘来看,这是一处与殷墟同时期的商代晚期大型族邑聚落与大手工业铸铜作坊。从出土的铜器上所铭族徽看,这里主要集中了以"天""戈"族为主体的商代晚期族群,这一族群在殷墟铁四路、戚家庄、刘家庄、大司空村等地都有发现。辛店村商代晚期文化遗址从地理位置上看不属于殷墟遗址范围内,但其文化内涵又与殷墟遗址内发现的文化内涵相同,也属于"大殷墟"文化。

在本次发掘区域内发现了与铸造青铜器有关的大量遗迹与遗物,是殷墟之外的商代晚期铸铜遗址的唯一考古发现。这个铸铜作坊与殷墟已发现的铸铜遗址相同,都是当时青铜礼器重要的生产基地。殷墟之外铸铜手工作坊的发现,表明青铜文明已深入影响到了殷墟附近重要的族邑聚落。同时也说明,在殷墟时期青铜器铸造技术得到推广,影响不断扩大,一批专门以青铜器铸造、销售与交换为职业的手工业生产族团逐渐形成。这也为殷商文化特别是青铜文化的影响、传播与交流提供了动力。

在M21和M41发现有大量的漆器,这也是发现商代晚期漆器最多的一次。虽然这些漆器胎质均腐朽,但外漆以朱、黑等为主体色彩的兽面纹、云雷纹基本保存完好,整体漆器纹饰精美,色彩艳丽,形状保存较好。且这批商代漆器均是与青铜礼器同出,是墓主人身份地位的象征。它为研究商代墓葬的等级制度、随葬风俗等提供了新的资料。

M21及其出土漆器、青铜器

368　黄淮七省考古新发现

烘范窑

出土陶范

阴范坑

房址

青铜觚　　青铜爵

Xindiancun Site used to be a place for bronze casting back in late Shang Dynasty. It is located in the southwest of Xindian Village, Anyang City, Henan Province. From 2016 to 2017, archaeologists from Anyang Institute of Cultural Relics and Archaeology carried out excavations on the site. The following are major outcomes of archaeological work done on Xindiancun Site. It has been preliminarily determined that Xindiancun Site, as old as the Yin Ruins, used to be a big city of clan settlement and a large-scale bronze casting workshop in late Shang Dynasty. Volumes of remains and relics of bronze casting have been discovered on the site. Xindiancun Site is the only bronze casting site of late Shang Dynasty that has been ever found except the Yin Ruins. A great number of lacquer ware, along with bronze ritual vessels, were revealed in two tombs dating back to Shang Dynasty, M21 and M41. These antiquities are new materials for the study on issues like tomb hierarchical gradation and sacrificial customs in Shang Dynasty.

# 煮海为盐　如玉如雪

## 近年来鲁北沿海地区盐业考古新发现

◎王子孟　党　浩

处于渤海南岸地带的鲁北沿海地区，地理范围涵盖今莱州湾沿岸、黄河三角洲地区，行政区划包括今潍坊市、东营市、滨州市、淄博市、德州市部分临海县区，是我国盐业考古重点关注的区域之一。2010年以来，山东省文物考古研究院在以课题为导向的主动性发掘和配合经济建设的基建考古中陆续发掘数处盐业遗址，主要包括：昌邑市火道—廒里遗址群01（唐央）遗址、寿光市机械林场盐业遗址、东营市广北农场一分场一队东南盐业遗址。

火道—廒里遗址群01遗址，原称"唐央遗址"，2014年10月至2015年2月我们对遗址西南部进行发掘，发现了丰富的东周时期文化遗存。遗址文化遗存可分为三期，时代从春秋中期延续至战国晚期。遗址具有多种功能，既可制盐，又可烧制生产和生活用陶器。这是该地区首次进行的考古发掘，极大地丰富了鲁北莱州湾地区盐业遗址的考古资料。

为配合黄水东调水利工程的施工建设，山东省文物考古研究院组成考古队于2017年4—6月对寿光市机械林场盐业遗址选择三个地点进行了发掘。第一地点和第三地点，相隔距离较近，文化堆积年代一致，从遗迹类型和出土器物以及形制分明的盐灶、盐井，附近大量的陶片堆积分析，这是东周时期的一处煮盐遗址。第二地点发现圆形、方形或椭圆形的灰坑，分布在盐灶的周围，表明这是处制盐工艺有别于其他两个地点的遗存。机械林场盐业遗址目前所获遗迹、遗物为探讨鲁北沿海东周至宋元时期的制盐工艺和流程提供了新的材料，也为我们深入研究盐业考古背后的环境和社会变迁提供了可能。

为配合省道改线工程的文物工作，2013年3—6月，对东营市广北农场一分场一队东南盐业遗址进行了考古勘探与发掘工作。本次发掘初步定性的遗迹有盐井、沉淀池、卤水沟，另范围广布的草木灰堆积可能是淋灰刮卤的摊场，其上密布的条状痕迹可能是车辙；集中分布的小坑可能是淋卤坑或储物坑。结合相关遗迹、遗物情况，遗址性质应为魏晋、北朝时期的煮盐作坊。开井取卤水，草木灰层可能起到摊场提纯卤水的作用，初步判断此时也用淋煎法生产食盐。作为鲁北地区首次发掘的魏晋、北朝时期盐业遗址，其所获材料为我们探讨历史时期山东北部沿海地区的制盐工艺、制盐规模、运作模式等盐业考古框架内的相关课题，提供了文献之外真实可靠的资料。

唐央遗址发掘近景（上西下东）

唐央遗址东周时期J2

唐央遗址东周时期制盐陶器

寿光机械林场第一地点东周时期H6

东营广北农场遗址J3出土木材

东营广北农场遗址
草木灰堆积

东营广北农场遗址盐井

寿光机械林场遗址
第二地点盐灶

寿光机械林场遗址第三地点东周时期H5发现大量陶片

The coastal area of northern Shandong Province, located on the south shoreline of the Bohai Sea, is among the regions that have attracted much archaeological attention of salt-making industry. Archaeologists from Shandong Provincial Institute of Cultural Relics and Archaeology have been conducting project-oriented successive excavations on several salt-making sites. These excavations were planned to be carried out before infrastructural projects of economic construction started. Discovered remains include salt wells, stoves used for separating salt from seawater, settling ponds and brine ditches. Apart from documentary records, these remains are reliable materials for archaeological studies concerning salt-making industry like craft, scale, operation mode in the coastal area of northern Shandong Province back in Eastern Zhou, Wei Dynasty, Jin Dynasty, Song Dynasty and Yuan Dynasty.

黄淮七省考古论坛

# 黄淮七省考古新发现
## （2011—2017年）下

河南省文物考古研究院
山东省文物考古研究院
安徽省文物考古研究所
江苏省考古研究所
河北省文物研究所
陕西省考古研究院
山西省考古研究所

编著

中原出版传媒集团
中原传媒股份公司
大象出版社
·郑州·

# 秦汉一统 雄风万里

秦汉王朝统一帝国的建立，开启了中国古代历史的新篇章，虽然不足500年的历史，但却给后人留下了不可估量的文化遗产。考古材料是诠释古代文明的重要依据，因此，考古新发现的及时公布具有非常重要的意义。黄淮七省近几年的考古工作开展得如火如荼，收获颇丰。考古内容方面，一如既往地重视城市考古、墓葬考古与手工业考古等，同时宗教考古与民族考古也有涵盖。

都城考古方面，秦都咸阳城的考古工作再次确认了宫殿区范围，新发现了府库区与手工制作区，为咸阳城的界域提供了新的线索；长安北渭桥遗址的发掘，再现了当时世界最大的木构桥梁建筑，对秦汉时期渭河河道的确认，以及汉长安城遗址的保护等均具有重要意义。章丘东平陵、即墨故城等诸侯国都城及郡治所城址的发掘，丰富了秦汉城市考古的内容；汉魏洛阳城太极殿宫殿形制的确认完善了我们对汉魏洛阳城核心区域布局的认识；统万城地处北部沙漠边缘，是十六国时期大夏国都城遗址，体现了中原与边疆政权、经济、文化的更迭与交流。除了都城等大中型城市，秦汉时期的小型聚落遗址也有重大发现，枣庄海子遗址是一处有一定布局规划的汉代居住遗址，性质可能属于汉代基层行政单位的"里"。

墓葬的考古发现能够较充分地体现当时社会的一统性及多样性。两汉帝陵、大云山江都王陵、定陶王陵等帝、王陵的勘探与发掘，丰富了两汉帝陵、诸侯王陵的研究内容；江淮地区土墩墓及晋北、陕北少数民族墓葬的发现，体现了文化的地域性差异及民族杂居与文化融合的现象。

凤翔雍山血池遗址属于秦汉时期祭祀类遗址的罕见发现，是从东周诸侯国到秦汉大一统国家祭祀活动的重要物质载体和实物体现。函谷关等"丝绸之路"考古项目的开展不仅重现了古代中国的政治实力与经济实力，而且具有浓郁的时代气息。此类考古工作的开展，无疑更进一步增强了我们的文化自信与民族自信。

该时期的考古工作还具有以下特点：1.以保护文化遗产为前提，田野调查与发掘充分与多学科相结合，尽可能地提取、保存考古材料中所蕴含的各方面的信息；2.对资料进行数字化管理，为考古资料的后期利用和信息传播奠定良好的基础；3.考古成果的及时公布与出版，不但能全面推动相关课题的深入研究，而且还能为我们的考古事业培养一支重要的科研力量；4.注重公众性与社会效益，并为此开展了很多工作，如为遗址规划提供专业的资料以及开展公众考古活动等。

# 丝路迢迢　雄关开道

## 河南新安县汉函谷关遗址考古调查与发掘

◎王咸秋

汉函谷关遗址位于河南省洛阳市新安县东，地处秦岭山脉东段的峡谷之中，南北两侧均为高山，皂涧河水由遗址的西侧绕至南侧，在东侧与涧河交汇后折向东流。从西汉武帝元鼎三年（公元前114年）楼船将军杨仆建关，至今已有2100多年的历史。遗址现存格局是一条狭长的通道，关楼遗址横亘在通道之上，是明清和民国时期多次重修的遗迹。关楼东侧，有两座汉代的夯土台基，俗称"鸡鸣台"和"望气台"。

2012年，汉函谷关遗址被列为"丝绸之路：起始段和天山廊道的路网"项目遗产点，为配合函谷关遗址保护规划的制定和申遗工作，洛阳文物考古研究院对遗址进行了考古调查和发掘。2012年至2013年，通过考古调查发掘，共发现夯土墙17条、古道路2条、夯土台2座、活动面9处，并对凤凰山和青龙山上的夯土长墙进行了勘探，遗址总体布局基本清楚。

关城东墙（Q1），位于望气台南侧，与关城南墙相交，保存较好。北部用夯土修筑，南侧用石头砌筑。东墙可分为早、晚两期，建筑年代均为汉代。在东墙发掘区还发现了护堤、排水渠及马道等重要遗迹。建筑遗址共发现两期，均为东汉时期。第一期建筑有通道、活动面、排水渠等遗迹。第二期建筑保存较差。

古道路共两条。L1，位于遗址中部，东西向贯穿遗址，从西汉建关时一直沿用到现代。L2，位于遗址南侧，时代为东周到西汉初期，是建关前古道，建关后被关城东墙阻断而废弃。

出土遗物以砖瓦等建筑材料为主，兵器有铁刀、铁戟、铁矛和铜镞。

函谷关遗址是一处东西狭长的小型城邑，城墙、道路和建筑遗址等要素均已发现。关城卡在峡谷之中，关城东墙与南北山上的夯土长墙相连接，达到军事防御和控制交通的目的。关城中部的古道路东西向贯穿关城，是唯一的通关道路；遗址南部、皂涧河北岸是主要的生活区。根据出土遗物和对遗迹的解剖，可以确定关城东墙、鸡鸣望气二台及台基西侧夯土墙为西汉建关时修建，关城南墙为汉代增建。在以往的考古工作中，对关隘的研究工作一直非常匮乏，对地位如此重要的内关进行系统的考古工作更是第一次。此次发现，为秦汉关隘制度的研究提供了重要的参考资料，也为函谷关遗址的保护提供了重要依据。

遗址全景（东—西）

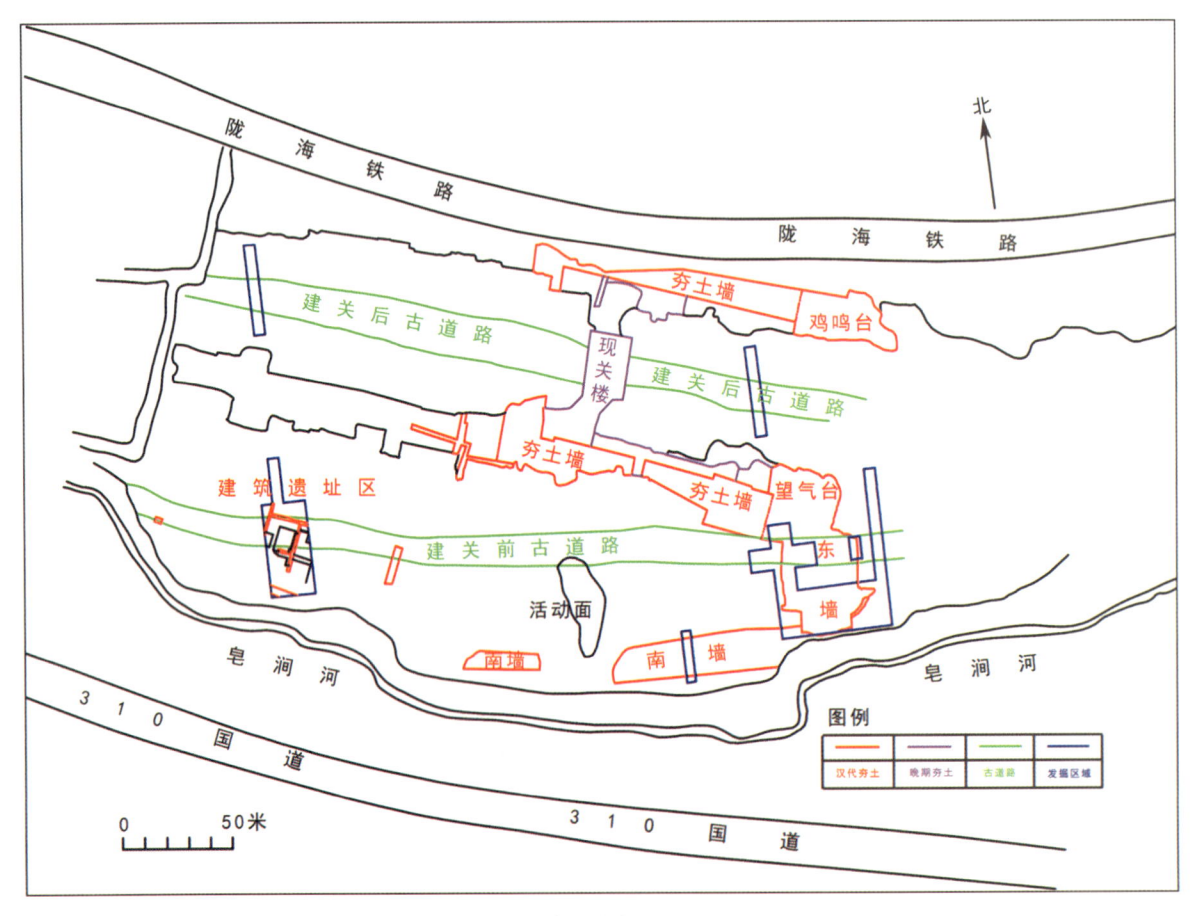

遗址分布图

关城东墙（Q1）北部（南—北）

关城东墙南部马道及排水渠（西—东）

"关"字瓦当　　　　　　　　"关"字铭文砖　　　　　　　瓦当

The Site of Hangu Pass, dating back to Han Dynasty, is located in the east of Xin'an County, Luoyang City, Henan Province. The gatehouse, right above the passageway, experienced maintenance and rebuilding many times during Ming and Qing dynasties and the Republic of China. On the east side of the gatehouse, there are two Han rammed earthen terraces, commonly known as "Terrace of Ji Ming" and "Terrace of Wang Qi". The following are major archaeological discoveries made this time. The Site of Hangu Pass actually consists of remains of a small east-west lying city covering a narrow strip of land. Vestiges of city walls, roads, architectures and others all have been discovered. The Pass is constructed in the valley of Qinling Mountains. Its east wall is connected with long rammed earthen walls built on mountains on both the south and north sides. Such a construction was meant for military defense and traffic control. The ancient road, going through the Pass in the middle, used to be the only passageway. In the south of the Pass, on the north bank of River Zaojian, there used to be the main residential area. According to analyses of unearthed relics and remains, it has been determined that the east wall of Hangu Pass, "Terrace of Ji Ming", "Terrace of Wang Qi", and a rammed earthen wall on the west side of the terraces were first built in Western Han, when the Pass was set up; while the south wall of Hangu Pass was constructed as an extension in Han Dynasty.

# 巍巍之城　尽显其荣

## 陕西西安市秦都咸阳城考古新进展

◎许卫红

从20世纪50年代开始，考古工作者就开始了对帝都咸阳城进行考古调查，"十一五"之后，咸阳城遗址名列国家大遗址重点保护项目名单，新一轮的咸阳城北区考古工作再次启动，主要取得了四方面的新进展。

1.首先是在北区开展建筑遗址数量、保存情况的核实，即"楼盘"清点。通过调查、勘探，核定了牛羊沟村以东至三义村东西分布的33处夯土遗迹。在牛羊沟村以西的聂家沟村、胡家沟村，新确定15组大型建筑。这些新发现的建筑遗址，根据位置可以确认和咸阳城有关的至少有14组，最近一处距离以往认为的"咸阳宫"西墙仅有6米。

2.2014年，为了寻找城墙、城界，考古队开始在咸阳北塬上广泛布置条形勘探带，并未发现符合条件的夯土迹象。但在海拔420~430米区域之间发现东西走向的线性堆积。线性堆积为水淤积土质，具体位置以高干渠为参照，依自然地势高低起伏，略呈东西走向的弓形；东部因近代取土已不可追踪，西部依走势并未和该区域的南北向自然沟会合，仍有延续的可能，现可见长度2902米。这条水淤积遗迹，高程落差与以往学者认为的成国渠故道流向明显抵牾，因而为咸阳城北区界域的确定提供了线索。

3.2014年冬季，在聂家沟村断崖边不到20平方米的范围内，采集到总量超过600千克的骨质遗物，原料取自不少于203头黄牛，种类包括骨料、坯料、废料、半成品以及各种铁质工具和磨石。骨质遗物有马镳、带具、博具棋子、琴轸、算筹、带钩以及大、小圆环。马镳、圆环等半成品表面刻有精致的图案。这处以骨质遗物为主的遗迹废弃时代不晚于西汉初期，属于制骨生产的次生堆积。这些资料不仅可以复原出完整的骨器生产工艺流程，也透露出当时生产管理的一些细节内容，从原料获取、生产组织到产品消费都有统一的管理。此外，调查采集遗物还包括石磬残块以及大量的冶铸遗物。

4.2016—2017年，秦都咸阳城遗址的主动发掘再次开始，确认了ⅡB1JZ2所在的胡家沟区域有与秦咸阳城北区主管国家或皇室物资生产、存放的官署机构，包括有大型府库类建筑。

382　黄淮七省考古新发现

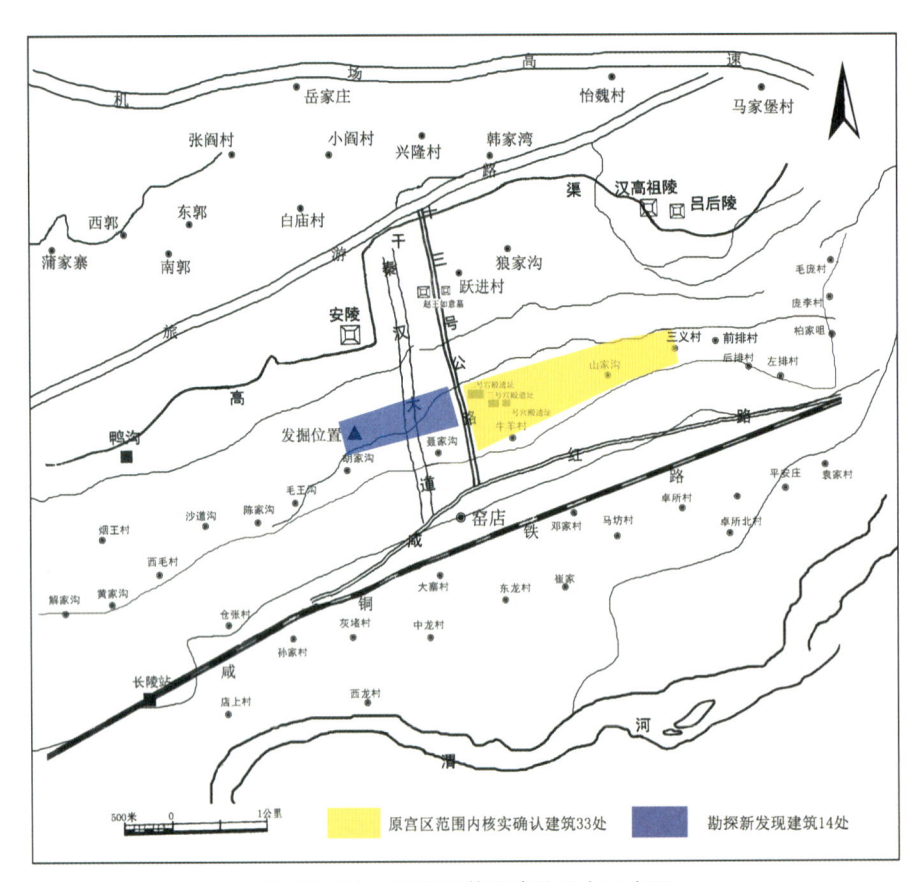

秦咸阳城宫区及附近范围建筑分布示意图

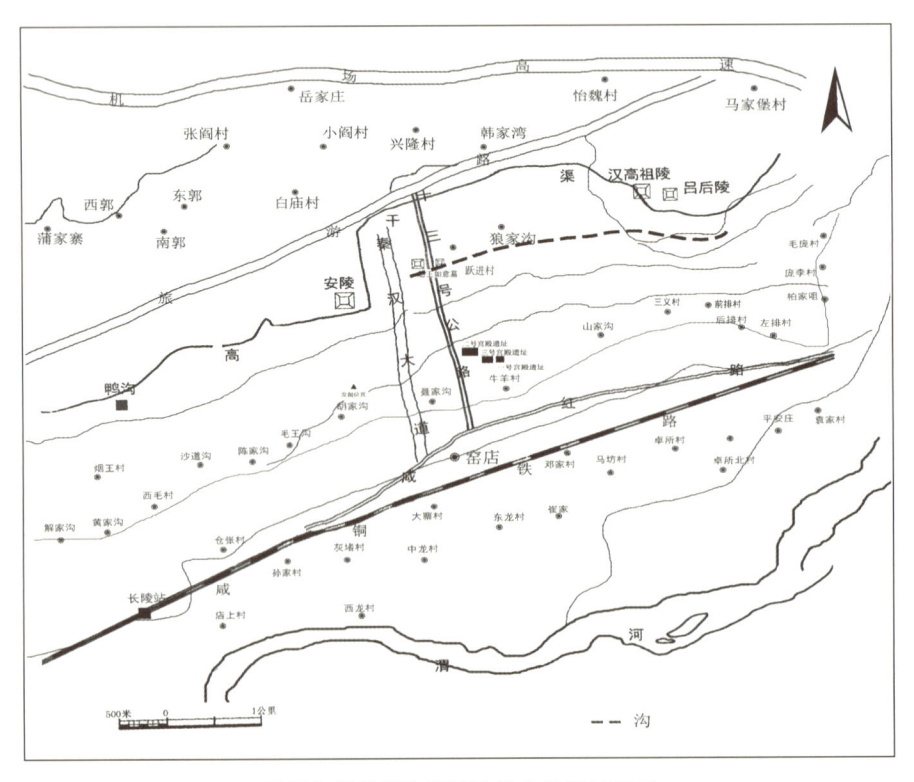

勘探条带发现沟类遗迹分布位置示意图

骨制品

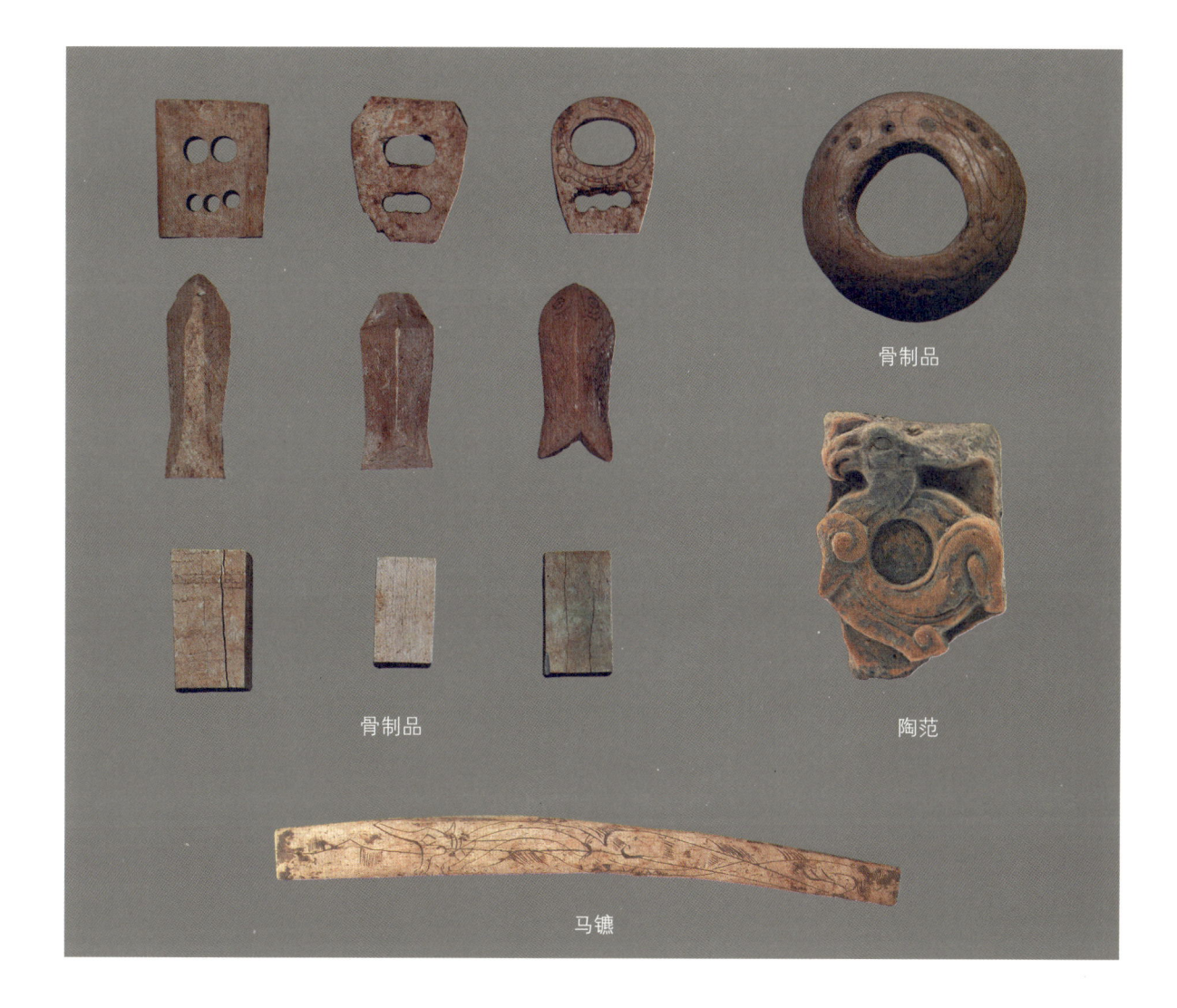

骨制品

陶范

马镳

Major discoveries can be summarized from four aspects. Firstly, as many as 33 east-west rammed earthen remains have been located in the area stretching from the east of Niuyanggou Village to Sanyi Village. In the west of Niuyanggou Village, in Niejiagou Village and Hujiagou Village, remains of 15 large-scale buildings, at least 14 of which are related with Xianyang, have been newly located. Secondly Linear marks left by silt have become a clue to the determination of the north boundary of the northern district of Xianyang. Thirdly, near a bluff in Niejiagou Village, a great number of bone remains, including curb chains, chess pieces, posts of a lute, counting rods, rings, have been discovered. Exquisite engravings are found on the surface of the curb chains and rings. These bone remains, deserted no later than early Western Han, were secondary deposits of bone implement production. Relics that have been collected also include broken pieces of stone chimes and a large number of remnants left after smelting and casting actives. Fourthly, architectural remains of the treasury of Xianyang, a large building that can be divided into four rooms of almost the same size lying in a east-west row, have been excavated. Many stone chimes have been unearthed. The treasury, deserted no later than early Western Han, was destroyed by a raging fire.

# 陕西西安市秦都咸阳城府库建筑遗址

◎许卫红

秦都咸阳城遗址胡家沟区域建筑基址北距安陵封土中心约1065米，东距20世纪发掘的一号宫殿约1150米，勘探确定有5组大型夯土建筑，其中4组按照东西一线分布，和以前发掘的一、二、三号宫殿遗址对应。按照大遗址考古工作虚拟分区，发掘建筑基址编号为ⅡB1JZ2。

该基址废弃堆积为大量板瓦、筒瓦、瓦当、龙纹空心砖等建筑材料，残碎严重。板瓦、筒瓦均装饰绳纹，其中筒瓦内壁纹饰约90%以上为麻点纹，可见清晰的泥条盘筑痕迹。

建筑结构基本清楚，平面呈曲尺形，四面垣墙厚2.50～3.20米，夹筑夯筑。内部隔有面积近等的四大间，按照由西向东次序分别编号为F1、F2、F3、F4，各间内有走向不同、长短不一的窄墙。F3东南另有一处附属设施，或为门廊（F7）。F4的南部还有部分建筑有待清理。

F1、F2内除发现建筑材料外，另在F2倒塌层中还发现一枚"大内（府）缯官"封泥，F3倒塌堆积中发现大量石磬残块。20余块石磬的鼓、股边部刻有文字，内容初步识读为"北宫乐府""右八""矢右商子""左徵""左终"等，字体以秦小篆为主，体现了石磬所属、排序编号及音阶，说明是成组的编磬。

出土的建筑材料与以往发掘的一、二、三号建筑相同，具有典型的战国晚期至秦代的特征。大量石磬刻字显示其ⅡB1JZ2与秦代"北宫乐府"有关，曾存放北宫乐府使用的器具。从隶属的关系看，封泥为"大府缯官"的可能性更大。

该组建筑毁于烈火，石磬残坏、散布的情景说明与人为破坏有关。多处墙体呈红烧土状，地面亦为青色硬面，木质类建筑材料化为炭末，石磬残块火烧后局部迸裂或呈白色。建筑的废弃时代不晚于西汉早期。

为进一步确定建筑周边遗址分布情况，在随后开展的调查中确定发掘区东南部300米处有大型建筑已被破坏，采集到大量遗物，包括建筑材料、"半两"钱模和与发掘出土石磬质地相同的石块、成型的石磬残块等。这些遗物的时代与发掘建筑同期。另还发现有L形排水沟和陶管道、大面积水相堆积和成型的石磬残块。初步判断ⅡB1JZ2东南为石磬的生产制作区域。

此次通过多种手段开展的工作可以确认，ⅡB1JZ2所在的胡家沟区域存在秦咸阳城北区主管国家或皇室物资生产、存放的官署机构，包括有大型府库类建筑。至今，该区域的考古工作仍在进行中，更多现象有待发现与公布。

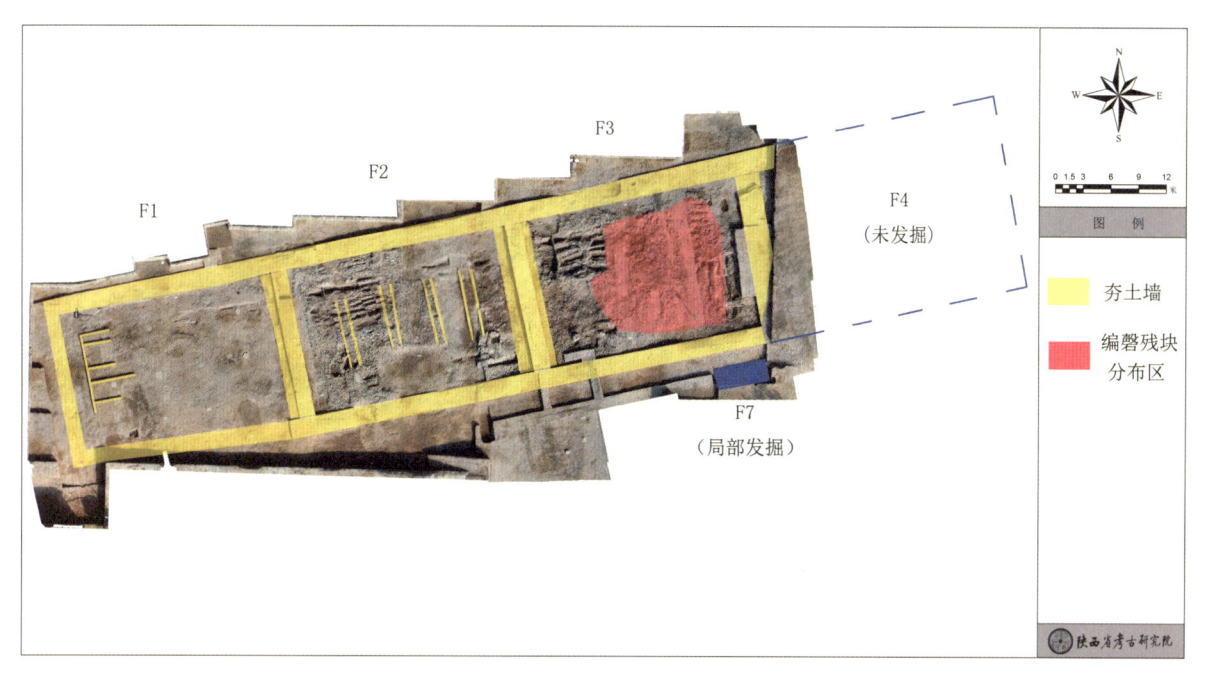

ⅡB1JZ2三维平面图

圆形陶管道

调查发现建筑材料残片

石磬残块上部分刻铭文字

"半两"钱模

龙纹空心砖残块

The major archaeological discovery made this time is an architectural site, whose ground plan is an 80-degree incline. The site, 100 meters long and 19.5 meters wide, can be divided into four large rooms, of almost the same size. From the west to the east, four rooms are respectively labeled as F1, F2, F3 and F4. Discovered pillars turn out to have been arranged in three rows and four lines. Walls were built by ramming earth between boards. Inside each room, remains of narrow walls with varied length and lying in different positions, have been revealed. In the southeast of F3, there is another auxiliary facility, possibly a porch. Apart from building materials, from F2, clay pieces that had been impressed with "Da Nei (Fu) Zeng Guan" have been unearthed. A large number of broken pieces of stone chimes, 20 of which were carved with characters, mainly small seal characters used in Qin Dynasty, showing their ownership, serial numbers and musical scale, like "Bei Gong Yue Fu", are found mixed in deposits of collapsed buildings. After researches, it has been determined that this site used to be a treasury of Xianyang, the capital of Qin. Deserted no later than early Western Han, it was destroyed by a raging fire.

# 陕西西安市汉长安城北渭桥遗址

◎王志友

渭桥遗址位于陕西省西安市未央区汉长安城遗址北侧的西席村、师道口村、唐家村和高庙村以北，2012年陕西省考古研究院、中国社会科学院考古研究所、西安市文物保护考古研究院成立渭桥考古队，开始对厨城门桥、洛城门桥进行抢救性的考古发掘。目前在西安地区已发现3组7座横跨原渭河的古桥：在厨城门外共发现5座古桥（分别编号为厨城门一至五号桥）；在洛城门外发现1座古桥（洛城门桥）；在汉长安城东北草滩镇王家堡发现1座古桥（王家堡桥）。其中以厨城门一号桥规模最大。

厨城门一号桥是1座用木、石材料构建的大型南北向木梁柱桥，自西汉时期建造以来，至魏晋时期经过多次维修。该桥宽约15.40米，南北长度约在880米左右；桥桩残长约6.20～8.80米，周长约0.50～1.50米。桥桩顺河流方向东西排列，间距不等，用材有桢楠、云杉、侧柏等树种。在一号桥中部以北均发现有大量不同形状、规格的大型石构件；较多的石构件上有一处或多处刻字或墨书题记，内容主要为编号、人名和制石机构性质，少量为位置、尺寸；从痕迹看，五边形石构件之间应以铁榫或白灰黏结在一起；此外，在少数石构件上发现有朱雀与青龙、朱雀与白虎的浮雕纹饰。从掩埋桥梁的上层淤沙中发现乾隆通宝铜钱的情况看，桥桩至此时尚露于水中，结合桥北端埽岸发现及渭河水文动力模拟结果显示，直到18世纪之前，渭河河道很可能还在渭桥位置。在厨城门一号桥北端发现的埽岸南侧，清理发现一艘汉代古船遗存，是渭河长安城段船舶考古的第一次发现。汉长安城北渭桥遗址出土的实用船只显示出成熟的木板船类型，采用的木榫板、木钉并联船板的技术在国内为首次发现。

厨城门桥可能即是文献所载的"中渭桥"遗址。以厨城门一号桥为代表的渭河古桥，是迄今为止所见规模最大的秦汉木梁柱古桥，也是现知同时期全世界最大的木构桥梁。多座渭桥位置的确定，为秦汉时期渭河河道南、北两岸的位置提供了确切资料，它们不仅是对汉长安城周边地区秦汉路网、水网系统研究的重要收获，而且对汉长安城遗址的保护、秦汉都城交通史的研究亦具有重要价值。

西安渭桥遗址位置图

厨城门一号2012—2014年发掘区域桥航拍照（西—东）

厨城门一号桥出土的石构件

厨城门一号桥北端埽岸以南出土的古船（西南—东北）

厨城门一号桥北端渭河堤岸与埽（西南—东北）

Seven bridges, in three groups, have been discovered in the north of Chang'an (now Xi'an City), the capital of Han Dynasty. Among these bridges, Bridge No.1 near Gate Chucheng is the largest. Bridge No.4, also near Gate Chucheng, was constructed in late Warring States Period. During the time from Western Han to Wei and Jin dynasties, Bridge No.1 was built several times. The bridge near Gate Luocheng was built during the epoch from late Western Han to early Eastern Han. Tang Dynasty witnessed the construction of Bridge No.3 near Gate Chucheng. After excavations, it has been found out that the course of River Weihe had not moved northward significantly until 18 Century. Constructed with wood and stones, Bridge No.1 near Gate Chucheng, approximately 15.4 meters wide and about 880 meters long, is a large north-south bridge supported by wooden piers. It had been repaired and rebuilt many times in history. At the north end of Bridge No.1, remnants of a bank have been discovered. On the south side of the bank, remains of a shipwreck dating back to Han Dynasty has been revealed. This is the very first discovery of ship archaeology along the segment of River Weihe near Chang'an.

# 山东即墨故城遗址近年考古工作收获

◎郝导华

即墨故城遗址位于山东省平度市东南约30千米的古岘镇大朱毛村一带，地跨古岘镇和仁兆镇，"故城临墨水，故曰即墨"。

为做好即墨故城遗址的大遗址保护规划工作，2011—2017年山东省文物考古研究院对遗址进行了大量的勘探和发掘工作，解剖了即墨故城遗址外城东南城墙。对即墨故城内城中北部建筑基址进行了发掘。主要收获是内、外城的确认和对外城东南城墙及城内大型建筑基址的发掘，经过以上工作，对遗址已经有了一个初步的认识。据考古发掘情况知，即墨故城遗址的主体是城址，城内则是由大型建筑（宫殿）基址、一般居住址、手工业作坊址、道路、水系等构成的统一体。

经过勘探，城址分为内、外城，主体均属汉代，是否存在更早的城墙有待发掘证实。外城东邻小沽河，西近墨水河，平面总体呈不规则的长方形，东南缺角，亦确认了北城壕。内城位于外城东南部，平面近长方形，确定了北、西、南城壕，南城墙中段距离南墙西端约390米处发现一处缺口，疑似城门类遗迹。对外城东南城墙地上存在的墙体南端进行了解剖，共发现城墙夯土3期，城墙分为地上城墙和地下基槽两部分；地上部分夯土质量较好，局部夯窝清晰可见，为平底夯；地下基槽部分，夯土质量较差，土质较软。另外，对内城中北部建筑基址亦进行了发掘，虽然只揭露了大型建筑基址的一部分，但发现了大型石柱础及与其对应的建筑基址。在内城勘探中发现多处建筑遗迹，主要属汉代，当时的运粮河（即今小沽河），经过东南城门洞，可直接与城内的贮货湾相通。还有就是，在外城东北部的纸房村内发现了炼铁炉群等遗迹。

即墨故城遗址是山东胶东地区最重要的古文化遗址之一。此次发掘，不仅对当地汉代考古学文化内涵、分期的研究有重要价值，而且有利于了解即墨故城城址建筑基址的结构及分布情况，进而对汉代城址的布局及演化过程等方面的研究亦具有重要的推动作用。

即墨故城遗址与六曲山墓群是胶东地区经历时间较长且规模最大的城址和墓群，对古代城市布局结构的研究具有重要意义。即墨故城地理位置优越，对其本身文化内涵的揭露，必将助推与周围相关地区古代文化及其关系的研究。

外城城墙

城墙夯窝剖面

内城中北部建筑基址大型石柱础分布（上为北）

瓦当

铺地砖

Site of Jimo City is located in the locality of Dazhumao Village, approximately 30 kilometers southeast of Pingdu City, Shandong Province. The site encompasses an area stretching from Guxian Town to Renzhao Town. The main part of Site of Jimo City is a city site. On this city site, there is a unity consisting of foundation sites of massive buildings (palatial architectures), average dwelling sites, handicraft workshop sites, roads, water systems, etc. Archaeologists from Shandong Provincial Institute of Cultural Relics and Archaeology have been conducting lots of archaeological reconnaissances and excavations on Site of Jimo City. Major outcomes include confirmation of the Inner City and the Outer City and excavations carried out on the foundation sites of both the southeast city wall of the Outer City and massive architectures inside the Inner City. Site of Jimo City and Liuqushan Tomb Cluster both have a relatively long history and they are respectively the largest city site and the biggest tomb cluster in eastern Shandong Province. They are of significance for the study on the layout and structure of ancient cities. Enjoying a favorable geographical position, Site of Jimo City used to be a transportation hub between the North and the South as well as the East and the West.

# 山东章丘东平陵城遗址 2009—2013 年考古发掘

◎ 张 溯

2008年山东省文物考古研究所、北京大学考古文博学院、济南市考古研究所三家单位联合申报《山东章丘东平陵故城遗址保护研究项目》专项课题，获得国家文物局批准。自2009—2013年，三家单位联合章丘市博物馆、城子崖遗址博物馆对东平陵城进行了考古测绘、勘探和发掘。发掘工作有三次，均位于制铁区（第Ⅴ区）和宫殿区（第十、十一区）。

制铁区经过两次发掘，2009年发掘东部，2012年发掘区位于2009年发掘区的西部。2009年发掘的第Ⅴ区的遗迹可分五期，其中以第二、三、四期遗存最丰富。

第二期发现有夯土地基、熔铁炉4座、建筑基址1座、灰坑80余个。熔铁炉呈东西向等距排列，间隔约3米，仅剩炉基，其中L1、L2号炉基保存较好，L4、L5只剩一小部分。熔铁炉均为圆形炉壁和圆形炉缸组成的双圈结构。F1为铸造活动的场所，建筑于夯土地基之上，位于4座熔炉北侧，主体由南侧的夯土墙与北侧的活动面两部分组成。

西汉晚期遗迹主要有烘范窑、储泥池、锻铁炉、取土坑、灰坑等，这些遗迹建造在熔铁炉废弃后的堆积之上或直接打破夯土地基。Y1被破坏得较严重，推测为烘范窑。L3建造在熔炉L1的倒塌堆积上，炉膛近似椭圆形，推测为锻炉。

与制铁相关的遗物有炉壁、鼓风管、铁材、铁器等。炉壁有砂质、泥质、草拌泥和复合材料四种，均是熔铁炉的炉壁。铁器可分为农具、工具、铁构件、兵器和其他5类。

2012年制铁区发现的主要遗迹有熔铁炉、蓄水池、灰坑、灰沟等。熔铁炉共6座，大体呈东西向排列，保存均较差，仅剩炉底部分，其中L6保存较好，尚存炉底和部分炉壁。

宫殿区共进行了三次发掘，主要发现为一座宫殿建筑（一号建筑基址）。该建筑位于平陵城的中轴线上，面阔9间，进深5间。墙外为回廊，回廊外为散水和甬道。推测该建筑为四阿重屋式宫殿建筑。始建年代大约为西汉中晚期，东汉时期仍沿用。

东平陵城制铁作坊的发现，是近几年发掘的重要收获。制铁作坊主要由夯土地基、熔铁炉、锻炉、烘范窑、储泥池及藏铁坑等遗迹组成，为研究汉代的冶金业提供了重要资料。整体上看，2009年发掘的制铁作坊早于2012年的，属于西汉中期。熔铁炉形制特殊，为首次发现。发现数件带"大四"字样的铸范。一般认为"大四"指泰山郡第四号冶铸作坊。文献记载泰山郡设置于嬴，汉嬴铁官位于莱芜市城子县，而平陵城在汉代属济南郡。可能泰山郡在东平陵城加工定做铁器，如是，该发现当为中国最早的代工产业。这一发现为汉代铁官制度及铁器生产和流通的研究提供了新的资料和思路。西汉晚期时，该区域内的熔铁炉被废弃，而主要用来制范和锻造等活动。属西汉晚期的烘范窑Y1的形制与河南南阳北关瓦房庄汉代冶铁遗址Y2类似。锻炉L3的形制与巩县铁生沟炉20、南阳北关瓦房庄汉代冶铁遗址发现的锻炉类似。西汉晚期时，熔铁炉迁至西部2012年发掘区，并一直沿用到东汉，其熔铁炉的形制也发生了一些变化。2012年所发掘的铸造作坊始建于西汉晚期，沿用至东汉，废于汉末，其时代与2009年发掘区的第3、4期遗存时代相当。

Y1（北—南）

L3

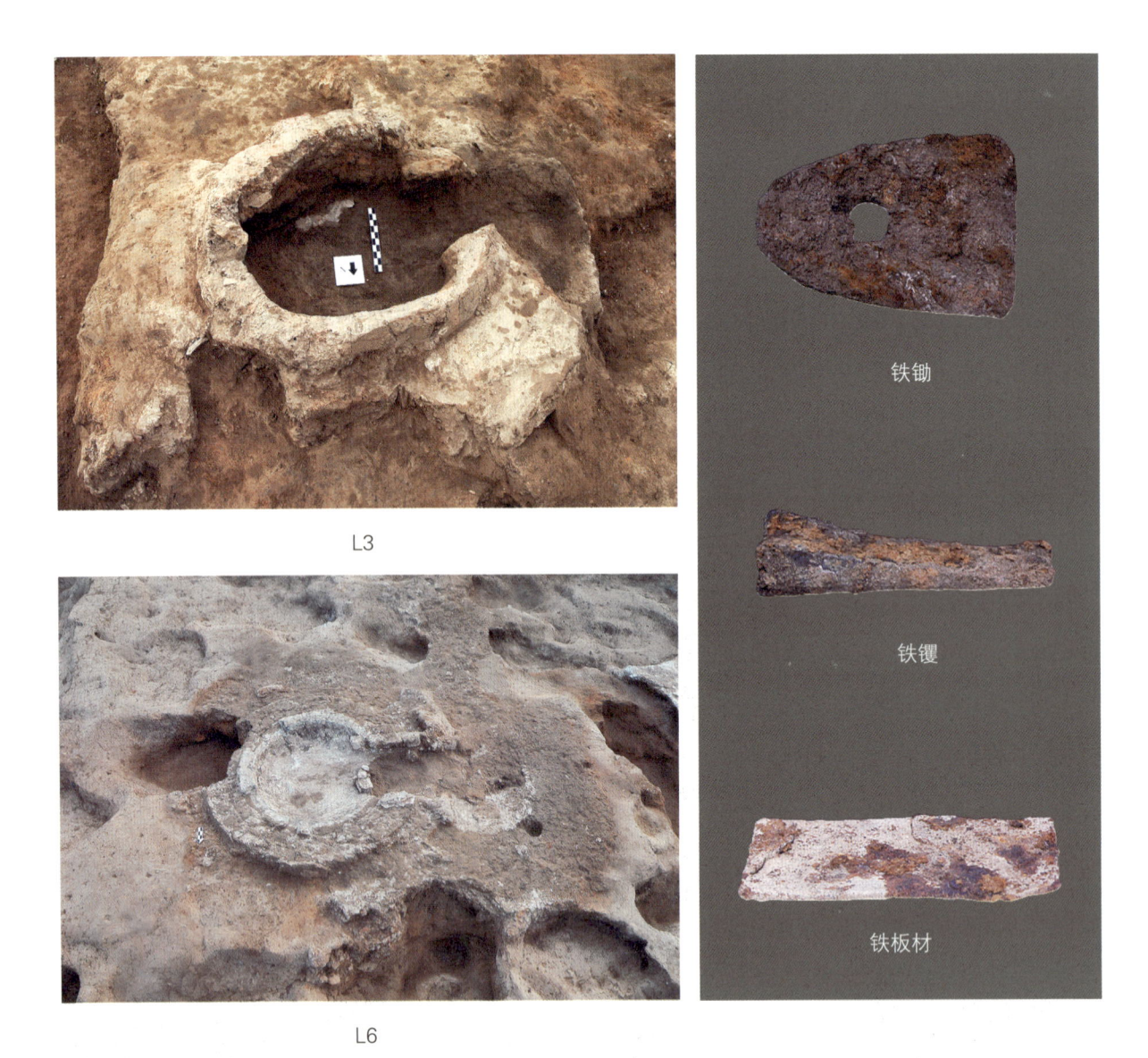

L6

铁锄

铁钁

铁板材

From 2009 to 2013, on the site of Dongpingling, archaeological work was mainly conducted in the zone of iron casting (Zone V) and the palace zone (Zone 10 and Zone 11). The site of the workshop including remains of rammed earthen foundation, iron casting, consisting of iron-smelting furnaces, forge furnaces, mold-baking kilns, mud ponds and pits containing deposited iron, is a major archaeological discovery made in recent years. It is the first time that iron-smelting furnaces in a special structure have been discovered. The iron-casting workshop revealed in 2009 dates back to the middle Western Han and it is older than the one excavated in 2012. The casting workshop whose remains were unearthed in 2012 was first constructed in the late Western Han and became deserted in the end of the Eastern Han. In the palace zone, the major discovery is a palatial architecture sitting on the central axis of Dongpingling. There is a double-eaved hip roof on the building. It was constructed during the middle and late Western Han and was still in use in Eastern Han.

# 河南汉魏洛阳故城 2012—2014 年考古新发现

◎钱国祥　刘　涛　郭晓涛　莫　阳

汉魏洛阳故城遗址位于河南省孟津县平乐镇金村南约1千米。为进一步推进汉魏洛阳故城遗址的发掘研究，结合国家大遗址保护和丝绸之路跨国申报世界文化遗产，2012年7月—2014年12月，中国社会科学院考古研究所洛阳汉魏故城队对北魏宫城太极殿遗址进行了全面勘察发掘。

太极殿遗址地处北魏宫城中部偏西，由铜驼街、宫城阊阖门、二号和三号宫门组成的北魏洛阳城建筑轴线上。勘察表明，太极殿遗址是由居中的主体建筑"太极殿"和东、西两侧的附属建筑"太极东堂""太极西堂"等构成的一组大型夯土台基建筑，是宫城内最大的殿址。太极殿台基南壁和东壁被破坏成沟槽状。但北壁保存较好，中段有向北凸出的凸台。凸台的东、西两端，也各设一条东西向踏道，太极殿台基南侧设有两条登台的漫道或踏道。凸台外壁砌筑包砖外，其余夯土壁面上直接涂抹白灰墙皮，部分墙皮上还涂有朱红色竖直条带。除凸台包砖北侧有砖铺散水外，其余均为素土地面。台基顶面已被破坏无存。在太极殿台基东侧为太极东堂的台基。在太极殿与东堂台基之间有夯土隔墙、门址和柱网等建筑遗迹。东堂北侧有廊房和夯土隔墙围合的独立院落，建筑规格较高。太极殿的营建主要可分为早晚三期：中间的主体部分夯土质量较好，为早期整体一次夯筑而成，始建于曹魏时期；中期至少有两次营建，是在主体夯土周边的增修和补筑，时代约为十六国和北魏时期；晚期则是在台基周边再次开挖沟槽重新改建和营修，但未完工，建造时代约为北周。

太极殿遗址发掘的学术意义有以下几个方面：第一，对汉魏洛阳城宫城太极殿庞大宫殿建筑群的平面布置有了明确认识，其主体部分是由中间的太极殿和两侧略小的太极东、西堂组成，形成三殿东西并列的布置；第二，解决了太极殿和东、西堂殿基的形制、规模和登台阶阶等问题；第三，解剖确认这座宫殿建筑群始建于曹魏，北魏和北周等时代相继有所增修或沿用，印证了相关文献记载；第四，魏晋至北魏太极殿位置的确定，进一步确认了北魏宫城是在魏晋宫城基础上的重修和沿用，对单一宫城制度出现于曹魏是重要的考古实据；第五，结合近年来宫城南区的勘察，从宫城阊阖门至太极殿前共设置有三道宫门，显然是符合中国古代都城门阙制度的建置，对《周礼》《礼记》所记"五门三朝制度"的研究具有重要的意义。

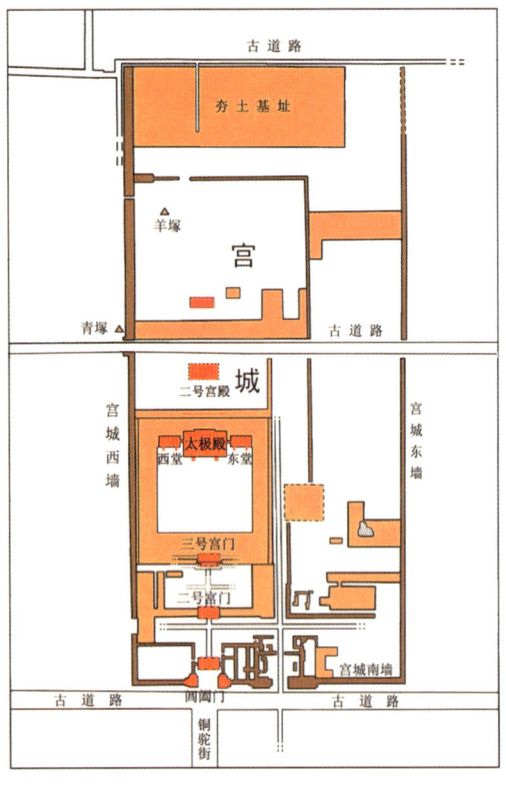

北魏洛阳宫城平面图（上北下南）

太极殿台基北侧三期遗迹（北—南）

太极殿北侧踏道遗迹（北—南）

太极殿与东堂之间东阁门遗迹（东北—西南）

After archaeological reconnaissances and excavations, the following are major discoveries concerning the site of the Han-Wei period capital in Luoyang. It has been found out that, in the palace, Hall of Taiji mainly consists of a main hall in the middle and two smaller halls, the east side hall and the west side hall. Three halls lie in a line. Issues concerning structure and scale of three halls mentioned above and stone steps leading up to the halls have been settled. Hall of Taiji, as a building complex, was first constructed in Cao Wei. When it comes to Northern Wei and Northern Zhou, maintenance, rebuilding and extension of the building complex, which was still in use, were carried out. The palace of Northern Wei turns out to be the one used in Wei and Jin dynasties, only after rebuilding. This fact has become a solid evidence proving the convention of building a single palace in one city started in Cao Wei. It has been confirmed that three gates were set up along the way from Gate Chang He to the front of Hall of Taiji.

# 陕西靖边县统万城遗址的考古发现

◎ 邢福来

统万城遗址位于陕西省靖边县北部，地处陕西与内蒙古交界的毛乌素沙漠南缘，无定河上游红柳河北岸的台地上，是十六国时期匈奴族后裔赫连勃勃建立的大夏国都城遗址。自2006年，为配合大遗址保护，我们对有关城市布局、周边墓葬、祭祀遗址等方面进行了重点调查与发掘。

统万城外郭城呈曲尺形，西北部凸出，城垣走向与东西城城垣基本一致。东、西城城门外均有瓮城，已探明五处。西城西门瓮城位于西城西垣偏南处，瓮城门面南，紧贴西城西垣。西门平面呈"亚"字形，门道内外两侧均有凸出的夯土台。唐代西门瓮城废弃后，西门内侧人为修筑夯土，隔断城内与瓮城的联系。东城大型建筑基址应该是东城的主体建筑之一，四面均有斜坡漫道。夯土台叠压唐代晚期地层，其建造年代当在晚唐五代时期。西城城垣外、东城南垣、东垣、北垣外均建造有马面或垛台，每面8~10个，将城垣外广场分成若干区域，便于守城将士从多面居高临下用弓箭、礌石等武器抗击攻城之敌。另外，城垣外设立虎落，地面撒铁蒺藜防范敌骑兵入侵。

与统万城作为大夏国都及唐宋时期中国北方重要城市有关的墓葬区，南至华家洼、东南至尔德井墓群、西至敖包墓群、北至瓦渣梁墓群，在这南北约10千米、东西约20千米的范围内清理出北朝、唐、五代、宋代墓葬40座，基本搞清了与统万城有关的墓葬年代、形制及各时代墓葬形制的演变序列。

与祭祀有关的遗址位于统万城东南及西北约2千米处。西梁夯土台基址位于统万城遗址东南，隔红柳河与城址相望。主要由围墙及围墙内的3个墩台等部分组成。查干圪台位于统万城遗址西城西北、外郭城内，共发现3座夯土台，此次发掘了1、2号夯土墩台。西梁和查干圪台两处夯土遗址均被隋唐时期墓葬打破，结合统万城历史沿革，我们认为其建造年代应与统万城同期，西梁和查干圪台两处大型夯土台基址分别位于统万城遗址东南郊与西北，从其建筑位置与统万城之间的空间布局关系看，应为两组礼制性建筑，可能与大夏国时期统万城的祭祀活动有关。

东城建筑基址（上北下南）

西梁夯土台基址

西城西门（东—西）

榆林靖边八大梁墓地M1壁画正射影像图

H11出土的礓石（东—西）　　　　　　　　　马面虎落（西—东）

Major archaeological discoveries that have been made on the site of Tongwan City since 2006 mainly concern city layout, nearby tombs, ritual sites, etc. In terms of city layout, it has been confirmed that the outer city of Tongwan City was in the shape of a carpenter's square, with a convex pointing to the northwest. Ramparts of the outer city, which used to parallel with those of the East City and the West City, enclosed 7.7 square kilometers. Archaeological surveys have proved the existence of barbican entrances, five of which have been located outside both the East City and the West City. Protruding battlements, or embattled towers, were constructs on the exterior of the ramparts of the the West City and the south, east and north ramparts of the East City. On the massive foundation site in the East City, there used to be a major regional building constructed during the epoch from late Tang to Five Dynasties. Distribution of tombs related with Tongwan City and features of funerary customs in Shaanxi Province have been determined. Dates of the tombs, their structures, and the evolutional sequence concerning the shapes and forms of tombs built in each era have been generally clarified. Remains made of rammed earth in Xiliang and Chagan Getai should be ritual sites related with sacrificial activities in Tongwan City in Xia Kingdom.

# 宏宏之穴　以象其生

## 河南三门峡市大唐火电厂墓地重要考古发现

◎马俊才　李　辉　杨树刚　曹艳朋

2014年3—10月，河南省文物考古研究院和三门峡市文物考古研究所组成考古队，对三门峡大唐火电厂基建区内的古墓葬进行了多学科大规模抢救性发掘，共发掘古墓葬802座，其中751座秦人墓是较为重要的发现。

这批秦墓数量众多，保存很好，排列密集有序，几乎没有打破关系，当经过详细规划，并有专人严格管理。时代从战国晚期至西汉早期不间断，许多墓葬有完整的随葬品组合，是不可多得的秦文化重要材料。墓葬类型丰富，大小有别，体现了等级差别和时代特征。墓葬绝大多数为竖井墓道侧向或顺向洞室墓，少数为长方形竖穴土坑墓，个别为成年瓮棺葬。墓道多为西向，少数为东向，个别为南北向。墓主头向多与墓道方向相同。侧向洞室墓和长方形竖穴土坑墓时代多为战国晚期，主要分布在北区，北区可能为战国晚期秦军人墓地，人殉的现象多出现在此区墓葬中。顺向洞室墓时代多为秦代和西汉早期，主要分布在南区。南区的墓葬中还有在墓穴四周开挖防水设施的围沟墓、瓮棺葬墓和积石墓。

一条东西向宽7米左右的空挡区将整个秦人墓区分为南、北两个大区，这个空挡区可能是神道遗址，但是由于上部地层已被破坏，无法确知其表面的具体情况。

一些小型顺向洞室墓的墓道内，还发现挖有U形半环状小沟，内有淤土，也是防水设施。

本次发掘揭示了本地秦人洞室墓掘墓、埋棺、放物、封墓门、墓道祭祀、封埋等流程。除传统的科学发掘清理外，为了研究秦文化内涵和汉民族形成等重要课题，同时进行了体质人类学、DNA、古人寄生物、古人食性、动物考古、金属文物保护、漆木器灰痕保护等多学科及时采样与现场鉴定，获取了数以千计的相关标本，为后续研究提供了物质基础。

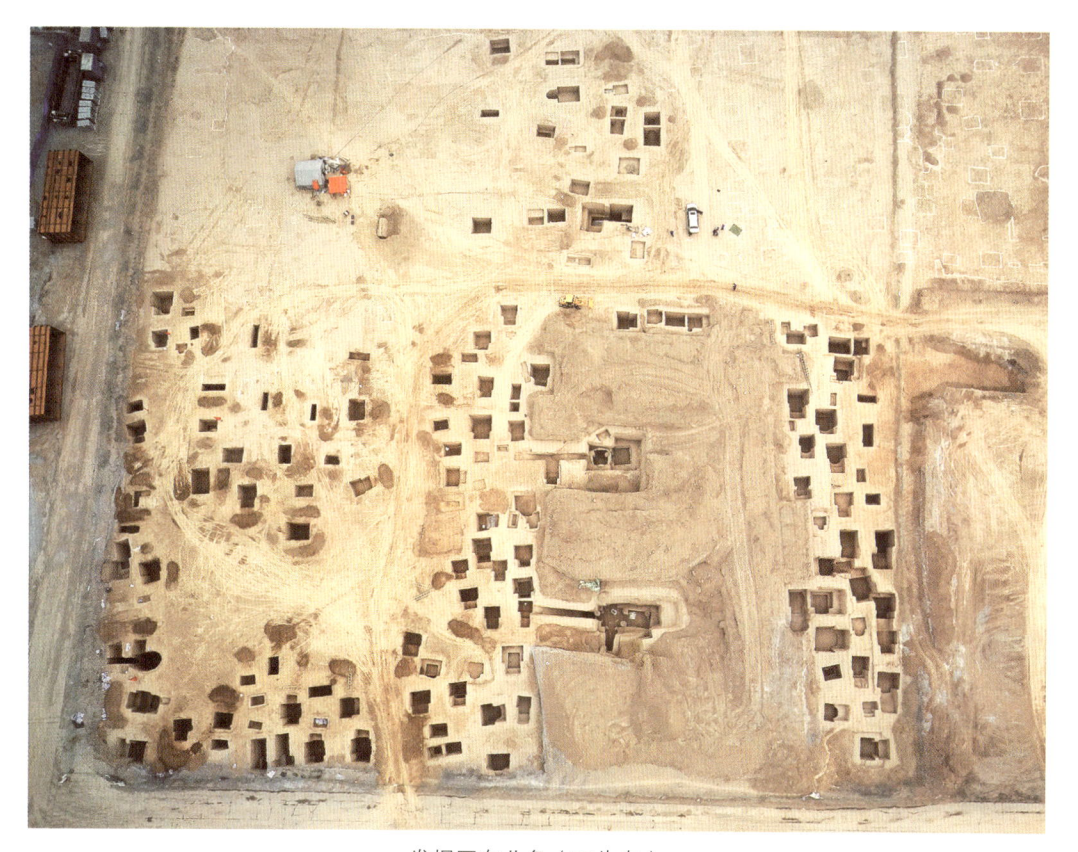

发掘区东北角（下为东）

战国秦人洞室墓M98（西—东）

西汉M335彩绘陶器(北—南)

秦汉M437瓮棺葬(东—西)

秦汉围沟墓M663全景（上北下南）

In 2014, as many as 802 tombs, distributed in a cemetery located in Datang Thermal Power Station in Sanmenxia City, were excavated. The discovery of 751 Qin tombs is the most important achievement. Firstly, the Qin tombs, numerous and well-preserved, were constructed during the time from late Warring States Period to early Western Han. Complete sets of funerary objects have been revealed from many of the Qin tombs. Secondly, the majority of Qin tombs are shaft tombs with a tomb tunnel pointing to the west. Thirdly, the Qin tombs were densely arranged probably according to a detailed planning, and almost none of them overlapped with another. In addition, an east-west seven-meter-wide open space, which could be a spirit road, divided the cemetery into two sections. Scattered with Qin tombs, most of which had a lateral entrance, a small-scale cemetery dating from Warring States Period was in the north section. Human sacrifices were unearned from tombs in this section. In the south section, there were tombs dating from Qin and early Western Han. Most of them were tombs with a tunnel, as the entry, digging into the ground. The discovery of this cemetery in Sanmenxia reveals the procedures concerning Qin shaft tombs such as digging, burying the dead, placing funerary objects, putting up a wooden tomb gate, conducting sacrificial rituals in the tomb tunnel and filling in and sealing the coffin pit.

# 山东龙口市西三甲墓群考古发掘重大收获

◎孙兆锋

西三甲墓地位于龙口市新嘉街道西三甲村村西、南以及东三甲村村东，墓地东西约2000米，南北宽约100米，部分压于现在村庄之下。2013年4月，烟台市博物馆考古队共发掘墓葬90座（另有1座清代墓），可分为三个时期：战国时期、西汉时期、东汉—魏晋时期。

战国墓共32座，均为长方形土坑竖穴墓，大部分带有熟土二层台，其中3座带壁龛，1座带脚坑，13座设腰坑。陶器的基本组合为鼎、罐、豆、壶，规格较高的墓还有仿铜器的匜、铏等陶礼器，多为彩绘陶。

西汉墓共51座，多为长方形土坑竖穴墓，大部分带有熟土二层台，仅2座墓带有生土二层台，其中13座带壁龛。1座为瓮棺。陶器的基本组合为罐和壶，多为素面和细绳纹，另有少数器物施彩绘。

东汉—魏晋墓共7座，均为带长斜坡墓道的砖室墓，穹隆顶，以菱形纹或鱼纹等花纹砖砌筑而成。随葬器物大多遗失或损毁，仅在填土和墓底发现少量残存的随葬器物。主要为白陶及釉陶器，器形有壶、耳杯、盘、勺等。

这批墓葬中的战国与西汉墓存在打破关系，时代序列较为紧密。与山东省内出土同时期墓葬进行比较，墓葬形制及随葬器物均有许多相同及相近之处，其中战国墓年代应为战国中、晚期；西汉墓数量多且分布广泛，西汉早、中、晚三期均有；东汉—魏晋墓数量较少，年代应为东汉晚期到西晋早期。

西三甲墓葬群的发现具有重要的学术意义：一、西三甲墓群年代从战国到魏晋延续700余年，与南侧1千米处的惤县故城时代相吻合，二者存在较密切的渊源，对研究胶东战国—魏晋时期的聚落关系、社会历史、丧葬习俗及演变具有重要意义。二、战国中晚期中小型墓的集中发现，在烟台地区尚属首次，特别是完整荒帷的出土，为检讨以往这个时期随葬的串饰品提供了新的依据。三、战国、西汉和东汉或魏晋在墓葬布局上存在明显的分区，一方面反映了当时这一带因惤县城的存在，人口密度较大；另一方面惤县的统治者在墓地的选择和分布上有较细致的区划。四、本次发掘的墓葬以中型墓葬为主，也有部分小型墓，按当时惤县的规模和等级，此处应存在更高等级贵族墓葬，这需要以后结合惤县故城聚落考古工作进一步分析和梳理。

战国墓（M66）

汉墓（M15）

东汉—魏晋墓（M30）

战国陶兽形鸟

汉代草叶纹铜镜

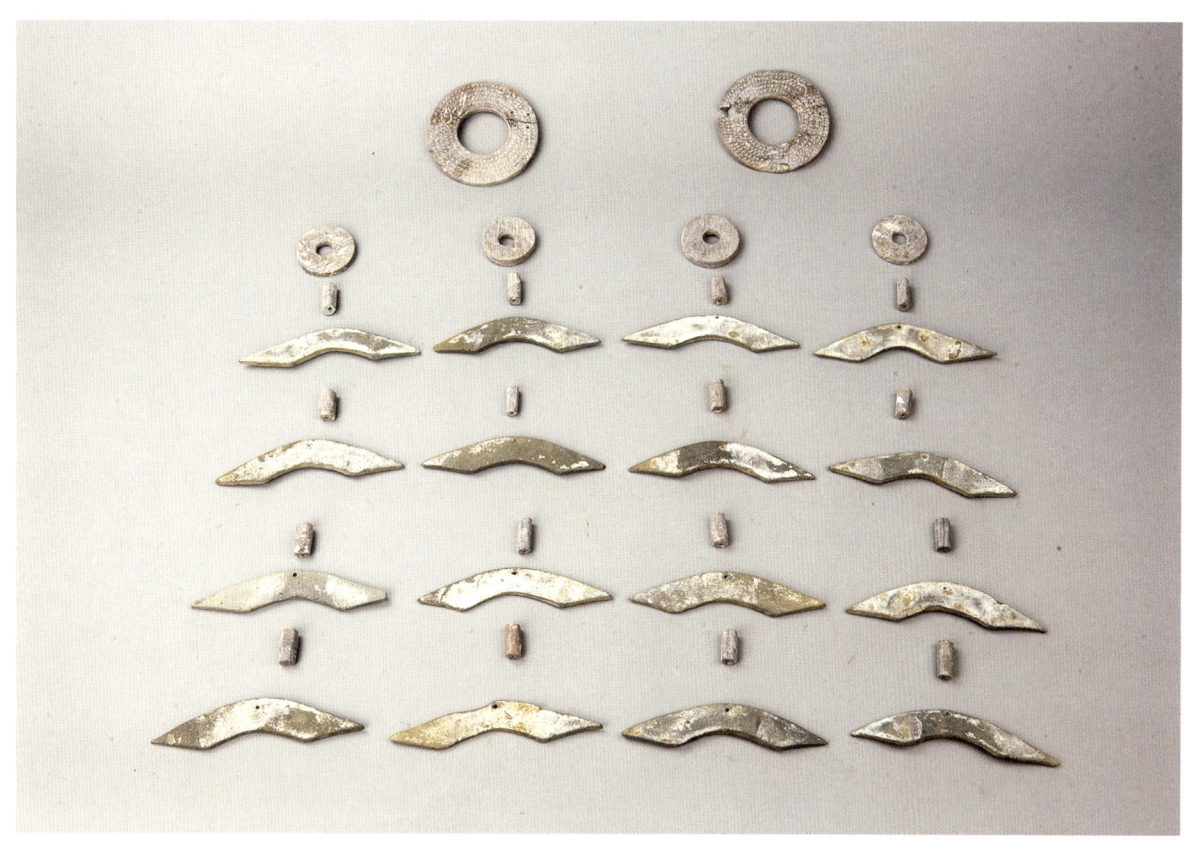

荒帷串饰

As many as 90 tombs have been discovered in a cemetery in West Sanjia Village. They were constructed during three periods, i.e. Warring States Period, Western Han and Eastern Han to Wei and Jin dynasties. Tombs dating from Warring States Period are all rectangular shaft tombs. The majority are north-south ones. The occupant of each tomb has been found buried in an extended supine position in a single lacquered coffin. Sets of unearthed potteries generally consist of Ding, jars, Dou, Hu, color-painted potteries imitating bronze ritual vessels Yi and He, and stringed ornaments on palls. The majority of Western Han tombs are east-west rectangular shaft tombs. Many occupants have been found buried in an extended supine position in a single coffin or in an inner coffin within an outer coffin. These coffins were usually lacquered. Sets of unearthed potteries generally consist of jars and Hu. Tombs dating back to the epoch from Eastern Han to Wei and Jin dynasties are all domed single-chambered or dual-chambered brick tombs with long sloping tomb tunnels. The majority are east-west tombs. West Sanjia Cemetery is closely connected with the nearby site of Jianxian since they are contemporaries. The discovery of West Sanjia Cemetery is of great significance for the study of relationships among settlements, social history, burial customs and evolutions concerned during the time from Warring States Period to Wei and Jin dynasties in Shandong district.

# 安徽六安市十里铺战国—西汉土墩墓

◎ 王　峰

十里铺土墩墓群位于安徽六安经济技术开发区，此地位于大别山的山前丘陵地带，多有隆起的岗地。安徽省文物考古研究所于2013年6—9月发掘了战国—西汉时期墓葬138座。其中有41座分别位于7个土墩内。土墩略呈椭圆形，包括一墩一墓1座、一墩二墓2座、一墩多墓4座，最多的7号墩内共有12座墓葬。

封土墩的发掘采用四分法，即以穿过土墩中心的正东西和正南北的两道隔梁为界线，将土墩分成四个区域进行发掘。由土墩堆土的层位关系，在几座一墩多墓的土墩内，均发现有明显早晚关系的墓葬。

一墩多墓的情况以1号墩（编号D1）为例，其内发现墓葬6座（M17～M22）。其中M17开口于④层下，M19开口于⑨层下，M18、M20～M22开口于⑩层下，6座墓葬的地层关系是M17→M19→M18、M20～M22。这6座墓葬中，M17、M19为带斜坡墓道的"凸"字形土坑竖穴墓，其余4座均为长方形土坑竖穴墓，有的设有头龛。出土陶器的组合为鼎、壶、钫、豆、敦、镟斗、罐、耳杯及灶等。初步判断M17、M19的年代为西汉早期，M18、M20～M22的年代为战国晚期。

一墩二墓的情况有2号墩（编号D2）和3号墩（编号D3）两座。这两个土墩内各自有并列的2座墓葬，每座墓葬的形制与1号墩的M17、M19略同，随葬品中陶器的组合也大致相同。不同的是，一组并列的两座墓葬中，其中一座随葬有铜剑，另一座却没有。据此判断同一墩内的两座墓葬具有性别上的差异，有剑者为男性，并列的则为女性，于是判断同一墩内的两座墓葬应为夫妻异穴合葬墓。

从此次发掘可以认识到一墩二墓与一墩多墓是两种性质有别的葬制。一墩二墓的情况其实就是夫妻异穴合葬，这在汉代的埋葬风俗中并不少见。而一墩多墓则是长江以南吴越地区先秦以来的文化传统，不见于北方地区。因此，安徽六安发现的战国—西汉时期的土墩墓，应当受到了吴越文化传统的影响。

D1封土剖面（东—西）及墓葬平面分布

D1M19随葬品（一）

D1M19随葬品（二）

D1M19随葬品(三)

In 2013, as many as 138 mound tombs, constructed during the time from Warring States Period to Western Han, were discovered in Shilipu Village, Lu'an, Anhui Province. 7 mounds contain 41 tombs in total. There are three types, i.e. a single tomb in one mound, two tombs in the same mound and multiple tombs in one mound. During excavation, the mounds were divided into four quadrants. In fact, building two tombs in the same mound and digging multiple tombs in one mound are two kinds of burial customs by nature. The former is a joint burial of a husband and wife. The latter reflects the cultural convention that had been passed down since the Pre-Qin Period in Wu-Yue Area south of the Yangtze River. Such a cultural convention was not adopted in north China. It can be concluded that the mound tombs discovered in Lu'an, Anhui Province, used to be influenced by Wu-Yue culture and traditions.

# 陕西西汉帝陵考古（2011—2017年）

◎焦南峰　马永嬴　杨武站　曹　龙　王　东　赵旭阳

2006年开始，陕西省考古研究院与中国社会科学院考古研究所、咸阳市文物考古研究所、西安市文物保护考古研究院联合组成汉陵考古队，展开了对西汉帝陵的考古调查、勘探与发掘工作。此次工作采取"全方位调查、大面积普探、重点地区详探、关键部位试掘、高精度测绘及资料数字化"的工作思路，田野工作与资料整理齐头并进，取得了较大成果。

先后对长陵、霸陵、平陵、杜陵、延陵等5座帝陵和汉太上皇陵、薄太后南陵、钩弋夫人云陵、许皇后少陵以及咸阳原上的司家庄战国秦陵园、严家沟战国秦陵园进行了考古调查、勘探、测绘，对阳陵帝陵陵园东门遗址、东司马门道建筑遗址、渭陵陵园园墙、围沟进行了部分发掘。发现陵园17座，确定陵邑5座，探明建筑遗址70余处、外藏坑1200余座、古墓葬550余座。确定了11座陵墓的陵区范围和基本布局，探明了各个陵园的结构、封土情况、墓葬形制、外藏坑、建筑遗址、陪葬墓等，发现了诸如多重陵园、陵区道路系统等新的遗迹现象，大致了解了文物遗存的性质、内涵。对研究中国古代帝陵，特别是汉代帝陵制度的发展演变具有重大意义。

西汉帝陵整体布局的厘清使我们基本掌握了西汉帝陵的平面形制、特点及其演变；大量外藏坑的发现，验证了史书中有关"外藏椁"的记载；汉文帝霸陵的考古新发现，使霸陵帝陵墓葬形制的历史之争尘埃落定；陵区道路、祔葬墓的发现与确认，为西汉帝陵研究增加了新内容；通过阳陵帝陵陵园东门遗址、东司马门道建筑遗址、渭陵陵园园墙、围沟的考古发掘，了解了西汉帝陵中的门阙制度及各类建筑的形制、营建方式；咸阳原战国秦陵园的确认，弥补了秦陵发展演变的缺环，为秦咸阳城研究提供了重要资料。

工作过程中，积极尝试使用新技术、新方法，如不同时期航空照片的对比判读、无损伤探测新技术等。

资料整理、研究与田野考古工作同步进行，取得了较多成果，积极推动了西汉帝陵、战国秦陵的深入研究，同时锻炼、培养了一批中青年专业人员，使他们成为秦汉考古领域的一支重要力量。另西汉帝陵大遗址考古工作开展以来，取得了显著的社会效益和较大的社会影响。

汉延陵帝陵封土（北—南）

汉延陵陵园内祔葬墓（东北—西南）

汉阳陵帝陵陵园东门遗址出土瓦当

汉阳陵帝陵东阙门遗址发掘现场（西北—东南）

汉阳陵帝陵陵园东门遗址踏步台阶（东南—西北）

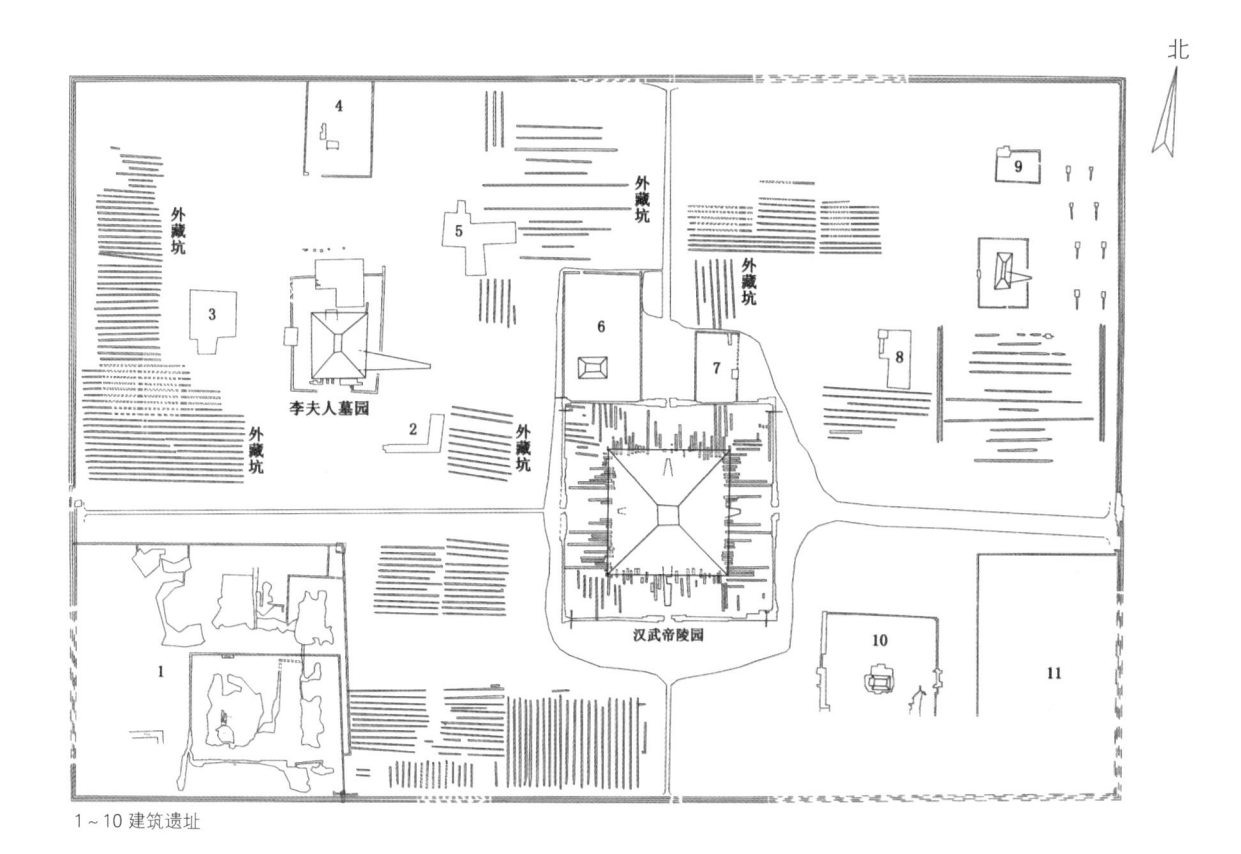

汉茂陵陵园平面布局图

Archaeological surveys, reconnaissances and excavations of mausoleums buried with emperors of Han Dynasty have been conducted since 2006. Field work and information sorting were carried out simultaneously. Major discoveries have been made after all-round investigations, large-scale general probes, intensive explorations in key regions, trial diggings in key sections, high-precision mapping and information digitalization. Outcomes of archaeological work done during 2011 to 2017 include determining the area and general layout of 11 Western Han imperial mausoleums and finding out the structure of each mausoleum, the tumulus in it, the structure of the burial, outer burial pits, architectural remains, satellite tombs, etc. Remnants that have been newly revealed are of multiple mausoleums and road systems within. Nature and significance of excavated relics have been generally understood. It is of great importance for the study of ancient imperial mausoleums in China and especially crucial for researches concerning the development and evolution of Han imperial mausoleums.

# 江苏盱眙县大云山江都王陵

◎李则斌

大云山汉墓位于江苏省盱眙县马坝镇云山村大云山山顶，海拔73.60米，西距盱眙县城30千米，南距汉代东阳城遗址1千米，西南与青墩山、小云山汉代贵族墓地相邻。2009年9月—2011年12月，南京博物院对大云山汉墓区进行了全面勘探与抢救性发掘，揭示出一处比较完整的西汉江都王刘非陵园，出土了陶器、铜器、金银器、玉器、漆器等各类文物一万余件（套），许多文物均为首次发现。

陵园平面近似正方形，每边长490米。陵园内共发现主墓3座、陪葬墓11座、车马陪葬坑2座、兵器陪葬坑2座。其中，主墓均分布于陵园南部，陪葬墓均分布于陵园北部，车马陪葬坑位于陵园南部，兵器陪葬坑分部于陵园北侧，紧靠陵墙。

通过近三年的考古勘探与发掘，已基本明确了大云山西汉江都王陵园的基本结构和平面布局。出土的大量漆器、玉器、铜器、金银器等精美文物，尤其是编钟、编磬、玉棺、金缕玉衣等，学术研究意义重大。

陵园内的陪葬墓区经过精心设计与规划，所有陪葬墓布局整齐划一，墓葬规模、棺椁结构、随葬品种类与数量等皆以该墓距离主墓的远近逐次降低或减少，统一的营造模式显示出与墓主人之间明显的身份与等级差异。

一号墓墓主明确为西汉第一代江都王刘非，这改变了以往关于西汉荆国、吴国、江都国、广陵国诸侯王葬地的认识，为重新考虑诸如仪征庙山墓地的性质（以往一直认为庙山墓地为江都王墓地）等课题提供了新的资料。

此外，大云山西汉诸侯王陵园的确认，为重新认识东阳城遗址提供了契机。目前的发现表明东阳城除小城外存在着范围更广的大城，如此，陵园与东阳城之间的关系值得进一步探讨，东阳城的性质也需要重新评价。

大云山西汉江都王陵园的发掘，出土材料极为丰富，为进一步研究西汉诸侯王陵制度提供了重要资料，并为汉代考古的相关研究提供了新的方法，开拓了新的视野。

大云山汉墓陵园全景（上北下南）

一号墓与二号墓全景（上东下西）

二区下层编钟情况

三A区下层编磬出土情况

秦汉一统　雄风万里　425

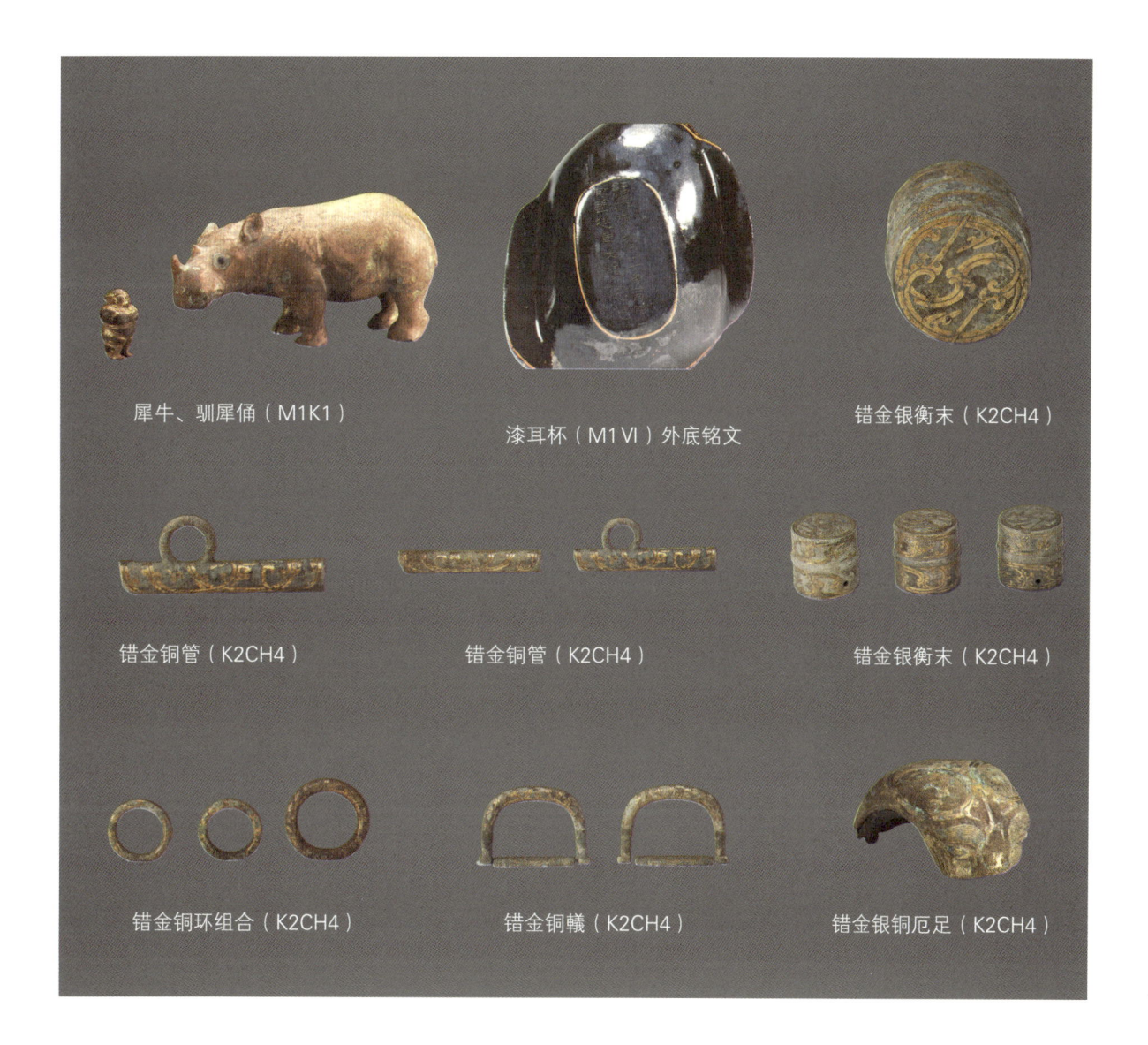

犀牛、驯犀俑（M1K1）　　　漆耳杯（M1Ⅵ）外底铭文　　　错金银衡末（K2CH4）

错金铜管（K2CH4）　　　错金铜管（K2CH4）　　　错金银衡末（K2CH4）

错金铜环组合（K2CH4）　　　错金铜軏（K2CH4）　　　错金银铜厄足（K2CH4）

On top of Mount Dayun, there is a walled mausoleum built for a marquis of Western Han. The plane layout of the mausoleum is almost a square. Inside the mausoleum, 3 major tombs, 11 satellite tombs, 2 chariot pits and 2 pits buried with weapons have been discovered. All the major tombs are in the southern part of the mausoleum, the satellite tombs are in the northern part, the chariot pits are also in the southern part and the pits containing weapons are in the northern part close to the wall. The structure and grade of the mausoleum, construction of the coffin chamber (concealed within in a frame structure made of cypresses), the jade coffin and jade garments, high-level funerary objects all indicate that the first Marquis of Jiangdu in Western Han, Liu Fei, is buried here.

# 江苏徐州市卧牛山 M2～M4 汉墓

◎刘 超

卧牛山位于徐州市泉山区火花村（现荣盛城小区）南侧，距城中心约5千米，海拔131.80米，由东、西两山头组成，M2～M4均位于西山北麓，惜古代均已遭盗掘。

卧牛山M2、M3于2010年4—9月发掘，为"凿山为藏"的大型横穴式岩洞墓，墓葬坐南朝北，墓向348°，墓葬上方依山势覆有斜坡状封土，封土以黄褐色、红褐色黏土相间夯实。两墓东西并列，中有门道互通，均由独立的墓道、甬道、壁龛、墓室等组成。墓道、甬道、门道及各墓室地面均凿有排水槽，且相互贯通，利用高低落差将积水排至裂隙或墓外。墓葬所在山体局部成岩作用较差，甬道、墓室四壁等岩溶裂隙处均以石板镶补。

M2各墓室（W1～W8）之间以门道或甬道相连接，因功用不同而形制各异。室顶结构有两面坡式、四阿式、四角攒尖式等。W3～W5、W8等墓室内均构建瓦木结构建筑，业已朽毁坍塌。部分墓室壁面残存横向或纵向红褐色漆线，应为搭构建筑或壁面装饰等所绘。W7室为前堂，墓室高大宽敞、置有方柱；W6室内出土辊轮，应为棺室所在。

M3墓室较M2墓室规格较小且低矮，墓室装饰技法与M2墓室相异，各室均未构建瓦木结构建筑，墓室髹饰精致，壁面多涂有数层澄泥，再髹以褐漆，最外层涂以朱砂或绘有壁画，惜已剥落殆尽，墓室顶部多髹褐色漆。所见墓室除E8室外，四壁顶端及室顶均嵌有铁环用以钩挂帷帐。

M4亦为横穴式岩洞墓，坐南朝北，墓向8°，由墓道及墓室两部分组成。墓室为狭长的长方形洞室，开凿不甚规整，墓口原有木质门板封堵。墓室中部残存棺漆痕迹及残碎墓主骨骸。

卧牛山M2、M3为典型的横穴式岩洞墓，两墓结构相异，M2墓室高大，部分墓室搭建瓦木结构建筑等形制，与中晚期楚王墓葬形制基本相同；M3墓室较矮，墓葬开凿规整细致，墓壁装饰等都明显带有早期楚王陵墓特点，两墓形制结构具有从早期向中期过渡的特点，其整体形制结构接近于西汉楚国第六代楚王刘注及王后墓，且在时代上应早于该墓，结合徐州西汉早期其他楚王陵墓形制特点，M2、M3或为西汉楚国第五代楚王刘道及其王后的合葬墓。M4为典型的横穴式岩洞墓，其规模较M2、M3相去甚远，徐州地区的岩洞墓墓主均为楚王或王后，列侯以下均为竖穴墓，故卧牛山M4墓主亦为王或后级别，另对出土盆骨确认，其墓主为女性，推测M4墓主或为楚王的早薨或后续王后。

M2W7室

M3E2室

M3E3室

Tomb M2 and tomb M3, discovered in Mount Wo niu, are large-scale horizontal cave tombs taking the advantage of a mountain. Both north-facing tombs, connected by a corridor, lie side by side. They each consist of a tomb tunnel, a passage, niches, eight coffin chambers, etc. On top of each tomb, there is a slope-like tumulus leaning against the mountain. The scale of tomb M2 is larger than that of tomb M3. They were probably constructed for the fifth marquis of Chu, Liu Dao and his wife, in Western Han. Tomb M4, which has a tomb tunnel, is also a horizontal north-facing cave tomb whose coffin chamber is a narrow rectangular. Tomb M4 is a small-scale tomb whose structure is simpler that those of tomb M2 and tomb M3. The occupant of tomb M4 is probably the spouse of Marquis of Chu who passed away very early.

# 河南南阳市百里奚西汉彩绘漆棺墓

◎王凤剑 翟京襄

百里奚西汉彩绘漆棺墓（M12）位于河南省南阳市百里奚路中段。此地俗称麒麟岗，地形为岗坡地，西高东低。

M12为"甲"字形斜坡墓道竖穴土坑墓，方向198°，墓室被盗。墓室平面为长方形，斜壁内收，距墓口3米处有生土二层台，中部为椁室及器物箱。椁室呈南北向放置，为两重椁，椁墙板、挡板皆为方木堆砌而成，椁板之间榫卯扣合，并用S形铁耙钉加固。椁室和南、北器物箱的上部及四周全部充填青膏泥。棺室分外棺和内棺，均为长方形，棺盖与棺体连接处凿有子母口，并用卯榫连接。外棺内侧刷有棕红色漆，外侧表面刷有较厚的黑色漆，上面施有红白彩绘。北侧绘有朱雀，东侧为白虎，南侧为玄武，西侧为青龙；棺盖上绘有阳乌和蟾蜍，主图四周绘有云纹加以修饰。内棺放置于外棺内，外侧表面刷有较厚的黑漆，内侧刷有红漆。棺内人骨一具，为仰身曲肢。棺内放置铜剑1件、铁削刀1件。M12虽经盗扰，仍出土陶、铜、铁、玉、木、骨等质地随葬品90余件套。陶器器表均施有黑漆，内施红漆。木漆器中耳杯较多，器表施有红漆。木漆盘表面施有红黑相间的纹饰，口沿镶嵌有银圈。在南侧器物箱出土玉印1方，正方形，正、反两面均雕刻有篆体印文，分别为"孔调"和"臣调"。

M12与相邻的M10时代均为西汉早期，M10下葬年代稍晚于M12，应该为共用同一墓塚的夫妻异穴合葬墓。特别值得一提的是M12出土四神图彩绘漆棺保存基本完好，黑底饰红白彩，四周画面丰富、精美，具有珍贵的史料价值。M12的墓主人应该为一个封秩千石或以上的地方官吏。这两座墓葬的考古发掘为研究中原地区汉代历史文化的发展及随葬习俗、埋葬制度等提供了新的实物资料。

彩绘漆棺发现以后，我们及时邀请相关单位文物保护专家，制定科学的文物保护方案，并运用3D扫描和红外照相技术对彩绘漆棺的相关信息进行完整记录，用X光探伤技术对棺内的文物分布及材质进行探测及内窥镜探视，为出土文物的科学保护打下了坚实基础。

M12外棺朱雀彩绘

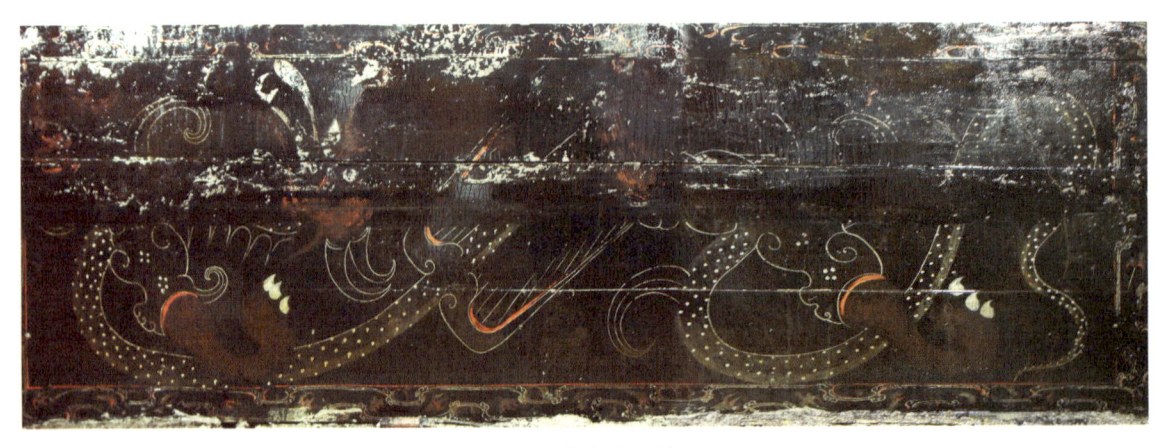

M12外棺青龙彩绘

秦汉一统 雄风万里 431

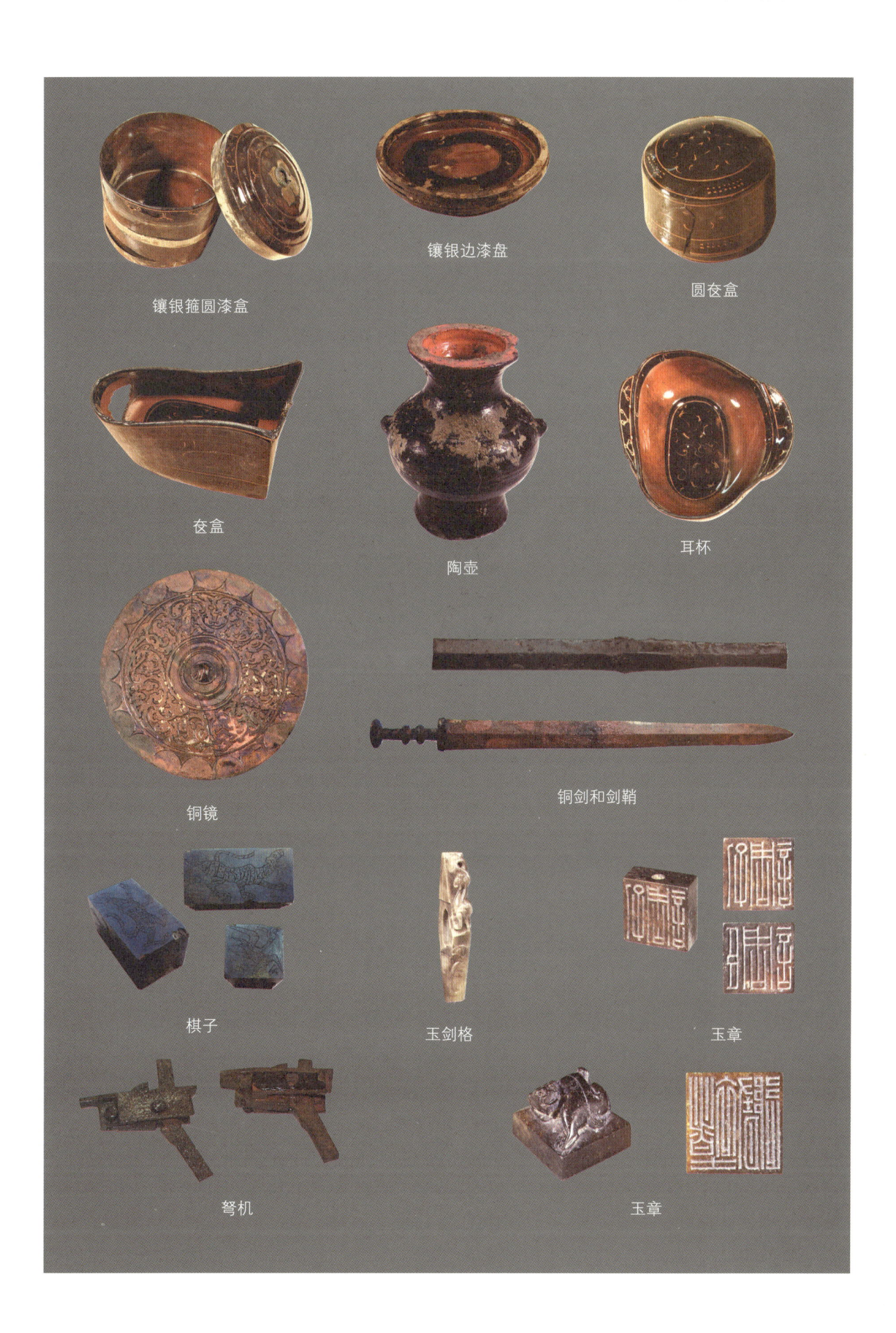

镶银箍圆漆盒　镶银边漆盘　圆奁盒

奁盒　陶壶　耳杯

铜镜　铜剑和剑鞘

棋子　玉剑格　玉章

弩机　玉章

M12全景

In 2014, two tombs, M10 and M12, dating from Han Dynasty were discovered near Bailixi Road in Nanyang City. Lying in the same position and paralleling with each other closely, both tombs are shaft tombs whose plane layout resembles the Chinese character "甲 (Jia)". One tomb was buried with a husband and his wife was the occupant of the other. In tomb M12, there is a double-layered inner coffin and a dual-layered outer coffin. The coffin chamber and the utensil box are concealed in black clay. The inner coffin, decorated with the colored Si Shen Pattern, is well-preserved. The tomb occupant of M12 should be a regional official ranking Zhi Qian Dan or higher in early Western Han.

# 山西蒲县曹家庄西汉匈奴墓

◎田建文 穆文军

曹家庄墓地位于山西省蒲县县城西南约5千米处的蒲城镇曹家庄村西北，2016年11月—2017年1月，山西省考古研究所共清理墓葬42座，其中土圹竖穴墓24座，洞室墓18座。洞室墓以洞室开口在墓道两端的正洞室墓为主，开口在一侧的侧室墓仅1座。

这批墓葬可分南、北两大区，北区以土圹竖穴墓为主，南区均为洞室墓。北大区又分两个小区，北1区自东北向西南可分5排，北2区自西北向东南也分5排；南大区墓葬头向没有规律可循，无法分排，只能按墓葬间距分为5个小区。

研究表明，这片墓地北大区早于南大区，是战国晚期以来魏国小贵族和平民墓，延续到汉武帝前期；南大区的洞室墓有8座墓随葬铜货币，除五铢钱外，M1、M29随葬大泉五十，时代从汉武帝后期到新莽时期。墓葬中的一些特殊葬俗和内蒙古、甘青地区的匈奴墓葬相同或相似，如随葬动物肢骨、狗，随葬铁鐎斗、小口罐，以及部分陶器底部有制陶过程中形成的方形垫痕等现象。据此，我们认为曹家庄墓地的洞室墓与匈奴人有关。

汉武帝元鼎五年（公元前112年）匈奴进犯位于今内蒙古鄂尔多斯的五原属国时，骑兵长驹几率领属国骑兵予以反击，抓获了乌维单于的从兄，被汉武帝封到河东郡北屈为列侯，称"骐侯"，从此北屈县一分为二，一为北屈，一为"骐县"。曹家庄墓地西汉中、晚期的洞室墓，印证了这段历史，并且部分得到体质人类学结果的支持。

中国境内西汉匈奴墓，有陕西长安客省庄、铜川枣庙、宁夏同心倒墩子、内蒙古伊克昭盟补洞沟、西沟畔墓地等，但这些墓葬多不出或没有发掘陶器，发掘陶器的墓葬也难以与中原地区的同期同类陶器做比较，而曹家庄的16座墓，无论是时间刻度，还是体质人类学，都是研究匈奴墓葬的绝好材料，这也是最偏东南的一处匈奴墓地。

M24铜器

M26壁龛内随葬器物

陶茧形壶  铜博山炉

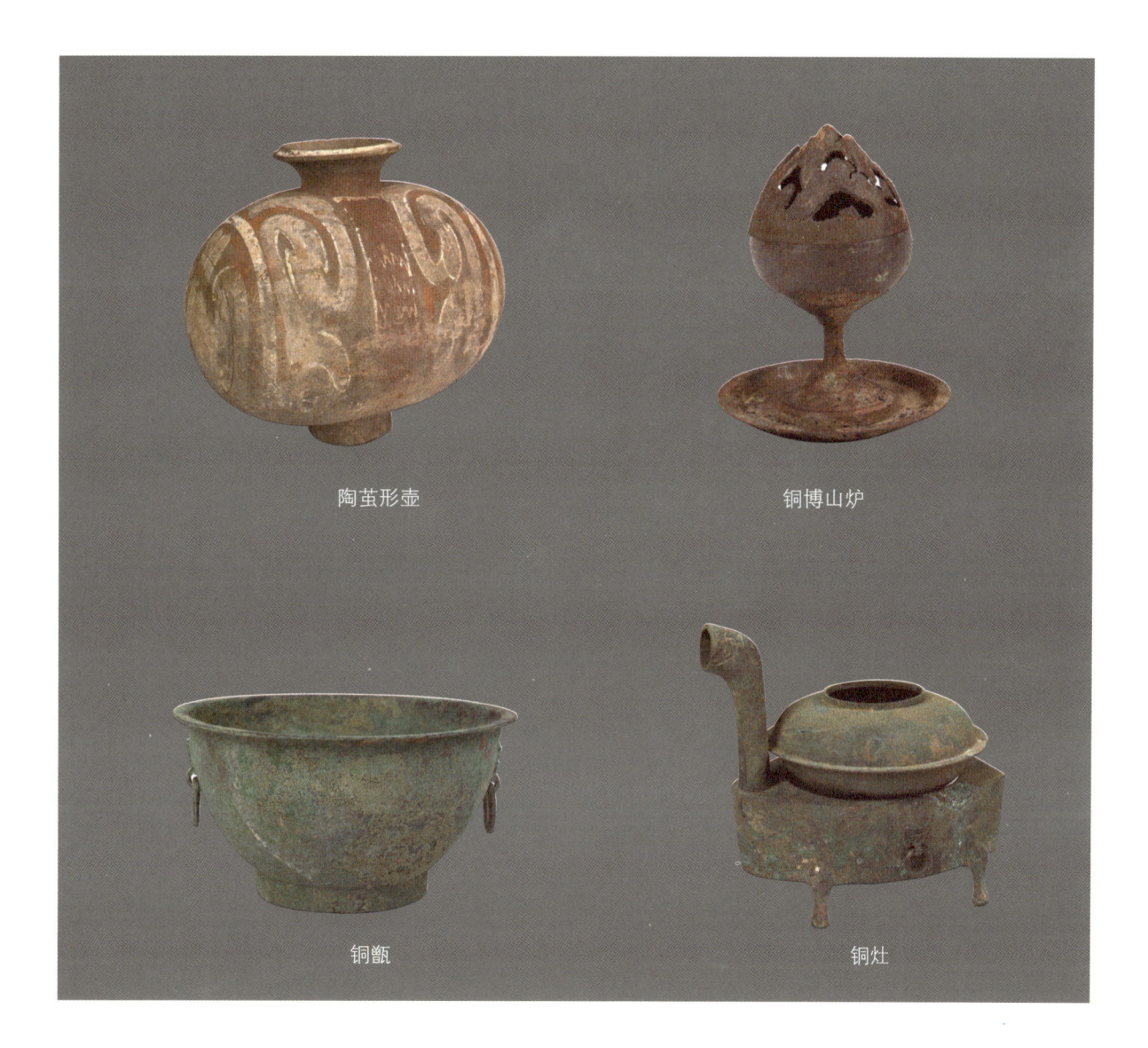

铜甑  铜灶

In Caojiazhuang Cemetery, as many as 16 tombs buried with Xiongnu people who lived during Western Han have been discovered in the south zone of the excavated area. Constructed during the time spanning from the final phase of Emperor Wu's reign in Han Dynasty to Xin Dynasty, they are cave tombs respectively with a sloping tomb tunnel. Funerary objects such as iron Jiao Dou and small-mouthed jars and square pad marks, left during production process, on the bottom of potteries are respectively the same as or similar with those discovered in Xiongnu tombs located in Inner Mongolia, Gansu and Qinghai provinces. After a comprehensive study basing on archaeological materials, documentaries and physical anthropological test results, it has been determined that Caojiazhuang Cemetery correlates with Xiongnu people.

# 河北石家庄市马鞍山汉代王侯墓

◎赵战护

马鞍山汉墓，位于石家庄市长安区南翟营村北，现存南、北两座墓葬，封土相连，形似马鞍，故而得名。2015年5月—2016年5月为配合石济铁路客运专线建设，河北省文物研究所联合石家庄市文物保护研究所对马鞍山汉墓M1（北侧之墓）进行了抢救性发掘。

通过勘探，未发现陵园沟、墙及陪葬墓、陪葬坑等遗迹，之后我们在采取措施保证石德铁路安全运营的前提下对墓葬南半部进行了解剖式发掘。这是一座多室双墓道砖石混筑墓，其先开凿一坑穴，采用预留墓道、南侧室、主室的方法夯筑而成。南侧室砖室墓壁顶部砌筑硬山顶；主室以石板砌筑墓壁，墓壁顶部砌筑硬山顶，上铺石板；主室与南侧室通过门相通。主室内壁砌筑夯土二层台，其上砌筑垂直墓壁的砖墙，砖墙上置石板，石板上再放置各类随葬器物，主室底部以木头铺底，其上再铺设石板。东西墓道皆为斜坡底，底部夯筑，东西墓道以墓门与主室相连，其中东墓道宽且长于西墓道，东墓门阔于西墓门，东墓道当为主墓道。

从这种墓葬结构来看，双墓道有西汉早期的特征，石板和砖混筑的方法，既有西汉早期的特征，又有东汉的特征，应是由石板向砖砌过渡的时期；仿厢结构这种葬制是由先秦、汉代的回廊发展而来，流行于西汉中晚期，由此判断这应是西汉中期至东汉早期的一座墓葬。从出土物来看，封土中出土了半两钱、五铢钱，也说明这是一座汉武帝以后的墓葬；再从随葬品来看，仿青铜礼器的陶壶、陶匜、陶钫数量较多，同时又未见陶厕、陶楼、陶猪等陶模型器，这也是西汉中期随葬器物的特点，另一方面出土器物与器形特征有着典型的西汉中晚期特征。综合以上，我们可以断定这是一座西汉中晚期的墓葬。关于墓主人的身份，首先从墓葬的规模和形制上来看，双墓道、阔墓室、仿厢结构，这是王侯常用的葬制；出土数量较多的陶器，尤其是仿铜礼器，与高庄汉墓、北新城汉墓、定州汉墓等是一致的；发现的木制建筑痕迹，满城汉墓大量采用。由此可见，这是西汉中后期的一座王侯墓葬。

陶壶　　　　　　　　　　　　　陶仓

陶奁　　　　　　　　　　　　　陶奁

陶耳杯　　　　　　　　　　　　陶匜

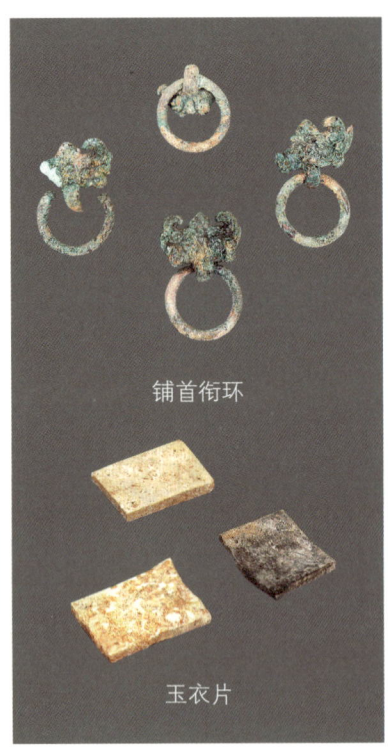

发掘区全正射影像（上北下南）

铺首衔环

玉衣片

Ma'anshan Han mausoleum is named after its saddle-like tumulus consisting of two mounds, one in the south and the other in the north. After excavation, it has been found out that the plane layout of tomb M1 resembles an east-west lying Chinese character "中 (Zhong)". Apart from the main chamber and symmetrical side chambers, there are twin tunnels leading to tomb M1. The tomb per se is a brick-chambered one. Stone slabs are piled as the walls of the main chamber; inside the main chamber, there is a two-tiered terrace made of rammed earth. On the terrace, stone walls perpendicular to the tomb wall were constructed to place stone slabs on which a diversified range of funerary objects were laid. Wood was used to cover the bottom; a layer of stone slabs was on top of the wood. The ceiling has been found out to be a wooden saddle roof without the overhang at the ends. The south side chamber, whose ceiling is the same as that of the main chamber, was constructed with bricks. Both tomb tunnels are slopes with a rammed base. The east tomb tunnel should be the main tunnel. Although the tomb had been raided before excavation, potteries, such as Hu, Fu, Fang and clay pieces that had been impressed by seals, bronzes, such as copper hanging stoves, decorative Pu Shou, bronze table legs and bronze eared cups, and jade pieces from a jade garment have been unearthed. After comprehensive analyses, it has been determined that Ma'anshan Han mausoleum should be constructed for a marquis during the middle and late Western Han.

# 山东青岛市土山屯汉墓群考古发掘

◎ 彭 峪

2011年、2016年和2017年，为配合基础工程建设，青岛市文物保护考古研究所联合黄岛区博物馆，对土山屯墓群部分区域进行了三次考古发掘。发掘工作中突出课题意识，积极探索鲁东南沿海汉代封土墓内涵及其与江浙一带的交流联系；严格执行田野考古操作规程，以寻找遗迹间时空关系为准则，灵活采用探沟和探方发掘方法；引入聚落考古理论，开展对周边遗址的调查，发现了同时期的城址、窑炉等相关遗迹；注重现代科技手段应用，配备无人机、RTK、图形工作站等设备，运用三维建模、红外扫描等技术提取资料；贯彻田野发掘与文物保护结合的理念，多次邀请文保专家到现场指导文物提取和保护；搭建多学科合作科研平台，开展植物考古、同位素分析、古DNA鉴定等多学科研究工作，取得了以下重要突破。

1. 土山屯墓群墓葬布局、封土、祭台、棺椁形制、出土文物等均保存较好，构成完整的有机整体，在汉代中低级贵族墓葬发掘资料中非常罕见。其封土下两座墓葬的结构，异于本地区发掘的胶州赵家庄汉墓、黄岛安子沟汉墓和日照海曲汉墓的"墩式封土墓"，为鲁东南沿海区域的这类封土墓研究提供了新的考古资料。

2. 墓群所在区域为秦汉时期琅琊郡范围，为秦汉时期琅琊郡或其下辖县（侯）地域。本次不仅发掘了一批"刘氏家族"墓葬，还在墓地北4千米处发现了一处同时期城址，该遗址调查发现大量汉"千秋万岁"瓦当、大型柱础石、双陶水管等重要迹象。墓群和遗址的发现，为进一步探寻盛极一时的琅琊郡地望等历史之谜提供了重要考古依据。

3. 土山屯墓群的墓葬形制及出土器物具有鲜明的吴越文化特色，大量原始青瓷器、扬州风格漆器和温明、玉席等葬具的发现，为研究汉代南北沿海地区经济文化交流和海上丝绸之路提供了翔实物证。

4. 遣册和"上计"文书牍等出土文献资料，非常珍贵。县级上计文书木牍的发现，是墓葬内发掘出土第一批完整的汉代县级上计文书牍。这批木牍保存完整、内容详尽、文字清晰，补文献之不足，对汉代行政制度、司法制度和书法史研究等具有重大意义，具有很高的文献价值和历史研究价值。

440　黄淮七省考古新发现

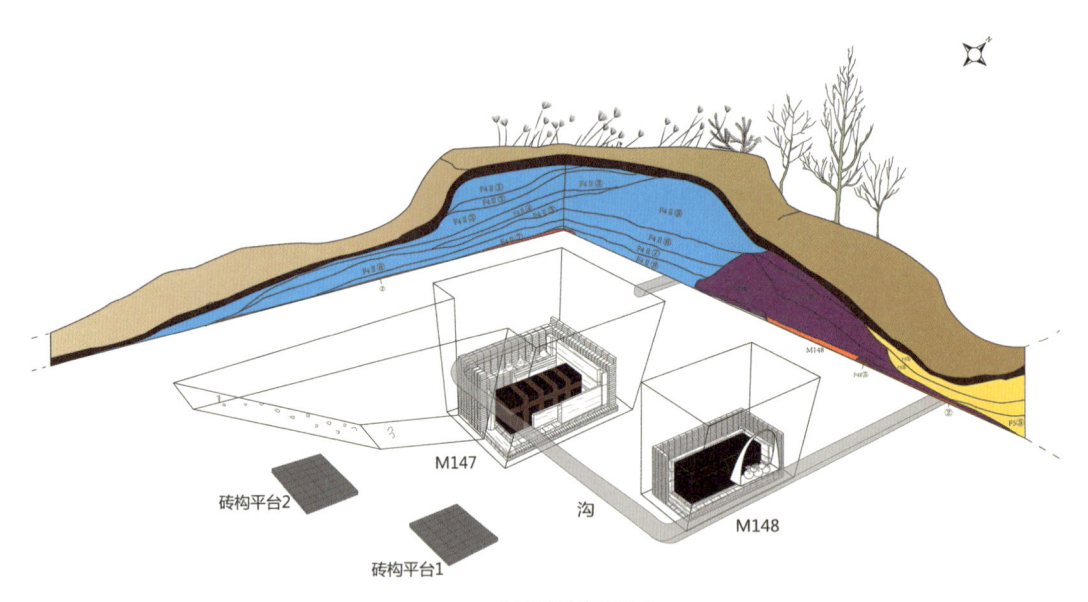

封4遗迹剖视图

封5前的祭台

封10前的祭台

秦汉一统　雄风万里　441

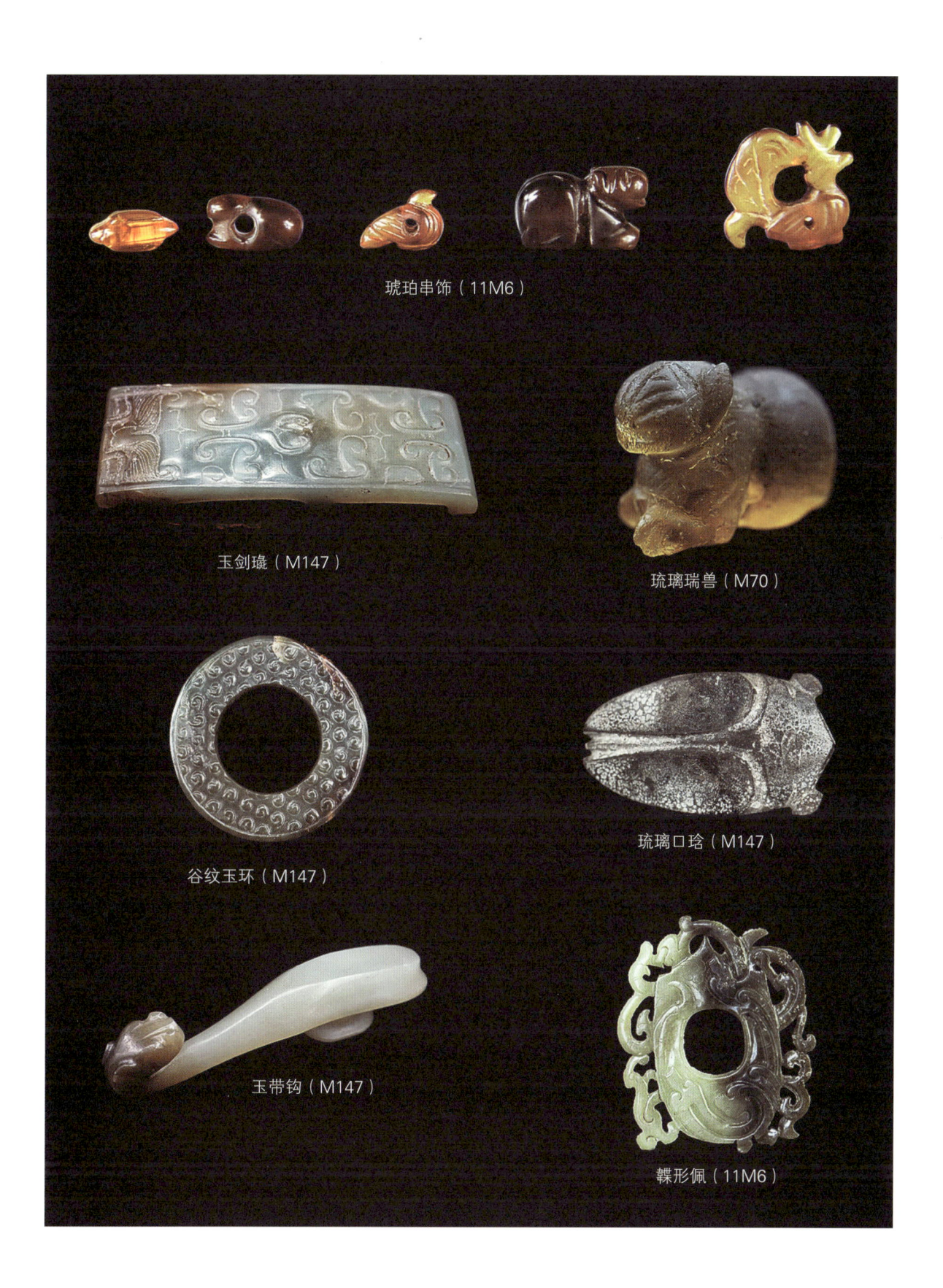

琥珀串饰（11M6）

玉剑璏（M147）

琉璃瑞兽（M70）

谷纹玉环（M147）

琉璃口琀（M147）

玉带钩（M147）

韘形佩（11M6）

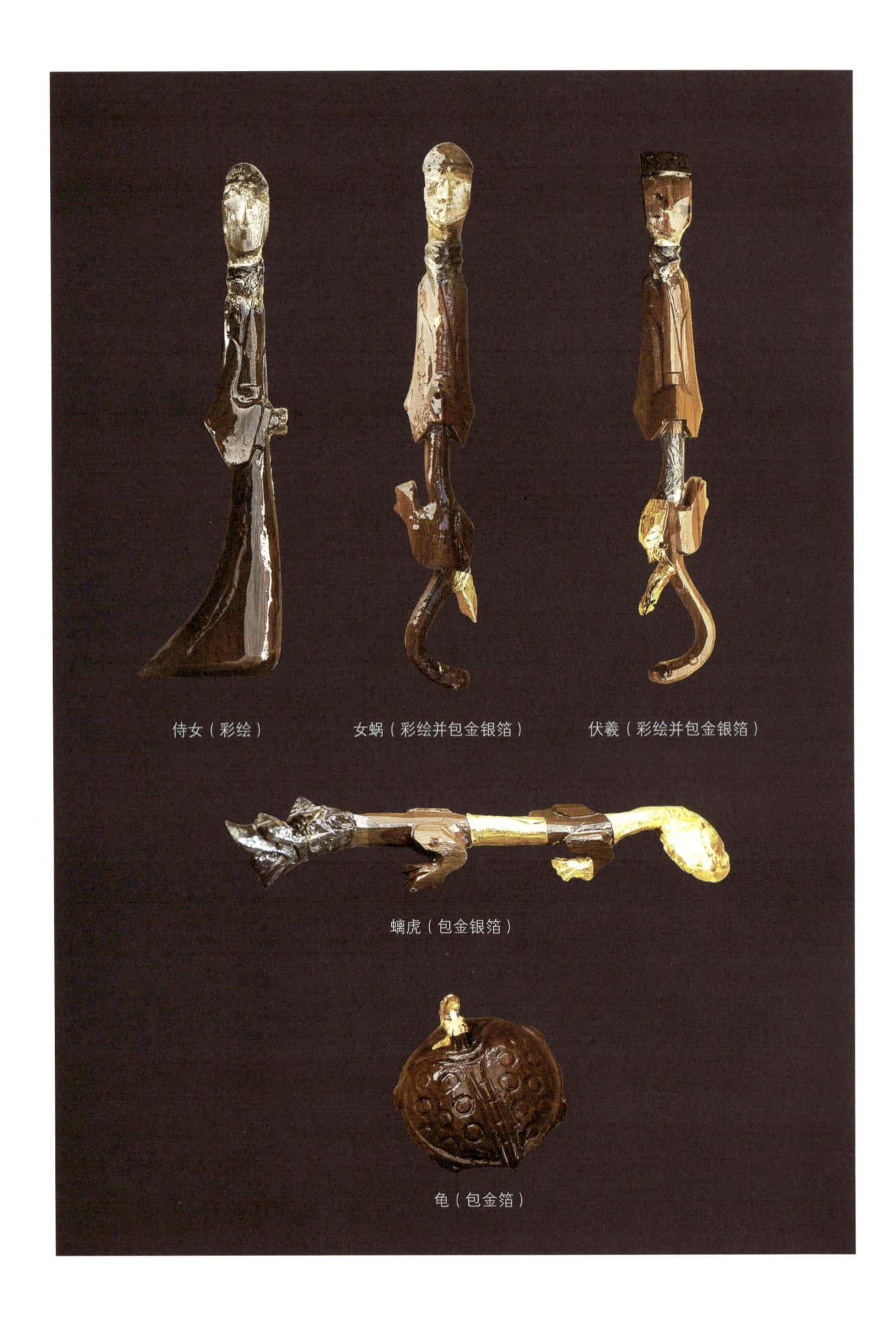

侍女（彩绘）　　女娲（彩绘并包金银箔）　　伏羲（彩绘并包金银箔）

螭虎（包金银箔）

龟（包金箔）

秦汉一统 雄风万里 443

玉席正摄影像及局部细节

保存现状  | 盝顶侧板内侧

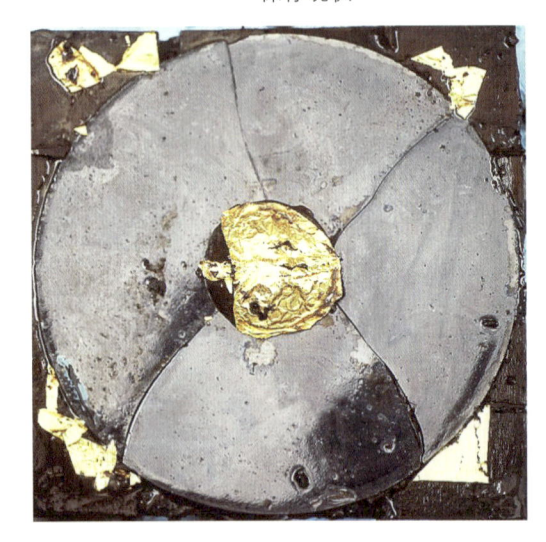

盝顶的玻璃盖和包金乌龟  | 温明内部虎头枕

壁板外侧  | 壁板内侧镶嵌的素面铜镜

玉温明（M147）

秦汉一统 雄风万里 445

鎏金铜盆（11M6）

漆案、漆盘、漆尊（M178）

嵌金七子奁（11M6）

凤鸟席镇（11M7）

四乳神兽铭文镜（M125）　七乳宴乐铭文镜（M170）

漆盒（M177）

玉具剑漆木剑鞘（M147）

双管毛笔（M157）

毛笔（M147）

板研盒（M140）　　漆刷　　木雕小瓶（M157）

堂邑令刘君衣物名（M147）　　左曹中郎刘仲子衣服疏（M157）　　名刺（M147）

M147棺椁结构及棺外侧的"棺束"

M177棺椁结构
——堂寝结构、搭建"人"字形椁顶立柱的横梁、栏杆

As many as 125 Han tombs, 18 tumuli and 7 brick terraces that were used as altars have been discovered in Tushantun Village, Qingdao, Shandong Province. The tombs are mainly shaft tombs in which the coffin chamber was constructed with bricks and wood in rock pits. Some of these tombs each have a tomb tunnel. In terms of the coffins, some have a dual-layered inner coffin and a triple-layered outer coffin; some have both dual-layered inner and outer coffins; the others have a double-layered inner coffin and an outer coffin. In some tombs, the outer coffin has been found concealed by a large number of pieces of pottery tiles. These tombs are named as "Ji Tao Mu (tombs surrounded by piled pottery pieces)". Over 1000 pieces/sets of relics have been unearthed. Jade seals carved with "Seal of Xiao Ling" and "Seal of Tangyi Ling", a mat made up of crystal and jade pieces, bamboo and wooden slips written with the list of funerary objects and "Shang Ji (a kind of administrative reports)", jade Wen Ming and jade pillow are the most important excavated antiquities. According to unearthed seals and records listing funerary objects, it has been speculated that the cemetery of Liu clan used to be here.

# 山东定陶王陵 M2 近年来考古发现

◎ 崔圣宽　王江峰

定陶王墓地（王陵）位于山东省定陶县马集镇大李家村西北约600米，原名"灵圣湖遗址"，自王陵内M2发掘后，2013年被国务院公布为"全国重点保护单位"，遗址名称遂定为"定陶王墓地（王陵）"。自2010年10月起，由山东省文物考古研究院、定陶区文物局联合组队，对M2进行抢救性发掘至今。墓地位于黄泛区，经多次历史时期的黄河淤积，致使墓葬封土被淤埋深达11米；且地下水位浅，这些均给发掘带来很大难度。

墓葬封土边长约160～180米，推算整个封土高度近20米。在墓圹四周发现了两个大型"回"字形夯土遗迹。内夯土台上柱洞与墓室积砂槽内立柱构成一大型高台建筑基址格局，其礼制性意义突显。夯土外台最早一期台边缘外，有一周排水沟。墓道东向，两壁版筑，底部铺垫青砖。在墓道中间发现一长方形坑，该坑两侧及顶部皆木板构建，盖板上发现4块有双孔玉璋。墓道东段南北两侧各有版筑夯土台，两夯土台形如阙台，皆黄褐花土夹杂青石碎片夯筑。

墓室在汉代地表起建，墓圹基本呈方形，墓圹内椁室外四周积砂槽内封填积砂。椁室略成方形，椁室顶部、四周、底部皆青砖封护。木椁墓室为大型"黄肠题凑"墓室，"亚"字形木椁墓室结构由前、中、后三室及耳室、甬道、门道、回廊、回廊外12侧室、三周题凑墙组成。各室皆有门。

遗物主要是一件竹笥，出土于中室甬道的前门口底板下长方形坑内。竹笥为子母扣盒，进行了髹漆，竹笥外丝带缠绕。内有一件女性长袍，长袍领背部有一块用十字花丝系结的玉璧。

M2封土下发现的版筑夯土内台、外台、墓道南北两侧阙台等遗迹现象，突显了其等级之高，与大体量高规格的"黄肠题凑"墓室相符。墓圹外版筑内台上围绕墓圹一周柱洞，构成了一组大型宫殿建筑台基。墓道两侧阙台上柱坑，以及墓道西端两侧立柱、角柱皆构成了相应的建筑布局，都具有特殊的礼制性功用。目前明确有墓上建筑结构的墓葬，仅在先秦时期的遗存中有零星发现。但目前封土下墓圹周边建筑台基式只有秦始皇陵封土结构与之相近。只是定陶王陵M2规模版筑内台小，且墓道两侧多出两个阙台以及外台而已。因此，M2封土结构堪称为"亚帝王"级墓葬封土结构。该墓葬封土结构对研究西汉帝王墓葬封土结构具有重要意义，也是解决大型封土结构堆筑方式的重要实例。

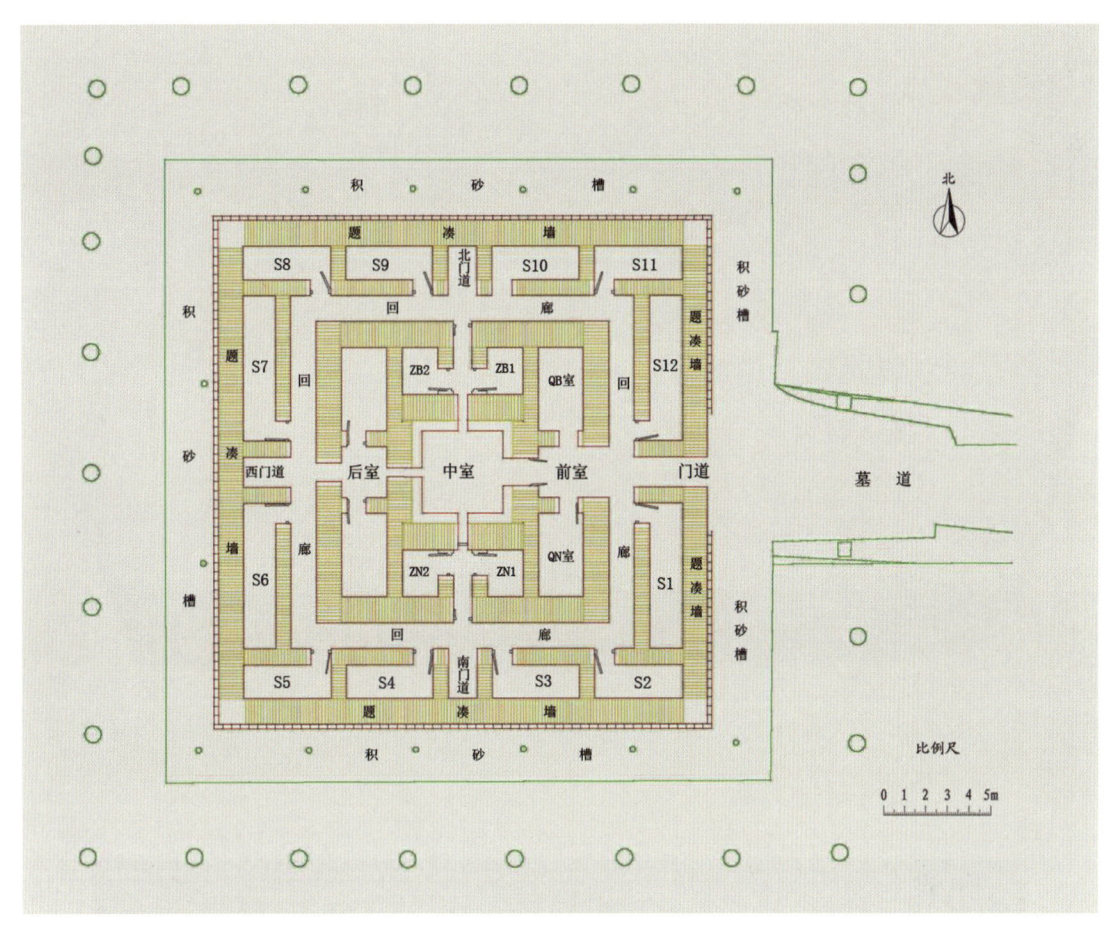

墓葬结构图

墓室"黄肠题凑"叠垒情况

竹笥

竹笥内汉袍缝制的玉璧

墓室周围积砂内及墓坑周围柱洞分布（东—西）

Mausoleum M2, buried with Marquis Dingtao, is a large-scale mausoleum above ground. Under the high tumulus, the coffin chamber, concealed within in a frame structure made of cypresses, is in the shape resembling the Chinese character "亚 (Ya)". The upper part of the vault is sealed with gray bricks and the outer coffin is concealed by accumulated sand. There is a rammed earthen terrace, whose plane layout resembles the Chinese character "回 (Hui)", surrounding the coffin chamber. On the inner square, there is a row of well-arranged postholes. The tomb tunnel points to the east; respectively on its south and north sides, there is a stamped earthen terrace in the shape of a side tower. Postholes are discovered on them. In Qinshihuang's Mausoleum, it has also been found out that terraces were constructed around the coffin chamber under the tumulus. Such a pattern is worthy further researches.

# 河南洛阳市东汉帝陵考古调查与发掘

◎王咸秋

东汉王朝共有12座帝陵,除献帝禅陵位于河南焦作修武县境内,其余11座帝陵均位于洛阳境内。洛阳境内的东汉陵区分为邙山和洛南两个陵区,北陵区位于孟津县内,南陵区位于今洛阳市伊滨区、偃师市境内。洛阳市文物考古研究院结合"邙山陵墓群考古调查与勘测"项目,从2005年开始对东汉帝陵及其陵园遗址进行了大规模的调查勘探。已经进行考古勘探工作的帝陵共7座,分别是:大汉冢、二汉冢、三汉冢、刘家井大冢、朱仓M722、朱仓M707、庞村镇白草坡村东汉帝陵。在帝陵封土周边发现了大面积的陵园建筑基址,集中分布在封土东侧或东北侧,陵寝建筑大体可以分为5个相对独立的建筑单元。并对朱仓M722、白草坡村M1030东汉帝陵陵园遗址进行了考古发掘。

朱仓M722东汉陵园遗址位于洛阳市孟津县朱仓村西部,地处邙山陵区内。陵园总体由两部分组成,暂称之为"内陵园"和"外陵园"。内陵园主要包括封土、地宫,以及东侧的1号台基建筑单元,在封土南侧还发现有部分建筑。外陵园位于内陵园东侧偏北,主要包括2号、3号台基建筑单元,和1号、2号院落建筑单元。出土遗物主要有绳纹筒瓦、板瓦、卷云纹瓦当、空心砖、方砖、条形砖等建筑材料,其中筒瓦、板瓦有戳印"南甄官瓦";日用陶器有盆、罐、碗等,以及各种铁质兵器,如戟、蒺藜、镞等。

白草坡村东汉帝陵属洛南陵区,墓冢编号M1030,位于伊滨区庞村镇白草坡村。目前主要发掘了村子北侧的夯土建筑、道路和灶坑等遗迹。封土正北还发现了阙台遗迹。

通过十余年来的考古工作,我们明确了东汉帝陵存在南、北两个陵区,明确了东汉帝陵墓冢的基本特征,对东汉帝陵陵园的布局有了较为清晰的认识,为今后研究东汉时期陵寝制度的内涵与演变,以及进一步探讨各陵墓主归属等问题,都提供了重要的参考资料,为今后洛阳东汉帝陵的保护工作提供了重要支撑。

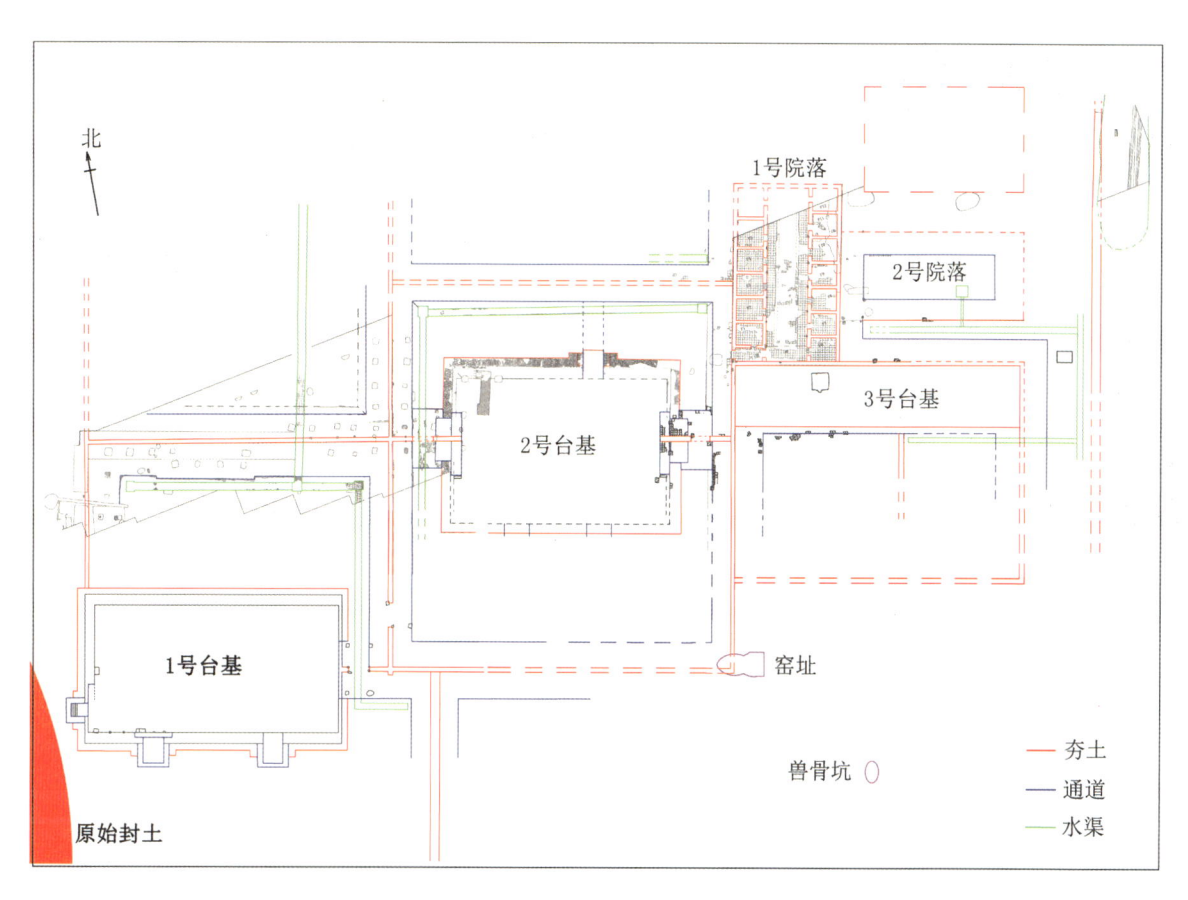

M722陵园遗址主要遗迹分布平面图

M722陵园遗址1号台基全景（南—北）

M722陵园遗址2号台基东门址与3号台基（西—东）

M722陵园遗址祭祀坑牛骨（西—东）

南甄官瓦   南甄官瓦

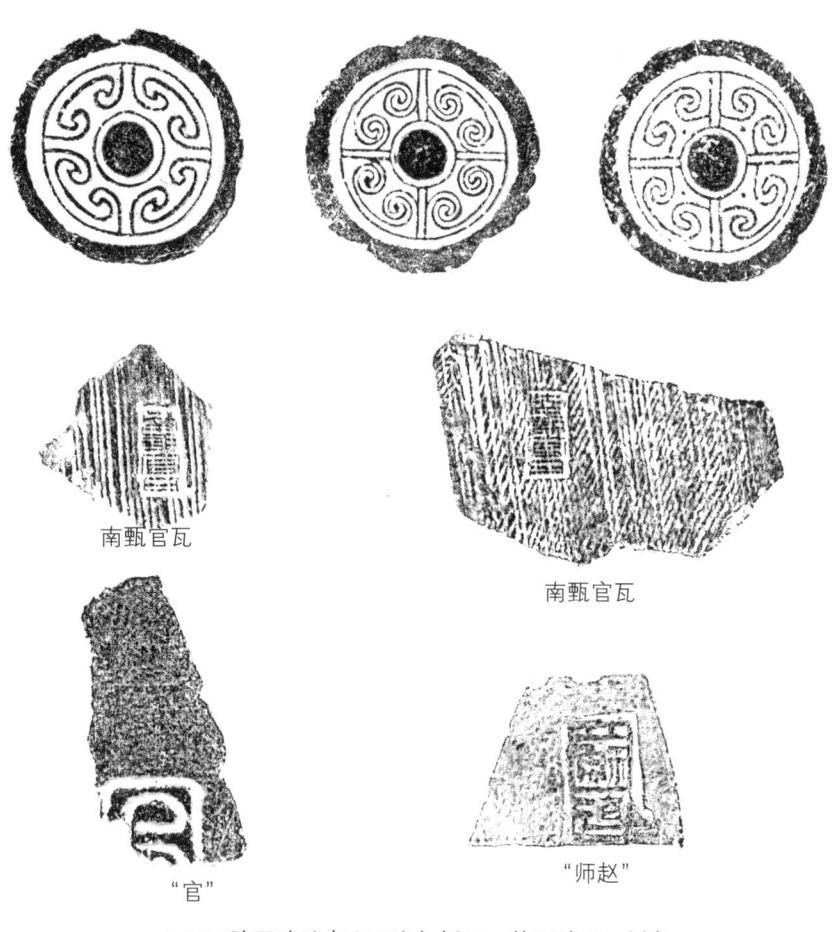

"官"   "师赵"

M722陵园遗址出土瓦当与板瓦、筒瓦戳印、刻字

As many as 7 imperial mausoleums have been excavated after archaeological reconnaissances since 2005. Mausoleum M722, which has been excavated, is located in Zhucang, in the locality of Mount Mangshan. This mausoleum has an inner yard and an outer yard. The plane layout of the inner yard, surrounded by foundations trenches filled with rammed earth, is a north-south rectangular. The round tumulus is in the center of the inner yard. Ground plan of the coffin pit resembles the Chinese character "甲 (Jia)". Terraces and some other constructions have also been discovered in the inner yard. The outer yard is located in the east by north direction outside the inner yard. Major architectural remains include bases of terraces and two courtyards. Mausoleum M1030, in which excavation is underway, is in Baicaopo Village in Luonan. The following are the major discoveries that have been achieved up till now. Roads surrounding the inner yard have been found on the east side and the north side of the tumulus. On the east side of the tumulus, there is a large-scale squarish rammed base of a terrace. On the northeast side of the tumulus, there are two sites of building complexes surrounded by rammed earthen ramparts, along the inner side of which there are drains. On the north side of the tumulus, remains of 50-plus stoves are arranged orderly. In the inner yard, between the north road and the tumulus, a pair of symmetrical rammed bases of terraces that could be remains of side towers have been discovered.

# 陕西靖边县杨桥畔渠树壕东汉壁画墓

◎段 毅

2015年5月，陕西省考古研究院对位于陕西靖边杨桥畔镇渠树壕的一座壁画墓进行了抢救性发掘，发掘地点东北距明代长城遗址烽火台约600米，位于国家重点文物保护单位渠树壕汉墓群范围内。

该墓系长斜坡墓道、砖券拱顶前后室直线形洞室墓，方向75°，水平总长26.50米，由墓道、封门、前室和后室四部分构成，墓室形制略呈"甲"字形。构筑方式是先在墓道底西端凿挖进拱顶土洞，再在土洞内用条砖暗箍砌筑前、后室，最后在前室和券顶壁面上绘制壁画。券顶在直壁之上用楔形子母砖相互对接砌合。该墓随葬品被洗劫一空，唯有珍贵的壁画遗存。

最引人注目的当属砖券拱顶的三垣二十八星宿天象图，这是中国天文考古学首次发现具有星形、星数、图像、题名四要素的二十八宿星象图。墓室的绘画大体可分为十四个单元，其他壁画内容还包括武士、车马出行、山林牧马、侍女、楼阁庄园、宴乐人物、祥禽瑞鸟等。

根据壁画中的伏羲女娲执规矩图、"黄道规"图出现的时间节点可判断该墓的年代上限不早于永元十五年（103年），定在东汉中晚期是比较适宜的。

渠树壕壁画墓天文图，呈现出围绕中心分布的"三垣二十八宿"的结构特征，提供了大量星形、星数与题名信息，表现"星"与"象"紧密结合的"星象"观念，显示诸宿与官星的"黄道内外"相对位置等，内涵十分丰富。壁画星图为探讨汉代天文学的发展状况，了解东汉时期与丧葬有关的观念习俗、宗教思想，以及研究先秦两汉时期的神话传说等提供了珍贵的实物资料。

执铩门吏图　　　骑马图　　　侍女图　　　侍女图

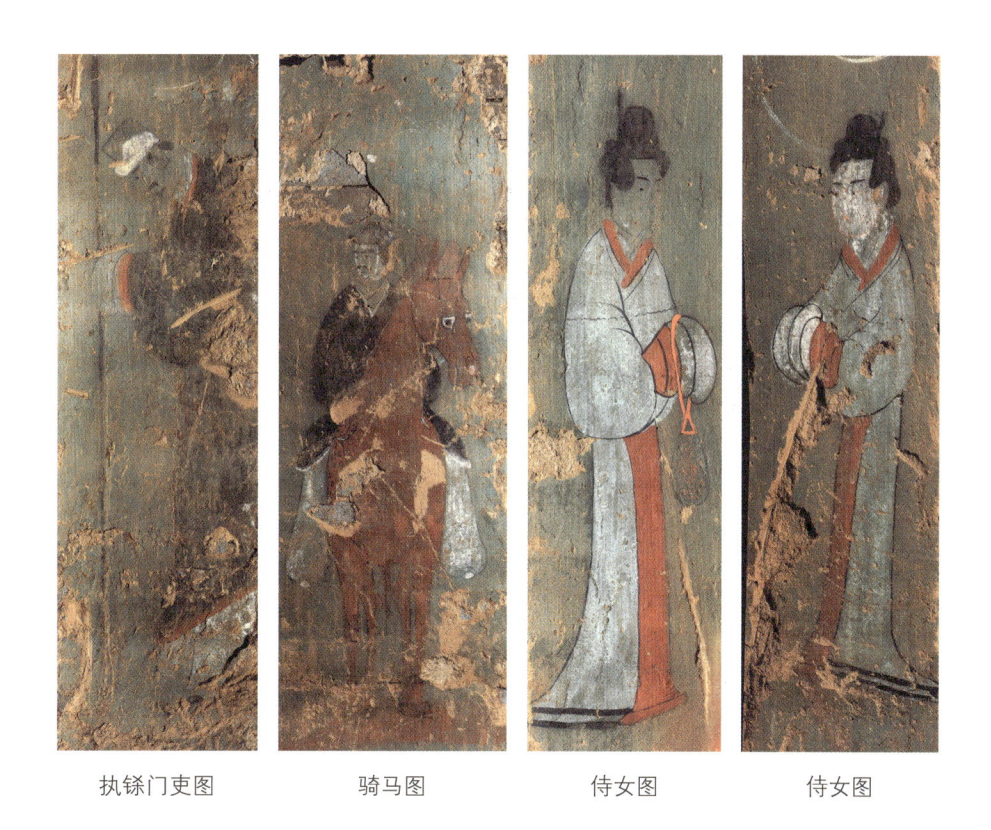

宴乐图

458 黄淮七省考古新发现

日（乌）

月（蟾）

车马出行图

    A mural tomb dating back to Han Dynasty has been discovered in Qushuhao Cemetery. The tomb consists of a brick dome-shaped vault, a front chamber, a rear chamber and a long sloping tomb tunnel. Apart from the south, north and west walls of the main chamber, murals, depicting constellations, spear-holding gate guards, outings on chariot and horses, maid servants, feasting and music, etc., have been discovered on the entire interior of the tomb. In particular, on the dome-shaped vault, there is an astrological map of the 28 mansions containing all four elements of information on star shape, star numbering, constellation images and naming. This map is the very first one of its kind to have been discovered in China. It has provided a scientific basis for interpreting the 28 mansions and understanding Zhong Wai Xing Guan. The murals show Sanyuan, Zhong Wai Xing Guan and relative positions of the ecliptic and the sun and the moon. The excavation of this mural tomb has provided valuable materials for studies concerning architecture, clothing, weapons, customs, myths, religion and art of Han Dynasty. Based on analyses of the astrological map and outings on chariot and horses painted on the wall, it has been preliminary determined that this mural tomb dates back to middle-late Eastern Han.

# 2012年河北安平县汉王公园东汉墓葬

◎张晓峥

安平县汉王公园墓葬位于河北省衡水市安平县城东南部，逯庄村西南约250米处，东距汉王路约210米。墓葬编号为2012AHM1（以下简称M1）。

M1为一座东汉时期多室砖室墓葬。由封土、飨堂、墓道、墓室几部分组成，墓道东向，盗扰严重。原封土整体形状应为覆斗状，未发现夯筑、夯面及夯窝现象。

飨堂位于封土东侧，中部开槽于封土之上，东半部延伸至原地表面，下压墓道东段。损毁严重，仅存部分台基及周边散水，上部建筑形状不详。

墓室为典型的砖砌多室墓，由墓门、甬道、前室、中室、后室组成。

甬道、中室及左右侧室的局部可辨有墨色绘画现象。

前室拱券顶壁面，局部可见炭黑、赭黄绘画遗痕，大部脱落残损。前室左侧室券顶局部残留古人书写的券砖位置编号，如"一、二、三、四、五、六、高、一、二、三、四、五、六"。为保证券砖的接缝密合性，用横面阴线及汉字"故"字来保证券顶砖的结合平行性。

后室扰土中残留有一些朱红漆皮碎片及碎朽木残渣。

该墓随葬品如楼、灶、奁、盒、案、耳杯、炉、猪圈和家禽等都是东汉墓葬中特别是中晚期所流行的，与安平壁画墓出土的器物也基本一样。据此，我们认为本墓的年代应定为东汉晚期，与安平壁画墓年代相同。墓主人身份可能不是官吏身份，应为当时安平地区的豪强地主阶级中的一员。

春秋、战国、两汉时期，墓葬周围开始有用于祭祀的飨堂出现并发展，级别越高、时代越晚，祭祀用飨堂类建筑物规模越大、越复杂。同时，飨堂的位置也不断发生变化，M1封土上发现的飨堂遗迹，在衡水地区两汉考古中尚属首次发现，为研究飨堂位置变化提供了新的实物资料。

墓葬及飨堂全景（东—西）

前室左侧室券顶部砖编号

扁壶　　铜牌饰　　陶俑　　陶俑

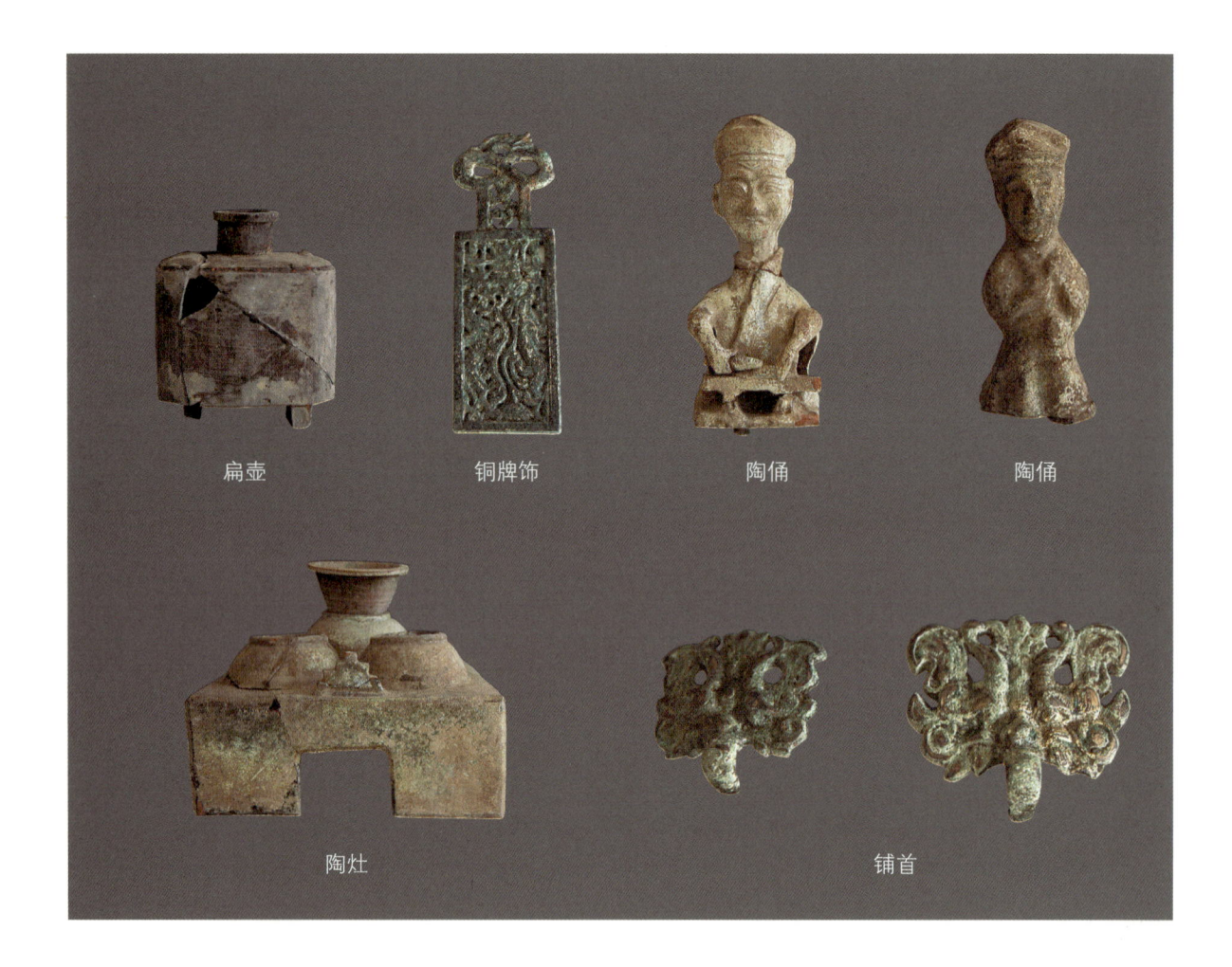

陶灶　　铺首

The Eastern Han tomb discovered in Hanwang Park is an east-west tomb whose plane layout resembles the Chinese character "中 (Zhong)". Its east tomb tunnel is the main tomb tunnel. Inside the tomb, there is a main chamber and side chambers. The tomb per se and its base were constructed with bricks and stones; the ceiling used to be a wooden saddle roof without the overhang at the ends. According to its structure and funerary objects, it has been concluded that this tomb should be constructed for a marquis during the middle and late Western Han. No auxiliary facilities, such as ditches and walls surrounding the graveyard, satellite tombs or satellite pits, have been discovered.

# 安徽广德县南塘汉代土墩墓

◎ 陈 超

南塘汉代土墩墓地位于安徽省东南部的宣城市广德县东南部南塘村，墓地主要分布在一座小土山丘之上，从山脚下一直到山顶端均有汉墓土墩分布。安徽省文物考古研究所于2011年先后发掘土墩汉墓共62墩。

土墩分为两类，甲类：一墩一墓；乙类：一墩多墓，包括一墩二墓、一墩四墓、一墩五墓、一墩六墓等，最多达一墩十八墓。现存土墩的形状有椭圆形、圆形，立面呈馒头状。

墓葬形制分为竖穴土坑墓和砖室墓两种。竖穴土坑墓分为有墓道和无墓道两种。有的土坑墓内还存有木椁和木棺葬具。砖室墓分为单室和多室两种。

此次发掘共出土随葬品上千件（套）。有铜、铁、玉石、（釉）陶、琉璃、鎏金器等材质。随葬品分布于墓主人旁一侧，比较规律，应该是随葬在椁室的边箱内。

我们根据土墩墓群分布特点、密集程度和地形特点可以将整个墓地分为五个区。而根据土墩墓密集程度、墩下墓葬分布情况和出土器物又可分为三个等级：第一等级是整个墓地，第二等级应为家族墓葬，第三等级应为家庭墓葬。土墩下的墓葬根据墓葬形制、大小和随葬品可以判断长幼尊卑的关系；而土墩下墓葬的数量则代表家庭内的人数，说明血缘相同；那种后期打破土墩的墓葬死者应该和土墩内的死者的血缘关系不大。大土墩和周围的小土墩组成了家族墓区，这是一种血缘纽带维系的社会关系的体现。

土墩墓是南方江、浙、沪、皖地区商周时期吴越族属主要的墓葬形式。本次发现的汉代土墩墓，数量多、范围大、分布有规律。有区域、等级、尊卑的差异，是进行聚落研究较好的材料。

D53M215器物组合

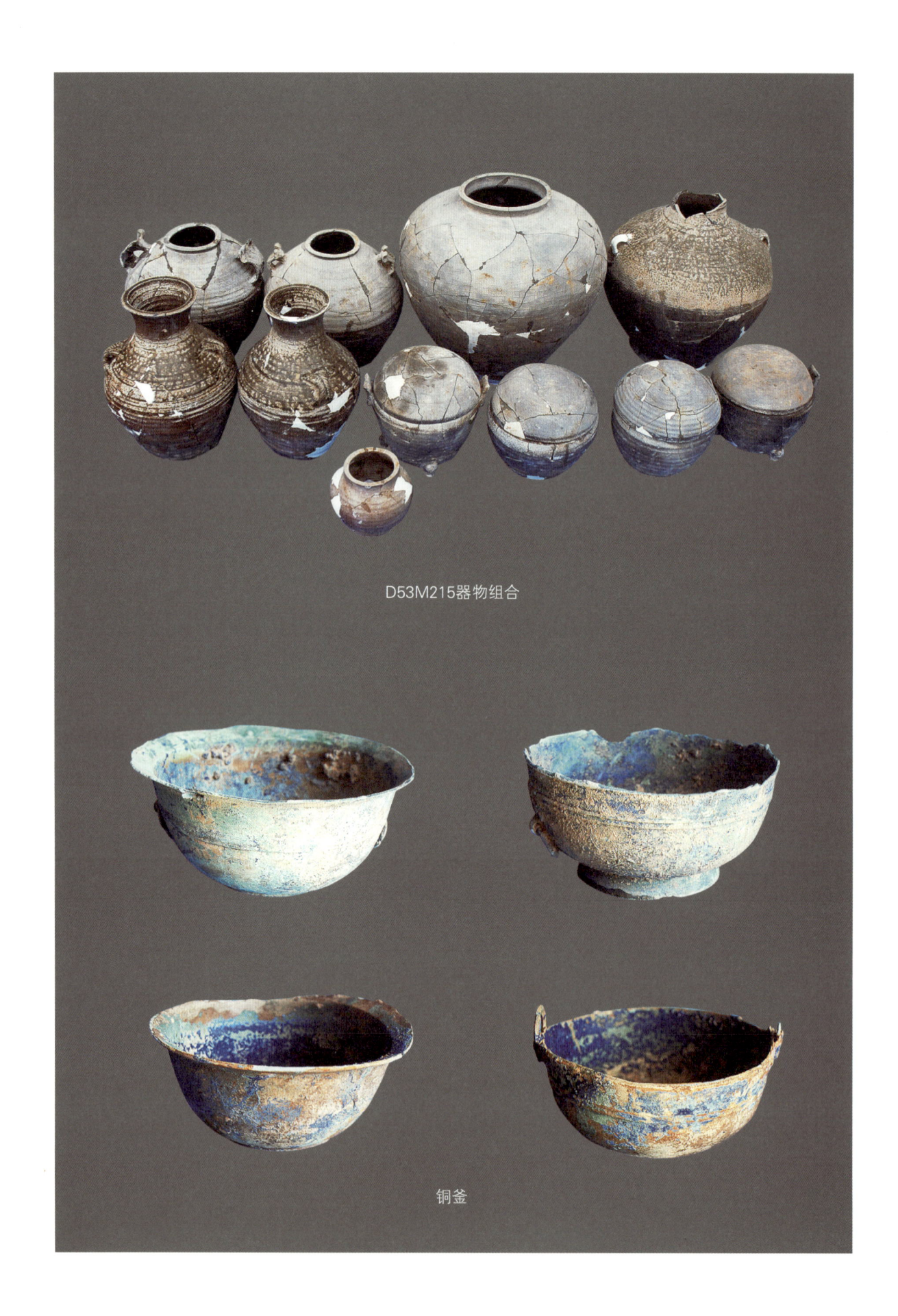

铜釜

秦汉一统 雄风万里

铜镜

铜钵　　　铜釜　　　铜罍

玉璧　　　玉琥　　　铜矛

印章

D61（西—东）

The majority of the Han tomb cluster discovered in Nantang Village is distributed on a small hill. There are 62 mound tombs. Over 1000 pieces/ sets of relics have been excavated, including bronzes, iron implements, jade ware, stone articles, glazed ware and colored potteries. According to their structures, the mound tombs can be divided into two categories, i.e. a single tomb in a mound and multiple tombs in the same mound. This tomb cluster can be partitioned into five sections and classified into the ranks. The first rank is the entire cemetery; the second rank consists of tombs of the same clan; tombs buried with occupants from a family constitute the third rank. Numerous mound tombs that have been discovered this time are distributed in a large area in a certain order. They illustrate differences of regions, hierarchical and social statuses. Therefore, these tombs are ideal materials for the study of settlements.

# 山西太原市开化墓地

◎马　昇　张光辉

开化墓地位于太原市晋源区罗城街道办事处开化村东北，汾河西畔，地处太原西山东麓丘陵地带，东南距晋阳古城北城墙约2.50千米，西南距著名的开化寺蒙山大佛约3千米。

2012—2013年共清理汉代墓葬26座，北齐墓葬21座。汉代墓葬以土坑竖穴墓居多，其次为土洞墓。墓向为东西向和南北向，分别位于发掘区东部和西部。根据墓葬形制及随葬品特征，初步确定这批汉墓的年代主要集中于西汉中晚期。北齐墓葬均为斜坡墓道拱顶土洞墓。墓向以东南向最多，以M20"赵信"墓为代表；西南方向其次，以M58"和公"墓为代表；西向墓葬仅发现M53和M65两座。

开化墓地为晋阳古城城北一处重要的墓区，为晋阳古城附近古代人群的构成和葬俗研究提供了重要材料。首先，开化汉墓多为土坑木椁墓和土洞木椁墓，时段集中于西汉中晚期。洞室木椁墓延续时间较长，是该区域汉墓的一个基本特征，而圆木木椁墓尤其值得注意，该类墓葬均在墓底以圆木或半圆木拼接椁室。这类圆木木椁墓是直接承袭中原地区土坑圆木木椁墓，还是受蒙古高原洞室圆木木椁墓的影响，是一个需要再讨论的问题。其次，开化北齐土洞墓的发掘，进一步明确了太原地区这类土洞墓的埋葬习俗。至今，开化村北已经发现"赵""和""贾""窦""侯""稿"等多个北齐单字姓氏，表明该北齐墓地应包含多个大家族。

M20、M58两座墓葬出土墓志均记载其先祖有在北朝为官的历史，这也是继（冯翊羌人）狄湛墓、（高车人）库狄业墓之后，在北齐陪都太原附近发现的又一批西北少数民族后裔墓葬。孝文帝汉化改制后的民族杂居和融合现象，从北齐陪都晋阳古城墓区死者的民族来源上也可窥见一斑。

汉代土坑木椁墓（M13）

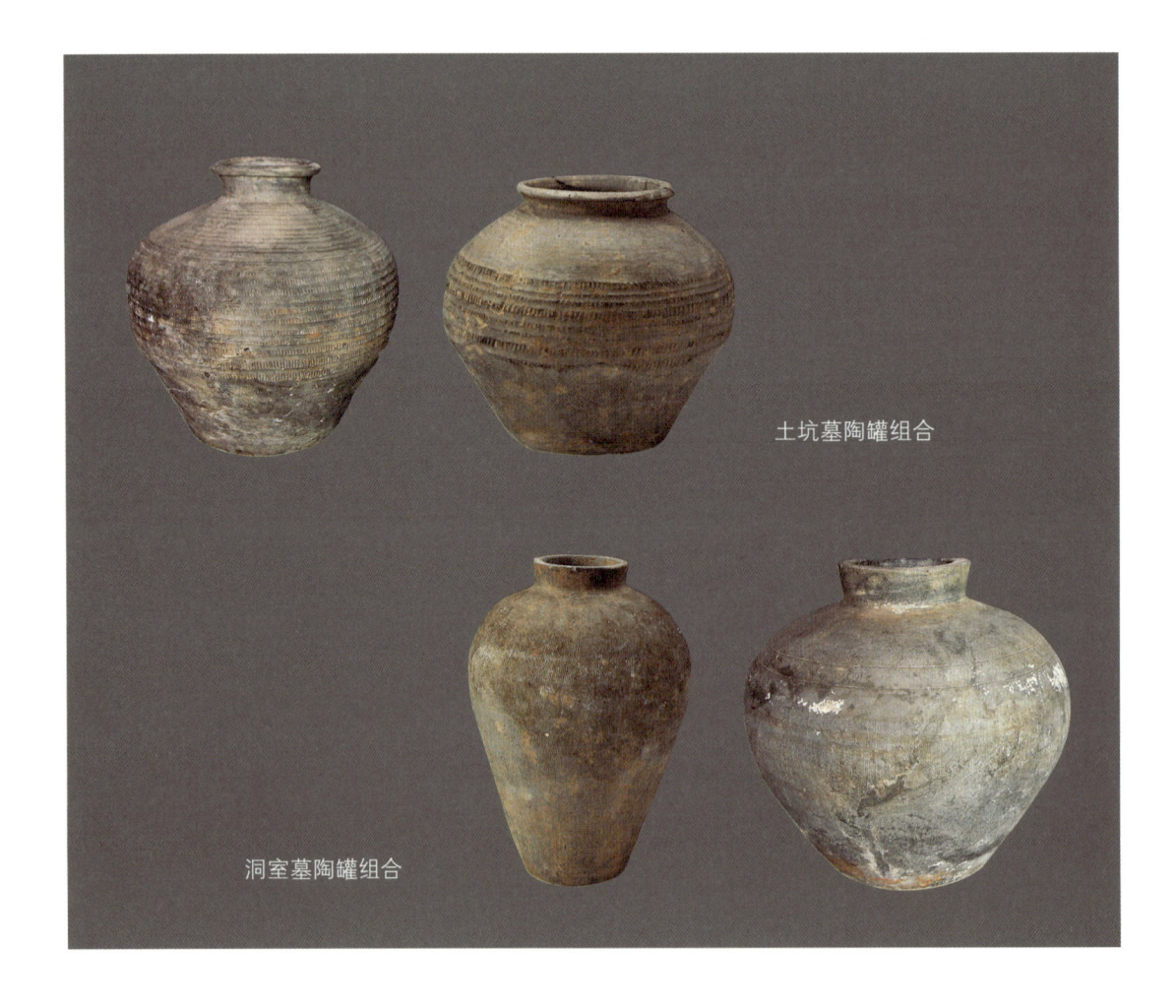

土坑墓陶罐组合

洞室墓陶罐组合

北齐墓M20

M20随葬陶俑

北齐墓M58随葬品

The tomb cluster in Kaihua constitutes an important cemetery in the north of the ancient city of Jinyang. During 2012 to 2013, as many as 26 tombs of Han Dynasty were successively excavated in this area. The majority are shaft tombs; some others are subterranean cave tombs. All 21 tombs of Northern Qi are arched subterranean cave tombs each with a sloping tomb tunnel. Tombs constructed during Han Dynasty, especially the middle and late Western Han, are mainly shaft tombs or cave tombs buried with wooden coffins. A primary feature of Han tombs discovered in this region is that those cave tombs containing wooden coffins were built over a considerable long time span. After the excavation of cave tombs dating from Northern Qi in Kaihua Cemetery, burial customs of this type of cave tombs in Taiyuan have been further clarified. Contents of the epitaphs unearthed respectively in tomb M20 and M58 record the phenomenon that different ethnicities living together and national amalgamation after Emperor Xiaowen implemented policies of sanitization.

# 河南洛阳市西朱村曹魏墓

◎王咸秋

西朱村墓葬位于洛阳市寇店镇西朱村南约650米，地处万安山北麓的缓坡上。北距汉魏洛阳城约18.30千米。共发现两座大型墓葬（编号M1、M2），两座墓葬东西排列，间距约400米，M1西侧距曹魏时期圜丘遗址（俗称"禹宿谷堆"）约2.50千米。两座墓葬和圜丘遗址处在一条东西轴线上，轴线方向约为东偏南4°。两座墓葬均未发现封土和陵（墓）园遗迹。

M1为长斜坡墓道明券墓，平面呈"甲"字形，墓道西向，方向274°。在墓葬土圹南北两侧和西侧共分布着39个柱础坑和3条排水沟，南北两侧的柱础坑排列规律，基本南北对称，这些柱础坑应该是修建墓葬时搭建临时性设施所遗留下的。墓葬由墓道、甬道、前室、后室组成。墓葬土圹东西全长52.10米，在墓道南北两侧壁留有7级水平生土台阶。墓室土圹近"凸"字形，东西长18.20米，南北最宽处15米，墓室土圹南、北、东三壁保存有6~7级水平或斜坡状台阶，在斜坡状台阶上部发现有明显的踩踏痕迹。墓葬口部距墓底深约10.80米。前室拱券形顶，顶部大部分已坍塌。在前室砖壁上发现有残存的壁画，仅残留数处人物、瑞兽、宴饮、祥云等图案。后室方形，顶部虽已坍塌，仍可以推断顶部是拱券形顶。

M1共出土文物500余件，包括陶器、铁器、铜器、漆木器和少量玉石器、骨器等。另外墓葬出土了大量刻铭石牌，石牌一面有隶书阴刻的文字，记载了墓葬内随葬品的名称、数量、质地和尺寸，每块石牌记载了一件或者一组随葬品，刻铭石牌所记述内容非常丰富，包括衣衾、器用、文房用具、梳妆用具、戏具、乐器、食物、丧仪类等十几个门类。

M1出土随葬品与洛阳正始八年墓、曹休墓部分器物有明显的相似之处，刻铭石牌此前仅见于西高穴曹操高陵，具有较为明显的时代和等级指向。M2未经发掘，其建筑形式与M1有相似之处，且两座墓葬与曹魏时期的圜丘处在同一条东西轴线上，因此初步推断两座墓的年代亦应为曹魏时期。

根据文献记载，曹魏明帝高平陵位于万安山地区，此次勘探发现的M2，其规模已达帝陵级别，初步推测墓主为曹魏明帝曹叡。曹魏时期的墓葬在全国范围内发现较少，此次考古发现，为复原曹魏时期高等级墓葬的葬制和丧葬礼仪提供了珍贵的资料。

部分墓砖戳印

刻铭石碑

秦汉一统　雄风万里　473

陶俑　　　　　　　　　　　琥珀雕件

玉器

石圭　　　　　　　　　　　石璧

墓葬位置图（上北下南）

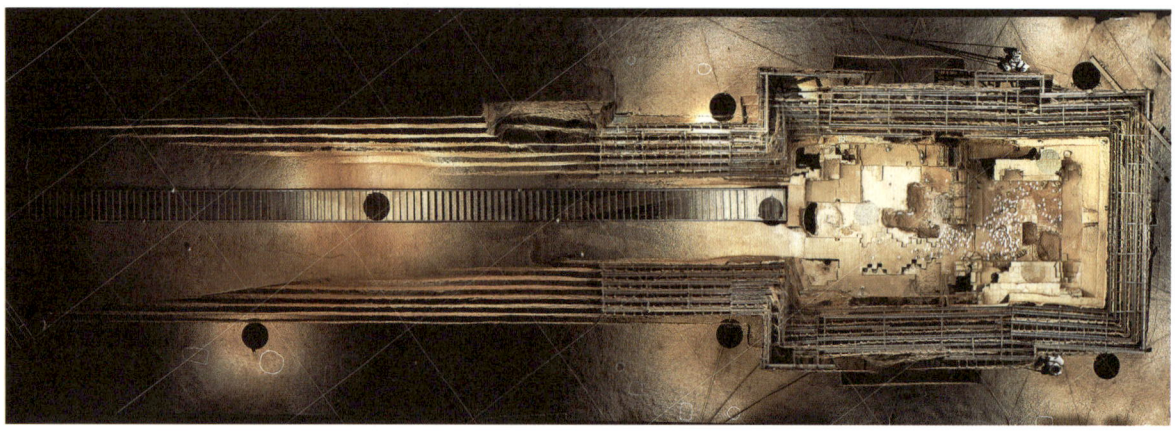

M1正射影像（上北下南）

Tomb M1 and tomb M2, dating back to Cao Wei, are located on the gentle slope at the foot of Mountain Wan'an in Xizhu Village. The plane layout of tomb M1, a shaft tomb with a long sloping tomb tunnel pointing to the west, resembles the Chinese character "甲 (Jia)". On the south, north and west sides of the coffin pit, there are 39 post bases and 3 ditches. The tomb consists of a tomb tunnel, a tomb passage, front and rear chambers. On both the north and south walls of the tomb tunnel, and the south, north and east walls of the coffin pit, there are stairs. Gates have been discovered in the middle of the tomb passage and between the front chamber and the rear chamber. Remaining murals have been found on brick walls inside the front chamber. More than 500 relics have been unearthed, including potteries, iron ware, bronzes, lacquerware, a small number of jade ware and bone implements. It has been preliminarily speculated that tomb M1 was a high-grade tomb constructed in Cao Wei. After archaeological surveys, it has been found out that the plane layout of tomb M2, which is also a shaft tomb but with a long sloping tomb tunnel pointing to the east, resembles the Chinese character "甲 (Jia)". It is highly possible that tomb M2 is related with Mausoleum Gaoping, buried with Emperor Ming of Cao Wei.

# 安徽当涂县"天子坟"孙吴墓

◎叶润清

"天子坟"位于安徽当涂县姑孰镇洞阳村，历史上多次被盗掘，2015—2016年，安徽省文物考古研究所会同马鞍山市文物局、当涂县文物管理所对该墓进行了考古发掘。

现存封土南北长47米，东西宽35米，高0～3.10米，夯筑而成。墓圹填土也为夯筑而成。该墓为前、后室四隅券进式穹隆顶结构砖室墓。斜坡墓道，方向165°。墓葬全长32.50米，最大宽13.10米，深3.60～4.10米。前室有东、西耳室与后室构成。前室四隅起券处各设石质牛头一个。在前室扰土中发现残覆顶石一块。

虽经多次盗掘，该墓仍在墓门前的唐代盗洞底部、前室、西耳室和甬道位置发掘出土各类精美随葬品181件/套，包括漆木器装饰件、女性饰品、车马器构件、兵器、日用品、佛像、俑、神兽构件、钱币九大类，涵盖金、银、铜、铁、陶、瓷、石、琉璃、玻璃、漆器等不同质地。由此可以想见，该墓中原应有大量珍贵随葬品。

通过与本地及南京、湖北、江西等地同时期的墓葬形制及随葬青瓷器、陶器比较，可以判断该墓年代为东吴晚期。唐代盗洞内出土一块隶书漆皮，释读为："永安三年□□日校尉□□□七寸铁镜合八枚□□□翠毛□□□□□尉薛□纪□……"此外还发现两块"永安四年"纪年文字墓砖。"永安"是吴景帝孙休使用的唯一一个年号，其在位时间为永安元年—七年（258—264年），"永安三年"和"永安四年"纪年文字的发现，说明该墓建造和使用年代应在永安四年或之后不长的时间内。

从史料记载、出土文字资料、"九鼎八簋"成套的陶礼器等多方面综合考证，当涂"天子坟"墓应是帝王陵墓级别的孙吴大墓，墓主身份与吴景帝孙休和朱夫人在多方面是高度吻合的。

476　黄淮七省考古新发现

墓室全景（南—北）

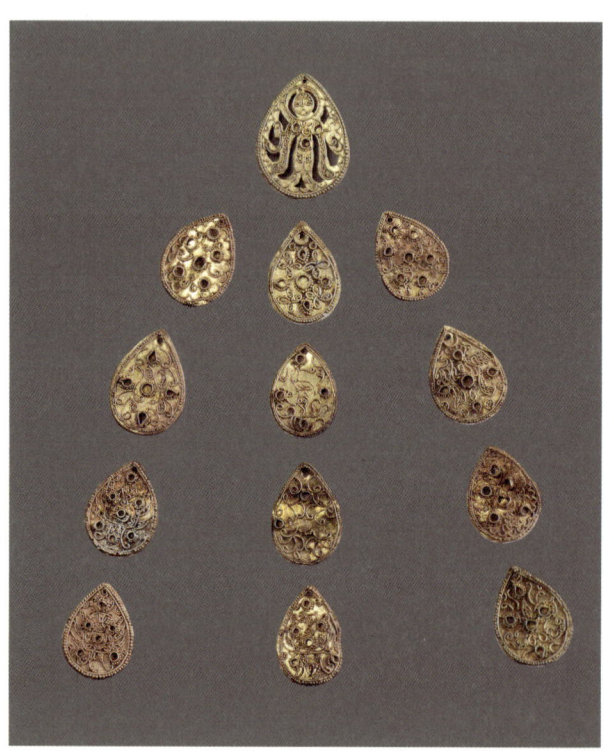

掐丝步摇金片

前室东北角石牛头

铜佛像

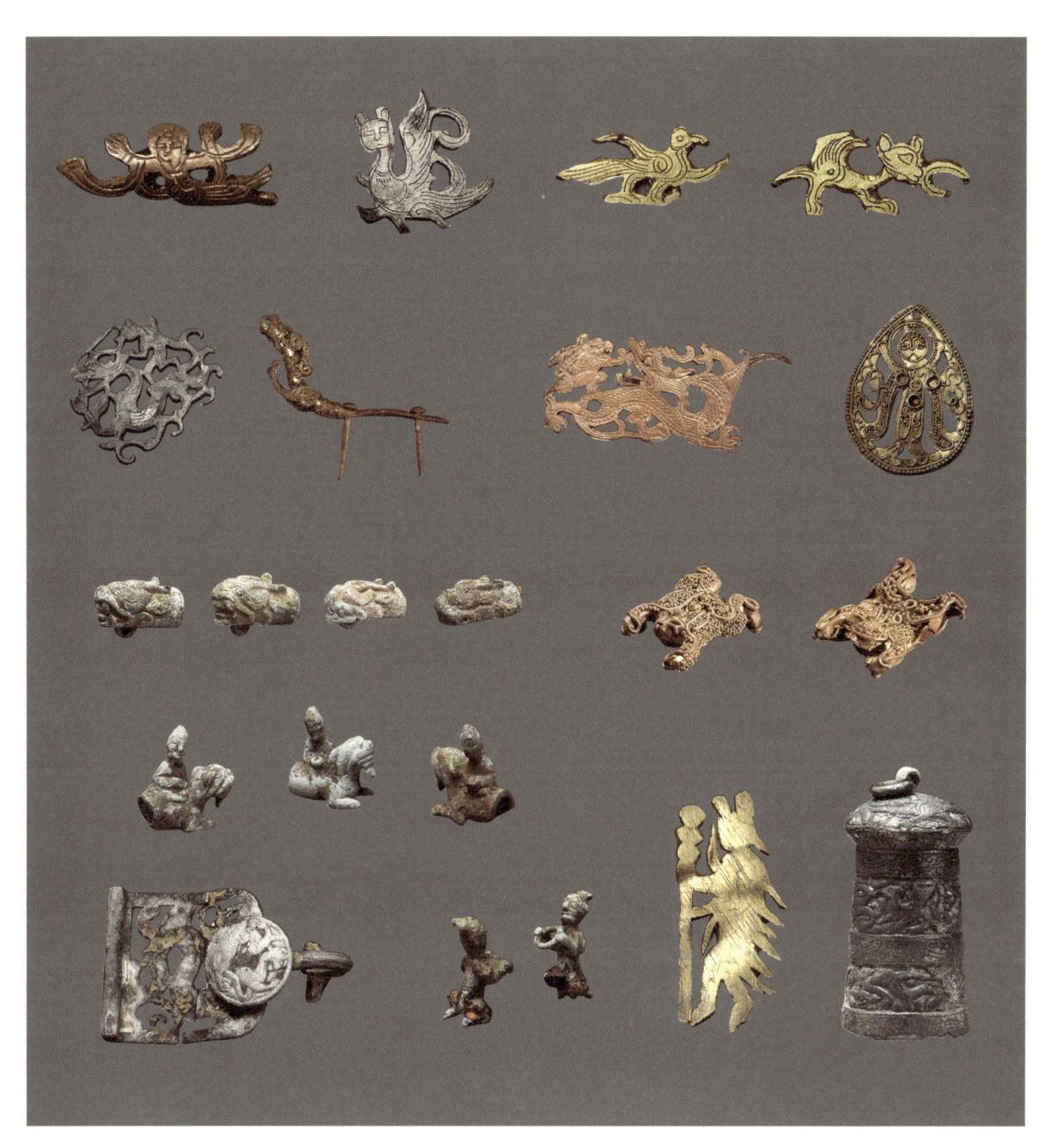

金、银、铜质随葬品

"Tianzi Fen" is a mausoleum with a high tumulus. There is a sloping tomb tunnel pointing to the south. Inside the coffin crypt, there is a front chamber, east and west side chambers and a rear chamber. The vault is a domed brick-chambered one with a ceiling whose four corners protruding inward. Among the funerary objects, there are chronicled textual materials. After analyses of these texts, it has been speculated that this mausoleum should be constructed for an emperor or a marquis of Eastern Wu. Identities of the occupants are highly consistent with those of Emperor Jing of Eastern Wu and his wife.

# 江苏邳州市新河煎药庙西晋墓地

◎马永强

煎药庙西晋墓地位于邳州市新河镇陈滩村煎药庙。2015年7月—2016年9月，南京博物院、徐州博物馆、邳州博物馆联合对其进行了调查、勘探与抢救性发掘。

墓地位于一块东西向椭圆形台地之上。煎药庙墓地共发掘墓葬9座，皆南北向，保存较好，形制结构完整，由墓道、前室、耳室、单后室或并列后室组成，墓道带斜坡，居北。砖室外用石灰包裹，内壁粉有石灰层。前室皆东西向，平面呈长方形。根据墓葬前室形制的不同可分为盝顶和券顶两种。墓地未经盗扰，随葬品摆放位置明确，出土了金、银、铜等随葬品300余件。

煎药庙墓地墓葬呈南、北两排分布，为东南—西北走向，皆为前后室墓，有前室盝顶后室券顶墓3座，包括并列双后室墓1座和单后室墓2座；前后室皆券顶墓6座，包括并列三后室墓3座和并列双后室墓3座，墓葬规模较大。个别墓葬前室有黑色影壁装饰，并有画像石。出土了鹦鹉螺杯、琉璃碗、贝类耳杯、金珰等随葬品，说明墓主身份较尊贵。出土的青瓷盘口壶、青瓷鸡首壶、青瓷谷仓罐、青瓷辟邪水注等，皆为西晋时期典型器物。结合其墓葬形制、墓葬中画像石的再利用等情况分析，墓地的时代应为西晋时期。据M8挡土墙中部发现的"下邳国县建忠里谋显伯仲伯孝伯"青砖之刻铭，推测墓地是一处西晋时期下邳国的高级贵族家族墓地。

煎药庙西晋墓地的发现弥补了徐州地区西晋考古的空白，使鲁南与苏南的西晋时期考古建立了地域空间上的联系。墓地保存完整，随葬品摆放位置与墓葬关系清晰，为西晋时期丧葬与埋藏制度研究提供了实证。随葬品中的鹦鹉螺杯与玻璃碗显示出了海上贸易与东西方文化的交流；南方青瓷与北方酱釉瓷器的共出反映了西晋时期南方青瓷的北传，以及以南北商品流转为代表的文化交流与融合。此外，墓地的发掘，对西晋下邳国历史的研究也具有重要意义。

煎药庙西晋墓地发掘后全景（上北下南）

M3二次扩建痕迹及东墓道台阶

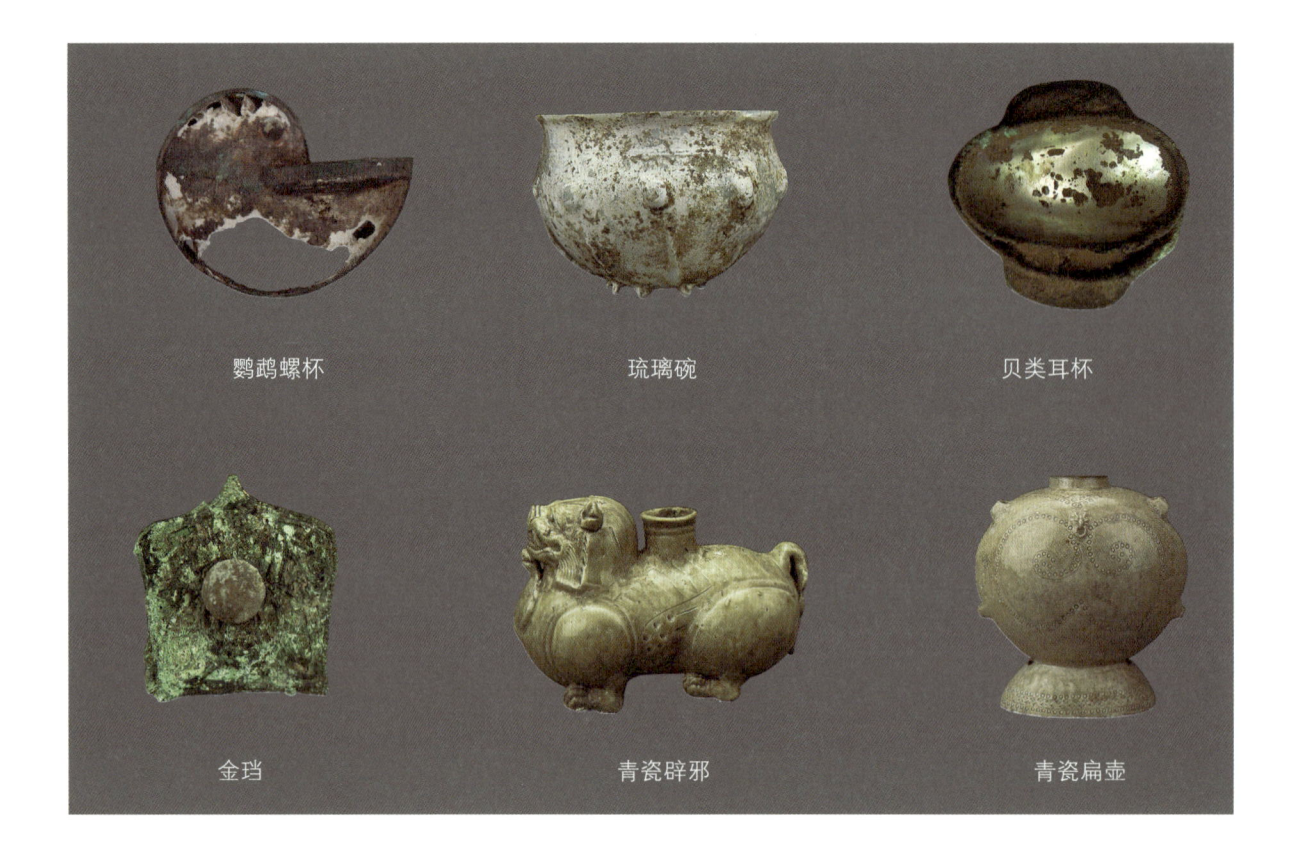

| 鹦鹉螺杯 | 琉璃碗 | 贝类耳杯 |
| 金珰 | 青瓷辟邪 | 青瓷扁壶 |

As many as nine tombs, comparatively well-preserved and intact, have been excavated from a cemetery near Jianyao Miao. Their tomb tunnels all point to the north. Each tomb consists of a tomb tunnel, a front chamber, side chambers and a single rear chamber or two symmetrical rear chambers lying side by side. Positioning in two rows running from the southeast to the northwest, these tombs are all relatively large ones. Each of them has a front chamber and a rear chamber. Decorative black screen walls, along with stone rilievo sculptures, have been discovered in some tombs. Excavated nautilus shell cups with handles, glass bowls, shell cups with handles, Jin Dang and other funerary objects all indicate the high level of the tomb occupant's status. Unearthed antiquities like celadon pots with a dish-shaped mouth are all typical artifacts of Western Jin. According to a comprehensive analyses of tomb structure, funerary objects, stone rilievo sculptures and engravings on bricks, it has been speculated that there used to be the cemetery of a supreme aristocratic family in the State of Xiapi in Western Jin.

# 天地鬼神　享礼之尊

## 陕西凤翔县雍山血池秦汉祭祀遗址

◎陈爱东　田亚歧

凤翔雍山血池遗址是目前我国秦汉时期"祭天"遗址中，与文献记载完全对应，由选址与地貌关系、坛场、祭祀坑、建筑、道路等内涵构成的完整的"畤"文化遗存。遗址位于陕西凤翔县柳林镇血池村，东南距秦雍城遗址约15千米。整个遗址区背靠一道东西向大山，分布于东西排列、南北走向的三道岇梁的阳坡一面。2016—2017年，对血池遗址进行了连续两年的发掘工作，发掘面积4000平方米，发掘祭祀夯土台、祭祀坑、建筑基址等各类遗迹250余处，出土玉器、青铜车马器等各类器物2600余件，同时也结束了数年来对这处总面积达470万平方米的大型遗址的考古调查工作，目前共确认相关遗迹包括各类建筑、场地、道路、祭祀坑等遗迹3200余处，调查和发掘工作均取得了重要收获。"坛场"夯土台所处的东侧山梁上的小山头之上，其北侧有一个更高的山头。台为圜丘状，围绕"夯土台"的是一个圜状"壝"，在"壝"的外侧有三重台阶平地。据文献，该处夯土台完全符合秦汉时期"西畤"的条件。

据出土器物类型学年代初步研究判断，血池遗址很可能即为西汉初期汉高祖刘邦在雍城郊外原隶属秦畤基础上设立的国家最高等级，专门用于祭祀天地及黑帝的固定场所——北畤。该遗址，是继礼县鸾亭山"西畤"相关遗迹后，首次在雍城发现与古文献记载吻合、时代最早、规模最大、性质明确、持续时间最长，且功能结构趋于完整的国家大型祭祀遗址；是关于"畤"遗存完整功能结构的首次发现，它以实际文化遗存印证了雍城历经秦代至西汉武帝时期，仍继续作为秦皇汉武时期"圣都"，以举行国家最高祭天礼仪活动之功能区的存在，填充了既往整个雍城遗址唯缺郊外以畤祭天遗存的空白，进一步明确了雍城遗址各功能区的空间分布与文化内涵。

对血池遗址的发现和发掘，不仅系正史记载中关于在雍地开展的一系列国家祭祀行为之印证，而且成为从东周诸侯国到秦汉大一统国家祭祀活动的最重要物质载体和实物体现，从"透物见人"的角度，此次考古发掘出的实物资料，对于深化秦汉礼制、秦汉政治、中国古代礼制文化等方面的研究均具有重要的学术价值。与此同时，通过今后以雍山血池遗址考古成果为契机，加强对文化遗产的保护、传承和利用，对于当代树立文化自信、增强对中华文明的自豪感与认同感同样具有重要意义。

血池遗址地貌环境与结构布局图（南—北）

"坛场"地貌特征

2016年发掘区祭祀坑及复原图

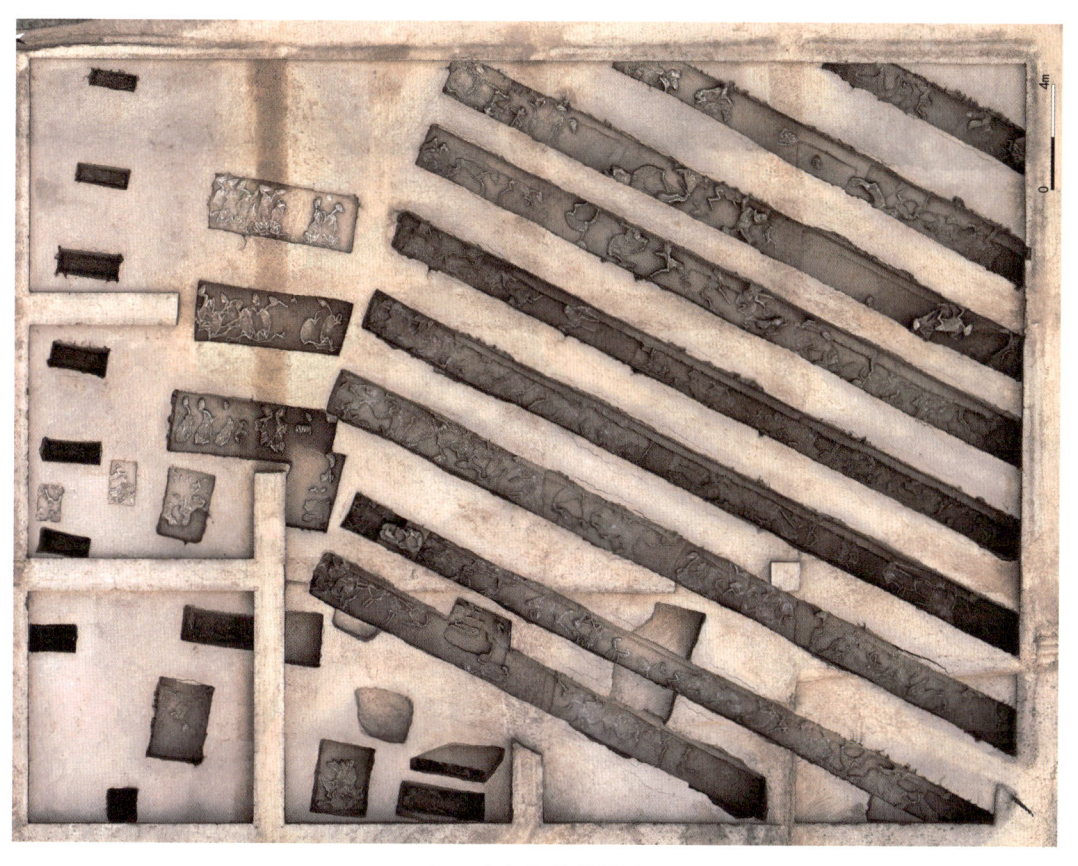

2017年祭祀坑发掘区

男性玉人

女性玉人

玉珩

玉琮

A diversified range of remains, whose total number exceeds 250, have been excavated. There is a rammed earthen terrace, pits for sacrificial rituals, and foundations of buildings, etc. The round rammed earthen terrace is enclosed in a surrounding circle, namely "Wei". Outside the "Wei", there is a triple-stepped platform, which perfectly matches the description of "Zhi" in documentary records written in Qin and Han dynasties. More than 2600 pieces of relics have been unearthed, including jade ware, bronze chariot and harness ornaments. According to their contents, the pits can be divided into two types. Some are buried with chariots while the others contain animals. Plane layout of the foundations of buildings, covering approximately 300 square meters, is squarish. It is highly possible that, on the Site of Xuechi, there was the North Zhi, set up by Emperor Gaozu of Han, Liu Bang in the beginning of Han Dynasty. The North Zhi, a supreme venue for national sacrificial ceremonies specially worshiping the heaven and the earth and Emperor Hei, was actually established on the base of what used to be Qin Zhi in the suburbs of Yongcheng. The North Zhi has been found out to be the oldest and largest venue where large-scale national sacrificial rituals were held. It was utilized for an explicit purpose for the longest time and its existence tallies with relevant historical documents. It is the first time that the site of such a venue has been discovered in Yongcheng.

# 灼铁烁金　铸刚锻韧

## 陕西杨凌邰城铸铁作坊遗址

◎赵艺蓬

杨凌邰城铸铁遗址位于陕西杨凌区法禧村西北农林科技大学所属苗圃基地西墙南段内、外两侧，2011年年初，陕西省考古研究院调查发现了252块陶范，以及少许铁炼渣、耐火材料等与铸铁相关的遗物，还有大量秦汉时期的陶器等。初步确认该地点应为一处铸铁作坊遗址，或与秦汉时期邰县治所有关。

随后的小规模试掘虽未发现炼炉、洪范窑、脱碳炉等与铁器生产活动直接相关的遗迹单位，但出土了相当丰富的与铸铁相关的遗物。器物种类包括：1.陶范与芯，铸器类别可辨者达数百件，主要是铧、锄、钁三类农业工具；2.炉壁与鼓风管残块；3.炼渣、炉渣、残铁块与木炭块等；4.附着有炼渣、铁锈的陶器与瓦片。另外，在两座灰坑内还出土了"半两钱"残石范4块。

根据出土遗物特征判断，该作坊可能为主要从事熔炼与浇铸活动的铸铁作坊，其产品构成主要是以农具为主，可能兼做铜钱。而就其可能生产钱币而言，其很可能属于一种官营作坊的性质。作坊所获遗存均为熔炼、浇铸环节遗物，显示作坊内部存在分工的可能，当属富兰克林所谓"规定式"的生产方式。

本次发掘所获遗存大多只是冶铸活动的废弃堆积，未发现直接与铸铁活动相关的窑炉等生产设施。因此，有关作坊规模、内部布局尚不明确。虽然如此，但其重要性与意义却不容忽视。第一，该作坊是迄今陕西唯一正式发掘的同类作坊，为今后探讨西汉都城附近铁器工业形态提供了新的素材；第二，弥补了先秦以迄汉代冶铁业研究的薄弱环节；第三，对探讨铁器生产分布格局与演变具有积极作用，有助于了解陕西地区西汉早中期铁器工业布局及格局演进；第四，杨凌铸铁作坊的发现与确认，对于进一步厘清秦汉时期邰城聚落的内部结构，进而研究秦汉郡县一级聚落的社会组织结构亦有积极作用。

镢范与芯　　　　　　　　锄范　　　　　　　　铧范与芯

炼渣　　　　　　　榆荚半两范模　　　　　　半两钱石范

From the site of an iron-casting workshop in Taicheng, Yangling, approximately 40 remains have been cleaned up. They are of ash pits, wells, etc. No vestiges of smelting furnaces, Hong Fan kilns or decarburization furnaces have been discovered. The following are unearthed relics. Firstly, there is a large number of pottery molds, including outer molds and inner molds. The majority of the molds were mainly used to produce farm tools like Hua, Chu and Jue. Molds of Chu are the most numerous. Secondly, remains of furnace walls and remnants of blast pipes have been revealed. Thirdly, slags, cinders, residual iron pieces and charcoals have been discovered. It is highly possible that the slags were left after smelting. Fourthly, potteries and tiles stained with slags and rust have been excavated. In addition, from two ash pits, four broken pieces of stone molds that were used to cast "Banliang Coin" have been unearthed. This workshop was in use no later than early Western Han. In most cases, smelting and casting of farm implements were carried out in this workshop; sometimes, coins were also minted here. As far as mintage is concerned, it is very likely that this workshop used to be run by the state. There might be division of labor since relics obtained from this workshop are all remnants left after smelting and casting.

# 亭里乡间　布衣炊烟

## 山东枣庄市海子汉代遗址考古发掘

◎吕　凯

　　海子遗址位于枣庄市山亭区山城街道办事处海子东村东北部，遗址西边缘靠近村庄，南邻海子村至东江村的乡间公路，北至一条现代灌溉渠，东至薛河支流西江西堤断崖。2017年由山东省文物考古研究院联合郑州大学考古专业共同进行考古发掘。重要发现是2座房址、8座溷厕（畜圈厕所）、2条道路、1条界沟（G1）和2个灶。

　　界沟（G1）呈南北向，文化遗存主要分布在沟东。沟内局部保存有较好的石砌墙基，性质可能为界墙。G1的中段石砌墙基西侧发现一条碎陶片铺成的道路。

　　本次发现的房址共有2座，为长方形地面式，保存均较差，仅余部分墙基或基槽，墙基均以石块砌筑，室内、外活动面均已完全破坏，半地穴式建筑物发现8座，平面均为长方形，保存相对较好。半地穴式建筑的做法为先于平地上挖出基坑，基坑坑壁多为斜壁，墙基贴坑壁构筑，主体多为石块及土相掺杂，砌筑不规整，内、外侧多处见竖立石板，亦有在坑壁上贴立石板的做法；多数于东侧或西侧有2块立石板构成的"通道"，"通道"底部向建筑内倾斜。建筑物内部堆积多分为上、下两层：上层为杂乱石块及残碎瓦片；下层均为深灰褐色填土，较疏松，含有大量黑灰及较多烧土、陶片等。底面多不平整，有的呈斜坡状。从形制上看，此类建筑物不适宜居住，应当另有他用；对下部堆积的取样化验显示来自人畜粪便的粪甾醇含量高，粪甾醇是构成堆积中土壤有机质的主要成分之一，指示了该建筑物可能具有厕所、畜圈和其他废弃物堆积区的功能，故而推测其性质为汉代的"溷厕"，即畜圈厕所。

　　通过本次发掘我们了解到，海子遗址是一处重要的，拥有一定布局规划的，围以界沟、界墙的汉代居住遗址，可能对应汉代基层行政单位的"里"，在以往考古工作中发现较少。海子遗址周围发现了多处数量众多的汉代墓地，综合这些材料，对于汉代中小型聚落研究有着非常重要的意义。本次发现的石砌房址及溷厕极少见于同时期其他遗址，尤其是其中半地穴式的房址所具有的特殊功能，具有比较重要的研究价值。

汉代界沟G1中段及北端（左南右北）

汉代溷厕F2及F3（上北下南）

Haizi Site is residential site dating from Han Dynasty. Constructed according to a planned layout, this site used to be surrounded by boundary ditches and boundary walls. Major remains that have been excavated include 10 dwelling sites, 2 roads, 1 boundary ditch, 2 stoves, 40-plus ash pits formed during different historical periods, and 9 tombs. The room sites can be divided into two types, i.e. the above-ground ones and half-dugouts. Both types of dwelling sites, whose wall bases are piled rocks, are interlaced with one another. The half-dugouts were probably toilets or pens. The discovery of Haizi Site is of great significance for the study of grassroots administrative units and medium-sized and small settlements in Han Dynasty.

# 唐风宋韵　气象万千

识。

  气象万千，谓景象宏伟绚丽，亦形容景色和事物多种多样，壮丽而多变化。宋范仲淹《岳阳楼记》云："朝晖夕阴，气象万千。"因此，用此词形容北朝以后的中国古代社会，颇为合适。随着经济发展，中外文化、贸易的交流以及科学技术的进步，自北朝起，至于元、明，我国古代社会发生了重要的转变，这种变化涉及政治制度、社会风俗、物质文化及精神文化等各方面，且文化与经济均呈现出多彩繁荣的态势。此外，随着少数民族入主中原及丝绸之路的通畅，民族交流与融合愈加深入，当时的物质文化亦随之具有丰富的民族信息。因此，考古遗存的面貌也深深烙上了这种社会转变、民族融合及文化交流的时代特征。2011—2017年黄淮七省关于北朝以后的重要考古发现收获颇丰，且以唐、宋、元、明时期的遗存为主，这些遗存充分体现了气象万千的时代特征。

  唐、宋经济之繁荣，离不了大运河与丝绸之路在交通上的支撑。京杭大运河是联通我国古代南北政治与经济的桥梁，海上丝绸之路则是沟通我国与世界的通道，隋代黎阳仓、回洛仓遗址，柳孜唐宋运河遗迹、海丰镇遗址以及樊村泾元代遗址等相继被发现，不仅对研究我国古代的水利设施与技术、航海技术具有重要意义，结合瓷窑址的材料，也使得我们对我国古代的陶瓷贸易、南北经济贸易以及海上中外贸易有了更为清晰的认识。而且，瓷窑址的发现亦丰富了我们对各地区瓷业面貌的认识，更新了我国的制瓷工程技术史。

  北朝以后，我国古代城市的布局、建筑群的布局及建筑风格均发生了显著变化。都城、行宫、地方城址以及聚落遗址的发现，是探讨城市规制布局，城址沿革、变迁的重要材料，而数量众多的建筑遗存，则为研究不同性质建筑的规格、布局、建筑工艺的发展提供了第一手资料。古人言"事死如生"，因此随着社会的变化，墓葬必然随之变化。除陵墓外，宋以后的墓葬的最大变化在于墓内装饰体现出更多的世俗性与生活化。陵墓、贵族墓及平民墓的发现，不仅为我们研究各等级、各地区的墓葬形制、葬俗及墓葬艺术提供了大量实物资料，其所蕴含的宗教、民族信息，与城址内发现的数量众多的寺庙遗存与生活遗存一起，亦全面丰富了我们对当时的宗教文化及民族融合等情况的认识。

# 运河悠悠　润千载文明

## 隋代大型仓储遗址的考古调查与发掘

◎刘海旺　王　炬

自2011年以来，河南文物考古工作者首次对隋代黎阳仓遗址和回洛仓遗址进行了较为全面的考古调查、勘探与发掘，基本上掌握了两处仓城遗址的范围、道路、仓窖、管理区等总体布局以及与漕运相关的情况。

隋代黎阳仓遗址位于河南省浚县城关镇东关村，东邻黄河故道，东北距黎阳城遗址约1千米。黎阳仓城依山而建，平面近长方形。仓城城墙为夯土筑成，护城壕位于东墙东侧，在东墙外侧还有另外一道壕沟。在仓城北中部发现一条南北向漕运沟渠，渠的南端发现有砖砌残墙遗存。在渠的西北侧，勘探出一夯土台基。从仓城的总体布局推断，仓城的西北部应为粮仓漕运和管理机构所在位置。目前已探明储粮仓窖84个，总体上看仓窖排列基本整齐有序，仓窖南北向大致有7排。仓窖皆为圆形，口大底小，口径大小不一。

另外，隋代黎阳仓废弃于唐初。在遗址中部区域发现叠压在废弃的隋代仓窖遗存之上的是一处具有大面积夯土基础的建筑遗存，推测这里可能是五代和北宋时期的官仓黎阳仓。

隋代回洛仓遗址位于隋唐洛阳城外的东北部，即洛阳市瀍河区瀍河乡小李村、马坡村西一带，向南与隋唐大运河通济渠相连。回洛仓仓城平面呈长方形，分为中部的管理区、东西两侧的仓窖区、道路和漕渠几部分。仓窖成组分布，排列整齐，经钻探确定的仓窖数量达到220座，推测整个仓城仓窖的数量在700座左右。已发掘清理的遗存包括完整的仓窖4座（C3、C46、C47、C140）、仓城内主要道路2条及仓城外北部道路4条。仓窖的形制结构相同，均呈口大底小的圆缸形。根据发掘情况，推测隋代回洛仓废弃的年代不晚于初唐。

作为代表隋代不同类型的大型国有粮仓——回洛仓遗址和黎阳仓遗址的同时发掘，为我们提供了研究隋代地下储粮技术的各个环节新的考古资料，并以超前丰富的考古新资料全面揭示了我国古代特大型官仓的概貌和当时的储粮技术水平以及储粮的种类，对于研究和复原隋代大型粮食仓储全过程具有前所未有的价值。

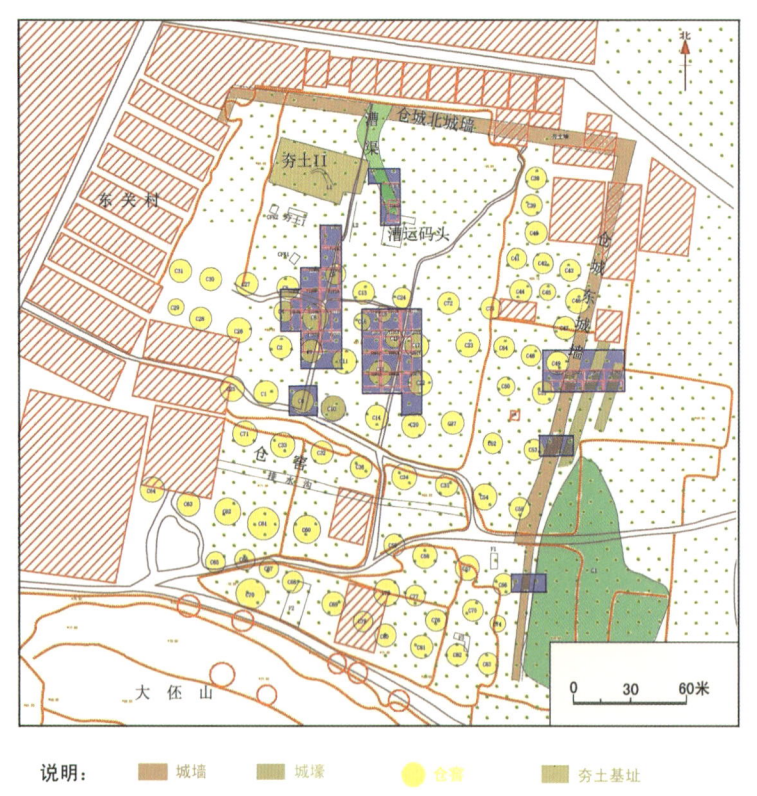

护城壕内柱洞

遗址全景俯瞰

遗址遗迹平面图

漕渠遗迹剖面

黎阳仓遗址

窖底与仓壁板灰遗迹（C6）

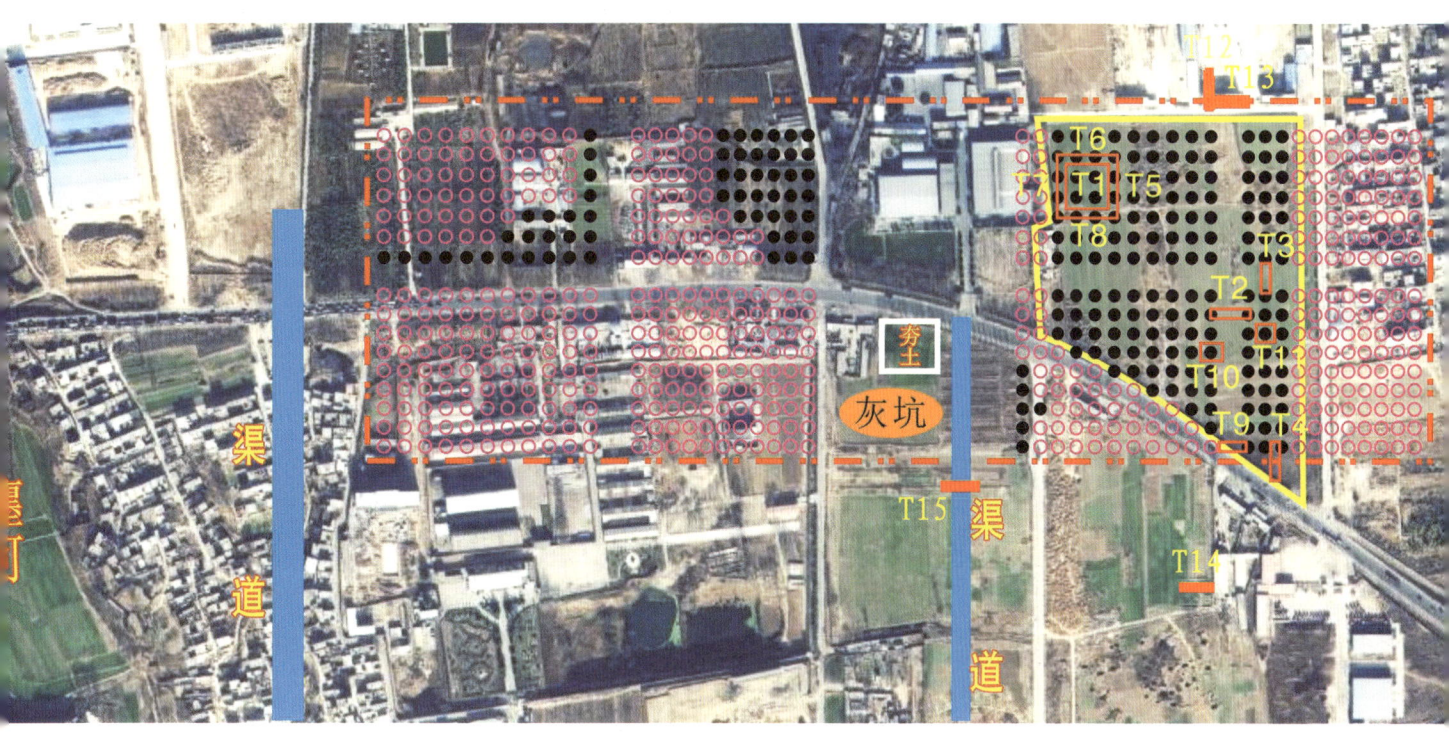

唐风宋韵　气象万千　495

回洛仓遗迹平面图

回洛仓C47
仓窖发掘现场

回洛仓漕运沟渠

回洛仓漕运沟渠
渠壁与淤泥

回洛仓窖壁烧烤状况　　　　　　　　炭化窖顶草秆（回洛仓C46）

壁木板灰痕迹（回洛仓C47）　　　　窖底席痕（回洛仓C3）

草秆遗迹（回洛仓C143）　　　　　窖壁席痕（回洛仓C3）

Liyang Granary Site of Sui Dynasty is located in Dongguan Village, Chengguan Town, Junxian County, Henan Province. Huiluo Granary Site is in the northeast of Luoyang City Site of Sui and Tang dynasties. To be exact, it is located in the area that is near Xiaoli Village and in the west of Mapo Village, Chanhe Township, Chanhe District, Luoyang City. Since 2011, archaeologists from Henan Province have been carrying out relatively comprehensive archaeological investigations, reconnaissances and excavations on both granary sites for the first time. Major unearthed remains include those of ramparts of the city in which the granaries used to be, moats, rammed earthen foundations, granary cellars, roads, canals and large-scale architectural foundations. What have been generally found out are years in which two granaries were deserted, their overall layout like range, roads, granary cellars and management areas as well as conditions of grain transportation via waterways. Now there is a general picture of exceptionally large official granaries, grain storage techniques and types of stored grain of the time when underground grain storage skills were well established in ancient China.

# 安徽柳孜唐宋时期运河遗址第二次考古发掘

◎陈　超

　　柳孜运河遗址位于安徽省淮北市濉溪县百善镇柳孜村。2012年2月—2013年6月安徽省文物考古研究所对其进行发掘，发掘面积2000平方米，发掘点位于1999年发掘区域的东侧并把原南岸石桥墩包括在内，发现的重要遗迹有运河河道、两岸的河堤、两岸的石筑桥墩、河道中间的石板路、道路、建筑址和木船等。

　　通过发掘，确认运河两岸河堤的堆积性质略有不同，北河堤是自隋唐时期一直沿用的，基本没有发生位移。南岸河堤的堆筑情况比较复杂，从解剖探沟可以看到其自唐代到宋代的堆筑技术和变化过程。为了增加河堤的稳固性和耐冲刷性，水工们采用阶梯状堆筑法，并结合大木桩的技术来修筑河堤。南河堤的宋代堤顶已不清楚，但唐代的堤顶尚存。探沟剖面的层位堆积说明当时水工是直接依托河道堆筑南河堤，且堆筑河堤的土较黏硬且纯净。

　　运河河道堆积共16层，其中第14层是河堤堆积，含有木岸，其下紧压黄沙层，从层位堆积可以判断出运河南堤有北移的现象。第16层是唐宋运河使用时的堆积。河底散落有大量石船碇，并发现了一艘残破的木船。沉船残损严重，船底朝上，船内出有崇宁通宝、崇宁重宝、熙宁元宝等，应该是储藏之物。

　　石筑桥墩均为长方体式墩身，北桥墩西侧存有保护桥墩的建筑遗迹，南岸石筑桥墩则依托河堤砌筑。两岸的石桥墩砌筑方式基本一致。首先是在河堤上挖出一个阶梯状大坑，然后铺石块，石块与石块之间用碎石子、土和石灰整平，即传统上的"支山"砌法。在北桥墩的北侧发现一条道路，为运河废弃之后修建的，根据层位关系推断石板路的时代为金代中后期。

　　此次发掘出土了大量的遗物，主要是生活用具、娱乐用具、武器、漕运遗物等。瓷器残片数以万计，可复原的遗物数量达7000余件。

　　柳孜运河遗址的二次发掘解决了很多关于通济渠的历史问题，厘清了运河在柳孜段的使用、管理及其淤废的过程，具有重要意义。

运河河道堆积（西向东）

沉船

出土瓷器

杂器

Liuzi Canal Site is located in Liuzi Village, Baishan Town, Suixi County, Huaibei City, Anhui Province. The first excavation was conducted in 1999. A series of important remains like those of shipwrecks and stone architectures were discovered and a number of valuable relics were unearthed. From February in 2012 to June in 2013, archaeologists from Anhui Provincial Institute of Cultural Relics and Archaeology excavated 2000 square meters of Liuzi Canal Site. Discovered remains include those of canals, embankments, stone bridge piers, roads paved with stone slabs in the middle of the river channel, sites of buildings, wooden boats. A large number of unearthed relics are mainly utensils for daily use, recreational equipment, weapons, vestiges of grain transportation via waterways, etc. After excavations, the age and accumulated deposit of Liuzi Canal Site as well as the way in which it was heaped up have been understood. The process in which the canal, in the locality of Liuzi Village, was in use and under management and then became deserted has been clarified.

# 江苏淮安市板闸遗址

◎ 胡　兵　赵李博

　　板闸遗址位于淮安市生态新城翔宇大道、枚皋路和里运河交会的三角地带，淮安市博物馆对其进行了两次抢救性发掘，确认板闸遗址是一处以水闸为核心，涵盖古河道、堤坝、码头、水闸、建筑基址、墓葬群、古粮仓、地面建筑三元宫等遗迹的明清时期大型遗址。

　　水闸遗迹总占地面积约2600平方米（含闸墩）。水闸整体大致呈对"八"字形，西南—东北走向，两端连接古运河。水闸两侧为闸墩，墩体上部土层较厚，下部土层较薄，上部与下部之间还有一层杂乱碎石和石料，这表明墩体并非一次形成。水闸主体由基础和闸墙两部分构成。

　　基础部分主要由地钉、龙骨木、底板和横梁等构成。闸墙系用条状青石错缝垒砌于底板之上而成，闸墙面石排列规整，里石则杂乱粗糙。按平面位置可将闸墙分为正身、上迎水雁翅和下分水雁翅三部分。

　　根据板闸遗址中水闸的结构和文献记载分析，其建造方法应为首先选址挖塘，底部筑三合土，再以桩木钉地，其上铺龙骨木和垫木，龙骨木与地钉则以榫卯结合。然后用成排枋木纵铺作为底板，以木梁横拦使整体形成梁板式基础，所有木构件之间均有铁钉加固，最后再于底板上垒砌条石。

　　水闸结构和用材的变化，反映了水闸的使用过程。在闸墙下部发现的转角条石，表明此前闸墙乃是向转角方向延伸的，现在所看到的这部分闸墙是经后期改向重建而成。另外，闸墙下部和上部之间也有多处不同。总之，闸体至少经历过两次重修，才变成现在的形状和结构。

　　与上海志丹苑水闸、江苏镇江京口闸、山东聊城土桥闸相比，淮安板闸的形制有较大的不同：其形状较为不规则，不见裹头与闸墙外衬河砖，且其底部为木料铺就，无石板衬底。另外，上海志丹苑水闸在底石和龙骨木之间还有衬石枋，而板闸则只在闸墙底下有衬石枋。

　　淮安板闸是目前全国唯一一座木板衬底的水闸遗址，结合文献资料和闸底出土遗物分析，水闸的年代上限为明代永乐十五年（1417年），下限应在明代晚期。

淮安板闸俯视图（上为南）

水闸正视图（北—南）

底板、牙石及关石桩

底板及横梁

西南雁翅墙体下的桩子

雁翅底部与衬石枋连接处的木护板

地钉及龙骨木

青花瓷碗　　　　　　　　　　　　龟趺碑座

Banzha Site is located in the New Eco-city of Huai'an City. The following are outcomes of excavations that have been carried out. The first is that it has been confirmed that this site is a large-scale one dating back to Ming and Qing dynasties. It consists of remains like an ancient river channel, a dyke-dam, piers, a lock, foundations of buildings, tomb clusters, ancient granary sites and an above-ground architecture, namely Sanyuan Palace. Remains of a water gate are the core of Banzha Site. The second is that it has been found out that the main body of the water gate is made up of two parts, the base and walls. The base mainly consists of stakes, a keel, a bottom floor and a beam. The walls can be divided into three parts, the body part, upstream wing walls and downstream wing walls. Building techniques, scales, shapes and structures of the water gate and its components like the base, walls and its body part have been found out. How the water gate was used can be observed from changes of its structure and materials. The water gate was built between 1417 A.D. to late Ming Dynasty. Banzha Site is of great value since currently it contains the only wooden-bottomed water gate in China.

# 京杭大运河山东段考古

◎李振光 吴志刚 王春云 吴双成

2008—2013年，山东省文物考古研究院联合枣庄、济宁、泰安、聊城、德州等地的文物管理部门对京杭大运河山东段河道及水工设施进行了调查、勘探、测绘，并对汶上县南旺枢纽遗址、阳谷县七级码头、七级闸，东昌府区土桥闸，临清市戴闸进行了全面的考古发掘，取得了丰硕的成果。

## 汶上县南旺枢纽遗址

1.南旺枢纽遗址的调查与勘探。对遗址的分布范围、结构布局、保存状况有了详细的了解，测算出了南旺湖、蜀山湖、马踏湖的周长和面积。对一些地表尚存的重要遗迹进行了测绘和勘探，绘制了南旺分水枢纽工程遗址分布示意图。

2.分水口、石驳岸与龙王庙核心区的发掘。石驳岸位于龙王庙北侧运河南岸，其基本构造是在南岸下深挖的河道内垒砌宽厚石墙，外侧用三合土夯打结实，平面呈曲线形，其对引入的小汶河来水起到顶冲、化解与分水的作用。

海漫石位于运河南岸，在分水龙王庙建筑群前发现较长的一段，顺河向东还有零星发现，用宽大石板平铺而成。石板顶面踩踏光滑，石板间接缝宽松，可能是长期使用破坏所致。海漫石向南延伸至龙王庙建筑群下，时代早于建筑群。

南岸大堤用花土、淤土夯打而成，大堤的北侧原有石块垒砌的石驳岸，被后期破坏仅存起石沟槽。石砌分水口设施位于汶运交汇处小汶河口两侧，向南与分水龙王庙古建筑群相对，用大石板垒砌，呈喇叭形。砖石堤岸位于运河北岸分水口以西，据砖上铭文，其应为明弘治十年或其后构筑。石筑台阶码头有4座，与砖石大堤一起垒砌而成，为堤岸向内嵌入式小码头。在砖石堤岸南侧河道内，发现成排的木桩挡板痕迹，应为挡沙板或缕水小堤。

分水龙王庙建筑群位于京杭大运河的南岸，坐南朝北，由东西并列的四组建筑组成。最东侧为分水龙王庙基址，其西为水明楼、禹王殿，向西为祠堂建筑群，最西为白大王庙建筑群。建筑群内发现多通明清时期的碑刻，碑文记载了建筑群及南旺枢纽的修建、改造历史。

3.邢通斗门。位于龙王庙建筑群西侧40米的运河南岸大堤上，为沟通运河与南旺湖的闸门。斗门由东西两侧的运河大堤和中间闸口组成。大堤用三合土夯打而成，其北侧有保护石墙。现存闸口的底部以密集木桩做基础，其上平铺木板，木板上再铺石板作为闸口底板。闸口底板的北侧砸4排直立木桩，木桩的北侧用斜立石板压住。此外，闸口的两侧还有用石块垒砌的直墙。

4.常鸣斗门。位于南旺镇三里铺村东运河的南岸大堤上，是连接运河与南旺湖的闸门。闸口呈"亚"字形，仅存底板和两层石墙，底部用石板平铺，底部石板凿有雁尾形槽，石板间用铁锔扣相连。每面立墙上各有一道闸槽。底板的北侧有一排保护木桩。北侧迎水雁翅两端的石墙被破坏，保存有较为密集的数排木桩，应为闸翅石墙的基础木桩。底部石板的南侧有4排保护木桩。

5.徐建口斗门。位于南旺分水枢纽分水口北侧2千米的小汶河西岸的徐建口村内，为沟通小汶河与马踏湖的闸门。石头闸门保存较好，闸门平面呈"亚"字形，由东侧的迎水雁翅、闸口，西侧的分水雁尾及东西两侧的保护木桩组成。闸口两侧立墙上各有两道闸槽，其建造方法为先在河底砸入密集的木桩做基础，在木桩上平铺石板，然后用石块砌筑两侧墩台立墙，石头间用铁锔扣连接。两侧直墙由里子石和外侧直墙组成。

6.徐建口西引水沟渠。徐建口斗门的西侧为南北向高岗，经勘探发现引水渠在徐建口村西150米处向北延伸，汇入十里闸村东北马踏湖内。引水沟渠呈口宽底窄的倒梯形，底部平整，为人工开挖而成，主要用于沉淀泥沙及对马踏湖实现供水平衡。

7.柳林闸。位于南旺镇柳林一村、二村、三村、四村的中间运河上。船闸呈"亚"字形，由闸口、墩台、迎水、雁翅、分水、雁尾、石砌码头、石头驳岸、底部基础木桩与保护木桩组成。

闸口底板保存较差，分为两期：早期用长方形石板铺成，晚期为长条形石板。墩台保存较差，用白灰三合土夯打而成，外表用石块垒砌直墙，可分为早、晚二期。闸口两侧南北两岸都筑有石驳岸，南岸保存较好。闸东南侧石驳岸分为早、晚二期，早期残存木桩和底部石墙，晚期驳岸呈中段外凸的弧形。闸东北侧石驳岸仅存底部木桩。

码头位于闸西南侧石驳岸的东端，东西两侧修筑台阶。闸口两侧的石墙及雁翅石墙用大石块垒砌而成。南侧雁翅向西砌筑有石墙以保护河岸。

8.寺前铺闸。位于南旺镇寺前铺村，始建于明正德元年（1506年），清乾隆年间重修。船闸呈"亚"字形，由闸口、墩台、迎水、雁翅、分水、雁尾、石驳岸、保护木桩等组成。

闸口平面呈长方形，底板用长方形大石板平铺而成，底板下用直立木桩做基础。墩台用白灰三合土夯打结实，外侧用大石块垒砌成直墙。闸门的东西岸边建有石驳岸，以石块横平铺设错缝叠砌而成。

## 阳谷县七级闸与七级码头

遗址位于阳谷县七级镇政府西北约200米。乾隆十年（1745年）重修。码头由石砌台阶状漫道、顶部平台及台阶下夯土平台组成。漫道由斜坡状边石与中部台阶组成。顶部平台用长方形大石板平铺而成，东侧与古街相接。平台的顶部用砖石垒砌有二座石垛。台阶下有夯土平台，平台上可见为固定船只残留的木桩及反复插入的木桩痕迹。

七级闸位于码头的西侧，2012年进行了清理，搞清了闸门的基本结构。

## 东昌府区土桥闸

遗址位于聊城市东昌府区梁水镇土闸村中，为京杭大运河的重要设施。土桥闸始建于明成化七年（1471年），清乾隆二十三年（1758年）拆修。

土桥闸船闸由大石块垒砌的迎水雁翅、闸口、分水雁尾、裹头、东西闸墩及南北侧底部的保护石墙和木桩组成。在闸北运河东岸发现减水闸一个，其北有一清代穿运涵洞，并发现"中华民国二十六年马颊河北支穿运涵洞"石碑一方。

月河，位于闸的东侧，呈南北长的不规则半圆形。大王庙，位于东侧闸墩上，坐东朝西，用青砖砌成。其东侧墙基内平铺一"康熙二十八年抚院明文"石碑。

聊城土桥闸是京杭大运河山东段首次发掘的船闸，也是大运河上完整揭露的第一座船闸，对于研究大运河的水工设施，认识大运河在我国古代交流与沟通中的作用具有重要意义。

## 临清戴闸

临清戴闸由迎水雁翅、闸口、分水雁尾组成，迎水雁翅位于东侧。闸口两侧直墙中间有闸槽，下有梯形石头门槛。闸口底板用长方形石板平铺而成，石头四边雕凿有雁尾形槽口，内用铁锔扣连接。闸槽内现保存有木头闸板，闸板的南北两端各有一条铁链，北侧铁链的下端拴有圆形大石坠，铁链和石坠对木板起到压镇和固定的作用。

闸的南侧为月河，在闸的东西两侧与运河连接。

戴闸与土桥闸相比有三个特点：一、规模大；二、雁尾部分的平面形制有别于土桥闸，雁尾中部存在一段南北向直墙，末端向东勾；三、在闸槽内保存较好的木头闸板，其作用应为闸口底部保持水位的闸板。

邢通斗门全景　　　　　　　　柳林闸

徐建口斗门　　　　　　　　祠堂建筑基址

**汶上县南旺枢纽遗址**

寺前铺闸

唐风宋韵　气象万千　509

石镇水兽　　　　　　　　　　　瓷碗

铁锔扣　　　　砖石堤岸、石筑台阶码头与木桩挡板

土桥闸北侧全景

船闸全景（由西向东）

闸门东侧底板

木头闸板（由东向西）

木板与闸槽间木楔

**戴闸**

闸底板及南侧立柱

寿字纹青花碗

青花瓷勺

镇水兽

青花瓷盘

闸槽与闸门槛石

土桥闸

From 2008 to 2013, investigations, archaeological reconnaissances and mapping were carried out along a segment of the Grand Canal in Shandong Province and its hydronic facilities. Comprehensive excavations were carried out on Nanwang River Bifurcation Site in Wenshang County, Qiji Pier and Qiji Lock in Yanggu County, Tuqiao Lock in the locality of Dongchang Prefecture and Daizha Lock in Linqing City. After excavations, firstly apart from an overall understanding of the preservation status and basic facilities of the canal, there is a deeper insight into facilities constructed along the canal in Nanwang County, structure and layout of the projects that divert water from Wenhe River to the Grand Canal, and balance and regulation of river waters. Techniques applied during the construction of hydraulic facilities that bifurcate Wenhe River to the North and the South and divert water to the Grand Canal are great achievements and they have been explicitly stated. Secondly, basic structure of Qiji Lock has been found out. It has been determined that Qiji Pier used to be a large stepped one, consisting of a stone stepped sloping access, a top platform and a rammed earthen platform at the bottom of this access. At last, there is a further understanding of the constructions, structures and layouts, functions, and operations of canal locks like Tuqiao Lock and Daizha Lock.

# 江苏镇江市中华路明清京口闸遗址

◎霍　强

京口闸，又名大闸、头闸，位于长江下游南岸，是历代千里漕运的"咽喉"。2012年8月，镇江博物馆考古人员对京口闸遗址展开了考古发掘工作，发掘面积2000平方米。经过近半年的考古发掘，先后揭示出了明清京口闸、码头、石岸、道路、碑亭等遗迹，并出土了一批民国至唐代时期陶瓷生活用品、祭祀供器等反映闸口文化特色的各类遗物。

1.京口闸

京口闸平面大致呈"八"字形，南北走向，北通长江，南接运河。全长54米，高6.25米，顶面海拔高度4.9~5.10米。清代京口闸的闸体是在明代闸体的基础上加修而成的，由闸口、迎水、雁翅、分水、裹头几部分构成。闸口平面呈长方形，其上设有闸身、闸槽、闸底石板、闸墩、绞关石。上迎水位于闸口北侧，平面呈北宽南窄的梯形，由上雁翅、上裹头组成。下分水位于闸口南侧，平面呈北窄南宽的梯形，由下雁翅、下裹头组成。

2.其他遗迹

清代石岸是在明代石岸的基础上分段加以修筑而成，其与上、下裹头相接，并继续向南、北延伸。石岸的建筑方法为采用不规则块石交错叠砌，自下而上逐渐收分，岸内侧填夯土，外侧底部设木桩挡护。

码头与上雁翅相接，平面为东西向长方形，采用黄色花岗岩铺砌，在底层台阶的外侧有按梅花式排列的杉木桩挡护。码头东西长11米，上口宽2.50米，下口宽3米，垂直高度2.50米，台阶17层。

碑亭遗迹西距闸体约5米，南距闸槽口14米。遗址平面呈方形，现残存一层用大小不一的块石砌筑的基址。在碑亭中央趴卧一尊石质龟趺座，龟首面向西侧，龟背中间设有一长方形碑座。

此次江南运河镇江段船闸遗址的发现，充分说明了我国古代建筑与治水工程技术具备相当高的水平，对于研究大运河的水工设施，运河沿岸的物质文化习俗，南北经济、运输、商贸等诸方面的交流与沟通有着重要意义。

京口闸遗址东闸体（北—南）

卵白釉花卉纹双耳瓷扁瓶　　　　　　　卵白釉龙凤纹双耳瓷扁瓶

青花云龙纹瓷香炉　　　　　　　青花海水龙纹瓷香炉

孔雀蓝釉云龙纹香炉　　　铁权

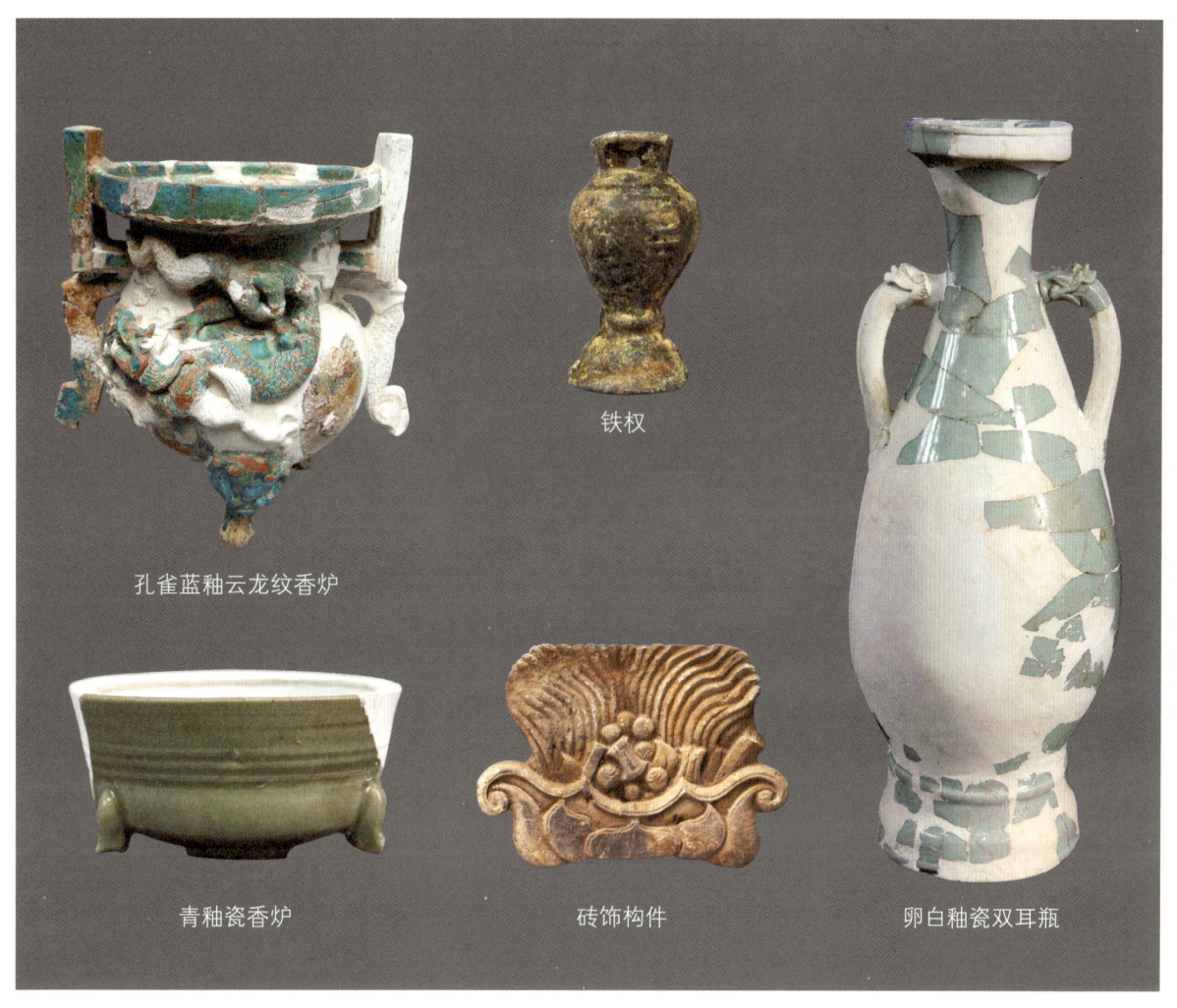

青釉瓷香炉　　　砖饰构件　　　卵白釉瓷双耳瓶

元代器物

In August 2012, archaeologists carried out excavations on Jingkouzha Lock Site. The excavated area is 2000 square meters. Remains were revealed one after another, including those of Jingkouzha Lock, pier, stone bank, roads and a pavilion built over a stone tablet which were constructed in Ming and Qing dynasties, river channel dug during the time from Tang Dynasty to Ming and Qing dynasties and river bank dating back to the same period. A number of relics that are remnants of a long time span from Tang Dynasty to the Republic of China were unearthed from the site, including those of ceramic utensils for daily use and vessels that were used to contain offerings. These relics reflect the cultural characteristics of a lock. After excavations, the age, scale, and structure of those revealed remains like Jingkouzha Lock, pier, stone bank, roads and the pavilion built over a stone tablet have been determined. Jingkouzha Lock Site is the first lock site that has been discovered along the Grand Canal in Zhenjiang prefecture in southern China. It is of great significance for the study of hydraulic facilities of the Grand Canal, material cultural customs along the canal and communication and exchanges in many aspects like economy, transportation and trade between the North and the South.

# 航琛越水　宝船佳瓷

## 河北黄骅市海丰镇遗址

◎雷建红　马小飞

海丰镇遗址位于河北省黄骅市东约25千米，处于羊二庄镇海丰镇村至杨庄村之间。遗址地处一中间高四周渐低的台地上，中心最高处为一东西向土岗，中心区面积约50万平方米。

通过对古柳河进行考古调查，确认古柳河河道大致呈西南—东北走向，在东光县西南联通南运河，于今黄骅关家堡村附近入海。调查中还发现遗址点60余处，其中包括毋兮城、古柳县、章武城、黄骅旧城、沧州旧城、南皮古皮城等城址，大多数遗址的年代为唐至元时期。

对海丰镇遗址东部濒海区域进行重点调查，发现遗址点6处，证明金元时期黄骅盐场附近可能分布有多处遗址点，此处为一个大的聚落群，是一处海上贸易出发地。

对海丰镇遗址的考古勘探将考古普探与对遗址东部与河道连接处进行重点勘探相结合，此外还采用地球物理方法进行考古调查。通过普探确认海丰镇遗址平面呈不规则形，发现踩踏面7处、道路3条、陶窑5座、灰坑2座、井1个及古河道一段。考古物探基本上确定了遗址东部古河道的具体位置，发现的重要遗迹有L3、踩7和Y1~5。

对海丰镇遗址的考古试掘分两个区域：Ⅰ区位于遗址中心，发掘面积300平方米，发现的元代遗迹数量较少，金代遗迹的数量、种类和保存状况都要明显好于元代，主要有道路、房址、火炕、灶、灰坑、灰沟及铺砖遗迹等。Ⅱ区位于遗址东部与河道接合处，疑似码头区域，重要收获即发现的一条东北—西南走向通往古柳河河道的金代道路。

海丰镇遗址以金代遗存为主，元代仍在沿用，遗址东部近河道处的大面积的踩踏面可能是仓货储存区，而古河道内的踩踏面极有可能是与航运相关的码头遗迹。房址集中分布在遗址的中北部，而且顺道路的走向而布局，应该是当时的居住区。通过对海丰镇遗址与大左庄遗址的比较研究，可以掌握海丰镇港口的历史变迁和发展脉络。而唐代煮盐遗迹，对研究海丰镇遗址早期以盐为对象的贸易形态具有重要意义。此外，古柳河的考古调查为开展河北境内古代各瓷窑址的水运交通线路研究和海丰镇港口遗址瓷器来源研究提供了支持。

总之，海丰镇考古的开展填补了北方濒海口岸遗址考古的空白，对研究金代北方海上丝绸之路的形成和发展及古代少数民族政权开展海运和对外贸易具有重大意义。

2016年布方、发掘后正射影像（右为北）

路面及类似路牙砖（东—西）

北侧路沟（东—西）

L1车辙痕迹（西—东）

L1剖面

Z8（南—北）

青釉梅瓶

酱釉器盖 　　　酱釉碗 　　　青釉碗 　　　酱釉碗

**遗迹与遗物**

白釉碗　　白釉碗　　白釉碗

白地黑花碗　　白地黑花碗　　扑满

Haifengzhen Site is 25 kilometers east of Huanghua City, Hebei Province. It is located between Hai-feng-zhen Village and Yangzhuang Village, Yang-er-zhuang Town. Its central area is approximately 500,000 square meters. From 2015 to 2017, archaeologists from Hebei Provincial Institute of Cultural Relics and other organizations carried out archaeological work on Hai-feng-zhen Site as well as other surrounding sites, discovering a large number of remains and relics dating back to Jin and Yuan dynasties. After archaeological work, it has been confirmed that Hai-feng-zhen Site is in an irregular shape with a maximum east-west length of about 1,600 meters and a maximum south-north width of about 1,600 meters. The site covers a total area of approximately 2,000,000 square meters. What have also been confirmed is the general direction of ancient Liuhe River and the distribution of ancient cultural remains along it. This is the basis for the study of ancient waterways for porcelain transportation, the provenance of porcelain unearthed from the port site in Haifeng Town, coastal settlement cluster back in Jin and Yuan dynasties Hebei Province and other issues. The application of geophysical (high-precision magnetic prospecting) archaeological exploration method is a try at combining traditional archaeological methods and geophysical prospecting means.

# 江苏苏州市太仓樊村泾元代遗址

◎张照根　张志清　孙明利

太仓樊村泾元代遗址位于苏州市太仓市城厢镇樊泾村小区西。2016年1月，苏州市考古研究所对遗址进行了初步勘探，已探明的遗址面积约30000平方米。2016—2017年，苏州市考古研究所、太仓博物馆、南京博物院组成考古队，以樊村泾古河道为界，分东、西两区展开发掘工作，合计发掘约13000平方米。

遗址发现各类遗迹现象430余处，主要有房址、道路、河道、灶台、水井、灰坑、灰沟、墙基、墓葬、河湾驳岸以及瓷片堆积等。以元代道路、河道等交通线为纵横框架，房屋基址密布其间，构成了遗址的核心文化遗存。遗址东发掘区内房屋基址规模较大，有大型围墙，内部建筑分组规划，道路布局规整，且发现大量瓷片堆积，初步推测该区为元代仓储及管理机构区域。遗址西发掘区内房屋建筑基址密集，规制相对东区较小，且叠压扰乱较为严重，初步推测该区为元代前店后坊式的商住生活区域。

遗址出土有瓷、陶、木、骨、铜、石、琉璃质等各类遗物。其中瓷片总量达150余吨，可复原器物不少于50000件，以元代中晚期龙泉窑青瓷为主，另有少量元代枢府瓷、青白瓷、青花和高丽青瓷出土，可辨瓷器器形有碗、盘、炉、瓶、盏、高足杯等40余类。窑口主要有龙泉窑、景德镇窑、磁州窑、铁店窑等。此次出土瓷器95%以上没有发现使用痕迹，结合太仓是元代新兴的一个港口城市，初步推测瓷器应当为商品在运输、转运过程中的损耗品。

根据遗址内发现的遗迹现象和遗物特征，初步推测遗址是大元王朝在江南地区经营的一处以龙泉窑青瓷为主的瓷器贸易集散地。该遗址主体年代为元代中晚期，下限为明代初年。遗址核心文化遗存可分三期：第一期为元代中晚期，第二期为元代晚期，第三期为元末明初。

太仓樊村泾元代遗址是目前发现的除龙泉窑址考古之外发现的规模最大的一处龙泉窑青瓷遗存，对补充元代龙泉窑青瓷标型器和建立元代龙泉窑青瓷标本库具有重要学术价值。通过与韩国新安沉船出水瓷器等比对，遗址出土瓷器有鲜明的外销特征，实证了太仓是元代海上丝绸之路重要港口和节点之一，为深入研究元明时期海运文化、配合海丝申遗提供了新材料。

遗址发掘区全景（上北下南）

东发掘区⑤层瓷片堆积（由北向南）

522　黄淮七省考古新发现

鬲式炉

鼓钉三足炉

荷花纹"至元四年"碗底

刻花缠枝牡丹纹荷叶盖罐

印花杂宝纹盘

刻花牡丹纹瓶

**元龙泉窑青釉瓷**

景德镇窑卵白釉"枢府"款盘

景德镇窑点褐彩堆塑螭龙纹转柄高足杯

景德镇窑青花缠枝花卉纹高足杯

大元通宝（八思巴文）

Taicang Fancunjing Site, dating back to Yuan Dynasty, is located in Fanjingcun Community, Chengxiang Town, Taicang City, Suzhou City. More than 430 remains, of a wide range, have been revealed, including house foundations, roads, river channels, stoves, wells, ash pits, ash ditches, wall foundations, tombs, riverbank revetments and piles of porcelain fragments. Unearthed relics are made of a wide range of materials, including porcelain, pottery, wood, bone, bronze, stone and glass. Porcelain and ceramic fragments, mainly celadons made in Longquan Yao, make up the majority of excavated antiquities. After excavations, core cultural remains of Fancunjing Site, whose major part is of late middle Yuan Dynasty, can be divided into three phases, respectively dating from late middle Yuan Dynasty, the late Yuan Dynasty and the end of Yuan Dynasty to the beginning of Ming Dynasty. According to their distribution pattern, the core cultural remains of Fancunjing Site undoubtedly used to be essential parts of institutional facilities inside Taicang City during Yuan Dynasty. It has been preliminarily inferred that Fancunjing Site used to be a state-run trading center and storehouse of porcelain, mainly celadons made in Longquan Yao, in southern China during Yuan Dynasty. Before the excavation of Fancunjing Site, no large-scale site of Yuan Dynasty had ever been discovered in southern Jiangsu Province. It is a great new archaeological find dating back to Yuan Dynasty in southern China.

# 绿堤春草　脉脉九河流

## 河北邢清干渠威县北宋"鲧堤"

◎佟宇喆

"鲧堤"遗址位于河北邢台市威县境内，长约20千米，南北走向，自威县邵固村南经全礼村西，过孙庄至南仓庄，再向北折至团堤村，而后入南宫境内。2013年5月—11月，河北省文物研究所考古队对"鲧堤"遗址进行了抢救性考古发掘。此次发掘的实际发掘面积近1300平方米，发掘区域位于威县县城东北约20千米常庄乡孙庄村西北的南水北调邢清干渠线路上。

经发掘，确认"鲧堤"堤体由三部分构筑而成，由上而下分述如下：

（1）二次扩筑部分。"鲧堤"两次夯筑所间隔的时间不长，因水患导致堤内淤积严重，因此二次夯筑时主要为加宽、加高堤体。目前残存的堤体二次扩筑部分，叠压于原堤体之上，宽度大于原堤体，西边一部分叠压于黄褐色自然淤积层之上。二次扩筑堤体剖面呈平行四边形，筑有两道土埂对堤体进行分割，堤体可分为三部分。夯层较为规整，共计9层。

（2）原筑堤体部分。叠压于大堤二次扩筑部分之下，剖面呈梯形，分东西7部分逐层夯筑而成，其下为夯土基槽。

（3）基槽。"鲧堤"堤体之下，开掘有基槽，剖面呈长方形，直壁平底，壁面粗糙。槽内用夯土填实，上为夯土堤体。

另在原地表与夯堤西边缘交界处及堤体西边护坡之上发现有柱洞若干，木柱直立插入，木柱已朽毁，仅存木灰痕迹，其为疑似防止大堤堤体被水流冲击而采取的保护措施所遗留痕迹。

"鲧堤"堤体夯筑较为规整，其内包含物较少，仅发现少量瓷器残片、陶器残片，器形有瓷碗、磨轮。

"鲧堤"堤体内出土器物较少，仅三件可修复的白釉瓷碗和少量瓷器残片。从瓷碗的器形和质量分析，推断"鲧堤"修建年代的上限为北宋中晚期。"鲧堤"遗址西边紧临沙河河道，北宋元丰四年（1081年）四月，黄河第二次北流（小吴北流）时，曾经借道沙河。综合以上两方面，可推断出"鲧堤"为北宋中晚期抵御黄河第二次北流所修建，修正了"鲧堤"为鲧所修建这一说法。

堤体全景（东南—西北） 　　　　　　　　　堤体剖面全景（东北—西南）

堤体剖面 　　　　　　　　　　　　　　　堤体剖面

两次修建堤体间淤积层

夯窝遗迹剖面　　　　　　　　　　　　堤体夯窝遗迹

堤体夯窝遗迹　　　　　　　　　　　　堤体中段胶泥部分剖面

起夯用的垄沟　　　　　　　　　　　　堤体底部木头柱洞痕迹

"Gun Di", an embankment, is in Weixian County, Xingtai City, Hebei Province. As a segment of South-to-North Water Diversion Project, a west-east major canal, running from Xingtai to Qinghe, pierces through it. From May to November in 2013, archaeologists from Hebei Provincial Institute of Cultural Relics carried out salvageal excavations on a segment of "Gun Di" which was enclosed in the construction site of the canal. After excavations, it has been found out that "Gun Di" was made up of segments of rammed earth that had been tampered twice. Foundation trenches have been discovered. It has been inferred from unearthed relics that "Gun Di" was constructed to resist the second northward flow of the Yellow River in middle and late Northern Song.

# 灵明宝藏　收在水晶宫

## 河北水下文化遗产保护

◎雷建红

河北是我国北方海洋大省之一，地处河海交汇处，水路发达，自古以来就是渤海湾北路重要的航运通道。特别是隋朝大运河开通后，大大便利了南北交通，加强了京都和河北、江南地区的水上运输。唐宋以降，随着水上航运技术的成熟以及海上贸易的日渐繁荣，为河北内陆水域和海域内蕴藏着丰富的水下文化遗产创造了得天独厚的优势。

"十二五"期间，河北省水下文化遗产保护工作稳步向前推进，河北省文物研究所围绕渤海湾海域开展了一系列的水下考古调查工作，并取得了可喜的成绩：

（一）机构和队伍建设。2012年起，河北省正式启动水下文化遗产保护工作。2013年河北省文物研究所增设水下考古研究室，专职负责河北省水下文化遗产保护工作，并对业务人员进行出水文物保护培训和水下考古培训。

（二）开展沿海水下文化遗产资源调查。2014—2015年，河北省组织专业人员完成了沧州、唐山、秦皇岛三市沿海14个县、区的水下文化遗产陆上调查工作。经调查，初步确认水下文物点70处，其中海防及航海设施15处、沉船点18处、古船坞1处、贝壳堤等海洋自然遗产2处及滨海古遗址34处。

（三）协作开展唐山东坑坨沉船水下重点调查。2013—2015年，水下考古研究室与国家文物局水下文化遗产保护中心合作，连续三年重点对东坑坨Ⅰ号沉船进行了水下考古调查，包括沉船潜水探摸、沉船遗址水下考古测绘、遗址周边海域物探调查等。初步查明东坑坨Ⅰ号沉船为一艘近代初期建造，沉没于民国时期的木肋木壳外包铜皮兼用铁木混合结构的蒸汽动力沉船。东坑坨Ⅰ号沉船是我国发现的为数不多的、保存较好的近代早期沉船遗址，是研究中国近代史的重要实物资料。

2014年东坑坨沉船水下考古启动仪式

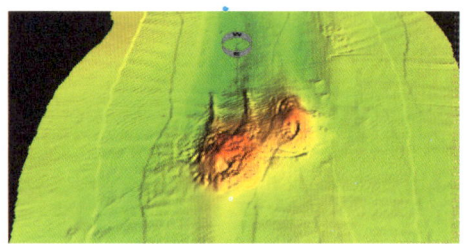

东坑坨沉船多波束影像

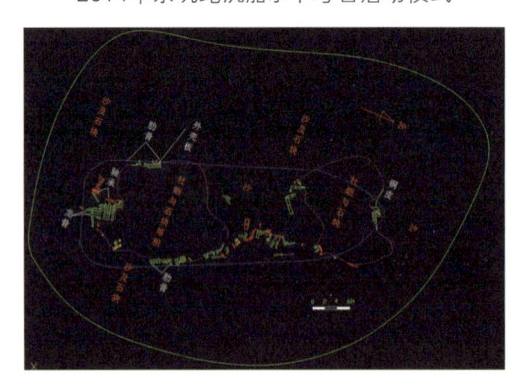

东坑坨沉船遗迹分布

布置（订）基线近照

东坑坨沉船铜皮

东坑坨沉船木板

There are abundant underwater cultural heritage sites in Hebei Province. A provincial underwater cultural heritage protection project was officially launched in 2012. Since then, archaeologists from Underwater Archaeology Division of Hebei Provincial Institute of Cultural Relics have been conducting a series of underwater archaeological investigations in Bohai Bay area. From 2014 to 2015, onshore investigations of underwater cultural heritage were carried out in 14 counties and districts of three coastal cities, Cangzhou, Tangshan and Qinhuangdao. There are 70 sites of underwater remains, including 15 sites of coastal defense and navigation facilities, 18 shipwrecks, 1 ancient dock, 2 sites of marine natural heritage like a naturally formed shell dyke and 34 seashore ruins. From 2013 to 2015, the Division cooperated with Underwater Cultural Heritage Protection Center of National Cultural Relics Bureau. A three-year intensive underwater archaeological investigation was carried out on Dong-keng-tuo Shipwreck Ⅰ. It has been preliminarily determined that Dong-keng-tuo Shipwreck Ⅰ should be a steam-powered ship built in early modern period.

# 万里江山　自古竞繁华

## 山西蒲州故城遗址发现北朝至唐代城墙

◎刘　岩　赵　辉

蒲州故城遗址位于山西南部永济市西15千米的蒲州镇境内，以发现唐代黄河大铁牛而闻名。遗址分为东、西两城，东西长2.49千米，南北宽1.71千米，占地面积4.26平方千米。

2012—2016年，山西省考古研究所持续对蒲州故城遗址开展了考古工作，完善了现有东城的平面形制，理清了地表城墙的始建年代，并对部分古建筑基址进行了发掘清理。最为重要的收获是在东城内发现了唐代地层，在西城内西北部找到了北朝至唐代时期蒲州故城的城墙遗迹。2015—2016年在西城内西北部进行了大面积的发掘，发现大规模夯土基址遗存，并对该夯土基址进行了较大范围揭露和局部解剖，确认夯土从北向南可分为6部分，并编号为夯1~夯6。

依据各部分夯土的遗迹现象，确定该夯土基址遗存为一段城墙遗迹。该城墙位于地表1.50米以下，东西走向，长约130米，主体宽8~10米，自身厚4~6米，夯筑质量高。最早修筑城墙时利用了原有的生土高台，将生土台稍作修整后作为墙芯，再依次在生土台的南侧夯筑夯3、夯4和夯5，形成城墙的主体。其中，夯3为城墙的原筑夯土，夯4、夯5为补筑、增筑形成，有规整坡面。此后在城墙南部增筑夯6，在城墙北部增筑夯2和夯1。综上，结合出土遗物判断，城墙始建于北朝，唐代沿用并在局部进行了大规模的增筑。宋金时期该段城墙墙体功能废弃，在平面和高度上对城墙均进行了扩建，发现的遗迹有房址、水道、水井等，此时夯土作为建筑基址使用，性质发生了"由墙到台"的转变。

在夯土城墙以南发现6方青石质的方形柱础石，从柱网的平面布局看，柱础石同属一座建筑，房址为东西向，面阔三间，进深两间。根据层位关系，此建筑的时代不晚于唐代。此外，还发现了唐代的水道、水井、灰坑等与房址相关联的遗迹。出土了数量较多的陶片、砖、瓦及石像底座、铜钱等遗物。

蒲州故城遗址新发现的城墙证实了唐代蒲州城的存在，其年代可上溯至北朝时期，早于蒲州故城地表现存城墙，它的发现为确定北朝至唐代蒲州城的位置、分布范围提供了十分重要的线索和依据。

530　黄淮七省考古新发现

发掘区全景及不同夯土的分布范围

发掘区地形地貌航拍（上为北）

探沟5与发掘区距离

探沟5内夯3、4、5叠压关系(东—西)

夯土墙体

唐代房址、灰坑、水道

瓦当　　　　陶盆　　　　柱础

From 2015 to 2016, on the City Site of Puzhou, archaeologists from Shanxi Provincial Institute of Archaeology conducted excavations in the northwestern part of its west district. The excavated area is a stretch of land of 3000 square meters. A large-scale rammed earthen foundation site was discovered, completely revealed and then partially dissected. It has been confirmed that, from north to south, the rammed earth that made up the ramparts can be divided into six parts. According to unearthed relics, it has been determined that the ramparts were first constructed in Northern Dynasties. When it came to Tang Dynasty, the ramparts were still in use and there were partial large-scale add-up constructions. During Song and Jin dynasties, there was no longer a rampart. Instead, the rampart was turned into a terrace.

# 江苏南京市花露岗唐至五代遗址的考古发掘

◎李 翔

花露岗位于南京老城区的西南部，北至集庆路，南至明城墙，东至鸣羊街，西至凤游寺，面积约20万平方米。该区域的地形呈现北部和东南部高，中部自北向南平缓降低的态势。经考古勘探与试掘，证明北部高地为自然形成的原始山体，东南部高地为人工堆筑而成，可能与明清时期愚园内湖面的开挖和疏浚有关。

2013年5月—2014年5月，南京市博物馆对愚园西侧进行了勘探、局部试掘和发掘，发掘面积总计约4400平方米。此次考古发掘中，发现的遗迹极多，有灰坑、房屋建筑、院落建筑、水井、墓葬及排水沟等。现仅对本次考古发掘发现的唐至五代的建筑加以介绍：

F2位于整个发掘区的北部，开口于第⑤层下。由磉墩、带砖砌散水的院落及墙基组成。磉墩共35个，磉墩上口为方形，其形状大小均有差异。由于早期被严重破坏，目前仅北部及东部断断续续保留了一部分墙基。从目前发现的这些遗迹现象推测，F2为一座南北向的"工"字形建筑，南北各建有一组东西五间、南北三进的建筑，两组建筑之间由一道廊道连接，廊道两侧为带砖铺散水的小院落。

F3位于整个发掘区的南部，开口于第⑤层下。由磉墩、带砖砌散水的院落、墙基组成。磉墩共17个，形制大小基本与F2的磉墩相同。F3西侧为一座砖砌大院落，被破坏严重，仅保存有东南角的砖砌部分。大院落东侧有一座四进四间的建筑，推测大院落西侧格局与之相同。

从目前已经发掘的情况看，该建筑群规模宏大、格局基本完整，从出土遗物及叠压地层推测其时代为唐至五代。根据文献资料记载，该建筑群可能与南唐时期合署办公有关，对于研究南唐时期南京历史文化具有重要的意义。

房址航拍图（上南下北）

白瓷碗

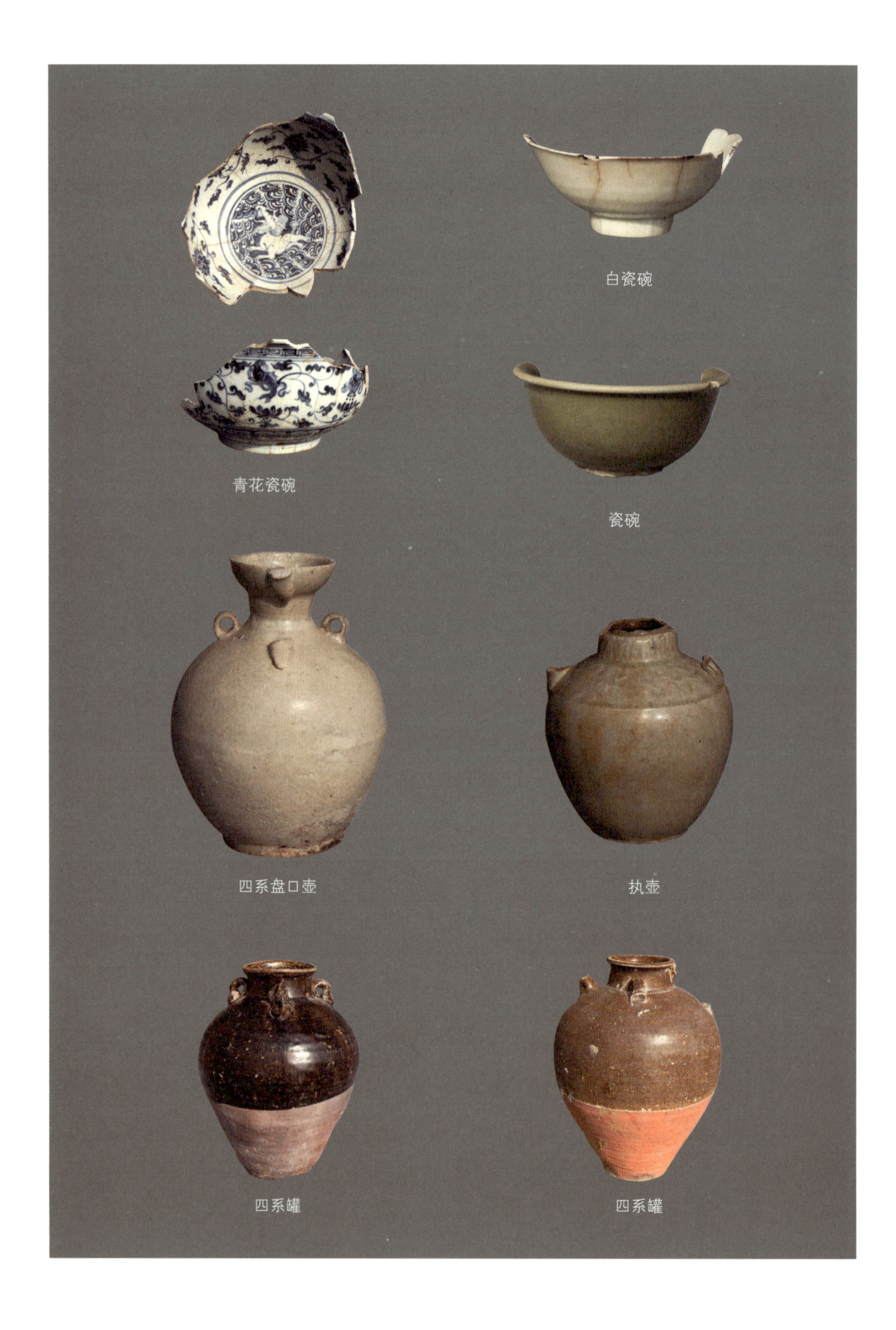

青花瓷碗

瓷碗

四系盘口壶

执壶

四系罐

四系罐

双系罐　　　　　　　　　　　陶罐

黑釉碗　　　　　　　　　　　陶碾

From May 2013 to May 2014, archaeologists from Nanjing Museum carried out archaeological reconnaissances and local trial diggings in the western area of Yuyuan Garden. Excavation shows that cultural deposits here can be divided into six phases. Apart from an foundation site of an ancient building complex between the south hill and north hill, there are remains of ash pits, wells, tombs, drains, etc. A great number of relics dating from Eastern Wu to Qing Dynasty have been excavated, including porcelain, potteries, stone implements and tiles. At present, excavation shows that the scale of discovered building complex is large and its layout is relatively complete. It has been inferred that this building complex, which might be related to office integration in Southern Tang, appeared during Tang Dynasty and Five Dynasties. This discovery is of great significance for studying and exploiting the history and culture of Nanjing in Southern Tang.

# 江苏盱眙县泗州城唐代至清代遗址

◎朱晓汀　甘恢元

泗州城遗址，位于盱眙县西北部淮河北岸的狭长滩地上。南京博物院考古研究所于2010年11月初启动了泗州城遗址的考古工作，至2014年，共发掘28,500平方米。

经钻探，汴河大致呈西北—东南向贯穿城址，向北经北门附近出城，向南经香华门附近出城。泗州城的内城垣大致呈椭圆形，面积约为2.4平方千米。外城垣形状与内城垣相似。内城垣有五座城门。

汴河发掘区位于遗址的中部偏南，清理出明清时期房址76座、院落7处、道路8条，此外，还揭露出元、明、清时期汴河东侧河岸及石护坡。

经发掘证实，内城垣修建于明代，内城垣内部还有两期城墙，第二期城墙的建造年代不早于宋代不晚于元代，第一期城墙的建造年代更早。外城墙确为明代包砖石加固的"邵公堤"。

城内发现多处建筑基址，包括1、2、4、5号基址，另发现东、西向大街一条。

4号基址较为重要，主要包括塔基和塔基以南的一路三进房屋两进院落的建筑、西塔院、东塔院。根据清理出的碑额刻文可知，4号基址即为元代建造的灵瑞塔，是研究藏传佛教建筑难得的实例。在塔基月台上增筑的中轴线建筑以及叠压于塔基之上东、西塔院，应为万历年间所建。

1号基址位于泗州城西南部，应是经过多次修缮甚至重建后的"大圣寺"。推测该建筑自唐代建成以后一直沿用，毁于康熙年间的大水。2号基址位于泗州城城内西南部，为一三进院落，依清康熙《泗州通志》，注明2号基址为观音寺。观音寺基址亦是在原来建筑的基础上于明末天启年间重修，沿用至清初。从建筑布局推断，5号基址应为2号基址的临时性附属建筑。

泗州城是我国目前发现的唯一一座"州城"遗址，其内外城墙较好地保存于地下，为研究明清时期泗州城的城市布局、城防、防洪工程及不同性质建筑的规格、布局、建筑工艺提供了第一手研究资料。

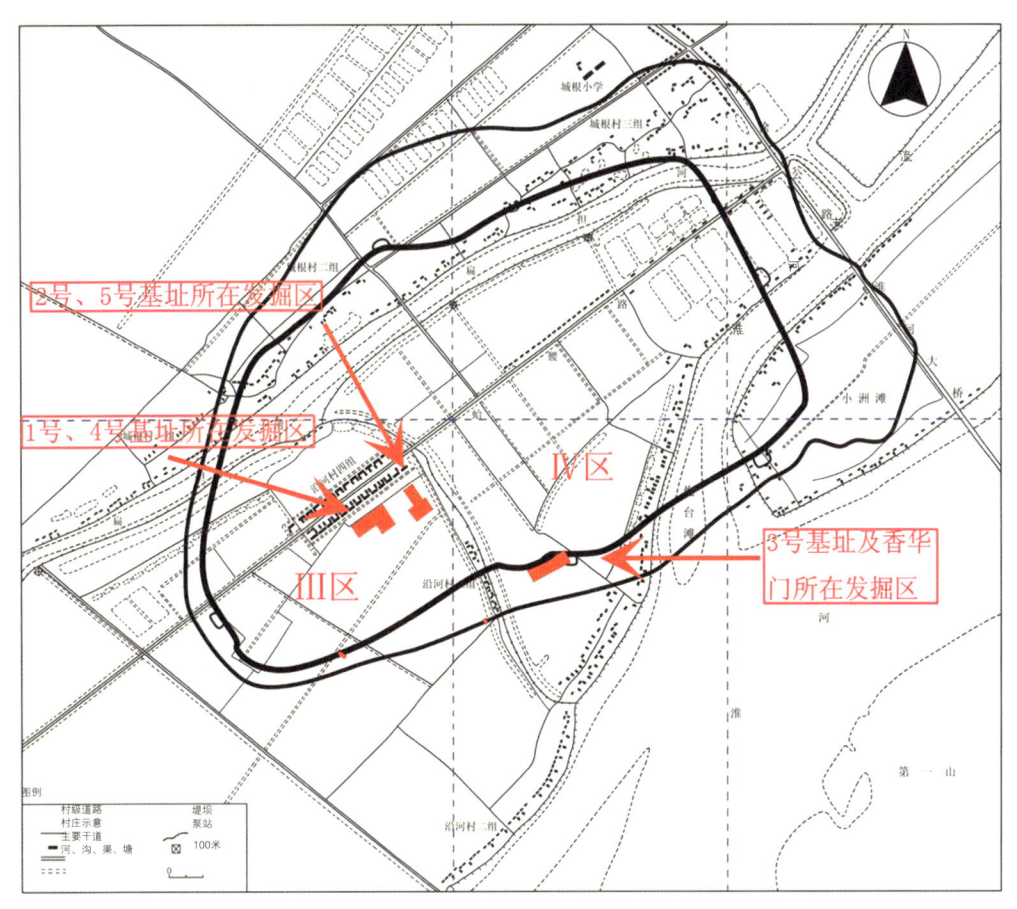

泗州城遗址简图

4号基址航拍图（上为东）

538 黄淮七省考古新发现

泗州城遗址1、4、2、5号（由右至左）基址航拍图

龙纹瓦当　　　　　3号基址出土抱鼓石　　　　　3号基址出土雀替

3号基址出土石构件　　　　　3号基址出土石构件

灵瑞塔塔基前侧龟趺座　　　　　建筑构件

Sizhou City Site is located on the north bank of Huaihe River, in the northwest of Xuyi County. After surveys and excavations, revealed remains are of ramparts, former river channel of Bianhe River, architectural foundations, roads, etc. Among them, the most important ones are vestiges of temple architectures. Unearthed relics including building components, stone implements, porcelain, potteries, stoneware, ironware, bronzes, bone implements and ivory ware. After excavations, it has been found out that Bianhe River, as a Golden Waterway during Tang and Song dynasties, gradually became silted up after Yuan Dynasty. Besides, positions of inner ramparts and outer ramparts surrounding Sizhou City have been located. Range, shape and structure of Sizhou City have also been determined. It is believed that the inner ramparts were built in Ming Dynasty while the outer ramparts were earthen ones piled during Song Dynasty. At present, as the site of a city where there used to be the administrative department of a prefecture, Sizhou City Site is the only one of its kind that has been ever discovered in China. Most of the relics, which are well-preserved, are first-hand materials for studies on layout, defense and flood control measures of Sizhou City during Ming and Qing dynasties as well as specifications, overall arrangement and building techniques of varied architectures. In particular, Foundation Site No. 4 is a rare example for the study of Tibetan Buddhist architectures of Yuan Dynasty.

# 河北肃宁县后白寺唐宋时期遗址

◎ 雷建红

后白寺遗址位于肃宁县梁村镇后白寺村西北100米处，西距小白河约500米，北距高家庄1500米。2013年8月—2014年1月，河北省文物研究所等对该遗址进行了考古发掘，发掘面积1700平方米，共清理遗迹165座，出土完整或可修复器物76件。文化遗存包括唐代、宋代及个别明清遗存。

该遗址地层堆积较为简单，分为两层，耕土层下即暴露出遗迹或生土。遗迹多数开口于②层下，部分开口于耕土层下。

唐代遗存主要是开口②层下的部分遗迹。遗迹较为单一，仅发现灰坑、灰沟、窑址三类，其中灰坑34座、灰沟2条、窑址1座。出土完整或可修复器物13件，其中陶器8件、瓷器3件、骨器1件、蚌器1件，另外还有大量陶瓷残片。

宋代遗存包括第②层及开口②层下的部分遗迹。遗迹共123个，其中灰坑102座、灰沟14条、井5眼及墓2座，墓葬均为埋葬儿童的砖棺墓。出土完整或可修复器物共63件，其中陶器21件、瓷器26件、石器2件、铜钱10枚、骨角器2件、银器1件及铜环1件。瓷器釉色有白釉、青白釉、黑釉、双色釉及酱釉等，瓷器窑口主要为定窑和磁州窑。

明清遗存仅发现5眼水井，均开口于耕土层下，为土圹圆形井。井内填土为黄褐土与红胶土混合成的花土，土质较黏。出土有青花瓷片。

通过发掘，我们认为该遗址是一处以唐、宋时期遗存为主的村落遗址，也有个别明清遗迹。由于发掘位置和发掘面积所限，未发现房基、路基等遗迹，出土遗物也相对较少，因此推测该遗址所处位置为村落的边缘地带。根据勘探结果推测，发掘区北侧100米处的地下遗存较为丰富，又据村民介绍，原来此处为一高约1.50米的土台，后村民盖房挖土形成现在的平地，该地曾出土大量的陶瓷器物，推测可能是村落的中心区域。

唐宋遗物

Houbaisi Site is located in the northwest of Houbaisi Village, Liangcun Town, Suning County. From August in 2013 to January in 2014, in coordination with the construction of a major canal, a segment of South-to-North Water Diversion Project that runs from Baoding to Cangzhou, archaeologists from Hebei Provincial Institute of Cultural Relics carried out excavations on Houbaisi Site. The excavated area is 1700 square meters and the total number of revealed historical remains reaches 165. Seventy-six pieces of antiquities, intact or repairable, were unearthed during excavations. Cultural contents of Houbaisi Site include remains dating back to Tang and Song dynasties and a small number of vestiges of Ming and Qing dynasties. It has been inferred that Houbaisi Site should be a village site where there are mainly remains of Tang and Song dynasties.

# 山西晋阳古城 2012—2018 年考古发现及主要收获

◎ 韩炳华

晋阳古城遗址位于山西省太原市晋源区晋源镇附近，西城墙紧挨大运高速公路，南城墙南接龙山大街，北城墙濒临蒙山大街，东城墙靠近汾河西岸，遗址面积约20平方千米。从2012年至今，山西省考古研究所等对晋阳古城遗址进行了考古调查与发掘，先后发现了一号、二号两处大型建筑基址。

一号建筑基址，整体平面布局呈南北向的长方形，该建筑基址可分为两期。第一期为晚唐建筑，保存较差。房屋东向，似为小型廊庑建筑。西庑以南为一倒座。第二期为五代建筑，房屋沿着纵轴线形成对称式院落布局坐落在一个台基上。大殿东西挟屋和月台为后来搭建。根据出土遗物和房屋建筑布局，确定该建筑始建年代为晚唐，废弃年代为宋初。晋阳古城一号建筑基址的发掘揭示了宋初晋阳城被毁的实际状况和晚唐至宋初时期建筑的基本布局。

二号建筑基址是一个复杂的建筑群体，分为东、西两组建筑基址。

西组建筑基址始建于唐，毁弃于宋初，保存基本完整。建筑南向，沿中轴线左右布局，由道路、三个庭院以及多处面阔三间的建筑组成。整组建筑由左右两侧房屋组成一个封闭的多进院落。根据遗迹现象，推测该建筑为大型寺庙建筑的一部分，修建年代为唐，可能在唐武宗时期受到破坏，五代后唐重新修葺，最终毁灭于宋初。

在西组建筑以东100米，发掘了东组建筑。整个建筑基址是一个由四周房屋围合而成的院落，最早一期建筑始建于东魏，经北齐、隋，最后废弃于初唐。建筑基址采用一种大面积"满堂红"地基处理方式，夯筑方法为平夯。该建筑基址之下为魏晋十六国文化层，经发掘确认有水井、窖穴、建筑台基等遗迹。魏晋十六国文化层以下为汉代文化层，发现有汉代遗迹，主要有水井、房址等。

二号建筑基址的发掘揭示了不同时代同一区域的不同类型建筑，尤其是唐五代大型寺庙建筑，其比较完整的建筑平面结构较为少见。根据发现的"隋之晋阳宫"残碑资料，推断发掘区可能是北朝和隋代晋阳宫所在区域。

一号建筑基址鸟瞰（上为东）

二号建筑基址鸟瞰（上为北）

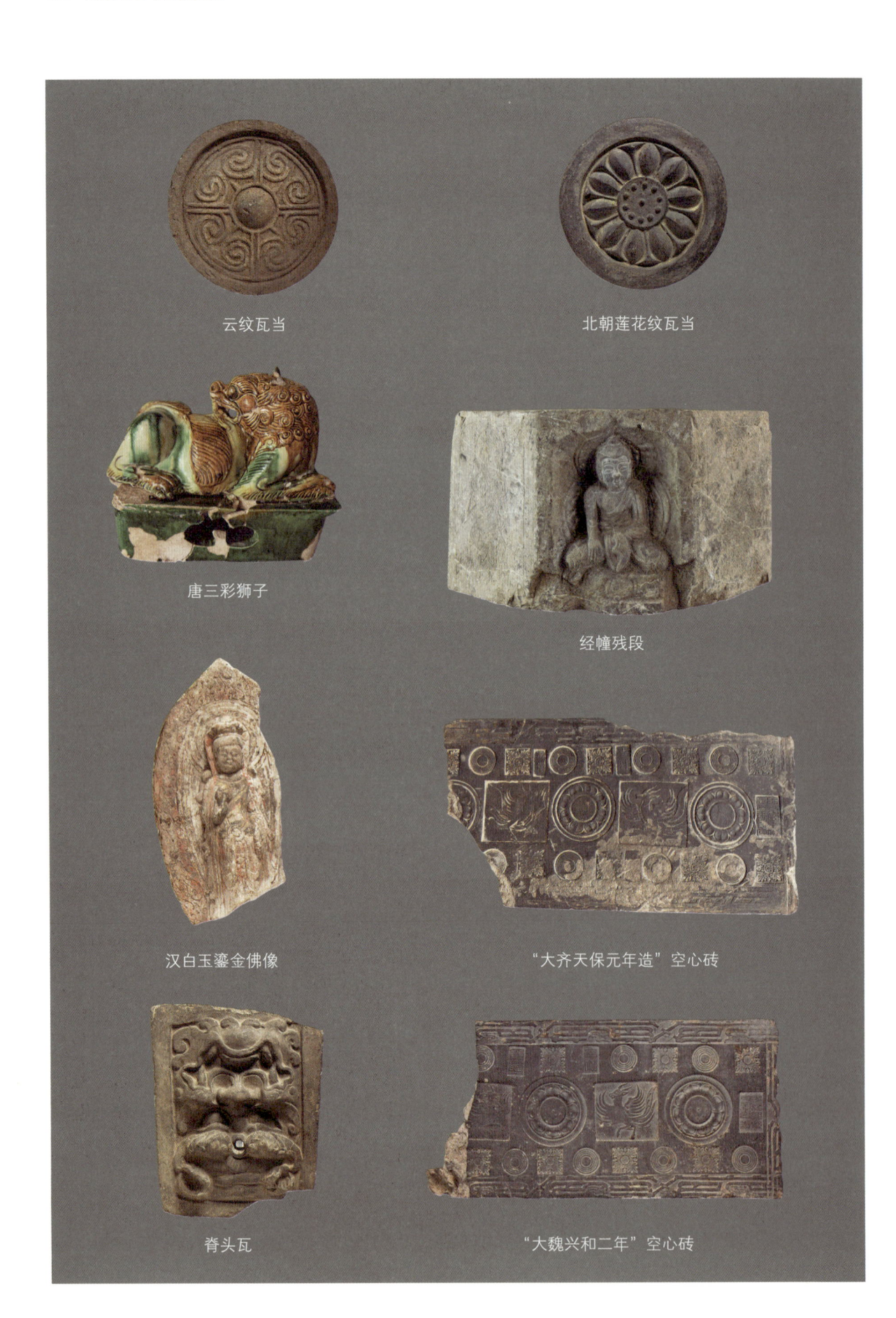

| | |
|---|---|
| 云纹瓦当 | 北朝莲花纹瓦当 |
| 唐三彩狮子 | 经幢残段 |
| 汉白玉鎏金佛像 | "大齐天保元年造"空心砖 |
| 脊头瓦 | "大魏兴和二年"空心砖 |

唐风宋韵 气象万千 545

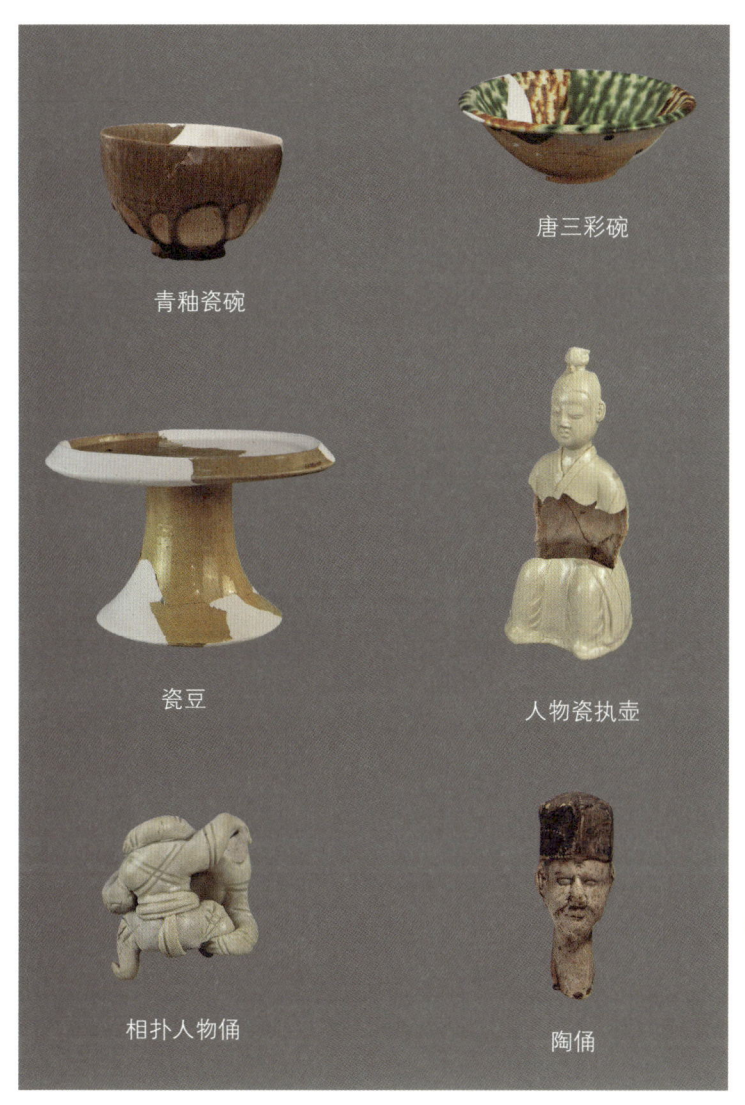

青釉瓷碗　唐三彩碗　瓷豆　人物瓷执壶　相扑人物俑　陶俑

残碑拓片

Archaeologists from Shanxi Provincial Institute of Archaeology and Taiyuan Institute of Culture Relics and Archaeology have been carrying out archaeological investigations and excavations on Jinyang City Site. Two large-scale architectural foundation sites, labeled as No.1 and No.2, have been discovered. The relatively complete plane layout of a massive temple architecture that used to be constructed on foundation site No.2 back in Tang Dynasty and Five Dynasties is rare. After archaeological work, the age, layout and structure and development of both architectural foundation sites have been basically figured out. According to a broken stone tablet with the inscription "Jinyang Palace of Sui", it can be inferred that there might be Jinyang Palace on foundation site No.2 back in Northern Dynasties and Sui Dynasty. Besides, unearthed relics are new subjects of the study on archaeological researches concerning sixteen states that formed during Wei and Jin dynasties in Shanxi Province, ancient porcelain-making techniques and cultural exchanges.

# 江苏东台市辞郎村遗址

◎高 伟 李光日

辞郎村遗址位于江苏省东台市辞郎村东约700米处，分布于泰东河两岸，遗址东距东台市市区7千米，北临东台镇西溪古街道。该遗址于2011年6月泰东河工程沿线考古调查时被发现，遗址总面积约8万平方米。2011年11月—2012年1月，南京博物院等单位对遗址进行了抢救性发掘，发掘面积共计约3535平方米。

唐代地层分布在西岸发掘区，东岸发掘区发现了唐代的灰坑和灰沟等遗存。出土遗物为生产生活用品，器类以瓷器为主，有少量釉陶器、陶器、石器、铁器和铜钱等。据统计，遗址东、西两岸共出土唐代瓷（器）片2900余件，胎质分为灰胎、褐胎、红胎、红褐胎、灰黄胎、灰褐胎等，釉色以青釉为主，青黄釉、酱釉其次，器物外壁施釉多不至底。另有少量白釉和素烧瓷器。器类可分碗、罐、执壶、盂、盏、盆、盒、灯盏等。以碗类最多，占出土瓷器的77%。瓷器多属越窑系产品，还有萧县窑、寿州窑等窑产品，有少量的长沙窑及宜兴窑产品。

宋代遗存分布于发掘区东岸第3层、西岸第3～4层，发现灰坑、灰沟、水井和墓葬等遗迹，出土遗物以瓷器为大宗，釉陶器、陶器、石器和铜器等数量较少。共出土宋代瓷器（片）3000余件，胎质分为灰黄胎、灰胎、灰白胎、灰黑胎等，釉色以青釉为主，青白釉次之，另有少量酱釉、黑釉瓷器，部分器物足底露胎。纹饰见有模印荷塘双鱼纹、回纹、莲花纹和弦纹等，器形有碗、盏、盘、瓷枕、杯式炉、执壶等。瓷器窑口有繁昌窑、龙泉窑、景德镇窑、吉州窑和建窑等。

此外，遗址出土的牛骨数量远大于人们日常食用的猪羊骨骼数量，很有可能是军队驻地的重要特征。

从遗址发掘区揭露的遗迹分布情况来看，东、西岸的遗存应是运河沿岸的生产生活遗存，由此可见遗址依河而生、临河而建之布局。遗址出土了大量晚唐至南宋时期的瓷器、陶器和少量建筑构件，以生产生活用品为主，反映了本地区晚唐至南宋这一时段的社会生产生活状况。

瓷碗（DG1:15）　　瓷碗（DG1:121）　　瓷碗（DG3:8）

瓷钵（XH11:1）　　瓷钵（XT1101⑦:6）　　瓷罐（XT1105⑤:5）

执壶（XG10②:7）　　执壶（DG3:6）

瓷罐（DG1:16）　　瓷罐（DG1:57）

**唐代遗物**

548　黄淮七省考古新发现

瓷碗（XTG1④∶25）　　　　　　　　　瓷盘（XT1120③∶12）

瓷碗（XT1016④∶6）　　　　　　　　瓷碗（DH1∶138）

瓷盏（XT1120③∶25）　　　　　　　瓷枕（DH1∶72）

杯式炉（XT1120③∶9）　　　　　　　执壶（XT1119④∶14）

宋代遗物

遗址发掘现场

Cilangcun Site is located approximately 700 meters east of Cilangcun Village, Dongtai City, Jiangsu Province. The site covers about 80,000 square meters. From November 2011 to January 2012, salvageal excavations were carried out on the site. Stratified deposits that accumulated in Tang Dynasty is found in the excavation area on the west bank. Unearthed relics are daily utensils and production tools. Vessels that have been revealed are mainly porcelain. There is just a small number of glazed earthenware, potteries, stoneware, ironware, copper coins, etc. Remains dating back to Song Dynasty, like ash pits, ash ditches, wells and tombs, are distributed on both the east and west banks of the excavation area. Apart from a relatively limited number of glazed earthenware, potteries, stoneware and bronzes, porcelain makes up the majority of antiquities that have been unearthed here. Excavation shows that remains found on the east bank as well as on the west bank should be remnants of production and activities of daily life along the canal. Unearthed relics, featured with typical characteristics of the era spanning from late Tang Dynasty to Southern Song Dynasty, represent contemporary local production and living conditions. It has been speculated that there used to be a military station here.

# 山西绛州州署遗址的考古发现

◎杨及耘 曹俊

绛州州署遗址位于山西省新绛县县城西部的一处高崖之上，坐北朝南，现仅存一座具有元代建筑风格的州署大堂和清代修建的二堂建筑。2013年3月—2015年7月，山西省考古研究所对绛州州署遗址进行了考古发掘和清理，发掘分为2个区域。

Ⅰ区发掘范围位于大堂前区域，建筑布局基本呈中轴线对称分布，轴线与现存大堂建筑的轴线相比略西。堂前院落由两条较长的南北向东西院墙和一条东西向的南院墙组成，略呈斗状，面积约2000平方米，我们认为该院落在绛州州署开始使用时就已存在。该院落中间即现存大堂建筑的南侧轴线位置，自北而南分别清理出三座由小而大的砖包月台、一条砖砌甬道、一座方形砖砌建筑的基址、一座内方外八的建筑基址及仪门建筑遗迹残存。在明清院落的砖铺地面下，清理出一条U形道路。院落内地层堆积较为简单，应系清代晚期短时间堆积而成，其废弃年代约在清光绪年后。

在现存大堂建筑基址的下面，发现两组被叠压的建筑基址，我们认为其分别系隋唐时期和五代北宋时期的州署大堂建筑遗存。在大堂院落西侧院墙外清理出部分夯土，其为一处面积较大的夯土基址，其年代应属隋唐时期，性质不明。两侧的附属院落的地层堆积可分为5层，遗迹保存较差，多为房址、道路、地面等遗迹，另有少量的窖穴、灰坑等。

Ⅱ区的发掘区域选择在二堂北面，其文化堆积至少分为5个时期，该区域内的建筑呈对称分布。发现的遗迹包括房址、道路、地面、排水、厕所及灰坑等。Ⅱ区发现的最重要遗迹为位于发掘区北侧轴线位置上的"思理池"遗存，在"思理池"南侧发现的建筑基址即为"知州宅"，其使用年代至少始自五代北宋，一直延续至明清时期。明清时期的"知州宅"基址以青砖砌筑，面阔三间，其内还清理出两座灶台，根据形制推测其应为房屋的取暖设施。此类灶台在Ⅰ区不见，而在Ⅱ区发现达十余处，这应该是与其建筑使用分区和功能有直接的关系。此外，Ⅱ区发现的遗物也多与生活有关。

通过对绛州州署遗址的考古发掘，可以肯定该遗址自隋唐时期始，直至民国时期都是作为州衙和县衙在使用，基本印证了文献记载。

绛州州署遗址整体（上北下南）

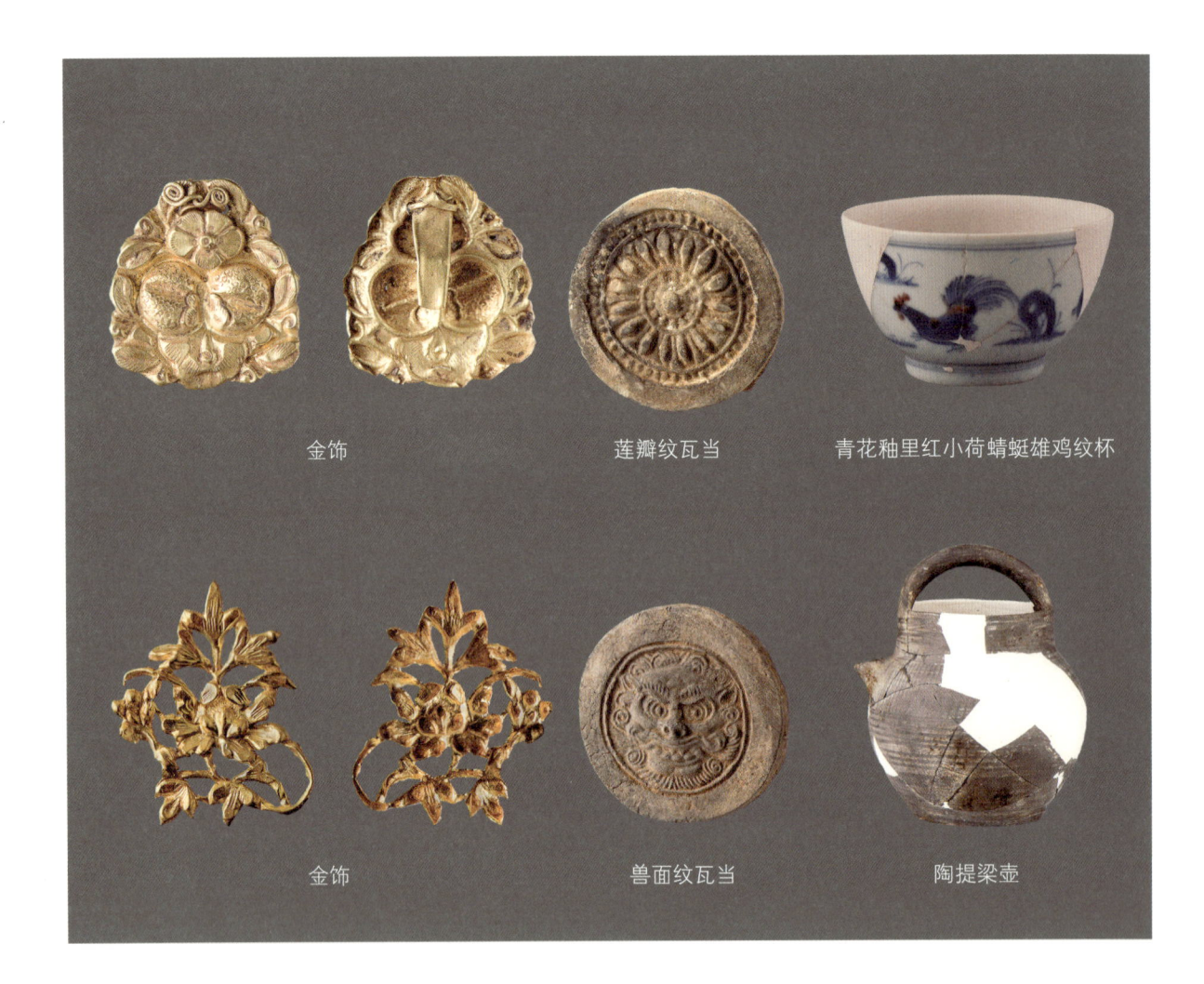

金饰　　　　　　　　　　　莲瓣纹瓦当　　　　青花釉里红小荷蜻蜓雄鸡纹杯

金饰　　　　　　　　　　　兽面纹瓦当　　　　陶提梁壶

From March in 2013 to July in 2015, archaeologists from Shanxi Provincial Institute of Archaeology carried out field archaeological excavations on a site that used to be the building of Administrative Department of Jiangzhou Prefecture. The excavated area is 6300 square meters. After excavations, it has been confirmed that, from Sui and Tang dynasties to the era of Republic of China, on the site there used to be the prefecture-level or county-level Yamen. It has also been found out that remains of such a government architecture possess diversified cultural features. The layout of a Yamen is usually described as "office in the front and living room in the back". This pattern was adopted on this site during every historical period. In addition, zoning occurred for the sake of different spatial uses.

# 河南开封北宋东京城顺天门遗址

◎ 葛奇峰

顺天门是北宋东京城外城西墙上的正门，位于河南省开封市金明区，东临夷山大街，北至晋安路，西接开封市金明中小学，南依汉兴路。2012年5月—2017年12月，河南省文物考古研究院等对顺天门遗址进行了大规模的调查勘探，并对主城门区域进行了考古发掘。本次发掘实际面积共2706平方米，清理出了五代、宋、金、元、明、清、近现代等各时期大量遗存。

顺天门是一座方形瓮城，门址平面呈长方形，"直门两重"，东西方向。瓮城西外侧有护城壕，城壕东距瓮墙15米。瓮城圈内以主城门中门道为轴线，南北对称，各分布有1座高台建筑。顺天门主城门平面为一门三道布局，由墩台、门道、隔墙、马道组成。

顺天门主体为夯土版筑，城门包砖。墙体分层夯筑，墙体中部夯窝较稀疏，两侧夯窝分布相对密集。城门修建在一座完整的高台上，高台下部为厚约0.50米的瓦片夯，上部为厚约1米的黏土夯。建筑方法是先在夯土上分割出墩台、门道和隔墙，并将这部分夯土剔除，接着再用瓦片夯的方式将基槽填平，没有打破下层的瓦片夯层。瓦片夯层中的瓦片经过筛选，黏土夯层中夯土的土质坚硬且纯净。

瓮城圈内发现了南北对称的高台建筑，面阔5间，进深2间，均未完全揭露。建筑基址台面平整，三面有砖墙围护，门前有台阶残迹。台基上分布有规整排列的边长1.40米的方形磉墩。

另外，还发现完全叠压在宋代顺天门之下的五代后周时期的迎秋门的西端面。端面显示，迎秋门城门包砖为单门道，东西方向。

顺天门是北宋东京城外城西墙上连接御道的正门，此次工作是首次对北宋东京城城门的发掘，明确了宋代瓮城的形制，城门的建筑结构、台基的夯筑工艺，清晰揭示出主城门一门三道的布局，找到了主城门包砖的范围，发现了瓮城内的两座重要建筑等。而且清理出宋代和五代后周相互叠压两个时期的城门，展现出城门从单门道到三门道的演变历程，以及瓮城从无到有的发展变化。

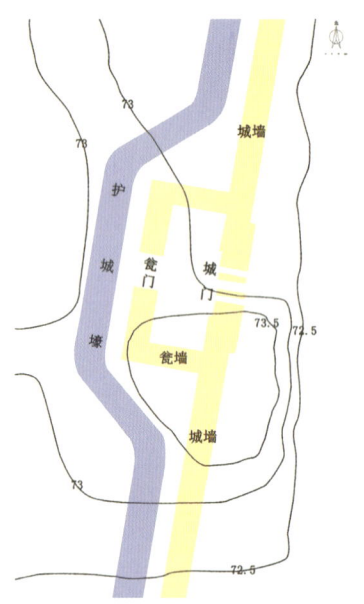

顺天门遗址平面图

顺天门遗址位置图

太湖石　　宋代磨喝乐

宋金时期的礌石　　宋代灰陶迦陵嫔伽和套兽

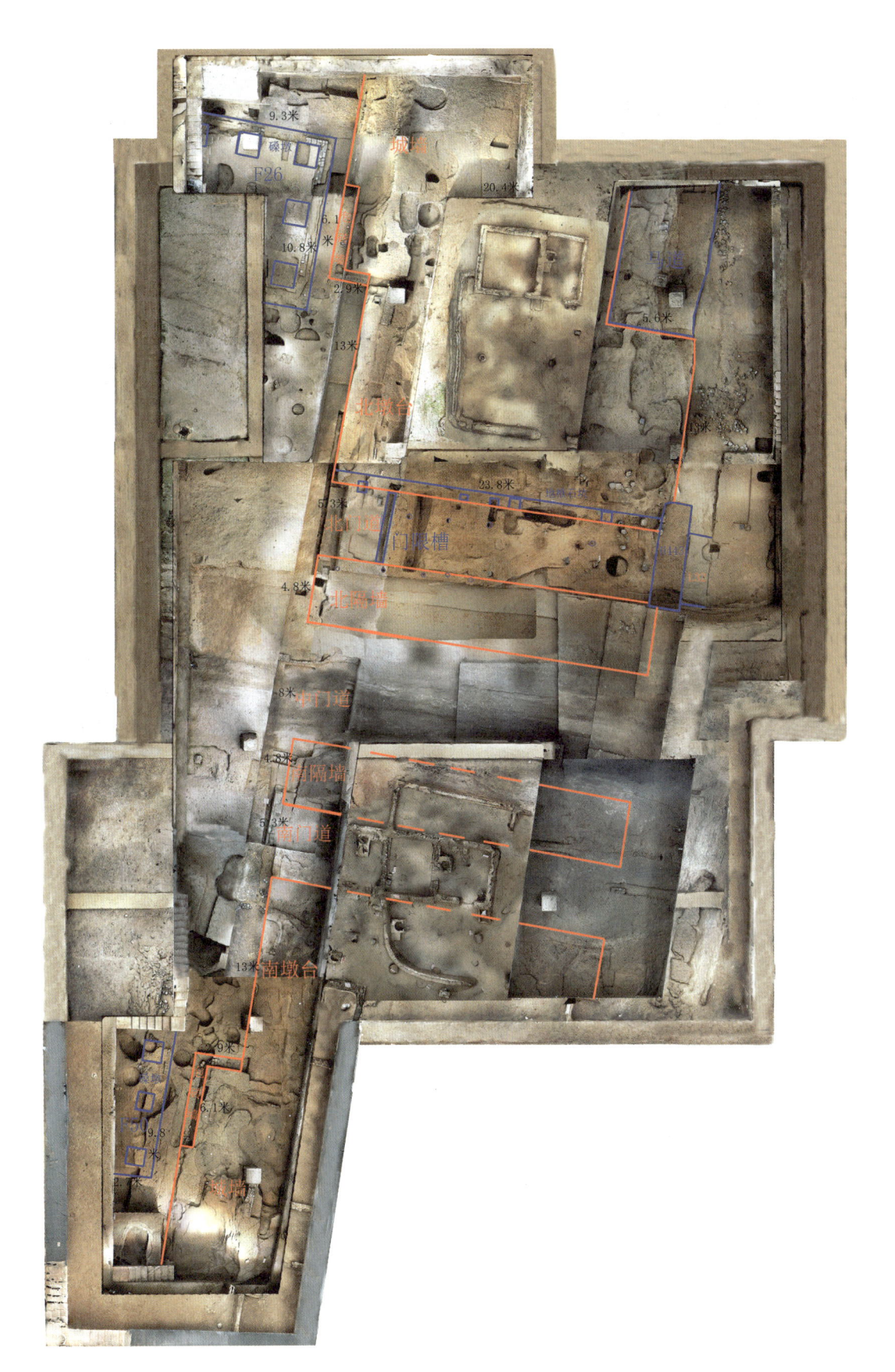

顺天门主城门发掘区全景正射影像图

宋代顺天门与后周迎秋门叠压关系　　　　　顺天门瓮城内北侧建筑

明代手工业作坊

    Shuntian Gate used to be the main entrance in the west wall of the outer city of Dongjing City, the capital of Northern Song Dynasty. It is located in Jinming District, Kaifeng City, Henan Province. From May in 2012 to December 2017, a joint team consisting of archaeologists from Henan Provincial Institute of Cultural Relics and Archaeology and other organizations carried out large-scale investigations and archaeological reconnaissances on the site of Shuntian Gate. Excavations were conducted in the locality of the main gate. Overlapped remains of city gates respectively dating back to Song Dynasty and Later Zhou of Five Dynasties as well as sites of two important architectures inside the barbican entrance were excavated. Layout of the main city gate, a three-way city gate, was clearly revealed. Position of the layer of bricks, as the skin of the main city gate, was located. The structure of barbican entrance constructed in Song Dynasty, the architectural structure of city gates and building techniques applied in the construction of the rammed foundation have been clarified. It has been found out that, in the rampart, there used to be a single-entrance gate before it developed into a triple-entrance one. What has also been revealed this time is the development process during which the barbican entrance emerged from nothing. Besides, excavations carried out this time were oriented by clear academic objectives. Revealed earthen ruins were fully and well protected. Multidisciplinary cooperation has made a considerable number of achievements.

# 河北张家口市崇礼太子城遗址金代行宫

◎黄 信 任 涛 魏慧平

崇礼太子城遗址位于河北省张家口市崇礼区四台嘴乡原太子城村村南，西距崇礼县城20千米。遗址四面环山，南、北各有一河流自东向西绕城而过后在城西汇合西流。

经勘探确认太子城遗址城址平面为长方形，现东、西、南三面城墙存有地下基址，北墙基址被河流破坏无存，残存三面墙体外均有壕沟，城址西墙有2道，东西间距50米。钻探确认城内主街道基本呈T形，已发现南门1座，门外有瓮城。城内钻探共发现建筑基址28座，其中南北中轴线上有3组：南部正对南门的9号基址，中部1、2、3号组成的中心基址群，北部25号基址。

2017年河北省文物研究所等对4处遗迹进行了清理，重要发现有：1. 南墙、南门与瓮城。南墙两侧包砖，包砖内每隔3米立木柱，内芯以土石填筑。南门为单门道，东西两侧各有一墩台。瓮城位于南门外，营造方式与城址南墙基本相同。瓮城门位于瓮城南墙中心，与城址南门为一条直线，同为单门道。瓮城门外有宽约5米的壕沟。2. 西内墙、西门与西院落。西内墙与西院落的营造方式与南墙相同，西门较南门规模小，单门道，门道两侧有墩台，西院落内共发现5组建筑基址。3. 9号建筑基址。位于太子城南北中轴线上，其为太子城遗址规格最高的建筑，平面布局为面阔三间，进深五间。在东、西、北各有一踏道通向基址上部。

太子城遗址出土遗物以各类绿釉琉璃或泥质灰陶建筑构件为主，其中大量青砖上戳印"内""宫""官"字。此外，白釉瓷器中已发现15件印摩羯纹碗盘底有"尚食局"款铭文，另有部分铜鎏金龙形饰件等。从出土遗物推测太子城遗址时代为金代中后期。

太子城遗址的发掘具有重要意义：1. "尚食局"款瓷器的发现，是在定窑窑址以外考古发掘出土该类产品最多的一次，据此推测该城址与金代皇室有关。2. 太子城遗址内发现大量戳印"内""宫""官"字砖，这是金代城址的首次发现。3. 经考古调查，推测太子城即《金史》中记载金章宗驻夏的泰和宫。

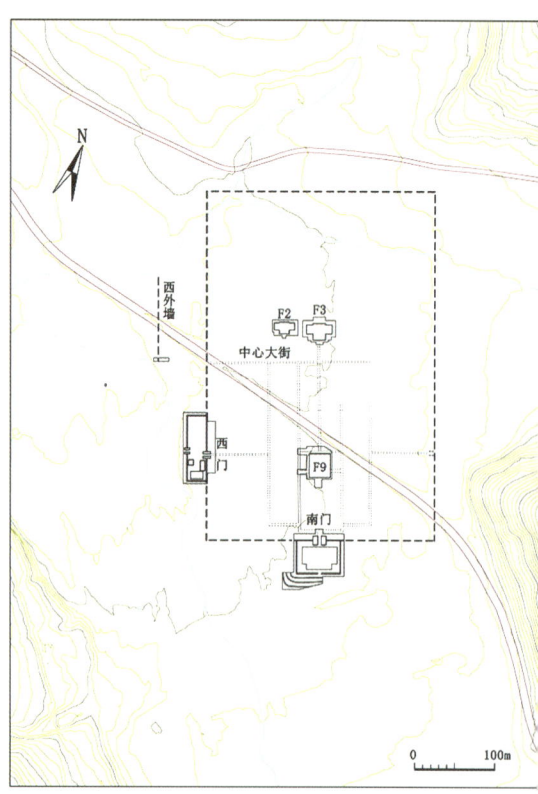

崇礼太子城遗址位置图（上为北）　　　　　　　　　　　　　　　　　　　　2017年发掘总平面图

"内"字方砖　　　　　　　　"宫"字砖　　　　　　　　"官"字砖

脊兽　　　　　　　　　　　脊兽　　　　　　　　　　　脊饰

唐风宋韵　气象万千　559

南门、南瓮城、壕沟（上为北）

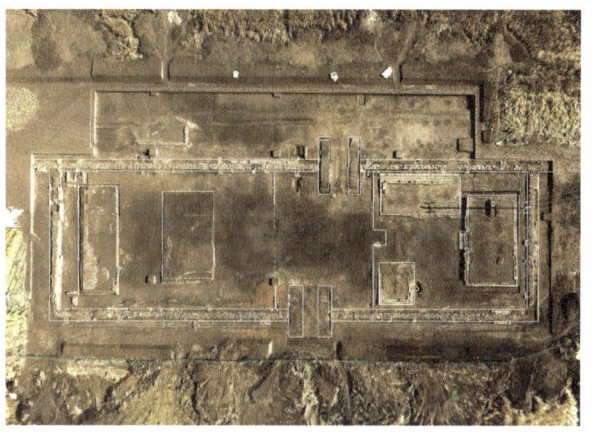

西门、西瓮城与瓮城内建筑基址（上为东）

9号建筑基址（上为北）

3号与2号建筑基址（上为北）

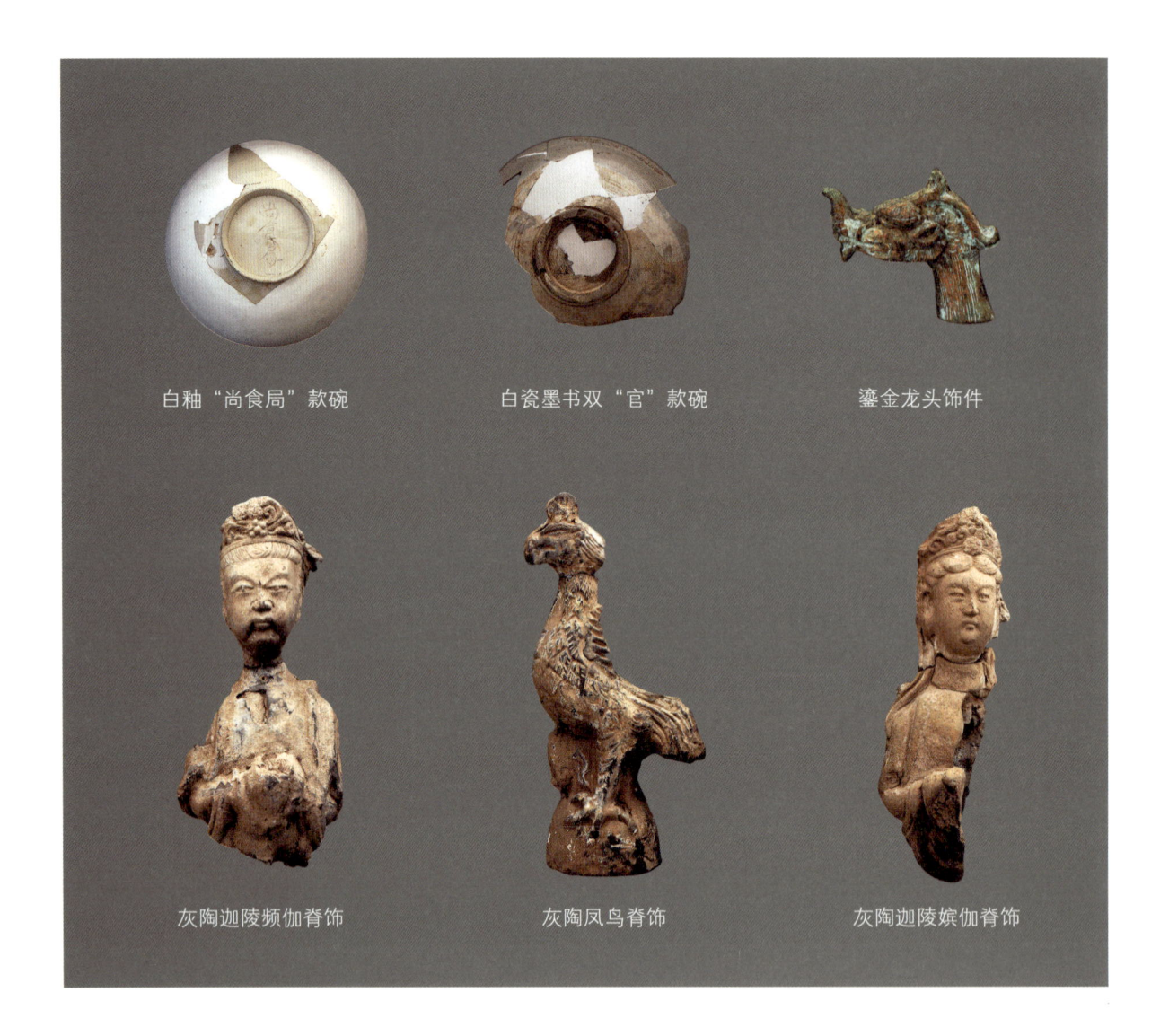

白釉"尚食局"款碗　　白瓷墨书双"官"款碗　　鎏金龙头饰件

灰陶迦陵频伽脊饰　　灰陶凤鸟脊饰　　灰陶迦陵嫔伽脊饰

Chongli Taizicheng Site is in the south of an area that used to be Taizicheng Village, Sitaizui Township, Chongli District, Zhangjiakou City, Hebei Province. Since May in 2017, archaeologists from Hebei Provincial Institute of Cultural Relics and other organizations have been carrying out comprehensive mapping, archaeological reconnaissances and excavations on Taizicheng Site. Remains of ramparts, barbican entrances, moats, architectural foundation sites, roads and others have been excavated. The majority of unearthed relics are architectural components. Discovered gray bricks are stamped with the characters of "Nei" "Gong" "Guan". "Shang Shi Ju" is found on those revealed white porcelain plates. After excavations, it has been confirmed that the plane layout of Taizicheng Site is a rectangular one. Scale of the city as well as structures and building techniques of the ramparts, gates, barbican entrances and architectural foundation sites have been generally found out. It has been inferred that on the site there was Taihe Palace where Zhangzong used to spend his summers in middle and late Jin Dynasty.

# 安徽凤阳县明中都遗址

◎ 王 志

明中都是明朝开国皇帝朱元璋营建的首座都城，位于安徽省凤阳县。安徽省文物考古研究所于2014—2017年先后三次对遗址开展勘探，2015—2017年又连续对遗址进行发掘。

近年的考古勘探主要在明中都遗址的宫城、禁垣范围内开展，勘探面积约210万平方米，发现宫殿、城墙、城门、河道、桥梁等遗迹，基本厘出宫城与皇城内建筑、水系布局的轮廓。发掘的遗址有"三大殿"遗址、承天门遗址和部分道路、水系，以及宫城东华门遗址、东南角台、东北角台、西华门顶部、午门门洞等处。

"三大殿"遗址位于明中都宫城的中心，基址的平面结构还未完全清晰，但其并非地表所呈现的"中"字形，基址由内外夯土构成，外圈夯土边缘残存有石构须弥座基础，并在基址外周发现踏道。另外，局部揭露了明代宫殿台基上的清代官学建筑和基址外围的明代晚期建筑基址。

承天门城台正中开有三个券门，在城台的两侧禁垣墙上又各开有一门，共五门。城台残存中间门洞和两侧墩台，墩台为内夯土芯外包砖结构。城台内夯土芯与其下夯土平台的夯筑方式基本一致，均采用一层砖瓦一层土的方式夯筑。承天门城台北侧两端各连接有条状夯土台，对称分布，与城台垂直，向北延伸，正对午门东西两观。承天门城台周边还发现了修筑城台时的排水沟渠等遗迹，在城门东侧存有早于城台修建的院落基址，并发现其南墙在修建城台和禁垣时有拆毁重建的现象。还发现城台和城墙外侧不同时段的民房、水井、道路等遗迹，展现出该门址的兴废历变轨迹。

东华门为三券门，清理出完整的城台基础。城台有南、北两个墩台，包砖砌法与承天门基本一致。城门洞内及边侧用砖砌筑须弥座。清理发现中、北门洞在早期便被封堵，仅留南门洞通行，其内保存有一条清代白玉石道路。东南角台和东北角台均为曲尺状城台，内夯土芯外包砖，夯土均为素土夯筑。午门门洞路面两侧设有排水浅沟，门洞北侧有散水，并设计了排水暗渠。此外，皇城内的道路、水系和西禁垣内窑址等处的发掘也均取得了一定收获。

明中都是经过精心规划设计的都城，虽然没有最终完工，但城市轮廓已经形成，对南、北两京的城市布局产生了重要影响，在研究城市规划史方面具有很高价值。

承天门城台中间的三个门洞（上东下西）

承天门西部包砖及夯土墙芯（西向东）

承天门出土字砖

奉天殿外台沿大型螭首（西南—东北）

西华门城台顶部航拍图（上北下南）

东华门南门洞内白玉石路面（西向东）

东华门门洞俯视（西向东）

东华门北墩台（西南—东北）

奉天殿基址外圈夯土西南角包石边界（西向东）

The Central Capital of Ming Dynasty used to be the first capital of the dynasty. It is located in Fengyang County, Anhui Province. From 2014 to 2017, archaeologists from Anhui Provincial Institute of Cultural Relics and Archaeology conducted archaeological reconnaissances three times on the site. From 2015 to 2017, a succession of excavations were carried out here. The archaeological reconnaissance was mainly conducted inside the imperial palace and in the area enclosed by palace walls. Foundations and remains of palaces, ramparts, gates, channels, bridges and others have been discovered. Excavated sites are of "Three Great Halls", Gate for Receiving the Mandate of Heaven, some roads, water system, East Glorious Gate, southeastern corner platform, northeastern platform, the top of West Glorious Gate, the doorway of Meridian Gate, etc. After excavations, the layout of architectures inside the palace and the imperial city and a map of the water system have been basically clarified. Shapes and structures of many important buildings like the "Three Great Halls" and Gate for Receiving the Mandate of Heaven have been revealed. Building techniques that had been applied in the construction of these architectures and vicissitudes they had went through are now gradually coming to light. The basis for a comprehensive and accurate understanding of architectural layout inside the imperial city in the Central Capital of Ming Dynasty, evolution of building techniques, history and changes of the architectures mentioned and other issues.

# 山东济南市宽厚所街遗址明代郡王府

◎李 铭 房 振 郭俊峰

宽厚所街遗址位于济南市古城区的东南隅，其具体范围北至泉城路，南至黑虎泉西路，西至舜井街，东至黑虎泉北路。济南市考古研究所自2011年7月—2012年3月对济南市历下区宽厚所街遗址进行了考古勘探和发掘。

此次在宽厚所街遗址清理出的两座大型院落基址皆坐北朝南，东西相距70米。这两座院落的规模、等级和年代特征符合明代郡王府的特点，我们推测西侧靠近舜井街的大型院落为宁海王府基址，而东侧的大型院落为宁阳王府基址。两座王府的地上建筑物早已完全消失，王府院落内地面大都埋在现地表下2米左右。宁阳王府的东院墙残存最高处近2米，接近现地表。王府在修筑时曾将院落范围整体垫高、整平。

宁阳王府的布局基本完整，规模宏大，其院墙的范围南北长134米，东西宽83米，总占地面积约1.2万平方米。院墙保存基本完整，王府内共有房屋100余间，其布局设计遵守中国古建筑中轴对称的原则，由中轴院落、东路院落、西路院落及其他相关建筑构成。中轴线上为五进主院落，东路院有三进院落，西路院则有两进，另有厢房、回廊等建筑。王府内建筑基础的营造方式，多数采用在墙基下夯筑地脚的方式，但府内最重要的建筑物——后厅房，是在整座房屋下挖基槽（局部挖至生土）并逐层夯筑起台基。宁阳王府院内还发现了完善的排水设施，大门外南侧还发现一长方形石砌池状遗迹，可能为一渗水池。

宁海王府仅残留院落东北角，院内残留两处房址，另残存长13米的排水渠1条。宁海王府北墙上的排水孔采用了与宁阳王府相似的构筑方法，但结构更为复杂和巧妙。

两座明代郡王府的发掘，是国内第一次对明代郡王府的全面揭露。其完整的布局，对研究明代郡王府制和明晚期地方郡王府的实际样式，以及当时的建筑技术都有很高的参考价值。

566　黄淮七省考古新发现

宁阳王府航拍照
（上为西）

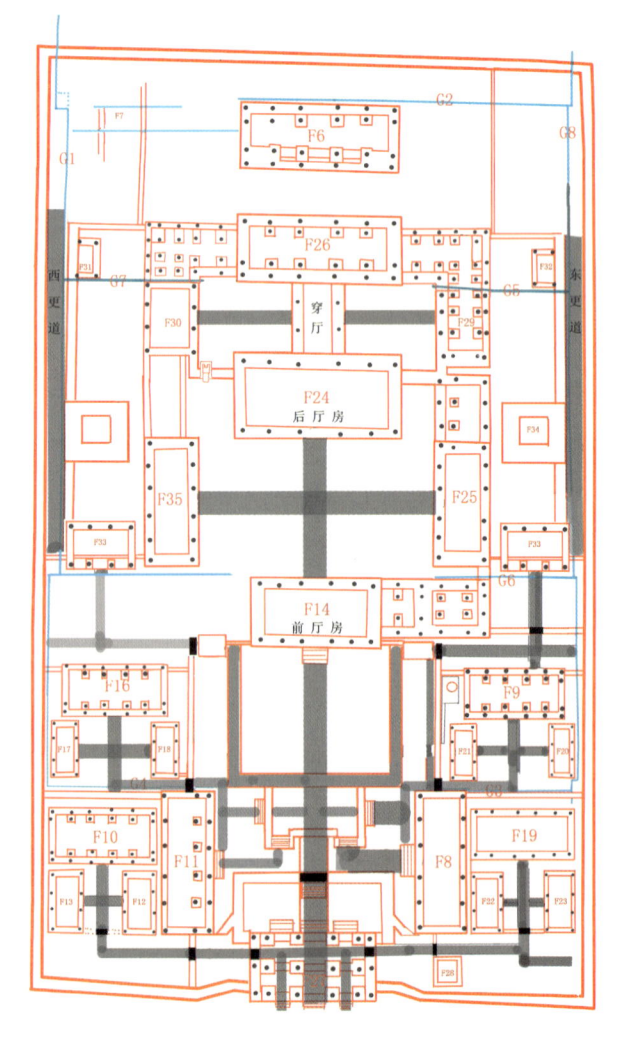

宁阳王府布局复原图（上为北）

宁阳王府东路院中进院落之正房F9（东—西）

    Kuanhousuo Street is in the southeastern corner of the historical district of Jinan City. Archaeological sites discovered here were excavated from July in 2011 to March in 2012. Basic conditions of underground remains in this region have been recognized. A number of important materials have been obtained. Excavations of two mansions owned by commandery princes of Ming Dynasty, Ningyang Mansion and Ninghai Mansion, are the most important. After excavations, there has been a relatively clear understanding of the layout and building techniques of Ningyang Mansion. Excavating two mansions, especially excavating the foundation of Ningyang Mansion, is the first time that a commandery prince's mansion has been entirely revealed in China. The basically complete layout is a perfect example to refer to in the study of rules and structures of a commandery prince's mansion in Ming Dynasty, actual styles of a local-level mansion occupied by a commandery prince in late Ming Dynasty and contemporary building techniques.

# 梵庭钟磬音　职奉三清隐终南

## 山西大同市云冈石窟窟顶遗址发掘

◎ 白曙璋

为配合云冈石窟窟顶防渗水工程，由山西省考古研究所、云冈石窟研究院、大同市考古研究所组成的云冈石窟联合考古队于2010年在窟顶西区发掘了一处较完整的北魏佛教寺院建筑遗址，在东区发掘了一处北魏至辽金的建筑遗址及辽金铸造场所。

西区北魏佛寺遗址是一处较完整的塔院式结构的佛教寺院，包括房址20间（套）、塔基1处，另有北魏时期陶窑2座、灰坑1个。出土遗物有建筑构件、石刻、日用器物等。塔基位于遗址东南部，平面呈长方形，北高南低。塔基西南部和东南部有两个柱础石。塔基主体为夯土，由三部分组成，第一部分是砌在塔基四周的石片，第二部分是塔基外围的夯土，第三部分是塔基中部的细沙土。塔基上还发现7排东北—西南向柱洞，应是塔的立柱遗迹。塔基内未发现地宫或埋藏坑等遗迹。

东区寺院遗址呈南北向长方形布局，南部是一个平面为八角形的塔基；中部面积较大，发现北魏柱础、辽金铸造场所遗址（包含许多熔铁炉和铸造井台），还有建筑遗址、水井和灰坑；北部有建筑遗存和水井。东区遗址从南到北，出土了大量北魏和辽金时期的建筑构件和陶器、瓷器等，还有少量佛教造像残片。

此次发掘的收获主要有：1. 塔基遗迹是目前我国发现最早的塔基之一，与云冈石窟内雕刻的各种方形塔样式一样，两相参证，可证明塔基的时代与石窟建造时间相近。塔基中没有发现埋藏坑和埋藏物，说明塔基建造时间较早。塔基边长约为14米，可以推知塔本身高度不是太高。在塔基周围，带釉瓦和板瓦、筒瓦发现较多，也说明带釉瓦的使用建筑可能是塔，塔是该遗址最主要的建筑。它的发现，有助于了解北魏前期云冈寺院的布局和范围，引起研究者对云冈石窟山顶区域北魏寺院遗址的重视。2. 辽金的铸造工场在全国是首次发现。这次铸造工场的发现，一是首次发现熔铁炉环绕铸造井台的实物布局，二是首次发现煤做燃料的例证，三是发现最早的风箱等鼓风设备遗迹。这些发现为了解宋辽金铸造工场提供了完整的实物资料，对于研究中国冶金史都有极重要的意义。这样的工场出现在云冈窟顶，很有可能出于建寺需要，反映了辽金时代云冈寺院可能又进入了一个建设高峰。

云冈石窟窟顶西区佛教寺院遗迹（上南下北）

云冈石窟窟顶东区辽金冶铸遗址及塔基俯拍（上西下东）

瓦当　　　　　　　　　　　　瓦当　　　　　　　　　　北魏塔刹相轮

佛像　　　　　　　　　　　　　　　　石兽首构件

From 2010 to 2011, on top of Yungang Grottoes, archaeologists were excavating a relatively complete Buddhist monastery site of Northern Wei in the west zone, and a monastery site dating back to the epoch from Northern Wei to Liao and Jin dynasties and a foundry of Liao and Jin dynasties in the east zone. The site of the Buddhist monastery is a comparatively well-preserved one consisting of temples and courtyards. Major remains excavated from this site include 20 rooms/suites and a temple base, which is one of the oldest of its kind in China. The plane layout of the monastery site dating back to the epoch from Northern Wei to Liao and Jin Dynasties is a south-north rectangle. On the site, there is a temple base whose ground plan is an octagon in the southern part while in the middle, there is a foundry of Liao and Jin dynasties that consists of multiple melting iron furnaces, hearths and remains of buildings, wells and a large number of ash pits, and in the northern part, there are constructions and wells. It is the first time that a foundry of Liao and Jin dynasties has been discovered in Yungang Grottoes and also in China.

# 陕西西安市周陵镇杨家村发现北朝佛教造像

◎ 肖健一　胡松梅

该遗址位于西咸新区周陵镇杨家村（该村已经拆迁）西部、西北以及东部，南临空港新城管委会，西距208省道300米，东北距边防村2400米。发掘古代墓葬17座，清理灰坑20座、陶窑5座。出土文物共计100余件，其中Y2出土的彩绘泥塑佛像头72件，是一批重要的考古资料。

Y2位于发掘区北部，平面呈扇形，包括窑道、操作间、窑门、火膛、窑室、窑床、烟道几部分。Y2填土中出土石造像1件、鸱吻1件、石臼1件、陶帐座1件，在窑室后壁底部杂土下发现泥质俑头72个，被有意识摆放于窑床上及中间烟道与西北烟道附近。

Y2开口于二层下，窑室接近马蹄形，出土物未见绳纹板瓦，应不会早于南北朝，结合其形制推测窑址年代不会晚于隋唐。出土塑像泥质，模制，外敷彩。大部分为头部，仅见部分身躯及手掌残件。头部高约10～30厘米，背部扁平，推测应与躯干部分贴于墙上。颈至头部有方孔，或是与身躯部分以竹木相连。塑像可分为佛、菩萨、弟子、供养人，一般弟子面部施红彩，菩萨面部为白彩。佛头像高髻、窄脸、长直鼻、细颈，有北魏瘦骨清像的特点，部分颈部有较粗的特点，最晚年代应该不会晚于北周。陶窑填土中亦发现残石造像、石臼、帐座等，提示附近当有寺院。推测或为北周武帝灭佛时，泥质塑像被掩藏于陶窑中。

本次考古发掘的墓葬年代跨度长，从西汉持续到唐宋，遗址年代为北周及以后时期，为研究附近地区的丧葬习俗、墓葬制度等提供了翔实的实物资料。发掘的窑址保存较好，形制完整，全面揭示了窑址的结构特征，为研究北周、隋唐时期窑址的演变等提供了新资料。泥质造像的集中发现在陕西为首次，对北周武帝灭佛历史事件以及北周以前佛教造像的研究大有裨益。

北朝佛教造像

泥塑佛像出土全景

The site is located in Yangjiacun Village, Zhouling Town, Xixian New District. As many as 17 tombs, 20 ash pits and 5 kilns have been cleaned up. The total number of excavated relics exceeds 100. From Y2, the excavated 72 pieces of colored clay heads, whose slender and eleganct appearance is in the prevailing style during Northern Wei, are those of the Buddha, the worshiping donors, Ananda and Bodhisattvas. It is the first time in Shaanxi Province that such a large amount of clay figurines have been discovered. This discovery greatly contributes to studies of Emperor Wu's ban on Buddhism in Northern Zhou and Buddhist statues made before this era.

# 定国寺、龙兴寺、天齐大王行宫
## ——山东东阿大秦村北朝唐宋宗教遗址发掘概述

◎李宝军　郑同修

东阿大秦村遗址位于聊城市东阿县铜城街道大秦村东，遗址核心区域南北长约145米，东西宽约110米。本次发掘仅清理了属于五代宋初的地表遗迹，共清理墓葬1座、井2口、灰坑4个、排水沟1条、灶3个、房址21座、庭院13处及门址2处。根据碑文初步判断该遗址所在为北朝定国寺、唐代龙兴寺和后周宋初天齐大王行宫。此外，调查时发现行宫西北有一处唐宋时期的聚落遗址。

天齐大王行宫平面略呈曲尺形，四面有断续存在的土筑围墙，行宫内以前后主殿、广顺元年石香幢、香火坛、门址构成的中轴线为中心，主要建筑沿中轴线东西对称分布，中轴线东西两侧为厢房建筑群。其中主殿西侧为偏厢建筑群，可能为生活居住区；偏厢南部为西厢房建筑群。主殿东侧为一处偏殿建筑，偏殿南部为东厢房建筑群。行宫内房址前及庭院中可见成排树桩，疑为经过规划的绿化树。

行宫范围内出土遗物种类丰富，主要有功德碑、石佛像、陶瓦当、陶建筑构件、木制品、瓷片、铜钱及骨贝器等。从发掘情况初步判断行宫内的建筑大量重复使用前代物品，部分房址可能有改建现象。

唐代龙兴寺虽已不存，但行宫范围内出土较多与龙兴寺有关的遗物，龙兴寺至少应建立于初唐，可能毁于盛唐之后。据遗址内出土的一通刻于北魏永熙三年的功德碑，疑定国寺即北魏末年的遗址所名，推测定国寺在北魏末年就已出现，可能延续至北齐。

大秦村遗址是目前山东所见历时最长、规模最大的宗教遗存之一，历经多次兴废，最终废弃于五代宋初，从现场情况来看应属于有意识的毁弃，毁弃原因可能与自然水患有关。定国寺、龙兴寺的发现为研究北朝唐代寺院分布、唐代官寺制度增添了新的考古材料，而天齐大王行宫遗存在目前国内已公布的考古资料中属于首次发现，对于研究天齐信仰及其演化提供了新的内容。

天齐大王行宫航拍图（上北下南）

香火坛（上北下南）及坛内纸钱　　陶脊兽　　贴金石佛像

后殿前壁画（北—南）　　波斯萨珊银币　　墨书"龙兴寺"　　石佛头

    Dong'e Daqincun Site, excavated from November in 2016 to April in 2017, is located in the east of Daqin Village, Tongcheng Neighborhood, Dong'e County, Liaocheng City. Excavated remains include tombs, wells, stoves, dwelling sites, courtyards, gates. Discovered vestiges are Dingguo Temple of Northern Dynasties, Longxing Temple of Tang Dynasty and Palace of King Tianqi, which dates back to Later Zhou and the beginning of Song Dynasty. A wide range of cultural relics have been unearthed. Conditions of Dingguo Temple and Longxing Temple are not clear since only surface remains dating back to Five Dynasties and the beginning of Song Dynasty have been excavated and dealt with. After excavations, the layout of Palace of King Tianqi has been known to a certain extent. The plane layout of the palace is almost in the shape of a carpenter's square. Major buildings in the palace were constructed in an east-west symmetrical pattern. On the west of the main hall, the flanking building complex might be an residential area. Deserted during the time from Five Dynasties to the beginning of Song Dynasty possibly because of naturally formed disastrous flooding, Da-qin-cun Site is one of the oldest and largest religious sites that have ever been discovered in Shandong Province. The discovery of Dingguo Temple and Longxing Temple has filled in the blank in historical records. At present, remains of Palace of King Tianqi, which are the very first to have been revealed, have provided new materials for the study of belief in King Tianqi and evolution of such a belief.

# 河北正定县开元寺南广场遗址

◎陈 伟 翟鹏飞 佘俊英 房树辉

开元寺南广场遗址位于河北正定县古城中部偏南、开元寺现址的南侧和西侧。开元寺始建于东魏，唐开元年间更名为开元寺。开元寺南广场遗址面积约12000平方米。2015年8月—2017年4月，河北省文物研究所对其进行了考古勘察与发掘。

开元寺南广场遗址文化层堆积可划分为10层，分属于唐、五代、北宋、金、元、明、清等7个历史时期。共发现各类遗迹132处，可将之分别归类为开元寺寺庙建筑系统、晚唐五代城墙系统、唐五代宋金至明清民居建筑和街巷系统。

开元寺寺庙建筑系统集中发现于遗址东北部、开元寺现址南侧，目前已发现唐代、金元时期两个时代的遗存。唐代遗存为一处池沼遗存，编号为G3。金元时期遗存包括建筑基址一座（F2）、道路一条（L2）。F2推测为开元寺南门，其旁发现了开元寺的南院墙。F2在元末被破坏后，开元寺南墙及南门消失。明清时期开元寺建筑布局的南界与现在基本相同。

晚唐五代城墙系统，其主要遗存是一道东西向的夯土城墙（Q1）。Q1的建筑年代可分为两期，一期为夯土墙及城台，二期在夯土城台外侧包砖墙并对夯土墙进行局部修补。城墙系统在北宋时期已经遭到破坏并废弃。初步推测Q1为晚唐五代时期正定城的子城城墙。

唐五代宋金至明清民居建筑和街巷系统主要分布于发掘区中南部，遗迹以房址、水井、灰坑和窖藏为主。目前发现的房址的年代均属宋金元明时期，包括民居、商铺、民间庙宇等。

本次考古发掘共出土了跨越唐五代至明清时期的2000余件可复原器物，可分为日常生活用具、建筑构件、宗教遗物、手工业商业遗物四大类。

通过本阶段的考古发掘，我们获得了以下认识：首先，发现了不同时期开元寺寺庙遗存，明确了开元寺的南界自唐至今经历了一个不断向北退缩的过程。其次，城墙和民居建筑遗存的发现展现了由封闭里坊到开放型街巷的发展过程，为了解正定古城城市布局的演变提供了重要线索。最后，2000余件出土文物是本次考古发掘最为重要的收获之一，是研究华北地区晚唐至明清城市居民日常生活和探讨正定古城的商业活动以及当时的商贸路线的重要资料。

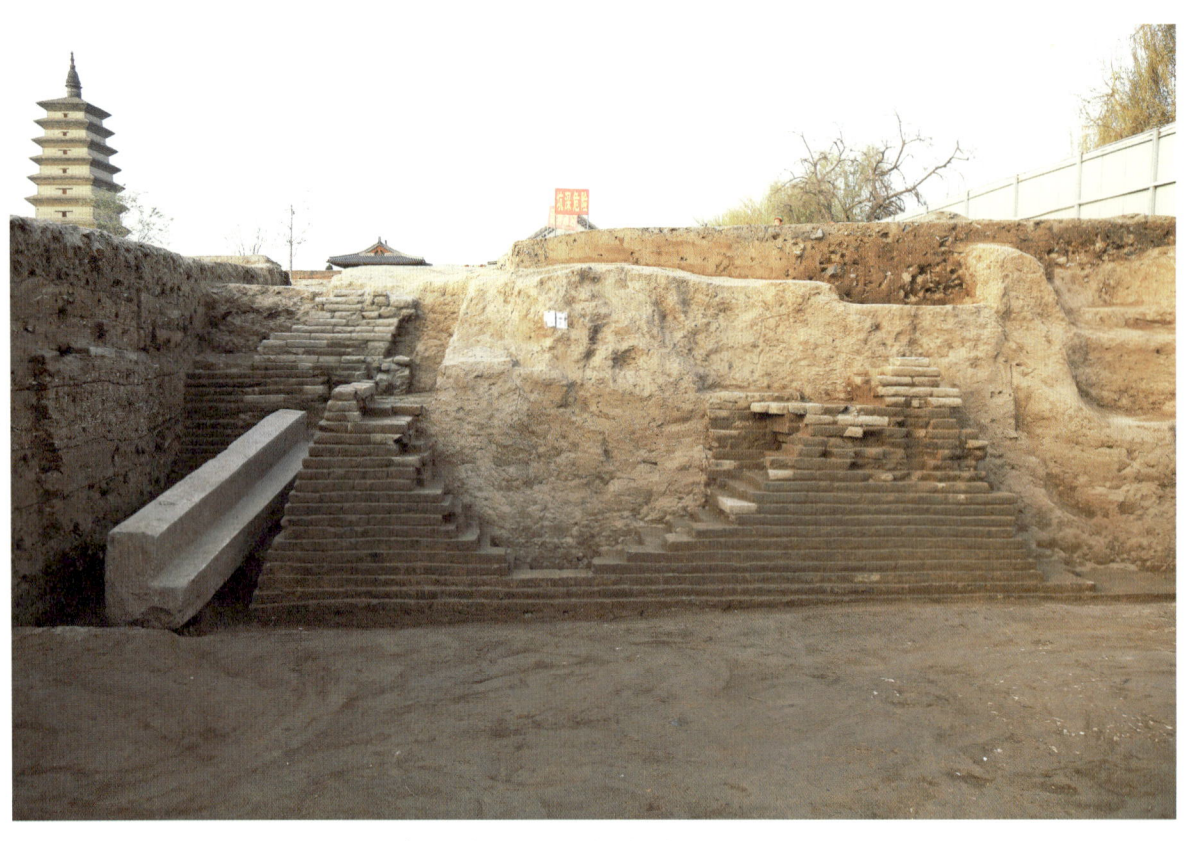

晚唐五代夯土城台及城台包砖（由南向北）

金元时期开元寺南门（由南向北）

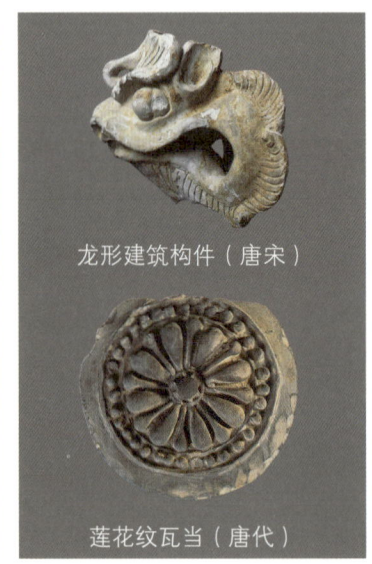

龙形建筑构件（唐宋）

莲花纹瓦当（唐代）

唐风宋韵 气象万千 579

白釉牡丹纹印花瓷盘（北宋）　　瓷罐（五代）　　孔雀戏牡丹图印花瓷盘（金代）

六瓣口折腹盘（金代）　　黑釉褐斑瓷盏（金代）　　黑釉深腹温碗（宋金）

童子扶鼓瓷塑（金代）

壁灯（宋金）　　黑釉执壶（宋金）　　黑釉组合灯（金代）

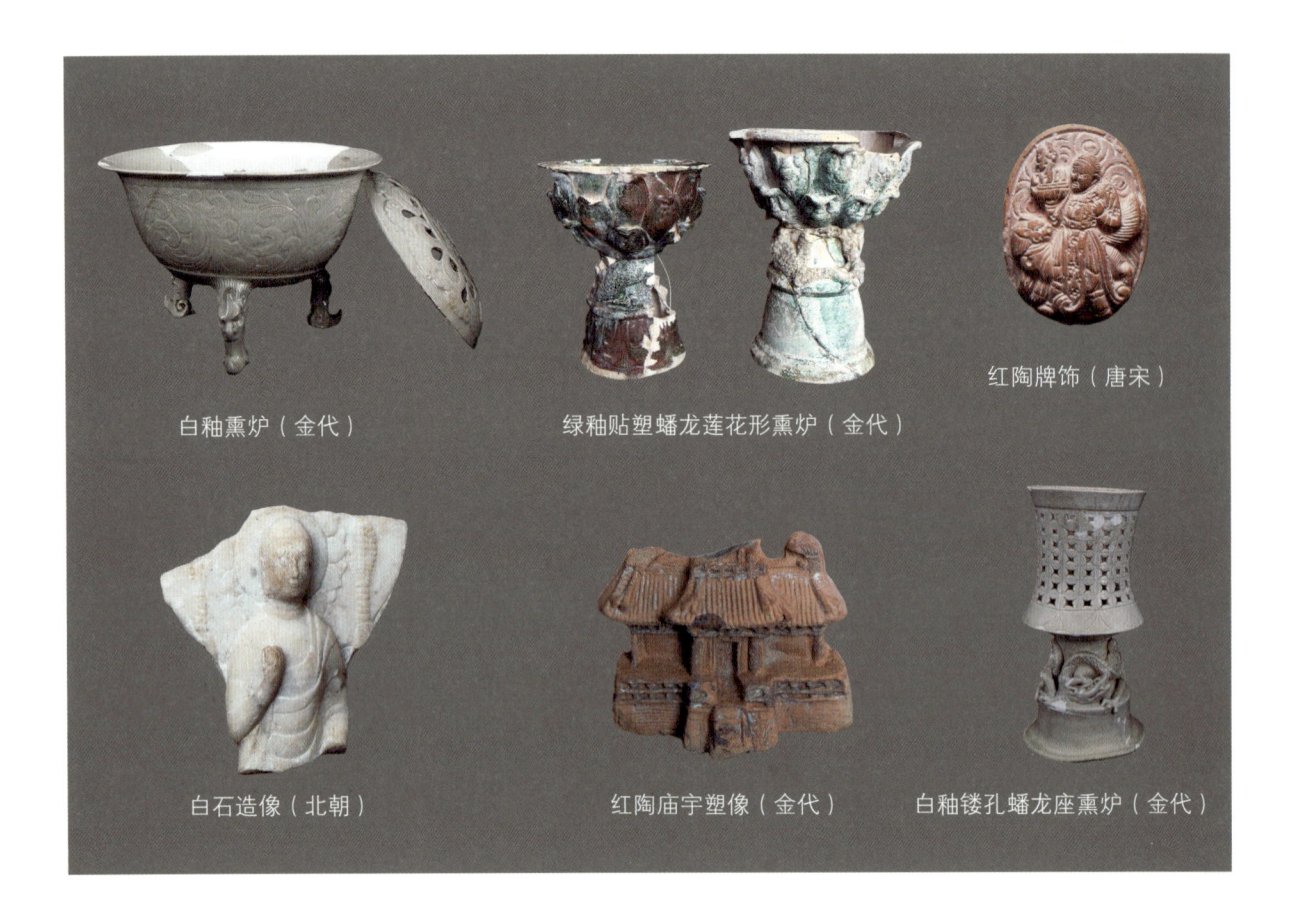

白釉熏炉（金代）　　　绿釉贴塑蟠龙莲花形熏炉（金代）　　　红陶牌饰（唐宋）

白石造像（北朝）　　　红陶庙宇塑像（金代）　　　白釉镂孔蟠龙座熏炉（金代）

There is a site on the south and west sides of modern-day Kaiyuan Temple, in the southern part of the ancient city of Zhengding. It covers approximately 12000 square meters. From August in 2015 to April in 2017, archaeologists from Hebei Provincial Institute of Cultural Relic carried out archaeological reconnaissances and excavations here. The site has been divided into ten phases. As many as 132 remains have been discovered. They are categorized into three types, namely temple architectures, defense facilities of city wall dating back to late Tang Dynasty and Five Dynasties and residential buildings and street systems dating from Tang Dynasty, Five Dynasties, Song and Jin dynesties to Ming and Qing dynasties. Unearthed antiquities can be divided into four types, namely daily utensils, building components, religious relics and remains of handicraft industry and commerce. These remains and relics are important materials for the study of daily life of city dwellers who lived during the time from late Tang Dynasty to Ming and Qing dynasties in North China as well as probings into commercial actives in the ancient city of Zhengding and contemporary trade routes. After excavations, it has been found out that the southern boundary of Kaiyuan Temple has been moving northward since Tang Dynasty. It is an important clue to finding out the layout of Kaiyuan Temple during the time from late Tang Dynasty to Ming and Qing dynasties, street systems of the ancient city of Zhengding as well as changes and evolution of city layout.

# 江苏南京清凉寺遗址考古发掘

◎龚巨平

清凉寺位于南京市鼓楼区清凉山，最早创建于南朝。2013年7月，南京市考古研究所对清凉寺遗址进行发掘，发掘面积1200平方米。发现的遗迹属于明代清凉寺的主要有4座建筑基址（F1～F4）、道路及4条附属排水设施等，另发现南唐塔墓一座。

F1（大佛殿）为台基式建筑，为五开间、三进深。局部保存有砖铺地面。台基南侧包墙用城砖砌筑，保存较好。北墙外有散水，散水外有水沟一条。F1的月台在主体建筑的南部，平面呈长方形。在月台的东侧发现有砖砌包墙。在月台与主体建筑交接部的左、右两侧均设有东西向台阶。根据建筑形式和建筑材料推断，其始筑时代为明代，清代有补修。

F2位于F1北侧，为带月台的台基建筑。F2残存南墙，保存有2个石柱础。台基南壁用条石砌筑包墙，月台台基包墙中间设台阶。F3揭露部分仅存北墙、前廊局部及部分铺砖。F4基址发掘平面呈长方形，部分揭露，室内地面残留有铺砖，与大佛殿方向垂直。根据已发现的柱础及磉墩分布位置分析，F4为带前廊的四进深建筑。根据F4的形制，两座建筑沿中轴线对称分布。

在发掘区内发现有完备的排水设施。其中三道水沟较为重要，围绕大殿东、西、北三侧分布。

据《金陵梵刹志》卷十八《清凉寺》篇记载，基本可判定F1即为佛殿，F2为法堂，F3为伽蓝殿，F4为祖师殿。

南唐塔墓（TM1）位于发掘区西北，即法堂基址西侧。TM1为土坑圆形砖室墓，圆形墓坑，直壁平底，壁面较光滑。圆形砖室，在墓室底部铺砖之上放置三块石板，平面形状呈"品"字形，具体用途不详。根据出土墓志，墓葬时代为南唐保大九年，墓主为清凉寺高僧悟空禅师。

经过考古发掘，我们基本摸清了发掘区内明代清凉寺北部的总体布局。在今清凉寺还阳泉北部区域内，中轴线上主要分布有大佛殿、法堂两座殿宇，大佛殿左前侧为伽蓝殿，右前侧为祖师殿，对于复原明代寺院的建筑规模、布局具有重要意义。

另外，明代建筑皆筑于生土之上，最早的遗存为南唐时期的悟空禅师塔墓。据此推测南唐清凉大道场的建筑及孙吴时期石头城附属仓城分布在本次发掘区的南侧。

发掘区全景

F1全景

南唐墓葬

大殿东侧踏道

东侧排水沟

大殿后石砌挡土墙

东侧廊庑

排水沟全景

Qingliang Temple is located in Qingliang Mountain, Gulou District, Nanjing City. After excavations, revealed remains, dating from Ming Dynasty, are of Great Hall, Buddhist Chapel, Hall of Samgha-arama, Hall of Patriarch, four architectural foundations, roads, four auxiliary drainage facilities, etc. Besides, a tower tomb which was constructed in Southern Tang has also been discovered. After excavations, it has been determined that the remains dating from Ming Dynasty are remnants of the construction of Qingliang Temple, a project initiated by feoffee of Feoffment Zhou, Zhu Su, in early Ming Dynasty. In the excavation zone, overall layout of the northern part of Qingliang Temple as well as structures and building techniques of those architectural remains have been basically found out. These findings are of great significance for restoring the temple as what it looked like in Ming Dynasty, i.e. in the exact same scale and layout. Besides, it has been inferred that Qingliang Temple of Southern Tang and auxiliary buildings of Shitoucheng should be on the south of the area that has been excavated this time. The tower tomb of Wukong, a chan master, is of great significance for the study of the development of Buddhism in Nanjing district and the scale of Qingliang Temple in Southern Tang.

# 山东烟台市严因寺遗址发掘

◎朱　超　吕　凯

烟台严因寺遗址位于烟台市芝罘区黄务街道办东珠岩村村西200米处两山之间的台地上，整个遗址南北长140米，东西宽130米，总面积1.8万平方米。山东省文物考古研究所对遗址的东部进行了考古发掘，分南、北两个发掘区，发掘清理了塔基及地宫1座、房基18座、道路3条、墓葬1座、排水沟3条、灰坑4个及石灰池2个，遗存可分为三期：

第一期为宋代塔院遗迹，位于南部发掘区，包括塔基，地宫，塔基东、西、南三面的房基及墓葬，分别编号FT1、DG1、F17、F12、F18及M1。塔基平面呈八角形，塔基正北中部有一东西向长方形砖砌台基，此处应为塔门位置所在。塔身外围另存一个年代较塔基稍晚的八角形塔座，二层叠涩台形式。塔座南侧留有通道，其顶部形制不清。地宫内部平面近似八角形，地面原铺砌方砖，现仅西壁底部残留少许。甬道位于地宫南侧，甬道顶部石板内面雕刻仿木结构的椽，甬道南端有竖井式地宫入口，入口处原盖有石板，现已不存。

F12、F17、F18均正对塔基，其中F18被严重破坏，仅存地基北侧部分护砖。M1位于F12南侧，为六角形砖室墓，墓道位于墓室南侧。因被严重破坏，墓室顶部已无存。

第二期为明代早期寺院遗迹，分布于北部发掘区中、南部，其佛殿以南北两塔为中轴线呈南北向分布，地势自南至北逐渐抬升。发掘区内仅揭露出寺院南部的佛殿基址，自南至北依次为山门殿、天王殿、大雄宝殿，分别编号F15、F16、F19。大殿平面均呈东西向长方形，现仅存红色垫土台基。大殿之间均以砖瓦铺砌的道路连接。天王殿F16外侧另有3条砖砌排水沟，编号分别为G1~G3。于天王殿南侧偏东位置发现宣德六年重建严因寺碑及龟趺。

第三期为明代晚期至清代寺院遗迹，分布于发掘区最北部，自东向西由3个院落相连构成，院落间有道路相通。每个院落由正厅及两侧配房组成。第一院落和第三院落内各发现一个石灰池。

关于寺院的修建年代，结合文献与重建严因寺碑，确认严因寺原名朱庵寺，始建于唐贞观年间，历经北宋天禧、熙宁，明宣德、万历几次重修成此规模。

北区（南—北）

南区（北—南）

**遗址全景**

地宫（东—西）      M1（东—西）

釉陶菩萨俑头部    灰陶菩萨俑头部    瓷器残片    釉陶建筑构件

Site of Yanyin Temple is located in the west of Dong zhuyan Village, Huangwu Neighborhood, Zhifu District, Yantai City. Excavated remains are 1 temple foundation and underground chamber, 18 bases of dwelling sites, 3 roads, 1 tomb, 3 drainage ditches, 4 ash pits and 2 lime pits. Unearthed relics are of several categories, porcelain, potteries, copper coins, ironware, etc. The site has been divided into three phases. The first phase dates back to Song Dynasty. There are remains of a court and towers inside it. The second phase contains remains of temples and monasteries of early Ming Dynasty. From the third phase, remains of temples and monasteries constructed from late Ming Dynasty to Qing Dynasty are revealed. The continuous existence and development of Yanyin Temple from Song Dynasty to Qing Dynasty, its layout and structure, as well as building techniques of temple foundation and underground chamber dating back to Song Dynasty have been clarified after excavations. The discovery of Yanyin Temple has provided important archaeological information for studies on the spread and development of Buddhism and evolution and changes of temple layout on Shandong Peninsula. Besides, Yanyin Temple is a valuable example to refer to in the study on architectural form and structure of temples.

# 山东济南市神通寺遗址的勘探和发掘

◎房　振　郭俊峰　邢　琪　李　铭　王　峰

　　神通寺遗址位于济南市历城区柳埠镇东北约2千米的琨瑞山金舆谷中，原称朗公寺。其历史可以追溯至十六国时期，是山东地区开创年代最早的一处佛教寺院，延续时间达1500余年。济南市考古研究所于2013年5月—12月对其进行了考古勘探和发掘。

　　本次勘探和发掘的区域位于金舆谷中部，基本上属于遗址的核心区域，共发现房址15座（其中F1早年曾经发掘，此次重新清理；F15未予清理）、墙体3条、道路1条。房址绝大多数仅存最下部墙体或部分墙基（均为石块垒砌），少数残留有铺地砖（或石板）；个别房址有台基、月台等附属设施。发掘出土较多瓦当、滴水、板瓦、筒瓦、砖雕构件及脊兽残件，少量瓷片、铜钱，零星石刻残件、佛像等器物。

　　本次勘探和发掘的房址应为现存神通寺遗址的主体建筑，该寺庙基本遵守了中国古建筑中轴对称的布局设计，中轴线上自南至北共发现F4、F3、F1、F8、F11、F13等六座建筑，其中前三者应分别为山门殿、天王殿、大雄宝殿，后三者可能分别为千佛殿（或罗汉殿）、方丈、法堂。F4西侧之F5可能为鼓台（或鼓楼之台基）；F1东南之F2应为伽蓝殿，西南之F15应为祖师殿；F13东侧之F12可能为其配殿，东南之F10可能为其厢房（两者亦可能为文献所载斋廊等建筑的东半部分）。遗址北部诸房址平面均呈长方形，仅存最下部墙体，个别存有铺地砖，均为平地起建，房址等级可能较低。

　　F1位于遗址中南部，是遗址内面积最大、等级最高的房址。平面呈长方形，坐北朝南，面阔五间、进深三间，其下有大型台基，南有大型月台，北有高台甬路，南北两侧均设门址。室内沿后金柱设影壁墙，墙南设大台基，大台基东西两端南侧各有小台基，依东西山墙各有"凹"字形台基。殿内存有10方雕饰繁复精美之覆盆式柱础，以及4方素面覆盆式柱础，其余柱础为大型素面方石。

　　F8位于遗址中部，规模仅次于F1，其平面呈长方形，坐北朝南。面阔七间、进深三间，南北两侧均设门址。

　　根据出土遗物、文献记载和碑文内容，初步推测现存房址多为明代所建，后经多次重修。本次勘探发掘使我们对神通寺遗址现存基址有了初步认识，但此次发掘的建筑基址时代较晚，未见早期房址。早期建筑构件也只有零星几件，仍需要进一步的工作来解释此现象。

神通寺遗址远景（南—北）

神通寺遗址发掘区全景（东—西）

Site of Shentong Temple is located in Jinyu Valley in Kunrui Mountain, approximately 2000 meters northeast Liubu Town, Licheng District, Jinan City. From May to December in 2013, archaeological reconnaissances and excavations were carried out basically in the core zone of the site. Discovered remains include 15 dwelling sites, 3 walls and 1 road. A considerable number of tile-ends, triangle-shaped edges that used to be on tile ends, flat tiles, barrel tiles, brick building components decorated with carvings, broken pieces of sloping ridge animal ornaments have been excavated. A small amount of porcelain fragments, copper coins and scattered stone carvings and Buddha statues have been unearthed. After excavations, the axisymmetric layout of Shentong Temple has been basically recognized. Now there is a preliminary understanding of the layout and building techniques of those discovered dwelling sites. Natures of some dwelling sites have been determined. It has been preliminarily inferred that most existing dwelling sites were constructed in Ming Dynasty and had been rebuilt several times.

# 幽室冥冥　事死以象生

## 江苏南京市栖霞区狮子冲南朝陵园考古概况

◎ 许志强

南京市栖霞区狮子冲的农田里，东西相对坐落着一对南朝石兽。关于这对石兽的归属，历来有刘宋文帝长宁陵和陈文帝永宁陵两说。2012—2013年，围绕狮子冲南朝石刻周边区域的考古调查、勘探、发掘工作相继展开，并发掘了北象山南坡两座大型南朝墓葬。

两座大墓均坐北朝南（M1方向154°、M2方向155°），东西并列，相距不到10米。墓葬上部各有独立封土，两墓之间封土相接位置有叠压现象。两座墓葬均遭到过严重的盗掘。两墓形制基本相同，均为平面呈"凸"字形、带甬道的单室砖墓，墓室平面近椭圆形，墓室外壁四周与墓圹之间有放射状砖砌挡土墙，两墓的甬道内各设有两重石门结构。M1墓室西壁揭露出相对完整的"羽人戏虎"及半幅"竹林七贤"砖印壁画。"竹林七贤"砖印壁画共有四人，为阮咸、阮籍、山涛、嵇康。M2东壁保存有完整的"仙人持幡"砖印壁画。此外，两墓的墓室乱砖堆积中分别出土了一块纪年砖，M1出土"中大通弍年"纪年砖，M2出土"普通七年"纪年砖。

考古工作者还在两墓周边发现四条疑似夯土墙，依托原有山岭在局部低洼处进行堆筑。四条墙体将两墓包在其中，推测为两墓共用的陵墙。

经试掘确认，农田中的两石刻虽经过人工抬升，但仍保持原有位置，两石刻下均有砖砌台基。并在石刻台基中间发现宽14.90米的砖砌神道。

此次考古工作主要收获如下：1. 经过详细的考古工作，可以确认北象山南麓的两座大型砖室墓葬的时代均应为南朝萧梁时期。根据两墓出土的纪年砖及相关文献记载，初步推定两墓的墓主分别为梁昭明太子萧统及其生母丁贵嫔（M1为萧、M2为丁）。基本排除了传统观点认为该处为陈文帝永宁陵的可能性。2. 本次发掘的两座大型砖室墓与其西南约350米处的两座石刻存在直接的对应关系。墓葬、陵墙、石刻、神道同属一体，构成了一座南朝陵园。作为陵园的重要组成部分，本次考古发现的陵墙、砖砌石刻台基、神道设施等遗迹丰富了南朝陵园的内涵，对于同时期的陵墓研究具有极为重要的学术意义。从某种意义上来说，其重要性丝毫不亚于两座南朝大墓。3. 本次考古发现的两座南朝大墓、陵墙等重要遗迹，对于该处文物主体的重新定名及保护范围的划定具有关键性的意义。

M1西壁"竹林七贤"

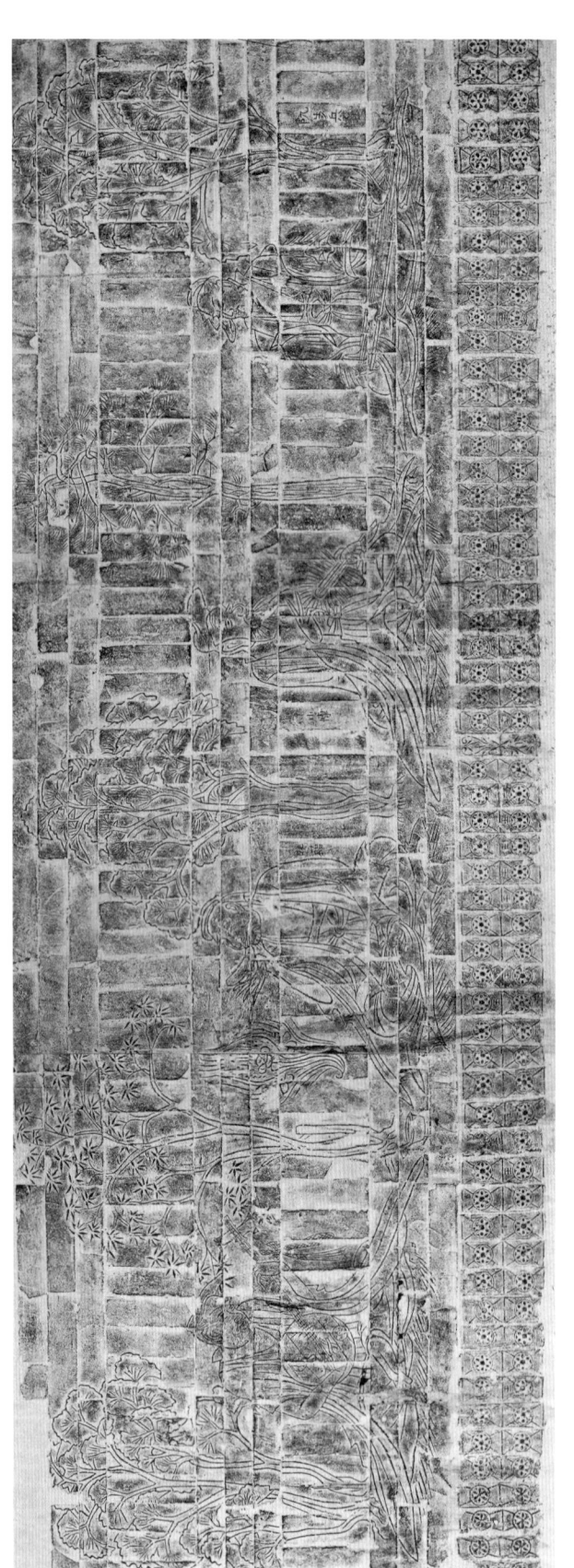

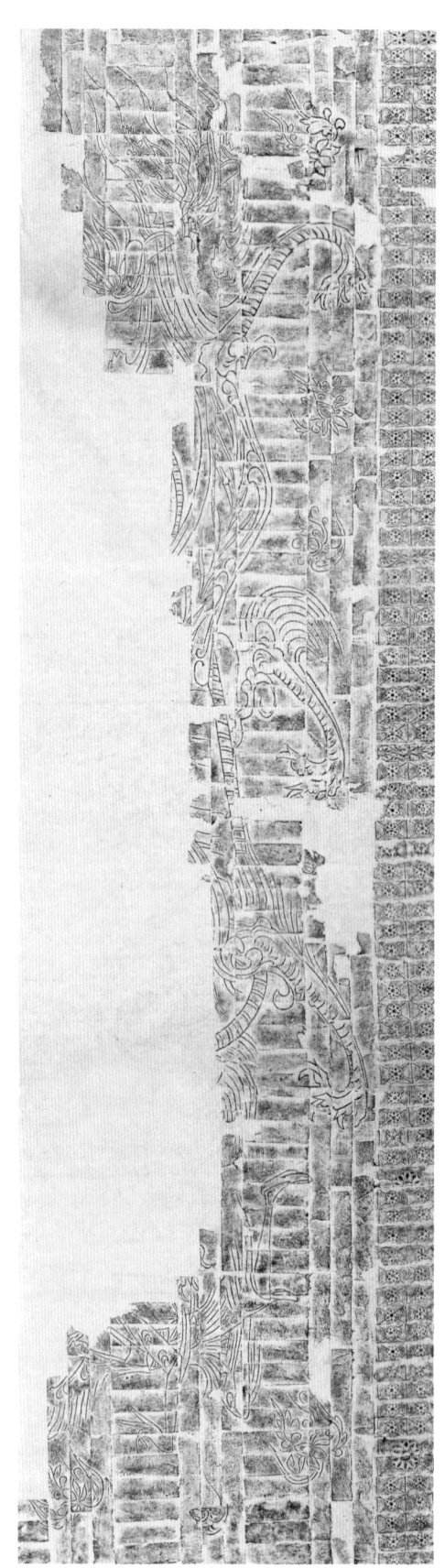

M1西壁"羽人戏虎"

唐风宋韵　气象万千　593

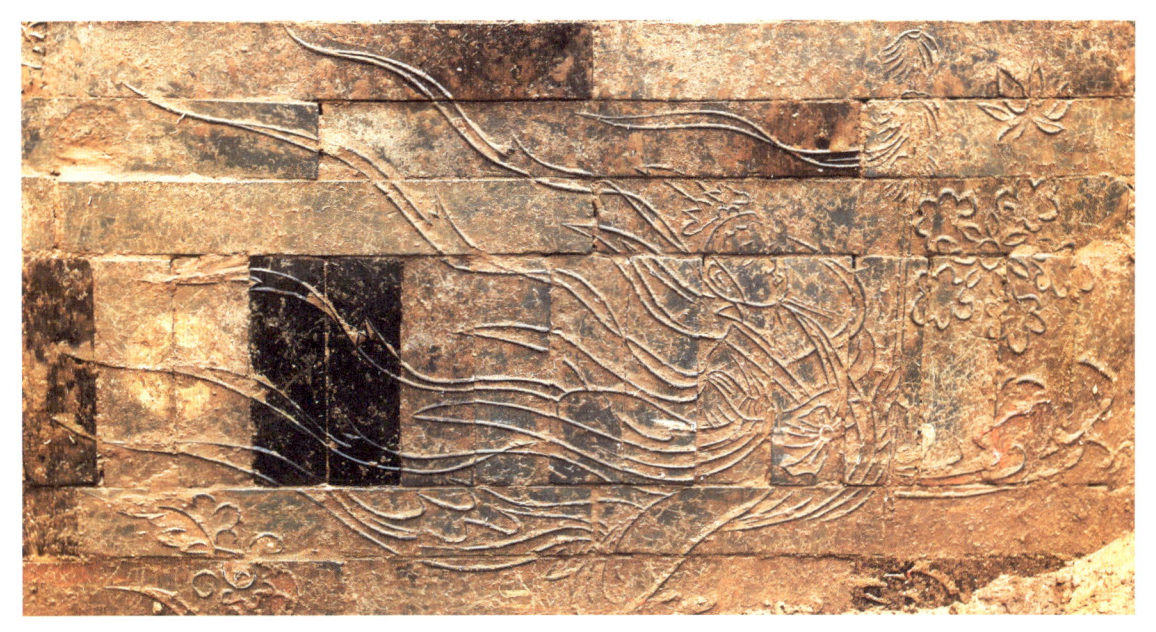

M2东壁"仙人持幡"

M1西壁"天人"

墓地全景（南—北）

　　Both large tombs are south-facing. On top of each tomb, there is a tumulus. The plane layouts of both tombs are the same, resembling the Chinese character " 凸 "(Tu). Each tomb is a single-chamber oval brick tomb with a tomb passage. Bricks engraved with the year in which they were produced have been unearthed from both tombs. "The Second Year of Zhongdatong" is found on bricks revealed in tomb M1, and "The Seventh Year of Putong" can be seen from bricks excavated from tomb M2. According to these engraved bricks and relevant documental records, it has been preliminarily determined that occupants of tomb M1 and tomb M2 are respectively Xiao Tong, Prince Zhaoming of Liang, and his biological mother, the Honored Court Lady Ding. In addition, remains, such as the mausoleum walls, brick terraces decorated with stone carvings, the spirit road, have been discovered. It is of great academic value for the study of contemporary tombs.

# 2015年山西侯马市新月小区北魏裴氏家族墓

◎王金平　段双龙

本次发掘位于侯马市高村乡虒祁村西北约1.50千米处，系虒祁遗址第九次发掘。重要的收获是发现了4座北魏墓，可分为砖室墓和土洞墓两种。

这4座北魏墓葬是继曲沃秦村北魏太和二十三年李诜墓后在晋南地区第二次发现的北魏墓葬，但墓葬形制与前者不同且保存完整，具有较高的研究价值。其中M1007更是山西发现的为数不多的北魏洛阳时代有明确纪年的墓葬。这4座墓葬从分布、墓葬形制及出土器物分析，应属于同一家族。其特征如下：

1. 从墓葬形制看，M1006为北魏时期实力最强时的斜坡墓道梯形土洞墓，M1007、M1008、M1024为迁洛后流行的带斜坡墓道的单室砖墓。值得注意的是本次发掘的M1007、M1008、M1024的墓室四壁均为直边方形。

2. 墓葬中的葬具仍沿用过去头大尾小的棺木，棺体前挡高阔，足挡低窄，这种形制具有浓郁的鲜卑民族风格。

3. 随葬品方面，墓葬中出现有北朝时期较为常见的陶灯及细颈壶。均没有发现陶俑，随葬容器或者延续着平城时代陶器的风格，或者使用南朝风格的鸡首壶等青瓷器。

4. M1006、M1007均有殉牲的习俗，其中M1006为鲜卑拓跋典型殉牲习俗，棺前布置有圆形漆案，上有动物骨骼。

5. 3座方形单室砖墓有典型的北魏洛阳时期风格，墓内出土鐎斗及青瓷器则具有南朝风格，同时M1006的长斜坡墓道梯形土洞墓、M1006及M1007墓内殉牲习俗又保留有典型的鲜卑风格。墓葬的砌筑方式及直边方形形制又具有自身特色，其远承魏晋，又华夷杂糅，既有民族传统，又兼收并蓄。其丰富的内涵及多样性反映出拓跋鲜卑民族文化与中原地区汉晋传统以及南朝文化相互影响而形成的"杂相糅乱"的文化面貌。

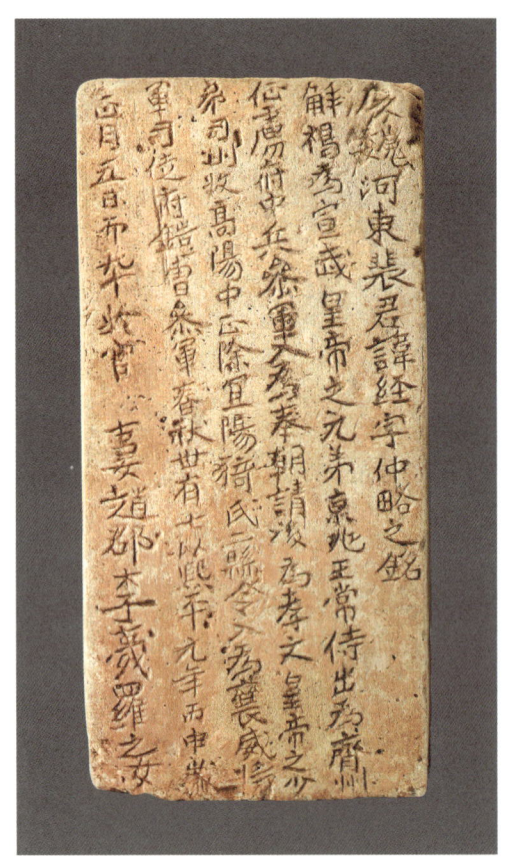

M1006　　　　　　　　　　　M1007墓铭砖

M1007

M1006、M1007、M1008随葬品

Four tombs of Northern Wei have been excavated. The occupants are members of the Pei's clan. One tomb is a subterranean cave tomb; the other three are brick-chambered ones. The cave tomb consists of a long sloping tomb tunnel, a passage, shafts and the coffin chamber. The tombs constructed with bricks are all domed single-chambered ones with a long sloping tomb tunnel each. From tomb M1007, a brick, engraved with the epitaph of Pei Jing, has been unearthed. The epitaph tells Pei's experiences as an official, the date of his death and details of his wife's family. These four tombs, with their diversified contents and varied Tibetan burial customs, illustrate miscellaneous and mixed cultural features under the interaction among the culture of Tuoba Xianbei, Han-Jin conventions prevailing on the Central Plains, and the culture of Southern Dynasties.

# 山西忻州市九原岗北朝壁画墓

◎ 白曙璋　张庆捷

忻州九原岗北朝壁画墓位于忻州市忻府区兰村乡下社村东北。2013年6月下旬，山西省考古研究所、忻州市文物管理处与太原市文物考古研究所联合组成考古队经过5个月的考古工作，共清理壁画约240平方米，出土大量陶俑残片、陶器、瓷器残片、铁质棺钉等，并且对壁画进行了及时的现场保护与信息采集。

该墓为带斜坡墓道的单室砖墓，方向177°，由墓道、甬道、墓室三部分组成。墓室上方残存封土堆，呈不规则圆形。墓道东、西两壁呈台阶状，可分为四层，甬道拱桥顶。墓室平面弧边形，穹隆顶，墓葬被盗，仅发现少量灶、井、仓等模型明器及瓷器残片等。

该墓葬发现大面积壁画，现存壁画主要集中于墓道东、西、北三壁及甬道两壁和墓室顶部。从壁画人物形象以及出土器物、陶俑观察，其年代应是北朝晚期，推测年代应为东魏至北齐早期。结合墓葬形制、规模、壁画内容和随葬品特征等推测，墓主人身份显赫、位高权重，应该是东魏或北齐统治集团的一位重要人物。该墓的发掘具有以下重要意义：

1. 从壁画内容及规模来看，无论是对地下世界的想象还是对现实生活的描绘都比同时期娄睿、徐显秀等墓葬的壁画内容更加丰富。第一层壁画内容充分揭示了北朝人丰富的精神世界；第二层狩猎图场面宏大，再现了北朝马上民族围猎练兵的历史；第三、四层的出行图规模很大，是北朝民族汇聚、部队勇猛善战的缩影。墓道北壁壁画中的木结构建筑在同时期墓葬中是首次发现，第一次用绘画的形式展现了北朝建筑的风采。并且，许多题材在同时期墓葬壁画中属首次发现，例如升天图、马匹贸易图、围猎图、大型门楼图等，都是研究北朝社会生活、历史文化和军事制度等方面的珍贵材料。

2. 该墓是忻州市发掘的首座北朝晚期墓葬。根据《北史》等文献记载，忻州地区是当时朝廷重臣活跃之地。该墓的发掘填补了忻州地区北朝墓葬资料的空白，而且对研究北朝社会生活、民族融合、绘画艺术以及我国古代建筑史都具有非常重要的意义。

唐风宋韵　气象万千　599

门楼图

东壁壁画局部

西壁壁画

东壁壁画疆良、风伯

Jiuyuangang mural tomb, dating from Northern Dynasties, in Xinzhou City was excavated in 2013. It is a south-facing single-chambered brick tomb consisting of three parts, i.e. a sloping tomb tunnel, a tomb passage and a coffin chamber. Large patches of murals, approximately 240 square meters, have been discovered in the tomb, mainly on the east, west and north sides of the tomb tunnel and on the ceiling of the tomb chamber. From top to bottom, murals painted on the east and west sides of the tomb tunnel can be divided into four sections; murals discovered in the tomb chamber were originally in three sections. These murals depict myths, hunting, outings, warriors, constellations, etc. As a tomb of Northern Dynasties discovered in Xinzhou district, the tomb per se is of exemplary significance. In addition, the excavation of this mural tomb greatly contributes to studies of social life, national amalgamation and the art of painting in Northern Dynasties, and the history of ancient Chinese architecture.

# 江苏苏州市虎丘路新村土墩砖室墓群

◎张铁军　何文竞

苏州市虎丘路新村土墩位于苏州市姑苏区虎丘路西侧，此次共发掘了M1、M2、M5、M6、M8等5座六朝早期砖室墓，M3、M4、M7等3座宋代砖室墓。

8座墓共处于一座土墩范围内。土墩上部因前期施工取土已遭破坏，相应范围内的文化遗存已不复存在。为了解M1和土墩的关系，分别在M1的东、南、西、北四面开挖探沟，确认M1、M2起筑于平台之上，土墩大部为其封土；现存封土东西长55米，南北宽50米，残高5米；M5、M6、M8打破土墩；M3、M4打破M5；M7打破M8。

通过此次发掘工作，我们主要有如下收获：

1. 通过比较，可以发现M1与南京上坊大墓和安徽马鞍山天子坟大墓平面结构相近、前后室均为穹隆顶；M1小于后两者，且与后两者在墓砖砌筑方式和构建穹隆顶的方法上存在明显差异。

2. M2因为早期顶部坍塌，客观上保护了墓室，随葬品没有被人为扰动，最大限度地保持了原貌。

3. M5出土了"吴侯"印文砖，为M1墓主人研究提供了重要线索。

4. 通过对虎丘路新村土墩的解剖，确认了M1、M2、土墩、M5、M6、M8之间的层位关系，对于深入研究M1、M2、M5、M6、M8的内涵提供了可能。

苏州地区曾是三国孙吴政权的早期政治中心。此次苏州市虎丘路新村土墩考古工作取得大量有效信息，其中遗迹间层位关系明确，出土文物精美、丰富，墓室体量巨大、保存基本完整，出土的"吴侯"印文砖等材料对孙吴早期器物学研究、三国孙吴早期宗室丧葬制度研究、六朝时期考古学研究以及长江南北文化交流研究都具有重要价值。

M1俯视（上北下南）

M5"吴侯"铭文砖

M6后室东墙砖手印

唐风宋韵　气象万千　603

M2陶仓

M1金兽

M2银碗

M2铜熏

M1瓷熏

M1石兽形器座

Major archaeological discoveries in the burial mound in Xincun, Huqiu Road, Suzhou City, are 5 brick-chambered tombs of early Six Dynasties and 3 tombs constructed with bricks and stones dating from Song Dynasty. All the tombs built in Six Dynasties are attached with tomb tunnels pointing to the north. In some tombs, there is a front chamber and a rear chamber. Some tombs are single-chambered ones. Side chambers are discovered in some other tombs. All these tombs have a dome or an arched ceiling. In tomb M5, a number of bricks are found engraved with characters "Wu Hou". All three tombs dating from Song Dynasty are damaged. They are east-west brick-chambered shaft tombs. The plane layout of each tomb is rectangular. No funeral objects have been discovered. The mound is the tumulus of tomb M1 and tomb M2. Other tombs of the Six Dynasties are not bound by the boundary of the mound; while tombs of Song Dynasty overlapped with those constructed during the Six Dynasties. The excavation of the burial mound in Xincun is of great significance for studies of archaeological culture of early Eastern Wu and cultural exchanges between the north and the south of the Yangtze River.

# 江苏扬州市隋炀帝墓

◎ 束家平

2012年12月至2013年11月，南京博物院等单位在扬州市西湖镇司徒村曹庄发掘了两座古代砖室墓，编号分别为2013YCM1、2013YCM2。经发掘，确认M1为隋炀帝墓，M2为萧后墓。

经全面勘探与发掘，隋炀帝墓与萧后墓为同茔异穴墓葬，隋炀帝墓周围没有发现与之相关的陵园遗迹。隋炀帝墓为斜坡墓道砖室墓，由封土、墓道、甬道、东耳室、西耳室及主墓室6部分组成。该墓出土了墓志、玉器、铜器、陶器及漆器等珍贵文物近180余件（套），其中"隨故煬帝墓誌"铭墓志、十三环蹀躞金玉带、鎏金铜铺首是墓主人身份最直接的证据。甲骑具装俑是迄今在扬州地区乃至南方地区首次发现，是流行于北朝至初唐北方地区高等级墓葬的随葬品，时代与地域特征明显。

萧后墓为短斜坡墓道腰鼓形墓，由墓道、甬道、东耳室、西耳室、主墓室五部分组成，主墓室由前室和后室两部分组成，东、西、北壁各有3个小壁龛。有两处盗洞。墓砖中有少量的龙纹砖与莲瓣纹砖。萧后墓随葬品丰富，出土陶器、瓷器、铜器、漆木器、铁器及玉器等200余件（套）。一套铜编钟（16件）、编磬（20件）及冠的出现预示着墓主人的皇室背景，玉璋、陶牛、陶猪、陶羊的随葬，表明唐太宗以一定的周礼下葬萧后。

隋炀帝墓的建筑方法是在土墩的中心挖浅穴、修砖室，同时堆筑夯土，夯土紧贴墓室砖壁，并预留墓道，下葬封门后在墓道内填土，最后封土形成土墩。隋炀帝墓位于土墩中心，而萧后墓偏于土墩东南隅，其墓圹打破土墩，是开挖土墩后下葬的。萧后墓晚于隋炀帝墓，与文献记载相符。这类"平地起封"的墓葬营造方式与西安、洛阳的土坑竖穴墓结构相比有着鲜明的地域特征。

隋炀帝墓的发掘，为研究隋唐高等级墓葬形制提供了实证资料，亦是中国历史上废弃帝王墓葬的难得的实物样本。一座封土下的两座墓葬，虽埋葬时间仅相差二十多年，但墓葬形制、随葬品风格却体现出地域性、朝代性的差异，这为研究隋末唐初的葬制演变提供了弥足珍贵的资料。隋炀帝和萧后墓的墓葬形制、随葬器物既有北方文化的特征，又有南方文化的因素，体现了隋唐时期南北文化的交流，是研究这一时期南北经济、社会、民俗、文化等传播融通的新素材。

隋炀帝墓与萧后墓（北向南）

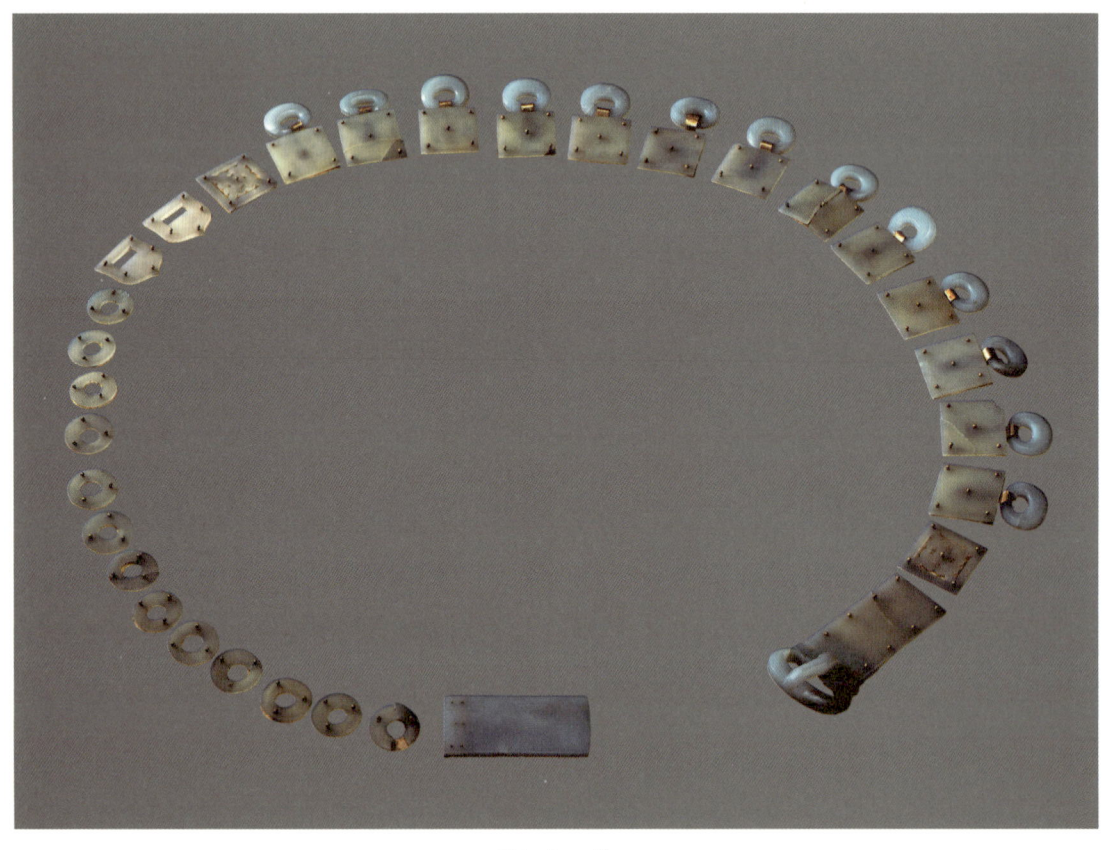

隋炀帝玉带

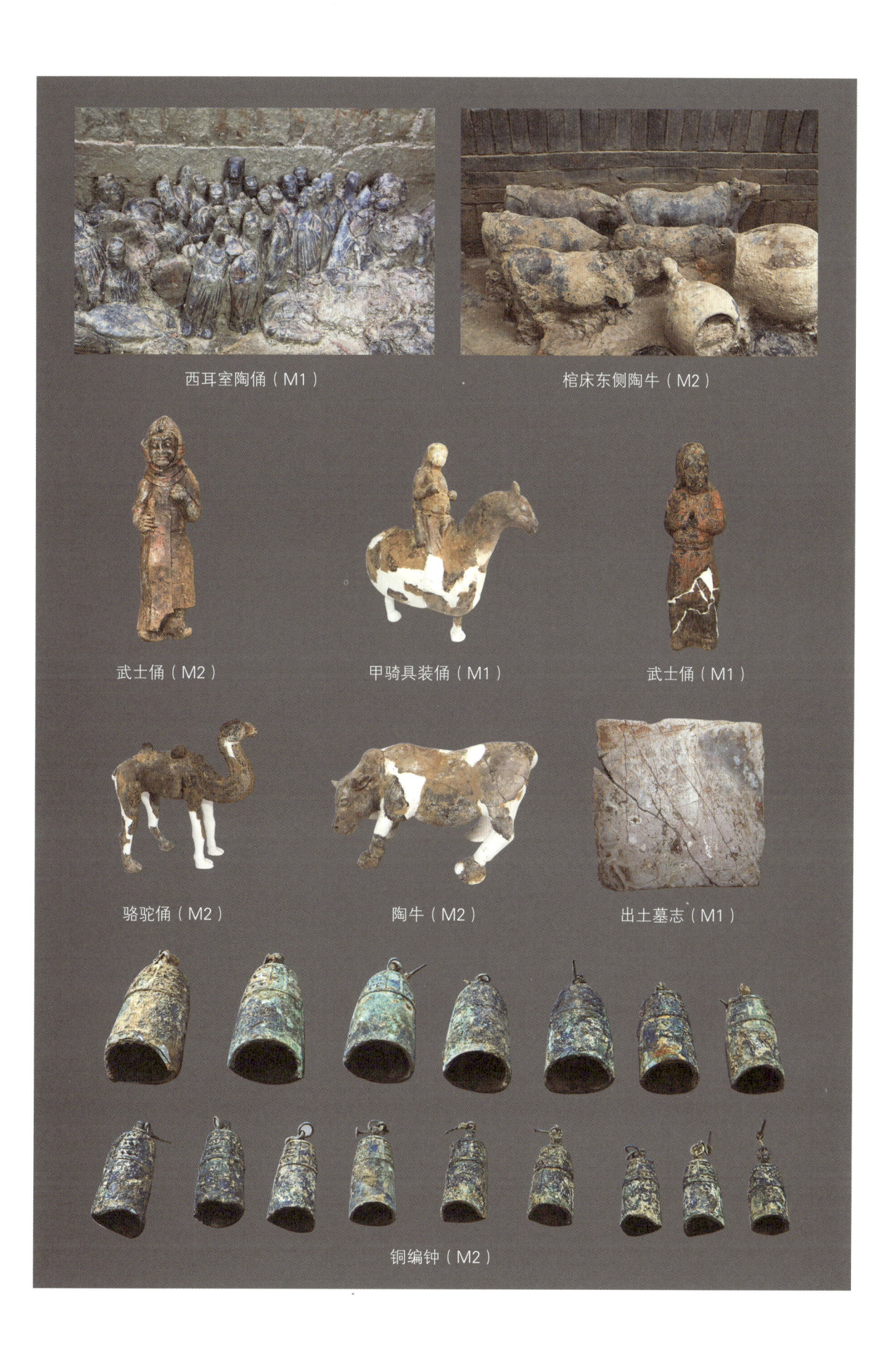

西耳室陶俑（M1） 棺床东侧陶牛（M2）

武士俑（M2） 甲骑具装俑（M1） 武士俑（M1）

骆驼俑（M2） 陶牛（M2） 出土墓志（M1）

铜编钟（M2）

三彩辟雍砚（M2）　　　　　　双人首蛇身俑（M2）

玉璋（M2）　　　　　　鎏金铜铺首（M1）

From December in 2012 to November in 2013, excavations were carried out in two ancient brick-chambered tombs, labeled as 2013YCM1 and 2013YCM2, in Caozhuang, Situ Village, Xihu Town, Yangzhou City. Both tombs are in the same mould but in different coffin pits. M1 is a square brick-chambered tomb with a long sloping tomb tunnel. M2, which is also a brick-chambered tomb, is in the shape of a waist drum and with a short sloping tomb tunnel. Precious antiquities have been unearthed from both tombs, including jade ware, bronzes, potteries and lacquerware. Figures of cavalrymen are the first ones that have been discovered in Yangzhou even in southern China. According to funeral objects like the epitaph and tomb structure, it has been confirmed that M1 is the mausoleum of Emperor Yang of Sui Dynasty. His wife, Empress Xiao, was buried in M2. Regional differences between the North and the South as well as dynastic differences represented by both tombs are new subjects for the study of evolution of burial conventions dating from the end of Sui Dynasty to early Tang Dynasty as well as diffusion and exchanges of contemporary economics, society, folk customs and cultures between the North and the South. The tomb, in which Emperor Yang of Sui Dynasty who was a dethroned emperor in Chinese history is buried, is a rare example of its kind. Excavations have brought to light soil evidence for the study of high-level tombs dating from Sui and Tang dynasties.

# 河北邢台市唐祖陵调查、勘探与发掘

◎ 郭济桥

唐祖陵为大唐高祖李渊第三代祖李天赐、第四代祖李熙的茔域，二陵共茔。陵区位于河北省邢台市隆尧县魏家庄镇王尹村北，北距县城6千米。唐陵主体由主陵区和光业寺两部分构成。主陵区自北向南为陵台、双阙、石像生，陵台到石像生南北长约200米，东西宽约80米。除石像生以外，其余遗迹地表无存，光业寺碑由县文保所保管。

经勘探，唐祖陵由两座主陵组成，分西北、东南方向排列。陵前置双阙，阙前分布石像生。在陵区东南方向有光业寺，在光业寺范围内有唐代砖瓦窑；西南方位可能存在下宫；东南部有陪葬墓。陵外有兆域围沟。通过考古勘探和发掘，关于陵园布局及建筑，现阶段最终确定的部分有：1. 两座主陵及陵后三座小墓；2. 陵前双阙；3. 双阙前神道及石像生；4. 唐代砖瓦窑。

陵前双阙为三出阙，双阙前有石蹲狮。围沟，推测为兆域界，其大小同于献陵"封内20里"规模，为李唐时期最高等级，均属帝王级形制，推测其范围为东西2000米，南北2300米左右。建初陵北侧的3座小型墓葬，不排除其为建初陵以前之上代祖先墓，为聚族而葬，唐陵附近应该即为李唐籍贯所在。陵前阙台、南端望柱坐落于唐代地面上，其余石像生坐落于宋代地面上，为宋代以后重修时从唐代地面提升而致，推测实施者为李氏后人。从石像生分布以及蹲狮造型分析，石像生的初立年代在唐高宗甚至唐玄宗以后。陵前阙台倒塌年代早于宋初，推测在唐末即已废弃。

出土遗物以建筑材料为主，包括长方形砖、方砖、磨砖、板瓦、筒瓦、莲花瓦当、鸱尾等。

经勘探，并未发现二陵共茔之周回围墙。以陵前双阙为基点，反复勘探，也没有见到围墙及角台迹象，推测当时围墙可能为植树等形式，为边长110米的方形建制。

乳台位置仅为勘探，仅发现西侧乳台部分夯土，推测隆尧唐陵司马院的范围为东西147米，南北394米。勘探未见墙基等建筑，应该也是采取植树等形式。按照陕西唐陵的情况，推测鹊台应该在陵前双阙中轴线上南约1300米。经勘探，该位置附近3米以下为粗河沙，东西向河道，其北见唐代地层，推测该处为唐祖陵兆域南边界，但鹊台情况不明。

东阙台

陵区文化层

光业寺唐代陶窑

祭台

附属墓葬

唐风宋韵　气象万千　611

石狮　　　　　　　　　　石狮　　　　　　　　　　武将

莲花瓦当　　　　　　双水波纹板瓦　　　　　　马头

鞍马

望柱基座

李伦墓志

  Zuling Mausoleum, in which ancestors of the emperors of Tang Dynasty were buried, is in the north of Wangyin Village, Weijiazhuang Town, Longyao County, Xingtai City, Hebei Province. From 2010 to 2016, archaeologists from Hebei Provincial Institute of Cultural Relics conducted surveys, archaeological reconnaissances and excavations in this mausoleum in Longyao County. Their archaeological reconnaissances covered 250, 000 square meters and the excavated area was 500 square meters. After archaeological reconnaissances, discovered remains include 2 major tombs, 3 minor tombs, twin side towers, spirit ways, Guangye Temple, kilns that used to produce bricks and tiles in Tang Dynasty. There is a wide range of unearthed relics, like stone carvings of animals and human figures and building materials. Revealed remains and relics indicate that Zuling Mausoleum, which became deserted at the end of Tang Dynasty, is made up of two major tombs, respectively located in the northwest and southeast. The surveys and excavations carried out in Zuling Mausoleum have made it possible for the confirmation of Jianchu Mausoleum and Qiyun Mausoleum, both of which were constructed in Tang Dynasty, the study on the origin of the Li family, namely the imperial family of Tang Dynasty, the layout of Zuling Mausoleum as well as comparative analysis of Zuling Mausoleum and mausoleums which are also of Tang Dynasty but have been discovered in Shaanxi Province.

# 陕西唐代帝陵近年来的工作和新发现

◎张 博

　　唐陵考古工作主要是对唐代18座皇帝陵园，以及李昺的兴宁陵、李虎的永康陵、以皇帝规格营建的顺陵等21座陵园进行全面的考古调查、勘探、测量和开展部分陵园建筑遗址的试掘工作。这些陵园分布于陕西关中地区渭河以北黄土高原二级阶地南端和北山山脉的南麓，南临渭河河谷、北依群山。截至2017年年底，已完成了全部陵园的考古勘探工作，并对17座陵园的部分建筑遗址进行了小面积的考古发掘。

　　唐代帝陵陵园按照其构造方式可分为封土为陵和因山为陵两种类型。封土为陵的陵园以献陵为代表。其他的封土为陵的陵园还有唐武宗端陵、唐敬宗庄陵、唐僖宗靖陵等。

　　因山为陵的陵园类型自昭陵开始，完善和定型于乾陵。乾陵的建造是唐帝陵形制变化的一个转折点，形成的"乾陵模式"对后来诸帝陵影响深远，为此后诸唐陵设计的楷模。

　　2011年对光陵东门门址、南侧列戟廊、南侧门阙进行了考古发掘，东门门址现仅存东半部分。门址为夯土台式建筑，平面呈长方形，为过厅式结构，面东背西，南北向面阔五间，东西向进深两间。两侧房间以隔墙隔断门址内外，中间三间为门道。光陵东门南侧列戟廊平面形状为长方形，面阔三间，进深一间，三面有墙，面向门址一侧敞开。光陵东门北侧门阙基础部分平面形状为梯形，主体为夯土结构的阙体，阙体由南向北分三次渐渐收窄，形成三出结构。

　　2016年对定陵下宫建筑基址1进行了考古发掘，发现定陵下宫宫墙外有围沟。宫城内多道夯土基址划分出两进三列共6个区域，每个区域的形状和内部格局不甚相同，中间两进区域应为核心区，前后两进内各有一个大型建筑基址。本次对建筑基址1位于北部中间位置的南侧边缘的基址进行了清理发掘，发现遗址由两个时代的建筑叠压形成，上部为一道东西向夯土台基，应该是宋代整修定陵下宫或者修建陵庙留下的遗迹。宋代建筑下为唐代大殿建筑的南侧台基边缘。

　　通过近年来的考古工作全面掌握了各个陵园的空间布局和范围结构，还搞清楚了陪葬墓的分布、数量、墓园形制和墓葬规格等信息，为深入研究唐代帝陵制度及其演变规律提供了大量客观且翔实的依据，将唐代陵墓考古研究推向更深层次和更高水平。

昭陵九嵕山

献陵南门遗址及封土（上为北）

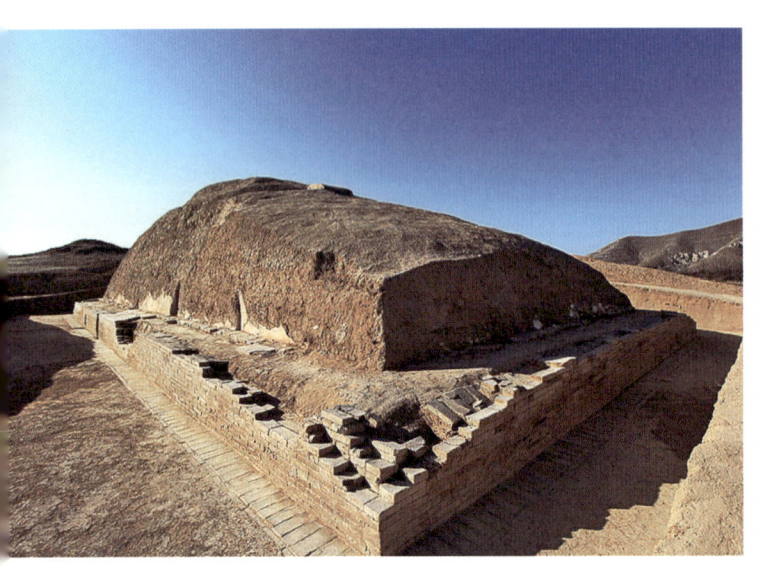

光陵东门南阙

唐定陵2016年下宫遗址发掘现场

唐定陵2015年南神道西侧新出土石人　　　　　　　　庄陵西侧翼马

Mausoleums of Tang Dynasty are distributed in an area stretching from the southern end of the second level of the Loess Plateau in the north of Weihe River on Central Shaanxi Plain to the southern piedmont of Beishan Mountain Range. By the end of 2017, archaeological reconnaissances have been carried out in all twenty-one mausoleums and partial excavations have been conducted on some architectural sites in seventeen mausoleums. According to their structures, mausoleums of Tang Dynasty can be divided into two types. Some mausoleums were constructed with a mould-like heap of rammed earth above the coffin pit. The others were hills before each one was turned into a mausoleum. After archaeological work, the spatial layout, range and structure of each mausoleum have been comprehensively learned. Their cultural connotations and development pattern have been grasped. The comprehensive assessment of the cultural value and preservation condition of these mausoleums provides basic information and scientific reference for protection and reasonable use of them.

# 陕西华阴市唐敦煌县令宋素墓

◎刘呆运　赵占锐

2014年3月中旬，陕西省考古研究院在华阴市夫水镇连村抢救性发掘了一座唐代墓葬。

该墓为带长斜坡墓道的单室砖室墓，坐北向南，墓葬由墓道、甬道、封门、墓室四部分组成。墓室为圆角方形，略呈铲形。目前已发现的唐代铲形单室砖墓较少，多出现于高宗时期，属五品以上官员的葬制。

墓室长期遭受水冲，所用葬具为木棺，原应纵向放置于墓室西部，前挡面北，形制与大小尺寸现已不详。墓主骨架已散乱，身高无法确定，推测西侧骨架为男性，东侧为女性。夫妇二人均为仰身直肢葬，头北足南。

宋素墓共出土随葬品70件（组），包括陶俑、陶器、铜器、铁器及石墓志等。在发掘清理时，墓室内有大量积水，随葬品散乱分布于墓室南部、东部及墓主骨架周围，集中分布的区域有：墓室西南角，以陶立俑为主；墓室入口处，以镇墓类陶俑和石墓志为主；墓室东壁下，以陶骑马俑、陶动物俑为主。铜、铁质器皿主要分布在墓主骨架周围。墓内出土的镇墓兽、武士俑、文官俑、陶骆驼、陶马等不仅制作精美，而且体格较大，高达六七十厘米。这些陶俑和关中地区常见的陶俑有所不同，但与河南洛阳的隋唐墓出土物较为接近，如偃师杏园李嗣本墓的随葬陶俑就与宋素墓所出陶俑颇为类似。

据墓志记载，墓主为沙州敦煌县令宋素与夫人王氏。墓主宋素卒于唐显庆四年（659年），咸亨元年（670年）五月与夫人王氏合葬于华州华阴县龙腹原。墓主宋素的最高官品为四品，与其墓葬规格是相符的。

宋素墓志记载了宋素的生平经历、家族谱系、宅葬地等情况，增补了史传文献的记载，对研究唐廷在沙州敦煌一地的遣官制度及其早期对敦煌的经营管理，探索隋至初唐时期科举入仕、辞官、又任官等基层文官的升迁，以及考察唐代洛阳和华州华阴县的史地等提供了珍贵的实物资料。另外，该墓志的发现对丝路的研究也有所裨益。

唐风宋韵　气象万千　617

风帽俑　　　　　双环髻侍女俑　　　　文官俑

武士俑　　　　　高髻侍女俑　　　　　毡帽俑

人面镇墓兽　　　　兽面镇墓兽

女骑马俑　　　　　　　　幞头骑马俑　　　　　　　　毡帽骑马俑

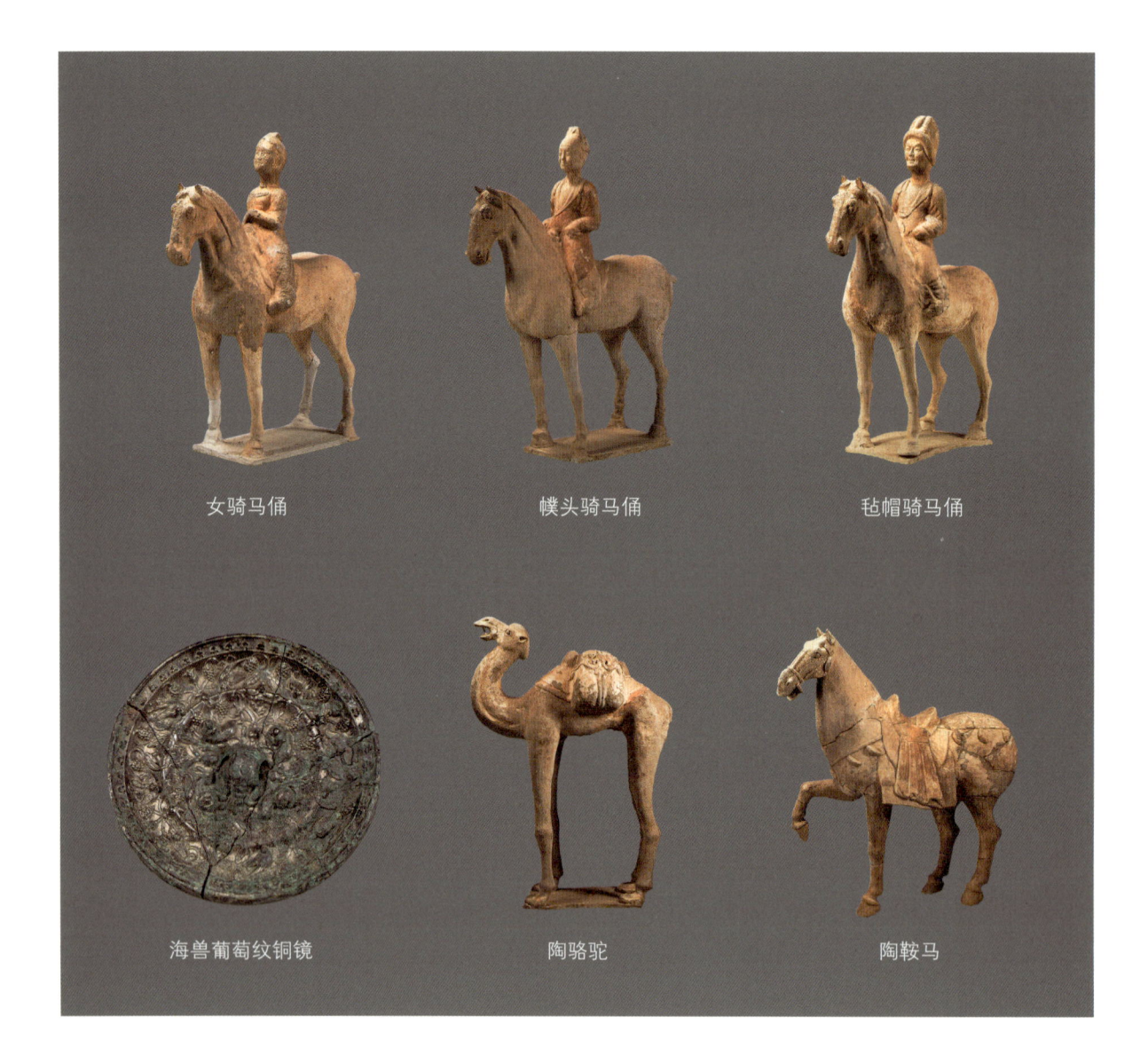

海兽葡萄纹铜镜　　　　　　陶骆驼　　　　　　　　　　陶鞍马

In mid-March 2014, archaeologists from Shaanxi Provincial Institute of Archaeology carried out salvage excavations in a tomb of Tang Dynasty in Liancun Village, Fushui Town, Huayin City. It is a brick-chambered tomb with a sloping tomb tunnel. Seventy pieces (sets) of funeral objects were unearthed, including pottery figurines, potteries, bronzes, ironware and a stone epitaph. According to the unearthed epitaph, it has been found out that the tomb's occupants are Song Su and his wife whose family name was Wang. This epitaph is of great significance for the study of early management of Dunhuang by Tang government. It also benefits the study of the Silk Road and promotes historical and geographic researches on Luoyang, which was the East Capital, and Hua-yin County of Huazhou Prefecture. Previously, there were relatively few historical records of Luoyang and Huayin County. Besides, a large number of antiquities, beautifully crafted, have been unearthed from the tomb. Among these antiquities, the pottery figurines are different from those discovered in Central Shaanxi Plain but similar to relics revealed in tombs of Sui and Tang dynasties in Luoyang, Henan Province.

# 陕西咸阳市唐昭容上官氏墓

◎李 明 耿庆刚

2013年8月至10月，陕西省考古研究院在陕西省咸阳市渭城区北杜镇邓村北发掘了一座带有五个天井的大型古代墓葬，并对墓葬周围进行了大面积勘探，并未发现神道碑、地面封土、墓园、石刻等地面标志。据出土墓志，该墓墓主是唐中宗昭容上官氏。

唐昭容上官氏墓系带天井和小龛的斜坡墓道单室砖券墓，坐北朝南，南北水平全长39米，深10.2米，由斜坡墓道、5个天井、5个过洞、4个壁龛、甬道和墓室等部分组成。过洞、甬道及墓室内残存有壁画痕迹。该墓第四天井以北的结构遭到大规模破坏。第四、第五天井于开口处被一形状不规则的扰坑打破，天井底部约1米以上的部分及它们的砖封门全部被破坏，然后水平向北破坏了甬道地面以上的绝大部分并直通墓室。

墓室内未出土随葬器物，壁龛和甬道内共出土随葬器物190余件，主要为陶俑和陶动物。陶俑的种类有骑马俑和立俑。立俑有幞头俑、风帽俑、仕女俑等，体型不大，高约20厘米，制作较为粗糙，几乎无彩绘。

据出土墓志载，墓主即唐代著名女诗人、政治家上官婉儿，葬于景云元年（710年）八月。

从该墓遭到的破坏程度和墓室的现状判断，如此程度的毁坏不似一般盗墓行为所致，应系大规模、有组织的破坏行为，很有可能是"官方毁墓"所造成的。另外，与同时代的墓葬相比，该墓随葬器物无甚特色甚至有些"寒酸"，似与墓主人正二品阶的身份有差距。

此次发掘最重要的发现无疑是"毁墓"迹象和出土墓志。结合墓志与史料记载，我们认为上官氏的礼葬、追赠谥号、文集编纂等都与太平公主有关，该墓的毁坏也应该在太平公主被赐死后不久，建墓与毁墓都是政治博弈的结果。该墓下葬时间具体，墓主人身份明确且系历史名人，出土文物较为丰富，能够使历史材料、出土文字材料、实物资料和考古学资料相结合，是一个难能可贵的研究标本。

墓葬剖视正射影像图（左为北）

墓室清理后情况（上南下北）

壁龛清理情况

第五天井西壁的典型扰动情况
（红线以上是扰坑）

唐风宋韵 气象万千 621

墓志拓片

陶骑马俑　　　　　　　　陶仕女骑马俑　　　　　　　陶立俑

陶立俑　　　　　　　　　陶鸡　　　　　　　　　　　陶马

From August to October in 2013, archaeologists from Shaanxi Provincial Institute of Archaeology excavated a large ancient tomb which is in the north of Dengcun Village, Beidu Town, Weicheng District, Xianyang City, Shaanxi Province. The tomb, a single-chambered one constructed with bricks, consists of a sloping tomb tunnel, shafts, an arched passage, niches, a path, a coffin chamber, etc. The tomb tunnel is featured with multiple shafts as well as small niches. As many as 190 pieces of funerary objects have been unearthed from the niches and path. Apart from an epitaph, revealed relics are mainly pottery figurines and pottery animals. Massive destruction of the tomb was the result of "sabotage initiated by the authorities". According to the epitaph, the occupant, buried in 710 A.D., should be Shangguan Waner, who ranked Zhaorong, namely a concubine of Emperor Zhongzong of Tang Dynasty.

# 山西临汾市西赵唐代墓葬

◎王金平　陈海波

　　西赵遗址位于临汾市尧都区尧庙镇西赵村西100米处，地处汾河东岸二级台地上，地势整体较为平坦，内有少量沟壑断崖。遗址范围南北长约2000米，东西宽约300米，总面积约60万平方米，是一处面积较大且内含较为丰富的古代遗址。2013年11月至2014年1月山西省考古研究所对西赵遗址进行了部分发掘，此次发掘区域位于遗址中部，共发现遗迹62处，清理遗迹52处，包括灰坑12个、墓葬40座。遗存的年代包括夏代、东周、汉代、唐代、元代和明清等多个时期。

　　唐代墓葬为本次发掘的最大收获，共有12座，均为单室墓，包括砖室墓8座、土洞墓4座。砖室墓由墓道、甬道和墓室三部分组成。墓道大体为斜坡状或阶梯状，墓室为弧边长方形或弧边方形，穹隆顶，墓主人多为二人合葬。土洞墓的墓道大体为长条形直壁斜坡状。葬具均为木棺，多为二人合葬，合葬时亦共用一棺，木棺的形体较大。出土器物包括彩绘陶罐、三彩瓶、各类陶俑、鎏金铜环、鎏金铜泡钉、银钗、玻璃器、铁器、石质或砖质墓志和钱币等，其中以M2、M3、M17和M45出土器物较为丰富。

　　M2位于发掘区东北部，方向195°，为砖室墓，出土有泥质陶俑、鎏金铜饰、铜镜、铜泡钉、铁器、兽面纹瓦当、玻璃器和石墓志等。此墓是山西地区首次发现玻璃器的唐代墓葬。M3位于发掘区东北部，方向190°，为方形砖室墓。根据墓葬形制及出土器物判断，墓中所出的带铭墓砖可能是当时唐代人修墓时利用了以前的旧砖。

　　目前山西省内发现的唐代墓葬主要集中在中部的太原地区和东南部的长治地区，晋北地区也有少量发现，晋南地区则很少发现唐代墓葬。本次发现的唐代纪年墓葬及其出土的器物不仅丰富了山西唐墓的资料，而且为我们进一步了解和研究山西地区的唐代墓葬提供了较为准确的参考。

三彩壶（M45：1）

陶俑（M2：9）

玻璃器（M2：13）

陶俑（M2：10）

志盖（M2：1）

墓志（M2：1）

墓志（M45：6）

**临汾西赵唐墓器物**

武士俑　　　　　　　　　镇墓兽

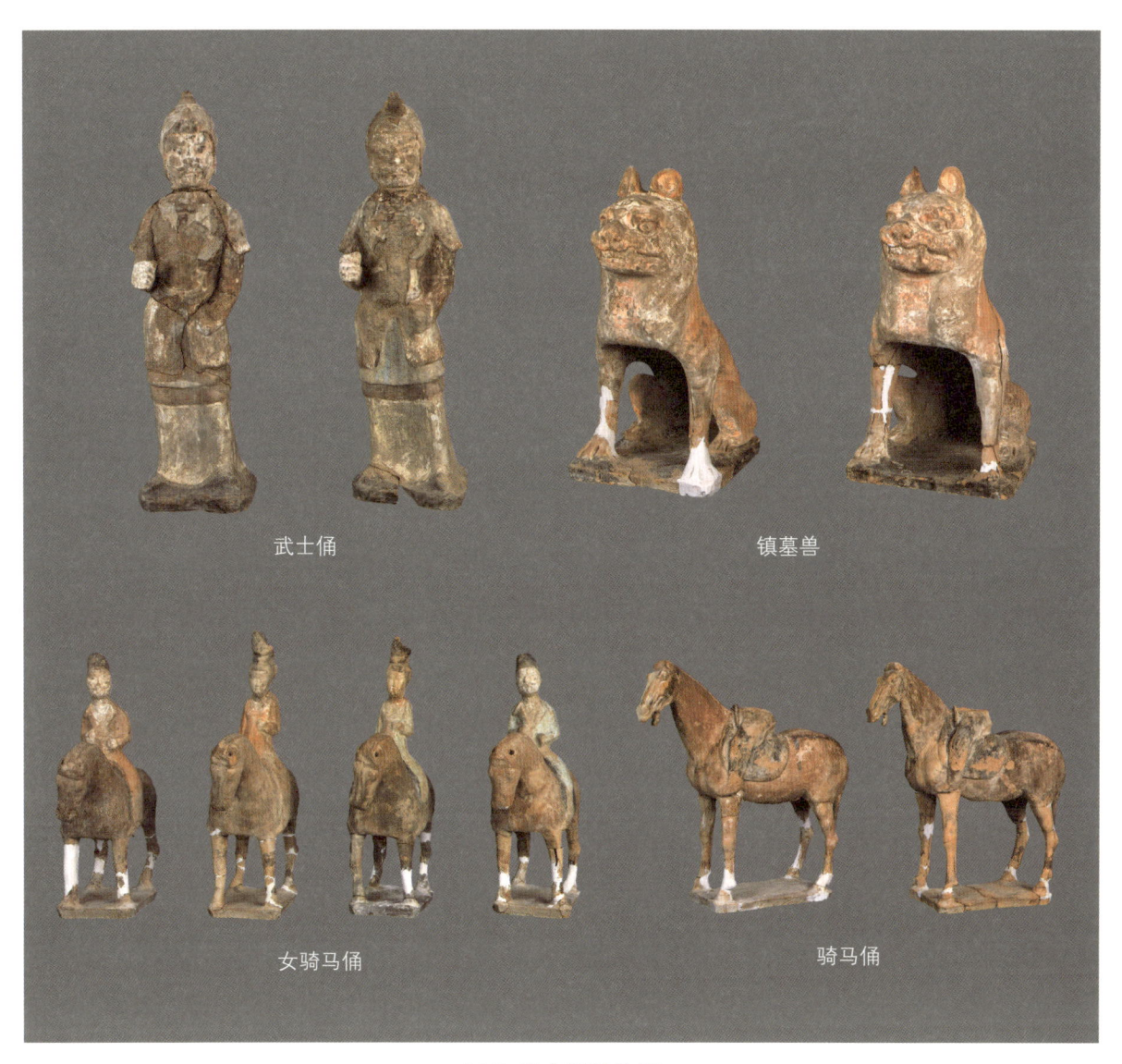

女骑马俑　　　　　　　　骑马俑

M17 出土彩绘陶俑

From November in 2013 to January in 2014, a joint team consisting of archaeologists from Shanxi Provincial Institute of Archaeology, Institute of Archaeology of the Chinese Academy of Social Sciences and Linfen Station of Culture Relics and Archaeology carried out a partial excavation on Xizhao Site. Unearthed remains and relics date back to various eras, including Xia, Eastern Zhou, Han Dynasty, Tang Dynasty, Yuan Dynasty, Ming Dynasty and Qing Dynasty. The discovery of twelve tombs dating back to Tang Dynasty is the greatest achievement made this time. From these tombs, revealed relics include colored potteries, tricolored ware, pottery figures, gilt bronzes, silverware, glassware, ironware, epitaphs and coins. The chronicled tombs of Tang Dynasty that have been discovered this time have provided a relatively accurate reference for further understanding and studies of tombs dating back to Tang Dynasty in Shanxi Province.

# 陕西长安郭庄唐宰相韩休墓

◎刘呆运　赵占锐

2014年3月，陕西省考古研究院等对长安郭庄唐代壁画墓进行了抢救性发掘。墓葬位于西安市长安区大兆街办郭庄村南100米处，西北距杜陵3千米。据出土墓志记载，该墓为唐宰相韩休之墓。

韩休墓为长斜坡墓道单室砖室墓，平面呈刀把形，坐北向南，方向175°。由墓道、5个过洞、5个天井、6个壁龛、甬道及墓室等部分组成。在墓室西部设置砖砌棺床，棺床北部部分砖已不存在。棺床东立沿及床面用条砖围砌，中间用夯土填实。葬具与葬式均已不清。墓葬的建造顺序和施工方法为：首先选好墓室位置，设计好大小尺寸，下挖口大底小的方形墓坑(坑四壁留坡面、四角留半圆形减力柱、对角留上下脚窝）；其次构筑砖墓室；再次逐层填土粗夯；最后地面以上强夯起封土。

墓内自墓道直至墓室原绘满壁画，其中以甬道和墓室壁画保存较好。各过洞入口收分处及洞顶边上，用红彩涂有影作宽带门洞口，在各过洞和天井的起券处用红彩影作宽带阑额。甬道顶部为如意状祥云图案，两壁为侍女图、抬箱图。墓室内顶部绘星象图，南壁绘朱雀图，西壁绘树下高士图，北壁西侧绘玄武图，北壁东侧绘山水图，东壁绘乐舞图。陕西历史博物馆工作人员对墓葬内的壁画进行保护揭取工作，同时邀请专业技术人员对墓葬进行三维激光扫描，记录壁画的原始状态。

该墓共出土随葬品186件（组），由于被盗扰破坏，器物原摆放位置已被扰乱。器类有：陶风帽俑、男立俑、仕女俑、风帽骑马俑、陶卧马、骆驼、牛、狗、猪、羊、鸡、鸭、陶塔式罐、灯盏；白釉瓷执壶、瓷盏；绿釉陶罐、陶钵；铁泡钉、铁环；石门一套、石墓志二合。

壁画是本次考古发掘的最重要的发现。特别是北壁山水图，为首次发现的独幅山水画，标志着山水画由纯粹的墓葬装饰壁画变为绘画作品，填补了山水画发展序列的空白，并将山水画的成熟期提至盛唐。同时，其绘画笔法、视角也为唐代山水画的鉴别提供依据。东壁的乐舞图，是目前首次考古发现的双乐队、双人合舞形式，体现了中西文化交流的生动场景。

唐韩休墓三维影像图（左北右南）

北壁东侧山水图

东壁乐舞图

陶鸭

墓室西壁树下高士图

侍女俑　　骑马俑　　石门正视图　　甬道东壁侍女图

In March 2014, a joint team consisting of archaeologists from Shaanxi Provincial Institute of Archaeology and other organizations carried out salvage excavations in a tomb of Tang Dynasty. The tomb, painted with murals, is located in the South of Guozhuang Village, Chang'an District. It is a single-chambered brick tomb with a long sloping tomb tunnel. This tomb consists of a tomb tunnel, a segmented arched passage, shafts, a gate sealed with bricks, a stone gate, a path, a coffin chamber, a coffin platform, etc. As many as 186 pieces (sets) of funerary objects have been unearthed, including pottery figurines, porcelain, ironware, a set of stone door planks and two steles carved with an epitaph. According to the epitaph, the occupant is Han Xiu, who was the Prime Minister of Tang Dynasty. After excavations, now there is a clear understanding of the construction sequence as well as construction methods of this tomb. Besides, the greatest archaeological achievement that has been made this time is bringing to light the murals painted in the tomb. Detaching and relocating these murals with protective measures and three-dimensional laser scanning is an attempt of combining traditional means and scientific methods.

# 河北平山县王母村唐代崔氏墓

◎ 韩金秋

王母墓地位于河北省石家庄市平山县平山镇王母村西约300米，东南距平山县治约4千米。

此墓为圆形竖穴土坑砖室墓。由墓道、墓门、甬道、墓室等四部分组成。墓内已被盗扰。

墓内除装饰仿木构件外，还饰有彩绘。墓壁上通体抹一层白灰，墓室前壁上绘有两幅侍女备茶和备食壁画。墓室内顶涂为青色，绘有白色星辰。

椁室在墓室的北部中间，下为须弥座，上有房形建筑。须弥座北紧贴墓室北壁，略向外弧。房形建筑平面为横长方形，内顶为叠涩顶。立颊两侧有斜面翼墙与墓壁衔接，翼墙上绘有人物。内壁涂有白灰，东、西壁各绘有一幅植物图，画面内容相同，竖式构图。北壁上绘一幅水墨山水画，横式构图，内容为秋天的山水景色，为一水夹两岸式构图。椁室内没有发现葬具。须弥座上置人骨一具，仅头骨较为完整，其他部分均已腐朽破碎。葬式为头西脚东。

随葬品集中置于须弥座上。出土瓷器有细白瓷碗1件、瓷碾1套、三足炉1件。另在墓室中出土8片碎小的瓷片。除瓷器外，还出土有铁器38件、漆器1件、铜钱86枚及墓志一盒。墓志分志盖和志石两部分，青石质。志盖为盝顶，顶面阴刻"太原郡霍氏夫人墓铭"。

墓主下葬于唐哀帝天祐元年（904年）。王母唐墓是我国晚唐中小型壁画墓的重要发现，树立了晚唐时期壁画墓的标尺，虽经盗扰，但具有重要的考古、历史、艺术价值，主要体现在以下几个方面：

1. 王母唐墓中的山水画是目前我国发现的年代最早的一幅通屏水墨山水画。王母唐墓山水画继承了以前山水画的主要风格和范式，是水墨山水画趋于成熟、开始成为一种独立绘画门类的标志，填补了唐、五代、北宋时期山水画发展序列的缺环，树立了中国早期山水画的标尺。

2. 王母唐墓中的房形椁室，前所未见。其与北朝隋唐时期中国北方地区常见的房形石椁差别很大，其应仿制了当时流行的单层四方塔造型。

3. 墓葬中壁画的题材丰富，一些题材如灯擎、备茶图等，可视为五代、辽、宋墓葬壁画的源头，具有承上启下的意义，更新了我们对墓葬艺术发展的认识。

棺床、房形椁及椁内山水壁画（南—北）

墓葬结构及壁画

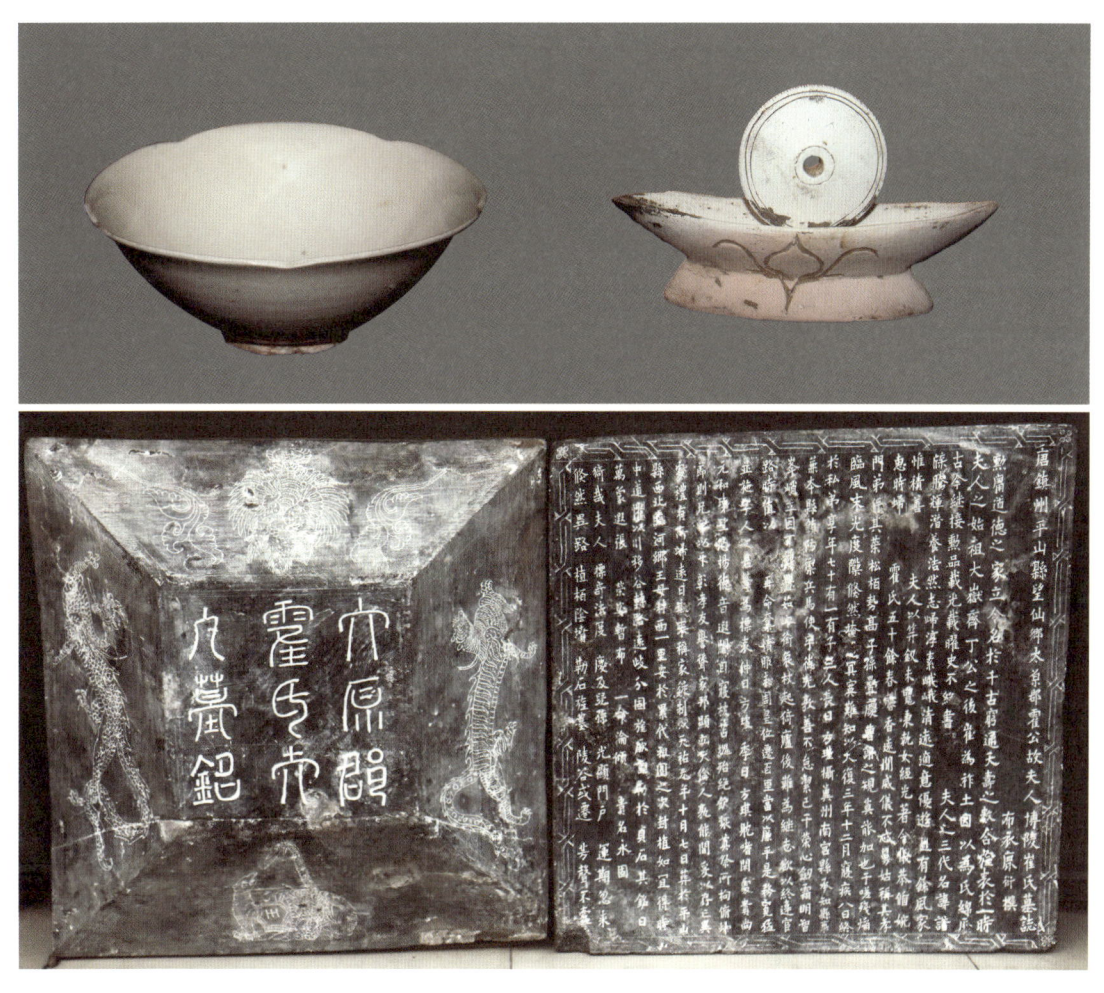

出土遗物

Wangmu Tomb is in the west of Wangmu Village, Pingshan Town, Pingshan County, Shijiazhuang City, Hebei Province. From May to December in 2016, archaeologists from Hebei Provincial Institute of Cultural Relics and Pingshan County Heritage Conservation Management Bureau carried out salvage excavations in the tomb. Wangmu Tomb, painted with murals and built with a stepped tomb tunnel, is a rectangular brick-chambered tomb. Although it had been harassed, funerary objects like porcelain and the epitaph were unearthed. The coffin chamber of the tomb is structured in a particular way that has never been seen before. Murals painted in the chamber vary in themes and they become a knot connecting the preceding and the following. As a benchmark of early Chinese landscape paintings, those depicting landscape have filled in the blank of the development sequence of landscape paintings in Tang Dynasty, Five Dynasties and Northern Song. According to the epitaph, the tomb's occupant was buried in 904 A.D. The excavation of Wangmu Tomb, which is of exemplary significance for mural tombs of late Tang Dynasty, is an important archaeological discovery of small and medium-sized mural tombs dating back to late Tang Dynasty.

# 河北曲阳县田庄大墓

◎张春长

田庄大墓位于河北省曲阳县南15千米。该墓倚山面水，坐北朝南，为一座带长斜坡墓道的大型砖室墓。墓葬分为地上、地下两部分，地上部分由墓上封土和墓前神道组成。地下部分以墓道、仪门、庭院、甬道、前室、后甬道、后室为中轴，左右分列10个侧室及2个大型龛。

墓葬南部地面有神道。神道两侧有四组石刻，自南向北依次为石柱、石虎、石羊、石人。东侧石羊坑北侧出土残碑榫1件，应为神道碑部件。神道北侧、墓道北段的东、西两侧各有"凸"字形坑一座。两座坑形状一致，左右对称，或为角阙基址。另外在神道南缘西侧发现长方形白灰碴堆积，可能为墓园西南角的标记。

墓道北端东西两侧相向伸出一段翼墙，墙体端面各竖立一砖柱，象征一道仪门，可能即为文献所言"乌头绰楔"，为考古发掘中首次发现。墓道北接庭院。庭院平面呈东西向长方形，底面平整。庭院东、西两侧砖墙上有券门通往东、西两侧室。庭院北侧有砖砌漫道连接墓门，田庄大墓的券门上方有仿木结构的门楼，门楼耸立于地表，背靠墓葬封土，是一座最为仿真的雕砖门楼。

后室内置石椁。石椁规模宏大，由棺形石椁和须弥座组成。侧室墓室平面为近圆形，穹隆形顶，墓壁多有仿木结构的砖雕，柱枋间有艳丽的彩绘，顶部绘有星宿图。

田庄大墓虽然经过多次盗扰，但仍出土了一批重要文物，其中以汉白玉造像和陶瓷制品尤为重要。另外墓葬中还出土有各种金、铜、铁、玉石等制品，其中的鎏金铜门钉、鎏金铜锁、鎏金蝴蝶合页、鎏金开元通宝以及滑石浮雕带饰等皆为不可多得的珍贵文物。

田庄墓葬的墓室为同期墓葬中结构最复杂、规模最大的砖筑墓室。墓葬结构及出土文物具有丰富的民族、地域和宗教信息。安史之乱后的河北，藩镇雄据，北方文化与河北地域文化、中原唐文化在此地相互影响、交融，发展成为一种新兴文化，田庄大墓正是这一历史背景的产物。另外田庄大墓按一定的规制和比例以墓砖为材构筑仿木结构，可能存在模数制度，从而为研究古代建筑模数制度的起源添加了珍贵的资料。

唐风宋韵　气象万千　635

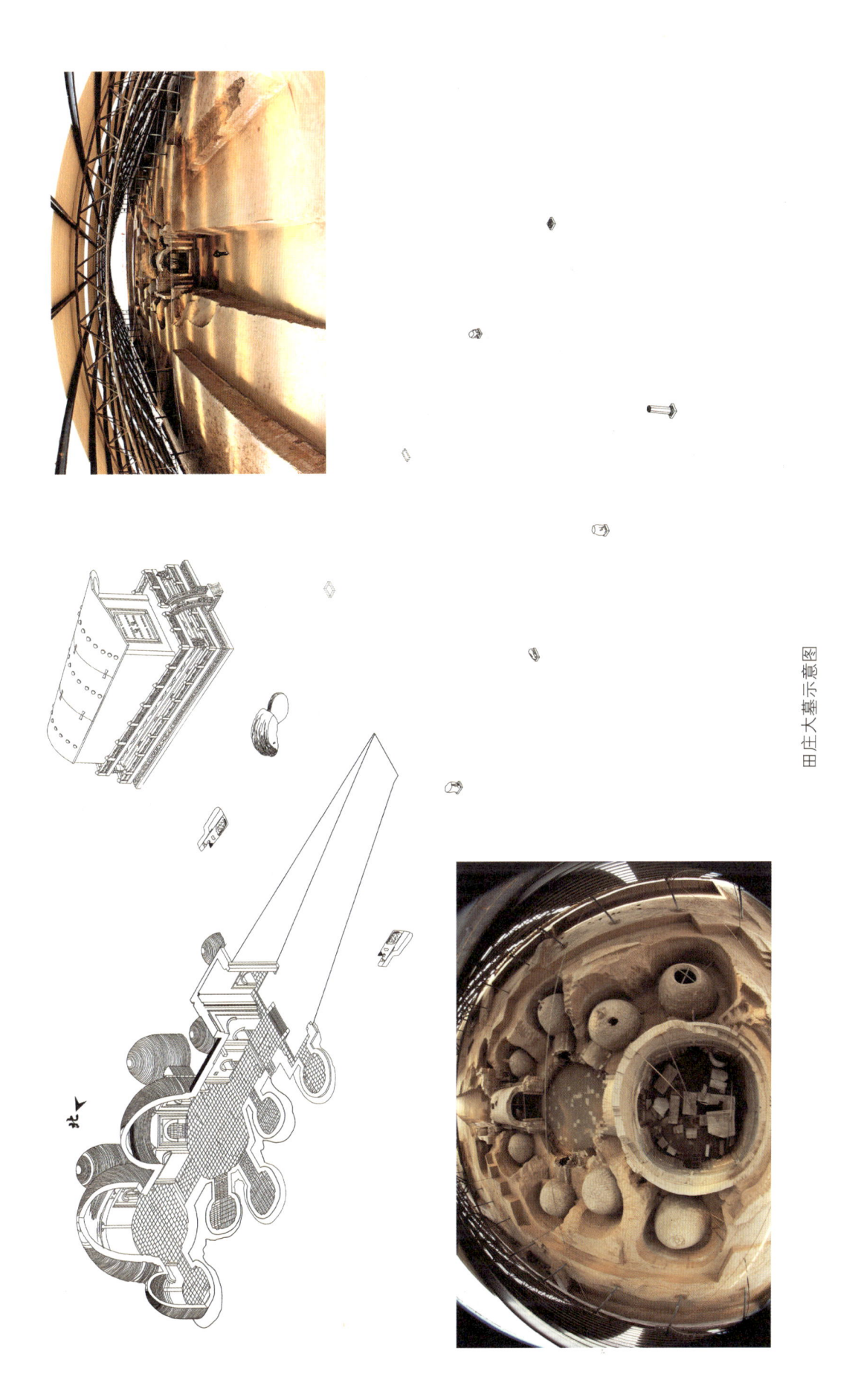

田庄大墓示意图

墓道壁画

抬棺力士

棺床壸门

石武官

棺床前圈桥子

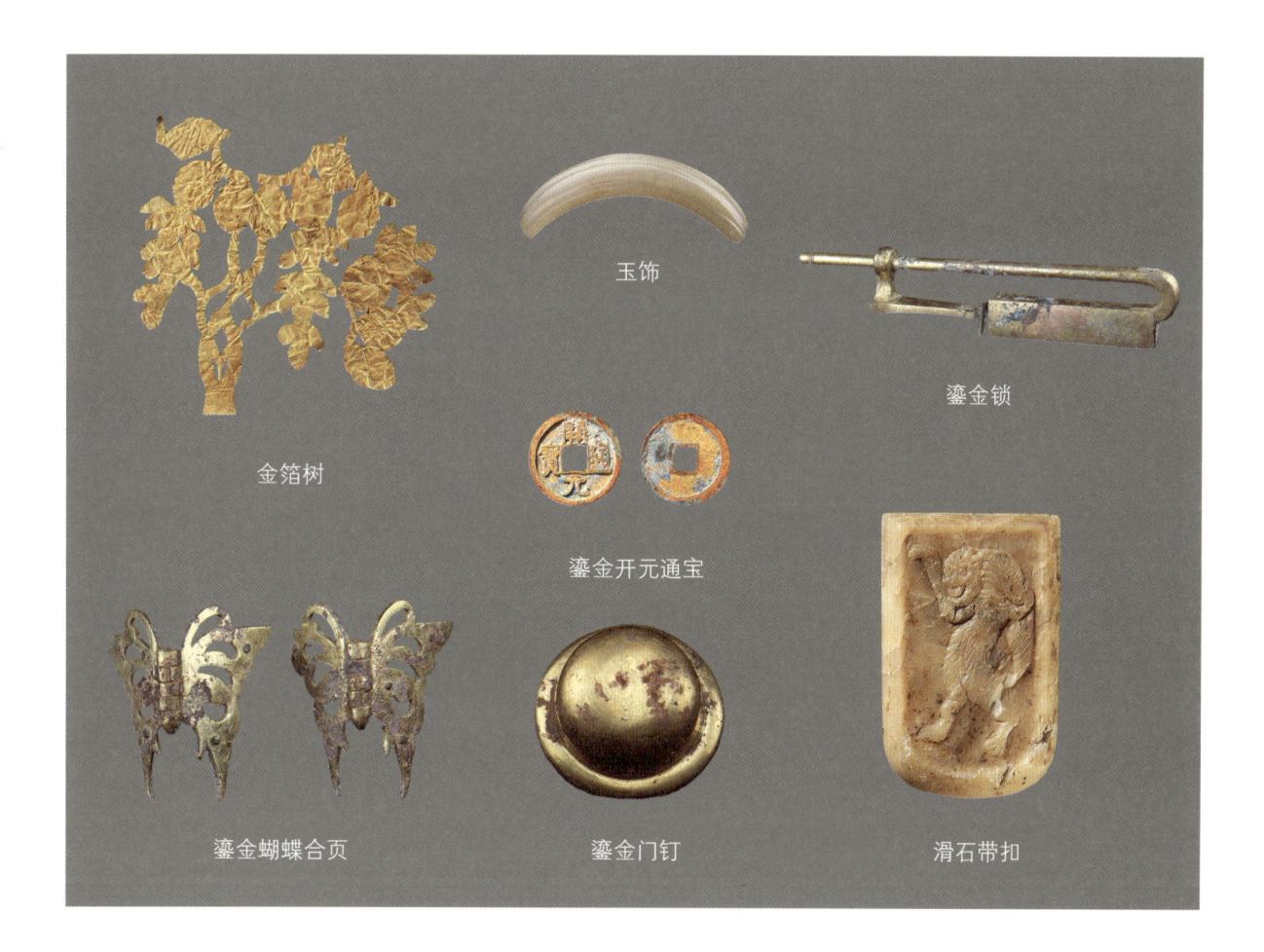

金箔树　　玉饰　　鎏金锁　　鎏金开元通宝　　鎏金蝴蝶合页　　鎏金门钉　　滑石带扣

Tianzhuang Tomb is 15 kilometers south of Quyang County, Hebei Province. From 2011 to 2013, archaeologists from Hebei Provincial Institute of Cultural Relics carried out excavations in it. As a large brick-chambered tomb built with a long sloping tomb tunnel, Tianzhuang Tomb consists of two parts, the above-ground part and the underground part. The above-ground part is made up of rammed earth piled on the coffin chamber and a spirit road leading to the tomb. The tomb tunnel, a secondary gate, a courtyard, a path, a front chamber, a backyard path and a rear chamber lined up underground, forming an axis on whose left and right sides there were 10 side chambers and 2 large niches. Although the tomb had been raided many times, a series of important relics, represented by white marble statues and ceramics, were unearthed during excavation. The structure of Tianzhuang Tomb and unearthed antiquities reflect abundant ethnic, regional and religious information. It has been inferred that the tomb dates back to the time of Tang Dynasty and Five Dynasties.

# 江苏南京市西天寺墓园宋墓

◎ 王　宏

2015年3月27日，在"南京市红十字会捐献遗体志愿者纪念林"项目施工过程中发现一座古代墓葬。南京市考古研究所随后派人进行现场勘查，并于2015年5月20日进场进行考古发掘。

该墓为仿木结构雕砖壁画墓，由墓室土圹、墓道、墓门、封门砖、墓室构成。墓道朝东，为斜坡墓道。墓门为仿木建筑结构。墓前壁砖墙分内、外两层，用青砖错缝砌筑。墓室券顶，券顶分内、外两层，券顶外部南北两侧紧贴券顶砌筑多层平砖予以加固。券顶内侧顶部有四个如秤钩状的铁钩，呈方形排列，间距约15厘米，分别挂有残断的铁环，原应为悬挂铜镜。内券顶与棺床及地面间砌筑仿木构建筑且饰有雕砖壁画。

棺床位于墓室西部，其中部有一金井，呈正方形。棺床前部偏北有一砖砌祭台，平面呈长方形，用青砖砌成。根据棺床上破损的棺木可以判断，棺床上原应放置两棺，随葬品集中置于棺床上，棺床上及棺床前各有一志石，字迹基本无存。悬挂在墓顶的铜镜落在棺床的一角，铜镜上铸有一圈墓铭"绍兴岁次乙亥壬午月甲寅日雁门郡开国侯御前中军统制高翊卫宅建亡妻恭人朱氏墓铭"。

墓铭载铸镜时间为南宋绍兴二十五年（1155年），墓主人为当时驻扎在建康府的御前中军的高姓统制官，具体姓名不可考。该墓形制结构独特，与南京发现的同时代的建中宋墓、清修秦熺夫妇墓截然不同，却与北方宋金时期的壁画墓类似，且墓顶悬镜的葬俗也多见于北方，尤其常见于辽宁、陕西、山西北部的辽金时期墓葬中。墓主所封开国侯的郡号为"雁门郡"，而雁门郡就位于今山西北部。综合各方面的因素，推测墓主人来自北方，籍贯或是在今山西北部一带。北宋靖康年间，金军南下攻破宋都东京汴梁，各地军马派兵进京勤王，后来这些军队随着政治中心的南迁而南下。南京在南宋时是建康府，曾是皇帝行都所在，军事地位极其重要，驻扎有大量的军队。西天寺宋墓这类具有北方因素的墓葬在南京的发现，应该就是这些南迁北人的传统丧葬习俗的反映和体现。

唐风宋韵　气象万千

墓葬全景（东—西）

墓门（东—西）

墓室南壁

墓室全景（东—西）

砖雕墓门

墓室北壁

金井与五色五方石

祭台

铜镜（背面—拓片—正面）

葵瓣纹铜镜　玛瑙饰件

水晶饰件　盾形铜镜

玉带饰　金环　水晶璧

瓷粉盒　瓷罐

剔犀漆盒

穿心盒

A tomb of Song Dynasty, sited in Xitian Temple Cemetery in Nanjing, was excavated in May, 2015. Imitating the structure of a wooden architecture, this is a mural tomb constructed with carved bricks and with a sloping tomb tunnel. More than 30 pieces of antiquities have been unearthed and they are made of gold, silver, jade, bronze, iron, tin, lacquer, crystal and stone. According to the epitaph engraved on the surface of a bronze mirror that was cast in 1155 A.D., the tomb occupants were Gao, who was a commander-general leading the major force of the imperial army stationed in Jiankang Prefecture, and his wife. This tomb, constructed in a particular structure that is different from its contemporaries that have been discovered in Nanjing, shows traditional burial customs brought along by people who had migrated from the North to the South. Excavations carried out in this tomb have brought to light precious remains and relics for the study of the composition of residents living in Nanjing during the transitional period from Northern Song to Southern Song as well as cultural diffusion and exchanges between the North and the South. The tomb per se is well worth further exploring.

# 安徽南陵县铁拐宋墓

◎张　辉

铁拐宋墓位于安徽省南陵县弋江镇奚滩村铁拐桥西约300米处的耕地之中，由两座古墓葬组成。两座墓葬相距约2米，均为竖穴土坑灌浆双棺墓，无墓道。灌浆由糯米浆、石灰、石子混合而成三合土。墓圹已遭破坏，暴露出三合土包浆层及外棺顶部。

M1的三合土包浆层长约4.80米，宽2.50米，残高1.70米。二重木棺，保存基本完整，木棺结构相同。重棺内外均髹朱漆，外棺朱漆已剥落。内棺靠近外棺尾部居中放置，内棺尾端设有托板。

M2为异穴合葬，西侧为M2A，东侧为M2B，二者以熟土墙间隔，相距约0.50米。三合土包浆层长约4米，宽3.70米，残高1.70米，顶部各有一处盗洞。M2A、M2B均为重棺，因遭早年盗掘损毁严重，棺木上半部已不存，残存结构基本与M1相同，只是M2B外棺前部加载横板设置头厢。

虽然此次发掘的两处墓葬规模不大，但出土遗物较为丰富，类型多样，制作精美，达200余件（套）：（1）金属类，有金银器、锡器、铁器、铜器，有金簪、银勺、银筷、首饰、配饰、锡钵、锡杯、锡碗、锡碟、铜钱、铜、对蝶、铜镜、铁剪、铁针等；（2）陶瓷类，有酱釉梅瓶、银扣茶盏、青白釉执壶等；（3）竹木类，有房屋模型、床榻及床架、衣架、家具、果实、木尺和伎乐木俑、仆从木俑、生肖木俑等；（4）纺织类，有棉织物、丝织物等及纸质类文物等。另有葬具类：灌浆保护层、墓砖、木棺及附属物等。并从发掘区附近采集到墓志铭（碑）4块。

从地层关系、墓葬形制、埋葬方式、随葬器物及相邻间距等方面综合分析，初步推断铁拐宋墓的年代应为北宋晚期，此处应为一处家族墓地，时间跨度不长。墓葬的建造方法应是采取先挖竖穴，整平后，底面刷浆加固，堆入石灰层以防潮，加铺青砖，安置外棺及内棺再自四周及顶部覆盖隔层后，随之灌入糯米浆、小石子、石灰三合土保护，最后封土成型的。

另外，如此众多的纺织物、完整的木俑及房屋、家具组合等随葬品在安徽尚是首次发现，填补了安徽宋元考古工作中的空白，反映了宋代本区域与其他区域的文化交流关系，为研究宋代社会结构、经济发展以及埋葬制度、民间风俗等提供了重要的实物资料。

唐风宋韵 气象万千 643

M1出土奉侍女俑组合

M1出土伎乐女俑组合

房模及内设桌椅组合

椅承组合

床榻架组合

M1出土女工组合

M1出土梅瓶　　M1出土锡台盏　　M1内棺盖顶贴画　　M1出土生肖狗俑

褶子（M1） 下衣（M1）

上衣（M1） 执壶（M1）

瓷碗（M1） 青瓷碗（M2） 青瓷盏（M2）

Tieguai Tombs, consisting of two tombs dating from Song Dynasty, are located in the farmland about 300 meters west of Tieguai Bridge, Xitan Village, Yijiang Town, Nanling County, Anhui Province. From June to the end of September in 2014, excavations were carried out here. Both tombs are grouted shaft tombs buried with two coffins. As many as 200 pieces (sets) of relics, which are of a wide range, have been unearthed, including gold and silver vessels, tinware, ironware, bronzes, porcelain, bamboo products and fabrics. Taking into account their stratal positions, structures, burial fashions, funerary objects, distance between each other and other issues, a comprehensive analysis of both tombs has been done. Building techniques applied in the construction of Tieguai Tombs have been found out. It has been preliminarily inferred that Tieguai Tombs, dating from late Northern Song, were sited in a family cemetery. Besides, relics like bamboo products and fabrics are of great significance since they have filled in the blank in archaeological discoveries of Song and Yuan dynasties in Anhui Province.

# 山西昔阳县宋金墓葬考古发掘

◎刘 岩 史永红

2013年5月到11月，昔阳县先后在松溪路、中医院旧址和澳垴山一带发现了7座宋金时期仿木构砖室墓葬。山西省考古研究所、昔阳县文物管理所和昔阳县博物馆联合对这些墓葬进行了发掘，并对其中的三座进行了异地搬迁保护。

松溪路扩宽工程中共发现了2座墓葬，均坐北朝南。1号墓为平面呈八边形的仿木构单室砖墓，整个墓室营造出前厅后室、东西院落的墓葬空间。该墓共埋葬3位墓主人，当为一夫二妻。该墓出土了一套陶器茶具，形象地展示了宋金时期的饮茶器具组合。

2号墓结构形制与1号类同，但墓室高大，设单棺床，墓内有精美的彩绘和壁画。其东北壁绘男女墓主人对坐图，其身后各有男女侍从。西北壁绘杂剧人物似正在做场。2号墓埋葬两位墓主人，当为夫妇合葬墓。

昔阳县中医院旧址在工程建设过程中勘探出4座墓葬。1号和4号墓为六边形单室砖墓，墓壁用白灰粉刷，无装饰。在狭小的墓室内合葬三至四人，仅随葬少量粗瓷碗、钵等。2号墓为八边形仿木构砖雕壁画单室墓，该墓埋葬2人，当为夫妇合葬。随葬陶、瓷、铜、骨等器物12件。3号墓为八边形仿木构砖雕壁画墓。墓壁上绘主人夫妇对坐图、庖厨图、放牧图等。东南壁下方绘有粮仓、石磨盘、石臼、公鸡和鸡笼等。该墓出土了木制供桌和木质买地券，上书"十七年岁次丁酉……大金国……"等字样。

澳垴山一带在修路取土时发现了一座保存完好的宋金砖墓。该墓为平面八边形仿木构砖雕壁画带耳室砖墓，坐北朝南。墓内共有6具骨架。该墓东北壁上绘出三对墓主人夫妇对坐图。结合墓内放置骨架数量和组合关系，推测该壁画就是反映三对墓主人生前生活的景象。此外，墓内还绘有蒸包子内容的庖厨图、放牧图、井、辘轳、石磨盘及杂剧、鼓乐图等。

鉴于松溪路1、2号墓和澳垴山宋金墓形制结构特殊，且壁画繁密精美，我们对其分别进行了拆迁异地复原和整体搬迁异地保护。

松溪路M1拆解过程　　　　　　　　　　　　　澳垴山公园墓葬整体加固

昔阳县中医院3号墓壁画

松溪路2号墓壁画　　　　　　　　　　　　　松溪路2号墓东北壁墓夫妇对坐图

夫妇对坐图（澳垴山宋金墓东北壁）

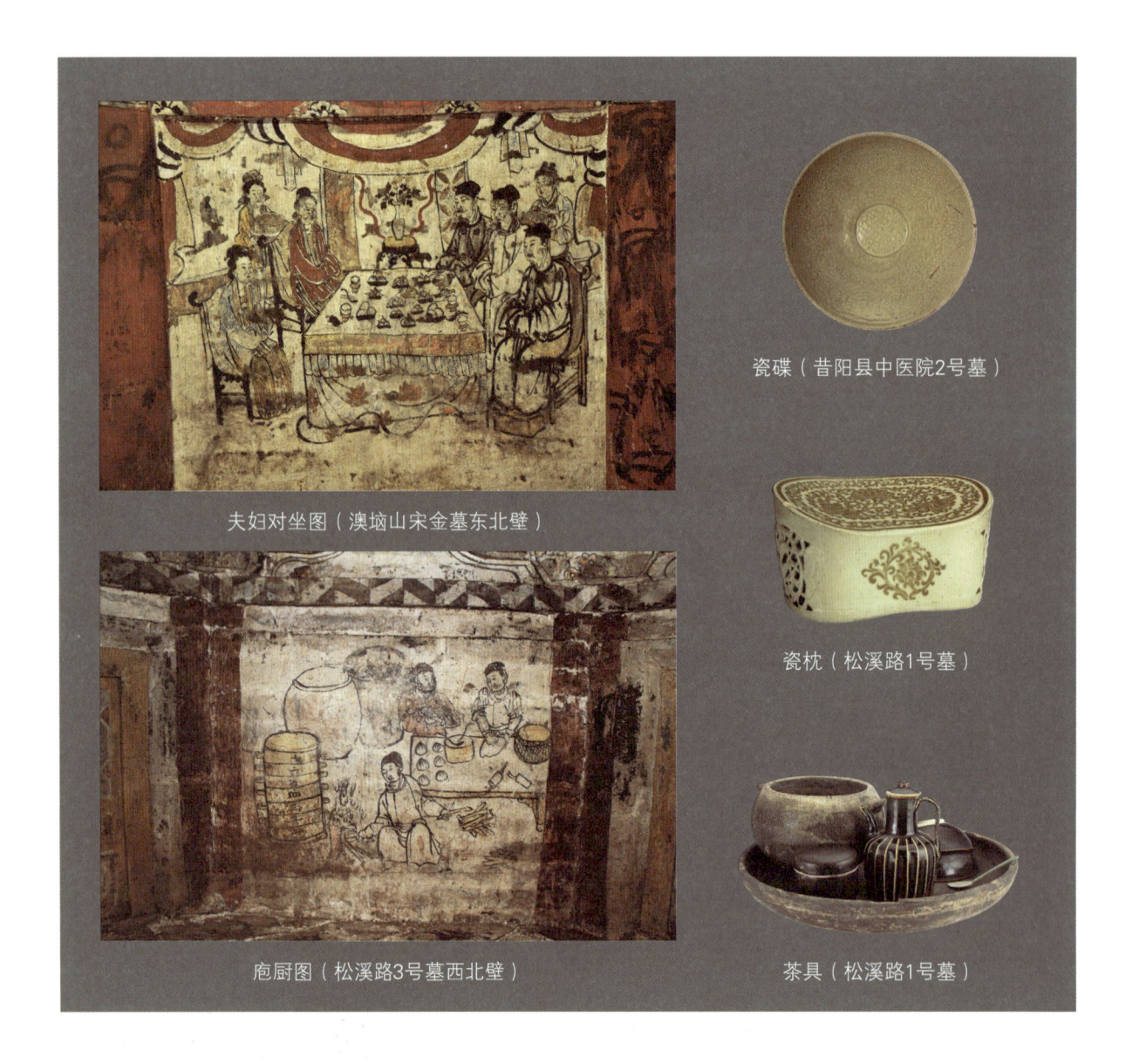

庖厨图（松溪路3号墓西北壁）

瓷碟（昔阳县中医院2号墓）

瓷枕（松溪路1号墓）

茶具（松溪路1号墓）

From May to November in 2013, seven brick-chambered tombs of Song and Jin dynasties, whose structure imitated that of a wooden building, were discovered in the area stretching from Songxi Road, former site of Chinese Medicine Hospital and Aonao Mountain, in Xiyang County. A joint team, consisting of archaeologists from Shanxi Provincial Institute of Archaeology, Xiyang Cultural Relics Management Bureau and Xiyang Museum, carried out scientific excavations in these tombs. A great number of murals painted in the tombs were revealed. Unearthed objects included potteries, porcelain, bronzes, bone implements, wooden furniture, title deeds. Among the seven tombs, three were relocated for protection since they were structured in a particular way and decorated with numerous exquisite murals.

# 山西长治县沙峪村宋至明清古墓群

◎ 杨林中

沙峪墓群位于山西省长治县县城东南约6千米处，西距沙峪村约800米。此次发掘面积共3300平方米，发掘古代遗迹38处，包括墓葬36座、水井1口、灰坑1个。宋代墓葬9座，坐北向南，除M1为正方形砖室墓以外，其余皆为长方形竖穴土洞墓。明代墓16座，坐西向东，除M3为长方形竖穴土洞以外，其余为斜坡墓道长方形砖室墓，墓室均为长方形、直壁、拱券顶，有井字形铺底砖，除墓门壁外，其余三壁设有暗耳室，墓顶绘有星宿图案。清代墓葬11座，东南朝向，均为长方形斜坡墓道土洞墓。水井为圆筒形竖井，井壁光滑，且有对称的脚窝，时代不详。灰坑的平面形状呈不规则形，出土遗物有明、清时期碎瓷片，砖、瓦碎片，时代应为明清。

M1为宋代仿木结构砖室墓，由墓道、甬道、墓门、墓室组成，平面呈"甲"字形。墓室、墓道采用条砖砌筑。墓道位于墓室的南部，竖穴墓道，底近平。墓门呈拱形，以条砖封门。墓室平面呈长方形，三面砌筑棺床。顶部结构为穹隆顶。该墓墓室浸满淤土，没有被盗扰的痕迹。

墓底骨架凌乱，腐朽严重，仅剩一些较大的头骨和肢体骨，可以清楚地辨认出为两具骨架。随葬品有2件，铜簪和瓷碗各1件。

M4为明代长方形斜坡台阶墓道砖室墓，方向250°，由墓道、墓门、墓室组成。墓室保存完整，置两棺，为夫妇合葬墓。人骨头向西，面向上，葬式仰身直肢。出土器物99件，琉璃器有俑、房、罐、灶、碾、猫、衣架、箱柜、衣柜、楼、盆架、盆、缸、鸡、磨、马、井台、香炉、灯台、壶、桌子、盘、杯、椅、帽及轿等，另有砂盆、瓷灯盏、铜镜、铜钱、瓷罐、铁牛、陶盒及陶罐等。

M11为清代长方形竖穴墓道土洞墓，墓道位于墓室东南部，平面形状呈梯形，墓底呈不规则形。墓室保存完整，置三棺。三副骨架，头向东北，面向上，葬式仰身直肢。出土的器物有铜簪、铜烟袋、银耳环、青花瓷碗、玻璃扣、铜扣、玉扳指、瓷灯盏、铜钱、瓷罐。

此次发掘所获取的墓葬形制结构、随葬品以及随葬品的制作工艺等综合信息，为研究该地区宋、明、清时期的生产力发展水平、生活方式等提供了宝贵的实物资料。

工地全景（由东向西）

M1南壁（由北向南）　　M4墓门封门石（由东向西）　M4墓门（由东向西）

M1西壁（由东向西）　　M1北壁（由南向北）　　M1东壁（由西向东）

唐风宋韵　气象万千　651

琉璃俑　　　　　　　　　　　　　琉璃房子

东壁（由西向东）　　　　　　　　南壁（由北向南）

西壁（由东向西）　　　　　　　　北壁上部（由南向北）

M4 壁画与遗物

琉璃家具（M4）

琉璃马（M4）　　　琉璃灶台及厨具（M4）　　　琉璃碾子（M4）

玉器（M7）　　　玉器（M11）　　　青花瓷碗（M11）

From October in 2010 to December in 2012, archaeologists from Shanxi Provincial Institute of Archaeology carried out excavations in Shayu Cemetery. Thirty-eight remains were excavated. Among the thirty-six excavated tombs, nine are of Song Dynasty, sixteen are of Ming Dynasty and eleven date back to Qing Dynasty. A wide range of relics were unearthed, including a large number of potteries, bronzes, porcelain, glazed ware and silverware. Excavations carried out this time have provided valuable materials for the study of productivity development, lifestyle and other issues during Song, Ming and Qing dynasties in Shangdang district.

# 山西汾西县郝家沟金代纪年壁画墓

◎ 武俊华

2015年8月，山西省考古研究所对一座金代壁画墓进行了抢救性发掘。此墓位于山西省汾西县永安镇郝家沟村北的山梁上，墓顶北部被施工破坏，墓室内已被扰乱，墓室壁画保存较为完整。

该墓是一座仿木构八角形单室砖室墓，由墓道、墓门、甬道、墓室组成，方向208°，墓道与墓室不在同一轴线，墓室略偏西。墓室系土圹内砌筑砖室，平面呈八边形，八角叠涩顶，顶部正中砌藻井，方砖铺地。棺床靠北铺设，与墓室等宽。

墓室内壁皆以白灰水刷大白，采用砖雕和彩绘相结合的装饰手法。砖雕用以表现仿木构建筑的门窗、铺作、檐枋、柱头、藻井等，其上兼施木作彩画，阑额、倚柱等则以影作彩绘方式表现。

除南壁开墓门外，北壁饰砖雕彩绘格子门，东南、西南壁饰砖雕彩绘花窗，东北壁、西北壁分别绘男、女主人宴饮图，东壁、西壁则绘妇人启门图。

墓室内葬具及人骨均已遭严重扰乱，保存极差，仅在东北壁下残存南北向棺木一具。葬式、性别、头向、面向等皆不能确定。因发掘前已被扰乱，仅出土白瓷盘、铜钗各1件。此外，发掘前在棺床靠北壁处采集砖质买地券1件，朱砂书写，字体潦草，录文如下：

维南赡部洲□□国□□平阳□」汾西县赵村保郝家庄郝□□」买到地捌分佳作□□□千□□□」九十文其身交付足东至青龙南至」朱雀西至白虎北至玄武上至苍天」下至黄泉其地四至分□故立文字」为据」大定廿二年后十一月十二□□□书□□□」□□□。由券文"大定廿二年后十一月"（1182年）字样确定墓葬年代。

墓主葬于金大定二十二年（1182年），该墓是临汾北部山区首次发现的金代纪年壁画墓，为金墓断代研究又提供了一座标尺型墓葬。此墓以砖雕、彩绘相结合的装饰手法构筑墓室，为了解北宋《营造法式》木构建筑彩画作制度在金中期的实践提供了对比材料。此外，墓中这种男、女主人不在同一画壁的夫妇对坐图较为特殊，在目前已发现的宋金时期墓葬中也极为少见。从绘画的角度看，墓壁上可见多处较为明显的起稿线痕迹，画中人物的比例也十分准确。最后，东、西两壁所绘妇人启门图及东壁妇人手持果盘的形象，为进一步探讨"妇人启门"题材的内涵提供了新线索。

654 黄淮七省考古新发现

墓室俯视图

墓室局部（由北向南）

墓室内顶彩绘

西壁仿木构彩绘

北壁补间铺作彩绘

唐风宋韵　气象万千　655

墓室局部（由南向北） 　　　　　　　　北壁格子门

西北壁壁画局部 　　　　　　　　东北壁壁画局部

西壁假门 　　　　　　　　东壁假门

白瓷盘

铜钗

买地券

In August 2015, archaeologists from Shanxi Provincial Institute of Archaeology conducted salvage excavations in a mural tomb of Jin Dynasty. The tomb is a octagonal single-chambered brick one, whose structure imitated that of a wooden building. Only a white porcelain plate, a bronze hairpin and a title deed made of brick were unearthed since the tomb had been harassed before excavation. According to the title deed, the tomb occupant was buried in the 22nd year of Dading Era of Jin Dynasty (1182 A.D.). As the first chronicled mural tomb of Jin Dynasty that has been discovered in northern mountainous area of Linfen City, this tomb is of great value for archaeological study of tombs constructed in Jin Dynasty.

# 河南荥阳市明代周懿王墓

◎ 孙 凯

2016年7月至12月，河南省文物考古研究院对荥阳市贾峪镇鲁庄墓地进行考古发掘时，发现了明代周懿王墓，该墓由主墓、祔葬墓和寝园建筑等多部分组成，其中主墓即周懿王及其王妃王氏的合葬墓。该墓是目前国内首次通过正式考古发掘的明代亲王级别的壁画墓。

寝园坐北朝南，由于早期被破坏，寝园建筑保存不佳，目前仅见享殿建筑基址，推测其形制应是面阔五间以绿色琉璃瓦覆顶的单檐歇山式建筑。东配殿仅见倒塌遗迹，推测配殿可能是以灰瓦覆顶的琉璃剪边式建筑。

从发掘情况来看，部分寝园建筑很可能是被大火焚毁的，可能与明末农民起义军在荥阳的活动有关。

享殿后端为周懿王墓，该墓坐北朝南，由长斜坡墓道和砖券墓室组成。墓道方向175°。墓室建于土圹之中，单室玄宫，墓室前部有琉璃瓦覆顶的单檐仿木门楼，门楼两侧为土坯垒砌的随门墙。

封门墙底部正中有方形砖龛，竖置汉白玉墓志一盒。根据志文得知，墓主为明代周懿王。值得一提的是，周懿王的墓志竟是用王妃的墓志改刻而成。虽然墓葬遭到盗掘，但墓室底部仍发现少量铜质明器，如炉、镜、火盆、剪、盘、熨斗、火箸等，墓室东南角发现铅质缸形"长明灯"一口。

墓内发现大量棺椁残片，内棺外壁以红漆髹饰，并沥金粉。内壁贴有织物，经鉴定为素绢。墓室地面北部有东西并列的青砖棺床，东侧应属周懿王，西侧属王妃王氏。

墓室内壁布满彩色壁画，其中顶部和北壁保存较好，画面整体表现的应该是西方极乐世界庄严圣境，与《佛说阿弥陀经》的记载比较相似。周懿王墓壁画整体具有写意特征，应是民间画匠所绘。

祔葬墓分列于主墓东西两侧，南北向排列。东侧祔葬墓共8座，西侧发现的祔葬墓包括1座砖券墓室和5座（部分位于厂房下）竖穴土坑墓，皆坐西向东。砖券墓室位于最北端，东部有长斜坡墓道，封门墙上端出土描金墓志一盒，墓主是周懿王夫人王氏。

周懿王墓的发掘表明，该墓园中祔葬墓排列在主墓前方的左右两侧，且两侧是相向而对。周懿王祔葬墓的排列方法系国内首见，至少目前为研究明代王墓制度提供了一个全新的材料。

墓葬布局（上为北）

唐风宋韵　气象万千　659

周懿王墓及部分祔葬墓出土遗物

明代周懿王墓

Mausoleum of Feoffee Yi who was granted with Zhou Feoffment in Ming Dynasty is located in Luzhuang Village, Jiayu Town, Xingyang City, Henan Province. It was excavated from July to December in 2016. The mausoleum consists of a main tomb, auxiliary burial pits and architectures in the yard, etc. The main tomb, a sing-chambered one, is a joint burial tomb of Feoffee Yi and his wife whose family name was Wang. Inside the tomb, large patches of relatively well-preserved colored murals depicting the solemn and holy land of the Western Paradise, have been found on the walls. Discovery of the Mausoleum of Feoffee Yi has provided brand new materials for the study of feoffees' mausoleums of Ming Dynasty, religious beliefs and other issues.

# 百卉千葩　巧艺夺天工

## 河北邢窑历次考古工作、收获与特点

◎ 王会民

邢窑是我国古代著名的制瓷窑口，自北朝后期登上历史舞台，历经隋、唐、五代、宋、金、元多个历史时期，前后延续了7个多世纪。

考古发现证明，邢窑制瓷遗存分布广阔，窑场众多。20世纪80年代于河北省临城县境首次发现邢窑遗址，之后又陆续在河北省内丘县、邢台县、邢台市和高邑县发现。1987—2011年，经考古调查、发掘，核定邢窑遗址31处，分布范围北起石家庄高邑县北焦，西南到邢台县西坚固，东至内丘县北光，南北长超过70千米，东西宽超过10千米。到2014年结束，考古工作先后共进行了8次，总发掘面积超过3000平方米。

初兴时期的邢窑产品一般胎体厚重，胎色多呈灰或灰白，不施化妆土，流釉、积釉、开片现象普遍。隋代以青瓷为主流产品，同时生产较多的细瓷产品和化妆土白瓷产品。唐代是邢窑的鼎盛时期，表现在窑场数量、瓷器产量的增加，化妆土的普遍使用，窑具和组合窑具的大量使用，以及产品质量的整体提升等方面。五代是邢窑走下坡路的阶段，此时邢窑的窑场和产品明显减少，白瓷釉面多白中泛黄，化妆土仍普遍使用。宋代处于维持时期，与唐代瓷器的圆润不同，棱角、花边、花口等器物占一定比例，并生产贡瓷。金代邢窑瓷器的生产和流通呈现出阶段性繁荣，但精品很少。元代的邢窑走向衰落。

装烧方法的演变过程反映了邢窑制瓷的发展历程。初始阶段，邢窑窑工主要使用筒形窑柱类作为支烧具，同时借鉴了釉陶烧制中的支钉间隔方法，大量使用瓷胎支钉、支具间隔器物。隋代主要使用蘑菇形、喇叭形窑柱和棚架式窑具裸烧器物，配以支钉、支具、垫圈等，并开始使用筒形匣钵装烧器物。唐代瓷器多为裸烧，渐少用窑柱，筒形匣钵多样，有漏斗形、盘形、盒形、碗形等，根据器形大小随意组合，五代依然。北宋及其后的金元时期，继续使用筒形、漏斗形匣钵等，并出现了较多的支圈、支珠、沙堆、泥垫、垫圈、涩圈叠烧等，与以前装烧方法有明显不同。

南北朝时期创烧于北方地区的邢窑，从最初的技艺模仿到掌握成熟的制瓷工艺，从生产不施化妆土的青瓷，至迟到隋代开始批量烧制白瓷，成为早期生产白瓷的代表性窑口，且以其为代表带动了北方诸窑的崛起，同时也为宋以后白瓷和色釉彩瓷的大发展、大繁荣奠定了基础。

盈款碗　　　　　花口盘　　　　　白瓷砚

北朝瓷碗　　　　白瓷碗　　　　　花口钵

隋三彩　　　　　透影白瓷标本　　白瓷莲座

Xing Yao is a well-known porcelain kiln in ancient China. Its site was first discovered in the 1980s in Lincheng County, Hebei Province. From 1987 to 2014, archaeological work were carried out eight times on Xing Yao Site. The total excavated area exceeded 3000 square meters. The existence of 31 kiln sites have been confirmed. After excavations, there has been a better understanding of the history, distribution, product types, porcelain features, firing techniques and other aspects of Xing Yao.

# 河北井陉县隋至清代瓷窑址

◎黄 信 胡 强

井陉窑遗址位于河北省井陉县与井陉矿区，目前共发现窑址12处，其中井陉县11处，井陉矿区1处。12处窑址集中分布于太行山东麓的陉里盆地、天护盆地、天长盆地及绵河、甘陶河、冶河及其支流上。2016年4—6月，河北省文物研究所与井陉县文物保护管理所组成联合考古队对井陉窑12处窑址进行了全面调查与勘探，并取得重要收获。

一、基本搞清了井陉窑瓷窑址的分布范围及每处窑址的烧瓷历史与产品特征。确认现存井陉瓷窑址的分布总面积约102万平方米，烧瓷历史基本可分为四大组：北陉、南陉、北防口、南防口窑址等4处窑址的时代为晚唐五代；井陉窑中心窑场——城关与河东坡窑址的时代为隋、晚唐五代、宋金时期；东窑岭与南秀林窑址的时代为晚唐五代、宋金时期；天护—冯家沟、北横口、南横口窑址的时代为金至民国，其中北横口窑址的时代可早至北宋末。

二、基本搞清了井陉窑窑业的发展历程。1.隋代后期创烧。井陉窑创烧于隋代后期（约600年以后），创烧地点为绵河流域的城关、河东坡窑址，早期产品主要为青釉碗、杯类瓷器，产品质量较差，器类单一。2.初唐至中唐空白期。一直未发现该阶段的遗存。3.晚唐五代高峰期。晚唐五代时期是井陉窑窑业发展的第一个高峰，烧瓷规模扩张，且出现大量高端细瓷器。4.北宋平稳发展期。此时生产规模较小，产品以白釉、黑釉等生活类器物为主，有大量粗胎类器物。5.金代高峰期。金代是井陉窑窑业发展的第二个高峰，烧瓷规模再次扩大，窑业堆积很厚，主要产品仍为白釉生活类器物，黑釉、酱釉等颜色釉瓷器在质量、种类与数量上占很大比例，且制作精美，其中剔花填彩、戳印填彩、刻划花填彩等装饰工艺为井陉窑窑址所独有。6.金代以后逐步衰落。此时窑口减少，天护—冯家沟、北横口、南横口、梅庄4处窑址继续烧造瓷器，但产品均变为磁州窑风格的民窑产品。

2016年的考古工作是对井陉窑12处窑址的首次全面调查与勘探，基本明确了各窑址的地表遗存现状与地下窑业堆积情况，确定了各窑址烧瓷品类、内涵、特征与时代延续情况等，对井陉窑的研究有重大推进作用。

城关青瓷碗（隋代）　　　　　　　南秀林化妆白瓷钵（晚唐）　　　　　　北防口化妆白瓷碗（晚唐）

Jingxing Kiln Sites are distributed in Jingxing County and Jingxing Mining Area in Hebei Province. Up till now, twelve kiln sites have been discovered, including eleven in Jingxing County and one in Jingxing Mining Area. These sites are scattered on a stretch of land that is 1,020,000 square meters. From April to June in 2016, archaeologists from Hebei Provincial Institute of Cultural Relics and Jingxing Heritage Conservation Management Bureau carried out a comprehensive investigations and archaeological reconnaissances in twelve kiln sites mentioned above. Results of investigation and archaeological reconnaissances indicate that Jingxing Porcelain Kilns were first put into use in late Sui Dynasty and they became to wane after Jin Dynasty. The history of porcelain firing can be divided into four phases. Besides, what have also been found out are the categories, connotations, features and continuation of fired porcelain from each kiln and other issues. As a result, studies on Jingxing Kiln Sites have been greatly promoted.

# 安徽萧县白土寨唐宋瓷窑址

◎蔡波涛

萧窑位于皇藏峪复背斜两条东北—西南走向的隆起褶皱所形成山丘中部的山间盆地内，倒流河从遗址中部由南向北穿过。2017年3月至8月，安徽省文物考古研究所等对白土寨窑址进行了主动性考古发掘，共清理出唐宋时期各类遗迹70处，包括窑址3座、料池4座、储灰池7座、房址10座、灰坑29个、柱洞类遗迹12个、灶类遗迹3处和路基2条。

窑炉遗迹集中分布在T0702和T0304内，均为马蹄形馒头窑。窑炉保存较差，由窑床、火膛和烟道组成，未发现操作坑。根据层位关系、窑炉形制、结构与方向等推断其应分为两个窑区。其中，Y1、Y3为一组联窑，Y1规模较Y3稍大，建于一座废弃的料池作坊之上，方向为东西向，窑门处于东部，窑门相连，皆为半地穴式马蹄形窑。火膛呈半月形，用耐火砖夹窑柱修建起来的墙体与窑床分隔开，二者高差为40～60厘米。窑床较平，存有一层较厚且不发硬的红烧土面，可见烧窑温度不高。此外Y1烟囱应是利用作坊F9的墙体搭建起来的。

料池类遗迹全为长方形，由垫板铺地，池边立砖，池底残存瓷泥。储灰池遗迹的平面形状多为长方形，直壁平底，池内包含大量草木灰，上层填土夹杂红烧土颗粒。

作坊区分为东、西两区，西部作坊区与东部烧造区仅一墙之隔，共有8座房址。东区作坊有F1、F9，F1应为专门保护料泥池C1而搭建，推测F9为一处练泥池遗迹，后改建为窑。除F3、F5、F7、F8外，其余房址皆配置有料泥池与储灰池类遗迹。

出土遗物丰富，保存完整的文物近800件，包括制料工具类、窑具类、生活用具类等。另晚期扰乱地层多出土酱釉深圈足涩圈碗、酱黑釉瓷罐、白地黑花瓷盆（部分带字"风花雪月"）等器物，实具金代风格。而早期唐代地层多出土青釉和黄釉的玉璧底碗、盏等，其施釉方法为蘸釉。

根据前期调查和发掘，可知萧窑始烧自隋唐，一直延续至宋元时期，其中欧盘窑址的年代最早，为隋至盛唐时期，白土村各窑址点的年代较晚，其发展历程似呈窑址点由北向南迁徙的趋势。本次发现丰富了我们对萧窑的认识，且碗形间隔具与船形间隔具等窑具的使用方式在这次发掘中有实物可以印证，对研究萧窑的装烧方式具有十分重要的意义。

发掘区遗迹分布图（上北下南）

唐风宋韵　气象万千　667

北宋时期F1（上北下南）

宋代瓷动物俑

宋代瓷人俑

北宋时期F4（上北下南）

唐代中晚期Y2（上北下南）

唐代青黄釉瓷碗　　　　　　　　　　　宋代白瓷枕

宋代白瓷瓜棱罐　　　　　　　　　　　宋代白瓷碟

金代酱釉双系罐　　　　　　　　　　　宋代刻划纹瓶

From March to August in 2017, archaeologists from Anhui Provincial Institute of Cultural Relics and Archaeology and other organizations carried out excavations on kiln sites in Baituzhai Village. As many as 70 remains, which are of a wide range, have been excavated and dealt with carefully. These remains, dating from Tang and Song dynasties, used to be kilns, slurry pits, lime paste storage pits, dwelling sites, ash pits, postholes, stoves, roadbeds, etc. A wide range of relics have been unearthed, including tools that were used to deal with slurry and paste, kiln furniture and daily utensils. After excavations, it has been determined that all kilns in Baituzhai Village were not constructed in a very early era. The workshop zone was divided into east part and west part. Development pattern of the kilns shows a trend that the kilns were relocating from the north to the south. Besides, the ways in which kiln furniture like bowl-shaped spacers and boat-shaped spacers were used have been confirmed by solid evidence that has been excavated this time. It is of great significance for the study of how biscuits were set and fired in Xiao Yao.

# 安徽繁昌县骆冲窑遗址

◎罗 虎 汪发志 徐 繁 崔 炜

骆冲窑遗址位于繁昌县城西郊约3千米的阳冲村骆冲村民组。2014年6—10月，安徽省文物考古研究所等对骆冲窑遗址进行了发掘，发掘面积300平方米，发现了较完整的龙窑1座（Y1）、房址1处、路面1条，出土了大量青白瓷器和窑具。

Y1位于骆冲窑遗址中部偏西南，为南方常见的龙窑，头南尾北，依山势自南往北逐渐抬升。Y1可分为窑室、窑门、窑尾等几部分，火膛和窑前操作间被破坏无存，Y1窑顶是用楔形窑砖东西向起券而成的券顶。窑床底面由砂、黏土和碎匣钵片混合铺成，局部烧结成灰褐色硬面，大部分较疏松。窑室内共发现四道隔墙，均为单墙，将窑室分为5段。根据倒塌的隔墙砖推断，隔墙的高度至少有7层窑砖。窑内堆积及包含物可分为两层。

出土遗物主要有青白瓷器、窑具和少量砖瓦，出自疑似龙窑Y2、窑业废弃堆积和房址内。出土瓷器器形有碗、碟、盘、盏、温碗、温壶盖、粉盒等。窑具数量众多，主要有匣钵、匣钵盖、匣钵座、支座、支钉和试烧片等。匣钵上的刻划字符多为数字，亦有姓氏、方位和年号等，而刻字位置多位于漏斗形匣钵的领部外表面或筒形匣钵外表面。

此次发掘，特别值得注意的是Y1内发现了4道隔墙，且隔墙与窑壁结合部位呈错缝咬合状砌筑。这种设置隔墙、窑内分室的做法与分室龙窑非常相似，但Y1内尚无独立的燃烧室和隔墙上的吸火孔，形态较原始。因此，我们判断骆冲窑遗址Y1应是分室龙窑的早期形式，或者说处于分室龙窑的起源阶段。

骆冲窑遗址的窑业废弃堆积较薄，暂未发现遗存有明显的阶段性变化，由此推断该遗址窑业的烧造时间应该不长，其应创烧于五代，且继承了皖南地区唐末至五代瓷器烧造工艺，而烧造时间应持续到北宋早期。

与繁昌窑遗址比较，骆冲窑遗址出土瓷器的釉色、瓷胎原料加工和装烧工艺均处于领先水平，但其持续烧造时间较短，产量较小，且迄今未发现制瓷作坊遗迹。另外，刻字匣钵出现的比例也明显高于繁昌窑窑址，且装烧窑具的种类亦明显增多。这些差异与窑场的市场定位、工匠群体的工艺传统以及当时南唐至宋初的社会政治、经济背景有何关系，值得我们进一步深入探索。

B型圈足盘

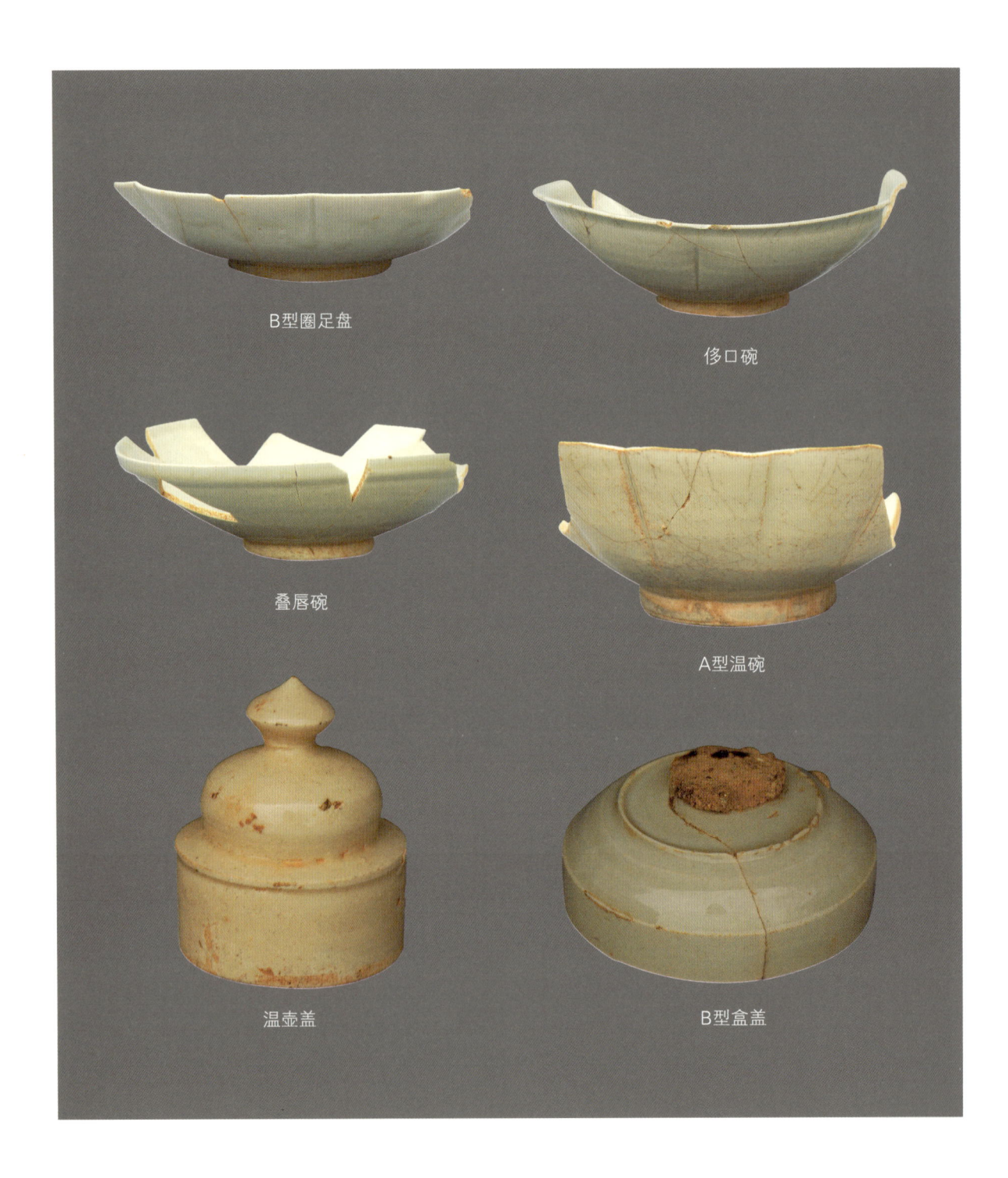

侈口碗

叠唇碗

A型温碗

温壶盖

B型盒盖

牡丹纹瓦当　　缠枝莲花纹

瓷枕　　束腰支座

如意云纹雕花砖　　桶状匣钵

Site of Luochong Kiln is located in Luochong Villagers' Group, Yangchong Village, approximately 3000 meters western suburb of Fanchang County. Discovered in the 1980s, the site covers about 1200 square meters. Two small-scale excavations were respectively carried out in 1996 and 2010. Kilns and deposits left by kiln industry are mainly in the western part of the hill; in the eastern part, there are few porcelain-making sites. From June to October in 2014, archaeologists from Anhui Provincial Institute of Cultural Relics and Archaeology and Fanchang Cultural Relics Bureau conducted a small-scale excavation on the site. Remains of a dragon-shaped long kiln, a house and a road were discovered. A great number of bluish-white porcelain and kiln furniture were unearthed. After excavations, it has been inferred that Luochong Kiln was constructed and first put into use during Five Dynasties. It had been in use until early Northern Song. No obvious phasic changes have been observed in products made in this kiln. Luochong Kiln didn't produce bluish-white porcelain for a long time. Kiln site Y1, in which there are compartments, should be an early form of partitioned dragon-shaped long kiln. Besides, there has been a basic understanding of Luochong Kiln, like its production techniques, production categories and features.

# 安徽繁昌窑柯家冲瓷窑遗址

◎ 罗 虎

柯家冲瓷窑遗址位于安徽省繁昌县城南郊的笠帽顶与毛竹山之间，窑址主要分布在繁阳镇铁门村高潮村民组和柯家冲村民组境内，遗址面积约1平方千米。2013年11月—2016年12月，安徽省文物考古研究所等对该遗址进行了持续发掘，发现了龙窑1座（Y2，早年曾于此地发现过一座窑址Y1）、作坊基址1处、工棚1处、排水沟和路面各1条。出土了大量青白瓷器和窑具，出土瓷器有碗、盏、碟、直壁盒、温碗、壶、盘、粉盒、砚台等，装烧窑具主要有匣钵、垫饼、垫圈和固定匣钵柱的窑柱等。

Y2位于窑包山南麓坡脚，为南方常见的龙窑，可分为窑前操作面、火膛、窑室、窑门、窑尾等几部分，窑床上保留有成排的匣钵或匣钵窝、青白瓷器和灰烬等。F2位于Y2以东约10米处，平面大体呈方形，其东南部发现有一处陶车基座和一个陈腐池。推测F2应是一处上覆瓦顶，外围出挑檐的作坊房址，可能是制作瓷器的成型区。C1澄泥池、C2淘洗池和G1排水沟均位于作坊区，且C2与G1相距不远，应是配合使用的作坊遗迹群。

另外，于Y1南侧发现道路一条，处于窑头和南二号窑门之间，应是装窑、出窑和烧窑等活动的通道。其上的车辙遗迹属于首次发现，推测应为独轮车车辙，为探索作坊内的运输工具及作坊布局提供了重要线索。

柯家冲瓷窑遗址是繁昌窑窑场分布的中心区，窑业废弃堆积厚达2～5米，此次发掘首次较完整地揭露了青白瓷成型作坊。根据地层堆积和出土遗物特征，可将目前发掘揭露的文化遗存初步分为两期。一期的年代相当于2002年繁昌窑遗址划分的第一期，为五代时期。产品整体风格与骆冲窑遗址类似，说明二者存在着密切的交流，同属于繁昌窑窑系。二期的年代为北宋早中期。器形特征与2002年繁昌窑遗址发掘划分的二、三期器物相似，在间隔窑具上，本期主要为垫饼，部分为垫砂，垫圈很少。本次发掘使得我们对于柯家冲窑址和骆冲窑址的创烧时代，二者在窑业生产技术、工艺传统等方面的相互关系都有了新的认识。

唐风宋韵 气象万千 673

遗迹分布图（镜向西北）

F2（东向西）

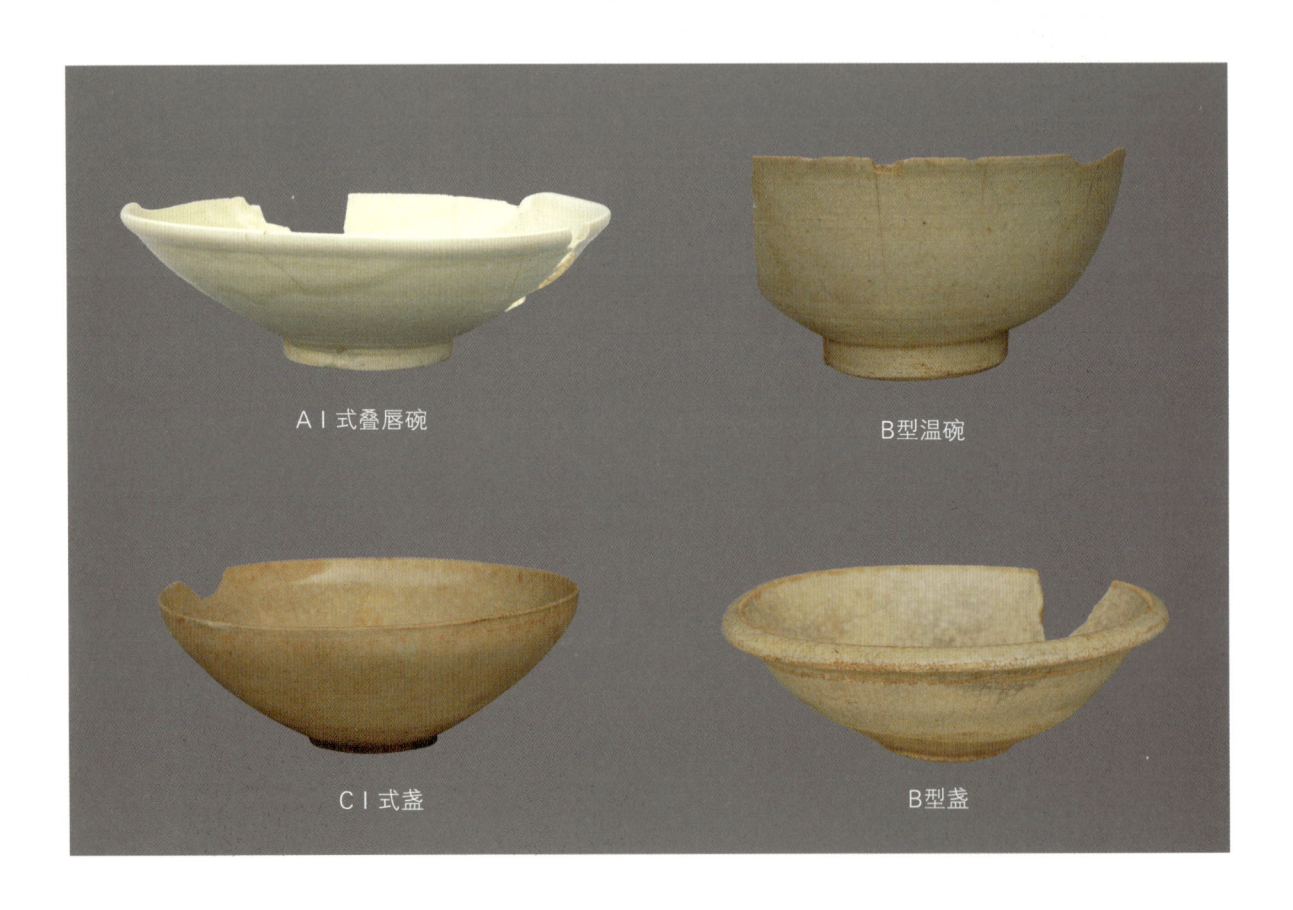

陶车基座　作坊房址（砾石块和黄地土硬面）
陶瓷沉淀池　　　　　　　　　　　　　柱洞
　　　　　　　　陶墙
　　　　　　　　　　　　　　　　　　柱洞
　　　　　糙缸？
　　　　　　　　　　　　柱洞　　陶洗池

AⅠ式叠唇碗　　　　　　　B型温碗

CⅠ式盏　　　　　　　　　B型盏

A型器盖　　　　　　　　　　　　　　C型盘

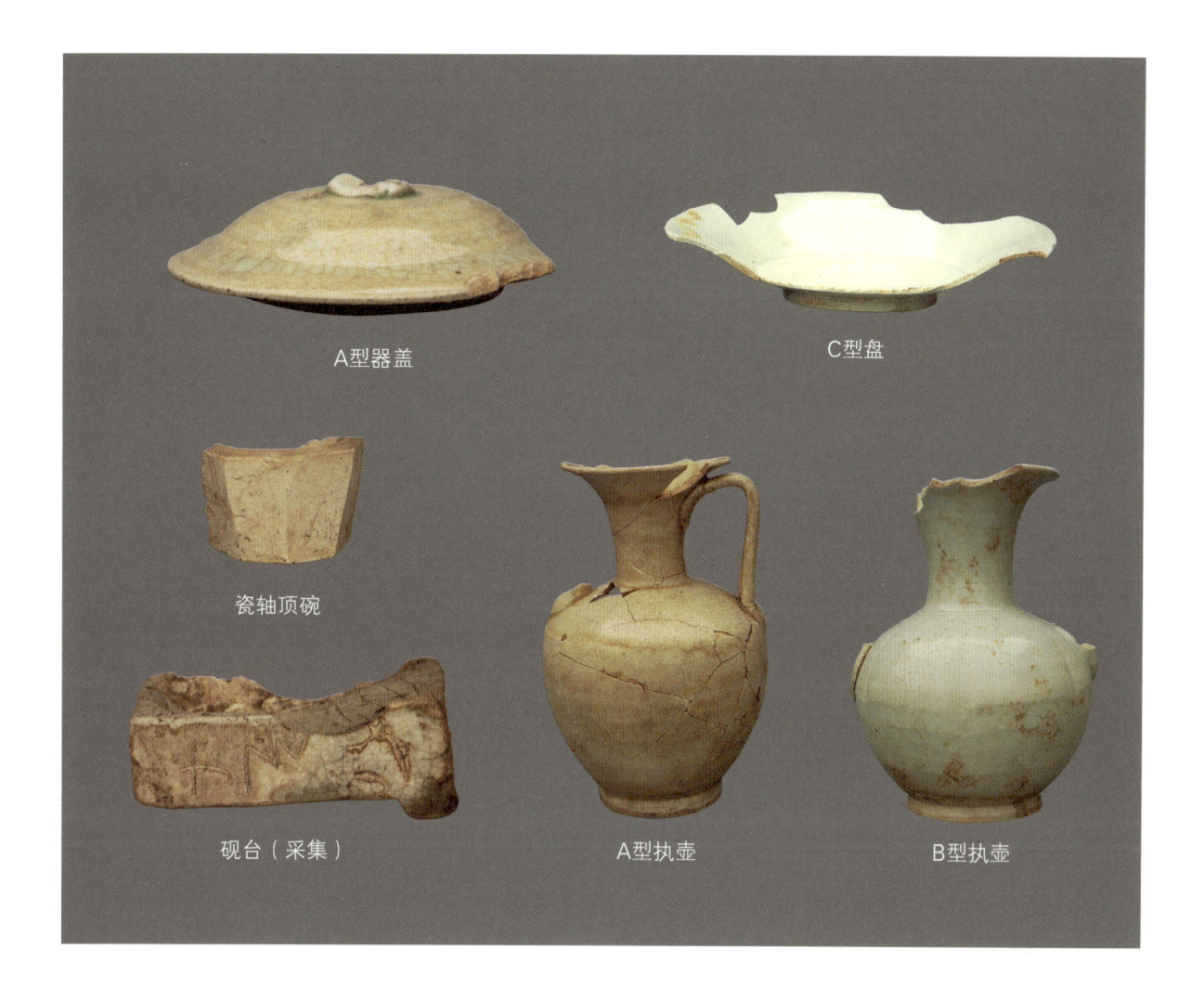

瓷轴顶碗

砚台（采集）　　　　　　A型执壶　　　　　B型执壶

Site of Kejiachong Kiln is located between Limao Mountain and Maozhu Mountain, 1.5 kilometers south of the suburb of Fanchang County, Anhui Province. Major kilns were distributed in the locality of Gaochao Villagers' Group and Kejiachong Villagers' Group, Tiemen Village, Fanyang Town. Discovered in the 1950s, the site encompasses about one million square meters. From November in 2013 to December in 2016, a joint team consisting of archaeologists from Anhui Provincial Institute of Cultural Relics and Archaeology and Fanchang Cultural Relics Bureau carried out excavations on the site. Remains of a dragon-shaped long kiln, foundation of a workshop, a shed, a drainage trench and a road were discovered. A great number of bluish-white porcelain and kiln furniture were unearthed. Layout and structure of the workshop zone on Site of Fanchang Kiln, as well as features of products made here in each period, have been basically recognized. Important materials are provided for the farther study of kiln production techniques, craftsmanship and conventions and the relationship between Kejiachong Kiln and Luochong Kiln.

# 山西河津市固镇宋金瓷窑址

◎高振华　王晓毅　贾　尧

固镇瓷窑址是晋南地区宋金时期重要的烧瓷窑场之一，位于河津市樊村镇固镇村。窑址主要分布于固镇村西、遮马峪东岸台地上。2016年3月至9月，山西省考古研究所等对固镇窑址进行了抢救性发掘，发掘工作分北涧疙瘩、上八亩和下八亩三个地点进行，清理制瓷作坊4处、瓷窑炉4座、水井1处、窑炉残渣及废品堆积坑35个，出土瓷片、窑具标本达6吨之多。

制瓷作坊及瓷窑炉的发现为本次发掘最重要的收获。在布局上，制瓷作坊紧邻窑炉，每处作坊对应一两座窑炉，是典型的小手工业作坊。作坊多为窑洞式，其中二号作坊为一处地窨式窑洞，门道与窑洞入口处设有天井，地域特色鲜明。作坊间存在明确的分工，据一号作坊内发现的淘洗池、陶缸，判断其应为练泥的场所；二号作坊内的石磨盘、瓷泥堆、大片的烧结面等遗存，反映其为制坯、晾坯的场所；而四号作坊底部整齐摆放的窑具，说明其可能为存放装烧具的场所。

发现的四座宋金瓷窑炉，均为半倒焰式馒头窑，由火膛、窑床、烟室等部分组成。其中北宋时期的Y1保存相对较好，烟室的总面积占整个窑炉面积的一半，这种特殊的烟室具备缓火、干燥等功能，在国内尚属首次发现。三座金代窑炉在结构上较北宋窑炉有所改进，因烧造产品的不同，其在通风口的设置、窑床的形制等方面又存在差别，对窑炉温度的掌控更加成熟。

固镇窑址生产的瓷器品类有粗白瓷、细白瓷、黑酱釉瓷和低温三彩釉陶，以白瓷为大宗。出土的北宋细白瓷，代表了同时期制瓷工艺的顶尖水平，独具风采的金代装饰瓷枕，明确了国内外大量同类馆藏和出土品的烧造窑口。另外，该窑址瓷器产品的装烧方法以覆烧和仰烧为主，根据间隔工具的不同，可分为三叉支钉叠烧、泥钉叠烧和涩圈叠烧。

固镇窑址的发掘，填补了山西地区无相关制瓷遗迹的空白，其成组的作坊与窑炉对探讨古代手工业生产的组织形式和管理体制以及区域经济形态具有重要意义。北宋窑炉Y1，极有可能掌握了利用窑炉余温进行晾坯的关键技术，此发现更新了制瓷工程技术史。

另外，河津窑在生产和装饰工艺上与周邻地区的登封窑、当阳峪窑、耀州窑、定窑、磁州窑相关联，博采众长而自成一体，是宋金时期北方地区制瓷工艺的集大成者。

唐风宋韵　气象万千　677

固镇瓷窑址地貌及发掘区示意图（上为北）

北涧疙瘩发掘区（上为北）

上八亩发掘区（上为西）

下八亩发掘区（上为北）

Y1（北宋　上为北）

二号作坊址及Y2（上为西）

Y4（金代　上为北）

四号作坊（上为西）

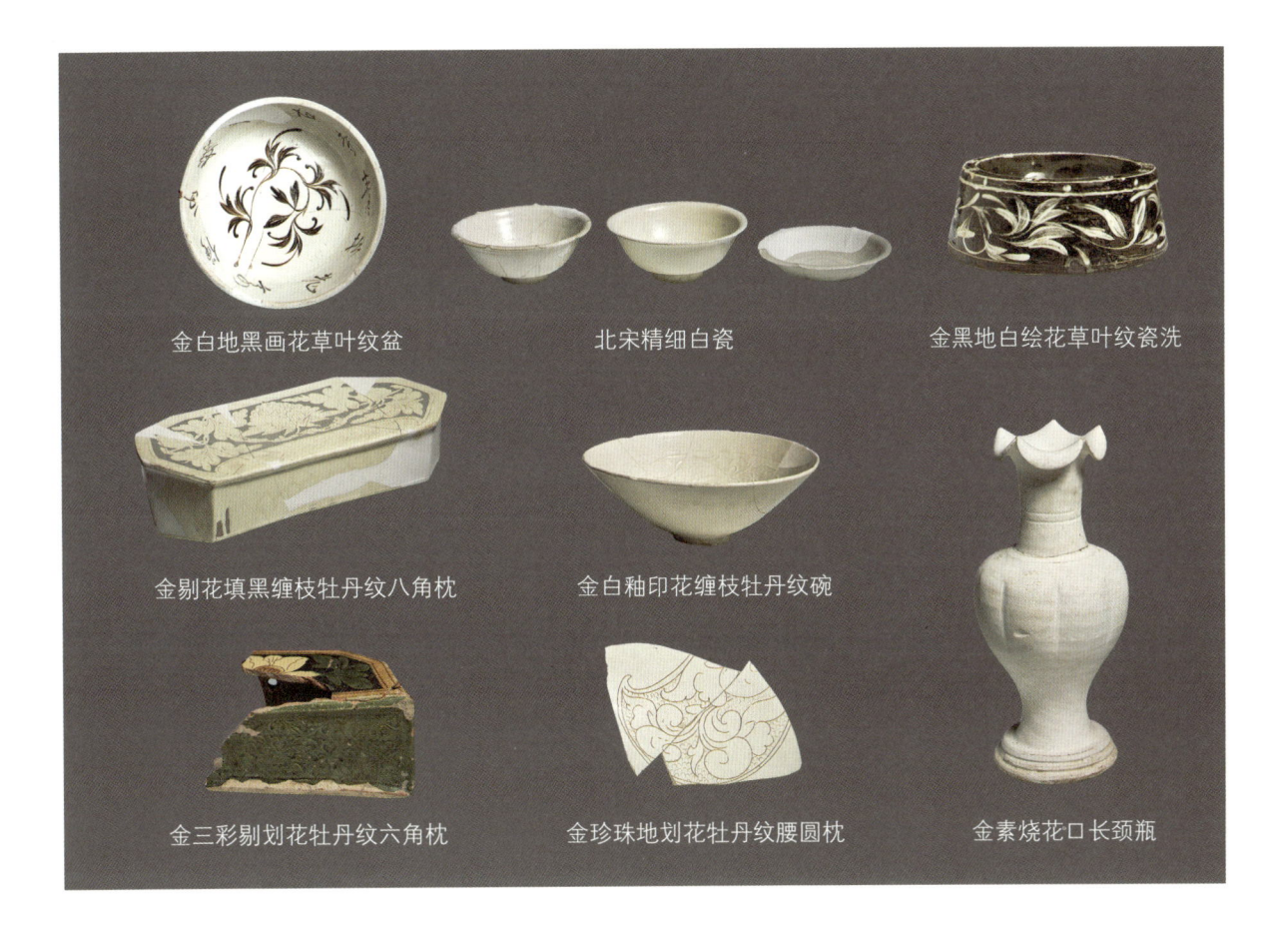

金白地黑画花草叶纹盆　　北宋精细白瓷　　金黑地白绘花草叶纹瓷洗

金剔花填黑缠枝牡丹纹八角枕　　金白釉印花缠枝牡丹纹碗

金三彩剔划花牡丹纹六角枕　　金珍珠地划花牡丹纹腰圆枕　　金素烧花口长颈瓶

From March to September in 2016, a team consisting of archaeologists from Shanxi Provincial Institute of Archaeology and Hejin Cultural Relics Bureau carried out salvage excavations on a kiln site in Guzhen Village, Fancun Town, Hejin City. As many as 44 remains have been cleared up, including porcelain-making workshops, kilns which date from Song and Jin dynasties and are in the shape of a steamed bun, wells, kiln residues, pits dumped with flawed products. A great number of relics like porcelain and kiln furniture have been unearthed. The excavated porcelain are coarse white porcelain, fine white porcelain, black glazed porcelain and low-temperature three-color glazed potteries. The following are major discoveries that have been made after excavations. Firstly, the discovery of a decorated porcelain pillow helps determine the provenance of a large number of similar porcelain pillows that have been distributed both at home and abroad. Secondly, the discovery of porcelain-making workshops and kiln furnaces have filled in the blank that none such sites were discovered in Shanxi Province. No kiln furnace like Y1, whose smoke chamber is in a special structure, has been discovered in China before. After the excavation of Y1, it has been inferred that, in Northern Song, the key technique of drying biscuits by using residual temperature of the kiln furnace might have been mastered. Thirdly, as a kiln occupied by small handicraft workshops, workshops and kiln furnaces were paired up here. It is of great significance for probings into production organization and management system of ancient handicraft industry as well as regional economies.

# 河南禹州神垕镇瓷窑发掘概况

◎李 辉

2013年3月，河南省文物考古研究院等对神垕镇建业"钧都新天地"项目第一期工程建设用地进行了考古勘探，勘探面积达10000平方米，发现了窑炉等众多制瓷遗迹。

从8月下旬开始，河南省文物考古研究院对该遗址展开抢救性发掘，发掘面积2120平方米，发现窑炉18座（其中较完整的13座）、作坊遗迹3处、灰坑126座、澄泥池13座、灶18座、灰沟3条及墓葬1座，出土大量瓷器残片和窑具残片，总数约数万枚。

发现十余座窑炉，除一座长方形分室窑炉和一座带有3个烟囱的椭圆形小窑炉外，其余窑炉平面均呈圆形。窑炉属北方地区常见的馒头窑，上部均已不存，仅保留火膛、窑床、落渣坑、出渣道、烟囱底部等部分。窑炉形制普遍较大，直径4~6米。Y1是唯一的一座长方形窑炉，时代应为金代。Y4、Y7、Y9应为元代窑炉。其余9座窑炉应为明代窑炉，其中Y8较为特殊，形制较小，平面椭圆形，带有3个圆形烟囱。

发现有澄泥池、储煤场、储釉缸、活动面等相关制瓷遗迹。澄泥池均为长方形，大小不一，大致分2类。一类以小青砖铺底，形制较小；另一类面积较大，四周以匣钵为壁。还有一些小坑，坑壁、坑底有涂抹白灰的痕迹，应为加工某种制瓷原料的地方。另外，还发现有两个作坊坑及数座小灶，灶似用于烘干新制坯体。

此次发掘，发现的窑址数量多、形制大、密度大，说明当时这里是一处规模较大的窑场。另外，众多配属设施的发现说明这里是集原料加工、坯体制作、入窑烧造等完整工艺流程于一体的窑场。

出土瓷片以白地黑花瓷占绝大多数，钧瓷、白瓷、黑瓷等也数量不少。该窑场烧造的产品品种十分丰富，金代的器形有天蓝红斑钧瓷盘、黑釉鸡心碗、白瓷碗，元代器物见有素烧白瓷碗、黑釉小瓷盏、白釉褐彩盆、青瓷罐等，明代则多见白地黑花罐和白地黑花点彩碗等。这些明代器物，具有北方磁州窑系的特点。

此次发现的窑炉，除金、元时期的以外，还有更多的明代窑炉。如此众多的明代窑炉的发现，在河南古瓷窑址考古发现中还属首次，对研究中原地区制瓷业的发展乃至中国北方的古代瓷器发展都具有重要意义。

Y1（西北—东南）

Y9（东北—西南）

Y5（西—东）

Y2（南—北）

Y6（西—东）

Y8（北—南）

H96　　　　　　　　　　　H83

宋代钧瓷盘残片　　　　　　明代白地黑花瓷

元代素烧碗　　　　　　　　明代白地黑花瓷

In August 2013, a joint team consisting of archaeologists from Henan Provincial Institute of Cultural Relics and Archaeology and Cultural Relics Exploration Team of Yuzhou City carried out salvage excavations in Shenhou Town. The excavated area used to be a construction site of the first phase of Jundu Xintiandi project, owned by Central China Real Estate Limited. A series of porcelain kiln sites of Jin, Yuan and Ming dynasties as well as a large number of porcelain fragments and other objects have been discovered. All of these indicate that, in this area, there used to be a large-scale kiln producing varied porcelain. Such a great number of kiln sites accurately dating back to Ming Dynasty are the first ones to have been discovered in Henan Province.

# 安徽凤阳县乔涧子明代琉璃窑遗址

◎罗 虎 唐更生 朱 江

乔涧子琉璃窑遗址位于安徽省滁州市凤阳县府城镇齐涧村乔涧子自然村南约1000米，面积约6万平方米。2013年7—10月底，安徽省文物考古研究所等对凤阳县乔涧子明代琉璃窑遗址进行了抢救性考古发掘，发掘明代早中期琉璃窑12座。

琉璃窑均为全倒焰窑，分为两种类型，一类为馒头窑，一类为马蹄窑。

馒头窑4座，平面近长勺形，形制基本相同，由操作坑、窑门、火膛、窑室和烟囱等五部分组成。操作坑平面近长方形，窑门平面近梯形，火膛平面略呈扇形，窑室平面为圆形。窑床一般用青砖平铺一层，也有的窑床底部不铺砖，仅有青灰色烧结硬面。推测燃料应为柴薪。

马蹄窑8座，构成同馒头窑，全长10～12米。操作坑平面近长方形，坑底残留有柱洞，沿两侧壁分布。窑室平面为马蹄形，窑床上有青灰色烧结面，有的窑床平面上还残留有一道道平行分布的灰白色或红褐色条状印痕，应为吸火孔痕迹。推测燃料应为柴薪。

出土遗物有瓦当、滴水、鸱吻、板瓦、筒瓦、花卉纹雕花砖、瓦当印模、青瓷碗、盘、香炉和动物骨骼等，亦有零星青花瓷片出土。瓦当分为陶和琉璃两类，以琉璃瓦当的素坯占绝大部分。瓦当纹饰有四爪或五爪团龙纹、花卉纹、乳丁纹、狮形兽面纹等，以团龙纹数量最多。滴水上有龙纹、牡丹纹、卷云纹、如意云纹等，其中龙纹和云纹数量占绝大部分。鸱吻上装饰有鱼麟纹。本次发掘的出土器物，以素坯最多，而琉璃成品则发现较少。这种现象可能与琉璃成品在当时多已转运和利用，而废弃的则多为第一阶段的残次品有关。

从陶窑形制结构及窑内出土器物判断，这些陶窑应为砖瓦窑，烧制琉璃素坯和琉璃成品。其中，马蹄窑的出土器物以瓦当和滴水占绝大部分，应为琉璃瓦窑，而馒头窑可能是砖瓦混烧的琉璃窑。

乔涧子琉璃窑遗址面积达6万平方米，规模大，窑址密集。在施工范围外，我们又发现了22座琉璃窑。乔涧子琉璃窑遗址出土的瓦当、滴水以及雕花砖，与明中都遗址出土的同类器基本雷同，且与南京聚宝山琉璃窑遗址出土的同类器也非常相似。从遗址规模、位置、出土遗物的特征并结合历史记载可推断，乔涧子琉璃窑址应为明代早中期为修建明中都和皇陵所建的官府窑场。

西部发掘区Y1~Y4平面分布（镜向东北）

东部发掘区Y5~Y8、Y11平面分布（镜向东南）

**安徽凤阳乔涧子琉璃窑址**

唐风宋韵　气象万千　685

Y3

Y3窑床

Y9窑床上的吸火孔印痕

Y10窑室出土灰陶瓦当和滴水

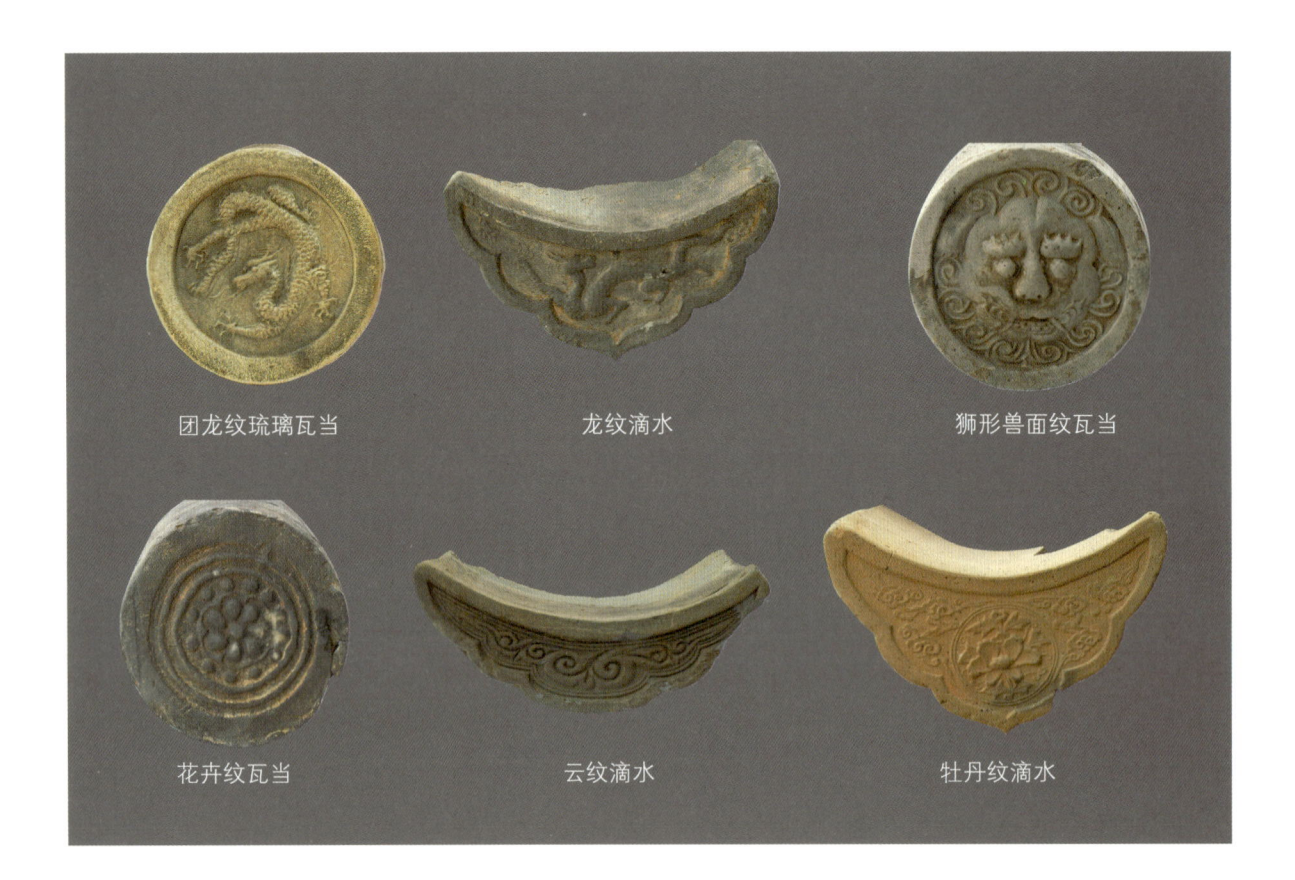

团龙纹琉璃瓦当　　　　　　龙纹滴水　　　　　　狮形兽面纹瓦当

花卉纹瓦当　　　　　　云纹滴水　　　　　　牡丹纹滴水

The site of a kiln that used to produce glazed earthenware is located about 1000 meters south of Qiaojianzi Unincorporated Village, Qijian Village, Fucheng Town, Fengyang County, Chuzhou City, Anhui Province. Commonly known as "Yao Ding Tou", this kiln site covers approximately 60,000 square meters. From the beginning of July to the end of October in 2013, a joint team consisting of archaeologists from Anhui Provincial Institute of Cultural Relics and Archaeology and Cultural Relics Management Institute of Fengyang County carried out salvage excavations here, discovering twelve kiln furnaces that used to produce glazed earthenware during early middle Ming Dynasty. After excavations, it has been found out that all these kiln furnaces were downdraught ones. They can be divided into two types. Some are in the shape of a steamed bun; the others are U-shaped. The majority of relics unearthed from the U-shaped furnaces that used to fire glazed tiles are tile-ends and triangle-shaped edges that used to be on tile ends. Furnaces that look like a steamed bun might be used to fire glazed bricks as well as glazed tiles. It has been inferred that, during early middle Ming Dynasty, there used to be an official kiln producing glazed earthenware needed for the construction of the Central Capital of Ming Dynasty and mausoleums. Therefore, the kiln site in Qiaojianzi, as the site of an official kiln that used to fire glazed earthenware in Ming Dynasty, has turned out to be the first of its kind that has been scientifically excavated in Anhui Province. It is of great academic value for kiln archaeology, the study of architectural history of the Central Capital of Ming Dynasty and contemporary mausoleums, etc.

# 江苏南京市栖霞区官窑村明代窑场遗址

◎杨平平

官窑村明代窑场遗址位于南京市栖霞区东北郊，分布于工农路以东的官窑山及其附近地区。

2016年6月至今，南京市考古研究院对该遗址开展了一系列的考古工作，发现文化遗迹219处，有窑114座、墓葬92座、烧坑10处及石头面（疑似石构码头）3处。遗址时代从六朝延续至明清，其中以明代遗存为主体，且明代窑基本集中分布在官窑山及其附近地区。

共试掘12座窑（编号Y15~Y26），皆位于山体近山脚的缓坡处，窑体沿山势下挖筑成。均为馒头窑，顶部不存，窑体结构保存完好，由窑门、火膛、窑室、烟道等构成。窑门外均发现有一略呈长方形的操作间，基本与原地表平齐。

出土遗物以砖瓦占大宗，偶见瓷器碎片等。砖的数量较多，但完整器较少，分为铭文砖和素面砖两类，素面砖占多数，少数为铭文砖。铭文砖两长端面均模印有阳文，一侧为"应天府提调官府丞王恪令史吴子名""上元县提调官县丞李健司吏方原吉"，另一侧为"总甲…甲首…小甲…造砖人夫…窑匠…""总甲""甲首""小甲""造砖人夫""窑匠"，铭文中的人名有所区别。瓦有板瓦、筒瓦和瓦当。瓷片大多出土于窑室及操作间的底部，具有典型元末明初的时代特征。值得注意的是，在官窑山山脚及Y19的操作间内还发现几件花卉纹的建筑构件。

窑内出土的铭文砖可在现南京城墙砖中找到实例，结合文献，Y15的操作间底部发现一枚"至正通宝"及Y22内的一块城砖热释光测年数值，推测该窑址的年代应为元末至明洪武间，而带有"府提调官""总甲""甲首"等铭文的城砖至明洪武十年才出现。因此，官窑村窑址发现的铭文砖应为明洪武年间烧制的，该处窑址的盛期亦为明洪武时期南京城建造的盛期，其应是明初应天府上元县为烧造砖瓦的官置窑场，主要烧制城砖，辅以烧制瓦类产品。

此次考古发掘的学术意义，主要有以下几个方面：首先，砖上丰富的铭文，为明初行政管理体制、户籍制度以及书法艺术等研究提供了重要材料；其次，各窑址为研究窑业技术丰富了材料；最后，疑似石构码头的石头面遗存和水系交通是该窑场整体布局的重要组成部分，大大丰富了窑场的面貌，对整个窑场系统原貌的恢复和研究提供新的材料。

南部发掘区

北部发掘区（Y15、Y16　上东下西）

中部发掘区

Y21、Y22　　　　　　　　　　　　　　Y20

Y26

铭文砖（Y16：7）　　砖铭文拓片（Y23：5）　　铭文砖（Y15：18）　　砖铭文拓片（Y21：2）

A kiln site dating back to Ming Dynasty in Guanyao Village is in the northeastern suburb of Qixia District, Nanjing City. An area of 3000 square meters has been excavated this time. Trial diggings have been conducted in 12 kiln furnaces, all of which are in the shape of a steamed bun. These kiln furnaces used to be made up of kiln gates, burners, kiln chambers, flues, etc. The majority of unearthed relics are bricks and tiles; only a very small number of porcelain fragments were occasionally revealed. It has been inferred that the heyday of this kiln was when the construction of Nanjing was in full swing during Hongwu Era of Ming Dynasty. The kiln, which has been confirmed to be an official kiln sited in Shangyuan Town of Yingtian Prefecture and designed to produce bricks and tiles in early Ming Dynasty, was mainly used to make bricks needed for the construction of Nanjing, the imperial capital of Ming Dynasty; sometimes, tiles were fired in it. After excavations, important materials have been provided to studies on kiln production techniques of Ming Dynasty, administrative management system as well as household registration system of an official kiln in early Ming Dynasty, calligraphy, etc. Besides, there are stone remains possibly of a stone pier and a water transportation system. As important parts of the entire kiln site, they are of great significance since their existence indicates a wider range of kiln features.

# 陕西渭南市尧头窑明清瓷窑遗址调查与发掘

◎于春雷

　　尧头窑遗址位于陕西省渭南市澄城县尧头镇尧头村，遗址的核心区位于梁塬顶部下至洛河之间的山坡与梁峁地带。尧头窑是一处规模宏大的烧造瓷器、砂器的民窑遗址，因独特的黑釉剔花工艺与粗犷大气的器形装饰，且窑火至今不熄，被誉为"瓷窑活化石"。

　　2013—2016年，陕西省考古研究院对该遗址进行了详细的考古工作。调查发现该遗址基本覆盖了尧头镇区，范围分布达8平方千米，共发现遗迹点319处/组，其中原料矿遗迹5处、加工场遗迹6处、作坊遗迹68处、窑炉遗迹130处、祠庙遗迹17处、古民居遗迹75处、废料堆积区6处、城址5处及其他遗迹8处（包括过街洞4处、戏楼1处、产品集散地1处、古水窖1处和道路遗迹1处）。多数窑炉遗迹为清代遗迹，有少量为民国窑炉，还有的晚至20世纪80年代。2016年度的发掘工作是对尧头窑遗址首次正式的考古发掘，揭露窑炉遗迹6处、耙泥池遗迹1处及其他遗迹4处，窑炉均为半倒焰式窑炉。出土器物包括窑具和瓷器产品两大类。

　　遗址可分为三期：第一期，21～23层，早期，相当于元末至明代初期。这一时期尧头窑烧造瓷器的技术特点是使用M形匣钵，但是产品为清一色的黑釉涩圈碗，产品形制规整，制作精良，另外还有砂器；第二期，15～20层，中期，包括Y5与Y6，相当于明初至明代中期。这一阶段的烧造技术是以使用支柱与搁板为典型特征，这类窑具与第一期的M形匣钵没有共存现象。产品以黑釉涩圈碗和小底瓮为主，产品粗糙，没有砂器；第三期，3～14层，晚期，包括Y1、Y2、Y3、Y4，以及地表看到的所有的窑炉遗迹，相当于明代中期至20世纪90年代。这一阶段的烧造技术以使用筒形匣钵为典型特征，其与支柱搁板有共存现象，产品种类繁杂，有砂器。

　　青釉器是尧头窑鼎盛时期的一种主要产品，烧造时间为明代中期至清代中期。青釉器全部是造型精美小件器物，文房用品所占比例较大，据此推断青釉器在尧头窑的生产是有文人参与的。尧头窑后期生产的产品以盆、瓮、海子等大型器为主，瓮窑区占整个窑区面积约三分之二。在清晚期及民国至20世纪90年代，缸瓮是其大宗产品。根据出土的器物及传世器物器形，瓷瓮可分为四期。

尧头窑耙泥池正射影像图（上南下北）

Y1、Y2、Y3（西—东）

Y5（南—北）　　　　　　　　　　　Y4（西—东）

砂器　　　　　青花碗　　　　　M形匣钵

白釉褐彩碗　　　支柱与搁板　　　晚期窑具

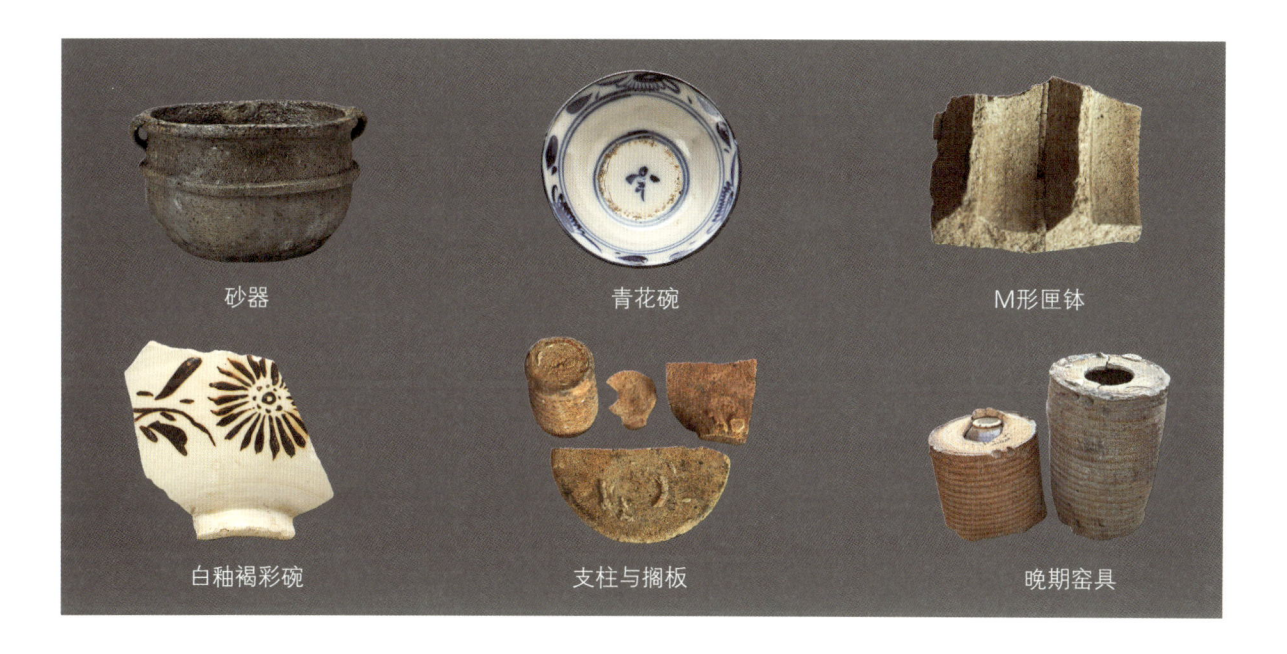

Site of Yaotou Kiln is located in Yaotou Village, Yaotou Town, Chengcheng County, Weinan City, Shaanxi Province. Chengcheng County is in the northeastern part of Central Shaanxi Plain, on the loess tableland of Weibei Plateau. Yaotou Kiln used to be a large-scale civilian kiln that produced porcelain and sandy ware. The kiln has been in use till modern days and is known as "the living fossil of kilns". In 2016, archaeologists from Shaanxi Provincial Institute of Archaeology carried out archaeological excavations on the site. The excavated area is 1000 square meters and revealed remains include kiln furnaces and mud pools. Unearthed objects can be divided into two categories, kiln furniture and ceramic products. After excavations, it has been confirmed that kiln furnaces of Yaotou Kiln used to be semi-downdraught ones. Yaotou Kiln, which has been in use from the time before the end of Yuan Dynasty and the beginning of Ming Dynasty to 1980s, can be divided into three phases. The kiln per se has provided new materials for the study of the distribution as well as technical development and exchanges of porcelain industry in North China.

# 汲井岁榾榾　出车日连连

## 河北黄骅市大左庄唐代盐业遗址

◎雷建红　马小飞　曹　洋

　　大左庄遗址位于河北省羊二庄镇杨庄村和大左庄村东北部盐场区域，东南距河北省黄骅市约30千米，西距海丰镇遗址约4千米。2016年6月6日，河北省文物研究所等单位在进行考古调查时发现该遗址。遗址东西宽约100米，南北长约200米，地表散布有较多的陶瓷片、动物遗存、砖瓦和红烧土。2016年10月，考古人员对遗址进行了考古勘探和抢救性发掘，勘探面积约为20000平方米，发掘面积约1400平方米。共计清理灰坑94座、灰沟11条、灶15座、井3口、刮卤摊场2处，并出土大量陶瓷器残片。

　　遗迹全部开口于表土层下，根据遗迹和出土遗物，结合打破关系，除G2、Z15等极少数遗迹外，遗址的主体年代应为唐代，推测这是一处唐代盐业遗址。根据遗迹现象，基本还原了一套完整的制盐工艺流程：取卤—输卤—沉淀—刮卤提纯—淋卤—储卤—上灶煮盐。

　　取卤：在发掘区的最北端发现了三口井，应是提取卤水的井。在J1和J3底部发现了芦苇和一些木构件残块，井底的芦苇可能是用来过滤卤水，预防和减少井内沙土上扬。

　　输卤：发现灰沟11条，灰沟填土包含有盐硝颗粒，推测其可能是用于输送卤水的沟渠。

　　沉淀：在发掘区中部偏南的位置有一块青绿色土区域，有可能是制盐过程中的沉淀池。

　　刮卤提纯：发掘区西南部有一块土质结构致密的区域，层理状堆积的次序为灰褐土—红烧土—草木灰—白色硬面（硬块）—灰绿土，其有可能是用来提取卤水的刮卤摊场。

　　淋卤和储卤：发掘的一些灰坑中，有一些较规整的方形、圆形或椭圆形坑，推测这些灰坑可能是淋卤坑或用于储存卤水和硝的。

　　上灶煮盐：通过发掘我们还发现了两座较大的灶，应为当时的煮盐之灶。

　　大左庄煮盐遗址是全国揭露的为数不多的盐业遗址之一，更是目前揭露的北方地区最为完整的唐代制盐作坊，其发现填补了河北地区盐业考古的空白。

大左庄煮盐遗址航拍图（上为西）

H9（储硝坑 东南—西北） 　　H10、H11（储硝坑 西—东） 　　J1上层发现的木架

Z6（西南—东北） 　　H24（淋卤坑 东南—西北） 　　J1底部残存木构件

H29（储卤坑 东—西） 　　沉淀过程形成的青绿色摊场 　　H23（左）、H17（右）（淋卤坑 西—东）

大左庄遗址出土器物

Dazuozhuang Site is in the locality of a salt field in the northeast of Dazuozhuang Village and Yangzhuang Village, Yangerzhuang Town, Hebei Province. It was discovered during archaeological investigation carried out by archaeologists from Hebei Provincial Institute of Cultural Relics and Huanghua City Museum in the salt field in the east of Haifeng Town on June 6, 2016. In October 2016, archaeologists from Hebei Provincial Institute of Cultural Relics and other organizations conducted archaeological reconnaissances and salvage excavations on Dazuozhuang Site. It has been preliminarily determined that Dazuozhuang Site used to be a salt-making site in Tang Dynasty. According to revealed remains, a complete process flow of salt-making has been basically restored. The steps include piping brine, transporting brine, leaving the brine to settle, scraping and purifying the sediment, extracting highly concentrated salty solution, collecting the solution and boiling it on the stove. Dazuozhuang Site is one of the few salt-making sites that have been excavated around China. More importantly, it is the most complete salt-making site of Tang Dynasty in northern China. The discovery of Dazuozhuang Site has filled in the blank in archaeological study of salt industry in Hebei Province.

# 编后记

  陕西、山西、河南、河北、安徽、山东、江苏七省，背靠群山，面向大海，连贯南北，穿越东西。这里气候适宜，物产丰富，不仅是中华文明的发祥地，哺育了中华民族的祖先，更蕴藏了我们的民族之根、文化之脉……

  在地图上七省被分成了几部分，但隐于其后的古代文化却依照当时的环境，或东或西，或南或北以动态的方式发展演变，在这片广袤的土地上先后创造了无数的辉煌。鉴于七省的古代文化在发展演变中的特性，我们在编排此书时，不囿于古代遗址现今的行政区划，而将其按自身的文化"基因"，分门别类地纳入所属"基因组"之中，以共性为链，串起各点，最大程度地再现其原貌，以期读者在阅读中能够站在一个全新的视角，重新审视七省在中国古代文明发展历程中的不断裂性及重要性。

  全书收录的上述七省考古发现及研究项目共178项，由各相关单位提供。资料翔实丰富，各类遗存异彩纷呈。因限于篇幅，只能对其进行概述。在编纂过程中，诸同人为编者解疑答惑，给予无私的帮助，在此诚致谢意！

  承担本书编纂工作的是华夏考古编辑部的辛革、张凤、余洁和刘亚玲。编者在2018年6月稿件基本收齐后，开始编排文图、提写摘要等编辑工作。由于时间紧迫，错误在所难免，敬请指正。

  还要感谢孙英民先生、郑同修先生、宫希成先生、林旒根先生、张文瑞先生、孙周勇先生、王万辉先生于百忙中给予了指导性建议，河南省文物考古研究院刘海旺院长更是对此书的出版付出良多，特致谢忱！

  马琬铮女士为此书翻译英文摘要，一并致谢。

编者<br>
2018年11月